MUIR'S
HISTORICAL ATLAS
ANCIENT AND CLASSICAL
Sixth Edition

EDITED BY

the late R. F. TREHARNE, M.A., PH.D.
PROFESSOR OF HISTORY, UNIVERSITY COLLEGE OF WALES, ABERYSTWYTH

AND

HAROLD FULLARD, M.Sc.
CARTOGRAPHIC EDITOR

BOOK CLUB ASSOCIATES   LONDON

CONTENTS OF
ANCIENT AND CLASSICAL ATLAS

Maps marked with an asterisk are coloured physically

*1 THE WORLD AS KNOWN TO THE ANCIENTS 1:70M.
World according to Herodotus c. 450 B.C.
World according to Eratosthenes c. 200 B.C.
World according to Strabo c. 18 A.D.
World according to Ptolemy c. 150 A.D.

2A THE CRADLES OF CIVILISATION IN THE XV CENTURY B.C. 1:25M.
B *Achaean Greece according to Homer c. 1200 B.C. 1:8M.*
C *Troy 1:500,000*
D *The Assyrian Empire in the First Half of the VII Century B.C. 1:15M.*

3A THE NILE AND EUPHRATES VALLEYS c. 1200 B.C. 1:10M.
B *Ancient Egypt 1:5M.*

4A ISRAELITE CONQUEST OF CANAAN 1:2M.
B *Jerusalem before the Exile 1:50,000*
C *Syria and the Hebrew Kingdoms 1:5M.*
D *Palestine in the time of Christ 1:2M.*
E *Jerusalem before 70 A.D. 1:50,000*
F *Paul's Missionary Journeys 1:30M.*

5A PHOENICIAN AND GREEK COLONIES 1:20M.
B *Persian Empire c. 500 B.C. 1:20M.*

*6-7 ANCIENT GREECE 1:2M.
A *Acropolis 1:15,000*
B *Ancient Athens 1:50,000*
C *The Shores of Propontis 1:3M.*
D *Crete 1:3M.*

8 GREECE AND THE AEGEAN IN THE V CENTURY B.C. 1:3M.

9A PELOPONNESIAN WAR 1:8M.
B *Empire of Alexander the Great 1:20M.*
C *Empires of Alexander's Successors c. 300 B.C. 1:40M.*

*10-11 ROMAN EMPIRE 1:15M.
A *Imperial and Senatorial Provinces c. 14 A.D. 1:40M.*
B *Roman Conquest of the Mediterranean 1:30M.*
C *Republican Rome 1:60,000*
D *Imperial Rome 1:60,000*

*12 ANCIENT ITALY: NORTHERN SECTION 1:3M.

*13 ANCIENT ITALY: SOUTHERN SECTION 1:3M.
A *Republican Forum 1:15,000*
B *Imperial Fora 1:15,000*

14A ITALY UNDER THE ROMAN REPUBLIC 1:5M.
B *Latium 1:2½M.*
C *Racial Distribution c. 400 B.C. 1:15M.*

15 WEST ROMAN EMPIRE IN THE TIME OF AUGUSTUS 1:10M.

16 EAST ROMAN EMPIRE IN THE TIME OF AUGUSTUS 1:10M.

*17 ROMAN BRITAIN: PHYSICAL 1:3M.
A *Britain according to Ptolemy*
B *Hadrians Wall 1:1,500,000*

18-19 THE REALMS OF CIVILISATION, c. 200 A.D. AND THE NATURAL CONDITIONS AFFECTING THEIR RELATIONS 1:30M.
A *The Empire of Asoka, c. 250 B.C. 1:50M.*
B *Gupta Empire, c. 400 A.D., and Iran 1:50M.*

20 EUROPE ON THE EVE OF THE BARBARIAN INVASIONS, c. 395 A.D. 1:25M.

George Philip and Son Limited
12-14 Long Acre London WC2E 9LP

First published 1938
Sixth Edition 1963
Reprinted 1966 1969 1971 1973 1974 1976
© George Philip and Son Limited 1963

This edition published 1976 by
Book Club Associates
By arrangement with George Philip
and Son Limited

PRINTED IN GREAT BRITAIN BY GEORGE PHILIP PRINTERS LIMITED, LONDON

INTRODUCTION

THE ANCIENT WORLD

Plate 1 shows the area within which the whole drama of ancient history was played—the development not only of the civilisation of the West, upon which our attention is mainly concentrated, but of the remote and independent civilisations of China and India. But by far the greater part of the area shown on this map—the whole of northern Europe and Asia and the whole of Africa south of the Atlas mountains, except the narrow valley of the Nile—was practically untouched by the influence of the various civilisations, and was known to them, vaguely, as the region from which incursions of barbarians broke into the more civilised regions.

The small maps at the foot of the page give a diagrammatic illustration of the expansion of human knowledge about the earth's surface among the Greeks and Romans between the time of Herodotus (c. 450 B.C.) and the time of Ptolemy (c. 150 A.D.). Herodotus knew of the existence of India, but knew nothing of its shape, and the great civilisation of China lay altogether beyond his horizon. Ptolemy knew that China existed, but no more than that. The expansion of knowledge about the world and its peoples among the Greeks and Romans was thus very slight during the six centuries covered by these diagrams.

The beginnings of civilisation in the western part of the region covered by the main map took place in the two riverine districts of Egypt and Mesopotamia. The relations between these two regions are more clearly illustrated in **Plate 3.** They were brought into contact with one another at an early date ; the wanderings of Abraham ranged from Ur of the Chaldees, which was probably the chief centre of the Sumerian or Euphratic civilisation, through Syria to Egypt. Which of these two centres of development was the older, scholars are not yet ready to affirm with confidence. They probably had independent beginnings, but contributed something to each other's development. Excavators are beginning to reveal to us a third riverine civilisation, on the lower Indus, which was probably an offshoot from Sumer, but it seems to have had almost no influence upon the development of Indian civilisation, which seems to have been of much later origin. In distant China another riverine civilisation grew up, in the basins of the Hwang-ho and (later) of the Yang-tse-kiang. No direct contact seems to be traceable between the civilisation of China and those of Egypt and Babylonia. Isolated by the huge mountain-mass which is shown on the map, and by the great deserts of the north-east, the marvellous civilisation of China seems to have had from the first an isolated existence, though its influence spread over the Indo-China peninsula to the south-west of China, and over Japan, Korea and Manchuria in the north.

In the west, the riverine stage of civilisation was followed by a marine stage, when first the Minoans (whose brilliant civilisation has only recently been discovered,) and later the Phœnicians, the Greeks and (to some extent) the Etruscans made the Mediterranean the centre of the rising European civilisation, which was to be unified by the conquests of Rome. Throughout the "classical" era, and down to the great discoveries of the fifteenth and sixteenth centuries, the Mediterranean

and the countries bordering upon it remained the arena of western civilisation ; these lands are, indeed, the only part of the wide area shown in the main map of which the classical geographers had any real knowledge.

Meanwhile, from Egypt, and still more from Babylonia, the impetus to progress in civilisation had passed to the uplands of the Near East : to the Hittites and the Lydians in Asia Minor, to the Assyrians in upper Mesopotamia, to the Persians and the Medians on the high ground that looks down upon Mesopotamia in the East. Here arose huge but short-lived empires which strove for the control of the Fertile Crescent that curves round the Syrian deserts from Palestine to Mesopotamia. With these wide empires first the Greeks and then the Romans were brought into contact and conflict ; and it was in struggles against them that the nascent European system of freedom-under-law underwent its first ordeals. For a time, under Alexander and his successors, this wide region of the Near East was brought under the influence of the European civilisation. But this influence was short-lived. The Romans only succeeded in preserving control over the western fringes of this area. But this was enough to ensure that Christianity, born in Palestine, should be one of the most powerful moulding influences in the development of the European civilisation.

As for India, the real beginning of her distinctive civilisation may be traced to the coming of the Aryans, about 2,000 years before Christ. But this civilisation, though it was temporarily influenced by the coming of Alexander, and by a series of barbarian irruptions from Central Asia, had its own independent existence, almost as isolated as that of China. There was, indeed, always a thin stream of trade between India and Europe, and an intermittent trickle even from China to Europe ; but the European civilisation in effect knew nothing of the great civilisations of the East, at any rate until the later middle ages.

If by the "Ancients" we mean the Greeks and the Romans, the world really known to them was but a small fragment of the wide area represented in this map.

Plate 2 illustrates the ancient civilisations of the Near East which preceded the rise of Greek and Roman civilisation. The date 1400 B.C. is chosen for the first map, 2a, because by that date the main powers of the Near East had got themselves into position. (1) *Egypt*, whose records date back to at least 4,000 B.C., had reached a great height of development in the Early and Middle Kingdoms before 2000 B.C. Its development had then been interrupted by the conquest of the Hyksos (c. 1800–1600), who were probably Hittites (*see* below) with a following of Semitic tribes. The expulsion of the Hyksos (1580 B.C.) was followed by a great imperialist period, when Egypt conquered Nubia and Syria, especially under Thutmose III., c. 1500 B.C. The Egyptian empire was at the height of its power under Amenhotep III. at the date of the map ; all the Semitic tribes of Syria were obedient to it ; and the other empires were all in relation with it. (2) In *Babylonia* the beginnings of civilisation were as ancient as in Egypt. The Sumerians, a non-Semitic people who lived near the mouth of the Euphrates, had invented cuneiform writing, which was adopted by all the peoples of the Near

East. Their power was subsequently merged in that of the Semitic Akkadians of Babylonia, whose empire reached its height under the great codifier Hammurabi, c. 2200 B.C.—the Amraphel of Genesis and the contemporary of Abraham. But the development of Babylon, like that of Egypt, had been checked by a barbarian irruption—that of the Aryan Kassites (c. 1800–1200 B.C.) : on all sides the barbarian irruptions of c. 1800 B.C. mark an epoch like the later barbarian irruptions into the Roman Empire. (3) The *Semitic* peoples, who probably sprang from Arabia, occupied the whole area (coloured green on the map) from the mountains of Persia and Armenia to the Mediterranean : a wide crescent of settled ground, from Palestine through Mesopotamia to the Persian gulf, curving round the great desert whence Bedouin movements continually sprang. Apart from Babylonia, the greatest of the Semitic peoples were the *Assyrians*, who were beginning to be active at the date of the map, and were later (*see 2d*) to unite nearly the whole Semitic area under their rule ; the *Amorites*, who stretched from Syria into Northern Mesopotamia ; the *Canaanites*, who occupied the coastlands of Syria, and were beginning to be active in trade in the Phoenician cities ; and a multitude of smaller tribes, among whom the Habiru (? Hebrews) are mentioned as giving trouble in the Amarna letters. The Semitic peoples drew their civilisation partly from Babylon, partly from Egypt, and linked the two. (4) The *Hittite* empire, whose greatness has only recently been disclosed by archaeological research, had its centre in south-east Asia Minor (Cappadocia) and the Taurus mountains, whence they waged frequent war against the

FIG. 1.—THE MINOAN CENTRES IN CRETE

Egyptians and other Powers. Their greatness was at its height at the date of the map, 1400 B.C. They had only recently emerged, and had probably been the chief disturbing factor in the irruptions of c. 1800 B.C. There were also scattered Hittite tribes in Syria and Palestine : Abraham bought his grave from a Hittite clan. It is not known to what stock the Hittites belonged, but they were not Semites. Their neighbours and rivals were the people of *Mitanni*, in North Mesopotamia—an Indo-European tribe, probably related to the Medes. (5) In Crete and the Aegean Sea a brilliant civilisation, known as *Minoan*, was at its height at the date of the map. Its existence has only been disclosed in the twentieth century by archaeological research. The Minoans were not Greeks ; their downfall was probably due to the invasions of the Greeks from the north ; but Greek civilisation owed much to them. *Cnossus*, in Crete, was the centre of a sea-empire of which Greek legends and Egyptian monuments preserve traces. *Mycenae* in European Greece was a secondary centre of Minoan civilisation, and *Troy* (2c), at the mouth of the Dardanelles, was another. The influence of the

Minoans spread as far west as Sicily and South Italy, where their relics have been discovered.

The second map, 2b, illustrates the geography of Greece as it is described by Homer, for the period of the Trojan War (c. 1200 B.C.). The first wave of Greek conquest, that of the " Achaeans," had displaced the Minoan kingdom, while still keeping its Greek centre, Mycenae, as its capital ; and the Trojan War was an expedition of all the Achaean chiefs. The second wave of Greek conquest, that of the Dorians (c. 1000 B.C.) brought about a complete reconstruction of the political geography of Greece, which governed the great age of Greek history. The Homeric poems (? c. 850 B.C.) preserve the memory of the older geography, here represented.

The third map, 2d, shows, at its height, the empire of the Assyrians, who were the dominating factor in the Near East from c. 1000 B.C. to c. 600 B.C., the older Powers of Egypt, Babylonia, and the Hittites having fallen into decrepitude. Between the date of the first map on this plate, and the date of this, the Israelites had settled in Palestine, and had reached the culminating point of their power in the empire of David (c. 1000 B.C. : *see* **Plate 4**). The history of the divided kingdoms of Israel and Judah was dominated by the struggle against Assyria, which forms the background of the greater part of the Old Testament. The great age of Assyrian history began with Tiglath-Pileser III. (745), and reached its height under Sennacherib (705) and Esarhaddon (681). These monarchs ruled over the whole of Mesopotamia and Syria, thus uniting the whole Semitic stock outside Arabia ; they also occupied Egypt for a time. Their most dangerous enemies were, in the north, the *Medes* (Indo-European peoples in the uplands of Iran), the kingdom of *Urartu* (in Armenia : another ancient Power recently rescued from oblivion by archaeology) ; and in the south the ancient realm of *Elam*, and the *Chaldaeans* who were reviving the civilisation of ancient Babylonia. At the end of the seventh century B.C. the Medes and the Chaldeans united and rapidly overwhelmed Assyria (fall of Nineveh, 612 B.C.), which was more completely ruined than any other empire in history. For a short time a Chaldaean Empire took the place of the Assyrians, reaching its height under Nebuchadnezzar (605 B.C.) ; while the Medes extended their conquests in the north, and overthrew the empire of *Phrygia*, which had been built up in central Asia Minor by invaders from Europe. But both the Median and the Chaldaean empires were short-lived ; in the middle of the sixth century both were overthrown and incorporated by Cyrus in the vast Persian empire (*see* **Plate 5b**).

Plate 3. This map gives a fuller treatment of the region in which the first civilisations arose, and the lands between them. It shows, in brown, the wide desert regions which separated Babylonia from Egypt—the most difficult of geographical obstacles to intercourse. The deserts were, of course, crossed by caravan routes, using the oases, some of which are marked on the map. Round them curves the Fertile Crescent, with its agricultural (green) and pastoral (yellow) regions, which was the home of the chief Semitic peoples. A glance at this map is enough to show why Palestine was the inevitable clash-point in the constantly renewed conflict between the Egyptian Empire and the successive empires of the Euphrates and Tigris valleys—Babylonia, Assyria, Persia ; and why Megiddo was the natural scene of their Armageddon.

The second map (3b) illustrates in greater detail the area of the Egyptian Empire ; though it is necessary to check this map by the main map, which shows how narrow was

the peopled region of Egypt south of the delta, and how inaccessible except from the north. Egypt, indeed, may be compared to a lily, with the well watered region of the delta as the flower, the Nile valley as the stem, and the region of the Fayoum, round lake Moeris, as a bud. The true Egypt—occupied by a white-skinned people who gave birth to the Egyptian civilisation—extended only as far south as the First Cataract, where " Nubia," the land of black-skinned peoples, began. During the period of the Egyptian Empire's greatest power, its sway was extended as far southwards as the Sixth Cataract, but this region (part of the modern Sudan) was never fully incorporated in Egypt. The flat and well-watered lands of the delta never played so great a part in history as the narrow valley of the river ; and there was always a clear distinction between Upper Egypt, with its capital at Thebes (temples of Karnak) and Lower and Middle Egypt, with its capital at Memphis (modern Cairo, where the pyramids declare the greatness of its rulers). But these two regions were, according to legend, united as early as the First Dynasty, perhaps 5,000 years B.C. Lower Egypt controlled the western part of the Sinai Peninsula, with its copper and turquoise mines ; upper Egypt had ports on the Red Sea, whence trade was carried on in gold, gems, spices and hides. From the ports of the delta trade was carried on with the peoples of Syria and the western Mediterranean, including the Greeks. Protected by the desert and the sea, Egypt could live an isolated life in security. The ambitions of her rulers tempted them to conquer an external empire, and for about 500 years, from the 17th to the 12th century B.C., they controlled most of Syria, and gave civilisation to its peoples. But this empire was broken by the attacks of the Hittites from the north, and of the " peoples of the sea " (probably Minoans) a section of whom, known as the Philistines, were allowed to settle on the coast of Palestine, under the nominal suzerainty of the Pharaohs. After this period of imperialism, Egypt was the victim of successive conquests, first by the Assyrians, then by the Persians, then by Alexander the Great and his Macedonians, and ultimately by the Romans. Egypt was drawn into the common life of the Mediterranean world, and her great Greek port in the Mediterranean, Alexandria, became one of the principal centres of Greek thought and later of Christianity. Her own civilisation became stagnant, though she contributed to the ferment of mystical religious thought which marked the first century of the Christian era. But through all these conquests the life of her people went on unchangingly.

Plate 4 illustrates the history of the Israelites down to the time of Christ.

The first map illustrates the slow conquest of parts of Palestine by the tribes of Israel, and their long struggles with the Semitic Canaanites, whom they gradually absorbed, and with the non-Semitic Philistines. Their piecemeal conquests divided them into four separate blocks. Two tribes, Judah and Simeon, seem to have come in from the southern desert : Simeon melted away among the Bedouin tribes ; Judah had a hard struggle to establish a foothold on the high ground above the Dead Sea, and could not even conquer Jerusalem from the Canaanites until the time of David. The other tribes entered the country from the east of the Jordan ; the tribes of Reuben and Gad, and half of the tribe of Manasseh settled on the further side of Jordan and formed a second block. The most powerful tribes—Ephraim, Benjamin and half of Manasseh—occupied the highlands round

Mounts Ebal and Gerizim, with Shechem as their holy place, but only slowly conquered the fertile plain of Jezreel and the sea coast. In the north—in Galilee and northwards—the four tribes of Dan, Naphtali, Issachar and Zebulun established themselves with difficulty. First Ephraim, under Gideon and Abimelech, then Benjamin, under Saul, strove to bring these divided clans under a single control, and to keep the surrounding tribes at bay. Finally, about 980, Judah under David established for the first time the unity of the Children of Israel.

The second map illustrates (a) the consolidated kingdom of David, with its capital in the recently conquered city of Jerusalem, and its control over neighbouring tribes ; (b) the wide extension of the Davidic empire under Solomon which almost amounted to a hegemony of Syria ; and (c) its rapid collapse after his death, and the formation of the tiny kingdoms of Israel and Judah.

The third map shows the political condition of Palestine at the time of Christ : it is now a Roman province, including several vassal States held by the family of Herod, one of which contained Galilee. Two small plans show respectively Jerusalem as it was under David and Solomon and down to the exile, and as it was in the time of Christ ; and a final small map shows the chief journeys of St. Paul.

Plate 5. The first map on this Plate (5a) illustrates the work of three sea-going peoples who brought the Western Mediterranean into contact with the civilisation of the Eastern Mediterranean. First among these, in order of time, were the *Phoenicians*—Canaanites from the cities of the Syrian coast, especially Tyre. Their greatest period was between the fall of the Egyptian Empire in Syria, and the conquest of Syria by the Assyrians—c. 1200–750 B.C. ; Solomon's ally, Hiram of Tyre, ruled at the period of their greatest splendour, c. 950 B.C. They are said to have established themselves in Southern Spain (Tarshish or Tartessus) as early as 1100 B.C. They planted colonies in Cyprus, Western Sicily, Malta, Sardinia, Corsica, and along the north coast of Africa. The greatest of these, Carthage, traditionally dates from 813 B.C. It became the centre of the Punic Empire when Tyre fell under the dominion of Assyria and Persia. There was constant conflict between the Phoenicians and the Greeks when the latter began (in the eighth century B.C.) to invade their monopoly of sea-going trade.—The *Etruscans* appear to have migrated from Asia Minor to Western Italy at an unknown date. The Greeks, in the eighth century, found them planted, with twelve thriving cities, in Etruria ; they also occupied the Po valley ; they later (seventh century) conquered Latium and Campania ; and their pirate-ships dominated the Tyrrhenian or Etruscan sea, where they frequently fought the Greeks.—The *Greeks* spread outwards from continental Greece in two great stages : (1) At a very early date, say from 1200 B.C. onwards, Achaeans and Aeolians, and later Ionians, settled in the Aegean islands and the coast of Asia Minor ; the Achaeans or Aeolians in the north ; the Ionians farther south (Phocaea, Chios, Samos, Ephesus, Miletus) ; after the Dorian migration into Greece, Dorian colonists spread to the southern islands, to Crete, and to the southern part of the west coast of Asia Minor. (2) Between 750 and 550 B.C. there was a remarkable outburst of colonising activities. Some hundreds of Greek colonies were planted (a) on the north shore of the Aegean (mainly by Chalcis and Eretria, cities of Euboea) ; (b) in the sea of Marmora, the Bosporus, and all round the Black Sea (mainly by Miletus and Megara) ; (c) in the Ionian Islands and the coast of Epirus (mainly by Corinth) ; (d) in Southern Italy, which came to be

known as Magna Graecia (mainly by the Achaeans of the Gulf of Corinth, but also by Chalcis, which founded Cumae, whence the alphabet spread to the Latins) ; (e) in Sicily (mainly by Chalcis in the north-east, and by Corinth, Megara, and other Dorian cities in the south-east and south) ; (f) in the Western Mediterranean, from the Alps to the Pyrenees, in Corsica and on the west coast of Spain, notably Massilia (Marseilles) (mainly Phocaean) ; (g) on the north coast of Africa, in Cyrenaica (the island of Thera).

The rapid expansion of these three naval Powers represents the first extension of civilisation into the west.

The second map (5b) illustrates the gigantic Persian Empire, which with incredible swiftness incorporated all the civilisations of the East in a single vast dominion, in the second half of the sixth century B.C. The Persians

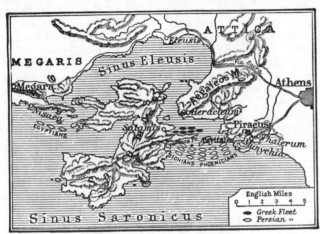

FIG. 2.—BATTLE OF SALAMIS

were an Indo-European people, akin to the Medes : their home, Persia proper, corresponds to the modern district of Fars. The Persian Cyrus, ruling over a little kingdom called Anshan, rebelled in 549 against the Medes, and made himself master of their whole vast empire ; overthrew and annexed the Lydian Empire of Croesus (546), with its capital at Sardes, and then came in contact with the Greeks of Ionia, whom he forced to submit ; captured Babylon (539) and made himself master of the whole Babylonian Empire, including Phoenicia and Syria where he restored the Jews to Jerusalem ; and also extended his sway widely over the countries to the east, possibly as far as Bactria and Afghanistan. Cyrus' son Cambyses conquered Egypt (525), and the whole eastern world was brought under a single rule. The next king, Darius (521–486), had at first to deal with revolts ; but he suppressed them and gave to his empire an efficient organisation under twenty satrapies or viceroyalties ; he extended his power eastwards as far as the Indus and sea of Aral ; he invaded Europe by the Bosporus, and crossed the Danube ; and it was this gigantic Power which, from 490 B.C. onwards, menaced the very existence of the little Greek states.

The double-page **Plate 6-7** is intended to illustrate the whole history of Greece proper. The boundaries shown are those of the fifth century B.C. The map is coloured physically, to bring out the mountain features which naturally split up continental Greece into a large number of separate city-states, each with its dependent country-side. The map shows the relationship of Greece Proper to the northern realm of Macedonia, which was to be the

means, under Alexander, of disseminating Greek culture over a great part of Asia. The map shows only European Greece : the islands of the Aegean and the Greek-settled coastland of Asia Minor, are shown in the next map, **Plate 8.**

The smaller maps on this plate show (a) the principal buildings of ancient Athens, clustered round the great fortified rock of the Acropolis ; on which stood the Parthenon and the Erechtheum ; (b) the extent of Athens in the time of Pericles, with the Long Walls, planned by Themistocles, which linked it to the port of the Piræus, thus making the centre of a maritime empire independent of attacks on the mainland ; (c) the Propontis, through which the main trade of Greece with the Black Sea passed, and the numerous Greek settlements on its shores. One interpretation of the Trojan war is that it was a struggle for the control of this important trade-route, which could be interrupted by Troy (Ilium) ; (d) the island of Crete, which was the centre of the prehistoric Minoan Empire, but played an unimportant part in Greek history.

Plate 8 is a supplement to **Plate 6-7**, showing not only continental Greece, but the islands of the Aegean and the wealthy Greek cities on the coast of Asia Minor, through which the Greeks were brought into conflict with the Persians. The map is coloured to show the four racial or linguistic groups which the Greeks recognised among themselves. Green is the colour of the Ionians, whose only representative on the mainland was Athens, the natural capital of the Ionian peoples, though in the earliest period this pre-eminence might have been claimed by the great colonising city of Miletus in Asia Minor. A mere glance at the distribution of the green colour in this map is enough to show why Athens became the capital of a maritime empire. Of these four races : (1) the *Achaeans* represent the ruling race of the heroic age, displaced by later migrations ; (2) the *Dorians* were the latest Greek immigrants in the tenth century B.C. ; Sparta, the greatest Dorian centre, retained leadership throughout the classic period ; (3) the *Ionians* were in the classic age the chief rivals of the Dorians and the chief source of Greek art and thought, first in Asia Minor and later in Athens ; they were probably, in the main, not only pre-Dorian but pre-Achaean ; (4) the *Aeolians* broadly represent all the other pre-Dorian Hellenic peoples. These divisions have not much historical value, except that they counted for a good deal among the Greeks themselves—especially the distinction between Dorian and Ionian, which was brought into sharp antithesis by the conflict of the Spartans and the Athenians.

Plate 9a shows the division of Greece between the two sides in the Peloponnesian War. The Athenian Empire, beginning as a confederacy of maritime states for common action against the Persians after the Persian invasion, developed into an empire when the treasury of the league was transferred from the sacred island of Delos to Athens (450 B.C.). Its members were later grouped into five districts, (1) Ionia, (2) Hellespont, (3) Thrace, (4) Caria, (5) the islands. Direct Athenian settlements or *cleruchies* were made in Euboea, Andros, Naxos, Aegina, Melos, Scyros, Imbros, Lemnos, Sinope, several cities in Chalci-dice, and the island of Lesbos. The critical struggle for Syracuse is illustrated by **Fig. 3.**

The principal map on **Plate 9b** shows the huge empire of Alexander, who brought all Greece under his sway and then conquered the Persian Empire (334–323 B.C.). This conquest was the means of extending the influence of Greek civilisation over the East, as far as the Indus valley ;

and this period of expansion is known as the "Hellenistic" period. Alexander's conquering march is shown on the map. An empire which was so swiftly created could not be expected to last long. It broke up into sections under

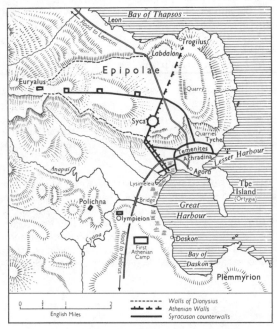

FIG. 3.—SYRACUSE

Alexander's generals, who are known as the Diadochi or successors. This division is shown in the smaller map, 9c. The chief of these kingdoms were: (1) Asia Minor and Syria under Seleucus and his successors the Seleucids; (2) Egypt under the Ptolemies; (3) Macedonia under the successors of Antigonus Gonatas; (4) Pergamum under the Attalids. It was with these Powers that the expanding empire of Rome was brought into conflict; their weakness made its conquests easier, and they were gradually merged in the Roman Empire.

Plate 10–11. This double-page plate is intended to illustrate the whole history of Rome and her Empire. On the main map, which is meant for general reference, note the way in which the empire was linked together by great roads, only the principal of which can be shown. It is probable that transport on these great roads was as swift and efficient as at any period in European history down to the coming of the railway; while the sea formed an equally valuable means of holding this Mediterranean empire together. Note, secondly, the distinction between the limits of the empire as they were when the empire was first systematically organised under Augustus, and the extensions subsequently made down to the time of Trajan: these extensions, shown by a scarlet line, include, in the west, Britain and Mauretania; in the centre, Dacia; in the east Cappadocia, Armenia, Mesopotamia and inland Syria. If Augustus' attempt to subjugate northern Germany had not been disastrously defeated, the Roman Empire might have had a shorter and more defensible frontier, along the line of the Elbe, the Bohemian mountains and the Carpathians.

The first of the smaller maps (11b) shows (a) the area of the Carthaginian Empire, which was the first external foe of Rome, then (240 B.C.) a purely Italian power; and (b) the stages in the growth of the Roman Empire. The

first advances were due to the Punic wars, of which the first gave to Rome the islands of Corsica and Sardinia, and the second Sicily and the Carthaginian coast of Spain. Then came a period of strenuous warfare, extending over eighty years (201–120 B.C.), which gave to Rome Cisalpine Gaul, bringing Italy up to the Alps, the greater part of Spain, south-eastern Gaul (Narbonensis), the home-territory of Carthage (which became the province of Africa), Macedonia, Greece, and the province of Asia (western Asia Minor): by this time (120 B.C.) Rome had become the dominant power in the Mediterranean. The third stage—the last century of the Republic, down to the death of Julius Cæsar, 44 B.C.—saw Cæsar's conquest of Gaul, the conquest of the African coast (Numidia and Cyrenaica), Syria, and the north and south coasts of Asia Minor. Before his death (14 A.D.) the emperor Augustus had completed the conquest of Spain, subjugated the Alpine regions of Rhaetia, Noricum and Pannonia, and the Balkan regions of Illyricum and Moesia, thus securing the whole line of the Danube as a frontier; he had annexed Egypt, and had brought the central part of Asia Minor under his control; the boundaries of the empire had been rounded off. His successors added Britain, Mauretania, Thrace, Cappadocia and inland Syria; the final conquests, which were to be impermanent, included Dacia, in Europe, and Armenia and Mesopotamia in Asia.

The second of the smaller maps (10a) shows how Augustus divided the empire between himself and the Senate for administrative purposes, keeping for himself the warlike frontier provinces where armies had to be maintained, and leaving to the control of the Senate the more peaceful provinces.

Finally, this Plate contains two plans of the city of Rome, one for the Republican, the other for the Imperial period.

Plate 12-13. This large double plate, like the corresponding plate of Greece, is intended for general reference in studying the whole history of Italy. It shows (by underlining) the numerous Greek colonies of "Magna Graecia." It also shows, in different symbols, the Roman and the Latin colonies by means of which the country was held down as it was conquered; and the great network of roads by which it was held together, and all its parts were made swiftly accessible. Note how the organising genius of Augustus extended the northern boundary of Italy, the heart of the empire, from the indefensible foothills of the mountains to the watershed.—The two plans, which show the forum of republican Rome, and the grandiose fora of imperial Rome, may be regarded as supplements to the plans of the city on the preceding plate.

Plate 14 is a politically coloured supplement to **Plate 12-13**, meant to illustrate, in particular, the methods whereby Rome conquered Italy. The process begins with the unification, after much fighting, of Latium, of which a more detailed map is given in the inset, **Plate 14b.** The second inset, **14c**, is meant to illustrate roughly the distribution of the racial stocks in Italy at an early date: the flood of conquered slaves which later poured into the peninsula turned it into a *colluvies gentium.* In the main map the Roman and Latin colonies are indicated, in most cases with the dates of their foundation. Note that Italy Proper excluded the whole valley of the Po and its tributaries. This, the most fertile part of Italy, had once been largely occupied by the Etruscans, while in the east and west the Venetian and Ligurian races remained distinct. Conquered by the invading Gauls, this district became known as Gallia Cisalpina, and even after it was

conquered, it was administered as a provincia until Augustus revised the imperial system. Its boundary was the little river Rubicon, which Cæsar crossed when he declared war upon the republic.

Plates 15 and **16**, coloured politically, show more clearly than is possible in **Plate 10–11** (with which they should be compared) Augustus' division of the Empire into provinces. The post-Augustan provinces are coloured buff. The whole coast of the Black Sea was under imperial control, but only the Crimean peninsula was organised as a province.

Plate 17, while primarily designed to illustrate the Roman occupation of Britain, also gives the names and distribution of the British tribes whom the Romans found in the island ; and, being coloured physically, it shows how hills, forests, and marshes broke up the country—obstacles which the Roman roads largely overcame. Though the Romans held Britain for nearly four centuries, little is known about their organisation : it is not even possible to give the boundaries of the provinces into which the island was divided. But note (1) the system of fortification against the northern savages—more fully shown in the inset, **17b** ; (2) the road-system, with London as its centre, because London was the lowest crossing-place on the Thames for the roads coming from the south-east coast ; (3) the location of the three main armies of occupation (legions), at York, Chester, and Caerleon ; (4) the few organised towns—Colchester, Gloucester, Lincoln, York, and St. Albans ; (5) the Saxon shore (from the Wash to the Severn), fortified during the fourth century as a protection against the German pirates.

Plate 18–19. This plate is intended to illustrate the geographical relations between western civilisation with the Roman Empire as its guardian, and the other civilisations which existed in the world before the breakdown of the Roman Empire began. The map is coloured to show broadly the character of the soil, and of its natural products. Note that there are three fertile and productive regions, each of which gave birth to a civilisation of its own—Europe in the west, India and China in the east. But note also that they are separated from one another by huge barriers of mountains, deserts, or semi-desert countries, which occupy the central area in the map. Out of this region nomadic tribes burst in at intervals upon each of the great civilisations, which strove in vain to keep them at arm's length. For this purpose, the frontier-fortresses of the Roman Empire may be compared with the Great Wall of China. About 200 A.D., the date of this map, the Chinese Empire, which was probably the most advanced of these civilisations, had extended its nominal sway over a vast region of Central Asia, in the hope of keeping the barbarians in check. India (then passing through one of her periodic phases of disorder), saw a large part of her richest territories under the control of a Central Asiatic dynasty ; Rome had pushed out her frontiers to the north and east in the hope of reducing the danger, but was soon to lose these gains. But between these rival civilisations—all threatened, from the same source, by a common danger—there was practically no contact.

The two insets show two stages in ancient history of India. In 250 B.C., when Rome had not yet begun the conflict with Carthage that was to make her the predominant power in the Mediterranean, almost the whole of India was under the enlightened and tolerant rule of the great Asoka, one of the noblest of monarchs. In 400 A.D., when the Roman Empire was already in ruins, a new Indian Empire had arisen under the Guptas and for

a moment it promised to reduce the whole sub-continent to subjection ; but before the English conquest India was never to know unity. At the same period of collapse in the west, the Sassanid kingdom, heir of the Parthians and of the Persians, was reviving past glories.

Plate 20 shows the "Lower" Empire, as it was reconstructed by Diocletian (286–305 A.D.) and Constantine (306–337 A.D.) after the first irruptions of the German barbarians in 250 A.D. and the following years. The frontiers have greatly shrunk, both in Europe (Dacia) and in Asia (Mesopotamia and Armenia). There is a sharp division between the western (Latin) and the eastern (Greek) halves of the empire. Constantinople has replaced Rome as the centre of supreme authority ; and the methods of government have become those of oriental despotism, save that the Roman system of law still prevails. The empire is now divided into four great Prefectures or satrapies, and the prefectures are in their turn divided into Dioceses. In the west, the Prefecture of Gaul includes the Dioceses of Britain, Gaul and Spain ; the Prefecture of Italy includes the Dioceses of Italy, Illyricum and Africa. In the east, the Prefecture of Illyria includes the Dioceses of Macedonia (including Greece) and Dacia ; the Prefecture of the east includes the Dioceses of Pontus. Asia, the Orient (Syria) and

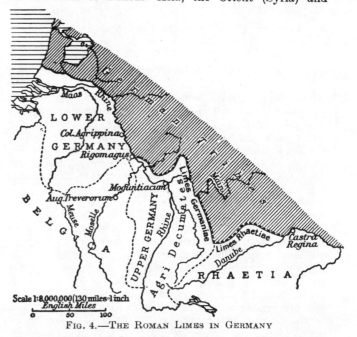

FIG. 4.—THE ROMAN LIMES IN GERMANY

Egypt. Along the weak northern frontier the German tribes are always dangerous and the fortifications of the Limes between the Rhine and the Danube have not availed to prevent the occupation of the angle between the two rivers by the Allemanni and Suevi. These barbarians were being enlisted in large numbers to fill the depleted ranks of the legions. Some of them had been converted to Christianity, which had become, under Constantine, almost the official religion of the empire. Their real veneration for the great structure of civilised society did not prevent them from desiring to enrich themselves by overrunning it ; and the downfall of the Empire under whose shelter the civilisation of Europe had absorbed the learning of Greece, the law of Rome, and the religion of Christianity was at hand. "Ancient" history had reached its term.

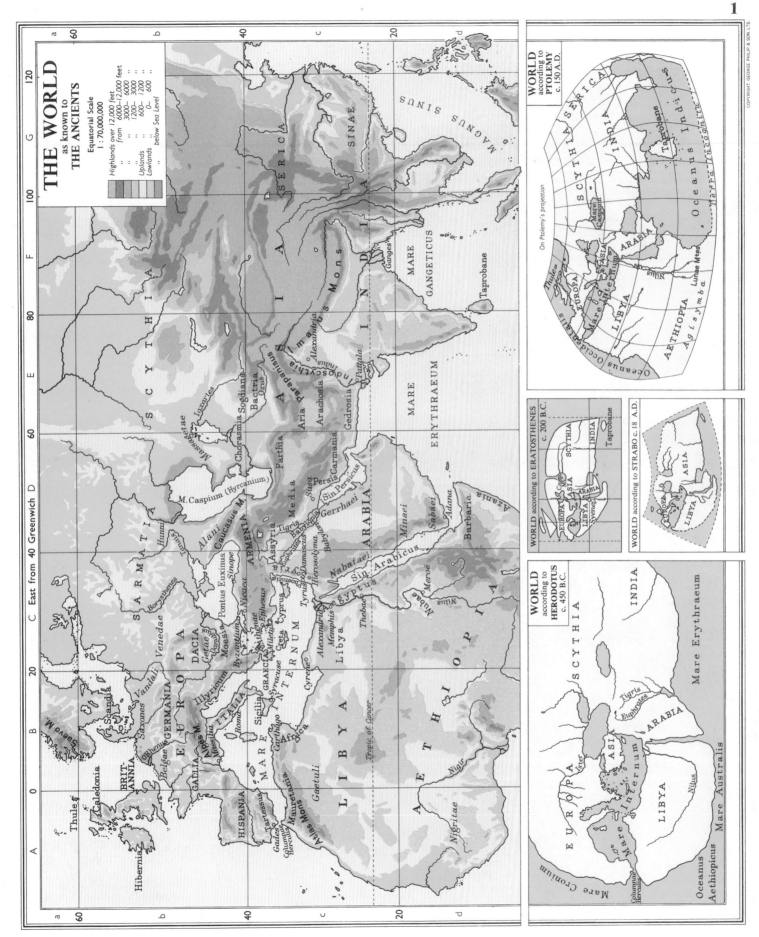

THE WORLD
as known to
THE ANCIENTS

Equatorial Scale
1 : 70,000,000

Highlands over 12,000 feet
from 6000–12,000 feet
" 3000– 6000 "
" 1200– 3000 "
Uplands " 600– 1200 "
Lowlands " 0– 600 "
below Sea Level

THE WORLD as known to THE ANCIENTS

Thule
Caledonia
Scandia
M. Sevo
BRITANNIA
Hibernia
Saxones
Orhenus
Vandali
Venedae
GERMANIA
Belgae
EUROPA
GALLIA
Alpes M.
Massilia
Roma
ITALIA
HISPANIA
Tartessus
Gades
Columnae Herculis
Mauretania
Atlas Mons
Africa
Carthago
Gaetuli
Sicilia
Syracuse
GRAECIA
Creta
Cyrene
MARE INTERNUM
Cyprus
Libya
LIBYA
Nigritae
Nigir

SARMATIA
DACIA
Getae
Danubs
Moesia
Illyricum
Byzantium
Nicaea
Athenae
Miletus
Ephesus
Pontus Euxinus
Sinope
Tanais
Humni
Alani
Caucasus M.
ARMENIA
Assyria
Tigris
Euphrates
Phoenicia
Tyrus
Hierosolyma
Damascus
Babylon
Babylonia
Susa
Media
Gerrhaei
ARABIA
Nabataei
Sin. Arabicus
Aegyptus
Damietta
Alexandria
Memphis
Thebae
Nubae
Meroë
Nilus
AETHIOPIA

SCYTHIA
Massagetae
Iaxartes
Chorasmia
Sogdiana
Oxus
Bactria
Paropanisus
Aria
Parthia
Persis
Carmania
Sin. Persicus
Minaei
Sabaei
Adana
Barbaria
Azania
MARE ERYTHRAEUM

SERICA
SINAE
I m a u s Mons
INDIA
Alexandria
Indoscythia
Indus
Pattala
Arachosia
Gedrosia
Gunges
MARE GANGETICUS
Taprobane

MAGNUS SINUS

M. Caspium (Hyrcanium)
Borysthenes

Tropic of Cancer

East from 40 Greenwich

COPYRIGHT. GEORGE PHILIP & SON, LTD.

WORLD according to PTOLEMY c. 150 A.D.

SCYTHIA
SERICA
INDIA
Taprobane
Oceanus Indicus
Terra Incognita
Thule
ASIA
Mare Caspium
ARABIA
EUROPA
Mare Internum
LIBYA
AETHIOPIA
Agisymba
Nilus
Lunae Mtes
Sinus
Oceanus Occidentalis

On Ptolemy's projection

WORLD according to ERATOSTHENES c. 200 B.C.

EUROPA
Casp.
M.Int.
ASIA
SCYTHIA
INDIA
LIBYA
ARABIA
Taprobane

WORLD according to STRABO c. 18 A.D.

EUROPA
ASIA
LIBYA
Syene

WORLD according to HERODOTUS c. 450 B.C.

SCYTHIA
INDIA
EUROPA
Ister
ASIA
Mare Internum
Tigris
Euphrates
ARABIA
LIBYA
Nilus
Mare Erythraeum
Columnae Herculis
Oceanus
Aethiopicus
Mare Cronium
Mare Australis

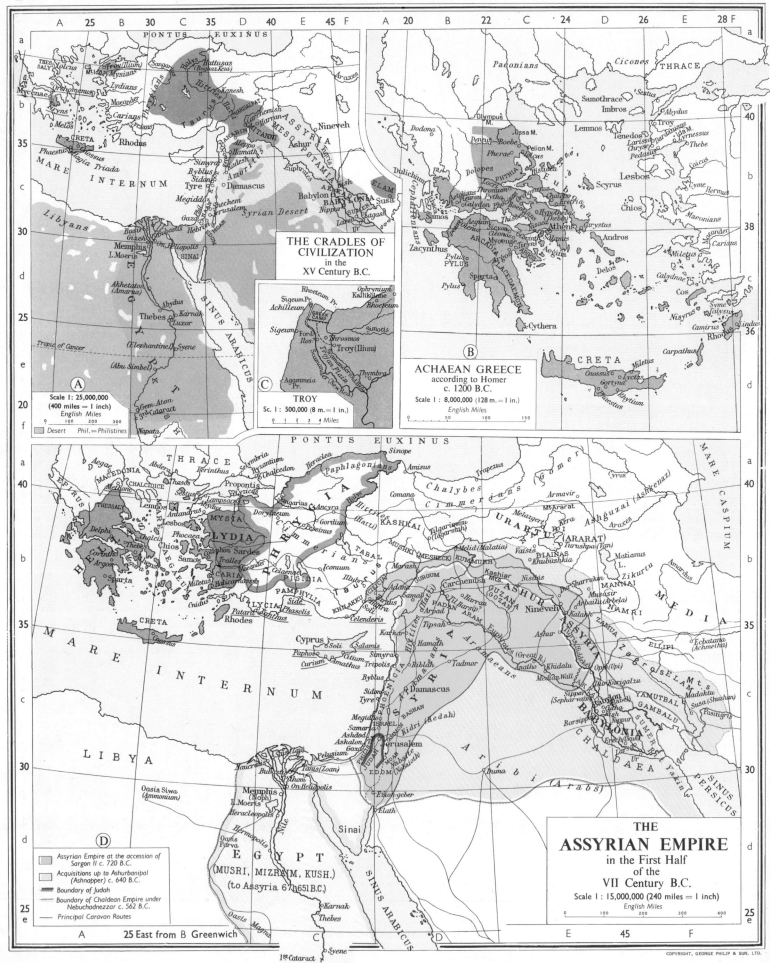

2

THE CRADLES OF CIVILIZATION in the XV Century B.C.

Scale 1 : 25,000,000
(400 miles = 1 inch)
English Miles
0   100   200   300

Desert   Phil.= Philistines

C TROY
Sc. 1 : 500,000 (8 m.= 1 in.)
0 1 2 3 4 Miles

B ACHAEAN GREECE according to Homer c. 1200 B.C.
Scale 1 : 8,000,000 (128 m.= 1 in.)
English Miles
0   50   100   150

THE ASSYRIAN EMPIRE in the First Half of the VII Century B.C.
Scale 1 : 15,000,000 (240 miles = 1 inch)
English Miles
0   100   200   300   400

D
Assyrian Empire at the accession of Sargon II c. 720 B.C.

Acquisitions up to Ashurbanipal (Ashnapper) c. 640 B.C.

Boundary of Judah

Boundary of Chaldean Empire under Nebuchadnezzar c. 562 B.C.

Principal Caravan Routes

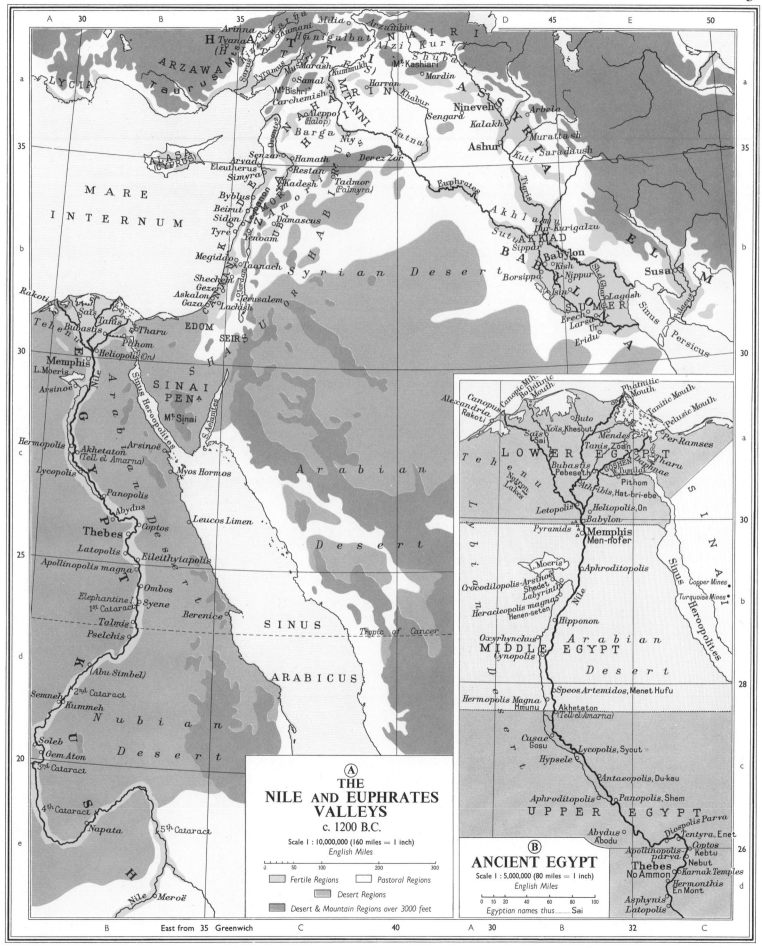

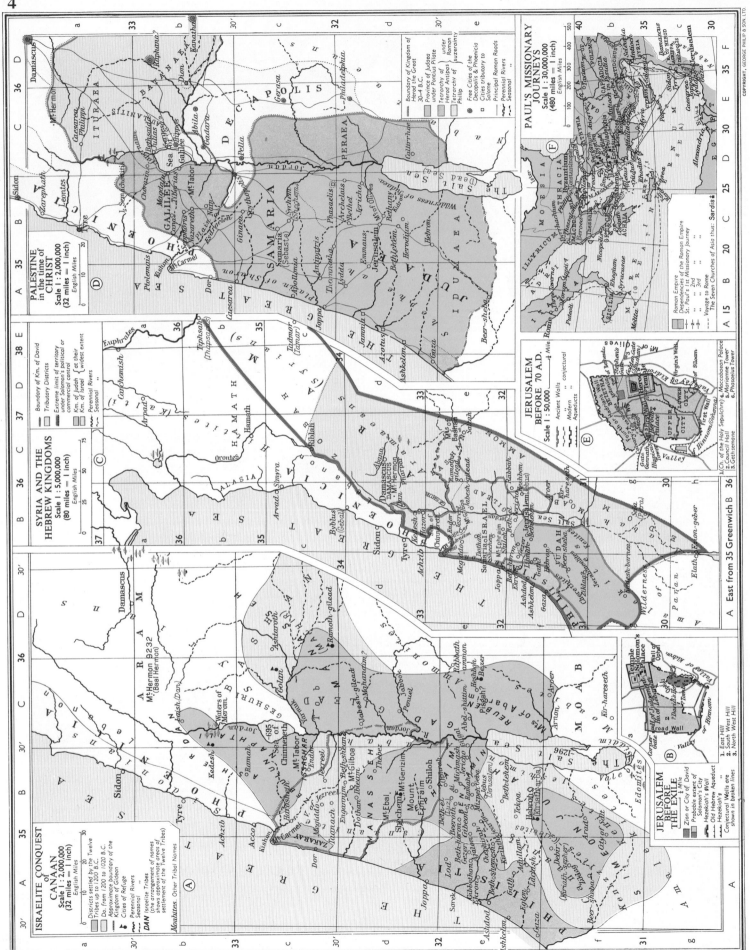

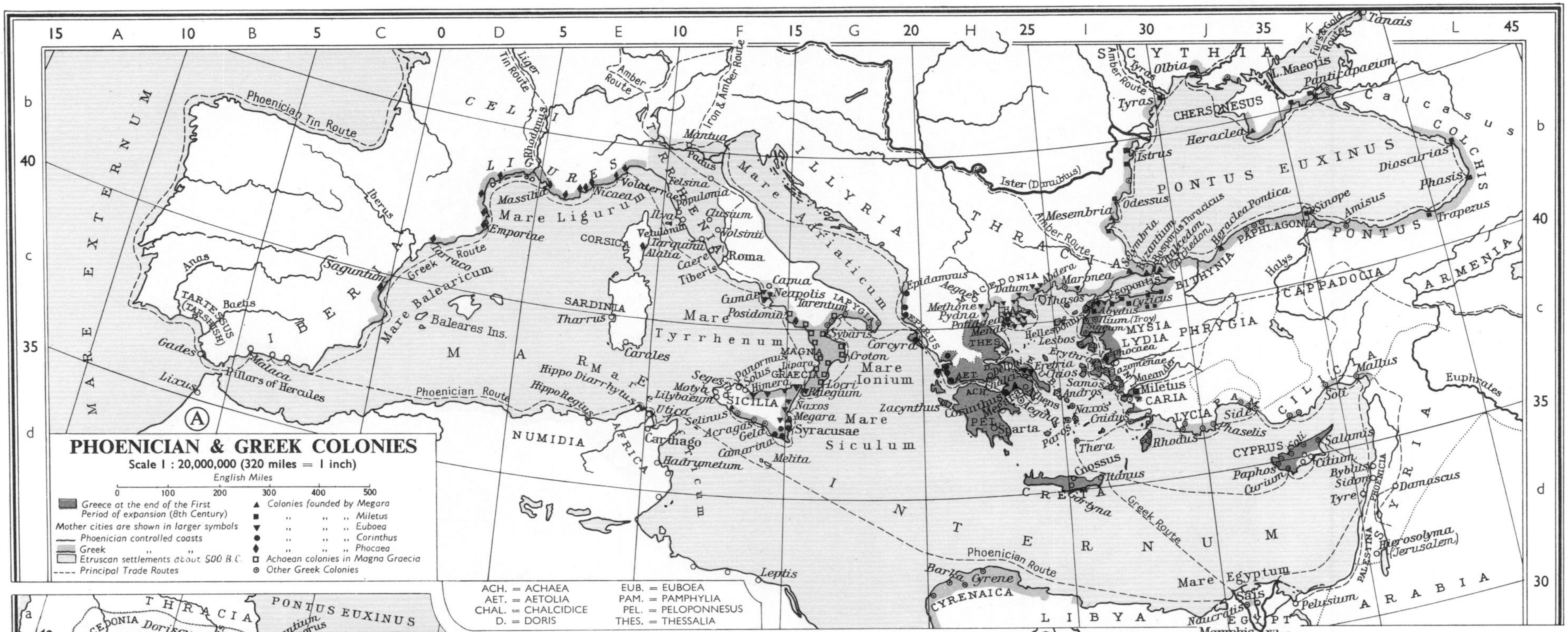

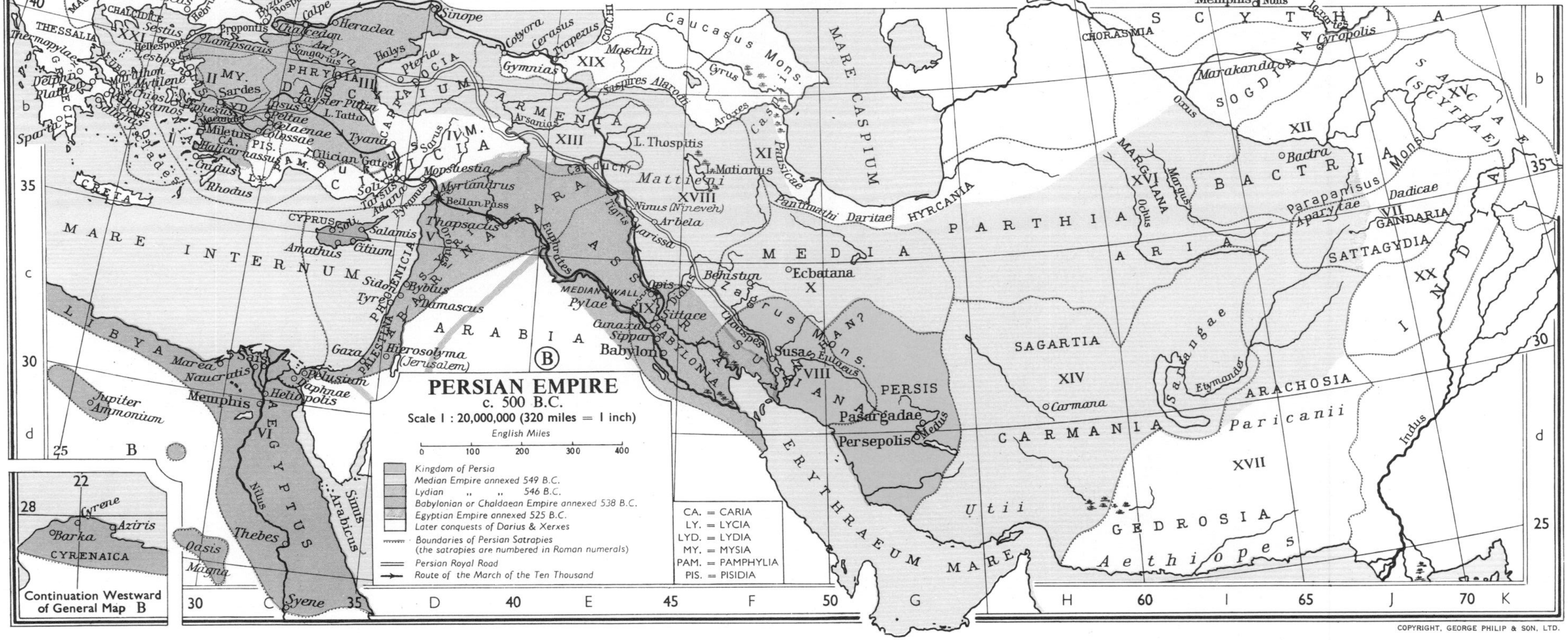

PHOENICIAN & GREEK COLONIES

Scale 1 : 20,000,000 (320 miles = 1 inch)

English Miles
100 200 300 400 500

Legend:
- Greece at the end of the First Period of expansion (8th Century)
- Colonies (founded by Megara ▲ Miletus ■ Euboea ▶ Corinthus)
- Mother cities are shown in larger symbols
- Phoenician controlled coasts
- Greek
- Etruscan settlements about 500 B.C.
- Achaean colonies in Magna Graecia
- Other Greek Colonies
- Principal Trade Routes

ACH. = ACHAEA	EUB. = EUBOEA	
AET. = AETOLIA	PAM. = PAMPHYLIA	
CHAL. = CHALCIDICE	PEL. = PELOPONNESUS	
D. = DORIS	THES. = THESSALIA	

(A)

PERSIAN EMPIRE
c. 500 B.C.

Scale 1 : 20,000,000 (320 miles = 1 inch)

English Miles
100 200 300 400

Legend:
- Kingdom of Persia
- Median Empire annexed 549 B.C.
- Lydian " 546 B.C.
- Babylonian or Chaldaean Empire annexed 538 B.C.
- Egyptian Empire annexed 525 B.C.
- Later conquests of Darius & Xerxes
- Boundaries of Persian Satrapies (the satrapies are numbered in Roman numerals)
- Persian Royal Road
- Route of the March of the Ten Thousand

CA. = CARIA	LY. = LYCIA
LYD. = LYDIA	MY. = MYSIA
PAM. = PAMPHYLIA	PIS. = PISIDIA

(B)

Continuation Westward of General Map B

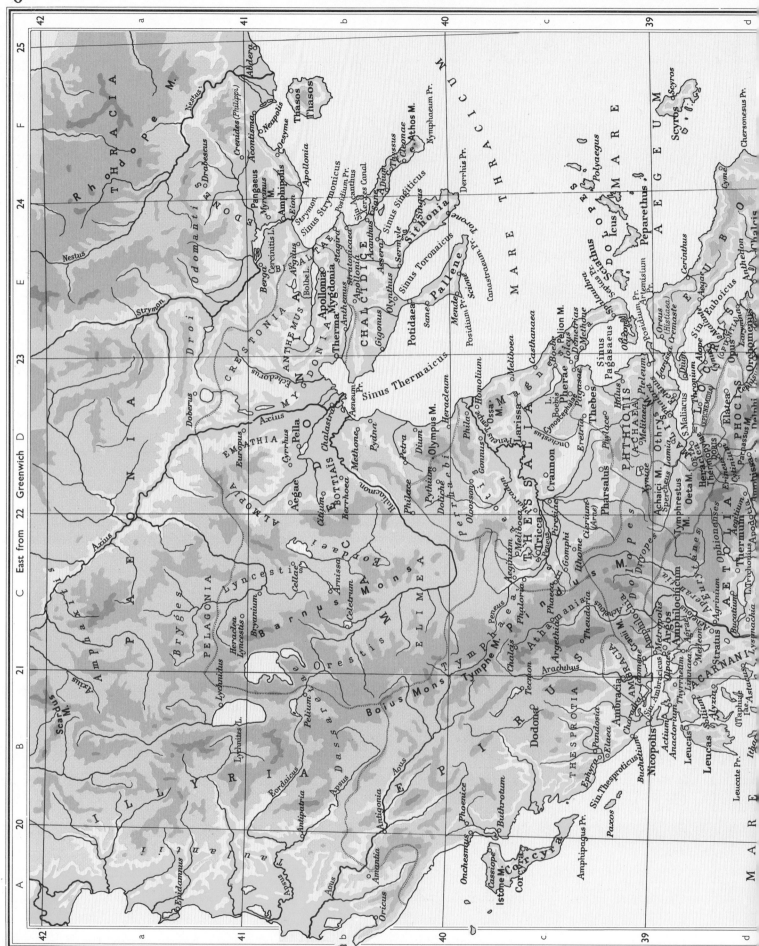

Map Labels

Grid references (top): 42, a, 41, b, 40, c, 39, d
Grid references (right/latitude): 25, F, 24, E, 23, D, 22, C, 21, B, 20, A

East from 22 Greenwich

THRACIA

Rhodope M.

ODOMANTI

Nestus

Strymon

Crenides (Philippi)
Acontisma
Neapolis
Oesyme
Apollonia
Amphipolis
Eion
Pangaeus M.
Myrcinus
Cercinitis L.
Berga
Argilus
Bisaltae
Bobel.
Stagira
Acanthus
Xerxes Canal
Stratonicea
Apollonia
Sane
Acrothoi
Athos M.
c. Nymphaeum Pr.
Derrhis Pr.
Singus
Sermyle
Assera
Olynthus
Sinus Singiticus
Sinus Toronaicus
Torone
Canastraeum Pr.

Thasos
Thasos

MARE THRACICUM

Posidium Pr.
Mende
Scione
Pallene
Potidaea
Gigonus
Sinus Thermaicus
Aenium
Methone
Pydna
Petra
Dium
Olympus M.
Heracleum

SITHONIA

CHALCIDICE

ANTHEMUS
Apollonia
Therma
Anthemus
MYGDONIA
CRESTONIA
Echedorus
Chalastra
Aloros
Cyrrhus
Pella
Axius
EMATHIA
Europus
Aegae
Citium
Berrhoea
BOTTIAIS
Mieza

Peparethus
Scopelus
SCIOPELODES

MARE AEGEUM

Scyros
Scyros

Sinus Pagasaeus
Pagasae
Pherae
Pteleum
Oleus
Demetrias
Methone
Casthanaea
Meliboea
Ossa M.
Boebe
Boebis L.
Pelion M.
Homolium
Gonnus
Larissa
Cynoscephalae
Pheneus
Crannon
Scotussa
Pharsalus
Atrax
Pharcadon
Pelinna
Phaloria
Gomphi
Tricca
Pirasiae
Aeginium
Ithome Cierium M.
Metropolis
Argos
Amphilochicum
Amphilochia

THESSALIA
PERRHAEBI
Phila
Pythium
Oloosson
Doliche
Phayttus

PHTHIOTIS
(ACHAEA)
Phthiotic Thebes
Phylace
Halus

Melitaea
S. Maliacus
Lamia
Thronium
Heraclea
Thermopylae
Oeta M.
Sperchius
Oetaei M. Othrys

DOLOPES
Ctimene
Dryopes
Angeiae
Phaeca
Ithome
Athamania
Argithea
Theudoria
TYMPHAEA
Pharoria
Chalais
Peneus
Tymphe M.

DORIS
PHOCIS
Cytinium
Apollonia
Tithronium
Lilaea
Parnassus M.
Trachis
Aegitium
Thermum
Trichonium
Lysimachia

AETOLIA

MOLOSSIS
EPIRUS
Dodona
Tecmon
Phoenice
Antigonia
Buthrotum
Oricus
Onchesmus
Istone M.
Cassiope
Corcyra
Corcyra

THESPROTIA
Ephyra
Pandosia
Eluea
Charadra
AMBRACIA
Ambracia
Arachthus
Argos
Amphilochicum

Nicopolis
Actium
Anactorium
Thyrrheum
Sin. Ambracicus
Olpae
Stratus
ACARNANIA
Metropolis
Palaerus
Alyzia
Sollium
Leucas
Leucas
Leucate Pr.
Ithaca
Taphiae
Astacus

Pr. Amphipagus
Paxos

MARE

ILLYRIA

Scardus M.
Axius
Epidamnus

Amphaxitis
PAEONIA

Lychnidus
Lychnitis L.
Heraclea Lyncestis
Brygium
Bryanium
Celetrum
PELAGONIA
Lyncestis
Barnus Mons
Orestis
ELIMEA
Bolus Mons
Peirum M.
Eordaicus
Dassaretae
ATINTANES
Apsus
Aous
Antipatra
Amantia

Bora Mons

Almopia
Haliacmon
Titarius M.
Tymphaeus M.

Oric us

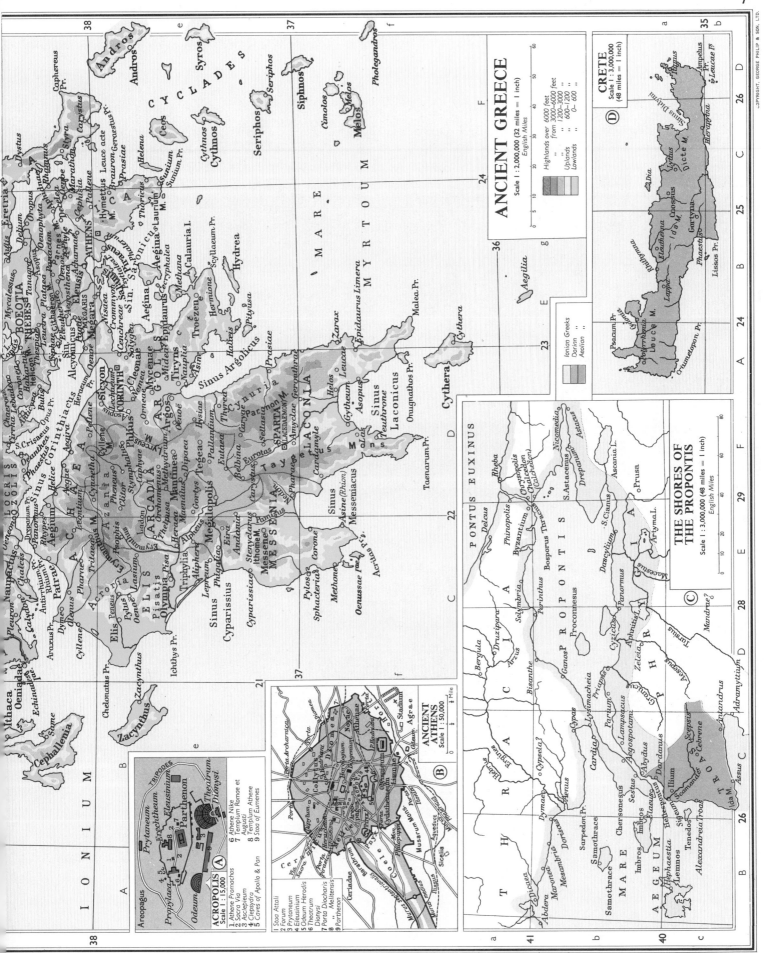

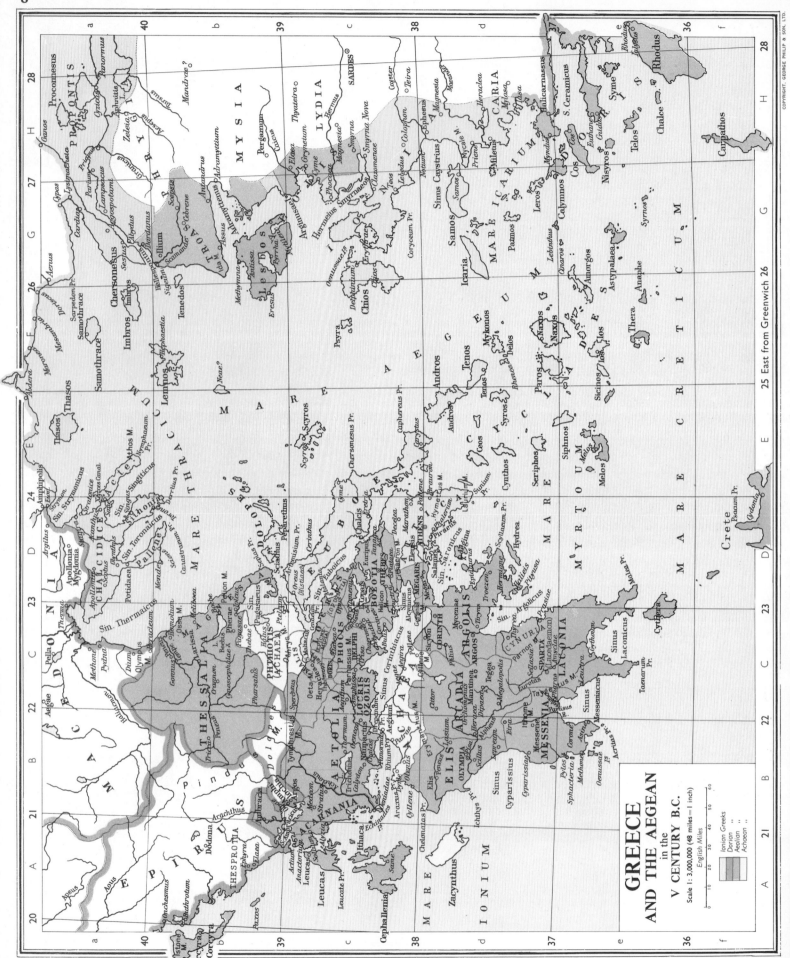

8

GREECE
AND THE AEGEAN
in the
V CENTURY B.C.

Scale 1: 3,000,000 (48 miles = 1 inch)

English Miles

Ionian Greeks
Dorian   „
Aeolian   „
Achaean   „

25 East from Greenwich 26

COPYRIGHT. GEORGE PHILIP & SON. LTD.

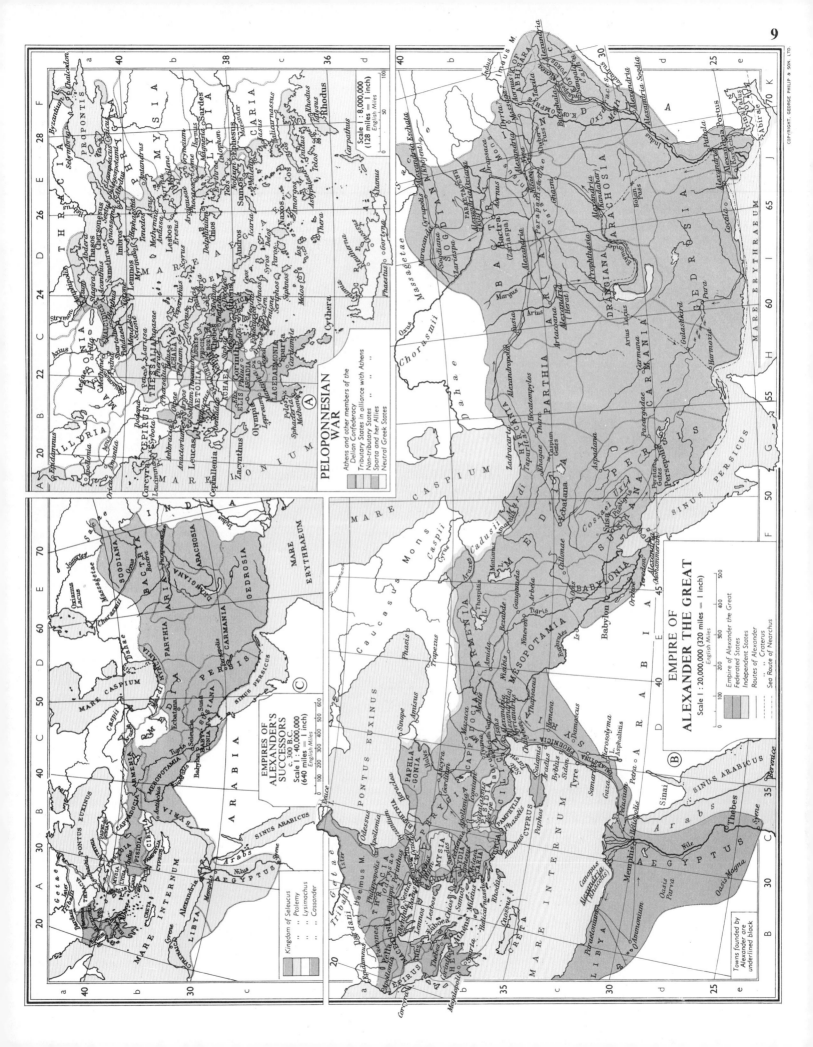

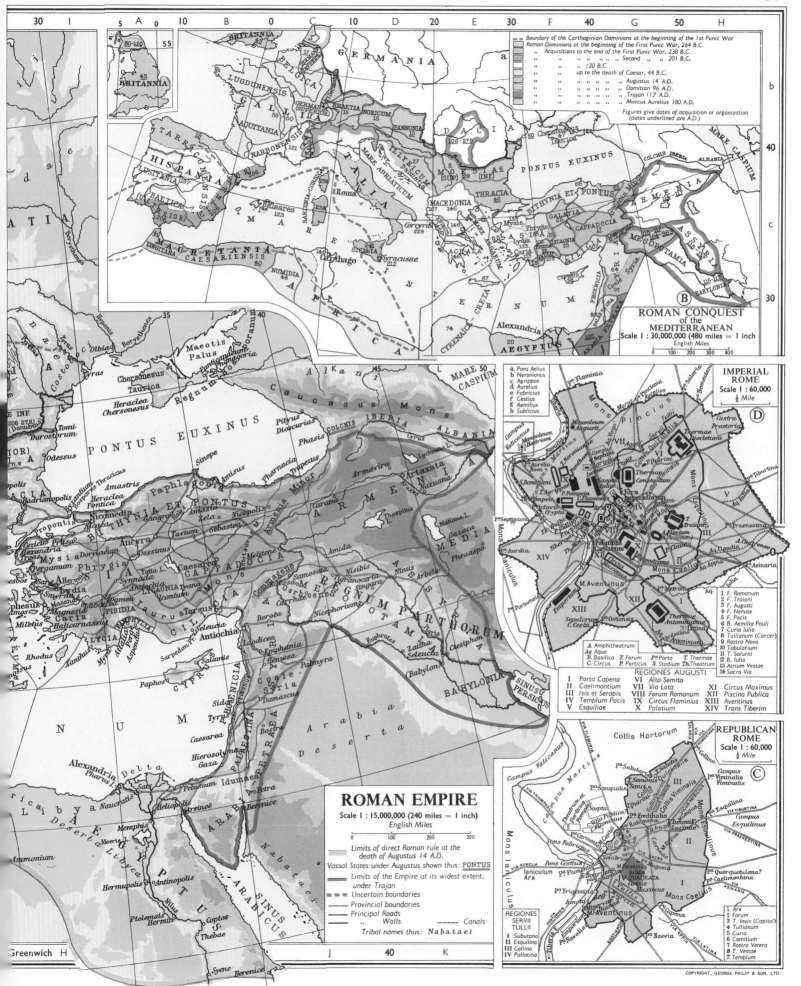

ROMAN CONQUEST of the MEDITERRANEAN

Scale 1 : 30,000,000 (480 miles = 1 inch)

English Miles

Boundary of the Carthaginian Dominions at the beginning of the 1st Punic War
Roman Dominions at the beginning of the First Punic War, 264 B.C.
"   "   Acquisitions to the end of the First Punic War, 238 B.C.
"   "   "   "   "   "   Second "   "   201 B.C.
"   "   "   "   "   120 B.C.
"   "   "   up to the death of Caesar, 44 B.C.
"   "   "   "   "   "   Augustus 14 A.D.
"   "   "   "   "   "   Domitian 96 A.D.
"   "   "   "   "   "   Trajan 117 A.D.
"   "   "   "   "   "   Marcus Aurelius 180 A.D.
Figures give dates of acquisition or organization
(dates underlined are A.D.)

IMPERIAL ROME

Scale 1 : 60,000
½ Mile

a. Pons Aelius
b. Neronianus
c. Agrippae
d. Aurelius
e. Fabricius
f. Cestius
g. Aemilius
h. Sublicius

A. Amphitheatrum
Aq. Aqua
B. Basilica
C. Circus
F. Forum
P. Porticus
Pa. Porta
S. Stadium
T. Thermae
Th. Theatrum

1 F. Romanum
2 F. Traiani
3 F. Augusti
4 F. Nervae
5 F. Pacis
6 B. Aemilia Pauli
7 Curia Iulia
8 Tullianum (Carcer)
9 Rostra Nova
10 Tabularium
11 Saturni
12 B. Iulia
13 Atrium Vestae
14 Sacra Via

REGIONES AUGUSTI

I Porta Capena	VI Alta Semita	XI Circus Maximus
II Caelimontium	VII Via Lata	XII Piscina Publica
III Isis et Serapis	VIII Forum Romanum	XIII Aventinus
IV Templum Pacis	IX Circus Flaminius	XIV Trans Tiberim
V Esquiliae	X Palatium	

ROMAN EMPIRE

Scale 1 : 15,000,000 (240 miles = 1 inch)

English Miles

Limits of direct Roman rule at the death of Augustus 14 A.D.
Vassal States under Augustus shown thus: PONTUS
Limits of the Empire at its widest extent, under Trajan
Uncertain boundaries
Provincial boundaries
Principal Roads
"   "   Walls
Canals
Tribal names thus: Nabataei

REPUBLICAN ROME

Scale 1 : 60,000
½ Mile

REGIONES SERVII TULLII

I Suburana
II Esquilina
III Collina
IV Pallatina

1 Arx
2 Forum
3 T. Iovis (Capitol)
4 Tullianum
5 Curia
6 Comitium
7 Rostra Vetera
8 T. Vestae
T. Templum

COPYRIGHT, GEORGE PHILIP & SON, LTD.

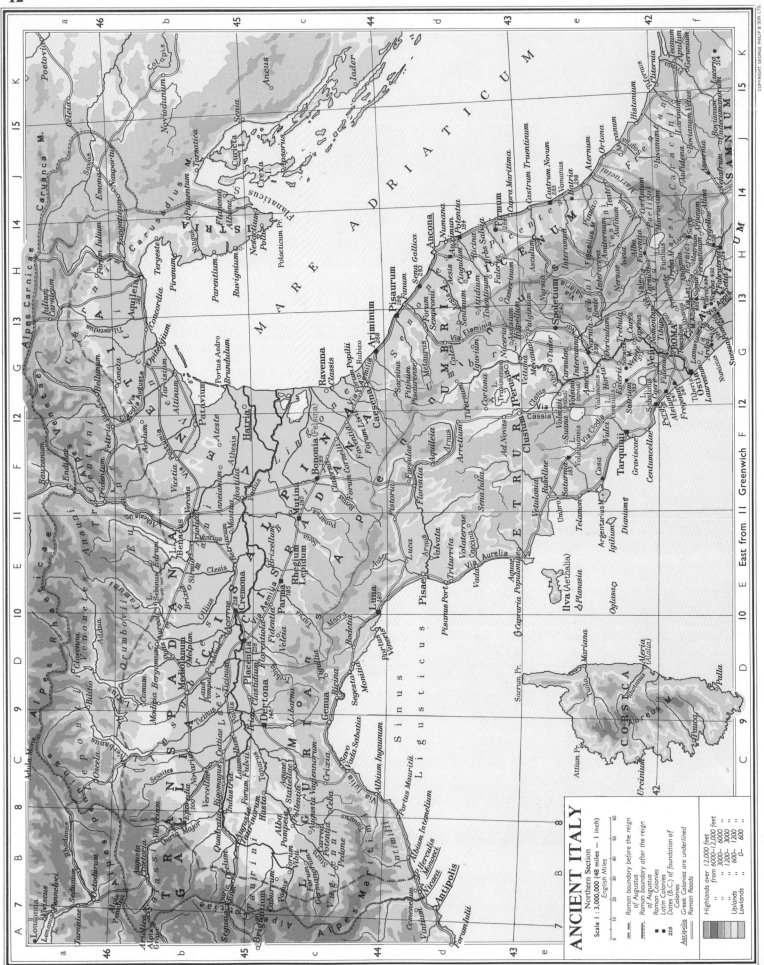

12

ANCIENT ITALY
Northern Section
Scale 1 : 3,000,000 (48 miles = 1 inch)
English Miles

Roman boundary before the reign of Augustus		
Roman boundary after the reign of Augustus		
Roman Colonies		
Latin Colonies		
Dates (B.C.) of foundation of Colonies		
Greek Colonies are underlined		
Roman Roads		

Highlands over 12,000 feet
from 6000–12,000 feet
" " 3000–6000 "
" " 1200–3000 "
Uplands " " 600–1200 "
Lowlands " " 0–600 "

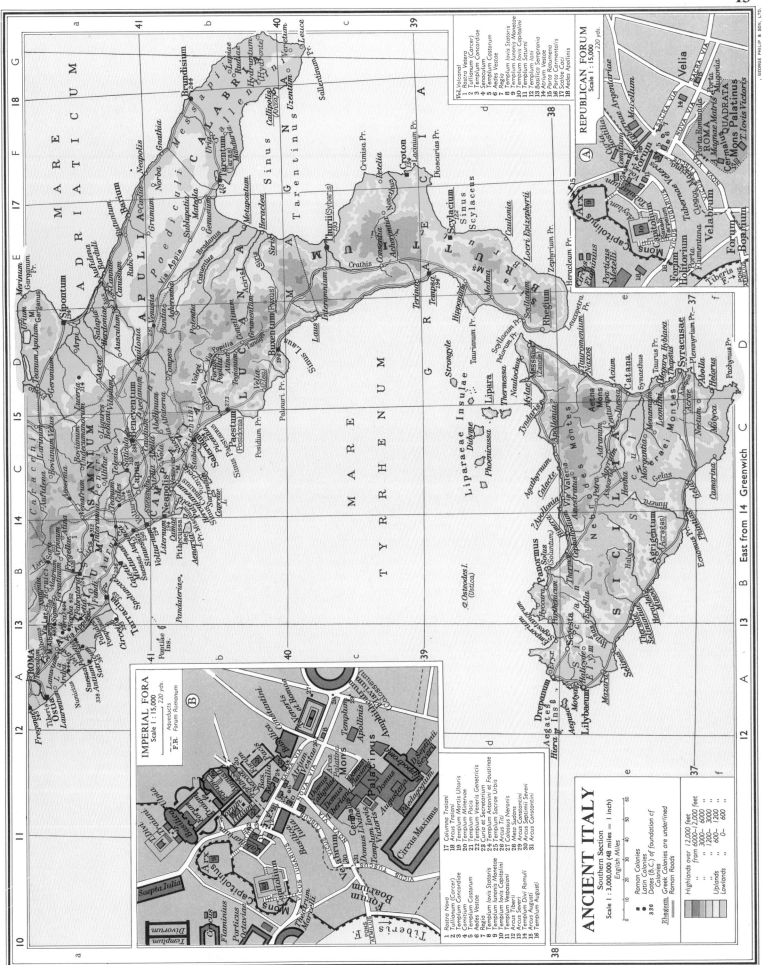

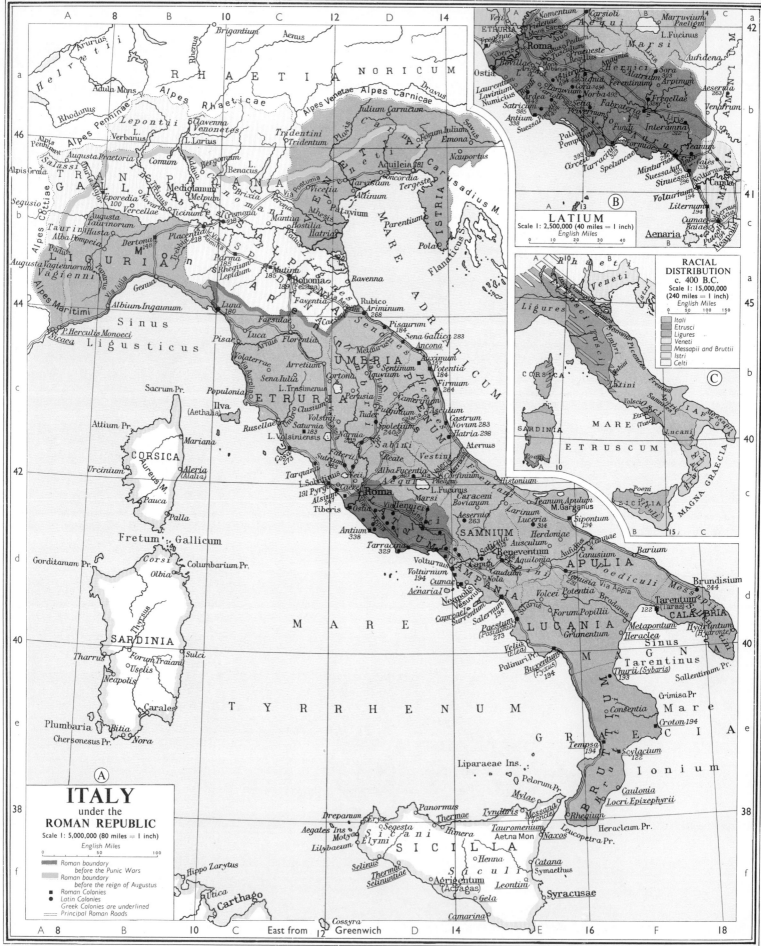

14

ITALY under the ROMAN REPUBLIC

Scale 1: 5,000,000 (80 miles = 1 inch)

English Miles

Roman boundary before the Punic Wars
Roman boundary before the reign of Augustus
■ Roman Colonies
● Latin Colonies
Greek Colonies are underlined
Principal Roman Roads

LATIUM
Scale 1: 2,500,000 (40 miles = 1 inch)
English Miles

RACIAL DISTRIBUTION c. 400 B.C.
Scale 1: 15,000,000 (240 miles = 1 inch)
English Miles

Itali
Etrusci
Ligures
Veneti
Messapii and Bruttii
Istri
Celti

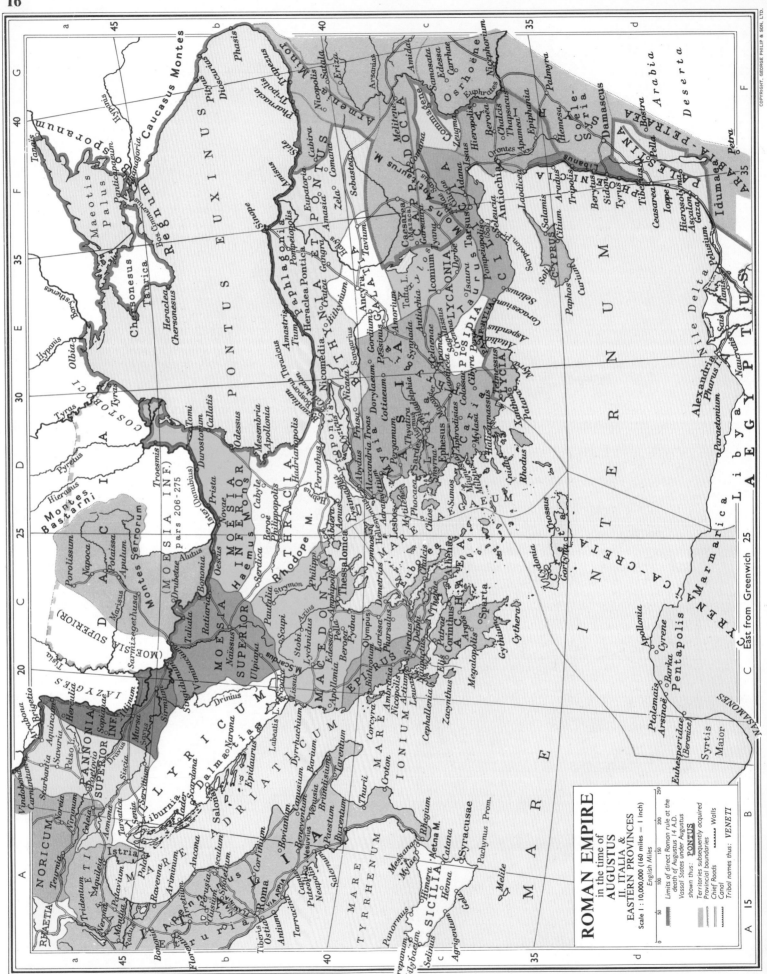

16

a
45
b
40
c
35
d

G

Caucasus Montes

Taurus
Tyras
Phasis
Dioscurias
Pityus

Bosporanum
Tanais

Maeotis
Palus

Hypanis
Bosp. Cimm.
Panticapaeum
Phanagoria

F
40

Regnum
Bosporanum

Trapezus
Tripolis

Armenia
Minor

Sinoe
Side
Polemonis
Eupatoria

Cappadocia

Melitene
Samosata
Edessa
Carrhae
Osrhoëne

Amida

Nicephorium
Palmyra

Euphrates
Beroëa

35

Chersonesus
Heraclea
Chersonesus
Tanrica

PONTUS EUXINUS

Amastris
Tium
Heraclea Pontica
Pompeiopolis
Amisus
Amasia
Zela
Sebastea
Comana

Cybira

Caesarea
Tyana
Nyanu
Adana
Tarsus
Seleucia

Hieropolis
Chalcis
Apamea
Epiphania
Hemesa
Orontes
Laodicea
Antiochia
Cyrrhus

Coele-
Syria
Damascus

Libanus

F
35

E
35

Olbia
Hypanis
Tyras

Nicomedia
Nicaea
Bithynium

Bithynia
Paphlagonia
Gangra

Galatia
Ancyra
Gordium
Pessinus
Tavium

Cappadocia

Cabira
Iconium
Derbe
Lycaonia

Cilicia
Pompeiopolis
Berytus
Sidon
Tyrus

Cyprus
Salamis
Citium
Aradus
Tripolis

Palestina
Caesarea
Pella
Hierosolyma
Ascalon
Gaza
Idumaea

Arabia-Petraea

E

Costoboci
Pyretus
Hierasus
Tyras

Montes
Bastarni

Dacia

Tomi
Callatis
Odessus
Mesembria
Apollonia

Moesia Inferior
(Moesia Inf.)
pars 206-275

Thracia
Bosporus Thracius
Byzantium
Perinthus
Propontis

Mysia
Pergamum
Adramyttium
Assus

Phrygia
Dorylaeum
Cotiaeum
Synnada
Apamea
Laodicea
Colossae
Sardes
Philadelphia
Thyatira
Smyrna
Ephesus
Magnesia
Tralles
Aphrodisias
Mylasa
Halicarnassus

Asia
Caria
Lycia
Xanthus
Patara
Myra

Rhodus

Paphos
Curium

D
30

Drobetae
Durostorum
Prista
Novae
Oescus
Ratiaria

Moesia
Superior
(Moesia Superior)

Haemus M.

Serdica
Beroe
Philippopolis
Hadrianopolis

Rhodope M.
Aenus
Abdera
Maronea

Lemnos
Lesbos
Mytilene

Aegaeum
Mare
Chios
Samos
Icaria
Miletus
Cnidus

Crete (Creta)
Cydonia
Gortyna

D
30

C
25

Porolissum
Napoca
Potaissa
Apulum

Marisus

Naissus
Ulpiana
Scupi
Stobi
Lychnidus
Axius
Scardus

Macedonia
Pautalia
Pella
Edessa
Beroea
Thessalonica
Amphipolis
Philippi
Strymon

Chalcidice
Olympus
Larissa
Pharsalus
Demetrias

Epirus
Nicopolis
Actium
Ambracia

Achaea
Thebae
Athenae
Corinthus
Argos
Sparta
Megalopolis
Elis
Patrae
Olympia

Gythium
Cythera

Mare Ionium
Cephallenia
Zacynthus

Apollonia
Ptolemais
Arsinoë
Cyrene
Barka
Berenice
Euhesperidae

Pentapolis

Marmarica

C
25

B
20

Sarmizegethusa

Montes Serrorum

Singidunum
Viminacium
Ulpianum
Sirmium

Drinius
Sirmium
Savus
Mursa
Drinus

Pannonia
Superior
Inferior

Iazyges

Siscia
Sisak
Tisia

Dalmatia
Narona
Scardona
Salonae
Epidaurus

Illyricum
Labeatis L.
Dyrrhachium
Apollonia

Adriaticum Mare

Corcyra

Mare
Ionium

Brundisium
Barium
Tarentum
Croton
Thurii
Rhegium

Sicilia
Messana
Mylae
Aetna M.
Catana
Syracusae
Himera
Selinus
Agrigentum
Gela
Camarina
Pachynus Prom.

Syrtis
Major

Nasamones

B

A
15

Noricum
Carnuntum
Vindobona
Brigetio
Aquincum
Savaria
Poetovio
Scarbantia
Emona
Aemona
Nauportus
Tergeste

Raetia
Tridentum
Aquileia
Patavium
Verona
Mutina
Bononia
Ravenna
Ariminum
Ancona

Liburnia
Istria
Pola
Iader
Senia
Tarsatica

Italia

Roma
Ostia
Tiberis
Antium
Tarracina
Puteoli
Neapolis
Vesuvius
Salernum
Paestum
Buxentum

Mare
Tyrrhenum

Melite

Drepanum
Lilybaeum
Panormus

A
15

ROMAN EMPIRE
in the time of
AUGUSTUS
II. ITALIA &
EASTERN PROVINCES

Scale 1 : 10,000,000 (160 miles = 1 inch)

English Miles
0 50 100 150 200 250

Limits of direct Roman rule at the
death of Augustus 14 A.D.
Vassal States under Augustus
shown thus: PONTUS
Territories subsequently acquired
Provincial boundaries
Chief Roads
Canal   Walls
Tribal names thus: VENETI

45
40
35

East from Greenwich 25

Aegyptus
Libya
Alexandria
Nile Delta
Paraetonium
Naucratis
Pharus I.
Pelusium

Mare Internum

COPYRIGHT, GEORGE PHILIP & SON, LTD.

INDEX

NOTE—Each Map in the Atlas is divided into Squares by the lines of latitude and longitude, and these Squares are indicated by Reference Letters in the map borders. These Reference Letters, following each name in the Index, indicate the Square, and the succeeding Numeral indicates the Number of the Map in which each place will be found. Thus:— "Babylonia, Fc, 9b" shows that Babylonia will be found on Map 9b, and in the Square indicated by the Reference Letters "Fc".

The following abbreviations are used:—A., *Amphitheatrum* (Amphitheatre); Aest., *Aestuarium* (Estuary); Aq., *Aquaeductus* (Aqueduct); C., *Castellum* (Castle); E., East(ern); F., Fl., *Flumen* (River); Ins., *Insula(ae)* (Island(s)); I(s). *Island(s)*; K., *Kingdom*; L., *Lacus* (Lake, Loch); M., *Mons* (Mountain); Mtes., *Montes* (Mountains); Mt(s). *Mountain(s)*; N., North(ern); Pa., *Porta* (Gate); Pr., *Promontorium* (Promontory); R., *River*; S., South(ern); Th., *Theatrum* (Theatre); Val., *Valley*; W., West(ern).

ABANA, R., Cd, 4c
Abarim, Mts. of, Ce, 4a
Abar-Nahara, Db, 5b
Abdera (Hispania), Be, 15
Abdera (Thracia), Hb, 5a; Da, 9a
Abella, Cb, 13
Abellinum, Cb, 13
Abel-shittim Ce, 4a
Abergavenny (Gobannium), Ce, 17
Abhira, Ec, 18b
Abila, Cb, 4d
Abirae, Je, 9b
Abodu (Abydus), Bc, 3b
Abolla, Df, 13
Abone, De, 17
Abu Simbel Bd, 3a
Abus, Cb., 15
Abus Fl., Fc, 17
Abydus (Abodu), Bc, 3b
Abydus (Mysia), Db, 16
Acanthus, Eb, 6
Acarnania, Cd, 6
Acco, Bc, 4a
Acelum, Fb, 12
Acerrae, Db, 12
Achaea, Cd, 7
Achaea, Phthiotis, Dc, 6
Achaia, Ed, 18
Achaici, M., Dd, 6
Acharnae, Ed, 7
Achelous, F., Cd, 6
Acherontia (Bruttium), Ec, 13
Acherontia (Lucania), Db, 13
Achilleum, Inset, 2c
Achmetha (Ecbatana), Fc, 2d
Achzib, Bb, 4a
Aciris, F., Eb, 13
Acium, De, 13
Acontisma, Fb, 6
Acrae, Ce, 13
Acragas, Fc, 5a
Acritas Pr., Cf, 7
Acropolis, Inset, 7a
Acroria, Ce, 7
Acte, Argolis, Ee, 7
Acte, Chalcidice, Fc, 15
Actium, Bd, 6
Ad Novas, Fd, 12
Adana, Arabia, Gf, 18
Adana, Syria, Dc, 2d
Addua, F., Db, 12
Adramyttenus, Gb, 8
Adramyttium, Cc, 7c
Adranum, Ce, 13
Adria, Ba, 4f
Aduatuca, Db, 15
Adula Mons, Ca, 12
Adullam, Ae, 4a
Aebudae, Inset, 17a
Aecae Da, 13
Aeclanum, Da, 13
Aedes Apollinis, Inset, 13a
Aedes Magnae Matris, Inset, 13a
Aedes Vestae, Inset, 13a
Aedui, Cc, 15
Aegae (Achaea), Dd, 7
Aegae (Euboea), Ed, 6
Aegae (Macedonia), Ca, 9a
Aegates, Ins., Ad, 13
Aegilia, Eg, 7
Aegina, Ee, 7
Aeginium, Cc, 6
Aegira, Dd, 7
Aegitium, Dd, 6
Aegium, Dd, 7
Aegospotami, Ea, 9a
Aegosthena, Ed, 7
Aegusa, Ae, 13
Ægyptus, Fe, 18
Aeminium, Ad, 15
Aemona, Aa, 16
Aenaria Ins., Bb, 13

Aeneum Pr., Db, 6
Aenus, Cb, 7c
Aenus, F., Ec, 15
Aeolis, Bb, 5b; Bb, 9b; Gc, 8
Aequi, He, 12
Aesepus, F., Dc, 7c
Aesernia, Ca, 13
Aesica (Great Chesters), Inset, 17
Aesis, Hd, 12
Aesis, F., Hd, 12
Aestii, Ha, 10
Aethalia, Ee, 12
Aethiopes, Id, 5b
Aethiopia, Bd, 1
Aetna M., Ce, 13
Aetolia, Bb, 9a
Aetolians, Bb, 2b
Africa, Dd, 18
Africa, Diocese of, Eg, 20
Africa (*vetus provincia*), De, 15
Agammeia Pr., Inset, 2c
Agathyrnum, Cd, 13
Agedincum, Cc, 15
Agger Servii Tullii, Inset, 11d
Aginnum, Cd, 15
Agisymba, Inset, 1
Agora, Inset, 7b
Agrae, Inset, 7b
Agraei, Cd, 6
Agri Decumates, Dc, 15
Agrigentum (Acragas), Be, 13
Agrinium, Cd, 6
Agrippae, Inset, 11d
Agyrium, Ce, 13
Ai, Be, 4a
Ajalon, Be, 4a
Ajodhya, Fc, 18b
Akhetaton (Tell-el-Amarna), Bc, 3b
Akhlamu, Db, 3a
Akkad, Db, 3a
Alalia (Aleria), De, 12
Alani, Gc, 18
Alasa (Cyprus), Ba, 3a
Alasia, Cb, 4c
Alatrium, Ba, 13
Alauna (Maryport), Cb, 17
Alba, Cd, 15
Alba Fucentia, He, 12
Alba Pompeia, Cc, 12
Albania, Gb, 11b
Albanus, L., Aa, 13
Albanus, M., As, 13
Albis, R., Fc, 20
Albium Ingaunum, Cc, 12
Albium Intemelium, Bd, 12
Albona, Jb, 12
Alchester, Ee, 17
Aleppo (Halap), Ca, 3a
Aleria (Alalia), De, 12; Dd, 10
Alesia, Cc, 15
Alexandreia Troas, Cc, 7c
Alexandretta (Alexandria), Db, 9b
Alexandria Aegyptus, Ed, 18
Alexandria, Asia, Ec, 1
Alexandria (Alexandretta), Db, 9b
Alexandria (Bactria), Ib, 9b
Alexandria (Gedrosia), Jd, 9b
Alexandria (Herat), Ic, 9b
Alexandria (India), Jb, Kd, 9b
Alexandria (Kandahar), Jc, 9b
Alexandria (Mohammerah), Fc, 9b
Alexandria (Porus), Kc, 9b
Alexandria (Rhacotis), Bc, 9b
Alexandria Eschata (Khojent), Ja, 9b
Alexandria Oxiana (Kilif), Jb, 9b
Alexandria Portus (Karachi), Jc, 9b
Alexandria Sogdia, Kd, 9b

Alexandria Troas, He, 11
Alexandropolis, Hb, 9b
Aliphera, Ce, 7
Allemanni, Ed, 20
Allifae, Ca, 13
Allobroges, Dc, 15
Almopia, Db, 6
Alope, Dd, 6
Alpes, Ed, 20
Alpes Carnicae, Ga, 12
Alpes Cottiae, Ab, 12
Alpes Maritimi, Bc, 12
Alpes Montes, Dc, 15
Alpes Penninae, Ba, 12
Alpes Rhaeticae, Ea, 12
Alpes Venetae, Ga, 12
Alpheus, F., C, 7
Alpis Graia, Ab, 12
Alpis Pennina, Bb, 12
Alsium, Gf, 12
Alta Semita, Inset, 11d
Altinum Venetia, Gb, 12
Altinum Pannonia, Ba, 16
Alutus, F., Gd, 10
Alyzia, Bd, 6
Alzi, Ca, 3a
Amalekites, Bf, 4a
Amantia, Aa, 9a
Amardus, F., Fb, 9b
Amasia, Fb, 16
Amastris, Cd, 11
Amathus, Cc, 5b
Ambracia, Bb, 9a
Ameria, Ge, 12
Amestratus, Ce, 13
Amida, Gc, 16
Amisia, F., Db, 15
Amisus, Fb, 16
Amiternum, He, 12
Ammon, Ce, 4c
Ammonites, Cd, 4a
Ammonium, Bd, 9b
Amor, Cb, 3a
Amorgos, Fe, 8
Amorites, Cb, 3a
Amorium, Ec, 16
Ampelus Pr., Da, 7d
Amphaxitis, Ca, 6
Amphilochia, Cc, 6
Amphipagus Pr., Bc, 6
Amphipolis, Ca, 9a
Amphissa, Dd, 6
Amphitheatrum Flavium, Inset, 13b
Amphylia, Eb, 4f
Amyclae, De, 7
Anactorium, Bb, 9a
Anagnia, Ba, 13
Anaphe, I., Fe, 8
Anapus, F., De, 13
Anas, R., Bf, 20
Anatho, Ec, 2d
Anauni, Ea, 12
Ancaster (Causennae), Fd, 17
Ancona, Hd, 12
Ancus, Kc, 12
Ancyra (Phrygia), Cb, 2d
Andania, De, 7
Andematunnum, Dc, 15
Anderida (Pevensey), Gf, 17
Anderida Silva, Fe, 17
Andhra, Jf, 19
Andhra, Kingdom of, Cc, 18a
Andros, Fe, 7
Angli, Ec, 20
Anglii, Db, 15
Anio, F., Gf, 12
Anneianum, Fb, 12
Anping, Nd, 19
Anshan, Fc, 5b
Antaeopolis (Du-kau), Bc, 3b
Antandrus, Eb, 9a
Anthedon, Ed, 6
Anthemus, Eb, 6

Antiachia, Ie, 11
Anticyra, Dd, 7
Antigonia, Bb, 6
Anting, Md, 19
Antinopolis, Ig, 11
Antioch (Pisidia), Eb, 4f
Antiochia, Fd, 18
Antiochia (Syria), Fc, 16
Antiochus, Kingdom of, Fb, 4f
Antipatria, Ab, 6
Antipatris, Ac, 4d
Antipolis, Bd, 12
Antirrhium Pr., Cd, 7
Antissa, Eb, 9a
Antitaurus M., Fc, 16
Antium, Aa, 13
Antonia, Inset, 4e
Antoniniana Aq., Inset, 11d
Anxa, Fb, 13
Anxanum, Je, 12
Aornus (Abhisara), Kc, 9b
Aornus (Bactria), Jb, 9b
Aous, F., Ab, 6
Apamea (Phrygia), Ec, 16
Apamea (Syria), Fc, 16
Aparytae, Jb, 5b
Aperantia, Cd, 6
Aphidnae, Ed, 7
Aphnitis, L., Db, 7c
Aphrodis ias, Dc, 16
Aphroditopolis (Middle Egypt), Bb, 3b
Aphroditopolis (Upper Egypt), Bc, 3b
Apodotia, Cd, 6
Apollinopolis magna Bd, 3a
Apollinopolis-parva (Nebut), Cd, 3b
Apollo and Pan, Caves of, Inset, 7a
Apollonia (Edones), Fb, 6
Apollonia (Illyria), Aa, 9a
Apollonia (Judea), Ac, 4d
Apollonia (Macedonia), Bb, 16
Apollonia ((Pentapolis), Cd, 16
Apollonia Phrygia, Cb, 9b
Apollonia (Sicilia), Cd, 13
Apollonia (Thracia), Db, 16
Apollonia Mygdonia, Eb, 6
Appia, Aq., Inset, 11d
Apsorus, Jc, 12
Apsus, F., Ab, 6
Apuli, Cb, 14c
Apulia, Ea, 13
Apulum, Ca, 16
Aquae, Inset, 17a
Aquea (Buxton), Ec, i7
Aquae Flaviae, Ad, 15
Aquae Populoniae, Ed, 12
Aquae Sextiea, Dd, 15
Aquae Statiellae, Cc, 12
Aquae Sulis (Bath), De, 17
Aquae Tarbellicae, Bd, 15
Aquileia (Etruria), Fd, 12
Aquileia (Rhaetia), Ec, 15
Aquileia (Venetia), Hb, 12
Aquilonia, Da, 13
Aquincum, Ba, 16
Aquitania, Dd, 20
Arabah, Bg, 4c; Cd, 4a
Arabia, Felix, Fe, 18
Arabia Deserta, Lh, 20
Arabian Desert, Bc, 3a; Cc, 3a
Arabia, Petraea, Fe, 18
Arabs (Aribi), Ec, 2d
Arachosia, Id, 18
Arachthus, F., Cc, 6
Arad, Bf, 4a
Aradus, Dc, 9b
Aram, Db, 4a
Aramaeans (Syrians), Cd, 4c
Arar, F., Cc, 15
Ararat, Mt., Eb, 2d

Ararat (Urartu), Eb, 2d
Arausio, Cd, 15
Araxes, F., Fb, 9b
Araxus, Pr., Cd, 7
Arbailu (Arbela), Eb, 2d
Arbela, Gd, 18
Arbela (Arbailu), Eb, 2d
Arcadia, Cc, 9a
Archelais, Bd, 4d
Arcus Augusti, Inset, 13b
Arcus Constantini, Inset, 13b
Arcus Septimii Severi, Inset, 13b
Arcus Severi, Inset, 13b
Arcus Tiberii, Inset, 13b
Arcus Titi, Inset, 13b
Arcus Traiani, Inset, 13b
Ardea, Aa, 13
Ardeatina, Pa., Inset, 11d
Arden, Forest of, Ee, 17
Arduenna Silva, Db, 15
Area Palatina, Inset, 13b
Arelate, Cd, 15
Areopagus, Inset, 7a
Argentarius, M., Fe, 12
Argentoratum, Dc, 15
Argethia, Cc, 6
Argilus, Eb, 6
Arginusae, Eb, 9a
Argolis, De, 7
Argos, De, 7
Argos (Amphilocia), Bb, 9a
Aria, Id, 18
Aribi (Arabs), Ec, 2d
Aricia, Ab, 14b
Ariminum, Gc, 12
Arinna, Ca, 3a
Ariolica (Transpadana), Ab Eb, 12
Arius, F., Ib, 9b
Arius Lacus, Hc, 9b
Arjunayana, Ec, 18b
Armavir, Ea, 2d
Armavira, Kd, 11
Armenia, Ke, 11
Armenia Minor, Fb, 16
Armorica, Bc, 15
Arne, Dc, 6
Arnissa, Cb, 6
Arnon, R., Cf, 4a
Arnus, F., Ed. 12
Aroer, Bf, 4c
Arpad, Da, 4c
Arpi, Da, 13
Arpinum, Ba, 13
Arrabona, Ba, 16
Arretium, Fd, 12
Arsaniưs, F., Db, 5b
Arsinoé (Aegyptus), If, 11
Arsinoé (Egypt), Bc, 3a
Arsinoé (Pentapolis), Cd, 16
Artacoana, Ic, 9b
Artaxata, Gc, 18
Artemisium, Ee, 6
Artyma, L., Eb, 7c
Arurias, F., Aa, 14a
Arvad, Bc, 4c
Arverni, Cc, 15
Arx, Insets, 13a, b
Arzanibiu, Ca, 3a
Arzawa, Ba, 3a
Arzus, F., Da, 7c
Ascania, L., Fb, 7c
Asclepieum, Inset, 7a
Asculum, He, 12
Ashdod, Ae, 4a
Asher, Bb, 4a
Ashguzai (Ashkenaz), Fb, 2d
Ashkelon, Ae, 4a
Ashkenaz (Ashguzai), Fb, 2d
Ashtaroth, Dc, 4a
Ashur, Da. 3a
Ashur (Assyria), Eb, 2d
Asia, If, 20
Asia, Diocese of, If, 20

Asinaria, Pa., Inset, 11d
Asine (Argolis), De, 7
Asine (Rhion), Cf, 7
Askalon, Bb, 3a
Asopus, Df, 7
Asopus, F., De, Ed, 7
Aspadana, Hd, 18
Aspendus, Ec, 16
Asphaltitis, L., Dc, 9b
Asphynis, Cd, 3b
Assera, Eb, 6
Assisium, Gd, 12
Assorus, Ce, 13
Assus, Be, 9a
Assyria, Da, 3a
Astacus (Acarnania), Cd, 6
Astacus (Phrygia), Fb, 7c
Atella, Cb, 13
Astigi, Ae, 15
Astures, Ad, 15
Asturica Augusta, Ad, 15
Astypalaea, I., Ge, 8
Asylum, Inset, 13a
Atalante, Ed, 6
Atavi, Cb, 18
Aternum, Je, 12
Aternus, F., He, 12
Ateste, Fb, 12
Athamania, Cc, 6
Athenae, Hf, 20
Athene Nike, Inset, 7a
Athene Promachos, Inset, 7a
Athens, Ancient, Inset, 7b
Athesis, F., Fb, 12
Athos, M, Fb, 6
Athribis (Hat-bri-ebe), Ba, 3b
Atina (Latium), Ba, 13
Atina (Lucania), Db, 13
Atlas, M., Cg, 20
Atrebates, Ee, 17
Atropatene, Mf, 20
Attalia, Db, 4f
Attica, Cb, 9a
Attidium, Gd, 12
Attium Pr., Ce, 12
Aufidena (Apulia), Ea, 13
Aufidena (Samnium), Ca, 13
Aufidus, F., Ea, 13
Aufinum, He, 12
Augusta Praetoria, Bb, 12
Augusta Rauricorum, Dc, 15
Augusta Taurinorum (Turin), Bb, 12
Augusta Treverorum, Dc, 15
Augusta Vagiennorum, Bc, 12
Augusta Vindelicorum, Ec, 15
Augustobona, Cc, 15
Augustobriga, Bd, 15
Augustodunum, Cc, 10
Augustodurum, Bc, 15
Augustonemetum, Cc, 15
Augustoritum, Cc, 15
Aulis, Ed, 7
Aunedonnacum, Cc, 15·
Aurasius, M., De, 15
Aurelia, Pa., Inset, 11d
Aurelia Nova, Pa., Inset, 11d
Aureliani, Dd, 20
Aurelius, Inset, 11d
Aureus M., De, 12
Aurunci, Ba, 13
Ausculum, Da, 13
Auser, F., Ec, 12
Australe Pr., Inset, 17a
Autricum, Cc, 15
Auximum, Hd, 12
Avaricum, Cc, 15
Aveia, He, 12
Avenio, Cd, 15
Aventicum, Dc, 15
Aventinus, Inset, 11d
Aventinus M., Inset, 11c; 11d
Avernuslacus, Cc, 14b
Aviones, Db, 15
Axius, F., Ca, 9a
Axylos, Ec, 16
Azania, Gg, 18
Azania, De, 7
Aziris, Inset, 5b
Azotus, Ad, 4d

BAAL HERMON (Mt. Hermon), Cb, 4a
Babel (Babylon), Ec, 2d
Babylon, Db, 3a
Babylon (Babel), Ec, 2d
Babylon (Cairo), Bb, 3b
Babylonia, Fc, 9b
Bactra, Jb, 5b; Jb, 9b

Bactria, Id, 18
Bactria (Zariaspa), Jb, 9b
Baetica, Ae, 15
Baetis, F., Ae, 15
Bagacum, Cb, 15
Bagistana, Gd, 18
Baiae, Cc, 14b
Bairat, Bb, 18a
Baithan, Jf, 19
Bakarei, Jg, 19
Baleares, Df, 20
Bannaventa, Ed, 17
Bantia, Db, 13
Bar Hill, Ba, 17
Barathrum, Inset, 7b
Barbaria, Gg, 18
Barbarike, Ie, 18
Barcino, Cd, 10
Barduli, Ea, 13
Barga, Ca, 3a
Barium, Ea, 13
Barka, Cd, 16
Barnus, M., Cb, 6
Bashan, Dc, 4a
Bashan, Mts. of, Ce, 4c
Basilica Aemilia, Inset, 13b
Basilica Constantini, Inset, 13b
Basilica Iulia, Inset, 13b
Basilica Sempronia, Inset, 13a
Basilica Ulpia, Inset, 13b
Bastarnae, Id, 20
Bastarni M., Da, 16
Bastetani, Be, 15
Basti, Be, 15
Bastuli, Be, 15
Batanaea, Db, 4d
Batava, Ec, 15
Batavi, Cb, 15
Bath (Aqua Sulis), De, 17
Bauxanum, Fa, 12
Beeroth, Be, 4a
Beer-sheba, Af, 4a
Behistun, Fc, 5b
Beilan Pass, Db, 5b
Beirut, Cb, 3a
Belbina, De, 7
Belgae, De, 17
Belgae, Bb, 1
Belgica, Cc, 15
Bellunum, Ga, 12
Benacus, L., Eb, 12
Benares (Kasi), Cb, 18a
Beneventum, Ca, 13
Benjamin, Be, 4a
Benwell (Condercum), Inset, 17
Berenice (Aegyptus), Cd, 3a
Berenice (Arabia-Petraea), Jg, 11
Berenice (Euhesperiade), Cd, 16
Berga, Eb, 6
Bergomum, Db, 12
Bergula, Da, 7c
Beroe, Db, 16
Beroea (Macedonia), Cb, 16
Beroea (Syria), Fc, 16
Berrhoea, Db, 6
Berytus, Fd, 16
Bethany, Bd, 4d
Beth-el (Luz), Be, 4a
Bethesda, Pool of, Inset, 4e
Beth-horon, Be, 4a
Bethlehem, Be, 4a
Bethsaida Julias, Cb, 4d
Beth-shean, Bd, 4a
Beth-shemish, Ae, 4a
Betriacum, Eb, 12
Bezabde, Eb, 9b
Bezer, Ce, 4a
Bezetha, Inset, 4e
Bhojas, Bb, 18a
Biainas, Eb, 2d
Bibracte, Cc, 15
Bibrax, Cc, 15
Bilbilis, Bd, 15
Bilitio, Da, 12
Birdoswald (Camboglanna), Inset, 17
Birrens (Blatobulgium), Ca, 17
Bisalate, Eb, 6
Bisanthe, Db, 7c
Bishri, Mt., Ca, 3a
Bit Yakin, Fc, 2d
Bitia, Be, 14a
Bithynia, Fc, 18; Je, 20
Bithynia-et-Pontus, Eb, 16
Bithynium, Eb, 16
Bituriges-Cubi, Cc, 15
Bituriges-Vivisci,·Bc, 15
Blatobulgium (Birrens), Ca, 17
Boderia Aest., Inset, 17a
Bodetia, Dc, 12

Bodh Gaya, Cb, 18a
Bodotria Aest., Da, 17
Boebe, Dc, 6
Boebis, L., Dc, 6
Boeotia, Cb, 9a
Boeotians, Cb, 2b
Boghaz Keui (Hattusas), Cb, 2a
Boii, Fc, 12
Boius, M., Bb, 6
Bokhara, Id, 18
Bolan Pass, Jd, 9b
Bolbe, L., Eb, 6
Bolbitinic Mouth, Ba, 3b
Bolerium Pr., Af, 17
Bononia (Felsina), Fc, 12
Bononia (Gesoriacum), Cb, 15
Bononia (Moesia), Cb, 16
Borcovicium (Housesteads) Inset, 17
Boreale Pr., Inset, 17a
Borsippa, Db, 3a
Borysthenes, R., Jd, 20
Bosporus Cimmerius, Fa, 16
Bosporus Thracius, Fa, 7c
Bostra, Jf, 11
Bottiais, Db, 6
Bovianum Undecumanorum, Ca, 13
Bovianum Vetus, Ca, 13
Bovillae, Ab, 14b
Bowness, Cb, 17
Bracara Augusta, Ad, 15
Bradanus, F., Eb, 13
Brancester (Branodunum) Gd, 17
Branodunum (Brancester), Gd, 17
Brauron, Ee, 7
Bravoniacum (Kirkby Thore), Db, 17
Bravonium, Dd, 17
Bremenium, Da, 17
Bremetennacum (Ribchester), Dc, 17
Brigantes, Db, 17; Inset, 17a
Brigantium, Ac, 12
Brigantium (Hispania), Ad, 15
Brigantium (Rhaetia), Dc, 15
Brigetio, Ba, 16
Britannia (Roman Diocese), Cc, 20
Brixellum, Ec, 12
Brixia, Eb, 12
Broad Wall, Inset, 4b
Brocavum (Brougham), Db, 17
Brough (Petuaria), Fc, 17
Brough (Verterae), Db, 17
Brougham (Brocavum), Db, 17
Bructeri, Db, 15
Brundisium, Ge, 20
Brundulum, Gb, 12
Bruttii, Ed, 13
Bruttium, Ed, 13
Bryanium, Cb, 6
Bryges, Ca, 6
Bubastis (Pebeseth), Ba, 3b
Bucatium, Cd, 6
Bucephala, Kc, 9b
Buchetium, Bc, 6
Bulis, Dd, 7
Burdigala, Ce, 20
Burgh by Sands, Cb, 17
Burgundiones, Fd, 20
Burrium, De, 17
Busiris, Cc, 3a
Buthrotum, Bc, 6
Butuntum, Ea, 13
Buxentum, Db, 13
Buxton (Aquae), Ec, 17
Buto, Ba, 3b
Byblus, Dc, 9b
Byblus (Gebal), Bd, 4c
Byzantium, Ib, 5a; Fa, 9a
Byzantium (Constantinopolis), Ie, 20

CABILLONUM, Cc, 15
Cabira, Fb, 16
Caburrum, Bc, 12
Cabyle, Db, 16
Cadusii, Fb, 9b
Caecina, Ed, 12
Caelia, Ea, 13
Caelimontana, Pa., Inset, 11c
Caelimontium, Inset, 11d
Caer Gai, Cd, 17
Caer Sws, Cd, 17
Caere, Ge 12
Caerleon (Isca), De, 17
Caernarvon (Segontium), Bc, 17
Caesar Augusta, Ce, 20

Caesarea (Cappadocia), Kf, 20
Caesarea I. (Gallia), Bc, 15
Caesarea (Judaea), Ab, 4d; Ed, 16
Caesarea (Mauretania), Df, 20
Caesarea (Mazaca), Fc, 16
Caesarea Philippi, Ca, 4d
Caesariensis, Ce, 15
Caesarodunum, Cc, 15
Caesena, Gc, 12
Caetobriga, Ae, 15
Caicus, F., Eb, 2b
Caieta, Ba, 13
Caistor, Fc, 17
Calabria, Fb, 13
Calacte, Cd, 13
Calagurris, Bd, 15
Calauria, I., Ee, 7
Calcaria (Tadcaster), Ec, 17
Calchedon (Chalcedon), Ib, 5a
Calebites (Kenizzites), Af, 4a
Caledonia, Ab, 20
Caledonii, Inset, 17a
Cales (Campania), Ca, 13
Cales (Umbria), Gd, 12
Calleva Atrebatum (Silchester), Fe, 17
Callinicum, Kf, 20
Callipolis, Fb, 13
Callirrhoe, Cd, 4d
Callonae, Fc, 9b
Calpe, Ca, 5b
Calpe, M., Ae, 15
Calydnae, Ec, 2b
Calydon, Cd, 7
Calymnos, Ge, 8
Camarina, Fc, 5a
Cambodunum, Ec, 15
Cambridge (Durolipons), Gd, 17
Camboglanna (Birdoswald), Da, 17
Camelon, Ca, 17
Camerinum, Hd, 12
Camirus, Ec, 2b
Campania, Cb, 13
Campus Agrippae, Inset, 11d
Campus Esquilinus, Inset, 11c
Campus Martius, Inset, 11c
Campus Vaticanus, Inset, 11c
Campus Viminalis, Inset, 11c
Camulodunum (Colchester), Ge, 17
Camuni, Eb, 12
Cana, Bb, 4d
Canaan, Dc, 2a
Canaanites, Af, Bd, 4a
Canastraeum Pr., Ec, 6
Cane, Gf, 18
Cannae, Ea, 13
Canopic Mouth, Ba, 3b
Canopus, Bc, 9b
Canovium, Cc, 17
Cantabri, Bd, 15
Canterbury (Durovernum), Ge, 17
Cantii, Ge, 17
Canusium, Ea, 13
Capena, Ge, 12
Capernaum, Cb, 4d
Capetani, Be, 10
Caphereus Pr., Fd, 7
Caphyae, De, 7
Capitol, Inset, 11d
Capitolinus, M., Insets, 13a, b
Capitolium, Insets, 13a, b
Cappadocia, Kf, 20
Capraria, Dd, 12
Capreae Ins., Cb, 13
Capsa, Df, 15
Capua, Ca, 13
Caracenii, Jf, 12
Carales, De, 15
Carana, Ke, 11
Carcer, Insets, 13a, b
Carchemish, Da, 4c
Cardamyle, Cc, 9a
Cardia, Cb, 7c
Cardiff, Ce, 17
Carduchi, Eb, 5b
Caria, Fc, 9a
Carians, Bb, 2a
Carina, Inset, 11c
Carlisle (Luguvalium), Db, 17
Carmana, Hc, 5b
Carmania, Hc, 9b; He, 18
Carmarthen (Maridunum), Be, 17
Carmel, Mt., Ac, 4a

Carmentalis, Pa, Inset, 11·
Carni, Ga, 12; Dc, 18
Carnuntum, Ba, 16
Carolis, Ef, 20
Carpathos I., Hf, 8
Carpatus Mons, Hd, 20
Carpetani, Bd, 15
Carpis, Ee, 15
Carrawburgh (Procolitia), Inset, 17
Carrea Potentia, Bc, 12
Carrhae, Fc, 16; Ab, 18b
Carriden, Ca, 17
Carsioli, He, 12
Carsulae, Ge, 12
Cartenna, Ce, 15
Carteia, Ae, 15
Carthago, Ff, 20
Carthago Nova, Cf, 20
Caruanca, M., Ja, 12
Carusadius, M., Hb, 12
Caryae, De, 7
Carystus (Euboea), Fd, 7
Carystus (Laconia), De, 7
Caspian Gates, Gb, 9b
Caspii, Fa, 9b
Cassanitae, Ge, 18
Cassiope, Ac, 6
Castell Collen, Cd, 17
Casthanaea, Dc, 6
Castle Flemish, Be, 17
Castlecary, Ca, 17
Castledykes, Ca, 17
Castlehill, Ba, 17
Castlesteads, Inset, 17
Castra Exploratorum, Ca, 17
Castra Praetoria, Inset, 11c
Castrense, A., Inset, 11d
Castrum Novum, He, 12
Castrum Truentinum, He, 12
Castulo, Be, 15
Casuentus, F., Eb, 13
Catana (Catane), De, 13
Cataractonium (Catterick Bridge), Eb, 17
Cathaei, Kc, 9b
Catterick Bridge (Cataractonium), Eb, 17
Catuvellauni, Fe, 17
Cauca, Bd, 15
Caucasus Mts., Fb, 16
Caudium, Ca, 13
Caulonia, Ed, 13
Causennae (Ancaster), Fd, 17
Cauvery, R., Jf, 19
Cayster, R., Hc, 8
Cayster Plain, Cb, 5b
Ceba, Cc, 12
Cebenna, M., Cd, 15
Cebrene, Cc, 7c
Cecryphalea, Ee, 7
Celaenae, Bb, 9b
Celeia, Ba, 16
Celenderis, Cb, 2d
Celetrum, Cb, 6
Cellae, Cb, 6
Celti, Da, 5a
Celtiberi, Bd, 15
Celtica, Cc, 15
Celtici, Ae, 15
Cemenelum, Bd, 12
Cenabum, Cc, 15
Cenaeum Pr., Cc, 8
Cenchreae, Ee, 7
Cenomani, Eb, 12
Centumcellae, Fe, 12
Centuripa, Ce, 13
Ceos, Fe, 7
Cephallenia Bd, 7; Cc, 16
Cephallenians, Bb, 2b
Cephalœdium, Be, 13
Cephisia, Ed, 7
Cephisus, Dd, 6
Ceramicus, Inset, 7b
Cerasus, Da, 5b
Cercinitis L., Eb, 6
Ceriadae, Inset, 7b
Cerinthus, Ed, 6
Cermalus, Insets, 13a, b
Cespius, M., Inset, 11c
Ceylon (Simkala), Fe, 18b
Ceylon (Tamraparni), Cd, 18a
Chaeronea, Dd, 6
Chalastra, Db, 6
Chalce, He, 8
Chalcedon, Ie, 20
Chalcedon (Calchedon), Ib, 5a
Fa, 9a
Chalcidice, Ca, 9a

Chalcis (Aetolia), Cd, 7
Chalcis (Epirus), Cc, 6
Chalcis (Euboea), Ed, 6
Chalcis, Syria, Fc, 16
Chaldaea, Ec, 2d
Chalybes, Da, 2d
Chalybon, Db, 9b
Chambal, R., Je, 19
Chang-an, Md, 19
Chang-Jeh, Md, 19
Charadra, Bc, 6
Charidemi Pr., Be, 15
Chatti, Cb, 18
Chauci, Db, 15
Chelonatus Pr., Ce, 7
Chephirah, Be, 4a
Chera, Jf, 19
Chera, Kingdom of, Ee, 18b
Cherethites, Af, 4c
Chersonesus (Thrace), Da, 9a
Chersonesus Cimbrica, Da, 10
Chersonesus Pr., Be, 14a
Chersonesus, Pr., Fd, 6
Chersonesus Taurica, Ea, 16
Cherusci, Db, 17
Chester (Deva), Dc, 17
Chesterford, Gd, 17
Chesterholm (Vindolanda), Inset, 17
Chester-le-Street, Eb, 17
Chesters (Cilurnum), Inset, 17
Chiang-Hsia, Nd, 19
Chiao Chow, Ne, 19
Chichester (Novio magus), Ff, 17
Ching-chao, Md, 19
Ching-chow, Nd, 19
Ching Chow, Nd, 19
Chinnereth, Sea of, Cc, 4a
Chios, Fc, 8
Choaspes, R., Fc, 5b
Chola, Jf, 19
Chola, K. of, Bc, 18a; Ed, 18b
Chorasmia, Hc, 18
Chorasmii, Ha, 9b
Chorazin, Cb, 4d
Chryse, Eb, 2b
Chrysopolis, Ie, 20
Cibalae, Gd, 20
Cibyra, Dc, 1b
Cicones, Da, 2b
Cierium, Dc, 6
Cilicia, Jf, 20
Cilicia (Khilakku), Cb, 2d
Cilician Gates, Cb, 5b
Cilurnum (Chesters), Inset, 17
Cimbrica Chersonesus, Da, 15
Ciminius, L., Ge, 12
Cimmerians, Cb, 2d
Cimmerians (Gomer), Ea, 2d
Cimolos, Ff, 7
Cinaros, Ge, 8
Cingulum, Hd, 12
Circeii, Ba, 13
Circesium, Lf, 20
Circus Flaminius, Inset, 13a
Circus Maximus, Inset, 13b
Cirrha, Dd, 7
Cirta, Ef, 20
Cispadana, Ec, 12
Citerior, Hispania, Be, 15
Cithaeron M., Ed, 7
Citium (Cyprus), Ed, 16
Citium (Macedonia), Db, 6
City of Salt, Bf, 4a
Clanis, F., Ge, 12
Clanoventa (Ravenglass), Cb, 17
Classis, Gc, 12
Clastidium, Db, 12
Claterna, Fc, 12
Claudia, Aq., Inset, 11d
Clausentum, Ef, 17
Clavenna, Da, 12
Clazomenae, Ic, 5a, Gc, 8
Cleonae (Argolis), De, 7
Cleonae (Chalcidice), Fb, 6
Clepsydra, Inset, 7a
Clesis, Eb, 16
Cliternia, Kf, 12
Clitor, De, 7
Cloaca Maxima, Inset, 13a
Clota Aest, Ba, 17
Clunia, Bd, 15
Clupea, Ee, 15
Clusium, Fd, 12
Cnidus, Ic, 5a
Cnossus, Dc, 16
Cocala, Jd, 9b
Coele, Inset, 7b
Coelesyria, Fd, 18

Colapis, F., Kb, 12
Colchester (Camulodunum), Ge, 17
Colchis, Kd, 11
Collina, Inset, 11c
Collina, Pa., Inset, 11c
Collis Hortorum, Inset, 11c
Collis Quirinalis, Inset, 11c
Collis Viminalis, Inset, 11c
Collytus, Inset, 7b
Colonia Agrippina, Ec, 20
Colophon, Eb, 9a
Colossae, Bb, 5b
Colosseum, Inset, 13b
Colossus Neronis, Inset, 13b
Columbarium Pr., Bd, 14
Columna Traiani, Inset, 13b
Columnae Herculis, Ae, 15
Comana (Bithynia), Fb, 16
Comana (Cappadocia), Fc, 16
Comitium, Insets, 13a, b
Commagene, Fc, 16
Compsa, Db, 13
Comum, Db, 12
Concordia (Venetia), Gb, 12
Condate, Bc, 15
Condercum (Benwell), Inset, 17
Coneta, Gb, 12
Confluentes, Db, 15
Conimbriga, Ad, 15
Consentia, Ec, 13
Consilium, Db, 13
Constantinopolis (Byzantium), Ie, 20
Contestani, Be, 15
Contrebia, Bd, 15
Copae, Ed, 7
Copais, L., Ed, 7
Coptos (Kebtu), Cd, 3b
Cora, Aa, 13
Coracesium, Ec, 16
Corcyra, Ac, 6
Corduba, Be, 15; Cf, 20
Corfinium, He, 12
Corinium, Inset, 17a
Corinium (Cirencester), Ee, 17
Corinth, De, 7
Corinthus, Ed, 18
Corioli, Ab, 14b
Coritani, Fc, 17
Corner Gate (Old Gate), Inset, 4b
Cornovii, Dd, 17
Cornus, Dd, 15
Corodamum Pr., Ie, 18
Corone, Cf, 7
Coronea, Dd, 7
Corsi, Bd, 14a
Corsica, Ce, 12
Corstopitum (Corbridge), Db, 17
Cortona, Gd, 12
Coryceum Pr., Gc, 8
Cos, He, 8
Cossaei, Fc, 9b
Cossura, I., Ee, 15
Costoboci, Da, 16
Cotiaeum, Dc, 16
Cotini, Dc, 18
Cotyora, Da, 5b
Cramond, Ca, 17
Cranii M., Cc, 6
Crannon, Dc, 6
Cratea, Eb, 16
Crathis, F., Ec, 13
Cremna, Ec, 16
Cremona, Eb, 12
Crenides, Fa, 6
Crestonia, Eb, 6
Creta, Hf, 20
Crete, Inset, 7d
Crexa I., Jc, 12
Crimisa Pr., Fc, 13
Crisa, Dd, 7
Criumetopon Pr., Aa, 7d
Crixia, Cc, 12
Crococalana, Fc, 17
Crocodilopolis-Arsinoe (Shedet), Bb, 3b
Crommyon, Ee, 7
Croton, Gc, 5a
Crypta, Inset, 11d
Ctesiphon, Kf, 11
Cularo, Dc, 15
Cullu, De, 15
Cumae, Fb, 5a
Cunaxa, Lb, 5a
Cunetio, Ee, 17
Cupra Maritima, Hd, 12
Cures, Ge, 12

Curia, Inset, 13b
Curia (Rhaetia), Dc, 15
Curia Hostilia, Inset, 13a
Curia Iulia, Inset, 11d
Curicta I., Jb, 12
Curium, Jd, 5a
Cusae (Gosu), Bc, 3b
Cutch, Ie, 19
Cutha, Ec, 2d
Cuttiae, Cb, 12
Cyclades, Ed, 8
Cydathenaeum, Inset, 7b
Cydonia, Cc, 16
Cyllene, Cd, 7
Cyllene M., De, 7
Cyme, Aeolis, Gc, 8
Cyme, Euboea, Fd, 6
Cynaetes, Ae, 15
Cynaetha, Dd, 7
Cynopolis, Bb, 3b
Cynoscephalae, Dc, 6
Cynossema, Ea, 9a
Cynuria, De, 7
Cynus, Ed, 6
Cyparissiae, Ce, 7
Cypas, Cb, 7c
Cypsela, Cb, 7c
Cyprus, Ec, 16
Cyrenaica, Ed, 18
Cyrenaica-Creta, Cd, 16
Cyrene, Hg, 20
Cyropolis, Jb, 5b
Cyrrhus, Db, 6
Cyrus, R., Fa, 2d; Ld, 11
Cythera, I., Df, 7
Cythnos, Fe, 7
Cytinium, Dd, 6
Cyzicus, Ha, 8

DACIA, Ca, 16
Dacia, Diocese of, He, 20
Dadicae, Kb, 5b
Dahae, Hb, 9b
Daix, R., Hb, 18
Dalmatia, Ge, 20
Damascus, Da; 4a
Damnonii, Ba, 17
Dan, Bd, 4c
Dan (Tribe), Ae, Cb, 4a
Danubius (Ister), F., Db, 16
Danum (Doncaster), Ec, 17
Daphnae, Cc, 3b
Dardani, Aa, 9b
Dardanians, Eb, 2b
Dardanus, Cb, 7c
Daritae, Gb, 5b
Dascylium, Cb, 5b
Dascylium, Eb, 7c
Dassaretae, Bb, 6
Datum, Hb, 5a
Davaka, Kingdom of, Fc, 18b
David's House, Inset, 4b
Debir (Kiriath-sepher), Af, 4a
Decapolis, Cb, 4d
Deceangli, Cc, 17
Decelea, Cb, 9a
Delcus, Ec, 7
Delium, Cb, 9a
Delos, Dc, 9a
Delphi, Hc, 5a
Delphi (Indraprastha), Ec, 18b
Delphinium, Gc, 8
Demetae, Be, 17
Demetrias, Dc, 6
Derbe, Eb, 4f
Der ez Zor, Da, 3a
Derrhis Pr., Fc, 6
Dertona, Cc, 12
Dertosa, Cd, 15
Deserta Libyca, Hg, 11
Dessinus, Ie, 11
Dertona, Cc, 12
Deva (Chester), Dc, 17
Devagiri, Ed, 18b
Devarashtra, Ed, 18b
Dhauli, Cc, 18a
Dia, Ca, 7d
Dialas, R., Fc, 5b
Dianium, Hispania, Ae, 15
Dianium, Italy, Fe, 12
Dicaea, Bb, 7c
Dicte M., Ca, 7d
Didyme, Cd, 13
Diogenium, Inset, 7b
Diomea, Inset, 7b
Dion, Db, 4d
Dioscoridis I., Hf, 18
Dioscurias, Lb, 5a
Dioscurias Pr., Fd, 13
Diospolis Parva, Cc, 3b
Dipaea, De, 7

Dipylum, Inset, 7b
Dium (Chalcidice), Fb, 6
Dium (Euboea), Dd, 6
Dium (Macedonia), Db, 6
Divodurum, Dc, 15
Divona, Cd, 15
Doberus, Da, 6
Dobuni, De, 17
Dodona, Bc, 6
Doliche, Db, 6
Dolopes, Cc, 6
Dolopes, Is., Ec, 6
Domus Augustana, Inset, 13b
Domus Caligulae, Inset, 13b
Domus Flaviana, Inset, 13b
Domus Liviae, Inset, 13b
Domus Septimii Severi, Inset, 13b
Domus Tiberiana, Inset, 13b
Doncaster (Danum), Ec, 17
Dor, Ac, 4a
Dorchester, Ee, 17
Dorchester (Durnovaria), Df, 17
Doris, Dd, 6
Doris, He, 8
Doriscus, Ba, 5b
Dorylaeum, Ec, 16
Dothan, Be, 4c
Drabescus, Fa, 6
Drangiana, Id, 18
Drapsaca, Jb, 9b
Dravus, F., Ba, 16
Drepanum (Phrygia), Fb, 7c
Drepanum (Sicilia), Ad, 13
Drepanum Pr., Cd, 7
Drinius, F., Bb, 16
Droi, Ea, 6
Droitwich (Salinae), Dd, 17
Drumburgh, Inset, 17
Druzipara, Da, 7c
Dryopes, Cc, 6
Dubris, He, 17
Du-kau (Antaeopolis), Bc, 3b
Dulichium, Bb, 2b
Duma, Dc, 2d
Dumnonii, Bf, 17
Duranius, F., Cd, 15
Durius, F., Ad, 15
Durnovaria(Dorchester), Df, 17
Durobrivae, Fd, 17
Durobrivae (Rochester), Ge, 17
Durocobrivae, Fe, 17
Durocortorum, Cc, 15
Durolipons, Gd, 17
Durostorum, Db, 16
Durotriges, Df, 17
Durovernum (Canterbury), Ge, 17
Durovigutum (Godmanchester), Gd, 17
Dymae, Cb, 7c
Dyme, Cd, 7
Dyrrhachium, He, 20
Dyrta Kb, 9b
Dystus, Fd, 7

EAST, DIOCESE OF THE (Orientis), Kg, 20
East, Prefecture of the, Jg, 20
East Roman Empire, If, 20
Ebal, Mt., Bd, 4a
Ebchester (Vindomora), Inset, 17
Eburacum (York), Eb, 17
Ebusus, Ce, 15
Ecbatana, Fc, 5b; Gd, 18
Ecbatana (Achmetha), Fc, 2d
Ecdippa, Ba, 4d
Echedorus, F., Db, 6
Echinades Ins., Cd, 7
Echinus, Dd, 6
Ecnomus Pr., Be, 13
Edessa (Macedonia), Cb, 16
Edessa (Syria), Fc, 16
Edetani, Bd, 15
Edom, Bg, 4c
Edomites, Bf, 4a
Edones, Ea, 6
Edrum, Eb, 12
Eglon, Ae, 4a
Egypt, Bc, 3
Egypt, Diocese of (Ægyptus), Ih, 20
Egypt (Musri, Mizraim, Kush), Cd, 2d
Eileithyiapolis, Bc, 3a
Eion, Eb, 6
Eira, Ce, 7

Eium, Ca, 9a
Ekron, Ae, 4a
Elaea, Aeolis, Hc, 8
Elaea, Thesprotia, Bc, 6
Elaeus, Ba, 9b
Elam, Eb, 3a
Elatea, Dd, 6
Elath, Ah, 4c
Elburz, Cb, 18b
Elea, Db, 13
Elephantine I., Bd, 3a
Eleusinium, Inset, 7a
Eleusis, Ed, 7
Eleutherae, Ed, 7
Eleutherna, Ba, 7d
Eleutherus, F., Cb, 3a
Elimberrum, Cd, 15
Elimea, Cb, 6
Elis, Ce, 7
Ellipi, Fc, 2d
Elymi, Ae, 13
Emathia, Da, 6
Emerita Augusta, Bd, 18
Emmaus, Ad, 4d
Emona, Ja, 12
Emporiae, Db, 5a
Emporium, Inset, 11c
Emporium Segestanorum, Ad, 13
En Mont (Hermonthis), Cd, 3b
Endidae, Fa, 12
Endor, Bc, 4a
Enet (Tentyra), Cc, 3b
Enganim, Bd, 4a
Entella, Be, 13
Eordaei, Cb, 6
Eordaicus, F., Bb, 6
Epeans, Bb, 2b
Ephesus, Hd, 8
Ephraim, Bd, 4a
Ephraim, Mt., Bd, 4a
Ephyra, Bc, 6
Epidamnus, Gb, 5a
Epidaurus (Argolis), Ee, 7
Epidaurus (Illyricum), Bb, 16
Epidaurus Limera, Df, 7
Epidium Pr., Aa, 17
Epiphania, Fc, 16
Epirus, Bc, 6
Eporedia, Bb, 12
Erandapalla, Ec, 18b
Erech, Eb, 3a
Erechtheum, Inset, 7a
Eresus, Fb, 8
Eretria (Euboea), Ed, 7
Eretria (Phthiotis), Dc, 6
Ergines, Ca, 7c
Eridu, Eb, 3a
Erineus, Dd, 6
Eriza, Fc, 16
Ermine Street, Fd, 17
Erymanthus, M., Ce, 7
Erythrae, Eb, 8
Erythraeum Mare, Gd, 5b
Eryx, Ad, 13
Esdraelon, Plain of, Bb, 4d
Esquiliae, Inset, 11d
Esquilina, Inset, 11c
Esquilina, Pa., Inset, 11c
Etruria, Fd, 12
Etrusci (Tusci), Bb, 14c
Etymander, R., Ic, 5b
Euboea, Db, 9a
Euganei, Eb, 12
Euhesperidae (Berenice), Cd, 16
Eulaeus, F., Gc, 5b
Eupatoria, Fb, 16
Euphrates, R., Db, 3; Gd, 18
Euripus, Dc, 8
Europa, Db, 1
Europus, Da, 12
Eurotas, F., De, 7
Eurytanes, Cd, 6
Eutaea, De, 7
Euthane, He, 8
Exeter (Isca Dumnoniorum), Cf, 17
Ezion Geber, Bh, 4c

FABRATERIA, Ba, 13
Faesulae, Fd, 12
Fair Havens, Cc, 4f
Faleria, Hd, 12
Falerii, Ge, 12
Fanum, Bd, 12
Faventia, Fc, 12
Felsina, Fc, 12
Feltria, Fa, 12
Ferentinum, Ba, 13
Fidenae, Gf, 12
Fidentia, Ec, 12

3

Filey, Fb, 17
Firmum, Hd, 12
Fiscellus, M., He, 12
Flaminia, Pa., Inset, 11d
Flanona, Jb, 15
Flaviobriga, Bd, 15
Flavium A. (Colosseum), Inset, 11d
Flevo L., Db, 15
Florentia, Fd, 12
Florentiola, Dc, 12
Flumen Senus, Inset, 17a
Flumen Vidua, Inset, 17a
Flumentana, Pa., Inset, 11
Folkestone, He, 17
Fontinalis, Pa., Inset, 11c
Forden, Cd, 17
Forest of Arden, Ed, 17
Forest of Dean, De, 17
Formiae, Bb, 14b
Forum Appii, Aa, 4f
Forum Augusti, Inset, 13b
Forum Boarium, Inset, 13b
Forum Cornelii, Fc, 12
Forum Fulvii, Cb, 12
Forum Germanorum, Bc, 12
Forum Holitorium, Inset, 13a
Forum Iulii, Dd, 15
Forum Iulium (Roma), Inset, 13b
Forum Iulium (Venetia), Ha, 12
Forum Livii, Gc, 12
Forum Nervae, Inset, 13b
Forum Pacis, Inset, 13b
Forum Popilii (Cispadana), Gc, 12
Forum Popilii (Lucania), Db, 13
Forum Romanum, Inset, 13b
Forum Sempronii, Gd., 12
Forum Traiani, Inset, 13b
Forum Traiani, Sardinia, Be, 14a
Forum Vibii, Bc, 12
Fosse Way, Ed, 17
Franci, Ec, 20
Fregellae, Ba, 13
Fregenae, Gf, 12
Frentini, Je, 12
Frento, F., Kf, 12
Fretum Gaditanum, Ae, 15
Fretum Gallicum, Cb, 15
Fretum Gallicum (Corsica), Dd, 15
Frisii, Ec, 20
Fucinus, L., Hf, 12
Fulaeus, F., Eb, 3a
Fulginium, Ge, 12
Fundi, Ba, 13

Gabaeum Pr., Bc, 15
Gad (Tribe), Cd, Ce, 4a
Gades, Bf, 20
Gaetuli, Bc, 1
Galatia, Jf, 20
Galilee, Bb, 4J
Galilee, Sea of, Cb, 4a
Gallaecia, Ad, 15
Gallia, Dd, 20
Gallia Cisalpina, Eb, 12
Gambalu, Fc, 2d
Gandaria, Kc, 5b
Gandhara, Jd, 19
Gandhara, Kingdom of, Eb, 18b
Ganganorum Pr., 17, Bd
Ganges, R., Je, 19
Gangra, Eb, 16
Ganos, Db, 7c
Garganum Pr., Ea, 13
Garganus, M., Da, 13
Gariannonum, Hd, 17
Garsaura, Ec, 16
Garumna, F., Bd, 15
Gath, Ae, 4a
Gaugamela, Eb, 9b
Gaul (Gallia), Diocese of, Dd. 20
Gaul (Gallia), Prefecture of, Dd, 20
Gaulanitis, Cb, 4d
Gaya, Fc, 18b
Gaza, Ae, 4a
Gazaca, Gd, 18
Geba, Be, 4a
Gebal (Byblus), Bd, 4c
Gedrosia, Ie, 18
Gela, Ce, 13
Gelas, F., Ce, 13
Gelligaer, Ce, 17
Gem Aton. Bd, 3a
Genath (Gate Genath), Inset, 4e
Geneva, Dc, 15
Genua, Cc, 12

Genusium, Eb, 13
Gepidae, Hd, 20
Geraestus Pr., Fe, 7
Gerania, M., Cc, 8
Gerasa, Cc, 4d
Gergesa, Cb, 4d
Gergovia, Cc, 15
Gerizim, Mt., Bd, 4a
Germania, Eb, 15
Germania Inferior, Db, 15
Germania Superior, Dc, 15
Geronthrae, Df, 7
Gerrha, He, 18
Gerrhaei, Ge, 18
Gerunda, Cd, 15
Gerunium, Da, 13
Geshuri, Cc, 4a
Gesoriacum (Bononia), Cb, 15
Getae, Ba, 9b
Gezer, Ae, 4a
Ghazni, Jc, 9b
Gibbethon, Ae, 4a
Gibeon, Be, 4a
Gigonus, Eb, 6
Gihon Sinnor, Inset, 4b
Gilboa, Mt., Bd, 4a
Gilead, Cd, 4a
Gilgal, Ce, 4a
Ginaea, Bc, 4d
Gionar Hill, Bb, 18a
Gizeh, Cc, 2a
Glenlochar, Bb, 17
Glevum (Gloucester), De, 17
Gloucester (Glevum), De, 17
Gnathia, Fb, 13
Gobannium (Abergavenny), Ce, 17
Godavari, R., Jf, 19
Godmanchester (Durovigutum), Gd, 17
Golan Cc, 4a ,
Golden Gate(Jerusalem),Inset,4e
Goldsborough, Fb, 17
Gomer (Cimmerians), Ea, 2d
Gomphi, Cc, 6
Gonnus, Dc, 6
Gorditanum Pr., Bd, 14
Gordium, Ec, 16
Gortyna, Id, 5a
Gortys, De, 7
Goshen (Egypt), Ba, 3b
Gosu (Cusae), Bc, 3b
Gozan (Guzana), Eb, 2d
Graecia, Ab, 5b
Granicus, Ba, 9b
Granicus, F., Db, 7c
Graviscae, Fe, 12
Great Chesters (Aesica), Inset, 17
Great Sea, The, Ac, 4a
Greece, 7
Greece (Achaea), Cb, 4
Grumentum Db, 13
Grumum, Eb, 13
Gryneium, Eb, 9a
Gujarat, Ec, 18b
Gulashkird, Hd, 9b
Gurgum, Db, 2d
Guttones, Db, 18
Guzana (Gozan), Eb, 2d
Gwalior, Ec, 18
Gymnias, Da, 5b
Gytheum, Df, 7

Habiru (Shasu), Cb, 3a
Habitancum, Da, 17
Hadrianopolis, Db, 16; Ie, 20
Hadrumetum, Ee, 15
Haemus, M., Ba, 9b
Hagia Triada, Bc, 2a
Halap (Aleppo), Ca, 3a
Haliacmon, F., Db, 6
Haliartus, Ed, 7
Halicarnassus, Bb, 5b; Ec, 9a
Halicyae, Ae, 13
Halieis, Ee, 7
Halton (Onnum), Ea, 17
Halus, Dc, 6
Halycus, F., Be, 13
Halys, R., Eb, 16
Hamath, Cb, 4c
Han Dominions, Nd, 19
Han-chung, Md, 19
Hanigalbat, Ca, 3a
Hardknot, Cb, 17
Harmozia He, 18
Harosheth, Bc, 4a
Harran, Ca, 3a
Hasta, Baetica, Ae, 15
Hasta, Liguria, Cc, 12
Hatra, Gd, 18

Hatria (Picenum), Je, 12
Hatria (Venetia), Gb, 12
Hatti (Hittites), Cb, Db, 2d
Hattusas (Boghaz Keui), Cb, 2a
Hazor, Bd, 4c
Hebron (Kiriath-arba), Be, 4a
Hebrus, F., Db, 16
Hecatompylos, Gg, 9b
Helena (Graecia), Fe, 7
Helice, Dd, 7
Helicon M., Dd, 7
Heliopolis (On), Ba, 3b
Hellas, Ab, 9b
Hellespontus, If, 20
Helorus, Df, 13
Helos, Df, 7
Helvetii, Dc, 15
Hemesa, Fd, 16
Henen-seten (Heracleopolis magna), Bb, 3b
Henna, Ce, 13
Hephaestia, Bc, 7c
Heraclea, Caria, Hd, 8
Heraclea Chersonesus, Eb, 16
Heraclea (Lucania), Eb, 13
Heraclea Lyncestis, Ca, 6
Heraclea (Malis), Dd, 6
Heraclea Minoa, Be, 13
Heraclea Pontica, Eb, 16
Heracleopolis magna (Henen-seten), Bb, 3b
Heracleum, Db, 6
Heracleum (Theseum), Inset, 7b
Heracleum Pr., Ee, 13
Heraea, Ce, 7
Heraei M., Ce, 13
Heraeum, Pr., Dd, 7
Herat, see Alexandria
Herculaneum, Cb, 13
Herculia, Ba, 16
Herculis Pr., Be, 17
Herdoniae, Da, 13
Hermeius Smyrnaeos, Gc, 8
Hermione, Ee, 7
Hermon, Mt., Cb, 4a
Hermonthis (En Mont), Cd, 3b
Hermopolis Magna (Hmunu), Bc, 3b
Hermunduri, Eb, 15
Hermupolis, Ig, 11
Hermus, F., Dc, 16
Hernici, Ba, 13
Herod Agrippa, Kingdom of, Fc, 4f
Herod's Palace, Inset, 4e
Herod's Temple, Inset, 4e
Herodium, Bd, 4d
Heruli, Jd, 20
Heshbon, Ce, 4a
Hestiaeotis, Cc, 6
Hiddekel (Tigris), F., Ec, 2d
Hiera, Ad, 13
Hierapolis, Kf, 20
Hierapytna, Ca, 7d
Hierasus, F., Da, 16
Hieropolis, Fc, 16
Hierosolyma, Fd, 18
Hierosolyma (Jerusalem), Dc, 5b
High Street, Db, 17
Himalaya Mts., Ba, 18a
Himera, Fc, 5a
Himera, F., Ce, 13
Hindu, Kush, Ba, 18a
Hinnom (Gehenna). Valley of, Insets, 4e, 4b
Hippicus Tower, Inset. 4e
Hippo Diarrhytus, Ec, 5a
Hippo Regius, Ec, 5a
Hippo Zarytus, De, 15
Hippodrome, Inset, 13b
Hipponium, Ed, 13
Hipponon, Bb, 3b
Hippos, Cb, 4d
Hirpini, Ca, 13
Hispalis, Ae, 15
Hispania, Ce, 20
Hispellum, Gd, 12
Histiaea, Ed, 6
Histonium, Je, 12
Hit, Bb, 18b
Hittites (Hatti), Cb, Db, 2d
Hittites (Hatti), Ca, 3a
Hittites (Kalti), Cb, 4c
Hmunu (Hermopolis Magna) Bc, 3b
Holyhead, Bc, 17
Homolium, Dc, 6
Honan, Nd, 19
Horncastle, Fc, 17

Horologium, Inset, 7b
Horta, Ge, 12
Horti, Inset, 7b
Hostilia, Fb, 12
Housesteads (Vercovicium), Inset, 17
Hsu Chow, Nd, 19
Huai, R., Od, 19
Hui-hi, Od, 19
Hunni, Db, 1
Huntcliff, Fb, 17
Hurmunduri, Db, 18
Hyccara, Bd, 13
Huntcliff, Fb, 17
Hydrea, Ee, 7
Hydronte, Gb, 13
Hydruntum, Gb, 13
Hymettus, M., Ee, 7
Hypanis, F., Ea, 16
Hypanis, F., Fa, 16
Hypsas, F., Ae, 13
Hypsele, Bc, 3b
Hyrcania, Hd, 18
Hyrcanium (M. Caspium), Db, 1
Hysiae, De, 7

Iader (Illyricum), Bb, 16
Ialysus, Fc, 9a
Iambia, Fe, 18
Ianiculum Arx, Inset, 11
Iapygia, Cb, 14c
Iasa, Hd, 8
Iasus, Ec, 9a
Iaxartes, F., Eb, 1
Iazyges, Ec, 18
Iberia, Cc, 5a
Iberia (Caucasus), Kd, 11
Iberus, R., Ce, 20
Ibleam, Bd, 4a
Icaria, Gd, 8
Iceni, Gd, 17
Ichthys Pr., Ce, 7
Iconium, Ec, 16
Icosium, Ce. 15
Ictis, Ab, 15
Icus, Ec, 6
Ida, M., Ba, 7d
Ida, R., Ic, 18
Ida, Mt. (Troy), Eb, 2b
Idomene, Cc, 6
Idumaea, Ae, 4d
Igilgili, De, 15
Igilium, Ee, 12
Iguvium, Gd, 12
Ilchester, De, 17
Ilerda, Cd, 15
Ilici, Be, 15
Ilissus, Inset, 7b
Ilium, Cc, 7c
Ilium (Troy), Bb, 2a
Ilkley (Olicana), Ec, 17
Illergetes, Cd, 15
Illubri, Cb, 2d
Illyria, Ba, 6
Illyria, Diocese of, Ge, 20
Illyria, Prefecture of, Hf, 20
Illyricum, Bb, 16; Gd, 20
Ilos, Inset, 2c
Ilva, Fb, 5a
Imaus Mons, Ec, 1; Kc, 9b
Imbros, Fa, 8
India, Fc, 1
Indoscythia, Ec, 1
Indraprastha (Delhi), Ec, 18b
Indus, R., Ie, 19
Industria, Cb, 12
Inessa, Ce, 13
Ingira, Cb, 2d
Insubres, Db, 12
Interacrea, He, 12
Interamna (Etruria), Ge, 12
Interamna (Latium), Ba, 13
Interamna (Picenum), He. 12
Interamnium, Ec, 13
Intimilii, Bd, 12
Inveravon, Ca, 17
Inveresk, Da, 17
Iol Caesarea, Ce, 15
Iolcus, Dc, 6
Iomnium, Ce, 15
Ionia, Gc, 8
Ioppe, Ed, 16
Ios I., Fe, 8
Ipsus, Bb, 9c
Irchester, Fd, 17
Iria, Dc, 12
Iria Flavia, Ad, 15
Irina Palus, Ke, 9b
Is, Ec, 9b

Isaura, Ec, 16
Isauria, Jf, 20
Isca (Caerleon), De, 17
Isca Dumnoniorum (Exeter), Cf, 17
Isca Silurum, Bb, 15
Iseum, Inset, 11d
Isin, Eb, 3a
Isis et Serapis, Inset, 11d
Israel, Dc, 2d
Israel, Kingdom of, Be, 4c
Issachar, Bc, 4a
Issus, Db, 9b
Istakr (Persepolis), Cb, 18b
Ister (Danubius), F., Hb, 5a
Istone, M., Ac, 6
Istri, Ba, 14c
Istria, Hb, 12
Istrus, Ib, 5a
Isurium, Eb, 17
Italia, Ed, 10
Italia, Diocese of, Fe, 20
Italica, Ae, 15
Italy, Ancient, 12-13
Italy, Prefecture of, Fe, 20
Itanus, Da, 7d
Ithaca, Bd, 7
Ithome, Cc, 6
Ithome, M., Ce, 7
Ituna Aest., Cb, 17
Ituraea, Ca, 4d
Iulia, Aq., Inset, 11
Iuliobona, Cc, 15
Iuliobriga, Bd, 15
Iuliomagus, Bc, 15
Iulium Carnicum, Ha, 12
Iunonis Reginae, Templum, Inset, 11
Iuvanum (Samnium). Jf. 12
Iuvavum, Ec, 15
Iverni, Inset, 17a

Jabbok, R., Cd, 4a
Jabesh Gilead, Be, 4c
Jalandhar, Eb, 18b
Jamnia, Ad, 4d
Jaugada, Cc, 18a
Jaxartes, R., Ic, 18
Jebus (Jerusalem), Be, 4a
Jericho, Be, 4a
Jerameelites, Af, 4c
Jerusalem, Jg, 4b, 4e, 20
Jerusalem (Hierosolyma), Dc 5
Jerusalem (Jebus), Bf, 4c
Jeshimon, Bf, 4a
Jezreel, Bc, 4a
Jezreel. Valley of, Bc, 4a
Joppa, Ad, 4a
Jordan, R., Cb, 3a; Cd, 4a
Judaea, Bd, 4d
Judaea, Wilderness of, Bd, 4d
Judah, Be, 4d
Judah, Kingdom of, Bf, 4c
Judgement, House of, Inset, 4b
Jumna, R., Je, 19
Junagarh, Ec, 18b
Jupiter Ammonium, Bd, 5b
Juti, Eb, 20

Kabul, Id, 19
Kadesh, Cb, 3a
Kadesh Barnea, Ag, 4c
Kalakh, Da, 3a
Kalinga, K. of, Cc, 18a
Kallikolone, Inset, 2c
Kalsi, Ba, 18a
Kalti (Hittites), Da, 4c
Kamarapura, Kingdom of, Gc, 18b
Kambojas, Ca, 18a
Kanatha, Db, 4d
Kanchi, Ed, 18b
Kanesh, Db, 2a
Kaplavasti, Cb, 18a
Karachi (Alexandria Portus), Je, 9b
Kara-shahr, Kc, 19
Karkar, Db, 2d
Karnak Temples, Cd, 3b
Kartripura, K. of, Eb, 18b
Kashgar, Jd, 19
Kashiari, Mt., Da, 3a
Kashkai, Db, 2d
Kashmir, Ba, 18a
Kasi (Benares), Cb, 18a
Katna, Dc, 12
Kaviripaddanam, Kf, 19
Ke Chow, Nd, 19
Kebtu (Coptos), Cd, 3b

4

Kedah (Kidri), Dc, 2d
Kedesh, Bd, 4c
Kedesh, Bb, 4a
Kenites, Bf, 4a
Kenizzites (Calebites), Af, 4a
Kera, Eb, 2d
Keralaputra, K. of, Bc, 18a
Khabur, F., Da, 3a
Khesout (Xois), Ba, 3b
Khidalu, Ec, 2d
Khilakku (Cilicia), Cb, 2d
Khojent (Alexandria Eschata), Ja, 9b
Khotan, Kd, 19
Khubushkia, Eb, 2d
Khyber P., Kc, 9b
Kidri (Kedah), Dc, 2d
Kidron, R., Bd, 4d
Kidron, Val. of, Insets, 4e, 4b
Kilif (Alexandria Oxiana), Jb, 9b
Kir-haraseth, Cf, 4a
Kiriath-arba (Hebron), Be, 4a
Kiriath-jearim, Be, 4a
Kiriath-sepher (Debir), Af, 4a
Kirkby Thore (Bravoniacum), Db, 17
Kish, Db, 3a
Kishon, R., Bc, 4a
Kistna, R., Jf, 19
Kizzuwatna, Ca, 3a
Kode, Cb, 3a
Konkan, S., Jf, 19
Korkai, Jg, 19
Kosala, K. of, Bb, 18a
Kottura, Fd, 18b
Kuang Han, Md, 19
Kuang-ling, Nd, 19
Kuang-Yang, Nd, 19
Kucha, Kc, 19
Kudal, Jg, 19
Kumani, Ca, 3a
Kummeh, Bd, 3a
Kummukh, Ca, 3a
Kurti, Da, 3a
Kush, Bd, 3a
Kushan Dominions, Id, 18
Kusinagara, K. of, Cb, 18a
Kuti, Da, 3a

Labeatis, L., Bb, 16
Labyrinth, Bb, 3b
Lacedaemon (Sparta), De, 7
Lacedaemonia, Cc, 9a
Lachish, Ae, 4a
Lacinium Pr., Fc, 13
Laconia, Df, 7
Lactodorum, Ed, 17
Ladon, F., Ce, 7
Laevi, Cb, 12
Lagash, Eb, 3a
Lagentium, Ec, 17
Laish (Dan), Cb, 4a
Lalita Patan, Cb, 18a
Lambaesis, De, 10
Lamia, Dd, 6
Laminium, Be, 15
Lampsacus, Ba, 2d; Cb, 7c
Lancaster, Db, 17
Langobardi, Fc, 20
Lanuvium, Aa, 13
Laodicea, Dc, 16
Laodicea (Syria), Fc, 16
Lappa, Ba, 7d
Larinum, Ca, 13
Larissa, Assyria, Eb, 5b
Larissa, Dardanians, Eb, 2b
Larissa, Thessalia, Dc, 6
Larius, L., Da, 12
Larissa Cremaste, Dd, 6
Larsa, Eb, 3a
Larymna, Ed, 6
Las, Df, 7
Lasea, Db, 4f
Lasium, Ce, 7
Latina, Aa, Inset, 11d
Latini, Aa, 13
Latium, Aa, 13
Latopolis, Cd, 3b
Laumellum, Cb, 12
Laurentum, Gf, 12
Lauriacum, Ec, 15
Laurium M., Ee, 7
Lauriya Araraj, Cb, 18a
Laus, Dc, 13
Laus Pompeia, Db, 12
Lavatrae, Eb, 17
Lebadea, Dd, 7
Lebanon, Ho. of, Inset, 4b
Lebanon, Mts., Cb, 3a
Lebedus, Gc, 8

Lebinthus, I., Gd, 8
Lechaeum, De, 7
Leicester (Ratae), Ed, 17
Lemanus, L., Dc, 15
Lemnos, Bc, 7c
Leontes, R., Ba, 4d
Leontini, Ce, 13
Leontium, Cd, 7
Lepontii, Ca, 12
Lepreum, Ce, 7
Leptis Magna, Ef, 10
Leptis Minor, Ee, 10; Ee, 15
Leros I., Gd, 8
Lesbos, Gb, 8
Letocetum, Ed, 17
Letopolis, Ba, 3b
Leuca, M., Aa, 7d
Leucae, Df, 7
Leucae Is., Db, 7d
Leucas, Bd, 6
Leucate Pr., Bd, 6
Leuce, Gc, 13
Leucimma Pr., Ab, 9a
Leucopetra Pr., De, 13
Leucos Limen, Bc, 3a
Leuctra, Boeotia, Ed, 7
Leuctra, Laconia, Ce, 8
Liang Chow, Md, 19
Liao-tung, Oc, 19
Libanus, M., Fd, 16
Libarna, Cc, 12
Libnah, Af, 4c
Liburnia, Bb, 16
Libya, Dd, 16
Libyans, Bc, 2a
Liger, R., Cd, 20
Ligures, Eb, 5a
Ligures Bebiani, Ca, 13
Liguria, Bc, 12
Lilybaeum, Ae, 13
Limes, Dc, 15
Limnae, Inset, 7b
Limnaea, Cd, 6
Limonum, Cc, 15
Lincoln (Lindum), Fc, 17
Lindinis, De, 17
Lindum (Lincoln), Fc, 17
Lindus, Fc, 2b
Lingones, Fc, 12
Lipara, Gc, 5a
Liparaeae Ins., Cd, 13
Liris, F., Ba, 13
Lissos Pr., Bb, 16
Lissus, Bb, 16
Liternum, Cb, 13
Littlechester, Ed, 17
Littus Saxonicum, Hd, 17
Lixus, Bc, 5a
Llandovery, Cd, 17
Llanio, Bd, 17
Locri (Magna Graecia), Gc, 5a
Locri, R., Cb, 2b
Locri Epizephyrii, Ed, 13
Locris (Epicnemidia), Dd, 6
Locris (Opuntia), Ed, 6
Locris Ozolis, Dd, 7
Lod, Ae, 4a
Logia Sinus, Ab, 17
Londinium, Ge, 17
Longaticum, Jb, 12
Loudoun Hill, Ba, 17
Lousonna, Aa, 12
Lower City, Inset, 4e
Lower Egypt, Ba, 3b
Loyang, Nd, 19
Luca, Ed, 12
Lucani, Cb, 14c
Lucania, Db, 13
Luceria, Da, 13
Lu-chiang, Nd, 19
Lucus Augusti, Ad, 15
Lugdunensis, Be, 15
Lugdunum, Cc, 15
Lugdunum Batavorum, Cb, 15
Lugii, Fb, 15
Luguvalium (Carlisle), Db, 17
Luae, Mtes., Inset, 1
Luna, Ec, 12
Lung-Hsi, Md, 19
Lupiae, Gb, 13
Lusitani, Ae, 15
Lusitania, Ae, 15
Lutetia, Dd, 20
Luxor, Cd, 2a
Luz (Beth-el), Be, 4a
Lycaonia, Fd, 18
Lychnidus, Ba, 6
Lychnites, L., Ba, 6
Lychnitus, L., Ld, 11
Lycia, Ed, 18

Lycians, Bb, 2a
Lycopolis (Syout), Bc, 3b
Lyctus, Dd, 2b
Lydda, Ad, 4d
Lydia, If, 20
Lydians, Bb, 2a
Lympne (Portus Lemanis), He, 17
Lyncestis, Cb, 6
Lyrceus M., De, 7
Lyrnessus, Eb, 2b
Lysimacheia, Cb, 7c
Lysimachia, Acarnania, Cd, 6
Lysimachia, Thracia, Aa, 9
Lyttus, Ca, 7d

Macae, He, 18
Macedonia, Cb, 6; Hf, 20
Macedonia, Diocese of, He, 20
Macestus, F., Eb, 7c
Machir (Manasseh), Dc, 4a
Macra, Dc, 12
Madaktu, Fc, 2d
Madraka, Eb, 18b
Madura, Ed, 18b
Maeander, F., Dc, 16
Maegaeum, Cb, 4f
Maenalus, De, 7
Maeonians, Eb, 2b
Maeotis, L., Ka, 5a
Maeotis Palus, Kd, 20
Magadha, Kingdom of, Fc, 18b
Magna Graecia, Gc, 5a
Magnae (Carvoran), Inset, 17
Magnesia (Caria), Hd, 8
Magnesia (Graecia), Dc, 6
Magnesia (Lydia), Dc, 16
Magnis, Dd, 17
Magnus Portus (Portsmouth Harb.), Ef, 17
Maha Kosala, Fc, 18b
Mahanadi, R., Ke, 19
Mahanaim, Cd, 4a
Mahendragiri, Mt., Fd, 18b
Maior, I., Ce, 15
Malaca, Cc, 5a
Malatia (Melid), Db, 2d
Malaya, Ec, 18b
Malea Pr., Ef, 7
Malis, Dd, 6
Mallus, Kc, 5a
Malwa, Je, 19
Mamucium (Manchester), Dc, 17
Manasseh (Machir), Dc, Bd, 4a
Manchester (Mamucium), Dc, 17
Mandrae, Ec, 7c
Manduria, Fb, 13
Manju Patan, Ke, 19
Mannai, Fb, 2d
Mansera, Ba, 18a
Mantinea, Cc, 9a
Mantua, Eb, 12
Maracanda, Jb 9b
Marakanda, Jb, 5b
Marash, Ca, 3a
Marathon, Ed, 7
Marcelli, Th., Inset, 11d
Marcellum, Inset, 13a
Marcomanni, Fd, 20
Mardi, Fb, 9b
Mardin, Da, 3a
Mare Adriaticum, Ge, 20
Mare Ægæum, If, 20
Mare Africum, Fc, 5a
Mare Australis, Inset, 1
Mare Balearicum, Dc. 5a
Mare Cantabricum, Bc, 18
Mare Caspium, Ne, 20
Mare Creticum, Ee, 8
Mare Cronium, Inset, 1
Mare Egyptum, Jd, 5a
Mare Erythraeum, Ec, 9c
Mare Etruscum, Bc, 14c
Mare Externum, Ac, 5a
Mare Gangeticum, Fd, 1
Mare Icarium, Gd, 8
Mare Internum, Dd, 18
Mare Ionium, Gf, 20
Mare Ligurum, Eb, 5a
Mare Myrtoum, Ef, 7
Mare Siculum, Gc, 5a
Mare Suevicum, Gb, 20
Mare Thracicum, Ec, 6
Mare Tyrrhenum, Ff, 20
Marea, Bc, 5b
Margiana, Id, 18
Margidunum, Fd, 17
Margus, F., Margiana, Ib, 5b
Margus, F., Moesia, Gd, 10
Mari, Db, 2a
Mariana, De, 12

Maridunum (Carmarthen), Be, 17
Marisus, F., Ca, 16
Marmarica, Cd, 16
Maronea, Ib, 5a
Marrucini, Je, 12
Marruvium, Hf, 12
Marsi, Hf, 12
Maryport (Alauna), Cb, 17
Massaga, Kc, 9b
Massagetae, Hc, 18
Massilia, Ee, 20
Mateola, Eb, 13
Mathura (Meerut), Ec, 18b
Matiana, L., Le, 11
Matianus, L., Fb, 2d
Mattieni, Eb, 5b
Mauretania, Df, 20
Mausoleum Augusti, Inset, 11d
Mausoleum Hadriani, Inset, 11d
Mazaca (Cæsarea), Fc, 16
Mazara, Ae, 13
Medeon, Cd, 6
Media, Gd, 18
Median Wall, Ec, 2d
Mediolanum, Db, 12
Mediolanum Santonum, Bc, 15
Medma, Dd, 13
Medus, F., Gc, 5b
Meerut (Mathura), Ec, 18b
Meerut (Mirath), Bb, 18a
Megalopolis, De, 7
Megara, Hc, 5a
Megara (Sicilia), Gc, 5a
Megara Hyblaea, De, 13
Megaris, Ed, 7
Megiddo, Bc, 4a
Melazgert, Eb, 2d
Meliboea (Hestiaeotis), Cc, 6
Meliboea (Magnesia), Dc, 6
Melid (Malatia), Db, 2d
Melita, Inset, Ab, 4f
Melitaea, Dc, 6
Melite, Ff, 20
Melite, Db, 9b
Melitene, Fc, 16
Melli, Kc, 9b
Mellte, Inset, 7b
Melos, Ff, 7
Melpum, Db, 12
Menaenum, Ce, 13
Menapii, Cb, 15
Mende, Hc, 5a; Ec, 6
Mendes, Ba, 3b
Menet Hufu (Speos Artemidos) Bc, 3b
Men-nofer (Memphis), Bb, 3b
Merinum, Ea, 13
Meroë, Cd, 1; Be, 3a
Merom, Waters of, Cb, 4a
Merv, Db, 18b
Mesambria, Bb, 7c
Mesembria, Ib, 5a; Db, 16
Mesheck (Mushki), Db, 2d
Mesopotamia, Eb, 9b
Messana, Gf, 20
Messana (Zancle), Dd, 13
Messapii, Fb, 13
Messene, Ce, 7
Messenia, Ce, 7
Meta Sudans, Inset, 13b
Metapontum, Eb, 13
Metaris, Aest, (The Wash), Gc, 17
Metaurus, F., Gd, 12
Metellinum, Ae, 15
Methana, Ee, 7
Methone (Macedonia), Db. 6
Methone (Messenia), Cf, 7
Methone (Thessalia), Fc, 6
Methydrium, De, 7
Methymna, Gb, 8
Metroni, Pa., Inset, 11d
Metropolis, Cd, 6
Mevania, Ge, 12
Michmash, Be, 4a
Midea, De, 7
Middle Egypt, Bb, 3b
Midia, Dc, 12
Miletus, Hd, 8
Miletus (Creta), Dd, 2b
Milid, Ca, 3a
Min Yueh, Ne, 19
Minaei, Gf, 18
Mincius, F., Eb, 12
Minius, F., Ad, 15
Minnagara, Ie, 19

Minor I., Cd, 15
Minturnae, Ba, 13; Bb, 14b
Mirath (Meerut), Bb, 18a
Misenum Pr., Cb, 13
Mitanni, Ca, 3a
Mitylene, Gb, 8
Mizpeh, Be, 4a
Moab, Cf, 4a
Moabites, Cf, 4a
Modicia, Db, 12
Moeris, L., Bb, 3b
Moesia Inferior, Db, 16
Moesia Superior, Cb, 16
Moguntiacum, Ec, 20
Mohammerah (Alexandria), Fc, 9b
Mona, Bc, 17
Monavia, Bb, 17
Monitia, Dc, 12
Mons Albanus, Ab, 14b
Mons Apenninus, Ed, 10; Fd, 12
Mons Caelius, Inset, 11c
Mons Esquilinus, Inset, 11d
Mons Ianiculus, Inset, 11d
Mons Pincius, Inset, 11d
Mons Sacer, Ab, 14b
Montes Bastarnici, Hc, 10
Montes Serrorum, Ca, 16
Monumentum Philopappi, Inset, 7b
Mopsuestia, Db, 5b
Morgantia, Ce, 13
Mosa, F., Dc, 15
Moschi, Eb, 5b
Mosella, F., Db, 15
Motya, Ae, 13
Motyca, Cf, 13
Mugonia, Pa., Inset, 11c
Munda, Be, 15
Murattash, Da, 3a
Mursa, Gd, 20
Murus Aurelius, Inset, 11d
Murus Hadriani, Cb, 20
Murus Medius, Inset, 7b
Murus Phalericus, Inset, 7b
Murus Septentrionalis, Inset, 7b
Musarum Mons, Inset, 7b
Musasir, Eb, 2d
Mushki (Mesheck), Db. 2d
Musri, Ca, 3a
Mutina, Ec, 12
Muziris, Jh, 19
Mycale, M., Hd, 8
Mycalessus, Ed, 7
Mycenae, Ce, 7
Mygdonia, Db, 6
Mykonos, Fd, 8
Mylae, Dd, 13
Mylasa, Bb. 9b
Myndus, Hd, 8
Myos Hormos, Bc, 3a
Myra, Ec, 16
Myrcinus, Eb, 6
Myriandrus, Db, 5b
Myrina, Db, 9a
Mysia, Ic, 5a
Mysians, Bb, 2a
Mytilene, Eb, 9a

Nabaite (Nebaioth), Dc, 2d
Nabataeans, Cd, 4d
Nabataei, Fe, 18
Naevia, Pa., Inset, 15c
Naharin, Ca, 3a
Nain, Bb, 4d
Nairi, Da, 3a
Naissus, He, 20
Namri, Fb, 2d
Nandangarh, Cb, 18a
Napata, Be, 3a
Naphtali, Cc, 4a
Napoca, Ca, 16
Nar, F., Ge, 12
Narbada, R., Je, 19
Narbada (Normada), R., Bb, 18a
Narbo, De, 20
Narbo Martius, Cd, 15
Narbonensis, Cd, 15
Narmada (Narbada), R., Bb, 18a
Narnia, Ge, 12
Narona, Bb, 16
Nasamones, Cd, 16
Natron Lakes, Ba, 3b
Naucratis, Cc, 5b
Naulochus, Dd, 13
Nauplia, De, 7
Naupactus, Cd, 6
Nauportus, Jb, 12
Navalia, Inset, 11d
Navalis, Pa., Inset, 11c

Navio, Ec, 17
Naxos, Euboea, Fd, 8
Naxos, Sicilia, Gc, 5a; Dc, 13
Naxuana, Le, 11
Nazareth, Bb, 4d
Neae, Fb, 8
Neaethus, F., Ec, 13
Neapolis, Be, 14a
Neapolis (Africa), Ee, 15
Neapolis (Apulia), Fb, 13
Neapolis, Campania, Cb, 13
Neapolis (Macedonia), Fb, 6
Neath (Nidum), Ce, 17
Nebaioth (Nabaite), Dc, 2d
Nebrodes Montes, Ce, 13
Nebut (Apollinopolis parva), Cd, 3b
Nedon, F., De, 7
Neetum, Cf, 13
Nemausus, Cd, 15
Nemea, De, 7
Nemetacum, Cb, 15
Nepal, Kingdom of, Fc, 18b
Nepete, Ge, 12
Nerium Pr., Ad, 15
Neronianus, Inset, 11d
Nersae, He, 12
Nervii, Cb, 15
Nesactium, Jc, 12
Nestus, F., Fa, 6
Newcastle (Pons Aelius), Inset, 17
Nicaea, Db, 16
Nicaea (Bactria), Jc, 9b
Nicaea (India), Kc, 9b
Nicaea (Liguria), Eb, 5a; Dd, 15
Nicephorium, Fc, 16
Nicomedia, Db, 16
Nicopolis (Armenia Minor). Fb, 16
Nicopolis (Epirus), Bd, 6
Nidum (Neath), Ce, 17
Nigir, R., Bd, 1
Nigliva, Cb, 18a
Nigritae, Ad, 1
Nile, R., Bc, 3a
Nilus, Ec, 4f
Nineveh, Da, 3a; Eb, 2d
Ningus, F., Hb, 12
Ninus, Lf, 17
Nippur, Eb, 3a
Nisaea, Ee, 7
Nishapur, Cb, 18b
Nisibis, Eb, 2d
Nisyros, I., He, 8
Nisyrus, Ec, 2b
Niy, Ca, 3a
No (Ammon, Thebes), Cd, 3b
Nola, Cb, 13
Nomentum, Ge, 12
Nomentana Pa., Inset, 11d
Noph (Memphis), Cd, 2d
Nora, Be, 14a
Norba (Apulia), Fb, 13
Norba (Hispania), Ae, 15
Norba (Latium), Aa, 13
Noreia, Ec, 10
Noricum, Fd, 20
Northern Hiung-nu, Kc, 19
Notium, Ec, 9a
Nova Via, Insets, 13a, b
Novae, Ie, 20
Novae Athenae, Inset, 7b
Novantae, Bb, 17
Novantarum Pr., Inset, 17a
Novaria, Cb, 12
Noviodunum, Kb, 12
Noviomagus (Chichester), Ff, 17
Noviomagus (Germania), Db, Dc, 15
Noviomagus (Lugdunensis), Cc, 15
Nubae, Cd, 1
Nubian Desert, Bd, 3a
Nuceria, Gd, 12
Nuceria Alfaterna, Cb, 13
Numana, Hd, 12
Numantia, Bd, 15
Numicius, F., Aa, 13
Numidia, De, 15
Nursia, He, 12
Nymphaeum Pr., Fb, 6
Nysa, Jc, 9b

OASIS MAGNA, Bd, 2d
Oasis Parva, Bd, 2d
Oasis Siwa (Ammonium), Bb, 2d
Oceanus Aethiopicus, Inset, 1
Oceanus Atlanticus, Ad, 20
Oceanus Britannicus, Bc, 18

Oceanus Germanicus, Db, 20
Oceanus Hibernicus, Bc, 17
Oceanus Indicus, Inset, 1
Oceanus Occidentalis, Inset, 1
Ocelum, Bb, 12
Ochus, F., Ib., 5b
Ocriculum, Ge, 12
Ocrinum Pr., Af, 17
Octapitarum Pr., Ae, 17
Octaviae, P., Inset, 11d
Octavii, P., Inset, 11d
Octodurum, Ba, 12
Octodurus, Dc, 15
Odessus, Db, 16
Odeum, Inset, 7a
Odomanti, Ea, 6
Odrysae, Ba, 9b
Oea, Ef, 10
Oeneon, Cd, 7
Oeniadae, Bb, 9a
Oenoe (Argolis), De, Ed, 7
Oenoe (Attica), Ed, 7
Oenoe (Elis), Ce, 7
Oenophyta, Ed, 7
Oenthea, Dd, 7
Oenussae, Is. Ionia, Gc, 8
Oenussae Ins., Messenia, Cf. 7
Oescus, Cb, 16
Oesyme, Fb, 6
Oeta, Dd, 6
Oglasa, Ee, 12
Olbia (Sardinia), Dd, 15
Olbia (Scythia), Ea, 16
Old Kilpatrick, Ba, 17
Olenus, Cd, 7
Olicana (Ilkley), Ec, 17
Olisippo, Ae, 15
Olives, Mt. of, Bd, 4d
Olizon, Ec, 6
Ollius, Eb, 12
Oloosson, Dc, 6
Olpae, Cd, 6
Olympieum, Inset, 7b
Olympia, Ce, 7
Olympus, Db, 6
Olynthus, Eb, 6
Omanitae, Hf, 18
Ombos, Bd, 3a
Omphis, Kingdom of, Kc, 9b
On (Heliopolis), Ba, 3b
Onchesmus, Bc, 6
Onchestus, F., Dc, 6
Onnum (Halton), Ea, 17
Onugnathos Pr., Df, 7
Ophel, Inset, 4b
Ophel, Wall of, Inset, 4b
Ophionenses, Cd, 6
Ophrah, Be, 4a
Ophrynium, Inset, 2c
Opis, Ec, 5b
Opis (Upi), Ec, 2d
Opitergium, Gb, 12
Oppius, M., Inset, 11c
Opus, Ed, 6
Opus, Pr., Dd, 7
Orcades, Inset, 17a
Orchoe, Fc, 9b
Orchomenus (Arcadia), De, 7
Orchomenus (Boeotia), Dd, 6
Ordovices, Cd, 17
Orestis, Cb, 6
Oreus, Cb, 9a
Oricus, Aa, 9a
Orneae, De, 7
Orontes, R., Cb, 4c
Oropus, Ed, 7
Ortona, Je, 12
Orumbovii, Db, 12
Osca, Bd, 15
Oscela, Ca, 12
Osci, Bb, 14c
Osii, Eb, 18
Osrhoene, Fc, 16
Ossa, M., Dc, 6
Osteodes, Ins., Bd, 13
Ostia, Gf, 12
Ostiensis, Pa., Inset, 11d
Ostrogothi, Id, 20
Otadini, Da, 17
Othona (Bradwell), Ge, 17
Othrys, M., Dd, 6
Ovilava, Ec, 15
Oxianus Lacus, Ea, 9c
Oxus, R., Ia, 9b
Oxydraces, Kc, 9b
Oxyrhynchus, Bb, 3b

PACHYNUS PR., Df, 13
Padan Aram, Db, 2d
Padmavati, Ec, 18b

Padus, F., Fb, 12
Paedagogium, Inset, 13b
Paeligni, He, 12
Paeones, Aa, 9b
Paeonia, Da, 6
Paeonians, Ca, 2b
Paestum, Cb, 13
Pagae, Ed, 7
Pagasae, Dc, 6
Paithan, Ed, 18b
Palaestina, Fd, 18
Palatinus, M., Inset, 13b
Palatium, Inset, 11d
Palatium Caesarum, Inset, 11d
Palestina, Cc, 5b
Palinuri Pr., Db, 13
Palla, Df, 12
Pallantia, Bd, 15
Pallantium, De, 7
Pallatina, Inset, 11c
Pallavas, Jf, 19
Pallene (Attica), Ed, 7
Pallene (Chalcidice), Eb, 6
Palma, Ce, 15
Palmyra, Kg, 20
Paludes Pomptinae, Ba, 13
Pamisus, F., Ce, 7
Pamphylia, If, 20
Panacton, Ed, 7
Panarus, F., Ec, 12
Pandateria, Bb, 13
Pandya, K. of, Bd, 18a
Pandosia, Bc, 6
Pangaeus, M., Fb, 6
Panjadada, Jd, 19
Pannonia (Interior), Ba, 16
Pannonia (Superior), Ba, 16
Panopolis (Shem), Bc, 3b
Panormus (Achaea), Cd, 7
Panormus (Phrygia), Db, 7c
Panormus (Sicilia), Bd, 13
Pantheon, Inset, 11d
Panticapaeum, Ka, 5a
Pantimathi, Fb, 5b
Paphlagonia, Je, 20
Paphlagonians, Ca, 2d
Paphos, Jd, 5a
Paraetacene, Jb, 9b
Paraetonium, Bc, 9b
Paran, Wilderness of, Ag, 4c
Parapanisadae, Jc, 9b
Parapanisus Mons, Jb, 9b
Parentium, Hb, 12
Paricanii, Jd, 5b
Parisi (Yorkshire), Fc, 17
Parium, Db, 7c
Parma, Ec, 12
Parnassus M., Dd, 6
Parnes M., Ed, 7
Parnon M., De, 7
Paropanisadai, Aa, 18a
Paros, Fd, 8
Parthenicum, Bd, 13
Parthenon, Inset, 7a
Parthia, Cb, 18b
Parthian Empire, Hd, 18
Parushapura, Jd, 19
Pasargadae, Gc, 5b
Pasitigris, F., Fc, 2d
Pataliputra, Cb, 18a
Patara, Dc, 16
Patavium, Fb, 12
Patmos I., Gd, 8
Patrae, Cd, 7
Pattala, Jd, 9b
Pauca, Cf, 12
Pausicae, Fb, 5b
Pautalia, Cb, 16
Pax Iulia, Ae, 15
Paxos, Bc, 6
Pebeseth (Bubastis), Ba, 3b
Pedasus, Eb, 2b
Pedone, Bc, 12
Pedum, Ab, 14b
Pelagonia, Ca, 6
Pelion M., Ec, 6
Pelium, Bb, 6
Pella (Macedonia), Db, 6
Pella (Palestina), Fd, 16; Cc, 4d
Pellene, Dd, 7
Pellene (Achaea), Db, 6
Peloponnesus, Hc, 5a
Pelorum Pr., Dd, 13
Pelso, L., Ba, 16
Peltae, Eb, 5b
Pelusic Mouth, Ca, 3b
Pelusium, Cc, 9b
Peneus, F., Cc, 6
Peneus, F., Ce, 7
Pennal, Cd, 17
Penneloci, Aa, 12

Pentapolis, Gf, 10
Pentri, Ca, 13
Penuel, Cd, 4a
Peparethus, Ec, 6
Peraea, Cd, 4d
Perga, Eb, 4f
Pergamum, Dc, 16
Perge, Cb, 9b
Perinthus, Ba, 9b
Per-Ramses, Ca, 3b
Perrhaebi, Dc, 6
Persarum Regnum, Mg, 20
Persepolis, Gd, 5b
Persian Empire, 5b
Persian Gates, Gc, 9b
Persis, Gc, 5b; Cb, 18b
Perusia, Gd, 12
Pessinus, Jf, 20
Petelia, Fc, 13
Petra (Arabia), Fd, 16
Petra (Graecia), Db, 6
Petra (Sela), Bg, 4c
Petra (Sicilia), Ce, 13
Petrianae, Cb, 17
Petuaria (Brough), Fc, 17
Pevensey (Anderida), Gf, 17
Phaeca, Cc, 6
Phaestus, Crete, Ba, 7d
Phaestus, Locris Ozolis, Dd, 7
Phalara, Dd, 6
Phalerum, Ee, 7
Phaloria, Cc, 6
Phanagoria, Fa, 16
Pharae (Achaea), Cd, 7
Pharae (Messenia), De, 7
Pharcadon, Dc, 6
Pharnacia, Fb, 16
Pharnaspa, Gd, 18
Pharos I., Dd, 16
Pharpar, R., Cd, 4c
Pharsalus, Dc, 6
Pharus I., Dd, 16
Phasaelis, Bc, 4d
Phaselis, Jc, 5a
Phasis, Gb, 16
Phatnitic Mouth, Ba, 3b
Pheneus, De, 7
Pherae, Dc, 6
Phigalia, Ce, 7
Phila, Dc, 6
Philace, Db, 6
Philadelphia (Asia), Db, 4f
Philadelphia (Palestine), Cd, 4d
Philippi, Aa, 9b
Philippi, P., Inset, 11d
Philippopolis, Cb, 16
Philistia, Ae, 4a
Philistines, Cc, 2a
Phinopolis, Ea, 7c
Phintias, Be, 13
Phlius, De, 7
Phocaea, Ic, 5a
Phocians, Cb, 2b
Phocis, Dd, 6
Phoenice, Bc, 6
Phoenicia, Fd, 18
Phoenicussa, Cd, 13
Pholegandros, Ff, 7
Phraaspa, Gd, 18
Phrygia, If, 20
Phrygians, Cb, 2a
Phthia, Cb, 2b
Phthiotis, Dc, 6
Phylace, Dc, 6
Phyle, Ed, 7
Picentes, Hd, 12
Picentia, Cb, 13
Picentini, Cb, 13
Picenum, Hd, 12
Picti, Cb, 20
Pictones, Bc, 15
Pillars of Hercules, Bc, 5a
Pinciana, Pa., Inset, 11d
Pindus, Mts., Cc, 6
Ping Chow, Md, 19
Pinna, He, 12
Piquentum, Jb, 12
Pir, Cc, 9a
Piraeus, Ee, 7
Piranum, Hb, 12
Piresiae, Dc, 6
Pisa (Graecia), Ce, 7
Pisae, Ed, 12
Pisanus Port, Ed, 12
Pisatis, Ce, 7
Pisaurum, Gd, 12
Piscina Publica, Inset, 11d
Pisgah, Mt., Ce, 4a
Pishtapura, Fd, 18b
Pisidia, Jf, 20
Pistoria, Ed, 12

Pithecussa Ins., Bb, 13
Pithom, Ba, 3b
Pitinum Pisaurense, Gd, 12
Pityus, Ke, 20
Pityusa, I., Ee, 7
Pityusae Ins., Ce, 15
Placentia, Db, 12
Planasia, Ee, 12
Plataea, Cb, 9a
Plavis, F., Ga, 12
Plemmyrium Pr., De, 13
Pleuron, Cd, 7
Plumbaria, Be, 14a
Pnyx, Inset, 7b
Poediculi, Eb, 13
Poeni, Be, Ac, 14c
Poetovio, Gd, 20
Pola, Hc, 12
Polacticum Pr., Hc, 12
Polemon, K. of, Fb, 4f
Pollentia, Bc, 12
Polyaegus, Fc, 6
Polyrrhenia, Aa, 7d
Pompaelo, Bd, 15
Pompeia, P., Inset, 11d
Pompeii, Cb, 13
Pompeii, Th., Inset, 11d
Pompeiopolis (Paphlagonia), Eb, 16
Pompeiopolis (Soli), Ec, 16
Pons Aelius (Newcastle), Eb, 17
Pons Aemilius, Inset, 13a
Pons Aeni, Ec, 15
Pons Aureoli, Db, 12
Pons Cestius, Inset, 11c
Pons Fabricius, Inset, 11c
Pontes, Fe, 17
Pontiae Ins., Ab, 13
Pontus, Jf, 20
Pontus, Diocese of, If, 20
Pontus Euxinus, Je, 20
Populonia, Fb, 5a
Porolissum, Ca, 16
Porta Archarnica, Inset, 7b
Porta Capena, Inset, 11d
Porta Carmentalis, Inset, 13a
Porta Diomea, Inset, 7b
Porta Flumentana, Inset, 13a
Porta Hadriani, Inset, 7b
Porta Itonia, Inset, 7b
Porta Mugonia, Inset, 13a
Porta Piraeica, Inset, 7b
Porta Ratumena, Inset, 13a
Porta Romanula, Inset, 13a
Porticus Metelli, Inset, 13a
Porticus Octaviae, Inset, 13b
Portsmouth Harb. (Magnus Portus), Ef, 17
Portuensis, Pa., Inset, 11d
Portus Adurni, Ef, 17
Portus Aedro, Gb, 12
Portus Cale, Ad, 15
Portus Herculis Monoeci, Bd, 12
Portus Itius, Cb, 15
Portus Lemanis (Lympne), He, 17
Portus Magnus, Be, 15
Portus Mauritii, Cd, 12
Portus Namnetum, Bc, 15
Portus Veneris (Gallia), Cd, 15
Portus Veneris (Italia), Dc, 12
Porus, Kingdom of, Kc, 9b
Posidium, Pr., Chalcidice, Eb, 6
Posodium Pr. (Italia), Cb, 13
Posidium Pr. (Pallene), Ec, 6
Posidium Pr. (Phthiotis), Ec, 6
Posidonia (Paestum), Cb, 13
Potaissa (Lucania), Db, 13
Potentia (Picenum), Hd, 12
Potidaea Ca, 9a
Praeneste Gf, 12
Praenestina, Pa., Inset, 11d
Prarjuna, Ec, 18b
Prasiae (Attica), Fe, 7
Prasiae (Laconia), De, 7
Prayaga, Cb, 18a
Priapus, Db, 7c
Priene, Hd, 8
Prista, Db, 16
Privernum, Bb, 14b
Procolitia (Carrawburgh), Inset, 17
Proconnesus, Db, 7c
Prophthasia, Ic, 9b
Propontis, Ib, 5a
Propylaea, Inset, 7a
Provincia, Cd, 15
Prusa, Fb, 7c
Prytaneum, Inset, 7a

Psacum, Pr., Aa, 7d
Pselchis, Bd, 3a
Psophis, Ce, 7
Psyra, I., Fc, 8
Psyttalea, I., Ee, 7
Pteleum, Dc, 6
Pteria, Cb, 5b
Ptolemais (Pentapolis), Cd, 16
Ptolemais (Phoenicia), Bb, 4d
Ptolemais Hermiu, Ig, 11
Pura, Ie, 18
Puteoli, Cb, 13
Pydna, Ca, 9a
Pylae, Ec, 5b
Pylae Ciliciae, Ec, 16
Pylos, Bc, 9a
Pylus, Elis, Ce, 7
Pylus, *see* Pylos
Pyramids, Bb, 3b
Pyramus, F., Db, 5b
Pyrenaei Mtes., De, 20
Pyretus, R., Id, 20
Pyrgi, Ge, 12
Pyrrha, Gb, 8
Pythium, Db, 6
Pytho, Cb, 2b
Pyxus, Db, 13

Quadi, Gd, 20
Quadrata, Cb, 12
Querquetulana, Pa., Inset, 11c

Rabbah, Ce, 4a
Raeburnfoot, Ca, 17
Rakoti (Alexandria), Aa, 3b
Ramah, Asher, Bc, 4a
Ramah, Benjamin, Be, 4a
Ramoth Gilead, Dc, 4a
Rampurwa, Cb, 18a
Raphana, Db, 4d
Ratae (Leicester), Ed, 17
Ratiaria, Cb, 16
Ratumena, Pa., Inset, 11c
Ravenglass (Clanoventa), Cb, 17
Ravenna, Gc, 12
Ravenscar, Fb, 17
Reate, Ge, 12
Reculver (Regulbium), He, 17
Regia, Insets, 13a, b
Regillus, L., Ab, 14b
Regina, Ec, 15
Regma, He, 18
Regni, Ff, 17
Regnum Bosporanum, Fa, 16
Regnum Parthorum, Ke, 11
Regulbium (Reculver), He, 17
Remi, Cc, 15
Renus, F., Fc, 12
Rerigonius Sinus, Ba, 17
Resaena, Bb, 18b
Restan, Cb, 3a
Reuben, Ce, 4a
Rha, R., Md, 20
Rhacotis (Alexandria), Bc, 9b
Rhaeti, Ba, 14c
Rhaetia, Ed, 20
Rhagae, Hd, 18
Rhamnus, Fd, 7
Rheba, Fa, 7c
Rhegium (Bruttium), Dd, 13
Rhegium Lepidum, Ec, 12
Rhenea, Fd, 8
Rhenus, F., Ed, 20
Rhion (Asine), Cf, 7
Rhithymna, Ba, 7d
Rhium Pr., Cd, 7
Rhodanus, F., Cd, 15; Ee, 20
Rhodope, M, Fa, 6; Gd, 10
Rhodus, If, 20
Rhoeteum, Inset, 2c
Rhoeteum Pr., Inset, 2c
Rhotanus, F., De, 12
Rhypes, Dd, 7
Rhytium, Dd, 2b
Ribchester (Bremetennacum), Dc, 17
Riblah, Cc, 4c
Richborough (Rutupiae), He, 17
Ricina (Liguria), Dc, 12
Ricina (Picenum), Hd, 12
Rigomagus, Cb, 12
Ripuarii, Ec, 20
Robogdii, Inset, 17a
Robogdium Prom., Aa, 17
Rochester (Durobrivae), Ge, 17
Rockingham Forest, Fd, 17
Roma, Gf, 12
Roma Quadrata, Inset, 13a
Roman Britain, 17

Roman Empire, 10-11; 15; 16
Romanula, Pa., Inset, 11c
Rostra Nova, Inset, 13b
Rostra Vetera, Inset, 13a
Rotomagus, Cc, 15
Rough Castle, Ca, 17
Roxolaeni, Fc, 18
Rubi, Ea, 13
Rubico, F., Gc, 12
Rudiae, Gb, 13
Rugii, Fc, Hd, 20
Rummindei, Cb, 18a
Rupnath, Bb, 18a
Rusaddir, Be, 15
Rusellae, Fe, 12
Rusgonia, Ce, 15
Rutuli, Ab, 14b
Rutupiae (Richborough), He, 17
Ruvignium, Hb, 12
Ryknield Way, Ed, 17

Sabaei, Dd, 1
Sabatinus, L., Ge, 12
Sabini, Ge, 12
Sabrina Aest. (Severn), Ce, 17
Sabrina, F., Bb, 15
Sacae (Scythae), Kb, 5b
Sacra Via (Athens), Inset, 7a
Sacra Via (Roma), Inset, 13b
Sacrum Pr., Dd, 12
Saepta, Inset, 11c
Saepta Iulia, Inset, 13b
Saetabis, Be, 15
Saevo M., Ba, 1
Sagalassus, Cb, 9b
Sagartia, Hc, 5b
Sagrus, Je, 12
Saguntum, Cc, 5a
Sai (Sais), Ba, 3b
St. Albans (Verulamium), Fe, 17
Sais (Sai), Ba, 3b
Sais (Zau), Cc, 2d
Sakas, Je, 19
Salamis (Cyprus), Jc, 5a
Salamis (Graecia), Ee, 7
Salapia, Da, 13
Salaria, Pa., Inset, 11d
Salassi, Bb, 12
Salcah, Ce, 4c
Saldae, De, 15
Salernum, Cb, 13
Salii, Ec, 20
Salinae (Droitwich), Dd, 17
Salisbury (Sorviodunum), Ee, 17
Sallentini, Fb, 13
Sallentinum Pr., Gc, 13
Salmantica, Ad, 15
Salonae, Bb, 16
Salt Sea, The, Bf, 4a
Salutaris, Pa., Inset, 11
Samal, Ca, 3a
Samaria, Bc, 4d
Samaria (Sebaste), Bc, 4d
Samarobriva, Cc, 15
Samatata, Kingdom of, Fc, 18b
Same, Bd, 7
Samnites, Bb, 14c
Samnium, Ca, 13
Samos, Gd, 8
Samos (Cephallenia), Bb, 2b
Samosata, Je, 11
Samothrace, Fa, 8
Sane, Eb, 6
Sangala, Kc, 9b
Sangarius, Eb, 16
Sanqualis, Pa., Inset, 11c
Santones, Bc, 15
Saradaush, Da, 3a
Sarangae, Ic, 5b
Sardes, Dc, 16
Sardinia-Corsica, Dd, 10
Sardis, Inset, Db, 4f
Sarmatia, Jc, 20
Sarmizegethusa, Ec, 18
Sarnia, Bc, 15
Sarpedon Pr., Cb, 7c
Sarsina, Gd, 12
Sarus, F., Db, 5b
Saspires Alardoii, Ea, 5b
Sassanid Kingdom, Cb, 18b
Satala, Fb, 16
Saticula, Ca, 13
Satiyaputra, K. of, Bc, 18a
Satricum, Aa, 13
Sattagydia, Jc, 5b
Saturnia, Fe, 12
Saurashtra, Je, 19
Savaria, Ba, 16
Savo, Cc, 12
Savus, F., Ba, 16

Saxones, Ec, 20
Saxum Tarpeium, Inset, 13a
Scalae Caci, Inset, 13a
Scallabis, Ae, 15
Scamander, F., Cc, 7c
Scandia, Fa, 20
Scandiae Ins., Ea, 15
Scarbantia, Ba, 16
Scarborough, Fb, 17
Scardona, Bb, 16
Scardus, M., Ba, 6
Scepsis, Cc, 7c
Sciathus, Ec, 6
Scillus, Bd, 8
Scione, Ec, 6
Scodra, Bb, 16
Scoti, Bc, 20
Scotus, Da, 8
Scupi, Cb, 16
Scylacium, Ed, 13
Scyllaeum, Dd, 13
Scyllaeum Pr. (Argolis), Ee, 7
Scyllaeum Pr. (Bruttium), Dd, 13
Scyros, Fd, 6
Scyrus, Db, 9a
Scythae (Sacae), Kb, 5b
Scythia, Jb, 19
Scythopolis, Bc, 4d
Sebaste (Samaria), Bc, 4d
Sebastea, Fc, 16
Sebinus, L., Eb, 12
Secia, F., Ec, 12
Second Cataract of Nile, Bd, 3
Secretarium, Inset, 13b
Sedunum, Ba, 12
Segedunum (Wallsend), Ea, 17
Segelocum, Fc, 17
Segesta (Liguria), Dc, 12
Segesta (Sicilia), Ae, 13
Segestanorum, Ad, 13
Segobriga, Be, 15
Segodunum, Cd, 15
Segontium (Carnarvon), Bc, 17
Segovia, Bd, 15
Segusio, Ab, 12
Seir, Cb, 3a
Sela (Petra), Bg, 4c
Seleucia, Ec, 16
Seleucia (Mesopotamia), Kf, 11
Seleucia (Syria), Fb, 4f
Selgovae, Ca, 17
Selinus (Cilicia), Ec, 16
Selinus (Sicilia), Ae, 13
Sellasia, De, 7
Selymbria, Ea, 7c
Semachonitis, L., Ca, 4d
Semneh, Bd, 3a
Sena Gallica, Hd, 12
Sena Iulia, Fd, 12
Senaculum, Inset, 13a
Sengara, Da, 3a
Senia, Aa, 16
Senones (Gallia), Cc, 15
Senones (Italia), Gd, 12
Sentinum, Gd, 12
Senzar, Ca, 3a
Sepharvaim (Sippar), Ec, 2d
Sepias Pr., Ec, 6
Sepphoris, Bb, 4d
Septimania, Pa., Inset, 11d
Sepulcrum C. Cestii, Inset, 11d
Sequana, R., Dd, 20
Sequani, Dc, 15
Serdica, Cb, 16
Serica, Gc, 1
Seriphos, Fe, 7
Sermyle, Eb, 6
Servitium, Ba, 16
Sessites, F., Cb, 12
Sestus, Ba, 5b
Seteia Aest., Cc, 17
Setia, Ba, 13
Severn (Sabrina Aest.), R., Ce, 17
Shahbazgarhu, Ba, 18a
Sharon, Plain of, Ac, 4d
Shasu (Habiru), Cb, 3a
Shechem, Bd, 4a
Shechem (Sychem), Bc, 4d
Shedet (Crocodilopolis-Arsinoé), Bb, 3b
Shel Gharraf, Eb, 3a
Shem (Panopolis), Bc, 3b
Shephelah, Ad, 4d
Sherwood Forest, Ec, 17
Shiloh, Bd, 4a
Shubari, Da, 3a
Shushan (Susa), Fc, 2d
Shuster, Bb, 18b
Sicani, Ae, 13
Sicca, De, 15

Sicelia, Inset, 7b
Sicilia, Be, 13; Ff, 20
Sicinos, I., Fe, 8
Siculi, Ce, 13
Sicyon, De, 7
Siddapura, Bc, 18a
Siddim, Vale of, Bf, 4a
Side, Bithynia et Pontus, Fb, 16
Side, Pamphylia, Jc., 5a
Sidon, Dc, 5b; Dc, 9b
Sidonians, Bb, 4a
Siga, Be, 15
Sigeum, Ic, 5a
Sigeum Pr., Inset, 2c
Signia, Ba, 13
Sila M., Dd, 13
Silarius, F., Db, 13
Silchester (Calleva Atrebatum), Fe, 17
Siloam, Pool of, Inset, 4e
Silures, Ce, 17
Simeon, Af, 4a
Simkala (Ceylon), Fe, 18b
Simoeis, F., Inset, 2c
Simyra, Bc, 4c
Sinae, Gc, 1
Sinai, Mt., Bc, 3a
Sinai Pen., Bc, 3a
Sind, Ie, 19
Singara, Lf, 20
Singidunum, Cb, 16
Singus, Eb, 6
Sinope, Fb, 16
Sinuessa, Ba, 13
Sinus Acanthus, Eb, 6
Sinus Aelanites, Bc, 3a
Sinus Alcyonicus, Ed, 7
Sinus Ambracius, Bd, 6
Sinus Arabicus, Cd, 3a
Sinus Argolicus, De, 7
Sinus Astacenus, Fb, 7c
Sinus Aualites, Gb, 18
Sinus Caystrius, Hd, 8
Sinus Ceramicus, He, 8
Sinus Cianus, Fb, 7c
Sinus Corinthiacus, Dd, 7
Sinus Crisaeus, Dd, 7
Sinus Cumanus, Cb, 13
Sinus Cyparissius, Ce, 7
Sinus Didymi, Ca, 7d
Sinus Euboicus, Ed, 6
Sinus Flanaticus, Jb, 12
Sinus Heroopolites, Bc, 3a
Sinus Laconicus, Df, 7
Sinus Laus, Db, 13
Sinus Ligusticus, Dd, 15
Sinus Maliacus, Dd, 6
Sinus Messeniacus, Df, 7
Sinus Oxianus, Hc, 18
Sinus Paestanus, Cb, 13
Sinus Pagasaeus, Dc, 6
Sinus Persicus, Eb, 3a
Sinus Saronicus, Ee, 7
Sinus Scylaceus, Ed, 13
Sinus Singiticus, Eb, 6
Sinus Strymonicus, Eb, 6
Sinus Tarentinus, Fb, 13
Sinus Thermaicus, Db, 6
Sinus Thesproticus, Eb, 6
Sinus Toronaicus, Eb, 6
Siphae, Ed, 7
Siphnos, Ff, 7
Sipontum, Da, 13
Sippar, Ec, 5b
Sippar (Sepharviam), Ec, 2d
Siris, Eb, 13
Siris, F., Eb, 13
Sirmio, Eb, 12
Sirmium, Ge, 20
Siscia, Gd, 20
Sithonia, Eb, 6
Sitifis, De, 15
Sittace, Ec, 5b
Smyrna, Hc, 8
Smyrna Nova, Hc, 8
So-fang, Mc, 19
Sogdiana, Jb, 5b; Jb, 9b
Sogdiana, Ib, 9b
Soleb, Bd, 3a
Soli (Cilicia), Jc, 5a
Soli (Cyprus), Jc, 5a
Soli (Pompeiopolis), Ec, 16
Sollium, Bc, 6
Solomon's Palace, Inset, 4b
Soluntum, Bd, 13
Solus, Fc, 5a
Solygea, De, 7
Sopara, Bc, 18a
Sopianae, Ba, 16
Sora, Ba, 13

Soracte M., Ge, 12
Sorek, R., Ae, 4a
Sorviodunum (Salisbury), Ee, 17
South Shields, Inset, 17b
Southern Hiung-nu, Mc, 19
Spain (Diocese of Hispania), Ce, 20
Spalautra, Ec, 6
Sparta, De, 7
Spartolus, Ca, 9a
Speluncae, Ba, 13
Speos Artemidos (Menet Hufu), Bc, 3b
Spercheus, F., Dd, 6
Sphacteria, Bc, 9a
Spinis, Ee, 17
Spoletium, Ge, 12
Sravasti, Ke, 19
Srinagar, Ba, 18a
Stabiae, Cb, 13
Stadium (Athens), Inset, 7b
Stadium Domitiani, Inset, 11d
Stagira, Eb, 6
Stanwix, Inset, 17
Stenyclarus, De, 7
Stephen's Gate, Inset, 4e
Stoa Hadriani, Inset, 7b
Stoa of Eumenes, Inset, 7a
Stobi, Cb, 16
Stratonicaea, Eb, 6
Stratonice, Da, 8
Stratus, Cd, 6
Strongyle, Dd, 13
Strymon, F., Cb, 16
Stura, F., Bc, 12
Stymphalus, De, 7
Styra, Fd, 7
Suana, Fe, 12
Sublicius, Inset, 11d
Sublupatia, Eb, 13
Subura, Inset, 11c
Suburana, Inset, 11c
Sucro, F., Be, 15
Sudeti Mts., Eb, 15
Suessa Aurunca, Ba, 13
Suessa Pometia, Aa, 13
Suessula, Ca, 13
Suevi, Ed, 20
Suevi, Semnones, Db, 18
Sugambri, Db, 15
Suindinum, Cc, 15
Sulci, De, 15
Sumer, Eb, 3a
Sunium, Fe, 7
Sunium Pr., Fe, 7
Surashtra, Ec, 18b
Surrentum, Cb, 13
Susa, Fc, 5b
Susa (Shushan), Fc, 2d
Susia, Hb, 9b
Susiana, Fc, 5b; Gd, 18
Sutrium, Ge, 12
Sutu, Db, 3a
Syagros Pr., Hf, 18
Sybaris, Gc, 5a
Sybota, Bb, 9a
Sychem (Shechem), Bc, 4d
Syene, Cc, 5b
Symaethus, F., De, 13
Syme, Ec, 9a
Synnada, Ec, 16
Syout (Lycopolis), Bc, 3b
Syracusae, Gc, 5a; De, 13; Gf, 20
Syria, Dc, 9b
Syria Deserta, Gd, 18
Syrian Desert, Cb, 3a
Syrians (Aramaeans), Dc, 4c
Syrnos I., Ge, 8
Syros, Fe, 7
Syrtis Major, Gg, 20
Syrtis Minor, Fg, 20
Sze Chow, Nd, 19

Taanach, Bc, 4a
Tabal, Cb, 2d
Tabernae Argentariae, Inset, 13a
Tabernae Veteres, Inset, 13a
Tabor, Mt., Bc, 4a
Tabularium, Inset, 13b
Tadcaster (Calcaria), Ec, 17
Tadmor (Palmyra), Cb, 3a
Tadmor (Tamar), Ec, 4c
Taenarum Pr., Df, 7
Tagus, F., Ae, 15
Tai Yuan, Nd, 19
Taliata, Cb, 16
Talmis, Bd, 3a
Tamar (Tadmor), Ec, 4c
Tamesa Aest., Inset, 17a
Tamesis, F., Bb, 15

INDEX

Tamralipti, Cb, 18a
Tamraparni (Ceylon), Cd, 18a
Tanager, F., Db, 13
Tanagra, Ed, 7
Tanais, Ka, 5a
Tanais, R., Db, 1
Tanarus, F., Cc, 12
Tanis (Zoan), Ba, 3b
Tanitic Mouth, Ca, 3b
Taphiae Ins., Bd, 6
Taprobane, Fd, 1
Tapti, R., Je, 19
Tapuritae, Gb, 9b
Taras, Fb, 13
Tarentum, Fb, 13
Tarnaiae, Aa, 12
Tarquinii, Fe, 12
Tarracina, Ba, 13
Tarraco, De, 20
Tarraconensis, Bd, 15
Tarsatica, Aa, 16
Tarshish (Tartessus), Bc, 5a
Tarsius, F., Dc, 7c
Tarsus, Cb, 5b
Tartessus (Tarshish), Bc, 5a
Tarus, F., Dc, 12
Tarvenna, Cb, 15
Tarvisium, Gb, 12
Tatta, L., Cb, 5b
Taulantii, Aa, 6
Taurianum Pr., Dd, 13
Taurica, Jd, 20
Taurini, Bc, 12
Tauromenium De, 13
Taurus, Jf, 20
Taurus, M., Ec, 16
Taurus Pr., De, 13
Tavium, Ec, 16
Taxila, Eb, 18b
Taygetus, M., De, 7
Teanum, Ca, 13
Teanum Apulum, Da, 13
Teate, Je, 12
Tecmon, Bc, 6
Tegea, De, 7
Tegianum, Db, 13
Tehenu, Ba, 3b
Teira, Hc, 8
Tekoa, Be, 4a
Telamon, Fe, 12
Telesia, Ca, 13
Tell-el-Amarna (Akhetaton), Bc, 3b
Telmessus, Dc, 16
Telos, Ec, 9a
Tempe, F., Dc, 6
Temple (Jerusalem), Inset, 4b
Templeborough, Ec, 17
Templum Antonini et Faustinae, Inset, 13b
Templum Apollinis, Inset, 13b
Templum Athene, Inset, 13b
Templum Augusti, Inset, 13b
Templum Castorum, Insets, 13a, b
Templum Concordiae, Insets, 13a, b
Templum Dianae, Inset, 11c
Templum Divi Romuli, Inset, 13b
Templum Divi Traiani, Inset, 13b
Templum Divorum, Inset, 13b
Templum Iani, Inset, 13a
Templum Iovis Capitolini, Insets, 13a, b
Templum Iovis Statoris, Insets, 13a, b
Templum Iovis Victoris, Insets, 13a, b
Templum Iunonis Lucinae, Inset, 11c
Templum Iunonis Monetae, Insets, 13a, b
Templum Martis Ultoris, Inset, 13b
Templum Minervae, Inset, 13b
Templum Pacis, Insets, 13b
Templum Quirini, Inset, 11c
Templum Romae et Augusti, Inset, 7a
Templum Sacrae Urbis, Inset, 13b
Templum Salutis, Inset, 11c
Templum Saturni, Inset, 13a
Templum Semonis Sanci, Inset, 11c
Templum Veneris et Romae, Inset, 13b
Templum Veneris Genetricis, Inset, 13b
Templum Vespasiani, Inset, 13b
Tempsa, Ed, 13
Tena Aest., Inset, 17a

Tenebrium Pr., Ce, 15
Tenedos, Gb, 8
Tenos, Fd, 8
Tentyra (Enet), Cc, 3b
Teos, Eb, 9a
Teredon, Fc, 9b
Tergeste, Hb, 12
Terina, Ec, 13
Teurnia, Ec, 15
Teuthrone, Df, 7
Teutones, Db, 15
Thaenae, Ef, 15
Thalaba, Ge, 18
Thapsacus, Db, 5b
Thapsacus (Tiphsah), Eb, 4c
Thapsus (Africa), Ee, 15; Ff, 20
Thapsus (Silicia), De, 13
Thara, Gb, 9b
Tharrus, Ec, 5a
Tharu, Ca, 3b
Thasos, Fb, 6
Theatrum Dionysi, Inset, 7a
Theatrum et Porticus Pompeii, Inset, 11
Theatrum Marcelli, Inset, 13b
Thebae, Achaea, Cc, 16
Thebae, Libya, Cc, 1; Ig, 11
Thebe, Eb, 2b
Thebes (Boeotia), Ed, 7
Thebes (Hypothebae), Cb, 2b
Thebes (No, Ammon), Cd, 3b
Thebes (Phthiotis), Dc, 6
Thebez, Bd, 4a
Thelpusa, Ce, 7
Thera, Dc, 9a
Therma, Eb, 6
Thermae, Be, 13
Thermae Agrippae, Inset, 11d
Thermae Antoninianae, Inset, 11d
Thermae Constantini, Inset, 11d
Thermae Diocletiani, Inset, 11d
Thermae Neptuni, Inset, 11d
Thermae Neronianae, Inset, 11d
Thermae Quirini, Inset, 11d
Thermae Salurni, Inset, 11d
Thermae Selinuntiae, Be, 13
Thermae Solis, Inset, 11d
Thermae Traiani, Inset, 11d
Thermae Vestae, Inset, 11c
Thermessa, Cd, 13
Thermopylae, Dd, 6
Thermum, Cd, 6
Thespiae, Ed, 7
Thesprotia, Bc, 6
Thessalia, Dc, 6
Thessalonica, He, 20
Thessaly, see Thessalia
Theudoria, Cc, 6
Theveste, De, 15
Third Cataract of Nile, Be, 3a
Thisbe, Cb, 2b
Thoricus, Fe, 7
Thospitis, L., Eb, 5b
Thrace, see Thracia
Thracia, Fa, 6; Ie, 20
Thracia, Diocese of, Ie, 20
Three Taverns, Aa, 4f
Thronium, Cb, 9a
Throsmos, Inset, 2c
Thule, Inset, 17a
Thurii, Ec, 13
Thusdrus, Ee, 15
Thyateira, Hc, 8
Thyatira, Db, 4f
Thymbra, Inset, 2c
Thyrea, De, 7
Thyrrheum, Bd, 6
Thyrsus, F., Bd, 14a
Thyssus, Fb, 6
Tiberias, Bb, 4d
Tiberina, I., Inset, 11d
Tiberis, F., Gf, 12
Tibur, Gf, 12
Tiburtina, Pa., Inset, 11d
Ticinum, Db, 12
Ticinus, F., Cb, 12
Tifernum, Gd, 12
Tifernus, F., Kf, 12
Tigranocerta, Ke, 11
Tigris (Hiddekel), F., Ec, 2d
Tigris, R., Db, 3
Tigullia, Dc, 12
Til Barsip, Db, 2d
Tilaventus, F., Ga, 12
Tilgarimmu (Togarmah), Db, 2d
Tingis, Bd, 18
Tingitana, Bf, 15
Tingitania, Cg, 20
Tipasa, Ce, 15
Tiphsah (Thapsacus), Eb, 4c

Tipsah, Db, 2d
Tiryns, De, 7
Tisia, F., Ca, 16
Titulcia, Bd, 15
Tium, Eb, 16
Tob, Cc, 4a
Togarmah (Tilgarimmu), Db, 2d
Tolentinum, Hd, 12
Toletum, Bd, 15
Tolosa, De, 20
Tomen-y-mur, Cd, 17
Tomi, Hd, 11
Topra, Bb, 18a
Torone, Ec, 6
Towcester, Ed, 17
Tralles, Bb, 2d
Transpadana, Cb, 12
Trapezus, Ke, 20
Trans Tiberim, Inset, 11d
Trasimenus, L., Gd, 12
Treba, Hf, 12
Trebbia, F., Dc, 12
Trebula, Ge, 12
Treveri, Dc, 10
Triballi, Aa, 9c
Tricca, Cc, 6
Trichonius, L., Cd, 6
Tridentini, Fa, 12
Tridentum, Fa, 12
Trigemina, Pa., Inset, 11c
Trimontium, Da, 17
Trinovantes, Ge, 17
Triphylia, Ce, 7
Tripodes, Inset, 7a
Tripolis, Fg, 20
Tripolis (Phoenicia), Fd, 16
Tripolis (Pontus), Fb, 16
Tripolitana, Ef, 10
Tritaea, Cd, 7
Tritonis, L., Df, 10
Triturrita, Ed, 12
Troas, Db, 4f
Troesmis, Da, 16
Troezen, Ee, 7
Trojan Plain, Inset, 2c
Troy (Ilium), Bb, 2a
Tsang-Wu, Ne, 19
Tuder, Ge, 12
Tullianum, Insets, 13a, b
Tullum, Dc, 15
Tunes, Ee, 15
Tung-hai, Nd, 19
Tun-Huang, Ld, 19
Tuola, F., De, 12
Turdetani, Ae, 15
Turduli, Be, 15
Turushpa (Van), Eb, 2d
Tusci (Etrusci), Bb, 14c
Tusculum, Aa, 13
Tyana, Ba, 3a
Tymphaea, Cc, 6
Tymphe M., Cc, 6
Tymphrestus M., Cd, 6
Tyndaris, Cd, 13
Tyras, Ja, 5a
Tyras, R., Id, 20
Tyre, Bb, 4a; Kg, 20
Tyrrhenia, Fb, 5a
Tyrus, Fd, 18

Ubi, Cb, 3a
Ugarit, Dc, 2a
Ujjain, Je, 19
Ulpiana, Cb, 16
Ulterior Hispania, Ad, 15
Umbria, Gd, 12
Umbri, Gd, 12
Umbro, F., Fe, 12
Upi (Opis), Ec, 2d
Upper City (Jerusalem), Inset, 4e
Upper Egypt, Bc. 3b
Ur, Eb, 3a
Uraipur, Bc, 18a
Uraiyu, Jf, 19
Urartu (Ararat), Eb, 2d
Urbs Salvia, Hd, 12
Urcinium, Ce, 12
Uria, Fb, 13
Urium, Da, 13
Uruk (Erech), Fc, 2d
Uselis, Be, 14a
Ustica, Bd, 13
Utica (Africa), Cf, 14; De, 15
Utii, Hd, 5b
Uxantis, Ac, 15
Uxii, Gc, 9b
Uzentum, Gc, 13

Vaccaei, Ad, 15
Vada, Ed, 12
Vada Sabatia, Cc, 12

Vadimonis, L., Ge, 12
Vagienni, Bc, 12
Vaisis, Eb, 2d
Valabhi, Ec, 18b
Valentia (Gallia), Cd, 15
Valentia (Hispania), Be, 15
Vallis Murcia, Inset, 11c
Vallis Quirini, Inset, 11c
Vallum Antonini, Ba, 17
Vallum Hadriani, Da, 17
Valvata, Ed, 12
Van (Turushpa), Eb, 2d
Vandali, Gc, 20
Vanga, Cb, 18a
Vapincum, Dd, 15
Vascones, Bd, 15
Vectis, Ef, 17
Veii, Ge, 12
Velabrum, Insets, 13a, b
Veldidena, Ec, 15
Veleia, Dc, 12
Velia, Inset, 13a
Velia (Elea), Db, 13
Velitrae, Aa, 13
Veltae, Eb, 18
Venafrum, Ca, 13
Venedae, Ib, 20
Veneris et Romae, Inset, 11d
Veneti (Gallia), Bc, 15
Veneti (Italia), Gb, 12; Ec, 15
Venetia, Fb, 12
Vengi, K. of, Fd, 18b
Vengipura, Fd, 18b
Venonae, Ed, 17
Venonetes, Da, 12
Venta, Inset, 17a
Venta Belgarum (Winchester), Ee, 17
Venta Icenorum, Hd, 17
Venta Silurum, De, 17
Venusia, Db, 13
Verbanus, L., Ca, 12
Vercellae, Cb, 12
Vercovicium (Housesteads), Inset, 17
Veretum, Gc, 13
Verlucio, De, 17
Vernemetum, Ed, 17
Verona, Fb, 12
Verterae (Brough), Db, 17
Vertones Oretani, Ad, 15
Verulamium (St. Albans), Fe, 17
Vesontio, Dc, 15
Vestini, He, 12
Vesunna, Cc, 15
Vesuvius, M., Cb, 13
Vetera, Db, 15
Yettona, Ge, 12
Vetulonia, Ee, 12
Via Aemilia, Ec, Gc, 12
Via Appia, Aa, Eb, 13
Via Asinaria, Inset, 11c
Via Aurelia, Ed, 12
Via Cassia, Fe, 12
Via Claudia Augusta, Gb, 12
Via Clodia, Fe, 12
Via Dolorosa, Inset, 4e
Via Domitia, Cd, 15
Via Flaminia, Gd, 12
Via Galaria, Inset, 11c
Via Iulia, Cc, 12
Via Lata, Inset, 11d
Via Latina, Ba, 13
Via Nomentana, Inset, 11c
Via Ostiensis, Inset, 11c
Via Popilia, Db, 13
Via Portuensis, Inset, 11c
Via Postumia, Fb, 12
Via Praenestina, Inset, 11c
Via Sacra (Athens), Inset, 7b
Via Sacra (Rome), Inset, 11c
Via Salaria, He, 12
Via Tiburtina, Inset, 11c
Via Triumphalis, Inset, 11c
Via Valeria (Italia), He, 12
Via Valeria (Sicilia), Ce, 13
Viadua, F., Fb, 10
Viadua, R., Gc, 20
Vibinum, Da, 13
Vicetia, Fb, 12
Vicus Iugarius, Insets, 13a, b
Vicus Longus, Inset, 11c
Vicus Patricius, Inset, 11c
Vicus Tuscus, Insets, 13a, b
Vienna (Gallia), Cc, 15
Vienna (Vienne), Dd, 20
Villa Publica, Inset, 11c
Viminacium, He, 20
Viminalis, Pa., Inset, 11c
Vindelicia, Ec, 15

Vindobona, Ba, 16
Vindolanda (Chesterholm), Inset, 17
Vindomora (Ebchester), Inset, 17
Vindovala, Inset, 17
Vinovia, Eb, 17
Vinocladia, Ef, 17
Vintium, Bd, 12
Virgin's Well, Inset, 4e
Virgo, Aq., Inset, 11d
Viroconium (Wroxeter), Dd, 17
Virodunum, Dc, 15
Virunum, Ec, 10
Visigothi, Hd, 20
Vistula, F., Gb, 10; Hc, 20
Visurgis, F., Db, 15
Vitricium, Bb, 12
Viviscus, Aa, 12
Volaterrae, Ed, 12
Volcanal, Inset, 13a
Volcei, Db, 13
Volsci, Bb, 14c; Ba, 13
Volsiniensis, L., Fe, 12
Volsinii (novus), Ge, 12
Volsinii (vetus), Ge, 12
Volturnum, Ba, 13
Volturnus, F., Ca, 13
Volubilis, Af, 10
Vomanus, F., Je, 12
Vosegus, M., Dc, 15
Vulci, Fe, 12

Wadi Tumilat, Ba, 3b
Walls (Jerusalem), Inset, 4e
Wallsend (Segedunum), Ea, 17
Walton Castle, He, 17
Warrington, Dc, 17
Wash, The (Metaris Aest.), Gc, 17
Watling Street, Dd, 17
Western Satraps, Ec, 18b
Wigan, Dc, 17
Winchester (Venta Belgarum), Ee, 17
World (Eratosthenes), 1b
World (Ptolemy), 1a
World (Herodotus), 1a
World (Strabo), 1c
Wroxeter (Viroconium), Dd, 17
Wuchun, Nd, 19
Wu-Wei, Md, 19

Xanthus, Bb, 9b
Xerxes Canal, Eb, 6
Xois (Khesout), Ba, 3b
Xyniae, Dc, 6

Y Gaer, Cd, 17
Yamutbul, Fc, 2d
Yandheya, Ec, 18b
Yang Chow, Ne, 19
Yangtze R., Od, 19
Yarkand, Jd, 19
Yarmuk, R., Cc, 4a
Yavanas, Id, 18
Yenoam, Cb, 3a
Yih Chow, Md, 19
Ying-chuan, Nd, 19
York (Eburacum), Eb, 17
Yu Chow, Nd, 19
Yu-chang, Ne, 19
Yueh-Sui, Me, 19
Yun Chow, Nd, 19
Yun-chung, Nc, 19

Zacynthus, Hc, 5a
Zadadrus, F., Kc, 9b
Zadracarta, Gb, 9b
Zagros Mts., see Zagrus Mons.
Zagrus Mons, Fc, 5b
Zahi, Cb, 3a
Zaitha, Bb, 18b
Zakaray, Ac, 4a
Zama Regia, De, 15
Zamua, Fb, 2d
Zancle (Messana), Dd, 13
Zarax, Ef, 7
Zarephath, Ba, 4d
Zariaspa, Ib, 9b
Zariaspa (Bactria), Jb, 9b
Zau (Sais), Cc, 2d
Zebulun, Bc, 4a
Zela, Fb, 16
Zeleia, Db, 7c
Zephyrium Pr., Ed, 13
Zeugma, Fc, 16
Ziklag, Af, 4a
Zikurtu, Fb, 2d
Zilis, Ae, 15
Zoan (Tanis), Ba, 3b
Zobah, Cc, 4c

MUIR'S
HISTORICAL ATLAS
MEDIEVAL AND MODERN
Eleventh Edition

EDITED BY

the late R. F. TREHARNE, M.A., Ph.D.
PROFESSOR OF HISTORY, UNIVERSITY COLLEGE OF WALES, ABERYSTWYTH

AND

HAROLD FULLARD, M.Sc.
CARTOGRAPHIC EDITOR

First Edition 1911
Second Edition 1914
Third Edition 1917
Fourth Edition, Enlarged 1920
Fifth Edition 1923
Sixth Edition, Revised and Greatly Enlarged . . . 1927
Seventh Edition 1947
Eighth Edition 1952
Reprinted 1956
Ninth Edition, Revised and Completely Redesigned . 1962
Tenth Edition 1964
Eleventh Edition . . . . ©1969

George Philip & Son Ltd.

PRINTED IN GREAT BRITAIN BY GEORGE PHILIP PRINTERS LIMITED, LONDON

PREFACE

FIFTY YEARS afford a searching test of the qualities of any work designed to satisfy the needs of many thousands of teachers and students in universities and in the higher classes of schools and colleges, especially when the book is planned on a scale which, despite the utmost economy in production, necessarily implies a fairly substantial price. The present editors of Ramsay Muir's *Historical Atlas: Mediaeval and Modern*, may fairly claim that the work which they are now partly refashioning has triumphantly stood that test, amply justifying the pride which Ramsay Muir and George Philip felt in their original edition of it. The *Atlas* has now run through eight editions and many reprints, and has so fully satisfied the need which brought it into being that it still has no serious rival in the British market over its own range and at a comparable price. It is no exaggeration to say that the Ramsay Muir historical atlases, pioneer works at their first appearances, demonstrating for the first time how a modern study of historical geography might illuminate so much of the study of history, played a decisive part in establishing historical geography as an integral part of the study and teaching of history in Britain. In so doing they did much to shape the new canon of our present method of teaching historical geography, especially by their demonstration of the physical basis of the subject, and also by their systematic conventions for representing historical data on coloured maps in such a way as to facilitate comparison between successive maps over long periods of time. To attempt now to recast a work which has not only thoroughly established itself in our educational provision, but has actually helped to shape our thinking and teaching of history, is no light responsibility.

Yet, after fifty years, reshaping there must be: in 1927, after only sixteen years, Ramsay Muir and George Philip themselves drastically refashioned this *Atlas* for its sixth edition. Muir never claimed that the *Atlas* was in any sense a work of original research, save where, as on British India, his own special knowledge enabled him at one or two points to make it so; the present editors can claim no more for this ninth edition. To make an atlas of this kind a work of original research would entail employing a specialist to design each separate map: this work aspires only to render in map form the conclusions of the best modern authorities readily available to the editors at the time when their work of revision was in process. But even this entails change. There are always errors and omissions to be rectified: the inevitable slow accretion of too many names on the successive editions of certain maps requires periodic pruning: the appearance of new and authoritative books, whether monographs, standard histories or works of reference, and even of new maps and atlases, inevitably necessitates change if the work is to be kept up to date. Most of all, we must keep pace with History itself. The last thirty years have not only seen rapid and tremendous changes in the political maps of the more familiar parts of the world, but have also forced on our attention regions virtually ignored in common history teaching until today. So we have been compelled to make great changes in this standard instrument of teaching history, some of them changes which we adopted grudgingly, others which we know the original editors would themselves have wished to see.

Inflation and rising costs have imposed sharp limits on us. Seeking to keep the price of the *Atlas* within the reach of those for whom it was first designed, we can in fact claim that, allowing for the changes in money value, the *Atlas*, at its present price, is no dearer than it was in 1911. But this has been achieved only by sharp cuts. The stimulating letterpress introduction of the first edition disappeared in 1952. Now one or two familiar maps have been dropped, and a few others reduced from double to single-page size, though we venture to think that the practical value of the *Atlas* to students has not materially suffered thereby. All this, with other rearrangements designed to save space without sacrificing content, has been done to make room for ten totally new plates illustrating world history since 1926, and especially recording the course of the shattering upheavals wrought in the world in that quarter-century of wars and revolutions. The result has been drastically to change the geographical and the chronological balance of the *Atlas*, shifting it much nearer our own contemporary age, and also away from our former European preoccupations.

Even so, the present edition tells as much as did any earlier edition of the *Atlas* of the history of the world before 1926—in fact, considerably more. New maps show the Norman conquest of S. Italy and Sicily, the rise of the house of Luxemburg, the rise of the house of Burgundy, the decline of the Ottoman Empire, Russian expansion in Turkestan, and the south-eastern United States during the Civil War. Many more maps have been redesigned to make them more informative, not merely by adding new names, but also by employing new technical processes of colour-printing to make them tell a more detailed story of the stages of development in many lands and at many periods. In particular several maps of

the more familiar parts of the world—Western and Central Europe, France, Germany, Italy, England and Wales, Scotland, Ireland, North America, South America, South Africa—have been coloured politically in the present edition, whereas in earlier editions they had a basis of physical colouring. Lest this be thought a retreat from one of Ramsay Muir's basic principles in designing the original *Atlas*, the editors assert that in this respect Muir's teaching has by now succeeded so completely that, at a time when modern schools everywhere are teaching physical geography and providing their pupils handsomely with atlases of physical geography, it is no longer necessary to provide physically-coloured maps in a historical atlas except where the subject-matter of the map especially requires a physical basis for its understanding. This change, we think, fully justified by present circumstances, has enabled us to add greatly to the historical content of the present edition. In re-designing these maps and in reviewing the content of many others, thousands of entries have been made: in many maps new place-names have been added, new boundaries shown, in some overcrowded maps the amount of lettering has been reduced. The aim has been throughout to make the *Atlas* an efficient work of reference for the teachers and students, furnishing without overcrowding all the information which they could reasonably expect to find for any but the most specialised and detailed work. Revision of this kind is a never-ending process, and will continue to be recorded in future reprints and editions. The editors owe much to the helpful criticism of users who have reported omissions and errors or who have made other suggestions for improvement; these, whenever advisable, have been incorporated. Further suggestions and criticisms will be welcomed as hitherto, for no work of this kind can hope to attain perfection.

It remains to acknowledge our greatest debts. First of all to Ramsay Muir and George Philip, whose original design we inherited and have tried to preserve as far as we could in greatly changed conditions. The memory of their friendly guidance is a valued inspiration to one of the present editors, who was a pupil of the one and a junior colleague of the other of the makers of this *Atlas*. Then to the late Mr. George Goodall, editor of the seventh edition and joint editor of the eighth, who played a large part in planning some of the changes embodied in the present version—a steady counsellor and shrewd guide whose knowledge and practical experience were always freely given, and who understood the limits of the possible.

R. F. Treharne.

H. Fullard.

CONTENTS

1 THE REALMS OF CIVILISATION c.200 A.D. 1 : 50M.

2 EUROPE ON THE EVE OF THE BARBARIAN INVASIONS
c.395 A.D. 1 : 25M.
A *Europe c.476 A.D.* 1 : 40M.

3A ROMAN BRITAIN 1 : 3M.
B *Britain according to Ptolemy*
C *Hadrian's Wall* 1 : 1½M.

4A EUROPE c.526 A.D. 1 : 25M.
B *Europe c.600 A.D.* 1 : 25M.

5 ITALY c.600 A.D. 1 : 5M.
A *Rome in the Middle Ages* 1 : 100,000
B *Papal Lands c.800 A.D.* 1 : 8M.

6 THE CONQUESTS OF ISLAM 1 : 30M. 622–945
A *Iraq, Syria and Mesopotamia* 1 : 15M.
B *The Disintegration of Islam* 1 : 70M.

7A THE TEUTONIC INVADERS OF BRITAIN 1 : 8M.
B *England under Offa and Egbert* 1 : 6M.
C *The Treaty of 886 and the Reconquest of the Danelaw*
1 : 6M.

8 EUROPE IN THE AGE OF CHARLEMAGNE 1 : 20M.
A *The Partitions of Verdun 843 and Mersen 870* 1 : 20M.
B *The Growth of the Frankish Kingdom to 768*
1 : 20M.
C *Races of Western and Central Europe c.800* 1 : 40M.

9 EUROPE c.900 A.D. 1 : 20M.

10 GERMANY ABOUT THE YEAR 962 A.D. 1 : 5M.

11 FRANCE AND BURGUNDY ABOUT THE YEAR 1032 A.D.
1 : 5M.

12 ENGLAND AND HER VIKING INVADERS 1 : 8M.

13 ENGLAND ACCORDING TO THE DOMESDAY SURVEY 1086
1 : 2½M.

14 SCOTLAND c.500–c.1200 A.D. 1 : 2M.
A *Ecclesiastical Scotland c.1500* 1 : 8M.

15 IRELAND BEFORE THE ENGLISH INVASION 1 : 2M.
A *Ecclesiastical Ireland c.1500* 1 : 8M.

16 EUROPE AT THE TIME OF THE FIRST CRUSADE c.1100 A.D.
1 : 20M.
A *Advance and Divisions of Christianity to c.1096*
1 : 60M.

17 THE ANGEVIN EMPIRE AND THE KINGDOM OF FRANCE
1154–1220 1 : 6M.
A *Growth of the French Monarchy from Philip Augustus
to the Hundred Years' War* 1 : 10M.

18A SECOND AND THIRD CRUSADES 1 : 20M.
B *Fourth and later Crusades* 1 : 20M.
C *Christian States in Syria c.1100* 1 : 5M.
D *Jerusalem during the Crusades* 1 : 25,000
E *Constantinople* 1 : 200,000

19 EASTERN EUROPE c.1250 1 : 15M.

20–21 WESTERN AND CENTRAL EUROPE IN THE EARLY
THIRTEENTH CENTURY 1 : 6M.
A *Rise of the Norman Kingdom of Italy and Sicily*
1 : 6⅓M.
B *Germany under Frederick Barbarossa* 1 : 12M.

22 WESTERN AND CENTRAL EUROPE c.1500 : ECCLESIA-
STICAL PROVINCES AND MEDIÆVAL UNIVERSITIES
1 : 10M.
A *Suburbicarian District of Rome* 1 : 5M.

23A ITALY IN THE XI CENTURY 1 : 10M.
B *Italy in the XII and XIII Centuries* 1 : 8M.
C *Iberian Peninsula : the Reconquest 1037–1270* 1 : 10M.
D *Iberian Peninsula 1270–1492* 1 : 10M.

24 EUROPE c.1360 1 : 20M.

25 ASIA UNDER THE MONGOLS 1 : 45M.

26 THE BALTIC LANDS AND THE HANSEATIC LEAGUE IN
THE XIV, XV AND XVI CENTURIES 1 : 10M.

27 MEDIÆVAL ENGLAND AND WALES c.1399 1 : 2½M.
A *London* 1 : 75,000

28A WALES AND THE MARCHES IN THE XIII CENTURY
1 : 2½M.
B *The Scottish Borders* 1 : 2½M.
C *France at the Peace of Bretigny 1360* 1 : 9M.
D *France in 1429* 1 : 9M.

29A THE ALPINE BARRIER AND THE NEIGHBOURING
BATTLEFIELDS 1 : 5M.
B *Growth of the Swiss Confederation* 1 : 2M.

30–31 WESTERN AND CENTRAL EUROPE IN THE LATER
FIFTEENTH CENTURY 1 : 6M.
A *Rise of the House of Burgundy* 1 : 6½M.
B *Rise of the House of Luxemburg* 1 : 10M.

32A ITALY DURING THE RENAISSANCE 1 : 5M.
B *Italy in the XVII and XVIII Centuries* 1 : 10M.
C *Italy in the XIX and XX Centuries* 1 : 10M.
D *Growth of Venice* 1 : 5M.
E *Growth of Florence* 1 : 5M.

v

CONTENTS

33A GROWTH OF THE OTTOMAN EMPIRE 1 : 20M.
  B *Algiers* 1 : 30M.
  C *Growth of the Habsburg Dominions to 1914* 1 : 10M.

34 EUROPE IN 1519 1 : 15M.

35 THE WORLD IN 1490 1 : 165M.
  A *The World according to Ptolemy* : 150
  B *The World according to Edrisi* : 1154
  C *The World according to Fra Mauro* : 1459

36 ECCLESIASTICAL ENGLAND TO THE TIME OF HENRY VIII 1 : 3M.
  A *English Dioceses in the Anglo-Saxon Period* C.800 1 : 9M.

37A SCOTLAND IN THE XVI AND XVII CENTURIES 1 : 3M.
  B *Ireland before the Tudor Conquest* 1 : 3M.
  C *The English Plantation of Ireland* 1 : 8M.

38-39 WESTERN AND CENTRAL EUROPE 1555–1648 1 : 6M.
  A *Religions of Central Europe* C.1618 1 : 18M.
  B *Alsace-Lorraine during the Thirty Years' War* 1 : 3M.
  C *Ernestine and Albertine Lands in Saxony* 1 : 3½M.

40A THE WORLD AT THE TREATY OF SARAGOSSA 1529 1 : 165M.
  B *The World according to Behaim* 1492
  C *The World according to Schoner* 1523

41A PORTUGUESE TRADE EMPIRE IN THE FAR EAST C.1580 1 : 50M.
  B *South America* C.1650 1 : 50M.

42 THE WORLD 1588–1650 1 : 165M.
  A *The World according to Mercator* 1587
  B *Australia according to Tasman* 1643

43A WEST INDIES AND CENTRAL AMERICA 1 : 25M.
  B *Political Distribution in 1650* 1 : 50M.
  C *Political Distribution in 1763* 1 : 50M.
  D *Political Distribution in 1855* 1 : 50M.

44 EXPLORATION OF NORTH AMERICA 1 : 35M.

45A EARLY COLONISATION OF NORTH AMERICA 1607–1689 1 : 10M.
  B *New England and the Middle Colonies* 1620–1650 1 : 5M.

46A THE NETHERLANDS IN THE XVII CENTURY 1 : 2½M.
  B *Campaign of Waterloo* 1 : 1M.
  C *The Netherlands: Political Distribution in the later Middle Ages* 1 : 5M.

47 EUROPE AFTER THE PEACE OF WESTPHALIA 1648 1 : 15M.

48A ENGLAND DURING THE CIVIL WAR 1642–43 1 : 4M.
  B *England during the Civil War 1644–45* 1 : 4M.

49A SCOTLAND SINCE THE RESTORATION 1 : 3M.
  B *Ireland since the XVII Century* 1 : 3M.
  C *The Cromwellian Settlement in Ireland* 1 : 8M

50 CENTRAL AND EASTERN EUROPE IN 1667 1 : 12M.

51 CENTRAL AND EASTERN EUROPE IN 1795 1 : 12M.

52 THE WORLD AT THE TREATIES OF UTRECHT 1713–15 1 : 165M.
  A *India at the beginning of the XVII Century* 1 : 30M.
  B *Gilolo and Ternate* 1 : 2½M.
  C *The Moluccas or Spice Islands* 1 : 20M.

53 FRANCE AND WESTERN GERMANY 1660–1789 1 : 6M.
  A *Paris at the time of the French Revolution* 1 : 50,000

54 EUROPE IN 1740 1 : 15M.

55A THE NARROW SEAS 1 : 6M.
  B *The North Atlantic* 1 : 60M.

56 NORTH AMERICA 1689–1783 1 : 10M.
  A *Quebec* 1 : 250,000
  B *Boston* 1 : 1M.

57 NORTH AMERICA IN THE ERA OF CONFLICT 1750–1783 1 : 5M.
  A *West and South* 1778–1781 1 : 20M.
  B *New York*

58 THE WORLD AT THE TREATY OF PARIS 1763 1 : 165M.
  A *The World according to Homan* 1716
  B *The World according to D'Anville* 1772

59A INDIA IN THE TIME OF CLIVE AND WARREN HASTINGS 1 : 20M.
  B *Calcutta* 1 : 10M.
  C *India in 1805* 1 : 20M.
  D *Madras* 1 : 10M.

60A THE GROWTH OF BRANDENBURG-PRUSSIA 1 : 6M.
  B *The Growth of Prussia* 1 : 6M.

61 GROWTH OF THE RUSSIAN EMPIRE IN EUROPE UP TO 1914 1 : 20M.
  A *Partitions of Poland* 1 : 15M.
  B *Russian Expansion in Turkestan* 1855–1895 1 : 21¼M.

62 EUROPE UNDER NAPOLEON 1810 1 : 15M.

63 THE IBERIAN PENINSULA AT THE TIME OF THE PENINSULAR WAR 1 : 5M.
  A *Strait of Gibraltar* 1 : 2½M.
  B *The Lines of Torres Vedras* 1 : 1M.

CONTENTS

64 EUROPE AFTER THE CONGRESS OF VIENNA 1815
1 : 20M.

65A and B RECONSTRUCTION OF GERMANY BY NAPOLEON
1 : 10M.

   C *The German Confederation* 1 : 12M.
   D *Growth of the German Zollverein* 1 : 12M.
   E *German Empire* 1871 1 : 20M.
   F *Schleswig Holstein* 1864 1 : 5M.

66A ENGLAND BEFORE THE INDUSTRIAL REVOLUTION
C.1701 1 : 4½M.
   B *England after the Industrial Revolution* 1911 1 : 4½M.

67A PRINCIPAL ENGLISH CROWN GRANTS 1 : 25M.
   B *United States* 1783–1803 1 : 25M.
   C *United States* 1803–1830 1 : 30M.
   D *United States: Slavery and Emancipation* 1787–1865
1 : 30M.

68 SOUTH AMERICA IN THE XIX AND XX CENTURIES 1 : 30M.
   A *North West South America* 1 : 40M.

69A THE WORLD IN 1830 1 : 165M.
   B *Arctic Exploration* 1 : 100M.
   C *Antarctic Exploration* 1 : 100M.

70-71 THE GROWTH OF THE UNITED STATES AND BRITISH
NORTH AMERICA 1 : 20M.
   A *Alaska* 1 : 30M.
   B *Alaska Boundary Dispute* 1 : 10M.
   C *The Campaigns of* 1812–14 1 : 10M.
   D *Niagara Frontier* 1 : 1M.
   E *North East Boundary Dispute* 1 : 8M.
   F *Jackson's Campaign* 1813–18 1 : 10M.

72 SOUTH EASTERN UNITED STATES DURING THE CIVIL
WAR 1 : 10M.
   A *Atlanta and Chattanooga Campaigns* 1 : 5M.
   B *Eastern Campaigns* 1 : 5M.
   C *Vicksburg Campaigns* 1 : 2½M.

73 INDIA IN 1858 1 : 15M.
   A *Partition of Bengal* 1 : 25M.

74 EUROPEAN INFLUENCE AND RUSSIAN EXPANSION IN
ASIA UP TO 1914 1 : 50M.

75 PARTITION OF THE PACIFIC IN THE XIX AND EARLY XX
CENTURIES 1 : 100M.
   A *Singapore* 1 : 15M.
   B *Samoa* 1 : 15M.
   C *Fiji Is.* 1 : 15M.
   D *Hawaii* 1 : 15M.
   E *Philippines* 1 : 20M.

76 THE WORLD AFTER THE CONGRESS OF BERLIN 1878
1 : 165M.
   A *Franco-German War* 1870–71 1 : 5M.
   B *Russo-Japanese War* 1904–5 1 : 5M.

77 EXPLORATION AND SETTLEMENT OF AUSTRALASIA
1 : 30M.
   A *New Zealand* 1 : 20M.

78 BALKAN PENINSULA 1800–1914 1 : 6M.
   A *The Slavonic and Bulgarian Powers in the Balkan
Peninsula* 1 : 20M.

79 THE DECLINE OF THE OTTOMAN EMPIRE 1683–1924
1 : 15M.

80A EXPLORATION AND PARTITION OF AFRICA TO 1914
1 : 40M.
   B *Egypt and the Nile Valley* 1 : 16M.

81A SOUTH AFRICA SHOWING THE GROWTH OF BRITISH
POWER DURING THE XIX CENTURY 1 : 20M.
   B *South Africa before and after the Great Trek* 1 : 10M.
   C *West Africa to* 1914 1 : 20M.
   D *Natal and Zululand during the Boer and Zulu Wars*
1 : 4M.

82 EUROPE ON THE EVE OF THE GREAT WAR 1914 1 : 20M.

83 THE WORLD AT THE OUTBREAK OF THE GREAT WAR
1914 1 : 165M.
   A and B *The Western Front* 1 : 3M.

84 EUROPE IN 1923 1 : 20M.

85 EUROPE IN 1923: LINGUISTIC DIVISIONS 1 : 20M.

86 THE WORLD ACCORDING TO THE PEACE TREATIES OF
1919–1927 1 : 165M.
   A *The Salonica Front* 1 : 4½M.
   B *The Italian Front* 1915–1918 1 : 3M.
   C *Asiatic Fronts* 1 : 16M.
   D *The Dardanelles* 1 : 2M.

87 CENTRAL EUROPE IN 1939 1 : 10M.

88 EUROPE AT THE HEIGHT OF AXIS POWER OCTOBER 1942
1 : 22½M.

89 EUROPE AFTER THE SECOND WORLD WAR 1 : 22½M.

90 JAPANESE EXPANSION 1928–42 1 : 60M.

91 EASTERN ASIA 1945–1969 1 : 30M.

92 INDIA, PAKISTAN, BURMA AND CEYLON 1969 1 : 17½M

93 THE NEAR AND MIDDLE EAST 1939–1969 1 : 17M.

94-95 THE WORLD IN 1969 1 : 100M.
Political Groupings 1 : 300M.

96A ITALIAN EAST AFRICA 1936–41 1 : 40M.
   B *West Africa* 1969 1 : 25M.
   C *Africa* 1923 1 : 64M.
   D *Africa* 1969 1 : 64M.

CLASSIFIED LIST OF MAPS AND SUBJECTS

A

ABBASID Caliphate, 8, 9
Abbasids, Disintegration of Islam under the, 6B
Aden Protectorate, 93
Afghan Supremacy, 59A
Afghanistan, 61B, 74, 92
Africa, 1923, 96C
Africa, 1969, 94, 96D
Africa, Partition and Exploration of, 80A
Ahmadnagar, 52A
Alaska, 71A, 75
Alaska Boundary Dispute, 71B
Alban, Kingdom of, 14
Albania, 78, 82, 84, 85, 88, 89
Albertine Lands in Saxony, 39C
Albigensian Crusade, 20
Albuquerque, Track of, 40
Algeria, 24, 80A, 96C, 96D
Almohad Empire, 18
Alpine Barrier and the Neighbouring Battlefields, 29A
Alsace-Lorraine during the Thirty Years' War, 39B
Anatolia, 33A
Angevin Empire, 17
Anglo-Egyptian Sudan, 80A, 96C
Angola, 80A, 96C, 96D
Annam, 74
Antarctic Exploration, 69C
Antarctica, 95
Antioch, Principality of, 18C
Apulia and Calabria, Duchy of, 21A
Aquitaine, Duchy of, 17
Arab League States, 93, 94-95
Arabia, 1, 6, 25, 41A, 96C
Aragon, 24
Aragon, Kingdom of, 23C, 23D
Archbishoprics in the Baltic Lands, 26
Archbishoprics in England at the Domesday Survey, 13
Archbishoprics in France and Burgundy, 1032 A.D., 11
Archbishoprics in Western and Central Europe in the later 15th century, 30-31
Archiepiscopal Provinces in Western and Central Europe, c.1500, 22
Archiepiscopal Sees in England to the time of Henry VIII, 36
Archiepiscopal Sees in Ireland c.1500, 15A
Archiepiscopal Sees in Scotland c.1500, 14A
Archiepiscopal Sees in Western and Central Europe c.1500, 22
Arctic Exploration, 69B

Argentina, 68
Arles, Kingdom of, 20
Armenia, Kingdom of, 19
Ascanians, Lands held by the, 21B
Asia, 94
Asia, Eastern, 1945-69, 91
Asia, European Influence and Russian Expansion in, 74
Asia under the Mongols, 25
Asia Minor, 86C
Asiatic Fronts in the Great War, 86C
Asoka Empire, 1
Assam, 74
Atlanta and Chattanooga Campaigns, 72A
Australasia, Exploration and Settlement of, 77
Australia, 75, 95
Australia, Commonwealth of, 77
Australia according to Tasman, 42B
Austria, 50, 65A, 84, 85, 87, 88, 89
Austria-Hungary, 82
Austrian Empire, 64, 65B
Austrian Netherlands, 55A
Aversa, County of, 21A
Ayubites, Empire of the, 18B

B

BACHAN, 52C
Bahama Islands, 43A
Balkan Peninsula 1800-1914, 78
Balkan Peninsula, Slavonic and Bulgarian Powers in, 78A
Baltic Lands and the Hanseatic League, 26
Baluchistan, 74
Barcelona, County of, 11, 23C
Bartholemew Diaz, Track of, 35
Basutoland, 80A, 81B, 96C
Batavian Republic, 51
Bavaria, 10
Bechuanaland, 96C
Bechuanaland Protectorate, 80A
Belgian Congo, 80A, 96C
Belgium, 82, 83A, 84, 85, 87, 88, 89
Benevento, D. of, 23A
Bengal, 59A, 59C, 73, 74
Bengal, Partition of, 73A
Berlin, World after the Congress of, 76
Bhonsla's Lands, 73
Bhutan, 73, 74, 91, 92

Bihar and Orissa, 73
Bijapur, 52A
Bishoprics in the Baltic Lands, 26
Bishoprics in England at the Domesday Survey, 13
Bishoprics in England to the time of Henry VIII, 36
Bishoprics in France and Burgundy 1032 A.D., 11
Bishoprics in Ireland, 1150, 15
Bishoprics in Western and Central Europe in the later
        15th century, 30–31
Bohemia, 10
Bohemia, Kingdom of, 31, 39
Bohemia and Luxemburg, Lands of the House of, 24
Bohemia-Moravia, Prot. of, 87
Bolivia, 68, 68A
Botswana, 96D
Bosnia, 78, 79
Boston, 56B
Bourbon Lands, 34, 54
Brandenburg, 34
Brandenburg-Prussia, 47, 50, 54
Brandenburg-Prussia, Growth of, 60A
Brazil, 41B, 68
Britain according to Ptolemy, 3B
Britain, Roman, 3A
Britain, Teutonic Invaders of, 7A
British Columbia, 75
British Guiana Boundary, 68B
British Honduras, 75
British Isles, 88
British North America, Growth of, 70–71
British North Borneo, 74, 75, 90
British Somaliland, 80A
Brittany, County of, 11
Brunei, 74, 75, 90, 91
Bulgaria, 24, 78, 79, 82, 84, 85, 88, 89
Bulgaria, Kingdom of, 9, 19
Bulgarian Kingdom, 18B
Bulgarian Powers in the Balkan Peninsula, 78A
Burgundian Kingdom, 4A
Burgundy, Kingdom of, 11, 16
Burgundy, Lands of the House of, 30–31
Burgundy, Rise of the House of, 31A
Burma, 73, 90, 91, 92
Byzantine Territory in Italy c.1000, 23A

C

CABOT, Track of, 40
Cabral, Track of, 40
Calabria and Apulia, Duchy of, 21A

Calcutta, 59B
Caledonia, Pictish Kingdom of, 14
Calmar, Lands of the Union of, 34
Cambodia, 74, 91
Cameroon, 96D
Cameroons, 96C
Canada, 56, 69A, 75
Cape of Good Hope, 80A, 81A
Capua, Duchy of, 23A
Capua, Principality of, 21A
Carinthia, 10
Carolina, 67A
Carolingian Empire, 8
Carnatic, 59A, 59C, 59D
Carpini's Route, 25
Castile, Kingdom of, 23C, 23D, 24
Cathay, 25, 35
Central Africa, 96D
Central America, 43A, 94
Central America in 1650, 43B
Central America in 1763, 43C
Central America in 1855, 43D
Central Europe in 1939, 87
Central Europe, Religions of, 39A
Central Provinces, 74
Central and Eastern Europe in 1667, 50
Central and Eastern Europe in 1795, 51
Cephalonia, County of, 24
Ceylon, 52A, 59A, 59C, 73, 92
Chad, 96D
Charles, Kingdom of, 8A
Chile, 41B, 68
China, 41A, 74, 75, 90
China, Great Wall of, 1
Chinese Republic, 91
Christian States in Syria c.1100, 18C
Christianity, Advance and Divisions of, to c.1096, 16A
Church, States of the, 30–31, 32A
Church Lands, 19, 20, 24, 26, 30–31, 34, 38–39, 47, 50, 51,
                  53, 54
Cilicia, 18C
Cinque Ports, 27
Civil War, England during the, 48
Civil War, South Eastern United States during the, 72
Cochin China, 74
Colombia, 68, 68A, 75
Columbus, Track of, 40
Commonwealth Countries, 94–95
Communist Bloc, 94–95
Congo, 96D
Congo (former French), 96D
Constantinople, 18E

Cook's Voyages, 58
Cordova, Emirate of, 6, 8, 9
Cossack Penetration, Lines of, 42
Costa Rica, 75
Crete, 78
Crusades, 16, 18
Cuba, 43A, 43B, 43C, 43D, 75
Cyprus, 93
Cyprus, Kingdom of, 18A
Czechoslovakia, 84, 85, 89

D

DAHOMEY, 96B, 96D
Dalmatia, 34
Dalriada, Scottish Kingdom of, 14
Dampiers' Voyages, Track of, 52
Danelaw, Reconquest of the, 7C
Danish Towns in Ireland, 15
Dardanelles, 86D
Delhi, Sultanate of, 25
Denmark, 9, 12, 24, 26, 34, 47, 50, 51, 62, 64, 82, 84, 85, 87, 88, 89
Denmark and Norway, 54
Djagatai Empire, 25
Domesday Survey, England according to the, 13
Dominican Republic, 75
Drake's Voyage, Track of, 42
Dutch East Indies, 74, 75, 90

E

EAST Anglia, 12
East Pakistan, 91, 92
East Roman Empire, 2, 6, 8, 9
East Roman Empire, Themes of the, 9
Eastern Asia 1945–1964, 91
Eastern Association, 48A
Eastern Campaigns of the American Civil War, 72B
Eastern Empire, 16, 24
Eastern Europe, 19
Ecclesiastical England to the time of Henry VIII, 36
Ecclesiastical Fiefs in France and Burgundy 1032 A.D., 11
Ecclesiastical Provinces in Western and Central Europe c.1500, 22
Ecuador, 68, 68A, 75
Egypt, 79, 80A, 93, 96C, 96D
Egypt and the Nile Valley, 80B
Eire, 49B

El Cid, Dominion of, 23C
England, 24, 34, 47, 54, 55A, 62
England during the Civil War, 48
England according to the Domesday Survey 1086, 13
England, Ecclesiastical to the time of Henry VIII, 36
England under Edward the Confessor, 12
England before the Industrial Revolution c.1701, 66A
England after the Industrial Revolution 1911, 66B
England under Offa and Egbert, 7B
England, Treaty of 886 and Reconquest of the Danelaw, 7C
England and her Viking Invaders, 12
England and Wales, Mediæval c.1399, 27
English Dioceses in the Anglo-Saxon Period, 36A
Episcopal Sees in England to the time of Henry VIII, 36
Episcopal Sees in Ireland c.1500, 15A
Episcopal Sees in Scotland 500–1200 A.D., 14
Episcopal Sees in Scotland c.1500, 14A
Episcopal Sees in Western and Central Europe c.1500, 22
Er Riff, 88
Eritrea, 80A, 80B, 93, 96C, 96D
Estonia, 84, 85, 87, 88, 89
Ethiopia, 80A, 96C, 96D
Europe c.476 A.D., 2
Europe c.526 A.D., 4
Europe c.600 A.D., 4
Europe c.768–814, 8
Europe c.900, 9
Europe c.1100, 16
Europe c.1360, 24
Europe 1519, 34
Europe 1648, 47
Europe 1740, 54
Europe 1810, 62
Europe 1815, 64
Europe 1923, 84
Europe 1942, 88
Europe 1969, 89
Europe, Linguistic Divisions, 85
Europe, Races of Western and Central, c.800, 8C
Exploration of Africa, 80
Exploration of the Antarctic, 69C
Exploration of the Arctic, 69B
Exploration of Australasia, 77
Exploration of North America, 44

F

FEDERATED Malay States, 74
Federation of Arabian Emirates, 93
Ferrara, D. of, 32A

Fiji Is., 75c
Finland, 84, 85, 88, 89
Flanders, County of, 11
Florence, Growth of, 32E
Florence, Republic of, 30–31, 32A
Formosa, 91
France, 34, 47, 54, 64, 82, 84, 85, 88, 89
France c.1032 A.D., 11
France in 1429, 28D
France, Kingdom of, 12, 16, 17, 20–21, 24, 38
France at the Peace of Bretigny, 28c
France and Western Germany 1660–1789, 53
Franco-German War, 76A
Franconia, 10
Frankish Empire, 6, 8
Frankish Kingdom growth to 768, 8b
Frankish Kingdom, 4A, 4B, 7A
French Appanages, 20, 30
French Community, 94–95
French Empire, 62
French Equatorial Africa, 80A, 96c
French Indo-China, 75, 90
French Monarchy, Growth of the, 17A
French Royal Domain, 11, 16, 17, 20, 24, 30, 38
French Somaliland, 80A
French West Africa, 80A, 96c

G

GABON, 96D
Galloway, Pictish Sub-Kingdom of, 14
Gambia, 80A, 96B, 96c, 96D
Gascony, Duchy of, 11, 17
Genoa, Republic of, 30, 32A, 38
Genoese Dominions, 19
German Confederation, 64, 65c
German East Africa, 80A
German Empire, 82
German Empire 1871, 65E
German South-West Africa, 80A, 81A
German Zollverein, Growth of the, 65D
Germany, 84, 85, 87, 88, 89
Germany c.962 A.D., 10
Germany, Kingdom of, 16, 20–21, 21B
Germany under Frederick Barbarossa, 21B
Germany, Reconstruction of, by Napoleon 1803, 65A
Germany, Reconstruction of, by Napoleon 1807, 65B
Ghana, 96B, 96D
Gibraltar, 63
Gilolo and Ternate, 52B
Golconda, 52A

Gold Coast, 80A, 96c
Golden Horde, Khanate of the, 19, 24, 25
Granada, Kingdom of, 23c, 23D
Greater Antilles, 43A, 43c
Greece, 78, 79, 82, 84, 85, 88, 89, 93
Guatemala, 75
Guiana, 41B, 55B, 68, 68B, 75
Guienne, Duchy of, 11
Guinea, 96B, 96D
Guyana, 68D
Gwynedd, Principality of, 28

H

HABSBURG Dominions, Growth of the, 33c
Habsburgs, Lands of the, 24, 30–31, 34, 38–39, 53
Hadhramaut, 74
Hadrian's Wall, 3c
Haiti, 75
Han Dominions, 1
Hanseatic League, 26
Hawaii, 75D
Hindustan, 40A
Hispaniola, 43A, 43B
Hohenzollern, Lands of the House of, 30–31, 38–39, 50, 53
Holland, 82, 84, 85
Holy Roman Empire, 16, 20–21, 24, 30–31, 34, 38–39, 54, 65
Honduras, 75
Hungary, 16, 19, 24, 34, 47, 51, 54, 79, 84, 85, 87, 88, 89
Hungary, Imperial, 39
Huguenot Centres in France, 38
Hyderabad, 74

I

IBERIAN Peninsula 1037–1270, 23c
Iberian Peninsula 1270–1492, 23D
Iberian Peninsula at the time of the Peninsular War, 63
Iceland, 88, 89
Iconium, Kingdom of, 18A
Ifni, 96c
Ilkhan Empire, 25
Imperial Free Cities, 53
Imperial Hungary, 39
India, 35, 74
India in 1805, 59c
India in 1858, 73
India at the beginning of the XVII century, 52A

India in the time of Clive and Warren Hastings, 59A
India, Pakistan, Burma and Ceylon 1969, 92
Indies, 42
Indonesia, 91
Industrial Revolution, England before and after the, 66
Iran, 93
Iraq, 6A, 88, 89, 93
Ireland, 24, 34, 47, 54, 62, 89
Ireland since the XVII century, 49B
Ireland, the Cromwellian Settlement in, 49B
Ireland, Ecclesiastical c.1500, 15A
Ireland before the English Invasion, 15
Ireland before the Tudor Conquest, 37B
Islam, Conquests of, 6
Islam, Disintegration under the Abbasids, 6B
Israel, 89, 93
Italian East Africa 1936–41, 96A
Italian Front in the Great War, 86B
Italian Somaliland, 80A, 96C
Italy, 82, 84, 85, 88, 89
Italy, Kingdom of, 9, 16, 20–21, 62
Italy c.600 A.D., 5
Italy in the XI century, 23A
Italy in the XII and XIII centuries, 23B
Italy in the XVII and XVIII centuries, 32B
Italy in the XIX and XX centuries, 32C
Italy during the Renaissance, 32A
Italy and Sicily, Rise of the Norman Kingdom of, 21A
Ivory Coast, 96B, 96D

J

JACKSON'S Campaign, 71F
Jagellons, Lands of the, 26, 31
Jalayas, Dominions of the, 24
Jammu and Kashmir, 92
Japan, 74, 90, 91
Japanese Empire, 75
Japanese Expansion 1928–42, 90
Jerusalem, Kingdom of, 18C
Jerusalem during the Crusades, 18D
Jordan, 89, 93
Joscelin, Lordship of, 18C

K

KAMERUN, 80A
Kashmir, 73, 74
Kenya, 96C, 96D

Khazar Empire, 9
Khmer Empire, 25
Korea, 74, 75, 90, 91
Kublai Khan, Empire of, 25
Kushan Dominions, 1
Kuwait, 93

L

LAOS, 74, 91
Latin Empire, 19
Latvia, 84, 85, 87, 88, 89
Lebanon, 89, 93
Leon, Kingdom of, 9, 23C
Leon and Castile, Kingdom of, 16, 23C
Lesotho, 96D
Lesser Antilles, 43A, 43C
Liberia, 80A, 96B, 96C, 96D
Libya, 80A, 96C, 96D
Lithuania, 24, 84, 85, 87, 88, 89
Lombard Duchies, 23A
Lombard Kingdom, 5
Lombard Territories, 5
Lombardy, Kingdom of, 23A
London, 27
Lothar, Kingdom of, 8A
Lotharingia, 10
Louis, Kingdom of, 8A
Louisiana, 56
Lucca, Republic of, 30, 32A
Luxembourg, 89
Luxemburg, Rise of the House of, 31A

M

MADAGASCAR, 80A
Madras, 59D
Magellan, Track of, 40
Majapahit, 40A
Majorca, Kingdom of, 23D
Malagasy Republic, 96D
Malawi, 96D
Malay Peninsula, 75
Malaya, 90, 91
Mali, 96D
Mameluke Sultans, 24
Manchukuo, 90
Manchuria, 74, 75, 90
Marco Polo's Routes, 25, 35

Matilda, Lands of Countess, 23B
Mauritania, 96D
Mercia, 12
Mersen, Treaty of, 8A, 9
Mesopotamia, 6A
Mexico, 43A, 43B, 43C, 43D, 75
Mien, 25
Milan, Duchy of, 30, 32A, 38
Modena, Duchy of, 32A, 38
Mogul Empire, 41A, 52A
Mohammed Abtin, Dominions of, 24
Moluccas, 52C
Monasteries in England at the Domesday Survey, 13
Monasteries in England to the time of Henry VIII, 36
Monasteries in Ireland c.1150, 15
Monasteries in Scotland c.500–1200 A.D., 14
Monasteries in Western and Central Europe c.1500, 22
Mongol Il-Khans, Empire of the, 19
Mongolia, 74, 75, 90, 91
Montenegro, 78, 82
Moravian Empire, 9
Morocco, 24, 64, 80A, 96C, 96D
Mozambique, 80A, 96C, 96D
Mysore, 59A, 59C, 73, 74

Niger, 96D
Nigeria, 80A, 96B, 96C, 96D
Nigritia, 58
Nizam's Dominions, 59A, 59C, 73
Norman Kingdom of Italy and Sicily, 18A, 21A
Normandy, 12
Normandy, Duchy of, 11, 17
North America 1689–1783, 56
North America 1750–1783, 57
North America, Growth of British, 70–71
North America, Early Colonisation of, 45A
North America, English Crown Grants, 67A
North America, Exploration of, 44
North Atlantic, 55B
North Atlantic Treaty Organisation, 94–95
North East Boundary Dispute, 71E
North East New Guinea, 75
North West Provinces, 73
Northern Ireland, 49B
Northern Rhodesia, 80A, 96C
Northumbria, 12
Norway, 12, 24, 34, 82, 84, 85, 88, 89
Norway, Kingdom of, 9, 26
Novgorod, Republic of, 19
Nyasaland, 80A, 96C

N

NAPLES, Kingdom of, 24, 32A, 62
Naples and Sicily, Kingdom of, 23B
Narrow Seas, 55A
Natal, 80A
Natal and Zululand, 81D
Navarre, Kingdom of, 11, 23C, 30
Near and Middle East, 1939–1969, 93
Nelson's Track, 55B
Nepal, 73, 74, 91, 92
Netherlands, 53, 64, 87, 88, 89
Netherlands in the XVII century, 46A
Netherlands, Political Distribution in the Later Middle Ages, 46C
New England, 67A
New England and the Middle Colonies 1620–1650, 45B
New Guinea, Territory of, 77
New Holland, 42B
New York, 57B
New Zealand, 75, 77, 77A
Newfoundland, 45A
Niagara Frontier, 71D
Nicaea, Empire of, 18B, 19
Nicaragua, 75

O

ODOACER, Kingdom of, 2
Oman, 74, 93
Orange Free State, 80A, 81B
Orange River Colony, 81A
Orange River Sovereignty, 81B
Organisation of American States, 94–95
Ostrogothic Kingdom, 4
Ottoman Empire, 34, 39, 47, 50, 51, 54, 64, 74, 82
Ottoman Empire, Decline of the, 79
Ottoman Empire, Growth of the, 33A
Oudh, 59A, 59C, 62, 73

P

PACIFIC, Partition of the, 75
Pakistan, 92
Palestine, 6A, 88
Panama, 68, 75
Papal Lands c.800 A.D., 5B
Papal States, 24, 32B, 32C, 34, 39, 47

Papal States in XV century and early XVI century, 32A
Papal Territory in Italy c.1000, 23A
Papal Territory in Italy in the XII and XIII centuries, 23B
Papua, Territory of, 77
Paraguay, 68
Paris at the time of the French Revolution, 53A
Paris, World at the Treaty of, 58
Parma, Duchy of, 38
Parthian Empire, 1
Persia, 6, 41A, 74, 93
Peru, 68, 68A
Peru, Lower, 41B
Peru, Upper, 41B
Peru, Vice-Royalty of, 41B, 42
Philippine Islands, 74, 75, 90
Philippines, 75E, 91
Piedmont, Principality of, 38
Poland, 16, 34, 47, 50, 54, 74, 84, 85, 87, 88, 89
Poland, Kingdom of, 19, 21, 24, 31, 39
Poland, Partitions of, 61A
Polygars, 52A
Portugal, 24, 34, 47, 54, 62, 63, 82, 84, 85, 88, 89
Portugal, County of, 23C
Portugal, Kingdom of, 23D
Portuguese Guinea, 80A, 96B, 96C, 96D
Portuguese Trade Empire in the Far East c.1580, 41A
Prussia, 51, 62, 64, 65A, 65B, 65C, 65E
Prussia, Growth of, 60B
Prussia, Kingdom of, 65D
Punjab, 73, 74

Q

Qatar, 93
Quebec, 56A

R

Rajputana, 59A, 59C, 73, 74
Rhine, Confederation of the, 62, 65
Rhodesia, 96D
Rio de Oro, 80A, 96C
Roman Dioceses, 2
Roman Empire, 1, 2, 4A, 4B
Roman Prefectures, 2
Rome in the Middle Ages, 5A
Rome, Suburbicarian District of, 22A
Rubruquis' Route, 25
Rum, Kingdom of, 18A

Rumania, 78, 79, 82, 84, 85, 87, 88, 89
Rus, Kingdom of, 16
Russia, 34, 47, 54, 64, 74, 82
Russian Empire, 62, 74
Russian Empire in Europe, Growth of the, 61
Russian Expansion in Turkestan, 61B
Russian States, 24
Russo-Japanese War, 76B

S

Sabah, 91
Saladin and the Ayubites, Empire of, 18A
Salerno, Duchy of, 23A
Salerno, Principality of, 21A
Salonica Front in the Great War, 86A
Salvador, 75
Samoa, 75B
Saracen Lands in the Iberian Peninsula, 23C
Saracen Territory in Italy c.1000, 23A
Sarawak, 74, 75, 90, 91
Sardinia, Kingdom of, 32B, 32C, 51, 62
Saudi-Arabia, 93, 96D
Savoy, Duchy of, 30, 32A
Savoy, Lands of the Counts of, 23B
Saxony, 10
Saxony, Ernestine and Albertine Lands in, 39C
Schleswig-Holstein 1864, 65F
Scotland, 12, 24, 34, 47, 54, 62
Scotland c.500–c.1200 A.D., 14
Scotland in the XVI and XVII centuries, 37A
Scotland Ecclesiastical c.1500, 14
Scotland since the Restoration, 49A
Scottish Borders, 28B
Seljuk Empire, 16
Seljuk Empire of Rum or Iconium, 18B
Seljuk Kingdom of Rum or Iconium, 19
Seljuk Turkish Amirates, 19
Senegal, 96D
Sequeira, Track of, 40
Serbia, 78, 79, 82
Siam, 74, 75, 90
Siberia, 74
Sibir, Khanate of, 25
Sicily, County of, 21A
Sicily, Kingdom of, 19, 23B, 24, 62
Sicily and Italy, Rise of the Norman Kingdom of, 21A
Siena, Republic of, 30–31, 32A
Sierra Leone, 80A
Sikkim, 29, 91
Sind, 73, 74

Singapore, 75A
Sinkiang, 74, 75
Slovakia, 87
Somali Republic, 96D
Song Empire, 25
South Africa, Republic of, 96D
South Africa, Union of, 80A, 96C
South Africa before and after the Great Trek, 81B
South Africa showing Growth of British Power, 81A
South African Republic, 81B
South America c.1650, 41B
South America in the XIX and XX centuries, 68
South America, North West, 68A
South East Asia Collective Defence Treaty, 94–95
South Eastern United States during the Civil War, 72
South West Africa, 96C, 96D
South Yemen, 93
Southern Rhodesia, 80A, 96C
Spain, 34, 47, 54, 62, 63, 64, 82, 84, 88, 89
Spanish Guinea, 80A, 96C, 96D
Spanish Morocco, 96C
Spanish Netherlands, 38
Spanish Sahara, 96D
Spice Islands, 52C
Staufen, Demesne Lands held by the House of, 21B
Staufen, Duchies held by the House of, 21B
Stephen Dushan, Dominions of, 24
Stephen Dushan, Empire of, 24
Strathclyde, British Kingdom of, 14
Sudan, 96D
Swabia, 10
Swaziland, 80A, 96C, 96D
Sweden, 9, 24, 26, 34, 47, 50, 51, 54, 62, 82, 84, 85, 88, 89
Sweden and Norway, 64
Swiss Confederation, 30, 34, 38, 50, 51
Swiss Confederation, Growth of the, 29B
Switzerland, 47, 54, 64, 82, 84, 85, 87, 88, 89
Syria, 6A, 88, 89, 93
Syria c.1100, Christian States in, 18C

T

TAMURLANE, Empire of, 25
Tanganyika, 96C
Tanzania, 96D
Tasman's Voyages, Track of, 42
Ternate, 52B, 52C
Thailand, 91
Themes of the East Roman Empire, 9
Tibet, 73, 74, 91, 92
Tidor, 52C

Timur, Empire of, 25
Togo, 80A, 96B, 96D
Togoland, 96C
Tongking, 74, 75
Torres Vedras, Lines of, 63B
Trade Routes in Asia in the Middle Ages, 25
Trade Routes of the Baltic Lands and the Hanseatic League, 26
Trade Routes of the Portuguese Trade Empire in the Far East c.1580, 41
Transjordan, 88
Transvaal, 80A, 81A
Trebizond, Empire of, 19
Tripoli, 24
Trucial Oman, 93
Tunis, 24, 80A
Tunisia, 88, 89, 96C, 96D
Turkestan, 74
Turkestan, Russian Expansion in, 61B
Turkey, 82, 84, 85, 86, 88, 89, 93
Tuscany, 23B
Tuscany, Duchy of, 23A
Tuscany, Grand Duchy of, 32B, 32C, 38–39
Two Sicilies, Kingdom of the, 18B, 32B, 32C, 50, 51, 54, 64

U

UGANDA, 96C, 96D
Ukraine, 74
Union of South Africa, 80A, 96C
Union of Soviet Socialist Republics, 75, 84, 85, 87, 88, 89
United Arab Republic, 96D
United Kingdom, 55B, 64, 82, 84, 89
United Provinces, 46, 47, 50, 54, 55A
United Provinces, Republic of, 38
United States, 55B, 75, 76
United States 1783–1803, 67B
United States 1803–1830, 67C
United States, Growth of the, 70–71
United States Slavery and Emancipation, 67D
Universities, Mediæval, in Western and Central Europe c.1500, 22
Upper Burma, 74
Upper Volta, 96D
Uruguay, 68
Utrecht, World at the Treaties of, 52

V

VANDAL Kingdom, 2A, 4A
Vasco da Gama, Track of, 40
Venetian Territories in the XII century, 23B

Venezuela, 41B, 68, 68A, 74
Venice, 54
Venice, Growth of, 32D
Venice, Republic of, 30–31, 32A, 32B, 38–39, 47, 50, 51
Venice, Territories of the Signoria of, 19
Verdun, Treaty of, 8A
Vicksburg Campaigns in the American Civil War, 72C
Vienna, Europe after the Congress of, 64
Vietnam, 91
Villeneuve's Track, 55B
Virginia, 67A
Visigothic Kingdom, 2A, 4A

W

WALES, 34, 47, 54, 62
Wales, Principality of, 27
Wales and the Marches, 28A
Warsaw, Grand-Duchy of, 62
Waterloo, Campaign of, 46B
Welf, Demesne Lands held by the House of, 21B
Welf, Duchies held by the House of, 21B
Wessex, 12
West Africa to 1914, 81C
West Africa 1969, 96B
West Indies, 55B
West Indies and Central America, 43A
West Indies and Central America 1650, 43B
West Indies and Central America 1763, 43C
West Indies and Central America 1855, 43D
West Pakistan, 92
West Roman Empire, 2
Western Front in the Great War, 83A and B
Western Germany 1660–1789, 53
Western Samoa, 75B
Western and Central Europe in the early XIII century, 20–1

Western and Central Europe c.1500, 22
Western and Central Europe in the later XV century, 30–31
Western and Central Europe 1555–1648, 38–39
Westphalia, Europe after the Peace of, 47
Wettin, Lands of the House of, 30–31, 38–39
Wittelsbach, Lands of the House of, 30–31, 38–39
World 1490, 35
World 1588–1650, 42
World 1713–15, 52
World 1763, 58
World 1830, 69
World 1878, 76
World 1914, 83
World 1919–1927, 86
World 1969, 94–95
World according to Behaim, 40B
World according to D'Anville, 58B
World according to Edrisi, 35B
World according to Fra Mauro, 35C
World according to Homan, 58A
World according to Mercator, 42A
World according to Ptolemy, 35A
World according to Saragossa, 40A
World according to Schöner, 40C

Y

YEMEN, 93
Yugoslavia, 84, 85, 88, 89

Z

ZAMBIA, 96D
Zipangu, 25
Zululand, 81D

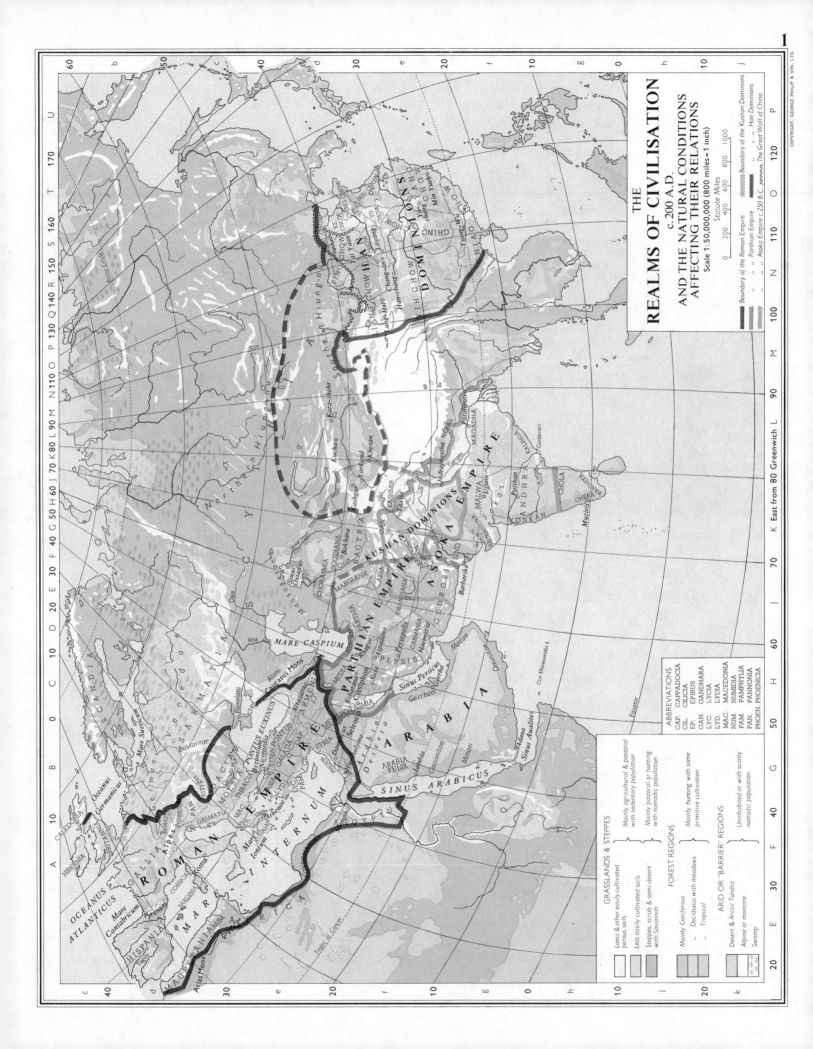

1

THE
REALMS OF CIVILISATION
c. 200 A.D.
AND THE NATURAL CONDITIONS
AFFECTING THEIR RELATIONS
Scale 1:50,000,000 (800 miles=1 inch)

Statute Miles
0   200   400   600   800   1000

Boundary of the Roman Empire
" " Parthian Empire
" " Asoka Empire c.250 B.C.
Boundary of the Kushan Dominions
" " Han Dominions
" " The Great Wall of China

ABBREVIATIONS
CAP. CAPPADOCIA	
CIL. CILICIA	
EP. EPIRUS	
GAN. GANDHARA	
LYC. LYCIA	
LYD. LYDIA	
MAC. MACEDONIA	
NUM. NUMIDIA	
PAM. PAMPHYLIA	
PAN. PANNONIA	
PHOEN. PHOENICIA	

GRASSLANDS & STEPPES
Loess & other easily cultivated porous soils
Less easily cultivated soils
Steppes, scrub & semi-desert with Savannah
Mainly agricultural & pastoral with sedentary population
Mainly pastoral or hunting with nomadic population

FOREST REGIONS
Mainly Coniferous
" Deciduous with meadows
" Tropical
Mainly hunting with some primitive cultivation

ARID OR "BARRIER" REGIONS
Desert & Arctic Tundra
Alpine or montane
Swamp
Uninhabited or with scanty nomadic population

OCEANUS ATLANTICUS

CALEDONIA
HIBERNIA
BRITANNIA
Londinium

OCEANUS GERMANICUS
Mare Suevicum
SCANDIA

GALLIA
Lutetia
Alpes
HISPANIA
Pyrenei
Tagus
Mare Cantabricum

ROMAN EMPIRE
CORSICA
SARDINIA
Roma
MARE INTERNUM

MAURETANIA
Atlas Mons
NUM.
AFRICA
Carthago

MARE TYRRHENIUM
SICILIA
Mare Ionium
Mare Adriaticum
DALMATIA
PAN.
NORICUM
RHAETIA
Vindobona
Danubius
MOESIA
DACIA
THRACIA
Byzantium
MACEDONIA
EPIRUS
Athenae

PONTUS EUXINUS
BITHYNIA
PONTUS
GALATIA
CAP.
ARMENIA
ASIA
LYD.
PHRYGIA
LYC.
PAM.
CIL.
Antiochia
SYRIA
CYPRUS
PHOEN.
Hierosolyma
Alexandria
AEGYPTUS
Nilus

CRETA

MARE INTERNUM
Tropic of Cancer

ARABIA
Desertum
ARABIA FELIX
SINUS ARABICUS
Minaei
Sinus Aualiles
Adana
Sabaei

SARMATIA
Rha
Bastarnae
Roxolani
Alani
Caucasus Mons
MARE CASPIUM
Daix

CHORASMIA
MARGIANA
Mossagetae
SOGDIANA
Bokhara
Oxus
BACTRIA
Jaxartes
Sinus Oxianus

PARTHIAN EMPIRE
MEDIA
Seleucia
Ctesiphon
Ecbatana
ASSYRIA
MESOPOTAMIA
Babylon
PERSIS
Persepolis
CARMANIA
Harmozia
Sinus Persicus
Gerrhaei
Gerrha
Omana
Macae
Dioscoridis I.

KUSHAN DOMINIONS
ARIA
ARACHOSIA
DRANGIANA
GEDROSIA
Kabul
GAN.
KASHMIR
Taxila
SIND
Barbariki
Barygaza

Kashgar
Yarkand
Khotan
Kucha
Kara-shahr
TARIM
Indus

Northern Hiung-nu
Southern Hiung-nu
An-hsi

ASOKA EMPIRE
NEPAL
Pataliputra
MAGADHA
Indraprostha
Ujjain
MALWA
Ganges
AVANTI
ANDHRA
Godavari
Baithan
Paithan
Yamuna
Kas
Kos
KONKAN
CHERA
CHOLA
Muziris
PANDYA
PROLEMAIA

Equator

HAN DOMINIONS
CHOW
CHINO
HAO
Lo-yang
Chang-an
Han-hsung
Min Yueh
Yü
TAI YUAN

Indian references within

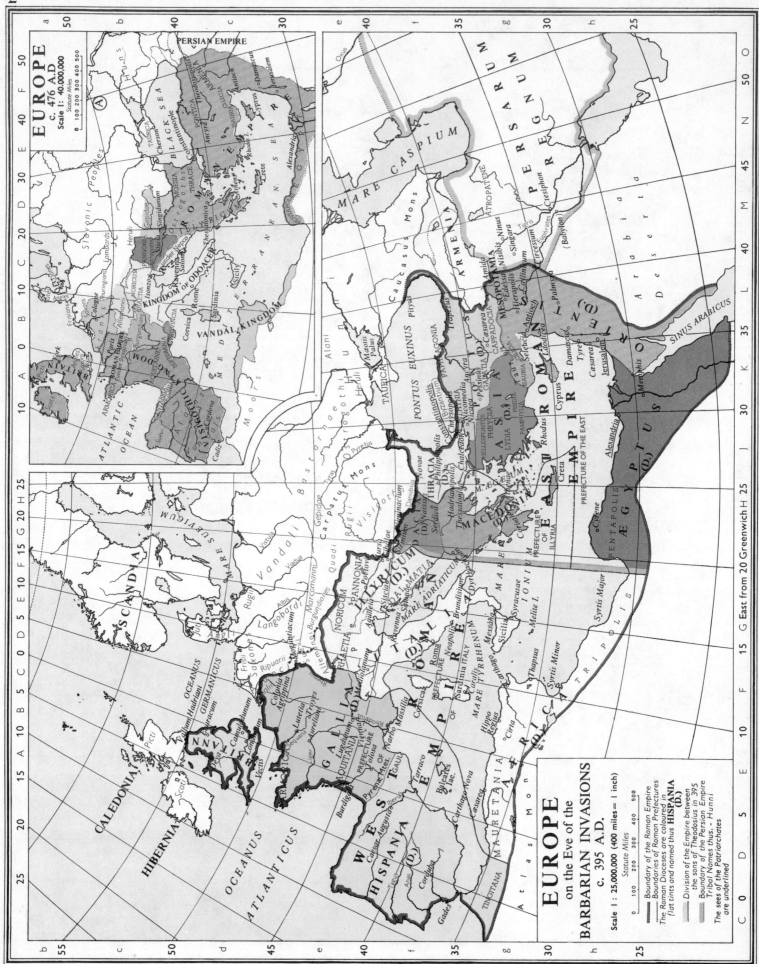

2

EUROPE
c. 476 A.D.
Scale 1: 40,000,000
Statute Miles
0 100 200 300 400 500
(A)

PERSIAN EMPIRE

Huns

Slavonic Peoples

R O M A N   E M P I R E

BLACK SEA

THRACE

KINGDOM OF ODOACER

VANDAL KINGDOM

MEDITERRANEAN SEA

ATLANTIC OCEAN

BRITAIN

VISIGOTHIC KINGDOM

CALEDONIA

HIBERNIA

OCEANUS ATLANTICUS

OCEANUS GERMANICUS

SCANDIA

MARE SUEVICUM

SUEVICUM

Vandali

Gepidae

Carpaty Mons

Bastarnethicum

Alani

Maeotis Palus

TAURICA

PONTUS EUXINUS

Constantinopolis

PAPHLAGONIA

PONTUS

GALATIA

CAPPADOCIA

ASIA (D.)

LYDIA (D.)

PHRYGIA

PISIDIA

PAMPHYLIA

ARMENIA

Caucasus Mons

MARE CASPIUM

MESOPOTAMIA

Nisibis Ninus
Edessa
Singara
Hierapolis
Amida
Carrhae

P E R S A R U M

R E G N U M

Ctesiphon
(Babylon)

Circesium
Euphrates
Tigris

ATROPATENE

S Y R I A (D.)

Damascus
Tyre
Caesarea
Jerusalem

Seleucia
Antioch
Laodicea

Palmyra

Cyprus

E A S T E R N

R O M A N

E M P I R E

PREFECTURE OF THE EAST

Rhodus

Creta

ORIENS (D.)

Arabia Deserta

SINUS ARABICUS

Alexandria

Pentapolis

A E G Y P T U S (D.)

Merothis

Cyrene

THRACIA (D.)

MACEDONIA (D.)

DACIA (D.)

Philippopolis
Hadrianopolis
Serdica
Novae
Naissus
Thessalonica
Corinthus
Byzantium
Chalcedon
Nicomedia
Nicaea
Pessinus
Ancyra
Myra
Tarsus
Seleucia

PREFECTURE OF ILLYRIA

Melite I.

IONIUM MARE

Syracusae
Messana
Sicilia

Thapsus

Syrtis Major

Syrtis Minor

TRIPOLIS

CYRENAICA (D.)

ILLYRICUM (D.)

PANNONIA

NORICUM

RAETIA

DALMATIA (D.)

Salonae
Singidunum
Sirmium
Siscia
Poetovio
Aquileia
Ravenna
Patavium

MARE ADRIATICUM

Brundisium
Neapolis
Roma
Corsica
Sardinia

PREFECTURE OF ITALY

I T A L I A

MARE TYRRHENUM

W E S T E R N

R O M A N

E M P I R E

MARE

Carthago
Hippo Regius
Cirta

AFRICA (D.)

MAURETANIA

TINGITANA

Atlas Mons

GALLIA

AQUITANIA (D.)

PREFECTURE OF GAUL

Lugdunum
Lutetia
Treveri
Colonia Agrippina
Vienna
Narbo Massilia
Tolosa
Burdigala
Arelate
Rhodanus

Quadi
Marcomanni
Burgundiones
Alemanni
Franci
Ripuarii
Saxones
Frisii
Langobardi
Rugii
Heruli
Gepidae
Visigothi

HISPANIA (D.)

Baleares Ins.
Tarraco
Caesar-Augusta
Corduba
Gades
Anas
Tagus

Albis
Viadua
Vistula

Pyretus
Tyras
Danubius

Picti
Scoti

Vallum Hadriani

Pyrenae Mtes.

EUROPE
on the Eve of the
BARBARIAN INVASIONS
c. 395 A.D.

Scale 1: 25,000,000 (400 miles = 1 inch)
Statute Miles
0 100 200 300 400 500

 Boundary of the Roman Empire
 Boundaries of Roman Prefectures
 The Roman Dioceses are coloured in flat tints and named thus HISPANIA (D.)
 Division of the Empire between the sons of Theodosius in 395
 Boundary of the Persian Empire
 Tribal Names thus.– Hunni
 The sees of the Patriarchates are underlined

3

ROMAN BRITAIN

Scale 1:3,000,000 (48 miles = 1 inch)

Statute Miles

0   10   20   30   40   50

Roman Roads thus
Tribal names — *REGNI*
Modern names within brackets
Forests
Marshes
Roman permanent forts
   " civil sites
Signal Stations

Highlands over 3000 feet
   "   from 1200–3000 feet
Uplands   "   600–1200   "
Lowlands   "   300– 600   "
   "   0– 300   "

BRITAIN according to PTOLEMY

Thule
Novantarum Pr.
Aebudae
Orcades
Fl. Vidua
Boreale Pr.
Cerigonius Sinus
Taexali
Vecturiones
Ituna Aest.
Clota Aest.
Caledonii
Fl. Serus
Damnonii
Boderia Aest.
Brigantes
Mona
Iverni
Ordovices
Eburacum
Australe Pr.
Seteia Aest.
Deva
Lindum
Ratae
Metaris Aest.
Octapitarum Pr.
Silures
Verulamium
Venta
Corinium
Camulodunum
Sabrina Aest.
Belgae
Tamesis Aest.
Isca
Dobunia
Herculis Pr.
Aquae
Bolerium Pr.
Vectis
Ocrium Pr.

HADRIAN'S WALL

Bowness
Magnis
Vercovicium
Housesteads
Borcovicus
Procolitia
Carrawburgh
Corbridge
Chesters
Onnum
(Halton)
Vindovala
Condercum
(Benwell)
Segedunum
(Wallsend)
(Drumburgh)
(Burgh by Sands)
Camboglanna
Birdoswald
Castlesteads
Vindolanda
(Chesterholm)
Corstopitum
(Corbridge)
Pons Aelius
(Newcastle)
Vindomora
(Ebchester)
(South Shields)
Luguvalium
(Carlisle)

Scale 1:1,500,000 (24 miles = 1 inch)

West from Greenwich

COPYRIGHT. GEORGE PHILIP & SON, LTD.

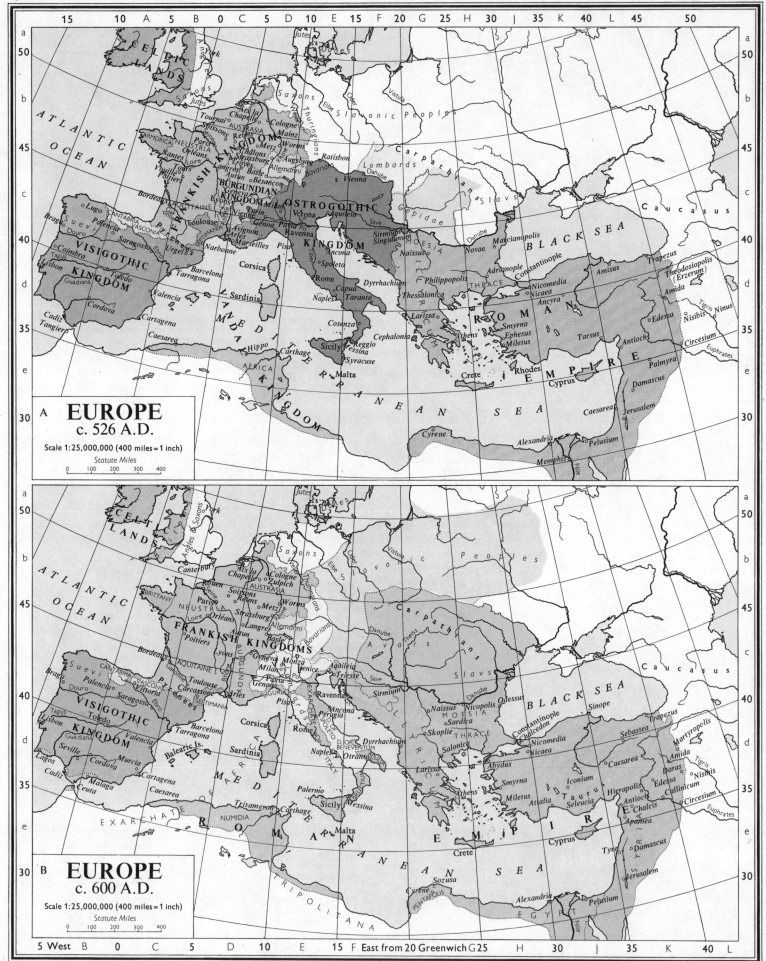

4

A EUROPE
c. 526 A.D.

Scale 1:25,000,000 (400 miles = 1 inch)

Statute Miles
0 100 200 300 400

B EUROPE
c. 600 A.D.

Scale 1:25,000,000 (400 miles = 1 inch)

Statute Miles
0 100 200 300 400

5

ITALY
c. A.D. 600
Scale 1:5,000,000 (80 miles=1 inch)
Statute Miles
0   50   100

——————— Lombard Territories
*Other lands owed a real or nominal
allegiance to the Eastern Empire*

PAPAL LANDS
c. A.D. 800
Scale 1:8,000,000
Statute Miles
0   50

Papal Lands
Before A.D. 754
754-774
774-814

(B)

Over 3000 feet
1200-3000 "
600-1200 "
0- 600 "

ROME
in the Middle Ages
Scale 1:100,000
Statute Miles
0   1

(A)

East from Greenwich

COPYRIGHT. GEORGE PHILIP & SON. LTD.

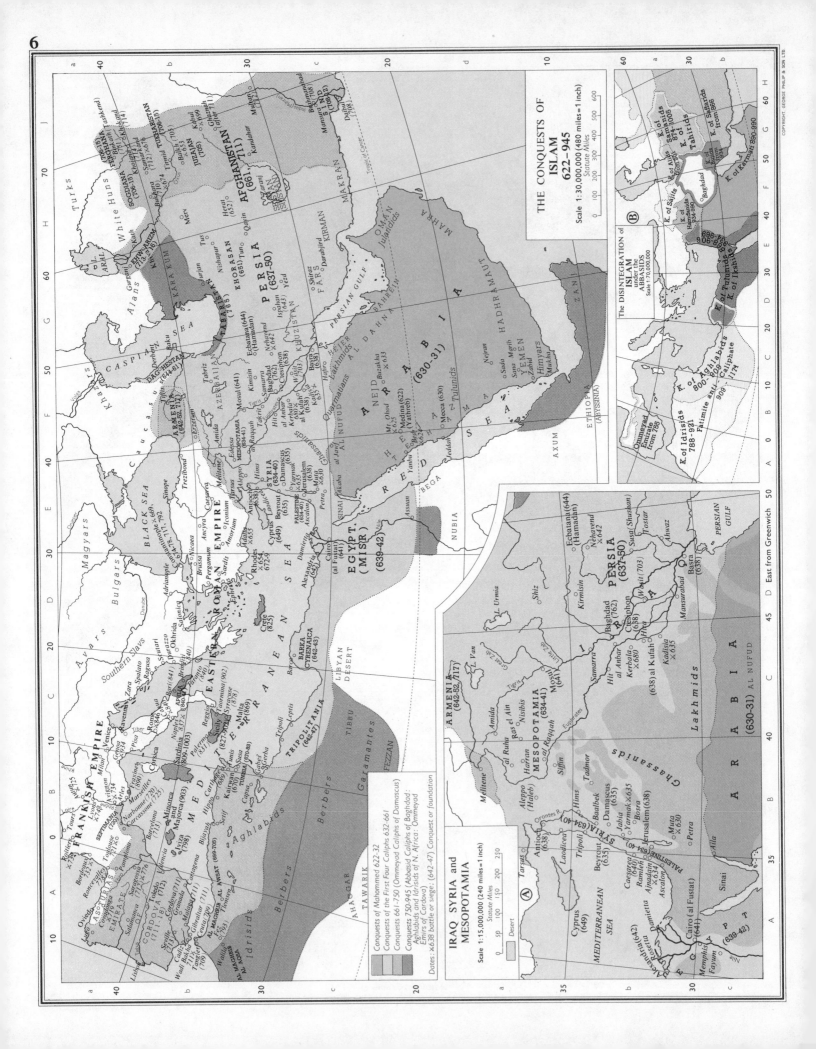

6

THE CONQUESTS OF ISLAM
622–945

Scale 1:30,000,000 (480 miles = 1 inch)
Statute Miles
0   100 200 300 400 500 600

B The DISINTEGRATION of ISLAM under the ABBASIDS
Scale 1:70,000,000

K. of Sajits
K. of Alids · Samanids from 901 · 874 1005
K. of Saffarids from 866
K. of Tahirids

K. of Hamdanids 934-990
Bujids
Baghdad
K. of Tulunids · K. of Ikshids
898-905 · 906

Ommeyad Emirate from 755
K. of Idrisids 788-921
K. of Aghlabids 800-909
Fatimite anti-Caliphate 909
SHIA Caliphate

IRAQ SYRIA and MESOPOTAMIA
Scale 1:15,000,000 (240 miles = 1 inch)
Statute Miles
50 100 150 200 250

Desert

Conquests of Mahommed 622-32
Conquests of the First Four Caliphs 632-661
Conquests 661-750 (Ommeyad Caliphs of Damascus)
Conquests 750-945 (Abbasid Caliphs of Baghdad; Aghlabids and Idrisids of N. Africa: Ommeyad Emirs of Cordova)
Dates: ×638 battle or siege: (642-47) Conquest or foundation

COPYRIGHT. GEORGE PHILIP & SON LTD.

A

ARMENIA (642-52, 717)
MESOPOTAMIA (634-41)
PERSIA (637-50)
ARABIA (630-31)

L. Van
L. Urmia
Shiz
Amida
Nisibis
Ras el Ain
al Ruha
Harran
Melitene
Aleppo (Haleb)
Hims
Siffin
Tadmor
Orontes R.
Antioch (638)
Laodicea
Tripoli
Beyrout (635)
Baalbek
Damascus (635)
Jabia
Bosra
SYRIA (634-40)
Muta ×630
Petra
PALESTINE (634-40)
Caesarea (640)
Ramleh ×634
Jerusalem (638)
Ascalon
Ajnadain ×634
Ailia
Sinai
Cyprus (649)
MEDITERRANEAN SEA
Damietta (642)
Alexandria
Rosetta
Nile
Cairo (al Fustat) (641)
Memphis
Fayum
EGYPT (639-42)

Ecbatana (644) (Hamadan)
Kirmisin
Nehavend ×642
Baghdad (762)
Ctesiphon (638)
Hira
al Anbar
Kufah
Kerbala ×680
al Kufah
Kadisia ×635
Basra (638)
Wasit (703)
Susa (Shushan)
Tostar
Ahwaz
Mansurabad
PERSIA (637-50)
PERSIAN GULF
Mosul (641)
Samarra
Hit
Great Zab
Little Zab
Tigris
Euphrates
Lakhmids
Ghassanids
ARABIA (630-31)
AL NUFUD

East from Greenwich

FRANKISH EMPIRE
Tours ×732
Poitiers 507
Bordeaux 732
Romegelier
Toulouse 721×
Narbonne 725
Carcassonne (713)
SEPTIMANIA (720)
Arles
Avignon 734
Marseilles 725
Rhine
Loire
Danube

Oviedo
Lugo
ASTURIAS
Coimbra
CORDOVA EMIRATE (711-8)
Toledo (712)
Cordova (711)×
Granada
Malaga (711)
Seville (712)
Cadiz (711)
Gibraltar (711)
Tangier (708)
Ceuta (711)
AL MAGHRIB AL AQSA
AL MAGHRIB AL AWSAT

White Turks
White Huns
Alans
Khazars
Volga
ARAL
L. ARAL
KHWARIZM (713-15)
SOGDIANA (706-15)
Bukhara 710
Samarkand ×676
Kath
FERGHANA (Tashkend) (714)
Khojend (714)
Firind
TUKHARISTAN (706-15)
Balkh ×653
Termid ×699
Kish
Merv
JUZJAN (705)
AFGHANISTAN (661, 711)
Herat (652)
Qayin
Ghaznin (711)
Kabul (705)
Kandahar
MAKRAN
Multan (Mukran)
SIND (708, 712)
Dabul (708)
Indus R.

CASPIAN SEA
Baku
Derbent
DAGHESTAN (644-61)
ARMENIA (642-52, 717)
Tiflis
Caucasus
Erzerum
Tabriz
AZERBAIJAN
TABARISTAN (765)
Tus
Nishapur
KHORASAN (651)
PERSIA (637-50)
Ispahan (643)
Yezd
Shiraz
FARS
Darabird
KIRMAN
OMAN Julandids
KARA KUM
Ecbatana (644) (Hamadan)
Nehavend (642)
Mosul (641)
Kimisin
Samarra
Baghdad (762)
Tokrit
Hit
Kerbala ×680
al Kufah
Kadisia (638)
Basra (638)
Wasit (703)
KHUZISTAN
PERSIAN GULF
BAHREIN
AL DAHNA
Hofuf
Lakhmids
Quarmathians
NEJD
A R A B I A (630-31)
AL NUFUD
Nejran
Sada
Marib
Sana
ZABID
YEMEN
Himyars
Mukha
HADHRAMAUT
MAHRA
ZANJ
Najran

EASTERN ROMAN EMPIRE
Constantinople 669, 674-8, 717, 792
Nicaea
Ancyra
Iconium
Amorium
Pergamum
Sardis
Ephesus
Brussa
Adrianople
Salonica
Spalato
Ragusa
Zara
Venice
Ravenna
Milan
Genoa
Pisa
Rome 846
Naples
Bari (841)
Brindisi
Tarento
Reggio
Sicily (827-902)
Palermo (831)
Syracuse (878)
Taormina (902)
Malta (869)
Crete (825)
Rhodes ×654, 672-9
Cyprus (649)
Amida ×655
Antioch ×638
Aleppo (634-40)
Hims
Damascus (635)
Beyrout (635)
SYRIA (634-40)
Yarmuk ×635
PALESTINE (635)
Jerusalem (638)
Ascalon
Muta ×630
Petra
SINAI
Amorium
Sinope
Trebizond
Treizond
Melitene
Tarsus
Edessa
Raqqah
MESOPOTAMIA (634-41)
Ctesiphon (638)
Euphrates
Tigris
BLACK SEA
Magyars
Bulgars
Avars
Southern Slavs
Svutari
Durazzo
Okhrida
Croats

BARKA
CYRENAICA (642-43)
Barca
Leptis
Tripoli
TRIPOLITANIA (642-47)
LIBYAN DESERT
NUBIA
Assuan
RED SEA
Mecca ×630
Medina (622) (Yathreb)
Mt. Ohod ×625
Yambu
Jeddah
Yanbu
Akaba
Tabuk
Dumat al Jandal
EGYPT (MISR) (639-42)
Alexandria (642)
Cairo (al Fustat) (641)
Damietta
ETHIOPIA (ABYSSINIA)
AXUM
BEGA

MEDITERRANEAN SEA
Sardinia (809-1003)
Corsica
Minorca and Majorca (903)
Iviza (798)
Balearic
Bougie
Bona
Tunis (670)
Kairouan (670-83)
Carthage (698)
Susa
Sfax
Gabes (670)
Cabes
Djerba
Tripoli
Berbers
Aghlabids
Idrisids
AHAGGAR
TAWARIK
FEZZAN
Garamantes
TIBBU
Berbers
AL NUFUD

Lisbon
Tagus
Barcelona (713)
Tarragona
Valencia
Cartagena
Bijaya
Tlemcen
Fez
Sidjilmessa
Wad Bukha
Walili (708)

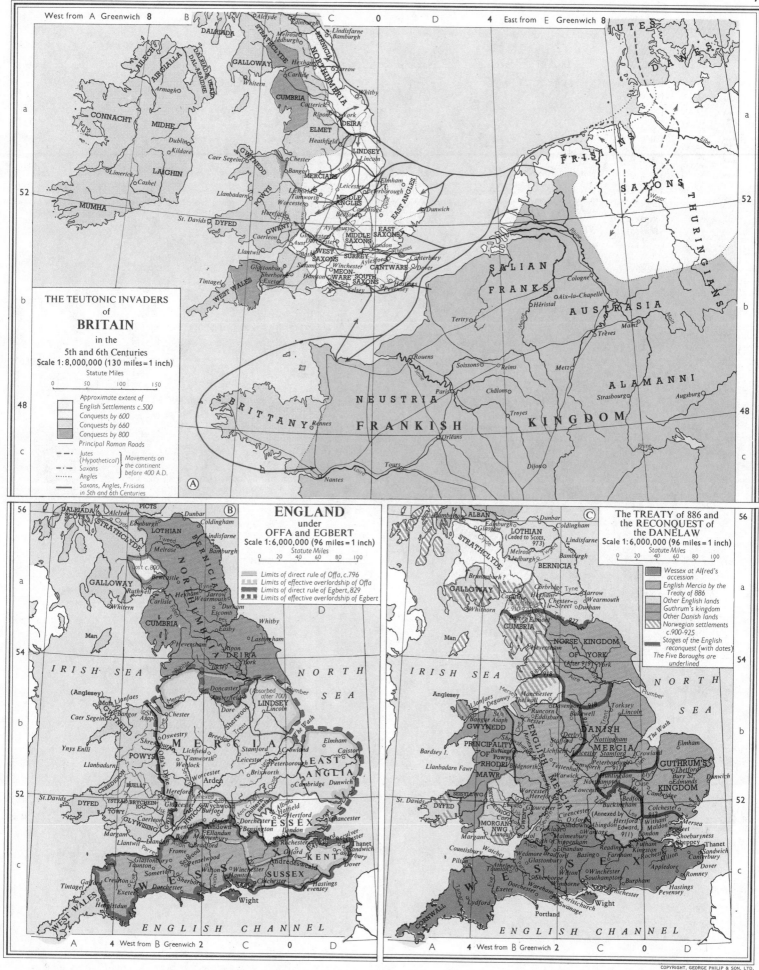

A

West from A Greenwich 8 · B · C · 0 · D · 4 · East from E Greenwich 8

THE TEUTONIC INVADERS
of
BRITAIN
in the
5th and 6th Centuries
Scale 1:8,000,000 (130 miles = 1 inch)

Statute Miles
0 · 50 · 100 · 150

Approximate extent of
English Settlements c.500
Conquests by 600
Conquests by 660
Conquests by 800
Principal Roman Roads

Jutes (Hypothetical) } Movements on
Saxons } the continent
Angles } before 400 A.D.
Saxons, Angles, Frisians
in 5th and 6th Centuries

DALRIADA · AILECH · AIRGIALLA · DÁLRIADA USCI · DÁLRIADA DÁLARAIDHE · Armagh · CONNACHT · MIDHE · Dublin · Kildare · LAIGHIN · Limerick · Cashel · MUMHA

Alclyde · Edinburgh · Melrose · Jedburgh · BERNICIA · Lindisfarne · Bamburgh · Hexham · Jarrow · STRATHCLYDE · DALRIADA · GALLOWAY · Whithorn · Carlisle · NORTHUMBRIA · Whitby · CUMBRIA · Catterick · Ripon · York · DEIRA · ELMET · Heathfield · Chester · LINDSEY · Lincoln · Caer Segeint · GWYNEDD · Bangor · MERCIANS · Leicester · Elmham · POWYS · Llanbadarn · Lichfield · Tamworth · MIDDLE ANGLES · Peterborough · EAST ANGLES · Dunwich · Worcester · Hereford · Bedford · Cambridge · St. Davids · DYFED · GWENT · Caerleon · Gloucester · MIDDLE SAXONS · London · Thames · EAST SAXONS · Llantwit · Bath · Cirencester · WEST SAXONS · SURREY · Canterbury · Dover · Glastonbury · Sherborne · Sarum · Winchester · Aylesford · CANTWARE · Tintagel · WEST WALES · Exeter · Hamton · MEON WARE · SOUTH SAXONS · Selsey · Pevensey · Hastings

JUTES · DANES · FRISIANS · Elbe · SAXONS · Weser · THURINGIANS · Rhine · SALIAN FRANKS · Cologne · Aix-la-Chapelle · Héristal · AUSTRASIA · Mainz · Meuse · Tertry · Trèves · Moselle · Rouens · Soissons · Reims · Metz · Châlons · ALAMANNI · Paris · Strasbourg · Augsburg · NEUSTRIA · Troyes · BRITTANY · Rennes · FRANKISH · KINGDOM · Orléans · Rhine · Dijon · Tours · Loire · Nantes

B

ENGLAND
under
OFFA and EGBERT
Scale 1:6,000,000 (96 miles = 1 inch)

Statute Miles
0 · 20 · 40 · 60 · 80 · 100

Limits of direct rule of Offa, c.796
Limits of effective overlordship of Offa
Limits of direct rule of Egbert, 829
Limits of effective overlordship of Egbert

PICTS · DALRIADA · Scots · Alclyde · Dunbar · STRATHCLYDE · Edinburgh · Coldingham · LOTHIAN · Tweed · Jedburgh · Lindisfarne · Melrose · BERNICIA · Bamburgh · GALLOWAY · lost c.800 · Newcastle · Ruthwell · Hexham · Tyne · Whithorn · Carlisle · NORTHUMBRIA · Jarrow · Wearmouth · CUMBRIA · Escomb · Whitby · Hevensham · Easby · Lastingham · Ripon · Ilkley · York · DEIRA · Man · IRISH SEA · Ribble · Doncaster · Austerfield · (Absorbed after 700) · Humber · (Anglesey) · Mon Llanfaes · Mersey · Dore · LINDSEY · Lincoln · Bangor · Chester · Dee · Sherwood · NORTH SEA · Caer Segeint · St. Asaph · Oswestry · Trent · GWYNEDD · Shrewsbury · Breedon · Stafford · Ynys Enlli · Offa's Dyke · MERCIA · Stamford · POWYS · Wenlock · Tamworth · Leicester · Elmham · Llanbadarn · Worcester · Brixworth · Peterborough · Crowland · EAST ANGLIA · Caistor · CEREDIGION · Arden · Hereford · Dunwich · Cambridge · BUELLT · St. Davids · DYFED · YSTRAD BRYCHEIN · Annexed 770 · TOWY · Gloucester · Wychwood · St. Albans · Hertford · Colchester · GLYWISING · Caerleon · Usk · HWICCE · Burford · Hatfield · London · Margam · Llandaff · Bath · Malmesbury · Ashdown · Dorchester · Benington · ESSEX · Parret · Bradford · Frome · Selwood · Reading · Oxford · KENT · Llantwit · Glastonbury · WESSEX · Sherborne · Wilton · Winchester · Andredsweald · Canterbury · Reculver · Thanet · Rochester · Dover · Tintagel · Gafulford · Hengestdun · Creedon · Taunton · Exeter · Dorchester · Hamton · SUSSEX · Hastings · Pevensey · WEST WALES · Wight · ENGLISH CHANNEL

4 West from B Greenwich 2

C

The TREATY of 886 and
the RECONQUEST of
the DANELAW
Scale 1:6,000,000 (96 miles = 1 inch)

Statute Miles
0 · 20 · 40 · 60 · 80 · 100

Wessex at Alfred's accession
English Mercia by the Treaty of 886
Other English lands
Guthrum's kingdom
Other Danish lands
Norwegian settlements c.900-925
Stages of the English reconquest (with dates)
The Five Boroughs are underlined

Humber · ALBAN · Edinburgh · Glasgow · Dunbar · LOTHIAN (Ceded to Scots, 973) · Coldingham · STRATHCLYDE · Clyde · Jedburgh · Lindisfarne · Bamburgh · BERNICIA · Brunanburh? · GALLOWAY · Corbridge · Tyne · Hexham · Chester-le-Street · Durham · Whithorn · Jarrow · Wearmouth · Carlisle · CUMBRIA · St. Eamont · 927 · Man · IRISH SEA · Heversham · 910-920 · NORSE KINGDOM OF YORK (After 919) · York · Ribble · 919 · Aire · Humber · Anglesey · Llanfaes · Deganwy · Thelwall · Manchester · Davenport 920 · Bakewell · Torksey · Lincoln · NORTH SEA · St. Asaph · Bangor · Runcorn · Eddisbury · Chester · DANISH · Nottingham · The Wash · GWYNEDD · Shrewsbury · Bridgnorth · Lichfield · ENGLISH MERCIA · MERCIA · Derby · Stafford · Leicester · Stamford · Crowland · Elmham · PRINCIPALITY OF RHODRI · Powys · Tettenhall · Tamworth · Peterborough · Bardsey I. · Warwick · Northampton · Ely · GUTHRUM'S · Llanbadarn Fawr · MAWR · Worcester · Hereford · Towcester · Bedford · Bury St. Edmunds · KINGDOM · Thetford · Dunwich · SEISYLLWG · Cambridge · Gloucester · Cirencester · Oxford · Hertford · Colchester · St. Davids · DYFED · MORGAN NWG · Llandaff · Bristol · Bath · Cricklade · Abingdon · Wallingford · Witham · Maldon · Mersea · BRYCHEINIOG · Ashdown · Reading · (Annexed by Edward, 911) · Shoeburyness · Margam · Chippenham · Wedmore · Bradford · Basing · Kingston · Rochester · Sheppey · Thanet · Sandwich · Countisbury · Watchet · Glastonbury · Wantage · Farnham · Milton · Appledore · Romney · Pilton · Athelney · WESSEX · Sherborne · Wimborne · Winchester · Southampton · Burpham · Dover · Lydford · Exeter · Dorchester · Wareham · Christchurch · Chichester · Hastings · Pevensey · CORNWALL · Portland · Swanage · Wight · ENGLISH CHANNEL

4 West from B Greenwich 2

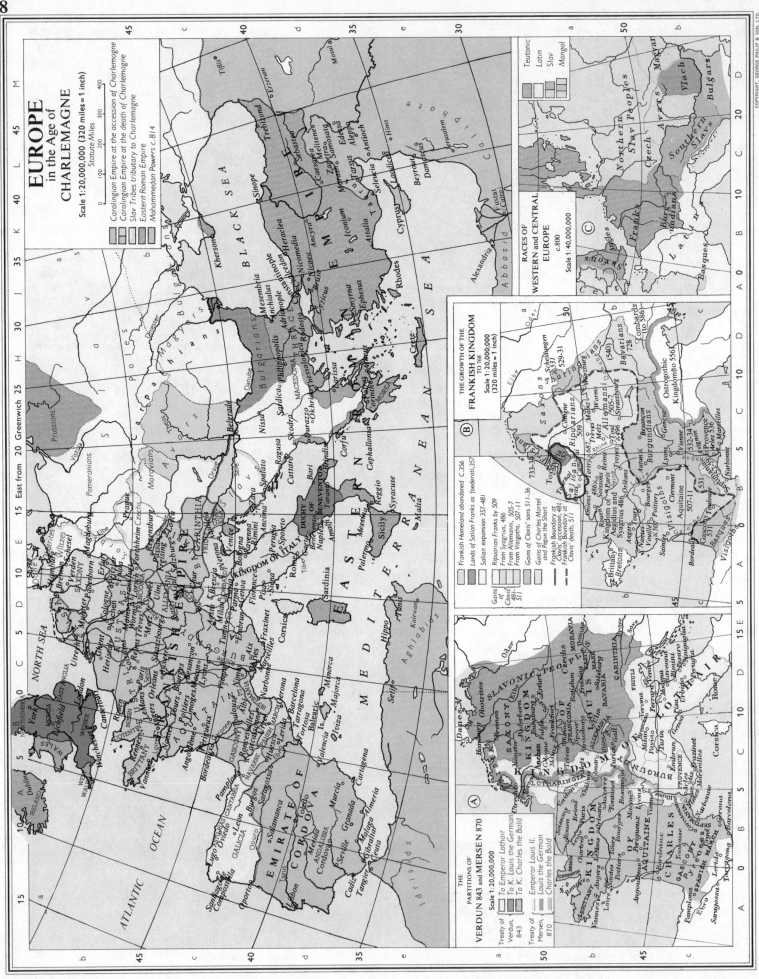

8

EUROPE
in the Age of CHARLEMAGNE

Scale 1:20,000,000 (320 miles=1 inch)

Statute Miles
0 100 200 300 400

Carolingian Empire at the accession of Charlemagne
Carolingian Empire at the death of Charlemagne
Slav Tribes tributary to Charlemagne
Eastern Roman Empire
Mohammedan Powers c.814

RACES OF WESTERN and CENTRAL EUROPE
c.800

Scale 1:40,000,000

Teutonic
Latin
Slav
Mongol

THE GROWTH OF THE FRANKISH KINGDOM
TO 768

Scale 1:20,000,000 (320 miles = 1 inch)

Frankish Homeland abandoned c.356
Lands of Salian Franks as foederati, 357
Salian expansion 357-481
Ripuarian Franks by 509
Gains of Clovis: From Allemanni, 505-7
From Visigoths, 507-11
Gains of Clovis' sons 511-36
Frankish Boundary at Clovis' accession, 481
Frankish Boundary at Clovis death, 511

THE PARTITIONS OF VERDUN 843 and MERSEN 870

Scale 1:20,000,000

Treaty of Verdun, 843:
To Emperor Lothair
To K. Louis the German
To K. Charles the Bald

Treaty of Mersen, 870:
Emperor Louis II.
Louis the German
Charles the Bald

COPYRIGHT, GEORGE PHILIP & SON, LTD.

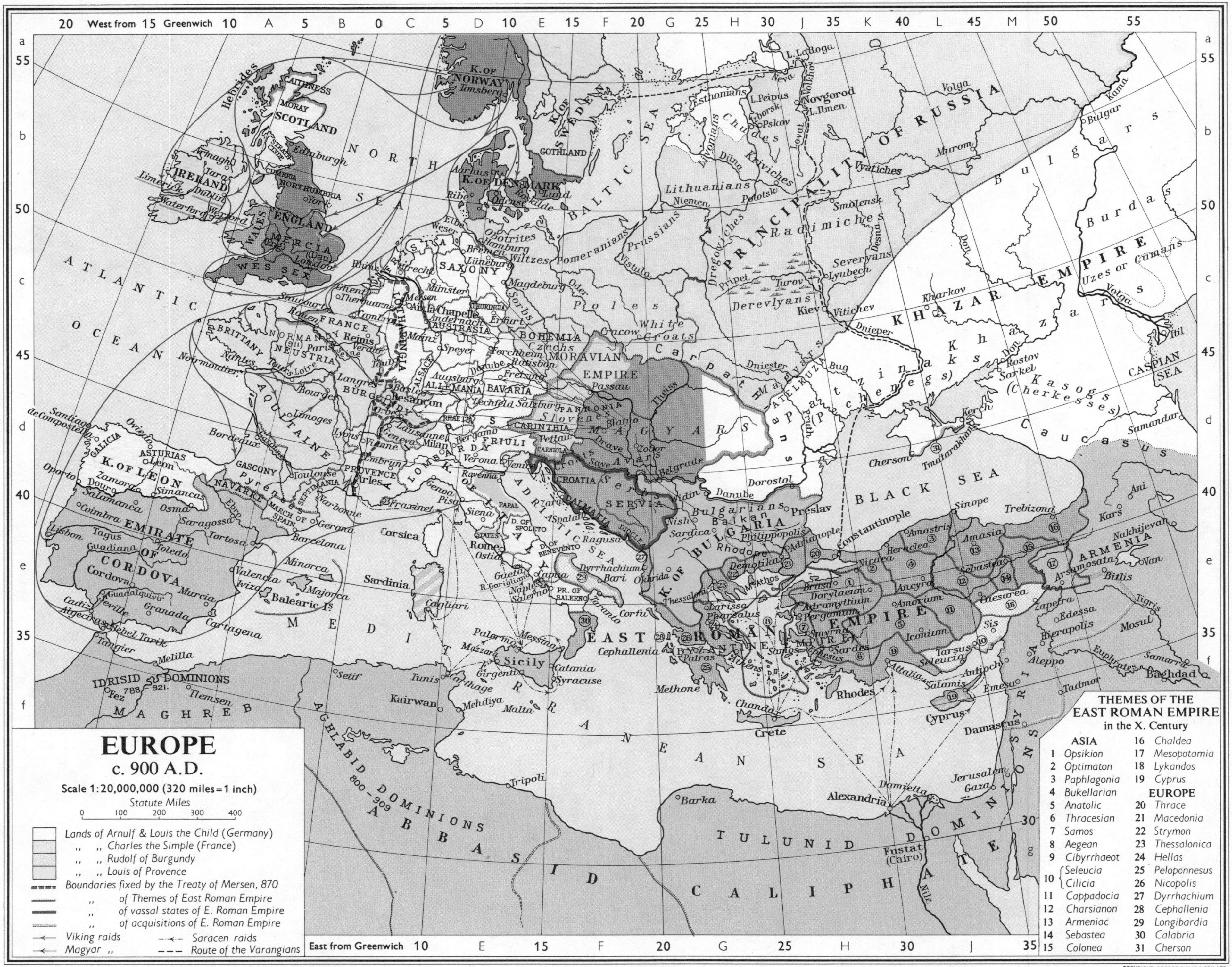

EUROPE
c. 900 A.D.

Scale 1:20,000,000 (320 miles = 1 inch)

Statute Miles

0 100 200 300 400

	Lands of Arnulf & Louis the Child (Germany)
	,, ,, Charles the Simple (France)
	,, ,, Rudolf of Burgundy
	,, ,, Louis of Provence

Boundaries fixed by the Treaty of Mersen, 870
,, ,, of Themes of East Roman Empire
,, ,, of vassal states of E. Roman Empire
,, ,, of acquisitions of E. Roman Empire

→ Viking raids   ··→·· Saracen raids
→ Magyar ,,   ---- Route of the Varangians

THEMES OF THE EAST ROMAN EMPIRE
in the X. Century

ASIA
1 Opsikion
2 Optimaton
3 Paphlagonia
4 Bukellarian
5 Anatolic
6 Thracesian
7 Samos
8 Aegean
9 Cibyrrhaeot
10 Seleucia
11 Cappadocia
12 Charsianon
13 Armeniac
14 Sebastea
15 Colonea
16 Chaldea
17 Mesopotamia
18 Lykandos
19 Cyprus

EUROPE
20 Thrace
21 Macedonia
22 Strymon
23 Thessalonica
24 Hellas
25 Peloponnesus
26 Nicopolis
27 Dyrrhachium
28 Cephallenia
29 Longibardia
30 Calabria
31 Cherson

West from 15 Greenwich 10

East from Greenwich 10

COPYRIGHT. GEORGE PHILIP & SON LTD.

GERMANY
about the year 962 A.D.

Scale 1:5,000,000 (80 miles = 1 inch)

Statute Miles

Boundary of the Kingdom proper
Boundaries of the Great Duchies and Marches

BALTIC SEA

KINGDOM OF DENMARK

Schleswig
SCHLESWIG

HOLSTEIN

Rügen I.

Colberg

Wollin (Jomsburg)
Usedom

POMERANIA
(Conquered by Germany 995)

Stettin
Garz
Pyritz

Lübeck
Obotrites
MECKLENBURG
Mecklenburg
Schwerin
Redarians
MARCH OF THE BILLINGS

Warnabians
Ukrians
Wiltzes
Lusatians

NORDMARK

Hamburg
Lüneburg
LANDS OF THE BILLUNGS
Bremen
Verden
Salzwedel
Werben
Havelberg
Walsleben
Hevellians

ENGERN
Aller
EASTPHALIA

Meseritz
Posen
Gnesen
Warthe

SAXONY

Brandenburg
Lebus
Spree
Oder

POLAND
(Tributary to Germany 963
Kingdom 1025)

Groningen
Norden
HOLLAND

Osnabrück
Minden (Duchy)
Brunswick
Magdeburg

WESTPHALIA

Utrecht
Deventer

Münster
Gandersheim
Detmold
Hildesheim
Halberstadt
Goslar
Harz
Wgnstein
Quedlinburg
Wolfeshott
Wettin
OSTMARK
LAUSITZ, LUSATIA
Milzienians
Glogau
SILESIA

Breda
Nimwegen
Xanten
Wesel
Dortmund
Ruhr
Paderborn
Nordheim
Nordhausen
Memleben
Merseburg
Halle
Leipzig
M. or
MERSEB.
Meissen
Bautzen
MARCH OF MEISSEN
Liegnitz
Breslau

Bruges
Ghent
Antwerp
FLANDERS
LOWER LOTHARINGIA (Duchy 959)
Maastricht
BRABANT
Louvain
Birthen
Kaisersworth
Cologne
Bonn
HESSE
Gerstungen
Erfurt
THURINGIA
Weimar
Flarchheim
Möllen
Hohen
M. OF
ZEITZ
Zeitz
Erz Gebirge
Leitmeritz
Giant Mts.

Namur
Liège
HAINAUT
Limburg
Andernach
Coblenz
Wetzlar
Labn
Fulda
Hersfeld
Meltrichstadt
Thuringian Forest
Eger

Cambrai
LOTHARINGIA (Duchy)
WESTER WALD
Frankfurt
FRANCONIA
Mainz
Tribur
EAST
Bamberg
Bleichfeld
Würzburg
WEST
DUCHY

BOHEMIA
(Tributary to Germany from 950
Under Poland 1003-4)
(Kingdom 1088)

Prague
Pilsen

M O R A V I A
(From 955 to Bohemia
Under Poland 1003-29)
Olmütz
Brünn

Bouillon
Luxemburg
Trèves
Böckelheim
Worms
UPPER LOTHARINGIA (Duchy 959)
Diedenhofen
Thionville
Metz
Verdun
Bar
Toul
Nancy
Speyer
Saarbrücken
Wimpfen
Weinsberg
Neckar
Nuremberg
MARGRAVIATE OF NORDGAU
(From Bavaria 976)
Ratisbon
(Regensburg)
Bohemian Forest

Clairvaux
Langres
Luxeuil
Strassburg
Lunéville
ALSACE
VOSGES
BLACK FOREST
Falkenstein
Zollern
Zähringen
Tübingen
WÜRTTEMBERG
Staufen
Waiblingen
SWABIAN JURA
Sigmaringen
Ulm
Danube
Iller
Augsburg
Freising
Passau
Linz
Krems
Vienna
Pressburg
MARCH OF
AUSTRIA
(Kingdom from 1000)
HUNGARY

KINGDOM OF FRANCE

COUNTY OF BURGUNDY
Besançon
Basle
Habsburg
THURGAU
(Duchy)
Constance
Zürich
St. Gall
L. of Constance
Lech-feld
Lech
BAVARIA (Duchy)
Mühldorf
Salzburg
Polling
TRAUNGAU
Altenburg
MARCH OF
Eppenstein
(MARCH)
CARINTHIA (Duchy 976)
STYRIA (MARCH)

Neuchâtel
BURGUNDY
Berne
Freiburg
UPPER
AARGAU
Lucerne
Engelberg
Chur
A L P S
Wilten
Brenner Pass
Meran
Brixen
Botzen
Villach
Mur
Drave

KINGDOM OF BURGUNDY
(ARELATE)
Geneva
Lausanne
Rhône
Simplon P.
St Gotthard Pass
Splügen P.
Rhine
FRIULI
Trent
Belluno
MARCH OF VERONA
(To Bavaria 952
to Carinthia 976)
Aquileia
Laibach
CARNIOLA (MARCH)
Trieste
ISTRIA (MARCH)
CROATIA

Lyons
Vienne
Cluny
Mâcon
Aosta
Little St. Bernard Pass
Gt. St Bernard Pass
LOWER
Grenoble
Mt. Cenis Pass
Turin
Ivrea
Como
Milan
Bergamo
Brescia
Lodi
Adda
Cremona
Pavia
Piacenza
Roncaglia
Po
KINGDOM OF ITALY
Treviso
Verona
Adige
VENICE
Venice
ADRIATIC SEA

COPYRIGHT, GEORGE PHILIP & SON, LTD.

FRANCE & BURGUNDY
showing
the Feudal Lordships
about the year 1032 A.D.

Scale 1:5,000,000 (80 miles = 1 inch)

Statute Miles

0   50   100

⚷	Archbishopric
⚶	Bishopric
(D)	Duchy
(C)	County
(V)	Viscounty
(S)	Seigneurie
(M)	Marquisate
	Boundary of France
	" of Royal Domain
	" of Burgundy
	" of Ecclesiastical Fiefs

East from Greenwich

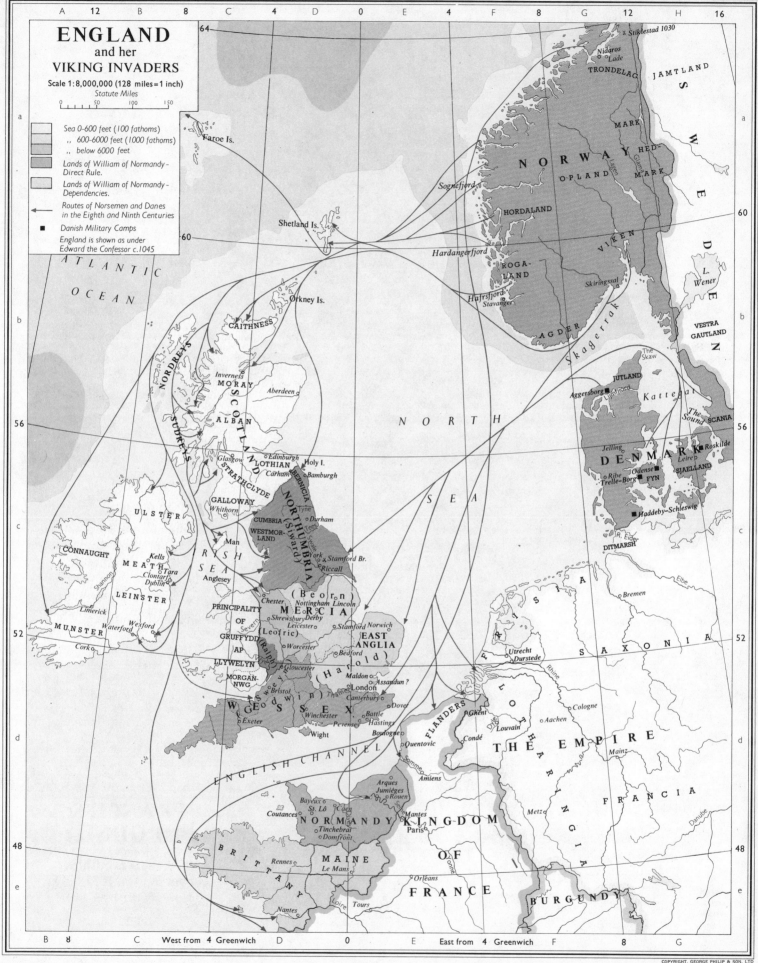

ENGLAND
and her
VIKING INVADERS

Scale 1:8,000,000 (128 miles=1 inch)

Statute Miles

	Sea 0-600 feet (100 fathoms)
	,, 600-6000 feet (1000 fathoms)
	,, below 6000 feet
	Lands of William of Normandy - Direct Rule.
	Lands of William of Normandy - Dependencies.
←	Routes of Norsemen and Danes in the Eighth and Ninth Centuries
■	Danish Military Camps

England is shown as under Edward the Confessor c.1045

ATLANTIC OCEAN

Faroe Is.

Shetland Is.

Orkney Is.

NORDREYS

CAITHNESS

Inverness
MORAY
Aberdeen

SUDREYS

SCOTLAND
ALBAN

Glasgow
LOTHIAN   Edinburgh
STRATHCLYDE   Holy I.
Carham   Bamburgh
GALLOWAY
Whithorn   BERNICIA

ULSTER

CONNAUGHT

Kells
MEATH   Tara
Clontarf
Dublin

LEINSTER

IRISH SEA

Man
Anglesey
Chester

MUNSTER

Limerick
Waterford
Wexford

Cork

NORTHUMBRIA
(Siward)
CUMBRIA   Tyne
WESTMORLAND   Durham
Tees
Swale   York   x Stamford Br.
Riccall

PRINCIPALITY
OF
(Leofric)
GRUFFYDD
AP
LLYWELYN
MORGAN-
NWG

(Beorn)
MERCIA
Nottingham   Lincoln
Shrewsbury   Derby
Leicester
Worcester   Stamford
Bedford
EAST
ANGLIA
(Harold)
Norwich

Severn
Gloucester
(Ralph)

Bristol
W.   Maldon   Assandun ?
(Godwin)   London
S   Thames   Canterbury
WESSEX   Dover
Winchester   Battle
Exeter   Pevensey   Hastings
Wight

ENGLISH CHANNEL

NORWAY

Stiklestad 1030
Nidaros
Lade
TRONDELAG   JAMTLAND

MARK

OPLAND
Lagen
Glamma   MARK

Sognefjord

HORDALAND

Hardangerfjord   VIKEN

ROGA-
LAND
Hafrsfjord   Skiringssal
Stavanger

AGDER

Skagerrak

SWEDEN

L.
Wener

VESTRA
GAUTLAND

The Skaw

JUTLAND
Aggersborg   Limfjord
Kattegat

The Sound   SCANIA

Jelling   DENMARK   Roskilde
Leire
Ribe   Odense
Trelle-Borg   FYN   SJAELLAND

R. Eider
DITMARSH

Haddeby-Schleswig

FRISIA

Bremen

Utrecht
Durstede

SAXONIA

Rhine

Elbe

NORTH
SEA

FLANDERS   Ghent
Louvain
Condé   Aachen
Quentovic
Boulogne   Somme
Amiens

Cologne

THE EMPIRE

LOTHARINGIA

Mainz

FRANCIA

Arques
Jumièges
Bayeux   Rouen
St. Lô   Caen   Mantes
Coutances   NORMANDY
Tinchebrai   Paris
Domfront   KINGDOM
OF
BRITTANY
Rennes
MAINE   FRANCE
Le Mans   Orleans
Yonne
Nantes   Loire
Tours

Metz

BURGUNDY

Danube

ENGLAND
according to the DOMESDAY SURVEY
1086

Scale 1:2,500,000 (40 miles = 1 inch)

Statute Miles
0 5 10 20 30 40 50

Legend

For modern spelling of Domesday names see Index

- English Shires
- Welsh Principalities
- Palatine earldoms surviving in 1086
- Forfeited palatinate of Hereford

Burgi and Civitates surveyed in Domesday Book are shown thus Eboracum others thus *Lundonia*

- Burgi and Civitates on the royal domain.
- Burgi and Civitates on mediate fiefs.
- Burgi and Civitates not named in Domesday Book.
- Royal castles named in Domesday Book.
- Royal castles not named in Domesday Book.
- Private castles named in Domesday Book.
- Private castles not named in Domesday Book.
- Archbishopric
- Bishopric
- Collegiate foundations
- Monastic foundations.

West from Greenwich

COPYRIGHT. GEORGE PHILIP & SON, LTD.

Regions and places (as labelled on map):

Berewic, Lindisfarna, Is. Farnea, Bebbanburh, NORTHUMBR, S.C.L., Alnwick, Redesdale, Morpeth, S.C.L., Bellingtun, Werc, Bewcastle, Munekeceastre, Tinemuthe, Hagustolham (Hexesham), Gateshevid, Gyrwe, Weremuthe, Carleo, Alston, Cuncacestre, Dunholm, CUMBRA, Appleby, Bowes, Brough, Derlington, Sedberuie, Ghillinges, Iarum, Muncaster, Bodele, Witebi, C. Alani, Clyveland, Catric, Nor-Treding, Elmeslac, Tresch, Pickeringham, Is. de Man, Daltune, Cherchebi, EVRVIC SCIRE, Ripun, Bretlinton, Loncastre, Crave, Chenaresburg, Stanfordbrycge, Skipsea, Scipone, Eboracum, Evvric, Poclinton, Heldernesse, Est-Treding, Fulford, Scireburne, Selebi, Beverlie, Hovedene, Ripa, Peneverdant, Wachefeld, Tateshale, Fornbi, INTER RIPAM ET MERSHAM, Mamecestre, Wes-Treding, Nor-Treding, Grimesbi, Mersha, Westderbei, Doneham, Dadisleia, Coningesburg, Ludes, Sud-Treding, Aberlleiniog, Deganwy, Roelant, Llanelwy, Tegeing, CESTRE, Heletune, Frotesham, Cinbretune, Pecfers, Bolsover, Blida, LINCOLESCIRE, Mon, Bangor, Caer Segont, Rhos, Rhufoniog, CESTRE SCIRE, Actune, Wich, Sudwelle, Lincolia, Stou, Holland, Bohnbroc, Nowerche, Wella, GWYNEDD, Maelor, Bangor, DERBY-SCIRE, Chetsteven, Edeyrnion Ynllaith, Luvu, Oswestry, Meresberie, Totebrie, STADFORD-SCIRE, Snotingham, Grantham, Belvedoir, Folchingham, St. Benedictus de Holme, Getnemuthac, Meirionydd, POWY, Sciropesberie, SCIROPESCIRE, Chirbury, Stantune, Stadford, Penkridge, Burtone, Derby, Medeltune, Stanford, Spallinge, Acra, Norwit, Cydewain, Montgomery, Wenloch, Licefelld, Tamworde, Roteland (to Snotingham), Gruiland, Wisbeche, NORDFULC, Arwystli, Quatford, Tettenhall, LEDECESTRE SCIRE, Ledecestre, Torp, Burg, Tetford, Beccles, Ceri, Ludlow, Dudelei, Coventreu, Rochingeham, TRENTEBRIGE SCIRE, Maelienydd, Lentaurde, Warwicscire, Warwic, NORTHANTONE SCIRE, Ramesyg, Elyg, Yxinga, S. Edmundi, Dunewic, Wigemor, Castle Ricardt, Leofminstre, WIRECESTRE SCIRE, Wiche, Wedone, Northantone, Huntedun, St. Ives, Grentebrige, SUDFULC, Clara, Gipewiz, Orford, Raddenore, Herdeslege, Clifford, HEREFORD SCIRE, Hereford, Persore, Medneltun, Evesham, Elnestow, BEDFORD SCIRE, Escewelle, Waledana, Sudberie, Haingeham, Colecestra, Buellt, Elfael, Teodekesberie, Wincelcumbe, Bochingeham, Merse, DEHEUBARTH, Dyfed, Dinevor, Ewias, Arcenefeld, Dene, Glowecestre, OXENEFORD SCIRE, Oxeneford, HERTEFORDSCIRE, Berchamstede, V. S. Albani, Herteforde, EXSESSA, Maldona, Brycheiniog, GWENT, Foresta, GLOWECESTRE SCIRE, Egleshom, Abbendone, Wicumbe, Waltham, Rageneia, Monemude, Nesse, Berchelai, Cirencestre, Crichelade, Walingeforde, MIDELSEXE, Lundonia, Barking, Deptford, MORGANNWG, Caerlean, Striguil, BERROESCIRE, Merleberge, Redinges, Westmonasterium, Stanes, Sudwerca, Roucestre, Cantuaria, Forewic, Seseltre, Llandaf, Caendydd, Malmesberie, Cauna, Certesyg, Sandwic, Mynyw, Ceredigion, Bristou, Bade, Bradford, Bedvinde, Basinges, SUDRIE, CHENTH, Dovere, Banwelle, Redinges, Goldilminge, Tonebridge, Folkestone, Cardigan, Alseberge, WILTESCIRE, Guerminstre, Ambresberie, HANTESCIRE, Gildeford, Heda, Romenel, Piltune, Portloc, Torre, Welle, Glastingeberie, Wiltunie, Sarisberie, Sceptesberie, Wintonia, Andredsweald, SUD SEXE, Rye, Ecclesia de Labatailge, Barnestable, SUMORSETE, Tantone, Lanporth, Adelinge, Givelcestre, Milebume, Scireburne, Rordesi, Hantune, Porcestre, Cicestre, Staynnges, Lawes, Ferle, Hastings, Baentone, Montagud, Creneburne, Rincoede, Nova Foresta, Tvinam, Harundel, Pevenesel, Borne, Cerneli, Winburne, Alwinestune, Is. de Wiht, DEVENESCIRE, DORSETE, Dorcestre, Warham, Warham (Corfe), Tintagel, Ochementone, Lideforde, Exonia, Bridport, Lym, Abedesberie, Dunhevet, Lansavetone, Tavestoche, Powderham, Beri, S. Carentochus, S. Neotus, Tremetone, S. Germanus, Bucfestre, CORNVALGIE, Plintone, Totenais, Combie, S. Michael, S. Pieranus, Achebrannus, S. Berrione, S. Probus, CORNVALGIE

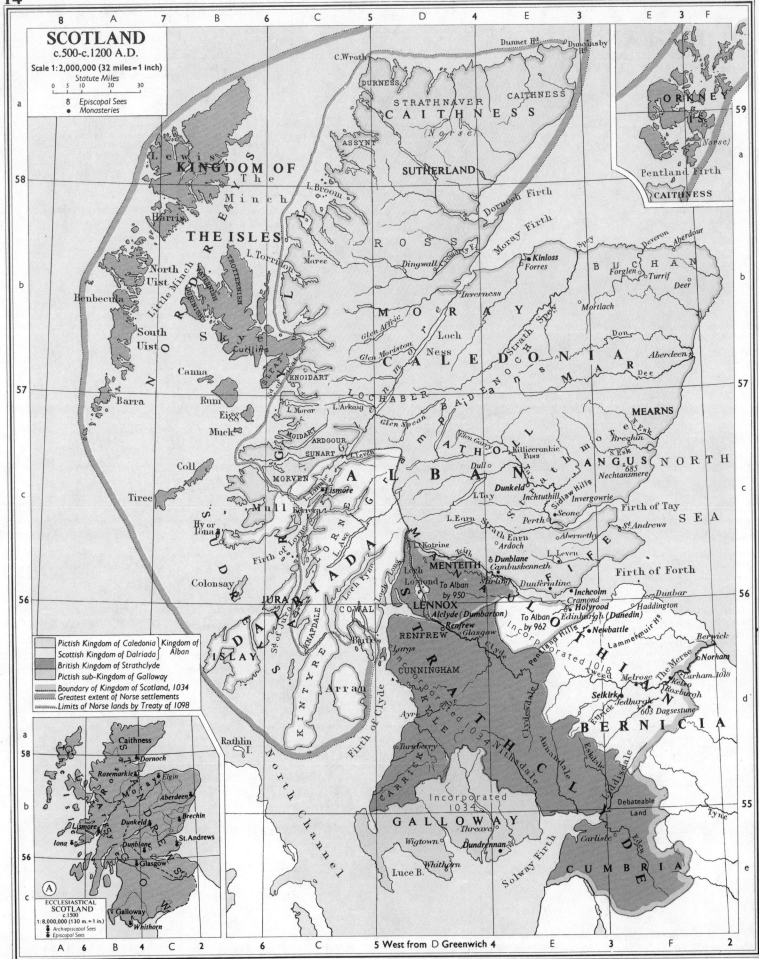

14

SCOTLAND
c.500–c.1200 A.D.

Scale 1:2,000,000 (32 miles=1 inch)

Statute Miles

 δ Episcopal Sees
• Monasteries

Legend:
- Pictish Kingdom of Caledonia
- Scottish Kingdom of Dalriada } Kingdom of Alban
- British Kingdom of Strathclyde
- Pictish sub-Kingdom of Galloway
- Boundary of Kingdom of Scotland, 1034
- Greatest extent of Norse settlements
- Limits of Norse lands by Treaty of 1098

ECCLESIASTICAL SCOTLAND c.1500
1:8,000,000 (130 m. = 1 in.)
- Archiepiscopal Sees
- Episcopal Sees

KINGDOM OF THE ISLES

ORKNEY IS. (Norse)
Pentland Firth
CAITHNESS

Dunnet Hd.   Duncansby Hd.
C. Wrath
DURNESS
STRATHNAVER   CAITHNESS
CAITHNESS   (Norse)
ASSYNT
SUTHERLAND
L. Broom
Dornoch Firth
Dingwall   Moray Firth
R O S S
L. Maree
Kinloss
Forres   BUCHAN
Forglen   Aberdour
Turriff   Deer
Inverness
M O R A Y   Mortlach
Glen Affric   Loch   Ness
Glen Moriston   STRATH   Spey   Don   M A R
C A L E D O N I A   Aberdeen
Dee

LEWIS
The Minch
NORDREYS
Harris
North Uist
Benbecula
South Uist   SKYE   SLEAT
Little Minch   TROTTERNISH
DUIRINISH   WATERNISH
L. Torridon
Cuillins
Canna
Barra
Rum
Eigg
Muck   L. Morar   L. Arkaig
Coll   MOIDART   Glen Spean
Tiree   ARDGOUR   SUNART
MORVEN   L. Leven
Hy or Iona   Mull   Lismore
Colonsay   Firth of Lorne

LOCHABER   BADENOCH   A T H O L L   Killiecrankie Pass
Glen Garry   Dull   Dunkeld   MEARNS
A L B A N   L. Tay   N. Esk   Brechin   NORTH
Inchtuthill   Sidlaw Hills   S. Esk   685   A N G U S
L. Earn   Invergowrie   Nechtansmere
Strath Earn   Scone   Firth of Tay
Ardoch   Perth   Abernethy   St. Andrews   SEA

DRUMALBAN
S. of Lorne   L. Awe   L. Katrine   Teith
ARGYLL   LORN   Loch   MENTEITH   Dunblane
JURA   Loch Lomond   Stirling   Cambuskenneth
KNAPDALE   Lomond   To Alban by 950   Dunfermline   Inchcolm   Dunbar
DALRIADA   Loch Long   LENNOX   F I F E   To Alban   Cramond   Holyrood   Haddington
Sd. of Jura   COWAL   Alclyde (Dumbarton)   by 962   Edinburgh (Dunedin)
ISLAY   Loch Fyne   RENFREW   Renfrew   Glasgow   L. Leven   L O T H I A N   Newbattle
KINTYRE   Bute   Incorporated 1018   Pentland Hills   Berwick
Largs   CUNNINGHAM   Clyde   Lammermuir Hs.   Norham
Rathlin I.   Arran   Melrose   The Merse   Carham 1018
S T R A T H C L Y D E   Ayr   Clydesdale   Tweed   Roxburgh
Incorporated 1034   CARRICK   Nithsdale   Annandale   Selkirk   Jedburgh   603 Dagsestune
North Channel   Turnberry   Incorporated 1034   Eskdale   Ettrick   Kelso
Firth of Clyde   G A L L O W A Y   Threave   Liddisdale   B E R N I C I A
Wigtown   Dundrennan   Debateable Land   Tyne
Luce B.   Whithorn   Solway Firth   Carlisle   Eden   C U M B R I A

59
58
57
56
55

a
b
c
d
e

8   A   7   B   6   C   5   D   4   E   3   E   3   F
5 West from D Greenwich 4

Inset (Ecclesiastical Scotland):
Caithness
Dornoch
Rosemarkie   Elgin
MORAY   Aberdeen
Lismore   Dunkeld   Brechin
Iona   Dunblane   St. Andrews
Glasgow
Galloway
Whithorn

COPYRIGHT. GEORGE PHILIP & SON, LTD.

15

ECCLESIASTICAL
IRELAND
c.1500
1:8,000,000 (130m = 1 in.)
Archiepiscopal Sees
Episcopal Sees

IRELAND
before the
ENGLISH INVASION
Scale 1:2,000,000 (32 miles = 1 inch)
Statute Miles

Bishoprics existing in 1150
Monasteries
Anglo-Norman Castles erected
during reign of Henry II
Irish Clans thus: *O'Dowd*
Danish Towns underlined in Red

Over 3000 feet
1200-3000 ,,
600-1200 ,,
0- 600 ,,

COPYRIGHT. GEORGE PHILIP & SON. LTD.

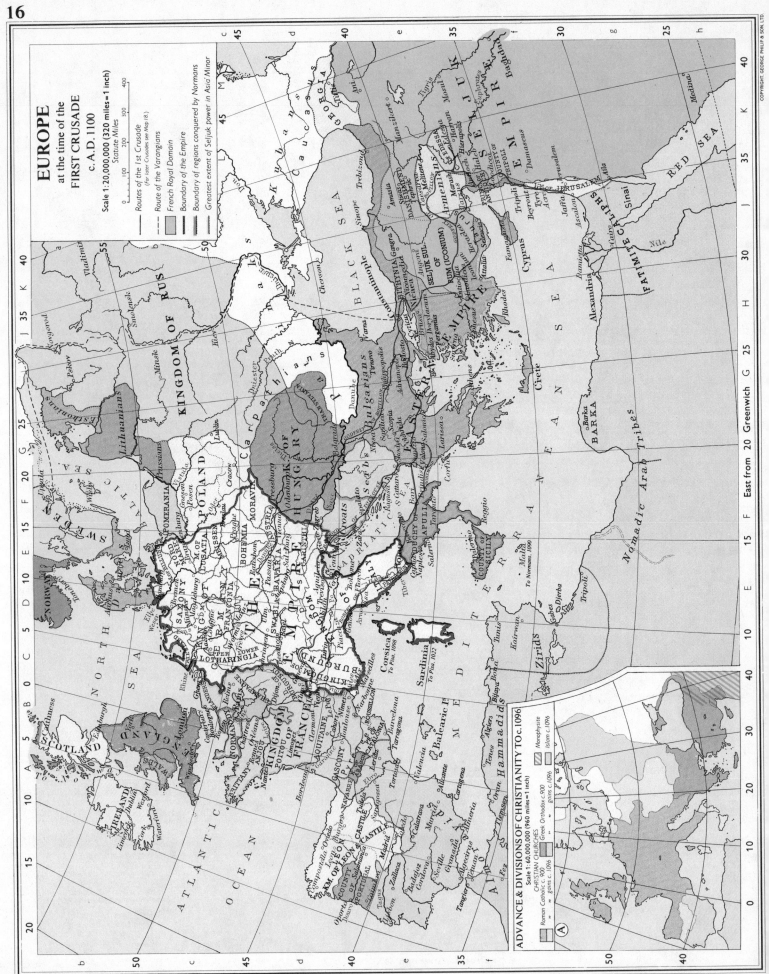

EUROPE
at the time of the
FIRST CRUSADE
C.A.D. 1100

Scale 1:20,000,000 (320 miles=1 inch)
Statute Miles

```
0   100   200   300   400
```

—————— Routes of the 1st Crusade
(For later Crusades see Map 18.)
- - - - Route of the Varangians
French Royal Domain
Boundary of the Empire
Boundary of French Royal Domain
Greatest extent of Seljuk power in Asia Minor

ADVANCE & DIVISIONS OF CHRISTIANITY TO c.1096
Scale 1:60,000,000 (960 miles=1 inch)

CHRISTIAN CHURCHES
Roman Catholic c.900
     "   gains c.1096
Greek Orthodox c.900
     "   gains c.1096
Monophysite
Islam c.1096

East from 20 Greenwich G

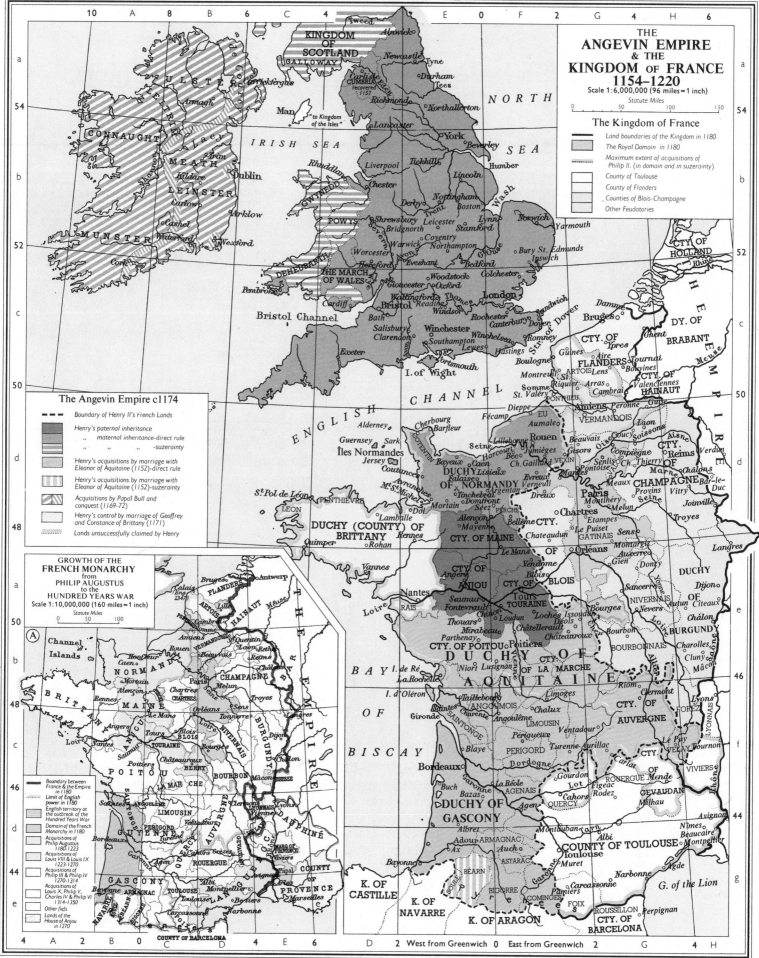

17

THE ANGEVIN EMPIRE & THE KINGDOM OF FRANCE 1154–1220

Scale 1:6,000,000 (96 miles=1 inch)

Statute Miles
0   50   100   150

The Kingdom of France

— Land boundaries of the Kingdom in 1180

The Royal Domain in 1180

······ Maximum extent of acquisitions of Philip II. (in domain and in suzerainty)

County of Toulouse

County of Flanders

Counties of Blois-Champagne

Other Feudatories

The Angevin Empire c1174

- - - Boundary of Henry II's French Lands

Henry's paternal inheritance

  "   maternal inheritance-direct rule

  "   "   "   -suzerainty

Henry's acquisitions by marriage with Eleanor of Aquitaine (1152)-direct rule

Henry's acquisitions by marriage with Eleanor of Aquitaine (1152)-suzerainty

Acquisitions by Papal Bull and conquest (1169-72)

Henry's control by marriage of Geoffrey and Constance of Brittany (1171)

······ Lands unsuccessfully claimed by Henry

GROWTH OF THE FRENCH MONARCHY from PHILIP AUGUSTUS to the HUNDRED YEARS WAR

Scale 1:10,000,000 (160 miles=1 inch)

Statute Miles
0   100

— Boundary between France & the Empire in 1180

······ Limit of English power in 1180

English territory at the outbreak of the Hundred Years War

Domain of the French Monarchy in 1180

Acquisitions of Philip Augustus 1180-1223

Acquisitions of Louis VIII & Louis IX 1223-1270

Acquisitions of Philip III & Philip IV 1270-1314

Acquisitions of Louis X, Philip V, Charles IV & Philip VI 1314-1350

Other fiefs

Lands of the House of Anjou in 1270

COPYRIGHT, GEORGE PHILIP & SON, LTD.

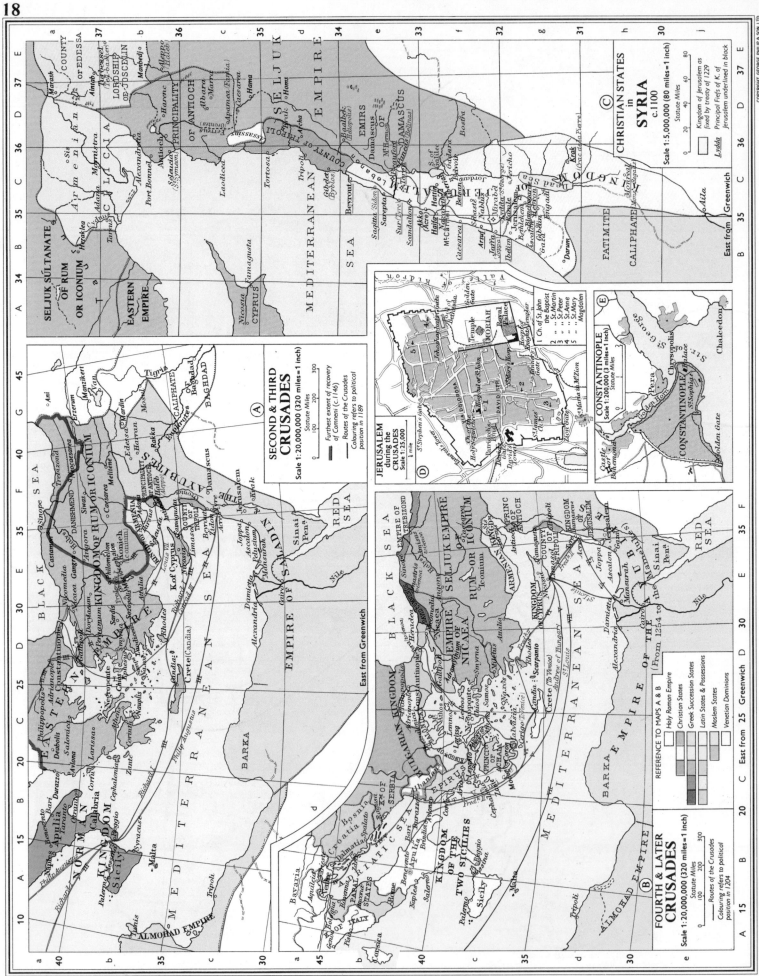

18

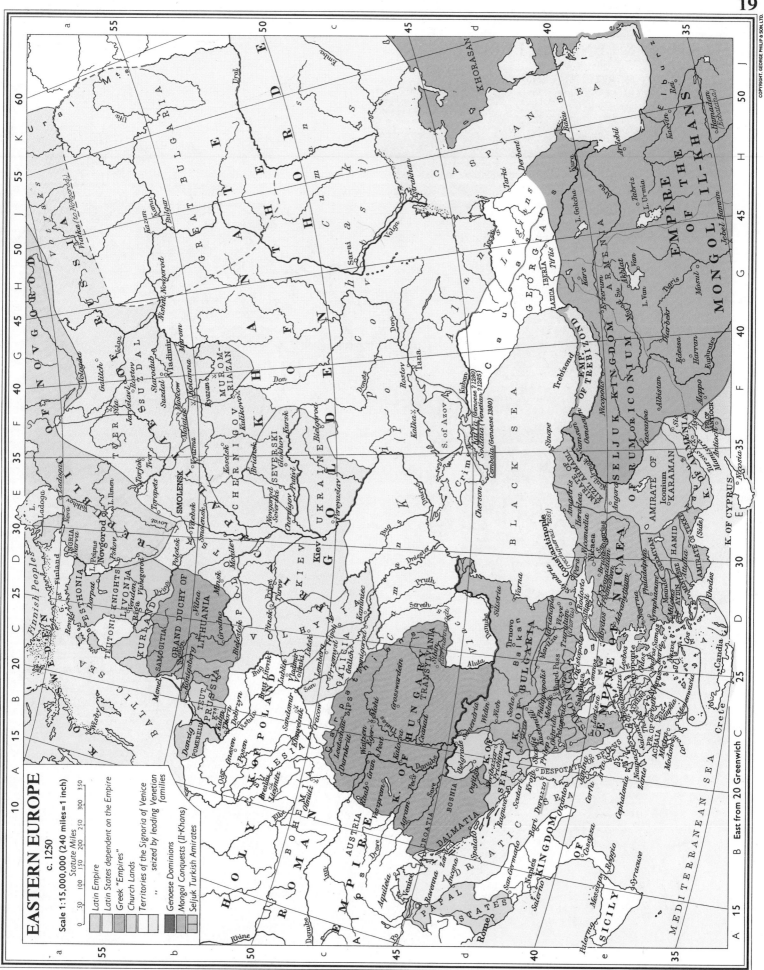

EASTERN EUROPE
c. 1250

Scale 1:15,000,000 (240 miles=1 inch)

Statute Miles

0   50   100   150   200   250   300   350

Latin Empire

Latin States dependent on the Empire

Greek "Empires"

Church Lands

Territories of the Signoria of Venice
"   "   seized by leading Venetian
families

Genoese Dominions

Mongol Conquests (Il-Khans)

Seljuk Turkish Amirates

EMPIRE OF THE IL-KHANS

MONGOL

KHORASAN

CASPIAN SEA

GREAT BULGARIA

THE GOLDEN HORDE

REPUBLIC OF NOVGOROD

SWEDEN

BALTIC SEA

TEUTONIC KNIGHTS
LIVONIA
KURLAND
ESTHONIA

GRAND DUCHY OF LITHUANIA
SAMOGITIA
TEUT. PRUSSIA
POMERELIA

K. OF POLAND

BOHEMIA

HOLY ROMAN EMPIRE

AUSTRIA

K. OF HUNGARY
TRANSYLVANIA

SILESIA

GALICIA

VOLHYNIA

KIEV
G. OF KIEV

UKRAINE

SEVERSKI

CHERNIGOV

SMOLENSK
TVER
SUZDAL
MUROM-RIAZAN

BLACK SEA

K. OF BULGARIA

SERVIA
BOSNIA
CROATIA
DALMATIA
DESPOTATE OF EPIRUS

PAPAL STATES
Rome

SICILY

K. OF NAPLES

MEDITERRANEAN SEA

Crete

K. OF CYPRUS

EMPIRE OF NICAEA

LATIN EMPIRE
Constantinople

SELJUK KINGDOM OF RUM OR ICONIUM

AMIRATE OF KARAMAN

ARMENIA
K. OF LESSER ARMENIA

EMPIRE OF TREBIZOND

GEORGIA
IBERIA

ALANS

Trebizond

Black Sea

S. of Azov

Crimea
Caffa
Soldaia
Cembalo

ADRIATIC SEA

Danube

Don

Volga

Ural

Dnieper

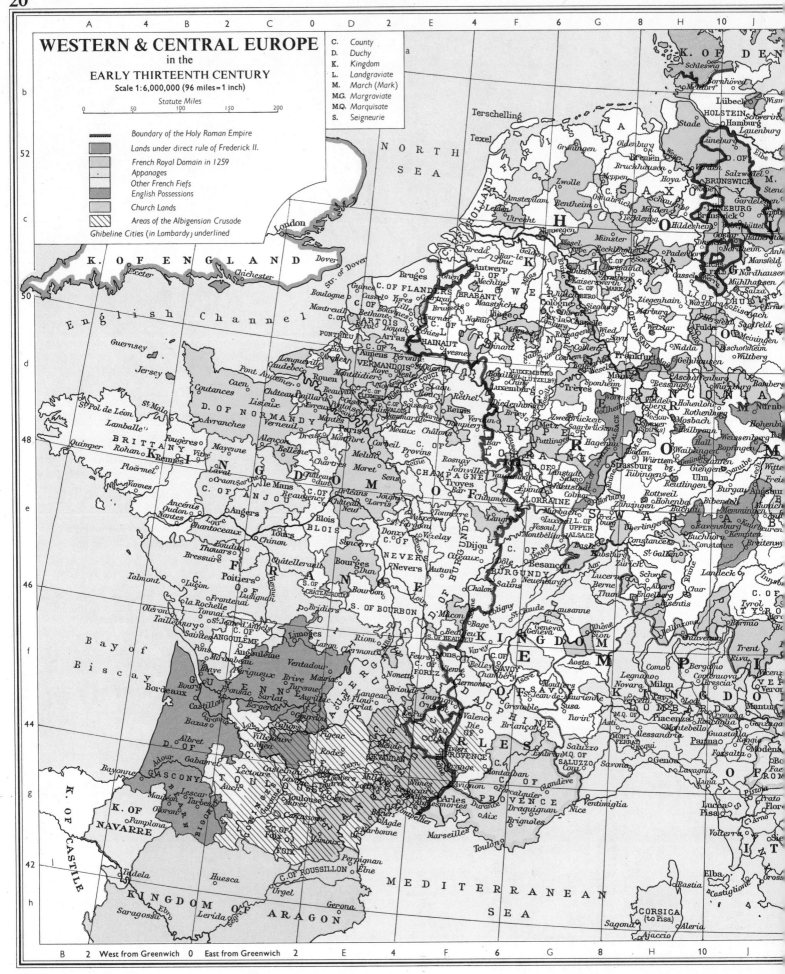

WESTERN & CENTRAL EUROPE
in the
EARLY THIRTEENTH CENTURY
Scale 1:6,000,000 (96 miles = 1 inch)

Statute Miles

0   50   100   150   200

C.	County
D.	Duchy
K.	Kingdom
L.	Landgraviate
M.	March (Mark)
M.G.	Margraviate
M.Q.	Marquisate
S.	Seigneurie

Boundary of the Holy Roman Empire
Lands under direct rule of Frederick II.
French Royal Domain in 1259
Appanages
Other French Fiefs
English Possessions
Church Lands
Areas of the Albigensian Crusade
Ghibeline Cities (in Lombardy) underlined

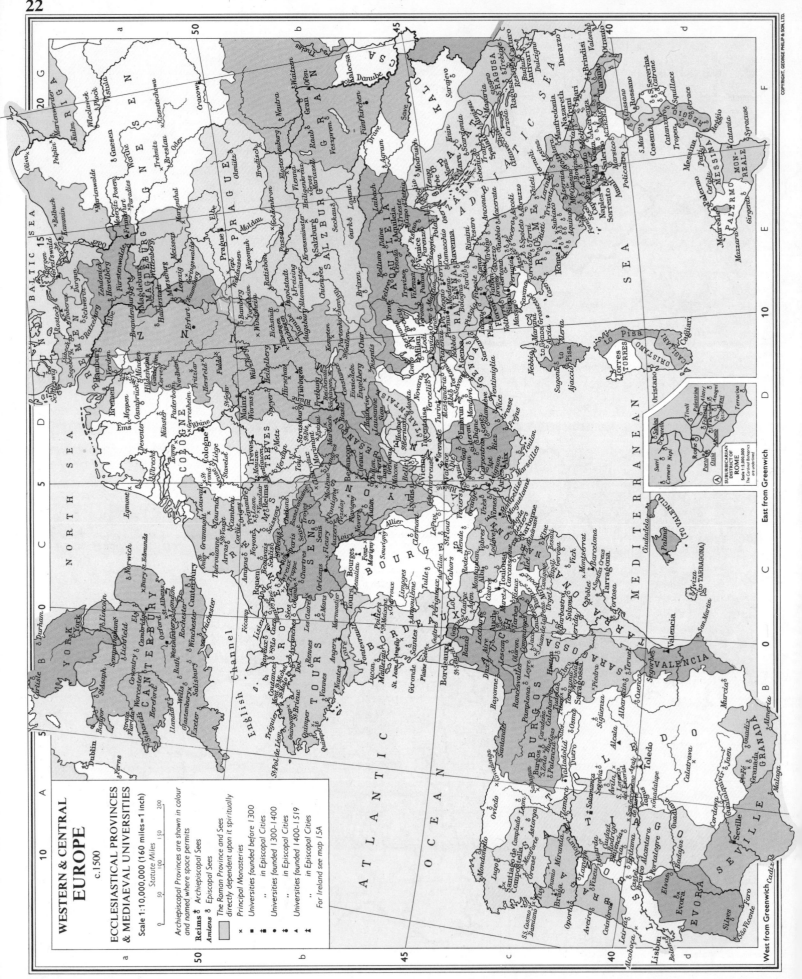

22

WESTERN & CENTRAL
EUROPE
c.1500

ECCLESIASTICAL PROVINCES
& MEDIAEVAL UNIVERSITIES

Scale 1:10,000,000 (160 miles=1 inch)

Statute Miles
0   50   100   150   200

Archiepiscopal Provinces are shown in colour
and named where space permits

Reims ‡ Archiepiscopal Sees

Amiens ∂ Episcopal Sees

The Roman Province and Sees
directly dependent upon it spiritually

Principal Monasteries   ×
Universities founded before 1300
  „ „ in Episcopal Cities
Universities founded 1300-1400
  „ „ in Episcopal Cities
Universities founded 1400-1519
  „ „ in Episcopal Cities

For Ireland see map 15A

SUBURBICARIAN DISTRICT OF
ROME
Scale 1:5,000,000
The Cardinal Bishoprics
are underlined

West from Greenwich   East from Greenwich

COPYRIGHT. GEORGE PHILIP & SON, LTD.

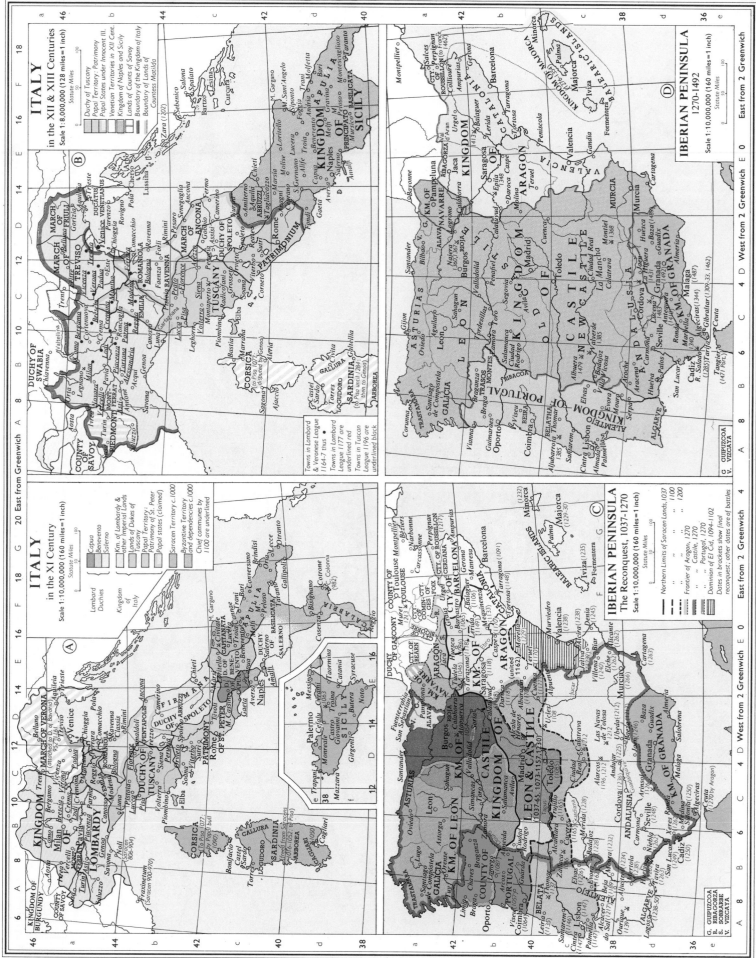

ITALY
in the XII & XIII Centuries
Scale 1:8,000,000 (128 miles=1 inch)

Duchy of Tuscany
Papal Territory: Patrimony
Papal States under Innocent III.
Venetian Territories in XII Cent.
Kingdom of Naples and Sicily
Lands of Counts of Savoy
Boundary of the Kingdom of Italy
Boundary of the Lands of
Countess Matilda

IBERIAN PENINSULA
1270-1492
Scale 1:10,000,000 (160 miles=1 inch)

East from 2 Greenwich

ITALY
in the XI Century
Scale 1:10,000,000 (160 miles=1 inch)

Capua
Benevento
Salerno

Lombard Duchies

Kingdom
of
Italy

Km. of Lombardy &
other Imperial Lands
Lands of Dukes of
Tuscany
Papal Territory
Patrimony of St. Peter
Papal states (claimed)

Byzantine Territory
and dependencies c.1000

Saracen Territory c.1000

Chief communes by
1100 are underlined

Towns in Lombard
& Veronese League
1164-7 thus
Towns in Lombard
League 1177 are
underlined red
Towns in Tuscan
League 1196 are
underlined black

IBERIAN PENINSULA
The Reconquest, 1037-1270
Scale 1:10,000,000 (160 miles=1 inch)

Northern Limits of Saracen Lands,1037
Frontier of Aragon, 1270
" " Castile, 1270
" " Portugal, 1270
Dominion of El Cid, 1094-1102
Dates in brackets show final
reconquest; other dates are of battles

COPYRIGHT. GEORGE PHILIP & SON, LTD.

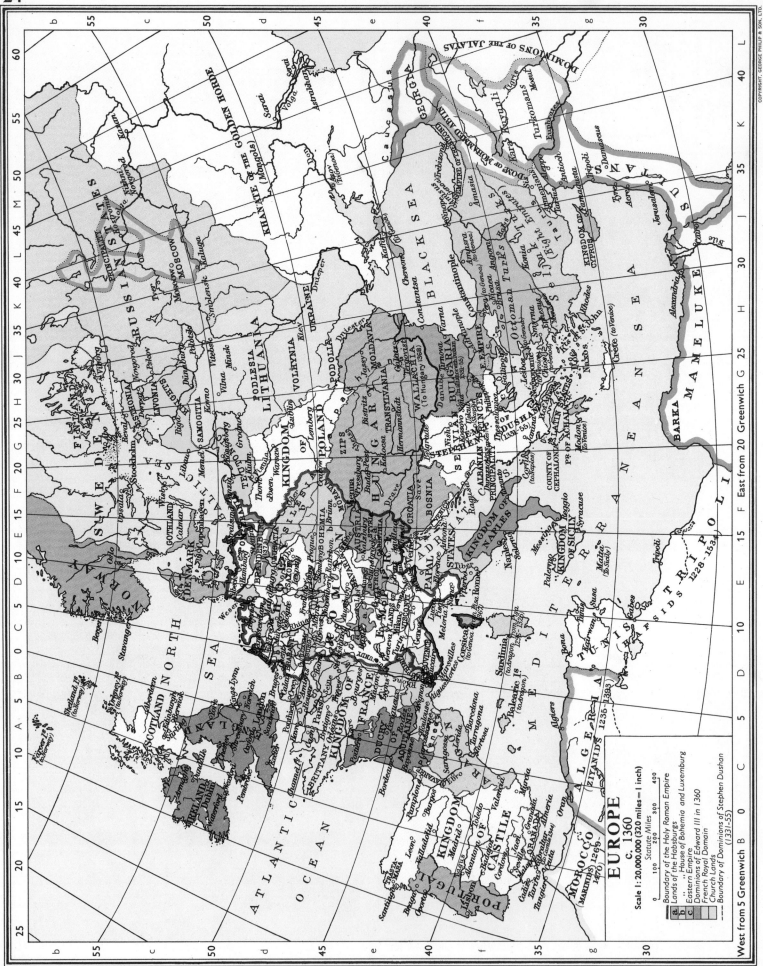

24

EUROPE
c. 1360

Scale 1:20,000,000 (320 miles=1 inch)

Statute Miles
0 100 200 300 400

—— Boundary of the Holy Roman Empire
a Lands of the Habsburgs
b ... House of Bohemia and Luxemburg
c Eastern Empire
Dominions of Edward III in 1360
French Royal Domain
Church Lands
----- Boundary of Dominions of Stephen Dushan

West from 5 Greenwich B   0   C   East from 5 Greenwich   D   E   F   East from 20 Greenwich G 25 H 30 J 35 K L

COPYRIGHT, GEORGE PHILIP & SON, LTD.

ATLANTIC OCEAN

NORTH SEA

BALTIC SEA

MEDITERRANEAN SEA

BLACK SEA

NORWAY

SWEDEN

FINLAND

DENMARK

SCOTLAND

IRELAND

KINGDOM OF ENGLAND

KINGDOM OF FRANCE

DUCHY OF AQUITAINE

BRITTANY

KINGDOM OF PORTUGAL

KINGDOM OF CASTILE

ARAGON

MOROCCO
(MARINIDS 1269-1470)

ALGERIA
(ZIYANIDS)

TUNIS
(HAFSIDS 1228-1534)

TRIPOLI

BARKA

MAMELUKE

RUSSIAN STATES

PRINCIPALITY OF MOSCOW

KHANATE OF THE GOLDEN HORDE
(Mongols)

LITHUANIA

PODLESIA

VOLHYNIA

UKRAINE

PODOLIA

POLAND

KINGDOM OF POLAND

SILESIA

BOHEMIA

MORAVIA

TEUT...

LIVONIA

ESTHONIA

SAMOGITIA

HUNGARY

AUSTRIA

TRANSYLVANIA

MOLDAVIA

WALLACHIA
(to Hungary 1368)

BULGARIA

SERVIA
STEPHEN DUSHAN
(1331-55)

BOSNIA

CROATIA

ZIPS

EMPIRE OF MAHOMMED AIDIN

GEORGIA

OTTOMAN TURKS

EASTERN EMPIRE

Constantinople

KINGDOM OF CYPRUS

KINGDOM OF NAPLES

KINGDOM OF SICILY

PAPAL STATES

CHURCH LANDS

ALBANIAN PRINCIPALITY

DOMINIONS OF THE JALAIRS

Jerusalem

DUSHAN
(1331-55)

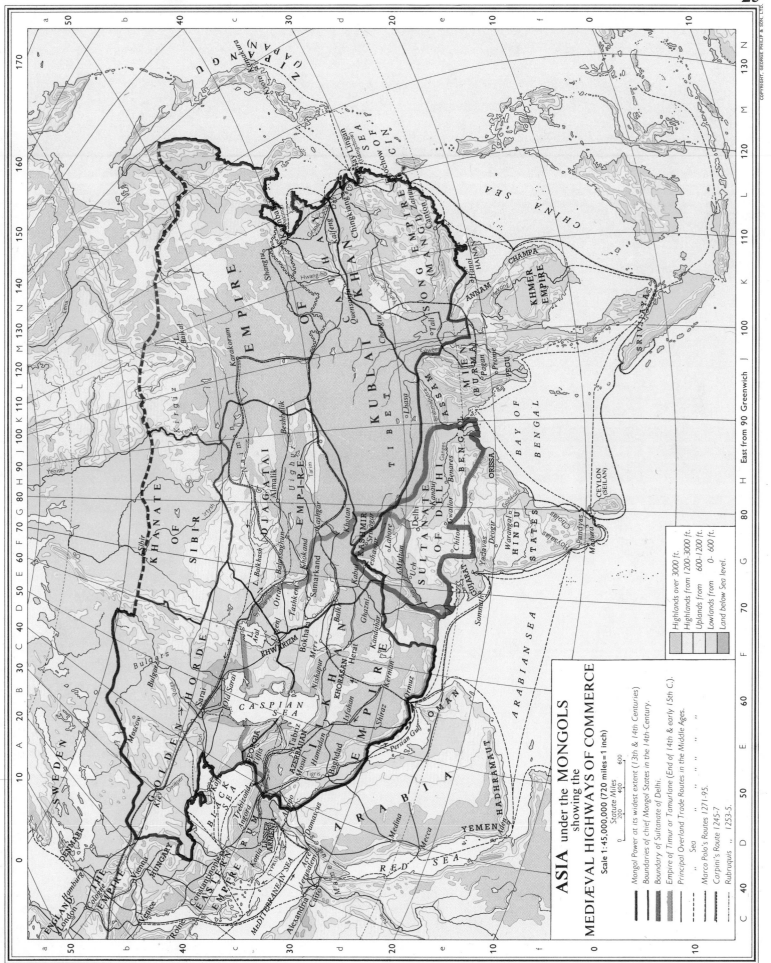

ASIA under the MONGOLS
showing the
MEDIÆVAL HIGHWAYS OF COMMERCE

Scale 1:45,000,000 (720 miles = 1 inch)

Statute Miles
0   200   400   600

Mongol Power at its widest extent (13th & 14th Centuries)
Boundaries of chief Mongol States in the 14th Century.
Boundary of Sultanate of Delhi.
Empire of Timur or Tamurlane (End of 14th & early 15th C.).
Principal Overland Trade Routes in the Middle Ages.
"   "   Sea
Marco Polo's Routes 1271-95.
Carpini's Route 1245-7
Rubruquis   "   1253-5.

Highlands over 3000 ft.
Highlands from 1200-3000 ft.
Uplands from   600-1200 ft.
Lowlands from   0- 600 ft.
Land below Sea level.

COPYRIGHT, GEORGE PHILIP & SON, LTD.

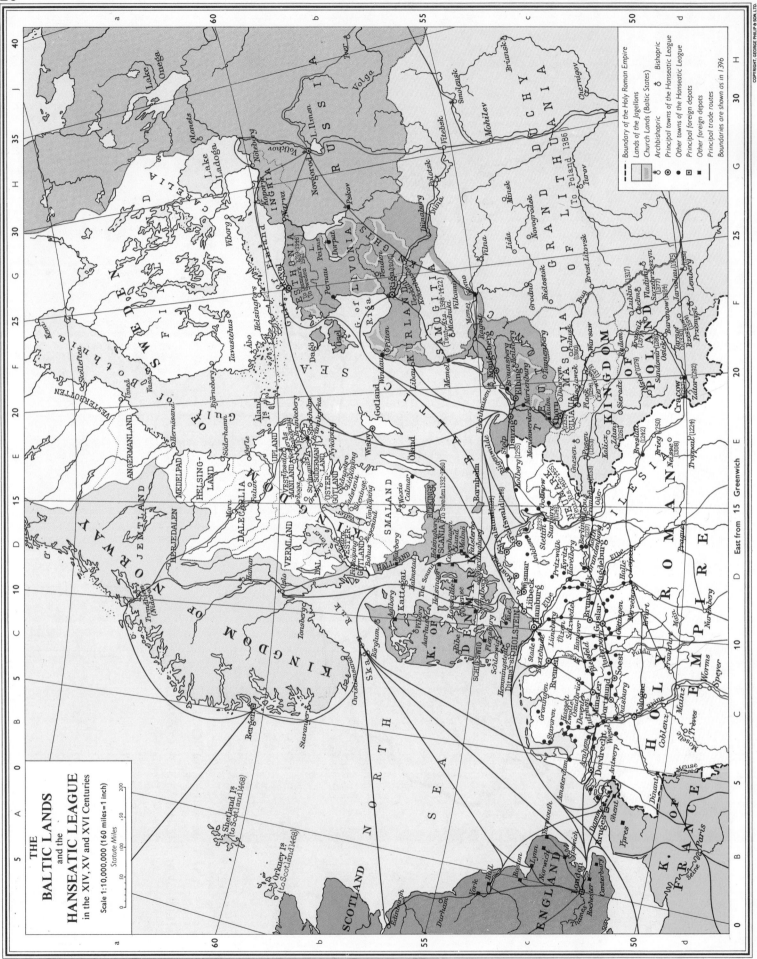

THE
BALTIC LANDS
and the
HANSEATIC LEAGUE
in the XIV, XV and XVI Centuries

Scale 1:10,000,000 (160 miles=1 inch)

Statute Miles

0   50   100   150   200

Boundary of the Holy Roman Empire
Lands of the Jagellons
Church Lands (Baltic States)
Archbishopric
Bishopric
Principal towns of the Hanseatic League
Other towns of the Hanseatic League
Principal foreign depots
Other foreign depots
Principal trade routes
Boundaries are shown as in 1396

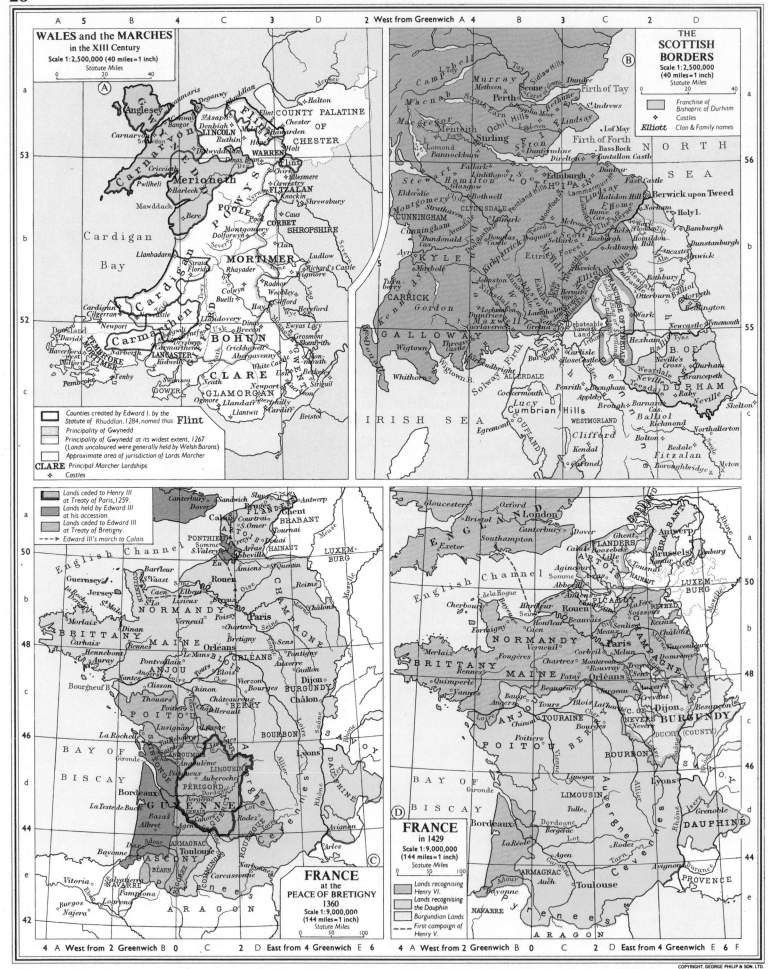

WALES and the MARCHES
in the XIII Century
Scale 1:2,500,000
(40 miles=1 inch)
Statute Miles
0   20   40

Counties created by Edward I. by the Statute of Rhuddlan, 1284, named thus **Flint**
Principality of Gwynedd
Principality of Gwynedd at its widest extent, 1267 (Lands uncoloured were generally held by Welsh Barons)
Approximate area of jurisdiction of Lords Marcher
CLARE Principal Marcher Lordships
⌖ Castles

THE SCOTTISH BORDERS
Scale 1:2,500,000
(40 miles=1 inch)
Statute Miles
0   20   40

Franchise of Bishopric of Durham
⌖ Castles
Elliott Clan & Family names

FRANCE
at the PEACE OF BRETIGNY
1360
Scale 1:9,000,000
(144 miles=1 inch)
Statute Miles
0   50   100

Lands ceded to Henry III at Treaty of Paris, 1259.
Lands held by Edward III at his accession.
Lands ceded to Edward III at Treaty of Bretigny.
- - - Edward III's march to Calais

FRANCE
in 1429
Scale 1:9,000,000
(144 miles=1 inch)
Statute Miles
0   100

Lands recognising Henry VI.
Lands recognising the Dauphin
Burgundian Lands
- - - First campaign of Henry V.

COPYRIGHT. GEORGE PHILIP & SON. LTD.

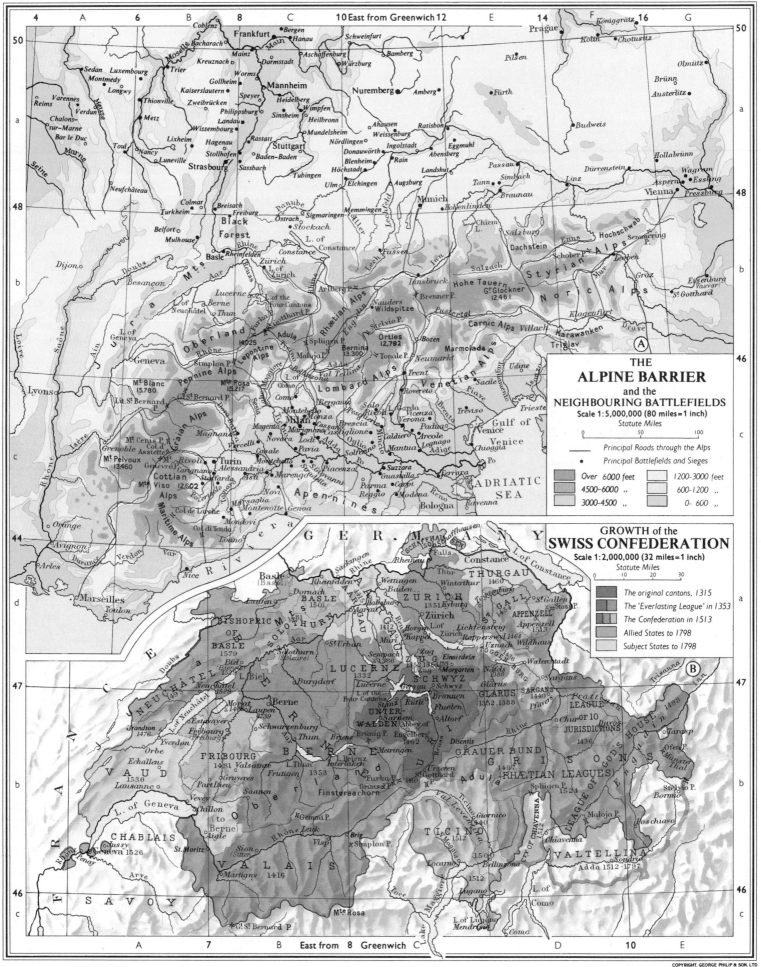

THE
ALPINE BARRIER
and the
NEIGHBOURING BATTLEFIELDS
Scale 1:5,000,000 (80 miles=1 inch)
Statute Miles
0   50   100

—— Principal Roads through the Alps
•   Principal Battlefields and Sieges

Over 6000 feet | 1200-3000 feet
4500-6000 „ | 600-1200 „
3000-4500 „ | 0- 600 „

GROWTH of the
SWISS CONFEDERATION
Scale 1:2,000,000 (32 miles=1 inch)
Statute Miles
10   20   30

The original cantons, 1315
The 'Everlasting League' in 1353
The Confederation in 1513
Allied States to 1798
Subject States to 1798

WESTERN & CENTRAL EUROPE
in the
LATER FIFTEENTH CENTURY

Scale 1:6,000,000 (96 miles 1 inch)

Statute Miles

0   50   100   150   200

Boundary of the Holy Roman Empire 1477
Boundaries of Electoral States within the Empire
Church Lands
Lands of the House of Hohenzollern
  "   "   "   "   "   Wittelsbach (Palatinate Branch)
  "   "   "   "   "   (Bavarian   "   )
  "   "   "   "   "   Wettin
  "   "   "   "   "   Habsburg
  "   "   "   "   "   Burgundy
Free Cantons of the Swiss Confederation
Allied
Imperial Free Cities

French Royal Domain 1461
Appanages
Other French Fiefs

AB   Archbishopric
B.   Bishopric
BUR. Burgraviate
C.   County
D.   Duchy
EL.   Electorate
K.   Kingdom
L.   Landgraviate
M.   Margraviate
      or Marquisate
PR.   Principality
R.   Republic
S.   Seigneurie
V.   Viscounty

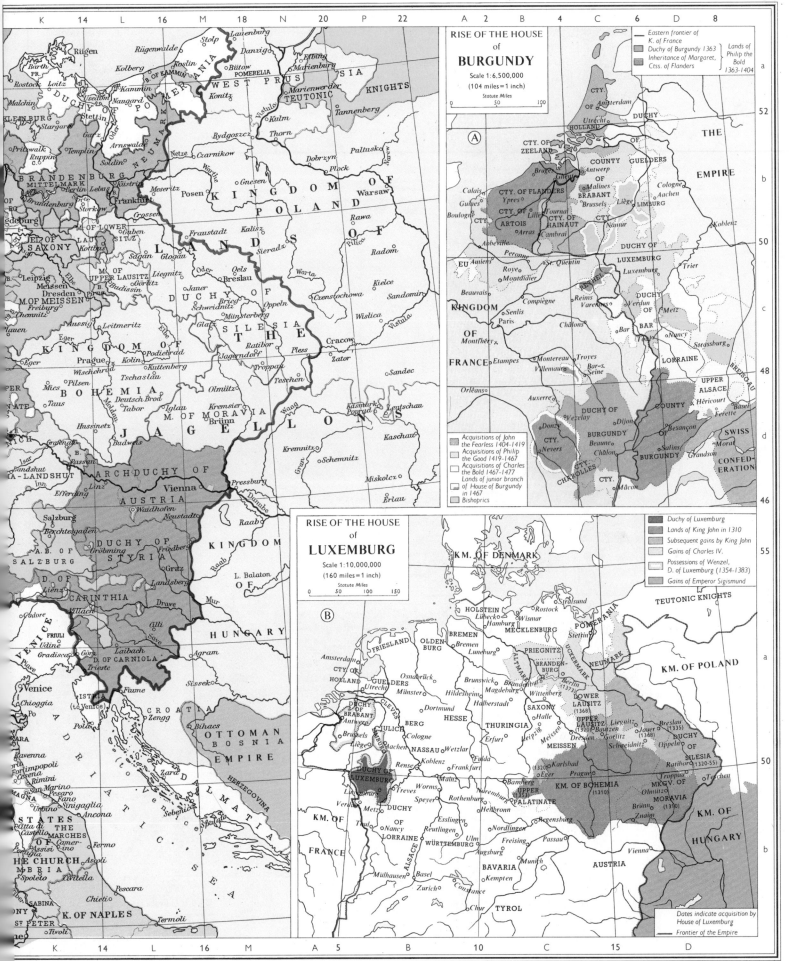

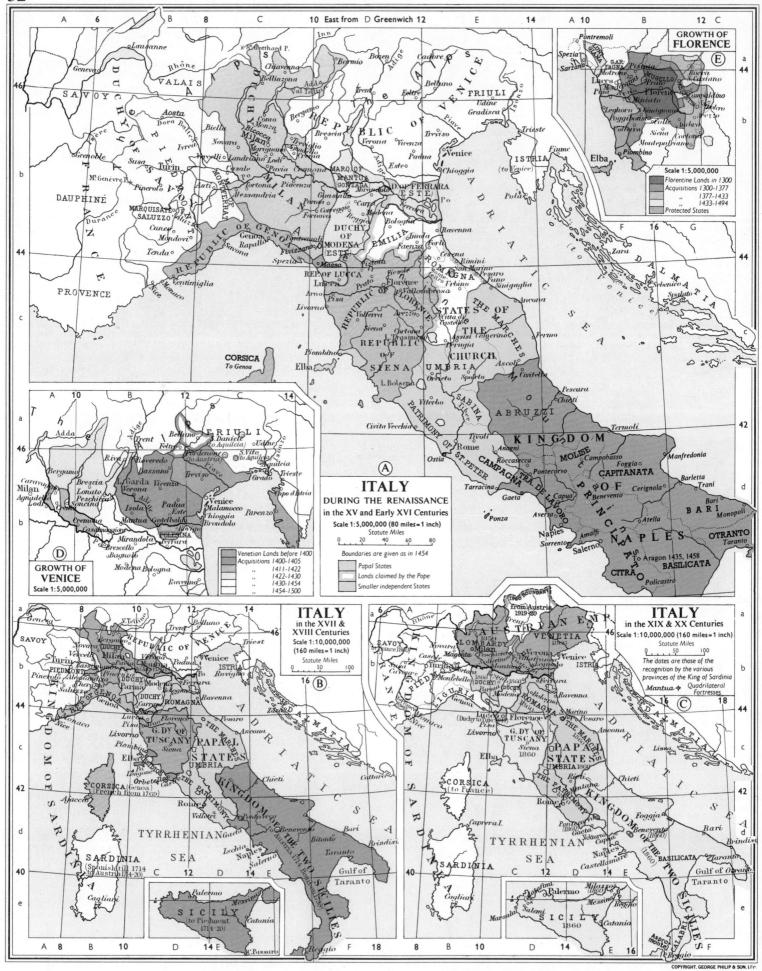

32

GROWTH OF FLORENCE

Scale 1:5,000,000

Florentine Lands in 1300
Acquisitions 1300-1377
,, 1377-1433
,, 1433-1494
Protected States

ITALY
DURING THE RENAISSANCE
in the XV and Early XVI Centuries
Scale 1:5,000,000 (80 miles=1 inch)

Statute Miles
0   20   40   60   80

Boundaries are given as in 1454

Papal States
Lands claimed by the Pope
Smaller independent States

GROWTH OF VENICE
Scale 1:5,000,000

Venetian Lands before 1400
Acquisitions 1400-1405
,, 1411-1422
,, 1422-1430
,, 1430-1454
,, 1454-1500

ITALY
in the XVII & XVIII Centuries
Scale 1:10,000,000
(160 miles=1 inch)

Statute Miles
0   50   100

ITALY
in the XIX & XX Centuries
Scale 1:10,000,000 (160 miles=1 inch)

Statute Miles
0   50   100

The dates are those of the recognition by the various provinces of the King of Sardinia
Mantua ✦ Quadrilateral Fortresses

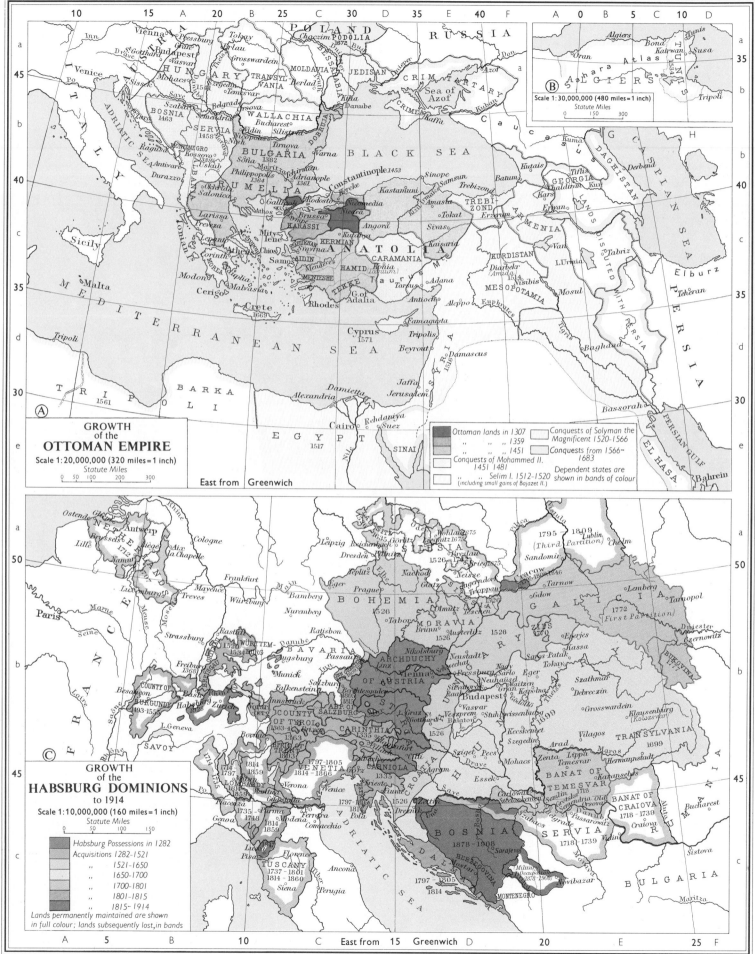

GROWTH of the OTTOMAN EMPIRE

Scale 1:20,000,000 (320 miles=1 inch)

Statute Miles
0 50 100 200 300

East from Greenwich

	Ottoman lands in 1307		Conquests of Solyman the Magnificent 1520-1566
	" " " 1359		
	" " " 1451		Conquests from 1566-1683
	Conquests of Mohammed II. 1451 1481		
	" " Selim I. 1512-1520 (including small gains of Bajazet II.)		Dependent states are shown in bands of colour

Scale 1:30,000,000 (480 miles=1 inch)

Statute Miles
0 150 300

GROWTH of the HABSBURG DOMINIONS to 1914

Scale 1:10,000,000 (160 miles=1 inch)

Statute Miles
0 50 100 150

	Habsburg Possessions in 1282
	Acquisitions 1282-1521
	" 1521-1650
	" 1650-1700
	" 1700-1801
	" 1801-1815
	" 1815-1914

Lands permanently maintained are shown in full colour; lands subsequently lost, in bands

East from 15 Greenwich

COPYRIGHT. GEORGE PHILIP & SON, LTD.

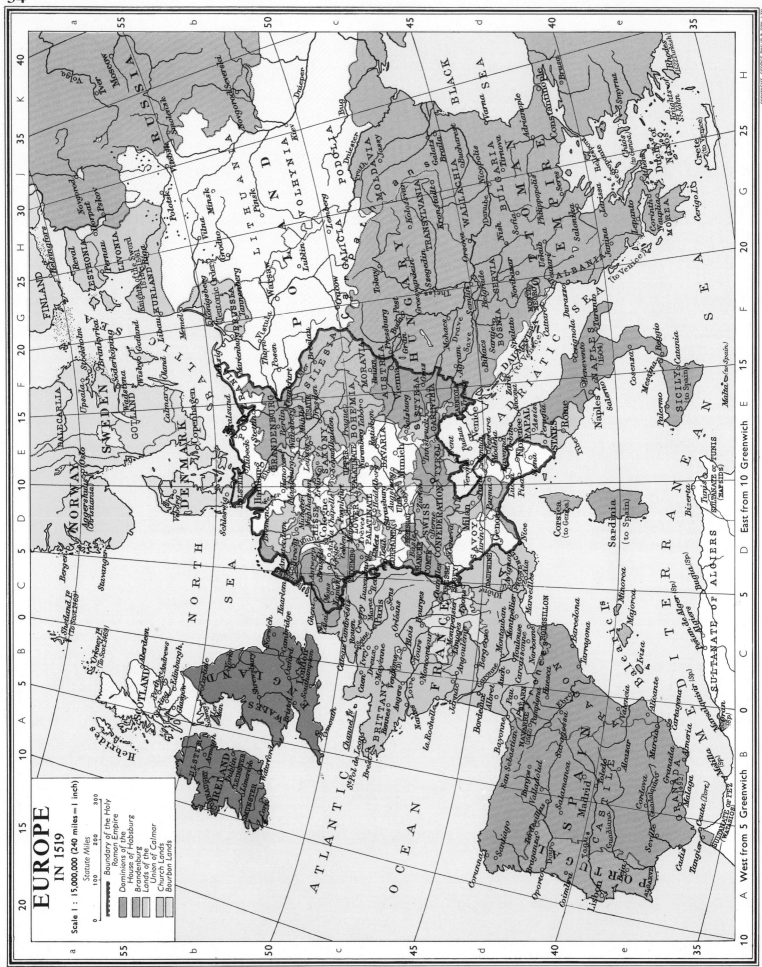

EUROPE
IN 1519

Scale 1 : 15,000,000 (240 miles = 1 inch)

Statute Miles
0   100   200   300

Boundary of the Holy
Roman Empire
Dominions of the
House of Habsburg
Brandenburg
Lands of the
Union of Calmar
Church Lands
Bourbon Lands

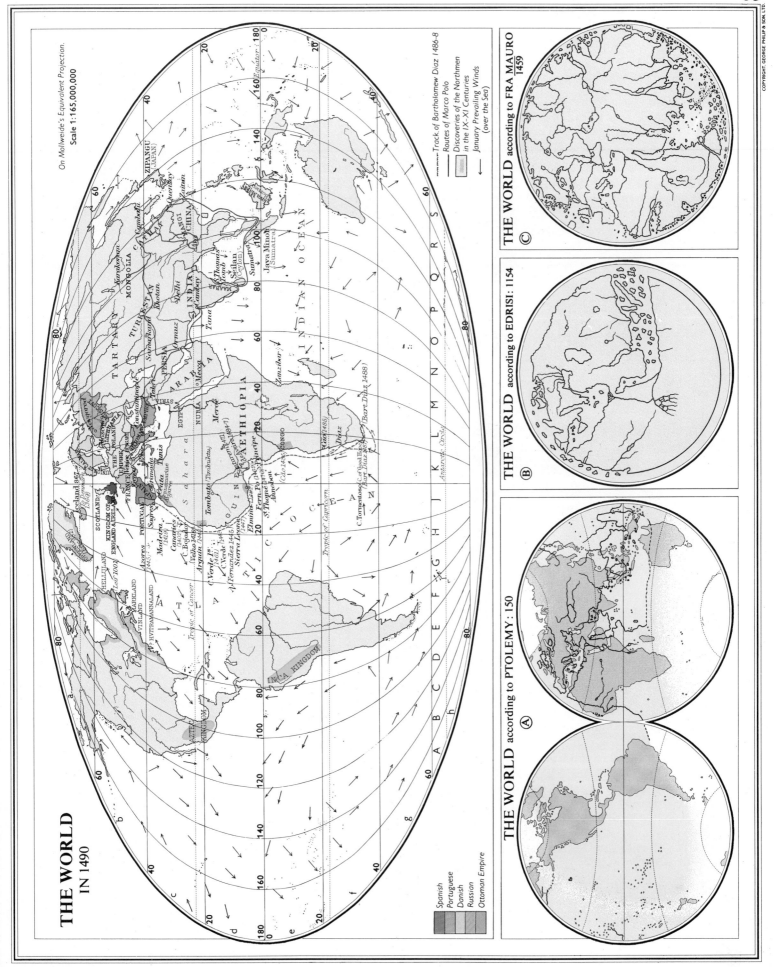

THE WORLD IN 1490

On Mollweide's Equivalent Projection.
Scale 1:165,000,000

_____ Track of Bartholomew Diaz 1486-8
_____ Routes of Marco Polo
☐ Discoveries of the Northmen in the IX–XI Centuries
→ January Prevailing Winds (over the Sea)

Spanish
Portuguese
Danish
Russian
Ottoman Empire

④ THE WORLD according to PTOLEMY: 150

⑧ THE WORLD according to EDRISI: 1154

© THE WORLD according to FRA MAURO 1459

ENGLISH DIOCESES
in the Anglo-Saxon Period
c.800
Scale 1:9,000,000 (150 miles = 1 inch)
Statute Miles
0   30   60

The boundaries of Old Bishoprics in 1291 are
shown in colours and named thus . . . . **DURHAM**
The boundaries of New Bishoprics (created by
Henry VIII) are shown by broad red lines
and named thus . . . . **Chester**
Dates of foundations of Dioceses thus **625**
Boundary between Provinces of Canterbury
and York . . . .
Archi-Episcopal Sees . . . . **York**
Episcopal Sees . . . . **Ely**
Parliamentary Abbeys represented in the
House of Lords . . . .
Greater Monasteries, dissolved 1538-40 . . . . .
Other Monasteries . . . .
In many towns there were several Monastic Houses.
The figure placed after the name represents the
number.

**ECCLESIASTICAL
ENGLAND
to the time of
HENRY VIII**

Scale 1:3,000,000 (48 miles = 1 inch)
Statute Miles
0   10   20   30   40   50

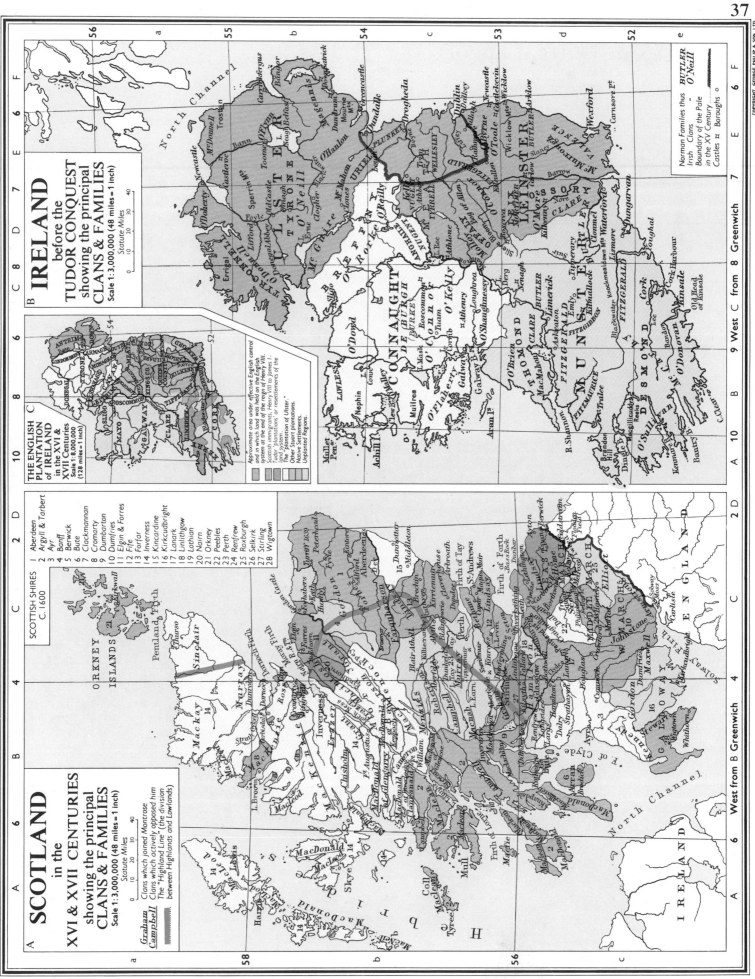

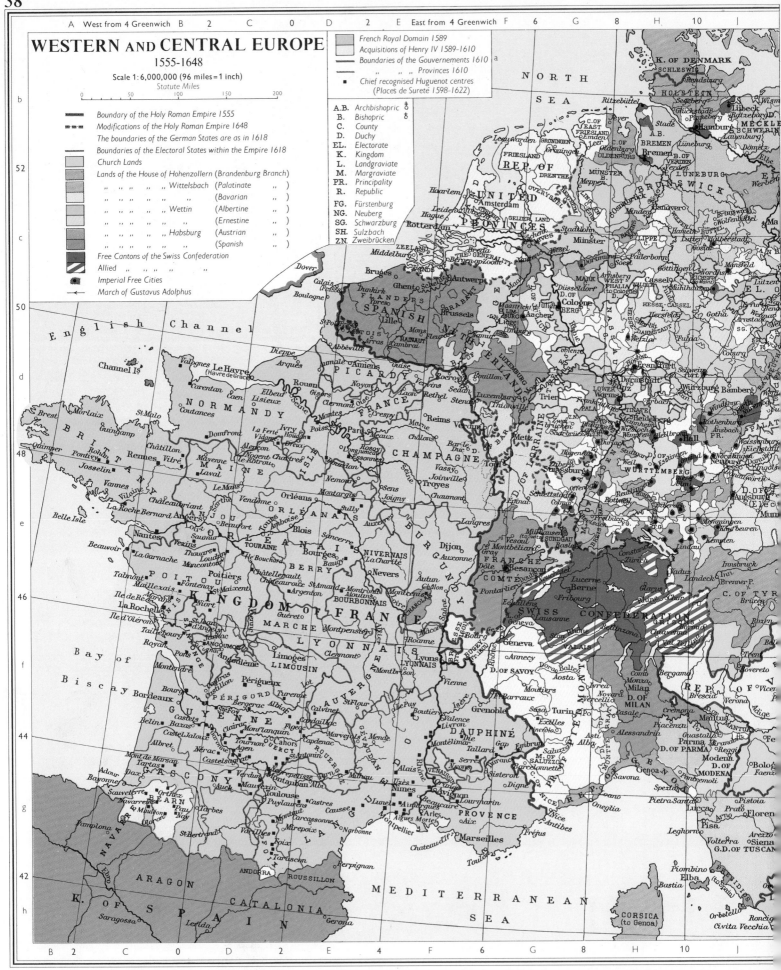

WESTERN AND CENTRAL EUROPE
1555-1648

Scale 1:6,000,000 (96 miles=1 inch)

Statute Miles

French Royal Domain 1589
Acquisitions of Henry IV 1589-1610
Boundaries of the Gouvernements 1610
" " " Provinces 1610
Chief recognised Huguenot centres
(Places de Sureté 1598-1622)

Boundary of the Holy Roman Empire 1555
Modifications of the Holy Roman Empire 1648
The boundaries of the German States are as in 1618
Boundaries of the Electoral States within the Empire 1618
Church Lands
Lands of the House of Hohenzollern (Brandenburg Branch)
" " " " " Wittelsbach (Palatinate ")
" " " " " (Bavarian ")
" " " " " Wettin (Albertine ")
" " " " " (Ernestine ")
" " " " " Habsburg (Austrian ")
" " " " " (Spanish ")
Free Cantons of the Swiss Confederation
Allied " " "
Imperial Free Cities
March of Gustavus Adolphus

A.B. Archbishopric
B.   Bishopric
C.   County
D.   Duchy
EL.   Electorate
K.   Kingdom
L.   Landgraviate
M.   Margraviate
PR.   Principality
R.   Republic
FG.   Fürstenburg
NG.   Neuberg
SG.   Schwarzburg
SH.   Sulzbach
ZN.   Zweibrücken

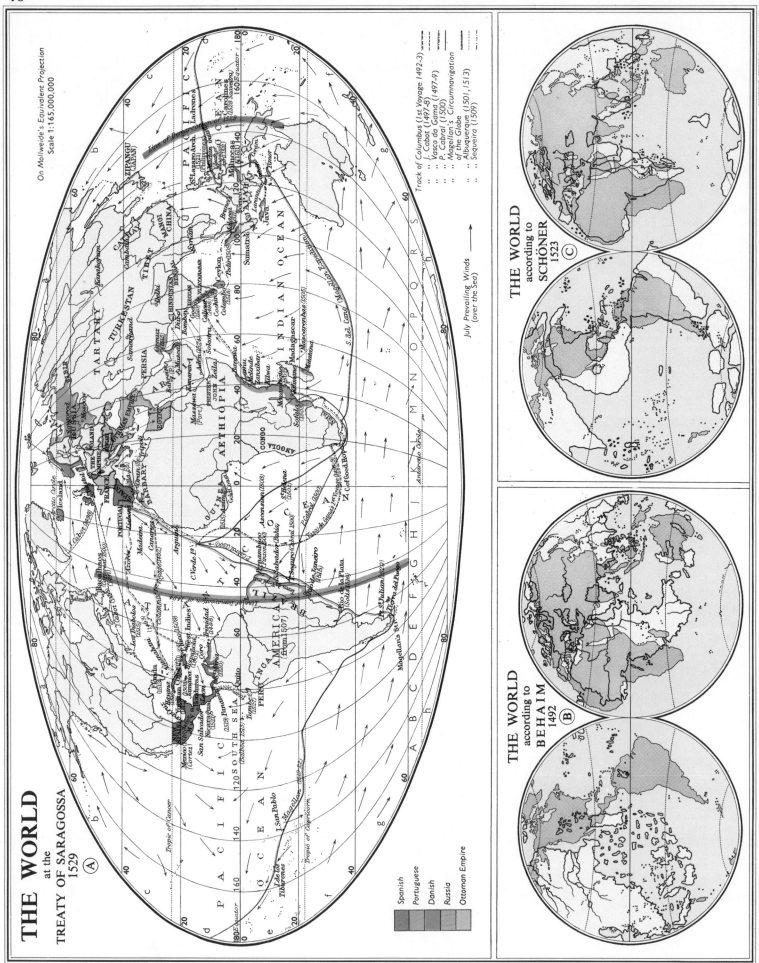

THE WORLD
at the
TREATY OF SARAGOSSA
1529 Ⓐ

On Mollweide's Equivalent Projection
Scale 1:165,000,000

Track of Columbus (1st Voyage 1492-3)
" " J. Cabot (1497-8)
" " Vasco da Gama (1497-9)
" " P. Cabral (1500)
" " Magellan's Circumnavigation
of the Globe
" " Albuquerque (1501, 1513)
" " Sequeira (1509)

July Prevailing Winds
(over the Sea)

Spanish
Portuguese
Danish
Russia
Ottoman Empire

THE WORLD
according to
SCHÖNER 1523 Ⓒ

THE WORLD
according to
BEHAIM 1492 Ⓑ

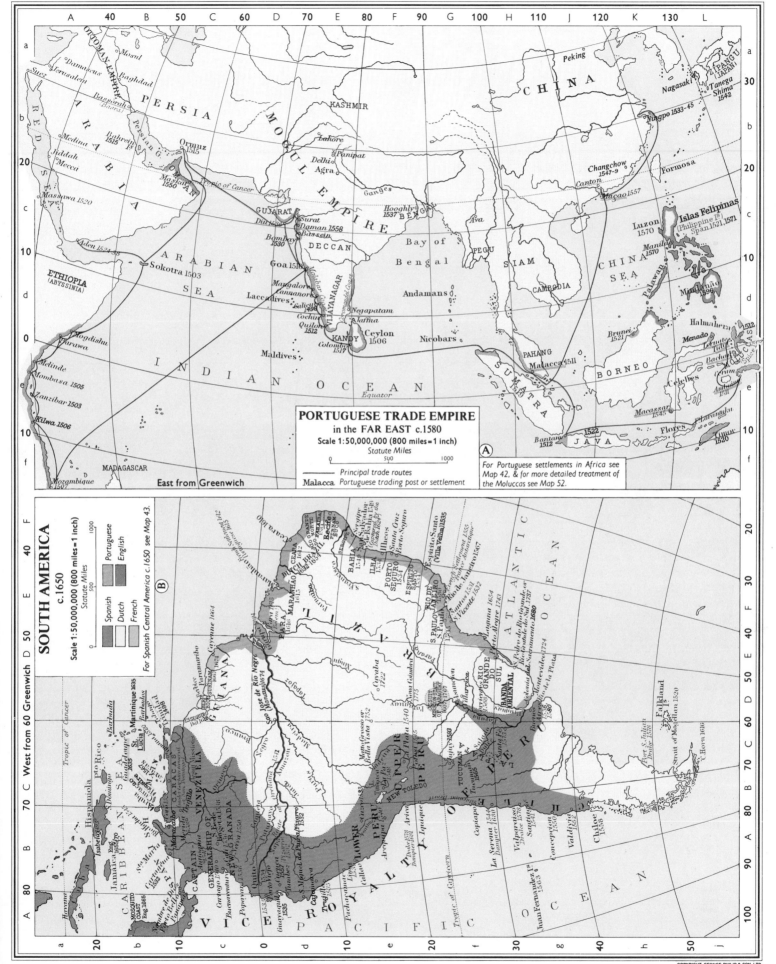

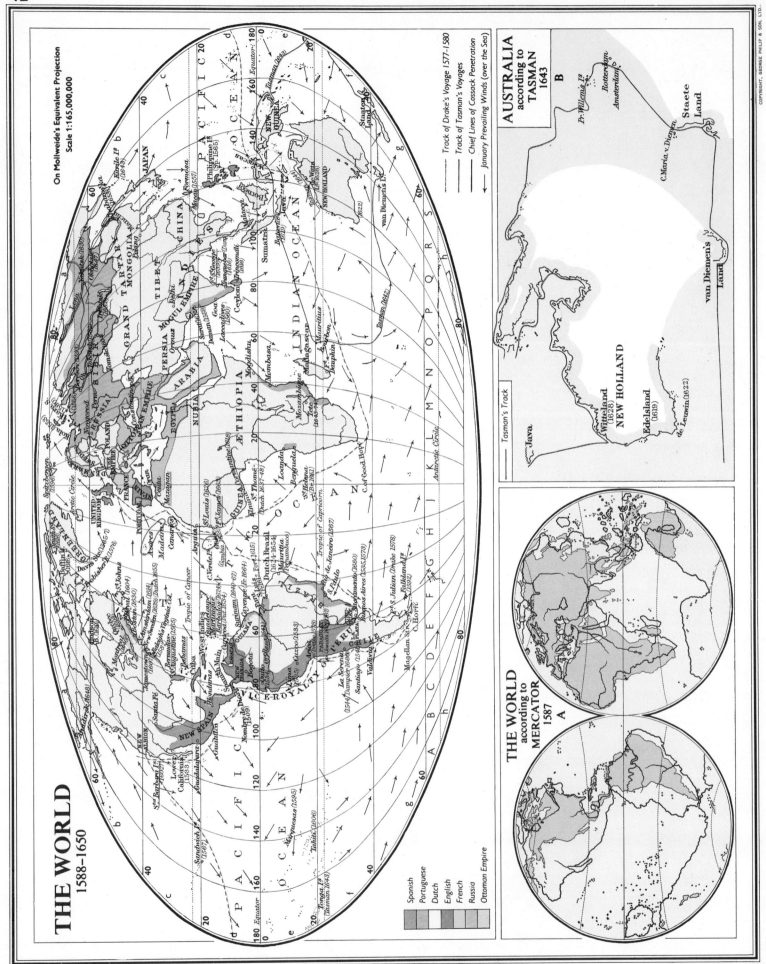

THE WORLD
1588-1650

On Mollweide's Equivalent Projection
Scale 1:165,000,000

	Track of Drake's Voyage 1577-1580
	Track of Tasman's Voyages
	Chief Lines of Cossack Penetration
	January Prevailing Winds (over the Sea)

Spanish
Portuguese
Dutch
English
French
Russia
Ottoman Empire

AUSTRALIA
according to TASMAN
1643

Tasman's Track

Java

Witteland (1628)
NEW HOLLAND
Edelsland (1619)
de Leuwin (1622)

Pr. Willems I.ᵈ
Rotterdam
Amsterdam
C. Maria v. Diemen

Staaten
Land

van Diemen's
Land

THE WORLD
according to MERCATOR
1587

A

B

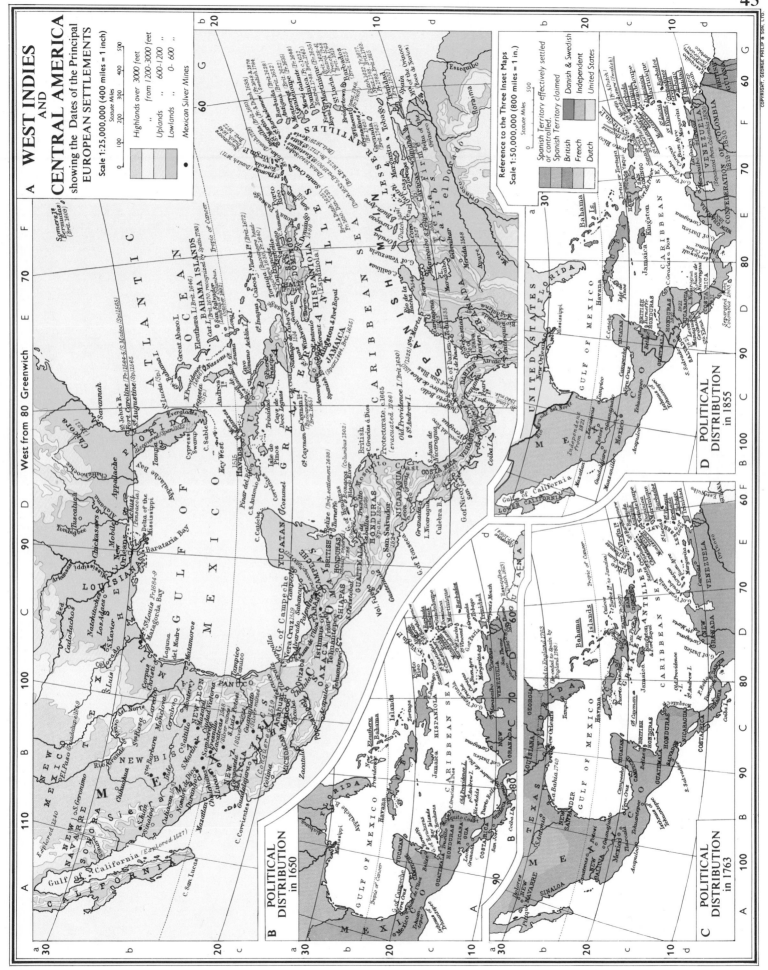

EXPLORATION OF NORTH AMERICA

Scale 1:35,000,000 (560 miles = 1 inch)

Statute Miles

0   200   400   600

EXPLORERS

Spanish
———— Ponce de Leon 1513
– – – – de Vaca 1528-36
–·–·– de Soto 1539-42
–×–×– Coronado 1540-42
············ Oñate 1598-1601, 1604

British
———— Hudson 1610-11
– – – – Baffin 1616
–·–·– Foxe 1631
–··–··– Hearne 1770-71
–·–·– Cook 1778
············ Mackenzie 1789-93
–·–·– Vancouver 1792-94
×××××× Ross 1829-32
·········· Franklin 1845

French
———— Cartier 1534
– – – – Cartier 1535
–·–·– Champlain 1603-15
–×–×– Jolliet & Marquette 1673
············ La Salle 1679-81
–·–·– La Vérendrye 1731-43

American
———— Lewis & Clark 1804-06
– – – – Pike 1806-07
–··–··– Smith 1826-29
–×–×– Frémont 1843-45

Others
———— Sverdrup 1898-1902
–·–·– Stefansson 1913-18

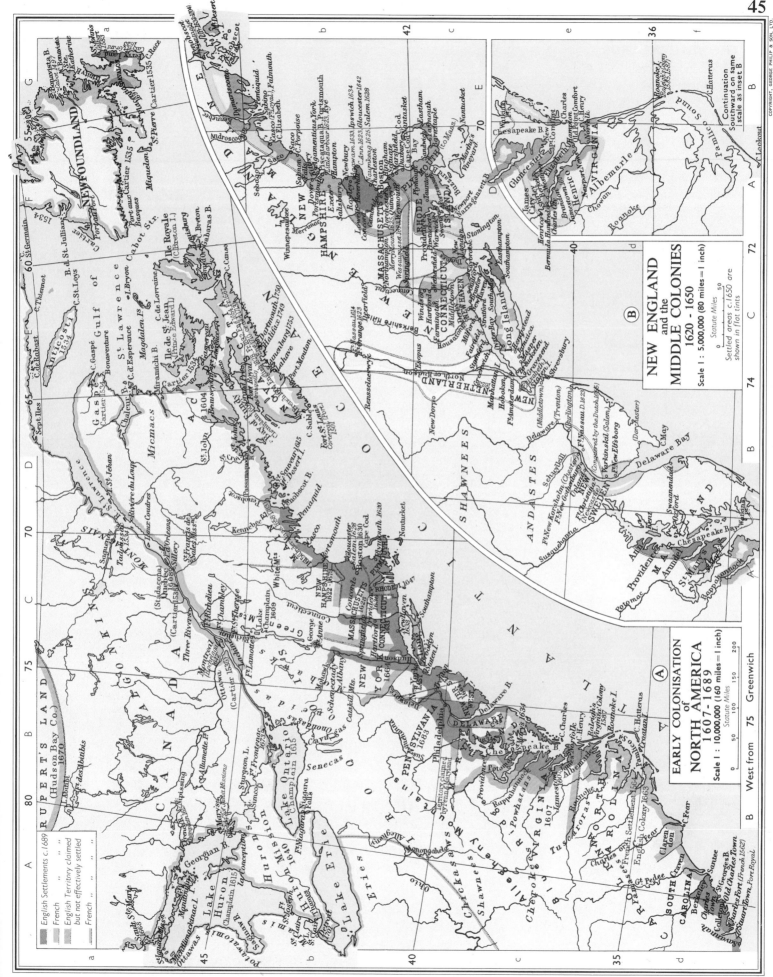

45

NEW ENGLAND
and the
MIDDLE COLONIES
1620 - 1650

Scale 1 : 5,000,000 (80 miles = 1 inch)

Statute Miles

Settled areas c.1650 are
shown in flat tints

EARLY COLONISATION
of
NORTH AMERICA
1607-1689

Scale 1 : 10,000,000 (160 miles = 1 inch)

Statute Miles

West from 75 Greenwich

English Settlements c.1689
French " " "
English Territory claimed
but not effectively settled
French " " "

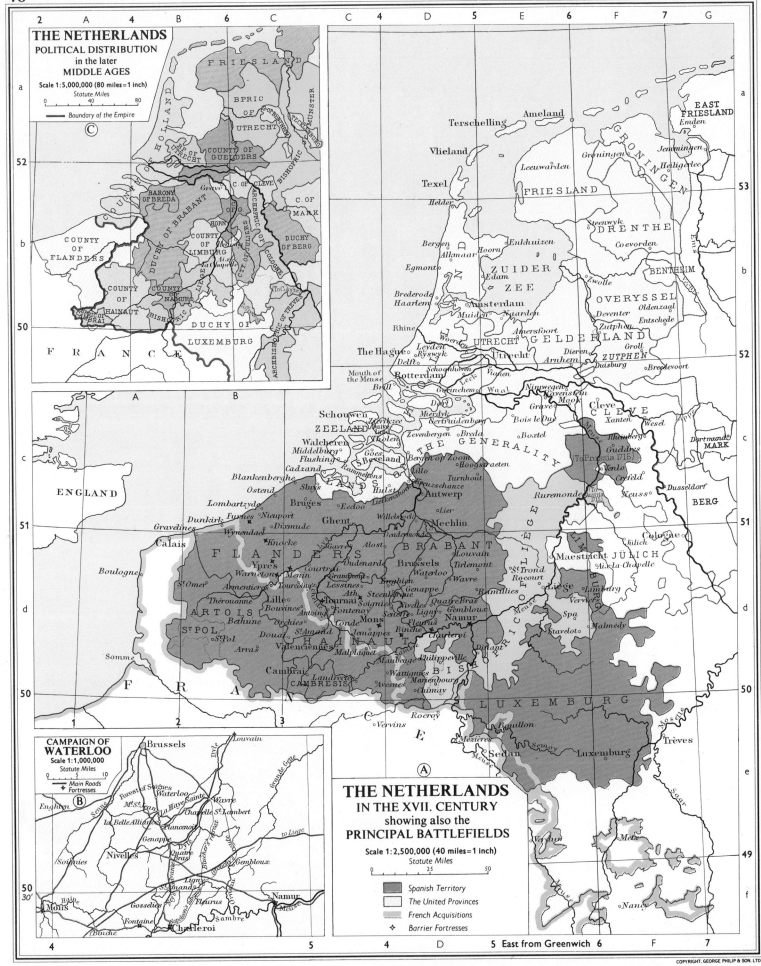

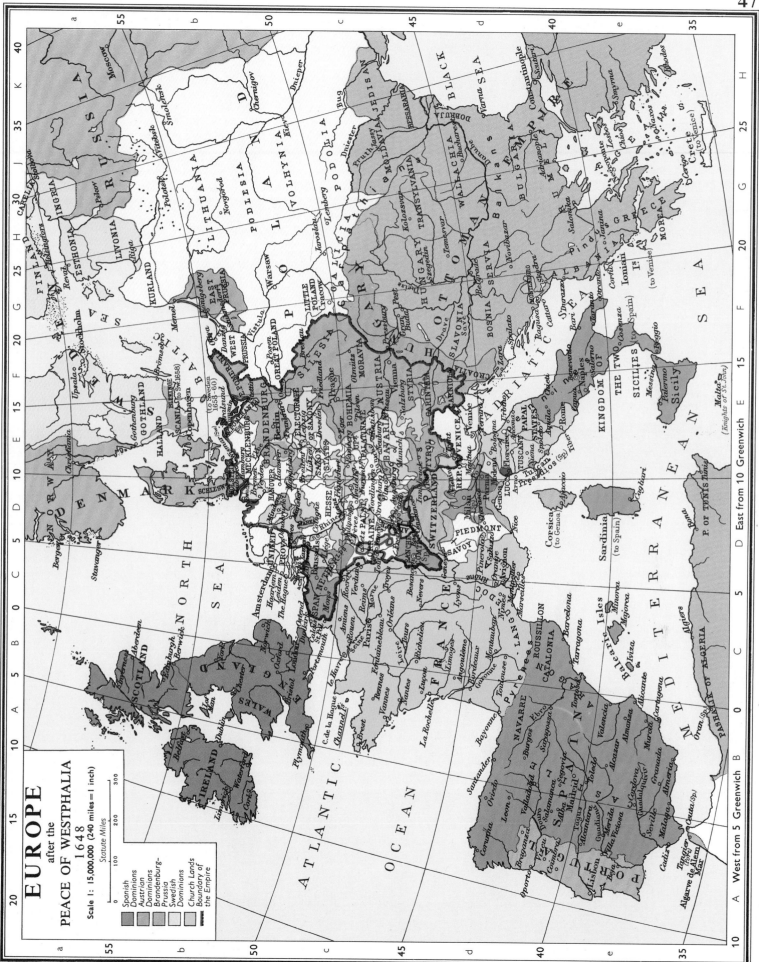

47

EUROPE
after the
PEACE OF WESTPHALIA
1648

Scale 1: 15,000,000 (240 miles=1 inch)

Statute Miles

0   100   200   300

Spanish Dominions
Austrian Dominions
Brandenburg-Prussia
Swedish Dominions
Church Lands
Boundary of the Empire

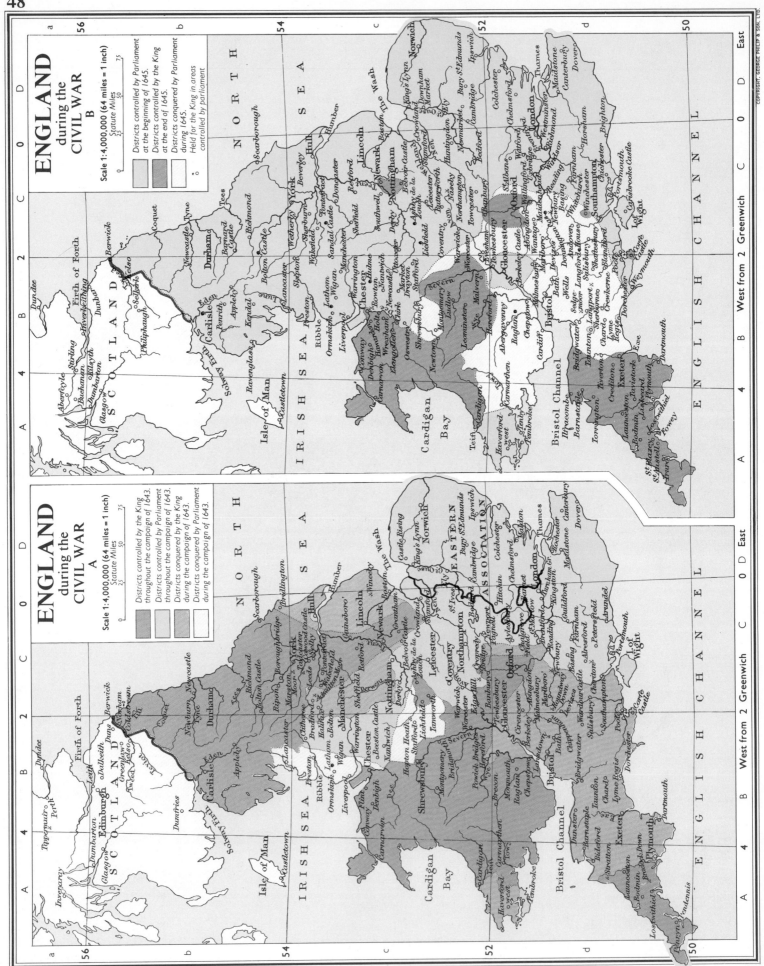

ENGLAND during the CIVIL WAR B

Scale 1:4,000,000 (64 miles = 1 inch)
Statute Miles

Districts controlled by Parliament at the beginning of 1645.
Districts controlled by the King at the end of 1645.
Districts conquered by Parliament during 1645.
Held for the King in areas controlled by parliament

ENGLAND during the CIVIL WAR A

Scale 1:4,000,000 (64 miles = 1 inch)
Statute Miles

Districts controlled by the King throughout the campaign of 1643.
Districts controlled by Parliament throughout the campaign of 1643.
Districts conquered by the King during the campaign of 1643.
Districts conquered by Parliament during the campaign of 1643.

COPYRIGHT. GEORGE PHILIP & SON, LTD.

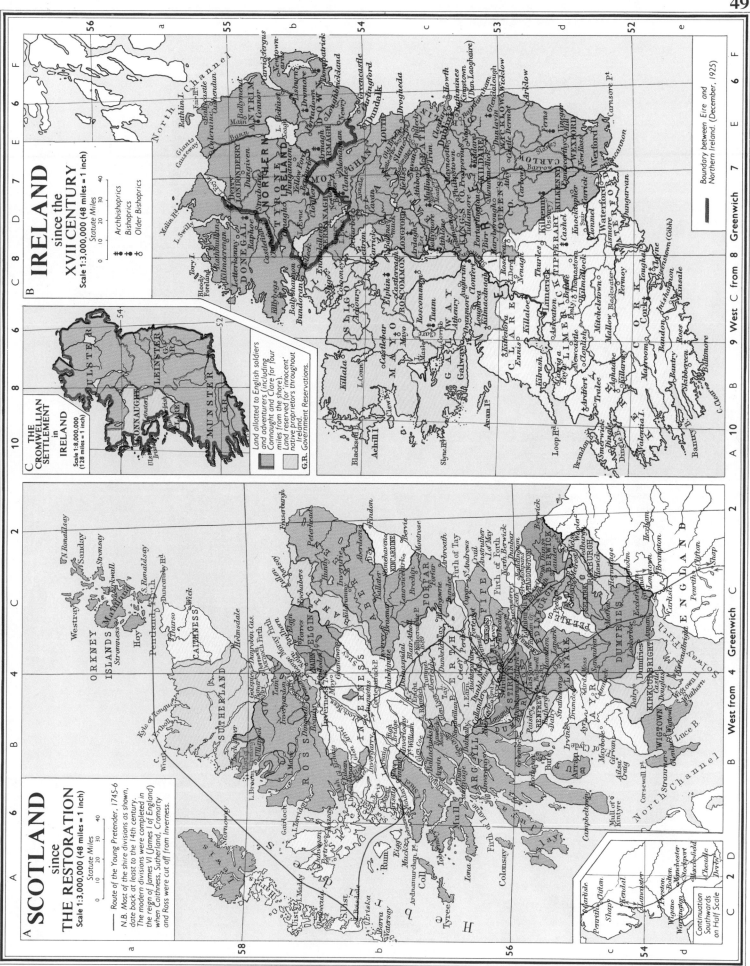

B IRELAND
since the
XVII CENTURY
Scale 1:3,000,000 (48 miles = 1 inch)

Statute Miles
0 10 20 30 40

✠ Archbishoprics
✚● Bishoprics
✝ Older Bishoprics

Boundary between Eire and
Northern Ireland. (December, 1925)

West C from 8 Greenwich

C THE
CROMWELLIAN SETTLEMENT
in
IRELAND

Scale 1:8,000,000
(128 miles = 1 inch)

Land allotted to English soldiers
and adventurers (including
Connaught and Clare for four
miles from the shore).

Lands reserved for innocent
native proprietors throughout
Ireland.

G.R. Government Reservations.

A SCOTLAND
since
THE RESTORATION
Scale 1:3,000,000 (48 miles = 1 inch)

Statute Miles
0 10 20 30 40

Route of the Young Pretender, 1745–6

N.B. Most of the shire divisions as shown,
date back at least to the 14th century.
The modern divisions were completed in
the reign of James VI (James I of England)
when Caithness, Sutherland, Cromarty
and Ross were cut off from Inverness.

West from 4 Greenwich

Continuation
Southwards
on Half Scale

20 East from Greenwich 25

	Austrian Dominions
	Spanish Dominions
	Hohenzollern Dominions (Brandenburg-Prussia)
	Swedish Dominions
	Church Lands
---	Boundary of the Empire

NORTH SEA

NORWAY
Trondhjem
TRONDHIEM (Sw. 1658-60)
Bergen
Christiania
Frederikssten

EMTLAND 1645
HARJEDALEN 1645
MEDEL PAD
HALSING-LAND
DALECARLIA
Skog
Gavle

SWEDEN
VARMLAND
VESTMAN LAND
UPPLAND
Upsala
Stockholm
SODERMANLAND
DAL
L. Wetter
NARKE
Linköping
Söderköping
OSTER GOTLAND
VESTERGOTLAND
Gothenburg
Elfsborg
HALLAND
SMALAND
Calmar
Öland
L. Wetter
Visby Gotland 1645

FINLAND
Storkyro
Gulf of Bothnia
Åland Is.
Abo
Helsingfors
Gulf of Finland
Reval

CARELIA 1617
Kexholm
L. Ladoga
Viborg
Nöteborg
Stolbova

INGRIA 1617
Narva
ESTHONIA 1561,2
Dagö 1582
Kurdis
Pernau
Dorpat
LIVONIA (From Poland 1629)
Wolmar
L. Peipus
Pskov

Novgorod
L. Ilmen

RUSSIA
Tver
Moscow

Skager Rak
Kattegat

DENMARK
Copenhagen
Roskilde
SCANIA 1658
BLEKINGE
Bromsebro
Knäred
Bornholm

BALTIC SEA
Rügen
Stralsund
Greifswald
Wolgast
Memel (Sw. 1629-35)
Pillau
Labiau
Königsberg
EAST PRUSSIA
Elbing
Danzig
Marienburg

G. of Riga
Windau
Riga
Libau
KURLAND
Mitau
Wallhof (1626)
Dvina
Polotsk
Vitebsk
Mohilev
Berestia
Ceded by Poland 1667
Smolensk
Andrusov
Kaluga

SCHLESWIG
HOLSTEIN
Lübeck
Wismar
MECKLENBURG
Stettin
POMERANIA
WEST PRUSSIA
Thorn
Posen
GREAT POLAND
Warsaw
Fraustadt
Kalisz
Pultusk
Bug
Brest Litovsk
Pinsk
Pripet
PODLESIA
BLACK RUSSIA
Grodno
Niemen
Minsk
Dnieper
LITHUANIA
Vilna
Kovno
Memel

UNITED PROVINCES
Amsterdam
Ryswick
Münster
Oldenburg
Bremen
Verden
Hanover
BRUNSWICK
Celle
Magdeburg
BRANDENBURG
Berlin
Damm
Warthe
Oder

SPANISH NETHERLANDS
Antwerp
Brussels
Maastricht
Dunkirk
Cologne
Aix la Chapelle
MARK
CLEVE
Liege

FRANCE
Reims
Verdun
Metz
Thionville
Strasbourg
Basle

SAXONY
Halle
Leipzig
Dresden
SILESIA
Breslau
Oppeln
Glatz
BOHEMIA
Prague
Marienburg
Ratisbon
MORAVIA
Olmutz
Brünn
Nordlingen
Frankfort
Würzburg
Ulm
BAVARIA
Augsburg
Munich
AUSTRIA
Vienna
Pressburg
Neuhausel
Salzburg
Innsbruck
TYROL
Trent
STYRIA
CARINTHIA
CARNIOLA
Trieste

SWISS CONFEDERATION
Zürich
Berne
Geneva
St. Gotthard

SAVOY
Turin
Staffarda
DAUPHINE
Milan
Casale
Mantua
PIEDMONT
REP. OF VENICE
Venice
Parma
Modena
REP. OF GENOA
Genoa
Lucca
TUSCANY
Florence
Lyons
Rhone
PROVENCE
Avignon
Marseilles
Toulon

GREAT POLAND
POLAND
Radom
Sandomir
Tissow
LITTLE POLAND
Lublin
Zamosc
Cracow
VOLHYNIA
Jitomir
Brody
Lemberg
RED RUSSIA
GALICIA
Zurawno
Buczacz
PODOLIA
Kaminiec
Choczim
Bug
UKRAINE
Kiev
Chigirin
Poltava
COSSACKS
Dnieper
JEDISAN
Kherson
Odessa
KHANATE
Bender
BESSARABIA

Poland 1667
Novgorod Severski
Chernigov
Baturin
Hadjach

Carpathian Mts.
BUKOVINA
Hungarian Ore Mts.
ZIPS
Kaschau
Munkacz
IMPERIAL HUNGARY
Gran Buda T 1664
Pest
TURKISH HUNGARY
BANAT OF TEMESVAR
Szatmar
Grosswardein
Klausenburg
Schässburg
TRANSYLVANIA
Temesvar
Carlowitz
Slankamen
MOLDAVIA (Turk. trib. from 1456)
Jassy
Pruth
Sereth

WALLACHIA
Transylvanian Alps (Turk. trib. 1391)
Bucharest
Silistria
DOBRUJA
Ruschuk
Sistova
Danube
BLACK SEA
Varna

ADRIATIC SEA
CROATIA
SLAVONIA
Save
Essek
Mohacs
Zenta
Peterwardein
Belgrade
Passarowitz
BOSNIA
Sarajevo T 1463
T 1483
SERVIA
Nish
Kossovopolye
MONTE-NEGRO
Ragusa
Cattaro
ALBANIA
Turk. 1416
Turk. 1479 T 1393
Preveza
Maura

Tirnovo
Sofia
BULGARIA
Uskub Turk. 1398
Philippopolis
Salonica Turk. 1479
Adrianople
Marliza
Constantinople (T 1453)
Bosporus
RUMELIA (Turk. 1371)
TURKISH EMPIRE
S. of Marmara
Angora
Konia
Taurus

IONIAN SEA
Negroponte
Chios
Smyrna
AEGEAN SEA
Athens
Morea
Nauplia
Tenedos
Dardanelles
Lemnos

CORSICA (To Genoa)
SARDINIA
Rome
PAPAL STATES
Ancona
S. MARINO
Chieti
Pontecorvo
Naples
Benevento
KINGDOM OF THE TWO SICILIES
Brindisi
Otranto
TYRRHENIAN SEA
SICILY
Messina
Reggio
Catania

CENTRAL & EASTERN EUROPE in 1667

Scale 1:12,000,000 (192 miles = 1 inch)

Statute Miles

0 50 100 200 300

CRETE
(To Venice 1212
Turk. 1669)
On same scale
Canea Candia

To Venice 1699-1718
Turk. 1460

Rhodes
Cerigo

20 East from Greenwich 25

Legend
- Austrian Dominions
- Kingdom of Prussia
- Swedish Dominions
- Church Lands
- Boundary of the Empire

NORWAY — Trondhjem — Bergen — Christiania — Fredrikshald — Upsala

SWEDEN — DALECARLIA — Gavle — Stockholm — Norrköping — L. Wener — L. Wetter — Linköping — Gothenburg — Karlskrona — Christianstad — Öland — Gotland

FINLAND — Gulf of Bothnia — Gulf of Finland — Wilmanstrand — Värälä — Anjala — Helsingfors — Åbo — Aland Is. — Sveaborg — Viborg 1721 — Kronstadt

DENMARK — Skager Rak — Kattegat — Aalborg — Aarhus — Zeeland — Copenhagen — Fünen — Bornholm — SCHLESWIG — Heligoland (To Denmark) — HOLSTEIN — Gottorp — Lübeck — Altona — Hamburg

NORTH SEA — BALTIC SEA

L. Ladoga — St. Petersburg — INGRIA — Narva 1721 — Reval — ESTHONIA 1721 — Dagö — Osel — L. Peipus — Dorpat 1721 — LIVONIA 1721 — Pskov — G. of Riga — Riga — KURLAND — Mitau — Libau — Memel — Novgorod — L. Ilmen — Tver — Volga — Moscow

WHITE RUSSIA — Polotsk — Vitebsk — Smolensk — Mscislaw 1772 — Mohilev 1772 — Minsk — Beresina — Dnieper — Kaluga

FRENCH REPUBLIC — Marseilles — Toulon — Lyons — Nice — Geneva — Berne — Basle — Strassburg — Vosges — ALSACE — Treves — Coblenz — Cologne — Aix-la-Chapelle — Liège — Brussels — Ghent — Antwerp — Malines — Düsseldorf — Crefeld — Münster — Amsterdam — BATAVIAN REPUBLIC

PRUSSIA — Berlin — Brandenburg — Magdeburg — Stettin — Mecklenburg — POMERANIA — SWEDISH POMERANIA — Stralsund — Wismar — Danzig 1793 — EAST PRUSSIA — Königsberg — Gross Jägersdorf — Elbing — Marienburg — Memel — WEST PRUSSIA 1772 — Kulm — Thorn — NETZE — Gnesen — Posen — Dobrzyn — MAZOVIA — Warsaw — Praga — HANOVER — Verden — Bremen — Oldenburg — Frankfurt — Cassel — SAXONY — Leipzig — Dresden — Cottbus — SILESIA — Breslau — Neisse 1742

SOUTH PRUSSIA — Kalisz 1793 — Radom — Sandomir — Szczekociny — Raslawice 1794 — Cracow

BOHEMIA — Prague — Eger — Nuremberg — Ratisbon — BAVARIA — Augsburg — Munich — Salzburg — MORAVIA — Olmutz — Brünn — Teschen — Neustadt

SWISS CONFEDERATION — Gotthard

TYROL — CARINTHIA — STYRIA — CARNIOLA — Klagenfurt — Graz — Vienna — Pressburg — Buda — Pest

PIEDMONT — KINGDOM OF SARDINIA — Turin — Milan — Savoy — Genoa — REP. OF GENOA — Parma — Modena — Mantua — REP. OF VENICE — Padua — Venice — Florence — TUSCANY — PAPAL STATES — Rome — Naples — KINGDOM OF THE TWO SICILIES — SICILY — Palermo — Messina — SARDINIA — CORSICA

HUNGARY — Tokaj — Theiss — TRANSYLVANIA — Transylvanian Alps — BANAT OF TEMESVAR 1718 — Temesvar — Mehadia — GALICIA 1772 — Carpathians — Lemberg — ZIPS — Munkacz — BUKOVINA 1775 — PODOLIA — Bar — Dniester

UKRAINE — Kiev — Poltava — LITTLE RUSSIA — Chernigov — Nemirov — Targowica — Yekaterinoslav — Kherson 1783 — Odessa — JEDISAN 1792 — Ochakov — Kinburn — BESSARABIA — MOLDAVIA — Jassy — Balta — Bug — Bender — Akerman

VOLHYNIA — Dubienka — Lublin — Czartorysk — Pripet

PODLESIA — Brest Litovsk — Radzyn — Maciewice — BLACK RUSSIA 1795 — Bialystok — Grodno — Niemen — Vilna — Kovno

CROATIA — SLAVONIA — DALMATIA — BOSNIA — Belgrade — Passarowitz — SERVIA — Nish — HERZEGOVINA — MONTENEGRO — Scutari — ALBANIA — BULGARIA — Sofia — Philippopolis — Adrianople — Varna — Silistria — DOBRUJA — WALLACHIA — Bucharest — Giurgevo — Braila — Ismail — Kilia — Danube — Ruschuk — Sistova

OTTOMAN EMPIRE — Constantinople — Bosporus — S. of Marmara — Dardanelles — Salonica — Monastir — ÆGEAN SEA — GREECE — Athens — MOREA — Smyrna — Angora — Konia — Taurus

ADRIATIC SEA — TYRRHENIAN SEA — IONIAN Is. — Corfu — Cerigo — Rhodes

CRIMEA — Kozlov (Eupatoria) — Bakhchisarai — Sevastopol — Kaffa — Perekop — BLACK SEA

L. Ladoga

CRETE (Turkish 1669) On same scale — Canea — Candia

CENTRAL & EASTERN EUROPE in 1795
Scale 1:12,000,000 (192 miles = 1 inch)
Statute Miles
0 50 100 200 300

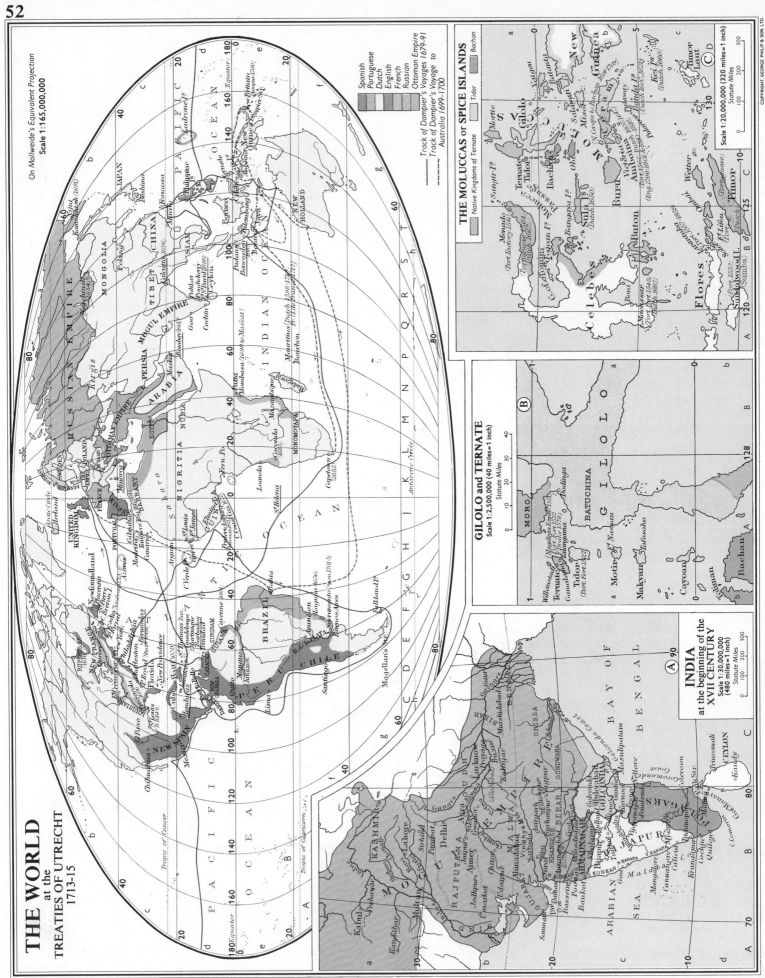

52

THE WORLD
at the
TREATIES OF UTRECHT
1713-15

On Mollweide's Equivalent Projection
Scale 1:165,000,000

Spanish
Portuguese
Dutch
English
French
Russian
Ottoman Empire 1679-91

Track of Dampier's Voyages 1679-91
Track of Dampier's Voyage to
Australia 1699-1700

THE MOLUCCAS or SPICE ISLANDS
Native Kingdoms of Ternate   Tidor   Bachan

Scale 1:20,000,000 (320 miles = 1 inch)
Statute Miles

COPYRIGHT. GEORGE PHILIP & SON, LTD.

GILOLO and TERNATE
Scale 1:2,500,000 (40 miles = 1 inch)
Statute Miles

INDIA
at the beginning of the
XVII CENTURY
Scale 1:30,000,000
(480 miles = 1 inch)
Statute Miles

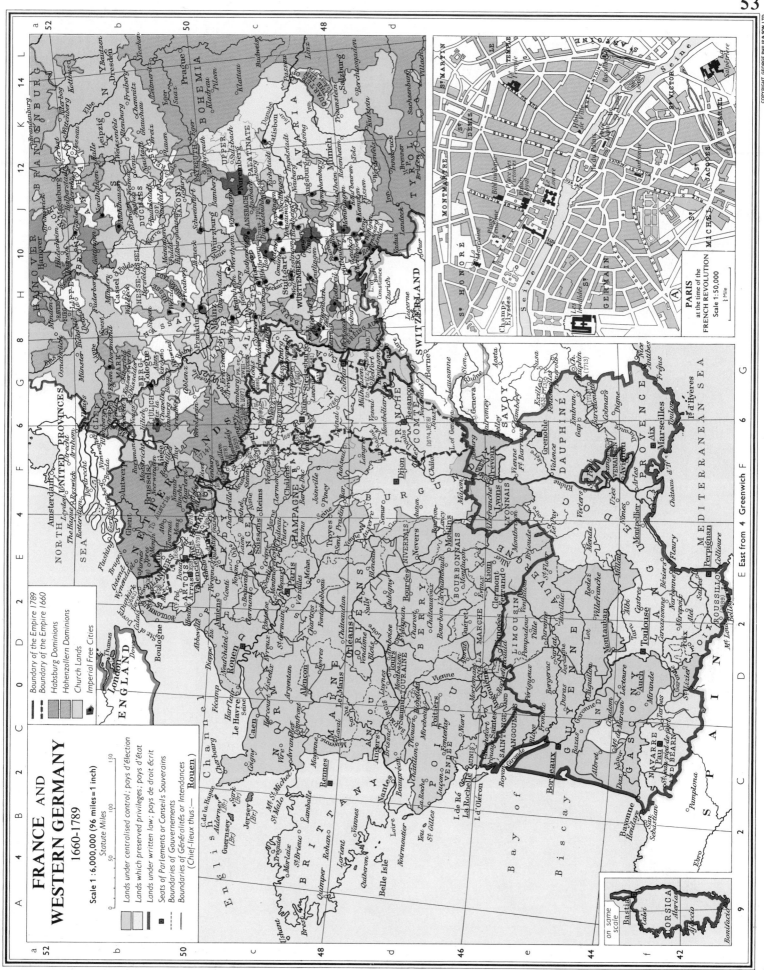

FRANCE AND WESTERN GERMANY
1660-1789

Scale 1 : 6,000,000 (96 miles = 1 inch)

Statute Miles

Lands under centralised control; *pays d'élection*
Lands which preserved privileges; *pays d'état*
Lands under written law; *pays de droit écrit*
Seats of Parlements or Conseils Souverains
Boundaries of Gouvernements
Boundaries of Généralités or Intendances
(Chief-lieux thus :— Rouen)

Boundary of the Empire 1789
Boundary of the Empire 1660
Habsburg Dominions
Hohenzollern Dominions
Church Lands
Imperial Free Cities

PARIS
at the time of the
FRENCH REVOLUTION
Scale 1 : 50,000

53

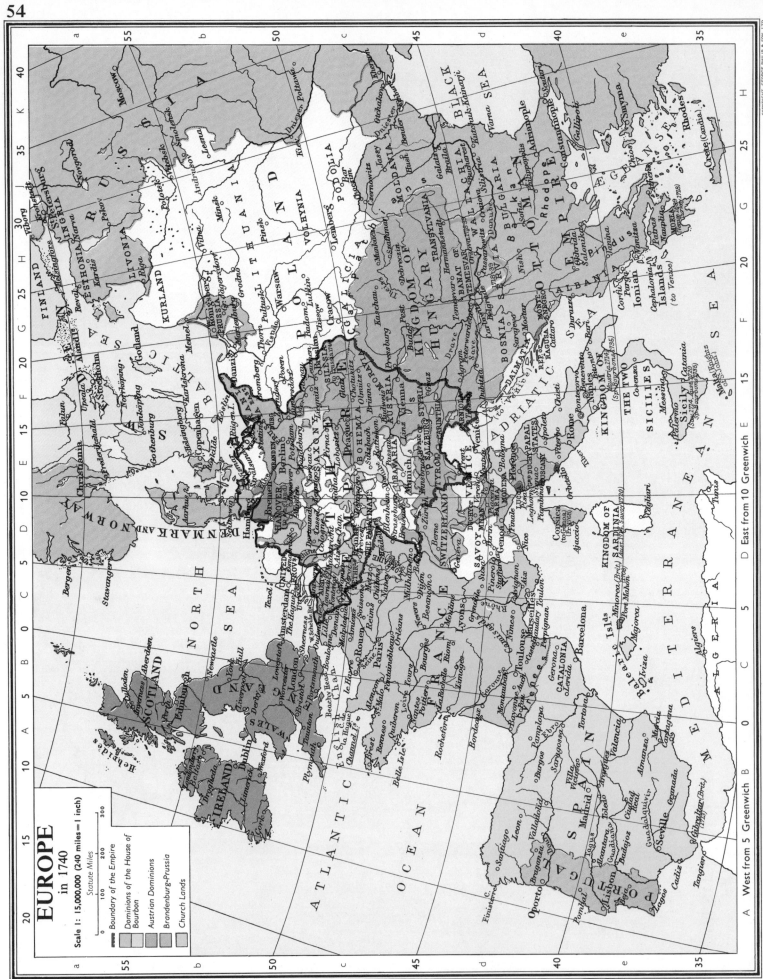

EUROPE
in 1740

Scale 1 : 15,000,000 (240 miles=1 inch)

Statute Miles
0 100 200 300

Boundary of the Empire
Dominions of the House of Bourbon
Austrian Dominions
Brandenburg-Prussia
Church Lands

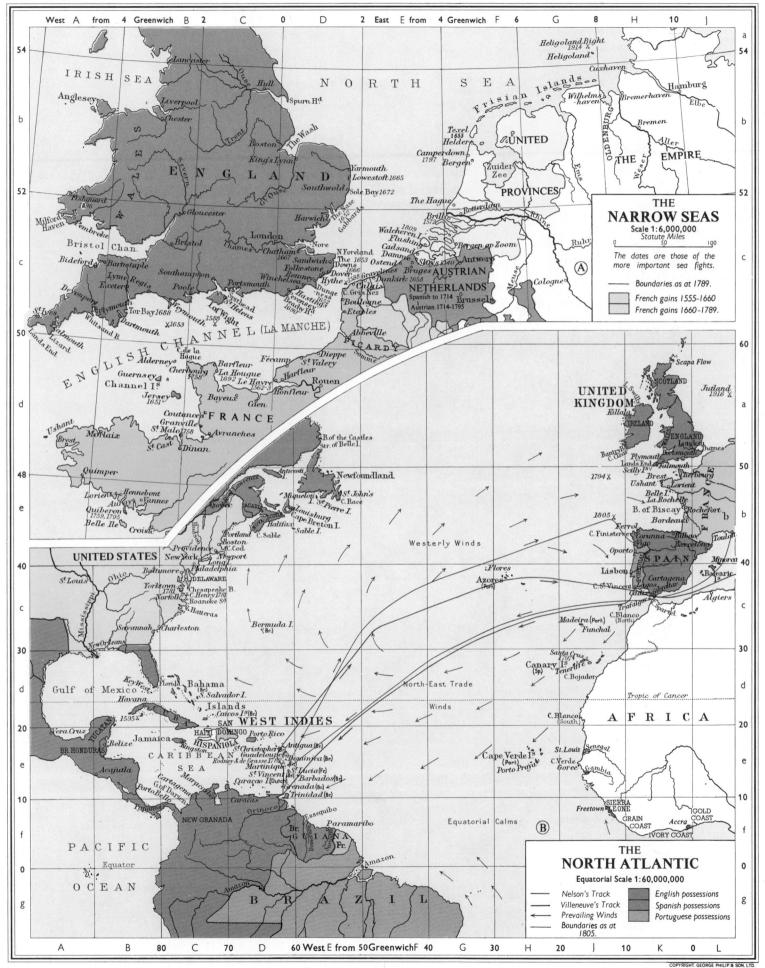

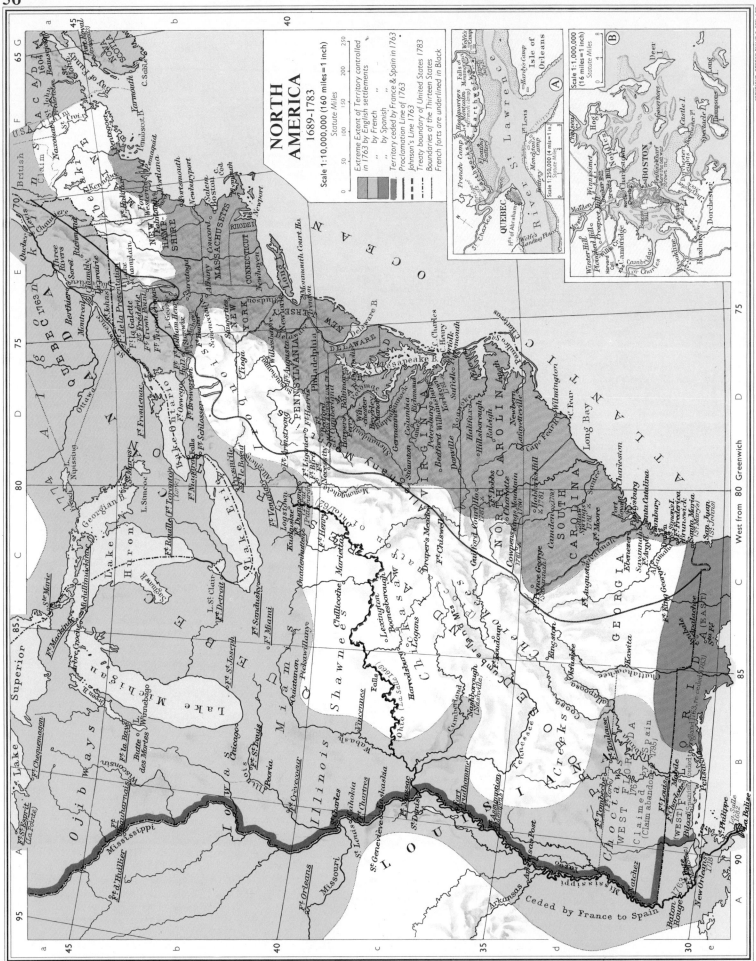

58

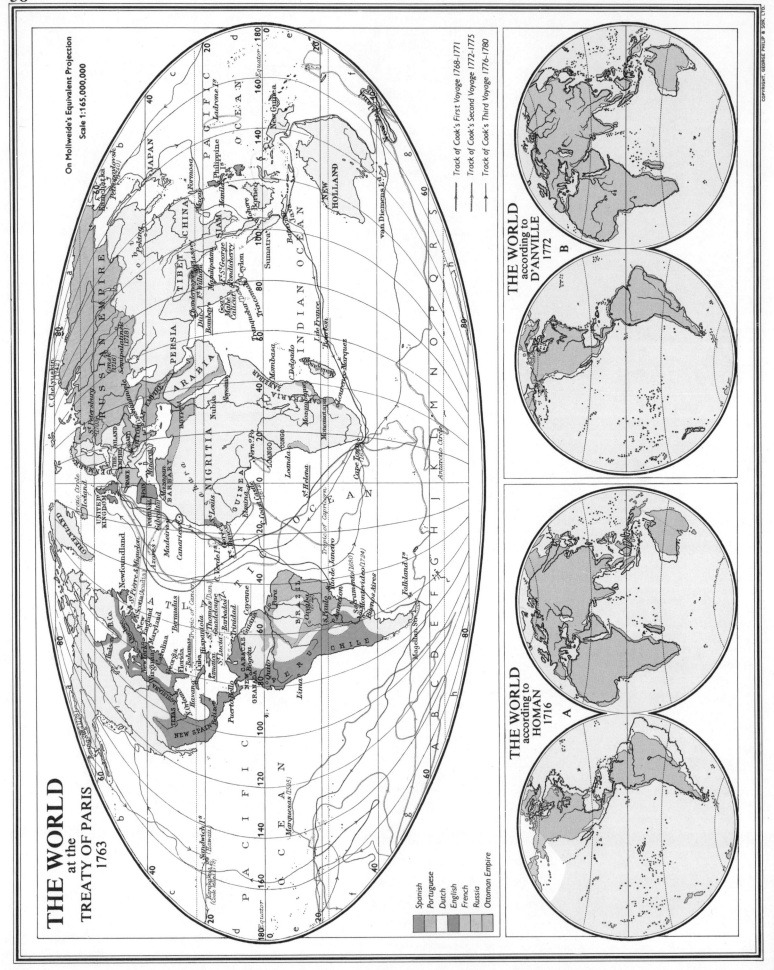

THE WORLD
at the
TREATY OF PARIS
1763

On Mollweide's Equivalent Projection
Scale 1:165,000,000

Track of Cook's First Voyage 1768-1771
Track of Cook's Second Voyage 1772-1775
Track of Cook's Third Voyage 1776-1780

Spanish
Portuguese
Dutch
English
French
Russia
Ottoman Empire

THE WORLD
according to
D'ANVILLE
1772

THE WORLD
according to
HOMAN
1716

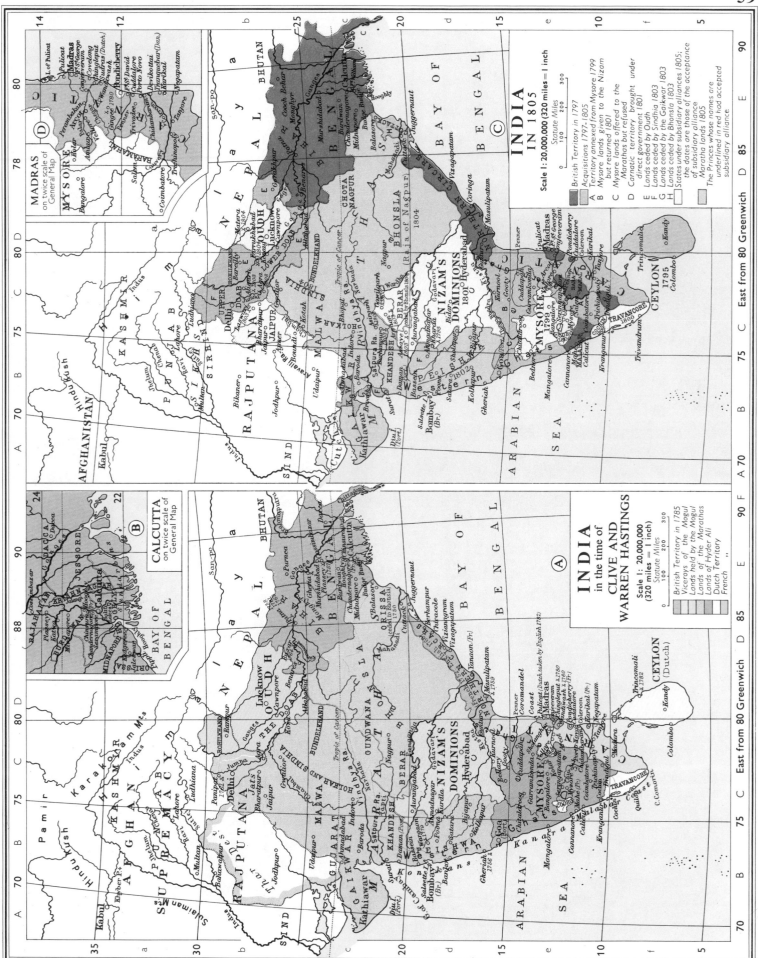

59

MADRAS
on twice scale of
General Map

MYSORE

INDIA
IN 1805

Scale 1 : 20,000,000 (320 miles = 1 inch)

Statute Miles
0   100   200   300

British Territory in 1797
Acquisitions 1797-1805
A Territory annexed from Mysore 1799
B Mysore lands given to the Nizam
     but returned 1801
C Mysore lands offered to the
     Marathas but refused
D Carnatic territory brought under
     direct government 1801
E Lands ceded by Oudh
F Lands ceded by Sindhia 1803
G Lands ceded by the Gaikwar 1803
H Lands ceded by Bhonsla 1803
States under subsidiary alliances 1805;
     the dates are those of the acceptance
     of the subsidiary alliance
Maratha lands 1805
The Princes whose names are
     underlined in red had accepted
     subsidiary alliance

COPYRIGHT, GEORGE PHILIP & SON, LTD.

East from 80 Greenwich

CALCUTTA
on twice scale of
General Map

INDIA
in the time of
CLIVE AND
WARREN HASTINGS

Scale 1 : 20,000,000
(320 miles = 1 inch)

Statute Miles
0   100   200   300

British Territory in 1785
Viceroys of the Mogul
Lands held by the Mogul
Lands of the Marathas
Lands of Hyder Ali
Dutch Territory
French   "

East from 80 Greenwich

THE GROWTH OF BRANDENBURG-PRUSSIA

Scale 1 : 6,000,000 (96 miles = 1 inch)

Statute Miles
0   25   50   75   100

- Brandenburg at death of Frederick I. 1440
- Acquisitions 1440-1608
- Acquisitions 1608-1624
- Acquisitions under the Great Elector, 1640-1688
- Acquisitions under Frederick III, (I. of Prussia) 1689-1713 & Frederick William I., 1713-1740
- Acquisitions under Frederick the Great 1740-1786
- Acquisitions under Frederick William II., 1786-1797
- Second Partition of Poland
- Third Partition of Poland
- Acquisitions under Frederick William III., 1797-1807

(A)

THE GROWTH OF PRUSSIA

Scale 1 : 6,000,000 (96 miles = 1 inch)

Statute Miles
0   25   50   75   100

- Prussia at the Treaty of Tilsit 1807
- Territory regained by the Treaty of Vienna 1815
- New territory acquired by the Treaty of Vienna, 1815
- Acquisitions 1815-1866
- *Bonn* University Towns

(B)

East from Greenwich

COPYRIGHT. GEORGE PHILIP & SON. LTD.

Map A labels: NORTH SEA, Heligoland (Dan. 1714-1807. Br. 1807-90), SCHLESWIG HOLSTEIN, BALTIC SEA, Memel, Tauroggen 1691,1793, Tilsit, Niemen, Stralsund, Rostock, Lauenburg 1657, Olivas 1793, Danzig, Pillau, Königsberg, Pregel, Gt. Jägersdorf, EAST PRUSSIA, Eylau, Friedland, Serrey 1691-1793, 1795, Kolberg, E. POMERANIA, KAMMIN 1648, 1657, Marienburg, Elbing, Heilsberg, ERMLAND, 1618, Grodno, E. EAST FRIESLAND 1744, Stade, Hamburg, MECKLENBURG, W. POMERANIA 1720, 1679, Draheim 1657, Stettin, Bahn, NEUMARK 1455, Marienwerder, Tannenberg, WEST PRUSSIA 1772 (First Partition), NEW EAST PRUSSIA 1795 (Third Partition), Emden, Bremen, Verden, Lüneburg, Lauenburg, Celle, PRIEGNITZ, UKERMARK, 1524 Ruppin, 1679, Zorndorf, Netze, Bromberg, Thorn, Vistula, Bug, Tingen 1702, 1707, B'PRIC OF MINDEN 1648, Hanover, Brunswick, ALTMARK Stendal, Fehrbellin, Spandau, MITTELMARK, Brandenburg, Berlin, Potsdam, Küstrin, Meseritz, Gnesen, Posen, SOUTH PRUSSIA, Warsaw, Tecklenburg, Osnabrück, RAVENSBERG 1614, Bielefeld, Hildesheim 1680, Magdeburg, Luckenwalde, Zossen, 1571 Frankfurt, Kunersdorf 1742, Warthe 1793, (Second Partition), Ravenstein, CLEVES, Wesel, Hamm, MARK 1614, Paderborn, Warburg, Wernigerode, HARZ, Halberstadt 1648, Wittenberg, Barwalde 1462, Cottbus 1462, LAUSITZ, Rothenburg, Kalisz, GUELDERS 1715,1801, Essen, Münster 1803, Crefeld, Jülich, Gimborn, HOHNSTEIN 1648, MANSFELD 1780, Merseburg, Rossbach, SAXONY, Halle 1680, Torgau, Hubertusburg, UPPER, Glogau, LOWER, Wohlau, Liegnitz, Leuthen, Breslau, Brieg, BERG, Cologne, Corbach, Cassel, Lutterberg, EICHSFELD 1803, Weimar, Erfurt, Gotha, Leipzig, Kesselsdorf, Bautzen, Görlitz, Hennersdorf, SILESIA, Mollwitz, Aix-la-Chapelle, Marburg, Fulda, Thuringian Forest, Chemnitz, Freiberg, Dresden, Pirna, Hochkirch, Pillnitz, GIANT Mts, Hirschberg, Landeshut, Hohenfriedberg, Schweidnitz, 1740, UPPER SILESIA, Coblenz, Rhine, Lahn, Frankfurt, Hanau, Dettingen, Ansbach, Maxen, Lobositz, Königgrätz, Soor, Neisse, Kosel, Beuthen 1603,7,10, NEW SILESIA 1795, Worms, Mainz, Würzburg, Bamberg, BAYREUTH 1420,40, 1470-86, Bayreuth 1591, Eger, Prague, Kolin, Chotusitz, AUSTRIAN SILESIA, Troppau, Jägerndorf 1603-7, 21, Teschen, ANSBACH 1415, 40,1470-86, 1791, LIMPURG 1713-42, Nuremberg, Pilsen, BOHEMIA, Czaslau, Pisek, AUSTRIA, Brünn, Olmütz, BAVARIA, Bohemian Forest, Ore Mts, Elbe, Neuchâtel 1707 (Pr.), Doubs

Map B labels: NORTH SEA, Heligoland (Ger. 1890, Prus. 1891), SCHLESWIG, Flensburg, Alsen, Kiel, HOLSTEIN, DENMARK, Malmö, Fehmarn, BALTIC SEA, Rügen I., Stralsund, POMERANIA, Greifswald, Rostock, Kolberg, Rep. of Danzig, Tilsit, Niemen, Königsberg, Eylau, Bartenstein, EAST PRUSSIA, Marienburg, Eider, Cuxhaven, Lübeck, Wismar, SCHWERIN, MECKLENBURG STRELITZ, WEST PRUSSIA, Marienwerder, United 1824-78, Emden, Bremerhaven, Hamburg, Lauenburg 1865, Lüneburg, Stettin, Kulm, Thorn, Ostrolenka, Pultusk, NETHERLANDS, PR. OF OLDENBURG 1834, Bremen, Celle, ALTMARK, Schönhausen, BRANDENBURG, Potsdam, Berlin, Spree, Küstrin, Frankfurt, POSEN, Posen 1815, Warthe, Warsaw, Cleves, Münster, Osnabrück, Detmold, Hanover 1866, Brunswick, Brandenburg, Magdeburg, Grossbeeren, Oder, Dennewitz, Wittenberg, LOWER LAUSITZ, Bug, Pilica, Kalisz, RUSSIA, WESTPHALIA 1815, HANOVER 1815, Halberstadt, Harz, ANHALT, Halle, Torgau, Glogau, Hainau, Crefeld, Düsseldorf, Elberfeld, RHINE PROVINCE 1815, Cologne, Bonn, HESSEN, Cassel, Langensalza, Weimar, Gotha, Erfurt, Lützen, Leipzig, Dresden, Chemnitz, Jena, SAXONY, UPPER, Bautzen, Wahlstatt, Breslau, SILESIA, Brieg, Schweidnitz, Aix, Marburg, Giessen, Thuringian Forest, Teplitz, Kulm, GIANT Mts, Reichenbach, Trautenau, Gitschin, Ems, Wetzlar, NASSAU, Wiesbaden, Ore Mts, Elbe, Münchengrätz, Sadowa, Sudetes, Oder, Mosel, Treves (to Oldenburg), Meisenheim 1866, Darmstadt, Frankfurt, HOHENZOLLERN 1849, Hechingen, Sigmaringen, Danube, Neuchâtel 1815-57 (Pr.), Doubs, Worms, Mainz, Würzburg, Prague, Königgrätz, Troppau, BOHEMIA

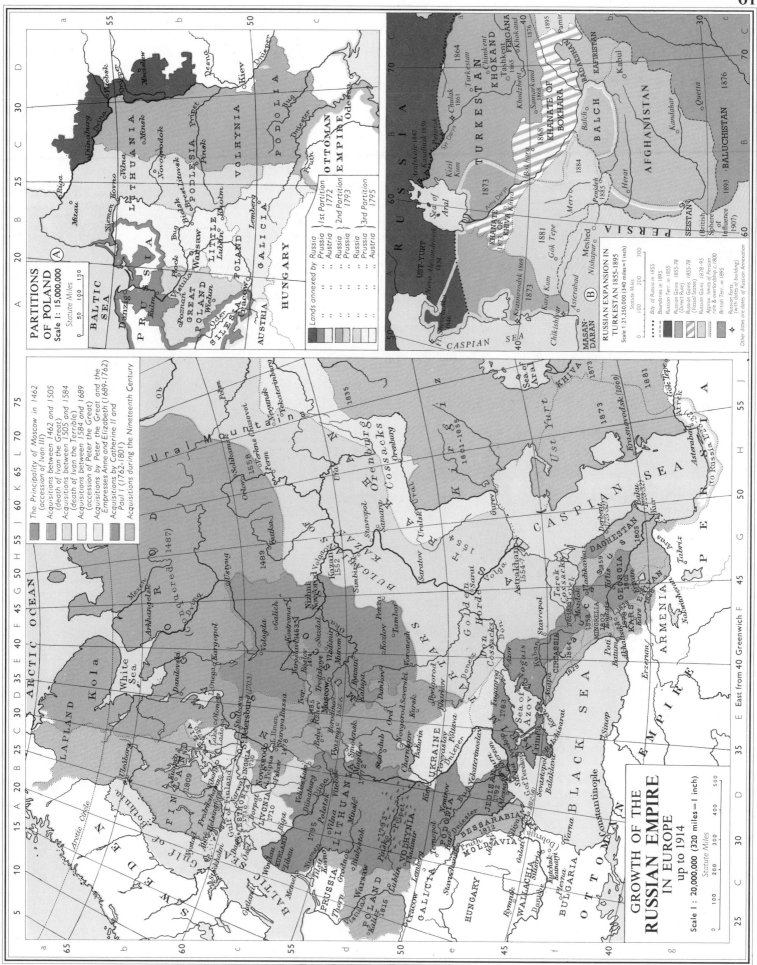

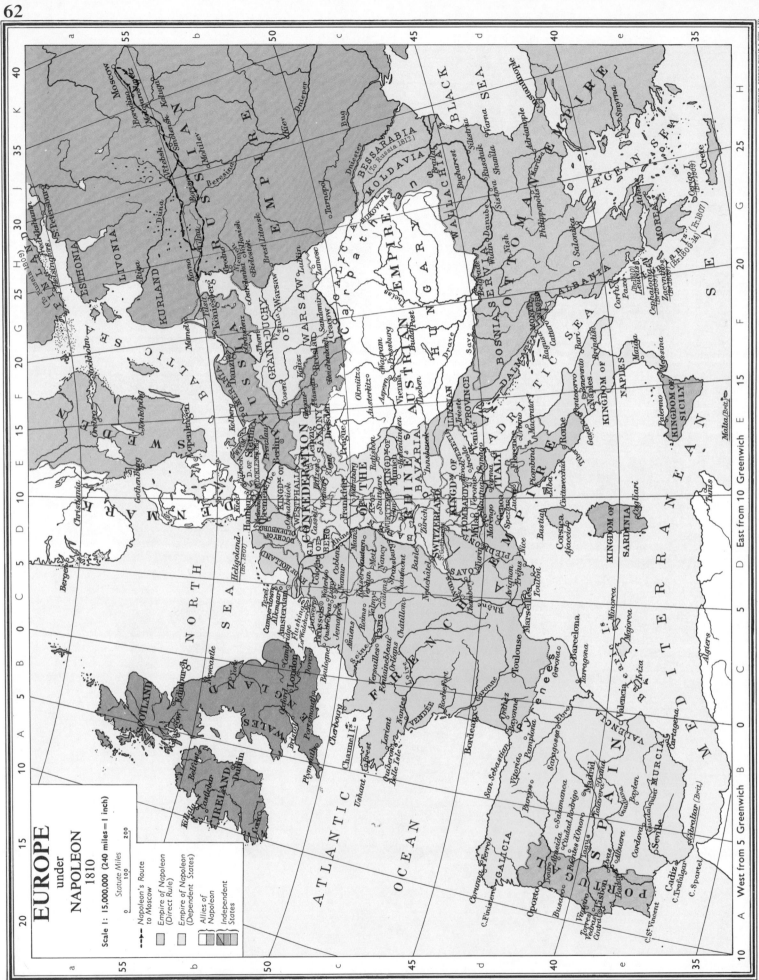

EUROPE
under
NAPOLEON
1810

Scale 1: 15,000,000 (240 miles = 1 inch)

Statute Miles

0   100   200

- - - ► Napoleon's Route to Moscow

Empire of Napoleon (Direct Rule)

Empire of Napoleon (Dependent States)

Allies of Napoleon

Independent States

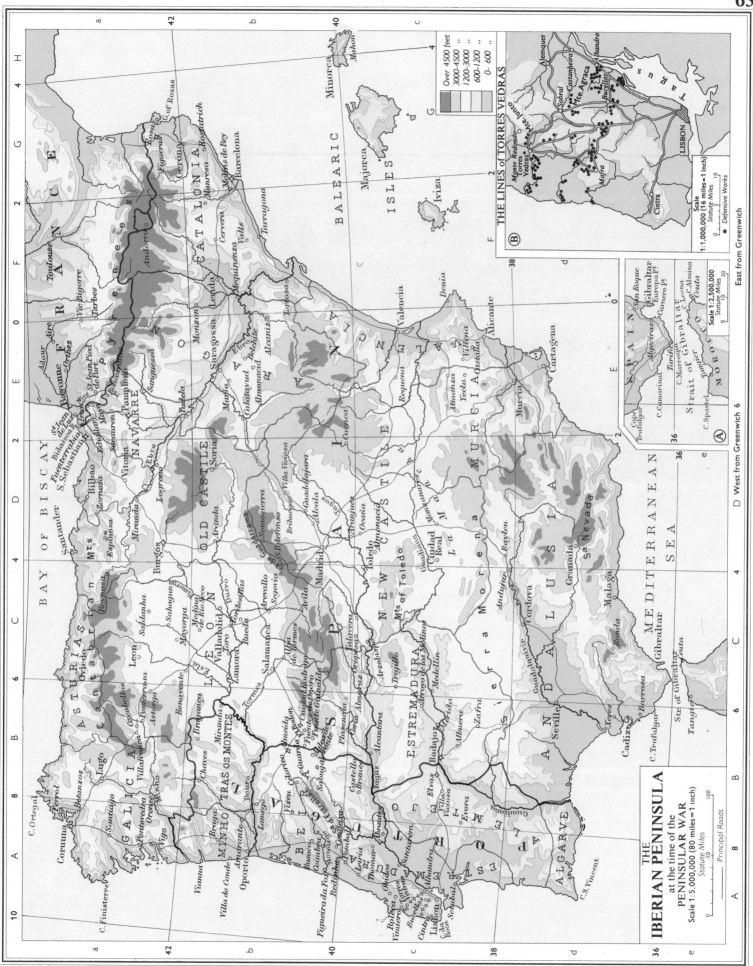

THE LINES OF TORRES VEDRAS

Over 4500 feet
3000-3000 ..
1200-3000 ..
600-1200 ..
0- 600 ..

Alemquer
Sobral
Castanheira
Mte. Agraca
Bucellas
Alhandra
Monte Redondo
Torres
Vedras
Mte. Junto
Mafra
Cintra
LISBON
TAGUS

Scale
1:1,000,000 (16 miles=1 inch)
Statute Miles
10
• Defensive Works

East from Greenwich

SPAIN
San Roque
Algeciras
Gibraltar
Europa Pt.
C. Marroqui
Tarifa
Strait of Gibraltar
Tangier
Carnero Pt.
C. Leona
C. Alnina
Ceuta
C. Comarinal
C. Trafalgar
C. Spartel
MOROCCO

Scale 1:2,500,000
Statute Miles
10   20

West from Greenwich

FRANCE
Toulouse
Vic Bigorre
Tarbes
Adour
Aire
Bayonne
Orthez
Vie.
St. Jean Pied
de Port
St. Jean
de Luz
Bidassoa
Fuenterrabia
S. Sebastian
Echallar
Maya
Sauveterre
Pamplona
Sanguessa
Tudela

BAY OF BISCAY

Santander
Bilbao
Espinosa
Zornoza
Vitoria
Miranda
Ebro
Logroño
Soria

ASTURIAS
Oviedo
C. Ortegal
Ferrol
Betanzos
Corunna
C. Finisterre
Santiago
Lugo
Pontevedra
Orense
Vigo
C. Finisterre

GALICIA

Mondonedo
Villafranca
Cacabellos
Leon
Sahagun
Mayorga
Benavente
Astorga
Braganca
Chaves
Braga
Villa do Conde
Oporto
Vianna
Minho
Douro
Lamego
Amarante

CANTABRIAN
Mts

OLD CASTILE
Burgos
Aranda
Medina
de Rio Seco
Valladolid
Toro
Zamora
Rueda
Tordesillas
Arevallo
Segovia
Guadarrama
S. Ildefonso
Avila

LEON
Salamanca
Alba
de Tormes
Ciudad
Rodrigo
Fuente Guinaldo
Tormes

PYRENEES
Andorra
NAVARRE
Puycerda
Figueras
G. of Rosas
Gerona
Mostalrich
Rosas

CATALONIA
Manresa
Cervera
Lerida
Monzon
Balaguer
Mequinenza
Valls
Tarragona

Saragossa
Ebro
Calatayud
Almonacid
Alcaniz
Batchite
Morella
Villa Viciosa

ARAGON

VALENCIA
Requena
Valencia
Denia
Alicante
Onstalla
Villena
Yecla
Almanza

MINORCA
Mahon

BALEARIC
ISLES
Majorca
Iviza

MURCIA
Murcia
Cartagena

NEW CASTILE
Guadalajara
Alcala
Brihuega
Madrid
Aranjuez
Ocaña
Toledo
Mts of Toledo
Talavera
Oropesa
Guadiana
Ciudad
Real
La
Mancha

SPAIN

Cuenca

ESTREMADURA
Arzobispo
Almaraz
Arroyo del Molinos
Medellin
Trujillo
Plasencia
Fonda
Merida
Badajoz
Elvas
Alcantara
Zafra
Albuera

SIERRA Morena
Andujar
Baylen
Cordova
Guadalquivir
Seville
Yepes
Ronda
Barrosa
Malaga
Granada
Sa Nevada
ANDALUSIA
C. Trafalgar
Cadiz
Str. of Gibraltar
Gibraltar
Tarifa
Tangier
Ceuta

MEDITERRANEAN SEA

MINHO
TRAS OS MONTES
Miranda
BEIRA
Tizeu
Viseu
Bussaco
Coimbra
Figueira
Foz
Pombal
Leiria
Thomar
Abrantes
Coria
Guarda
Almeida
La Boden
Fuentes d'Onoro
Castello
Branco
Sabugal
Tagus

ALEMTEJO
ESTREMADURA
Santarem
Cintra
Lisbon
Rolica
Vimiero
Torres Vedras
Obidos
Alcobaça
Mafra
Cintra
C. da Roca
Setubal
Redinha

ALGARVE
C. S. Vincent

Villa Vicosa
Evora
Elvas
Guadiana

THE
IBERIAN PENINSULA
at the time of the
PENINSULAR WAR
Scale 1:5,000,000 (80 miles=1 inch)
Statute Miles
50   100
—— Principal Roads

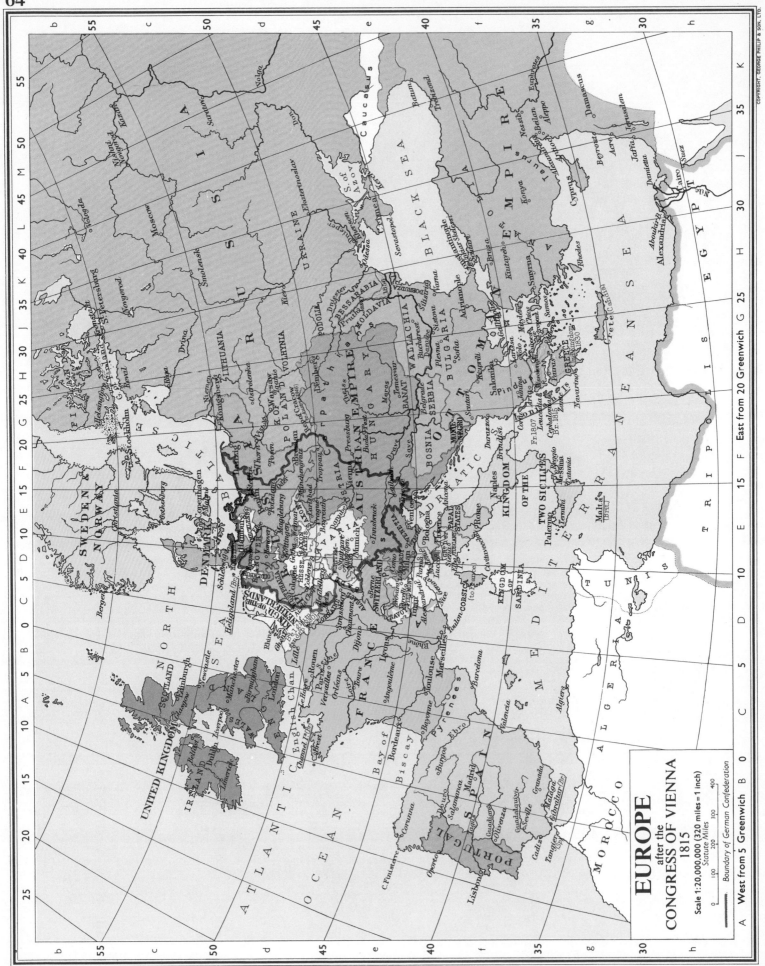

EUROPE
after the
CONGRESS OF VIENNA
1815

Scale 1:20,000,000 (320 miles = 1 inch)

Statute Miles

0   100   200   300   400

———— Boundary of German Confederation

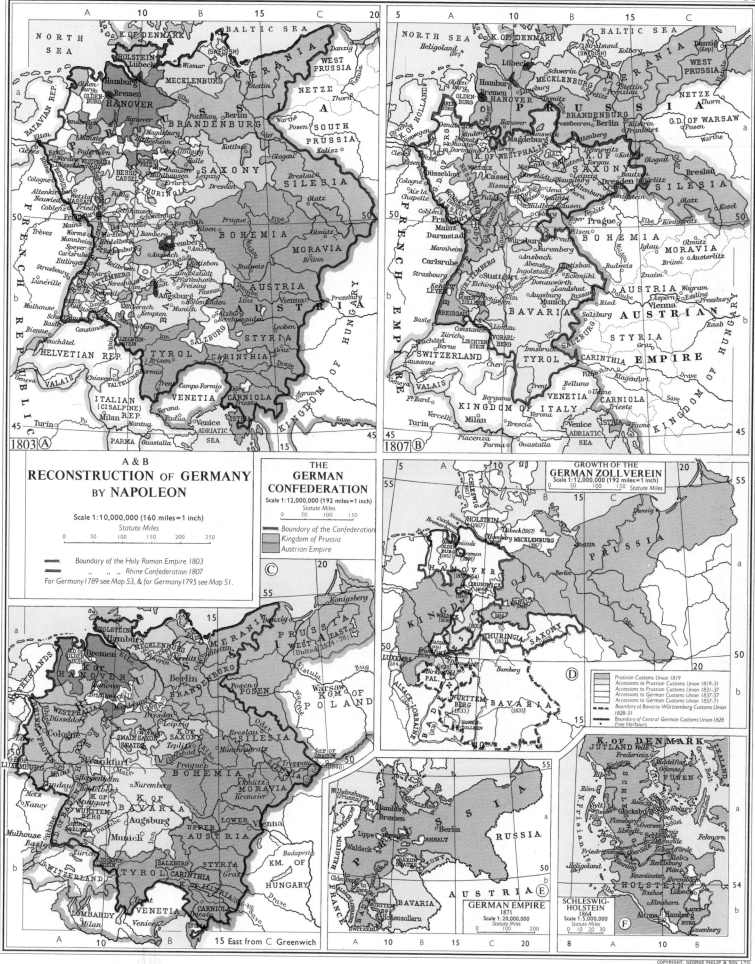

65

A & B
RECONSTRUCTION OF GERMANY BY NAPOLEON

Scale 1:10,000,000 (160 miles=1 inch)

Statute Miles
0   50   100   150   200   250

····· Boundary of the Holy Roman Empire 1803
····· „ „ „ Rhine Confederation 1807
For Germany 1789 see Map 53, & for Germany 1795 see Map 51.

THE
GERMAN CONFEDERATION

Scale 1:12,000,000 (192 miles=1 inch)

Statute Miles
0   50   100   150

Boundary of the Confederation
Kingdom of Prussia
Austrian Empire

GROWTH OF THE
GERMAN ZOLLVEREIN

Scale 1:12,000,000 (192 miles=1 inch)

Statute Miles
0   50   100   150

Prussian Customs Union 1819
Accessions to Prussian Customs Union 1819-31
Accessions to Prussian Customs Union 1831-37
Accessions to German Customs Union 1837-57
Accessions to German Customs Union 1857-71
Boundary of Bavaria-Württemberg Customs Union 1828-31
Boundary of Central German Customs Union 1828
Free Harbours

GERMAN EMPIRE 1871
Scale 1:20,000,000

Statute Miles
0   100   200

SCHLESWIG-HOLSTEIN 1864
Scale 1:5,000,000

Statute Miles
0   10   20   30

15 East from Greenwich

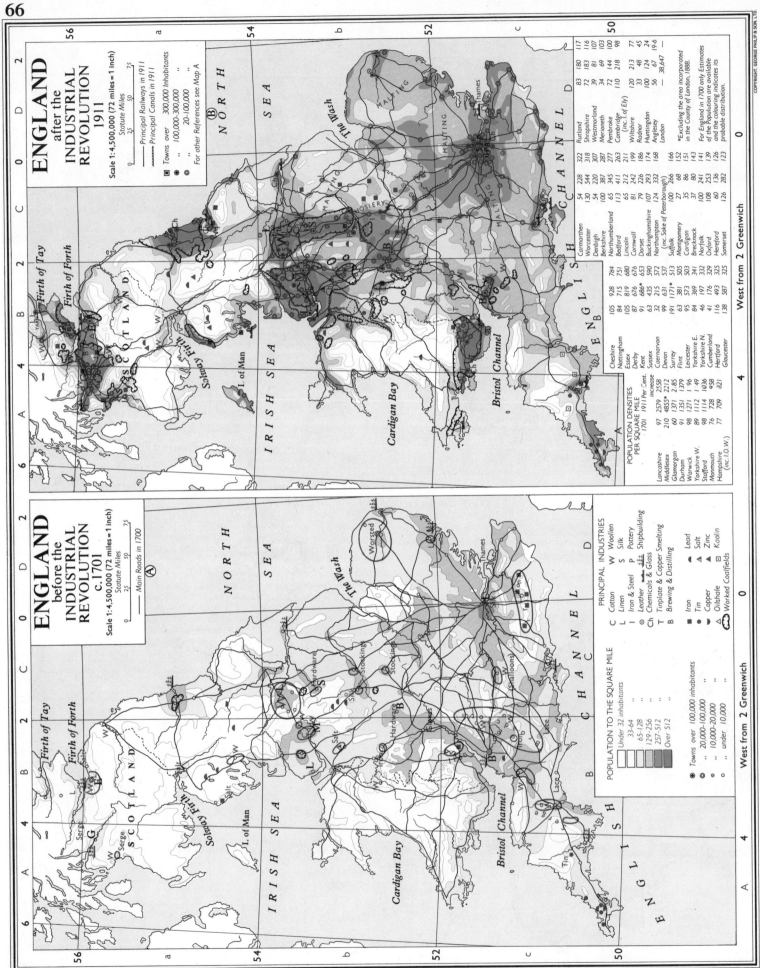

ENGLAND after the INDUSTRIAL REVOLUTION 1911

Scale 1:4,500,000 (72 miles = 1 inch)

Statute Miles
25 50 75

Principal Railways in 1911
Principal Canals in 1911

Towns over 300,000 Inhabitants
100,000–300,000 "
20,000–100,000 "

For other References see Map A

	1701	1911	Per Cent. increase
	POPULATION DENSITIES PER SQUARE MILE		
Lancashire	97	2579	2558
Middlesex	210	4855*	2212
Glamorgan	60	1371	2.85
Durham	91	1351	1379
Warwick	98	1271	1.96
Yorkshire W.	89	1112	1.49
Stafford	98	1114	1036
Monmouth	41	176	329
Hampshire (inc. I.O.W.)	76	728	958
	77	709	821

	1701	1911			1701	1911
Cheshire	105	928	784	Carmarthen	54	228	322
Nottingham	84	715	751	Worcester	130	544	318
Essex	105	819	680	Denbigh	54	220	307
Derby	87	676	676	Northumberland	65	345	277
Kent	91	686*	653	Bedford	113	411	263
Sussex	63	435	590	Lincoln	65	242	211
Caernarvon	32	215	572	Cornwall	81	242	199
Devon	99	631	537	Dorset	79	226	186
Surrey	191	1171*	513	Buckinghamshire	107	293	174
Flint	63	381	505	Northampton	124	332	168
Leicester	95	573	503	(inc. Soke of Peterborough)			
Yorkshire E.	84	369	341	Suffolk	100	266	166
Yorkshire N.	46	197	332	Montgomery	27	68	152
Cumberland	108	253	139	Cardigan	35	86	151
Hertford	116	493	325	Brecknock	37	80	143
Gloucester	138	587	325	Norfolk	100	241	141
				Oxford	108	253	139
				Hereford	60	136	126
				Somerset	126	282	123

	1701	1911
Rutland	54	117
Shropshire	72	116
Westmorland	39	107
Merioneth	34	100
Pembroke	110	98
Cambridge (inc. I. of Ely)	120	77
Wiltshire	33	45
Radnor	56	24
Huntingdon		
Anglesey		67
London	38,647	

*Excluding the area incorporated in the County of London, 1888.

For England in 1700 only Estimates of the Population are available and the colouring indicates its probable distribution.

West from 2 Greenwich

COPYRIGHT, GEORGE PHILIP & SON, LTD.

ENGLAND before the INDUSTRIAL REVOLUTION c.1701

Scale 1:4,500,000 (72 miles = 1 inch)

Statute Miles
0 25 50 75

Main Roads in 1700

POPULATION TO THE SQUARE MILE

Under 32 inhabitants
33–64 "
65–128 "
129–256 "
257–512 "
Over 512 "

Towns over 100,000 inhabitants
" 20,000–100,000 "
" 10,000–20,000 "
" under 10,000 "

PRINCIPAL INDUSTRIES

C Cotton — W Woollen
L Linen — S Silk
I Iron & Steel — P Pottery
⊙ Leather — ⌗ Shipbuilding
Ch Chemicals & Glass
T Tinplate & Copper Smelting
B Brewing & Distilling

▲ Iron — ▲ Lead
■ Tin — ▲ Salt
▲ Copper — ▲ Zinc
● Oilshale — ▲ Kaolin
⬭ Worked Coalfields

West from 2 Greenwich

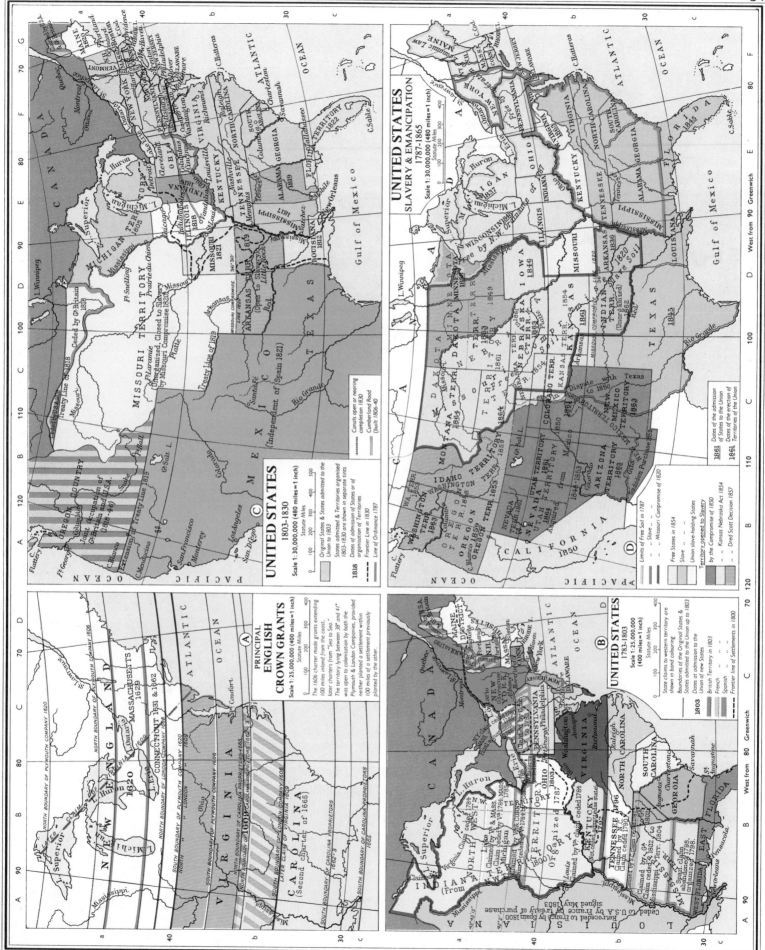

68

SOUTH AMERICA
in the
XIX & XX CENTURIES

Scale 1:30,000,000 (480 miles = 1 inch)

Statute Miles

0   200   400   600

——— Approximate Boundaries of States in 1830
- - - Boundaries subsequently & finally adjusted
▨▨▨ Boundary of Greater Colombia, 1819-30
▧▧▧ Boundary of Federation of Bolivia & Peru 1835-39

West from 50 Greenwich

GUYANA
BOUNDARY

Scale 1:24,000,000 (384 miles = 1 inch)

Statute Miles

0   100   200   300

——— Present Bdy. of Guyana
▨▨ Br. Guiana: Bdy. settlement 1899
——— Original Schomburgk Line
- - - Extension of Schomburgk Line
┊┊┊ Extreme Venezuelan Claim
▨▨▨ Extreme British Claim

NORTH WEST
SOUTH AMERICA
Conflicting Territorial Claims

Scale 1:40,000,000 (640 miles = 1 inch)

Statute Miles

0   200   400   600

——— Boundaries fixed by Treaty
*The conflicting claims of the various
states are shown by narrow bands of
their respective colours*

COPYRIGHT, GEORGE PHILIP & SON, LTD.

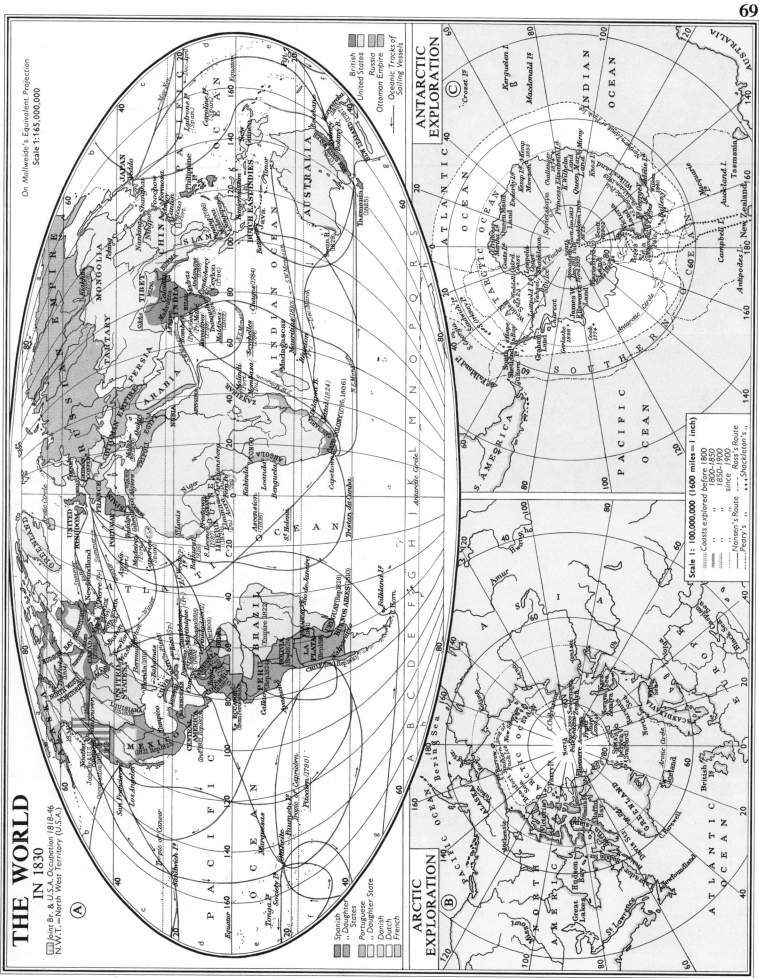

THE WORLD
IN 1830

On Mollweide's Equivalent Projection
Scale 1:165,000,000

Joint Br. & U.S.A. Occupation 1818-46
N.W.T. = North West Territory (U.S.A.)

British
United States
Russia
Ottoman Empire
Oceanic Tracks of
Sailing Vessels

Spanish   „ Daughter States
Portuguese „ Daughter State
Danish
Dutch
French

(A)

ARCTIC EXPLORATION

(B)

ANTARCTIC EXPLORATION

(C)

Scale 1: 100,000,000 (1600 miles = 1 inch)
Coasts explored before 1800
„   „   1800-1850
„   „   1850-1900
„   „   since 1900
Nansen's Route
Peary's „
Ross's Route
Shackleton's „

ALASKA 140 A 130 B 120 C 110 D 100 E 90 F 80 G 70 H

British North America

The Colonies in 1841
The Provinces of the Dominion
The Territories of the Dominion
Former boundaries of territories

Dates shown thus **1784** *are those of the organisation of the various colonies, and thus* **1867** *of the admission of the various provinces to the Dominion.*

Principal Trails & Mail Routes

══ OT ══ Oregon Trail
══ SFT ══ Santa Fé Trail
══ ST ══ Spanish Trail
══ PE ══ Pony Express
══ BOM ══ Butterfield Overland Mail

Principal Railroads

In operation up to 1848
" " 1848 to 1869
" " 1869 to 1890

C 110 D 100 West from E Greenwich 90 F 80

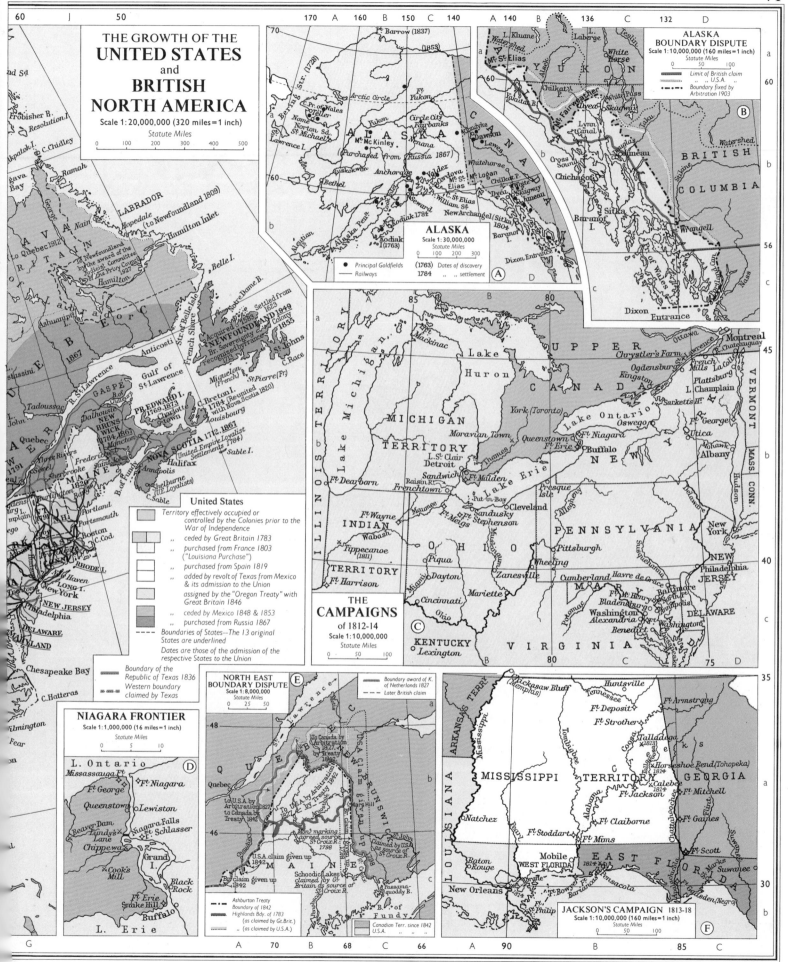

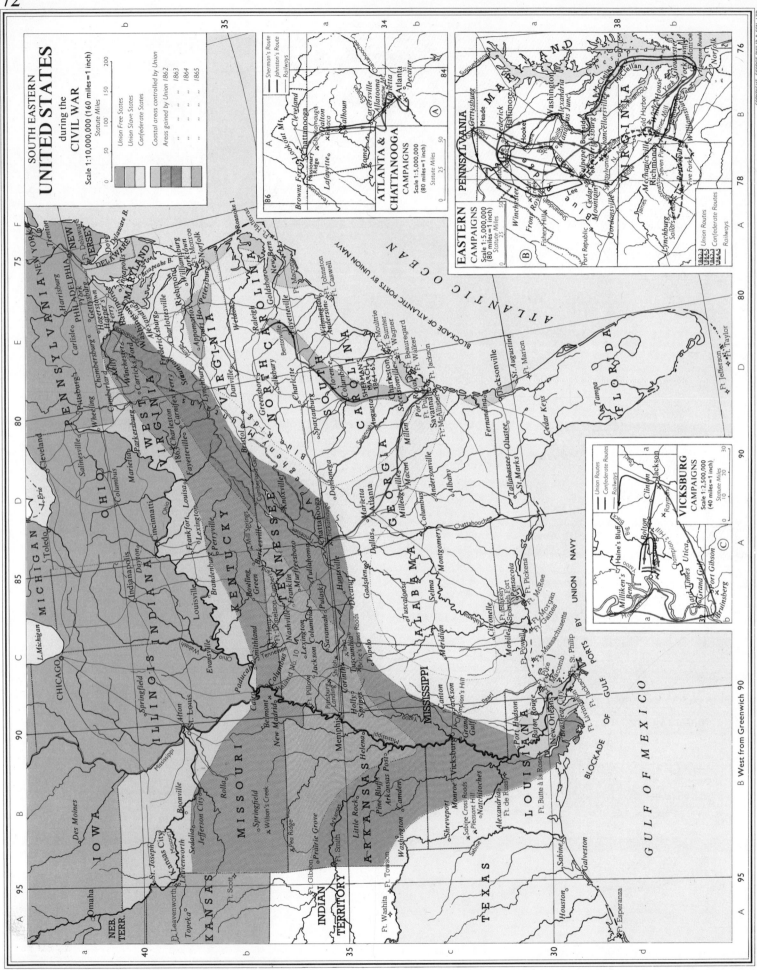

SOUTH EASTERN
UNITED STATES
during the
CIVIL WAR
Scale 1:10,000,000 (160 miles=1 inch)

Statute Miles

Union Free States
Union Slave States
Confederate States
Coastal areas controlled by Union
Areas gained by Union 1862
" " " 1863
" " " 1864
" " " 1865

ATLANTA & CHATTANOOGA CAMPAIGNS
Scale 1:5,000,000
(80 miles=1 inch)
Statute Miles

Sherman's Route
Johnston's Route
Railways

EASTERN CAMPAIGNS
Scale 1:5,000,000
(80 miles=1 inch)
Statute Miles

Union Routes
Confederate Routes
Railways

VICKSBURG CAMPAIGNS
Scale 1:2,500,000
(40 miles=1 inch)
Statute Miles

Union Routes
Confederate Routes
Railways

ATLANTIC OCEAN

GULF OF MEXICO

BLOCKADE OF ATLANTIC PORTS BY UNION NAVY

BLOCKADE OF GULF PORTS BY UNION NAVY

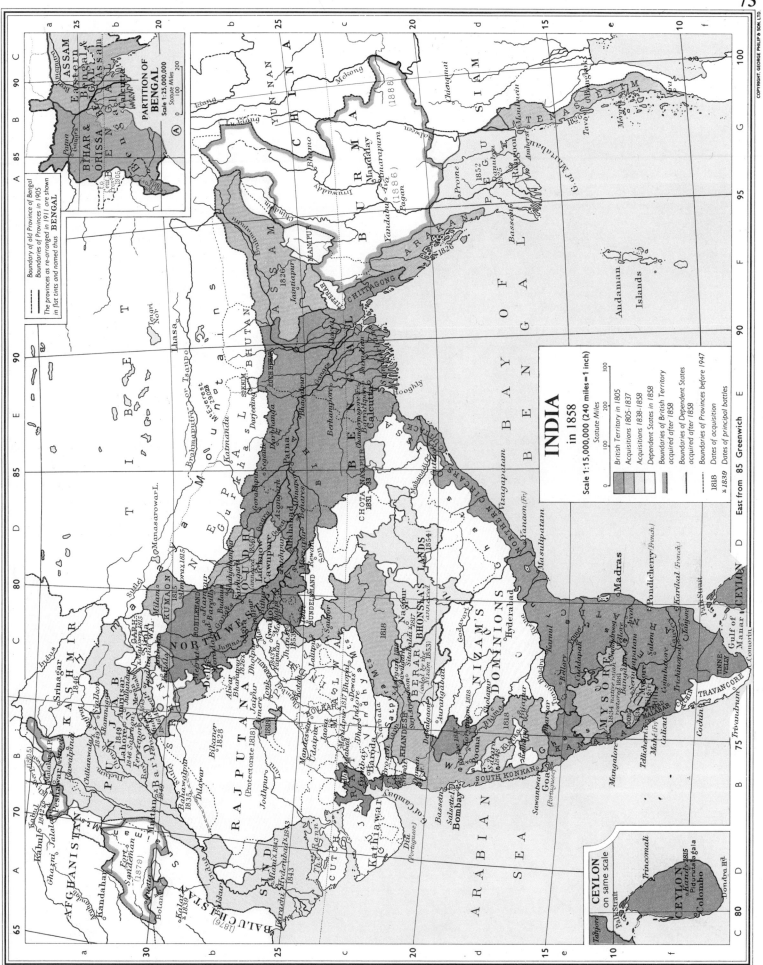

INDIA
in 1858

Scale 1:15,000,000 (240 miles = 1 inch)

Statute Miles

PARTITION OF BENGAL

Scale 1:25,000,000

CEYLON
on same scale

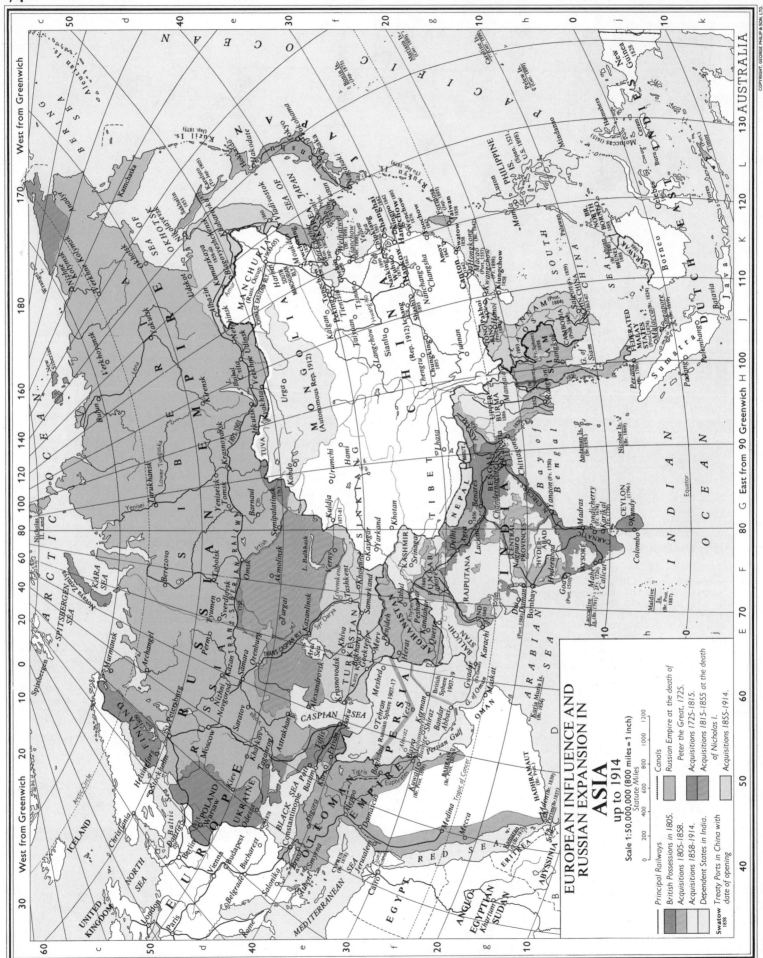

74

EUROPEAN INFLUENCE AND
RUSSIAN EXPANSION IN
ASIA
up to 1914

Scale 1:50,000,000 (800 miles = 1 inch)

Statute Miles
0   200   400   600   800   1000   1200

Principal Railways

Canals

British Possessions in 1805.

Acquisitions 1805-1858.

Acquisitions 1858-1914.

Dependent States in India.

Russian Empire at the death of
Peter the Great, 1725.

Acquisitions 1725-1815.

Acquisitions 1815-1855 at the death
of Nicholas I.

Acquisitions 1855-1914.

Swatow   Treaty Ports in China with
1858   date of opening

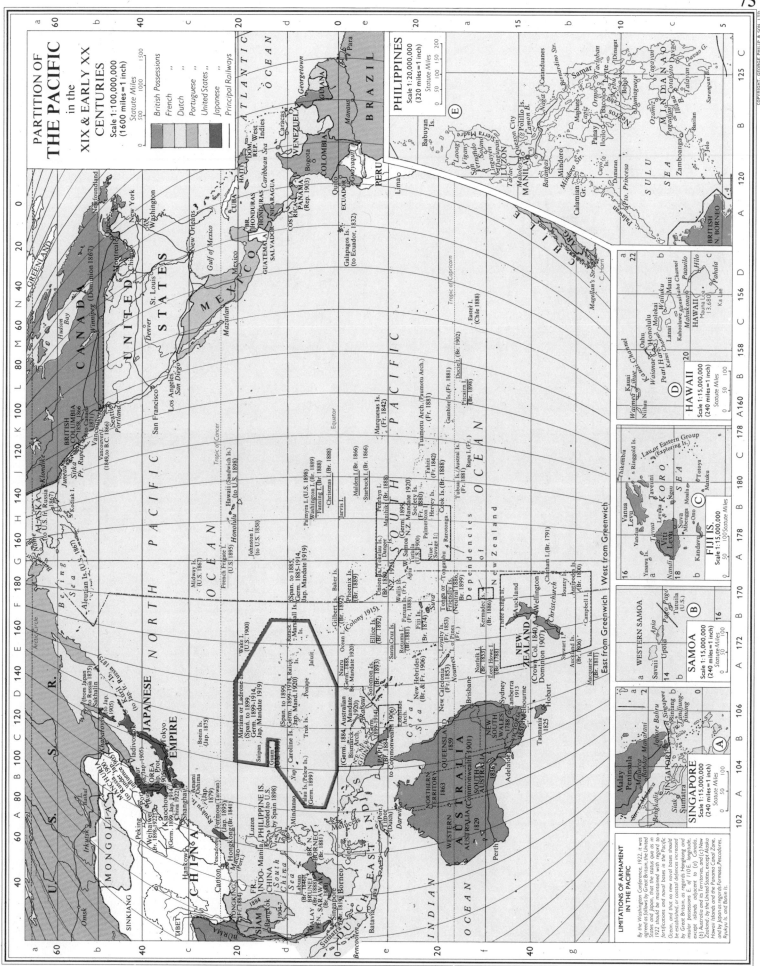

PARTITION OF THE PACIFIC in the XIX & EARLY XX CENTURIES

Scale 1:100,000,000
(1600 miles = 1 inch)

Statute Miles
0   500   1000   1500

British Possessions
French   "
Dutch   "
Portuguese "
United States "
Japanese   "
Principal Railways

PHILIPPINES
Scale 1:20,000,000
(320 miles = 1 inch)

Statute Miles
0 50 100 150 200

HAWAII
Scale 1:15,000,000
(240 miles = 1 inch)

Statute Miles
0   50   100

FIJI IS.
Scale 1:15,000,000

Statute Miles
0   50   100

SAMOA
Scale 1:15,000,000
(240 miles = 1 inch)

Statute Miles
0   50   100

WESTERN SAMOA

SINGAPORE
Scale 1:15,000,000
(240 miles = 1 inch)

Statute Miles
0   50   100

LIMITATIONS OF ARMAMENT IN THE PACIFIC

By the Washington Conference, 1922, it was agreed as follows by Great Britain, the United States and Japan, that the status quo as in 1922 should be maintained with regard to fortifications and naval bases in the Pacific Ocean, and that no new naval bases should be established, or coastal defences increased by Great Britain, as regards Hongkong and insular possessions E. of 110°E. longitude, except Australia and its territories and New Zealand;—by the United States, except Alaska, Hawaii Islands and the Panama Canal Zone, and by Japan as regards Formosa, Pescadores, Ryukyu Is. and Bonin Is.

COPYRIGHT, GEORGE PHILIP & SON, LTD.

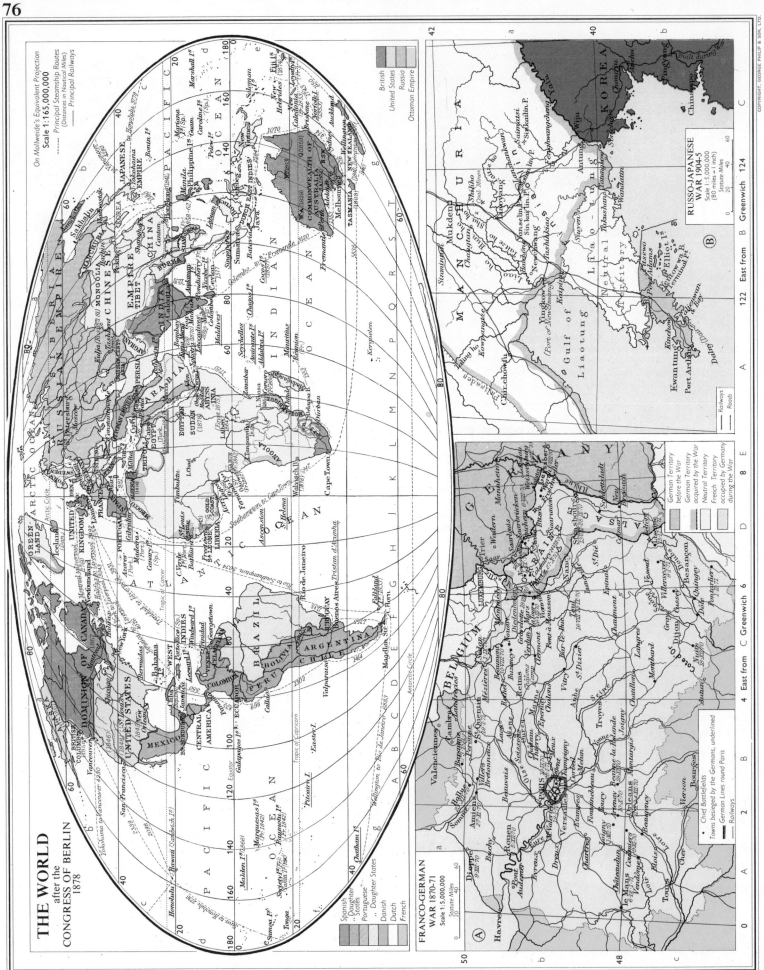

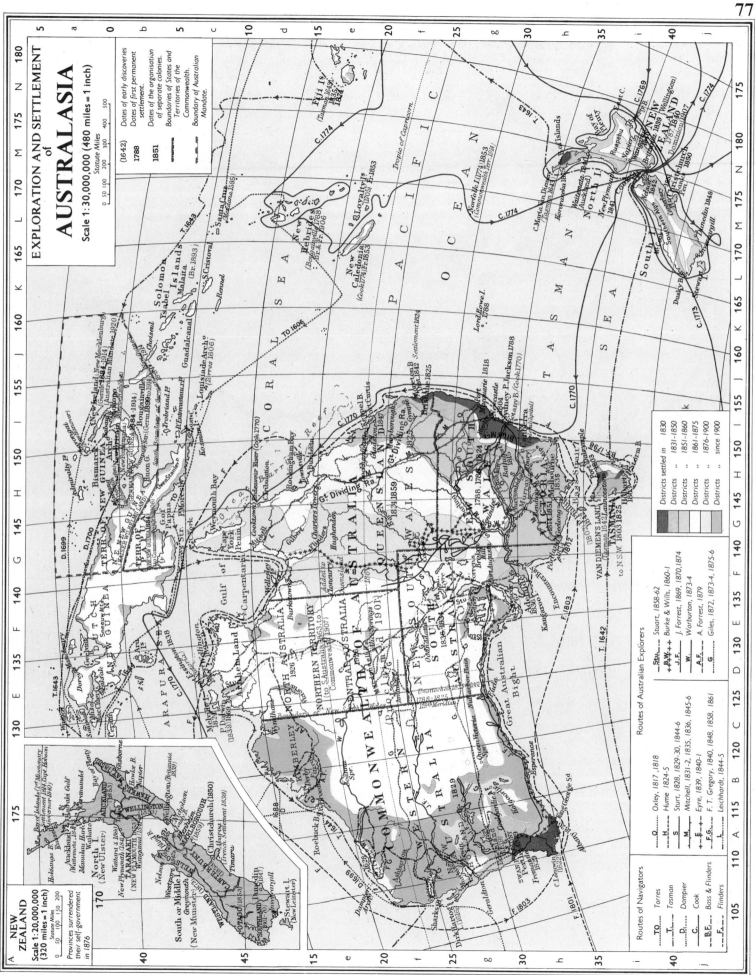

EXPLORATION AND SETTLEMENT
of
AUSTRALASIA

Scale 1:30,000,000 (480 miles = 1 inch)

Statute Miles
0 50 100 200 300 400 500

(1642) Dates of early discoveries
1788   Dates of first permanent settlement.
1851   Dates of the organisation of separate colonies.
————— Boundaries of States and Territories of the Commonwealth.
— ·· — ·· — Boundary of Australian Mandate.

NEW ZEALAND

Scale 1:20,000,000 (320 miles = 1 inch)

Statute Miles
0 50 100 150 200

Provinces surrendered their self-government in 1876

Routes of Navigators

T.O. ——— Torres
T. ——— Tasman
D. ——— Dampier
C. ——— Cook
B.F. ——— Bass & Flinders
F. ——— Flinders

Routes of Australian Explorers

O. ——— Oxley, 1817, 1818
H. ——— Hume 1824-5
S. ——— Sturt, 1828, 1829-30, 1844-6
M. ——— Mitchell, 1831-2, 1835, 1836, 1845-6
E. ——— Eyre, 1839, 1840-1
F.G. ——— F. T. Gregory, 1840, 1848, 1858, 1861
L. ——— Leichhardt, 1844-5
Stu. ——— Stuart, 1858-62
B.W. +++ Burke & Wills, 1860-1
J.F. ——— J. Forrest, 1869, 1870, 1874
W. ——— Warburton, 1873-4
A.F. ——— A. Forrest, 1879
G. ——— Giles, 1872, 1873-4, 1875-6

Districts settled in 1830
Districts ,, 1831-1850
Districts ,, 1851-1860
Districts ,, 1861-1875
Districts ,, 1876-1900
Districts ,, since 1900

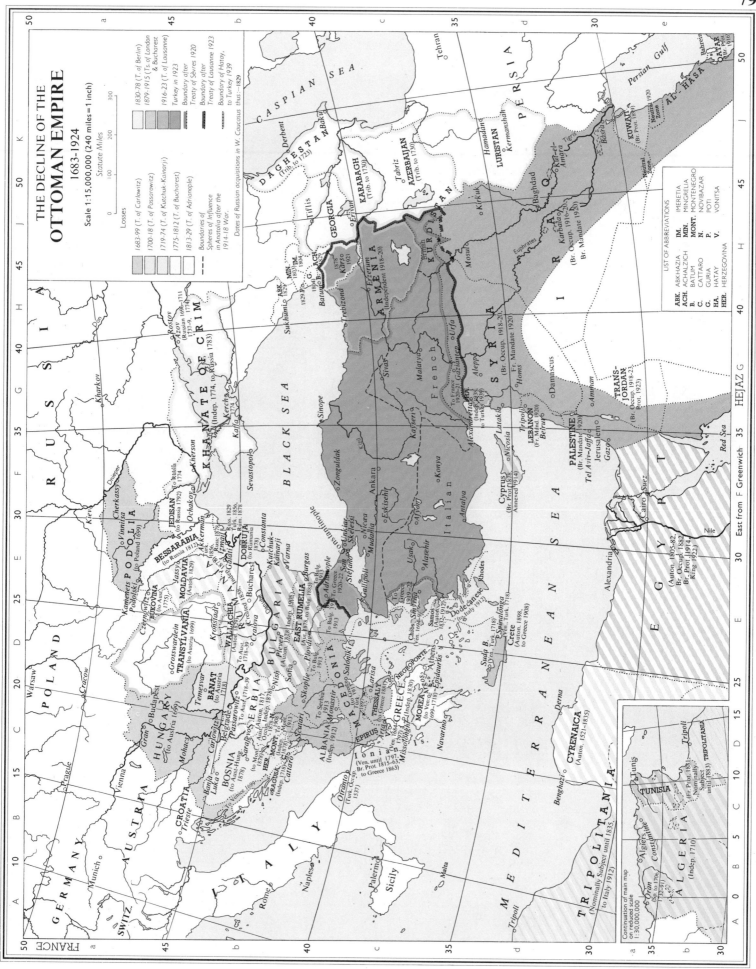

THE DECLINE OF THE
OTTOMAN EMPIRE
1683-1924

Scale 1:15,000,000 (240 miles=1 inch)

Statute Miles

0	100	200		300

Losses

1683-99 (T. of Carlowitz)
1700-18 (T. of Passarowitz)
1719-74 (T. of Kutchuk-Kainarji)
1775-1812 (T. of Bucharest)
1813-29 (T. of Adrianople)

1830-78 (T. of Berlin)
1879-1915 (Ts. of London & Bucharest)
1916-23 (T. of Lausanne)
Turkey in 1923

Boundary after Treaty of Sèvres 1920
Boundary after Treaty of Lausanne 1923
Boundary of Hatay, to Turkey 1939

Boundaries of Spheres of Influence in Anatolia after the 1914-18 War.

Dates of Russian acquisitions in W. Caucasus thus:—1829

LIST OF ABBREVIATIONS

ARK	ABKHAZIA	**IM.**	IMERETIA
ACH.	ACHALZICH	**MIN.**	MINGRELIA
B.	BATUM	**MONT.**	MONTENEGRO
C.	CATTARO	**N.**	NOVIBAZAR
	GURIA	**P.**	POTI
HA.	HATAY	**V.**	VONITSA
HER.	HERZEGOVINA		

Continuation of main map on reduced scale 1:30,000,000

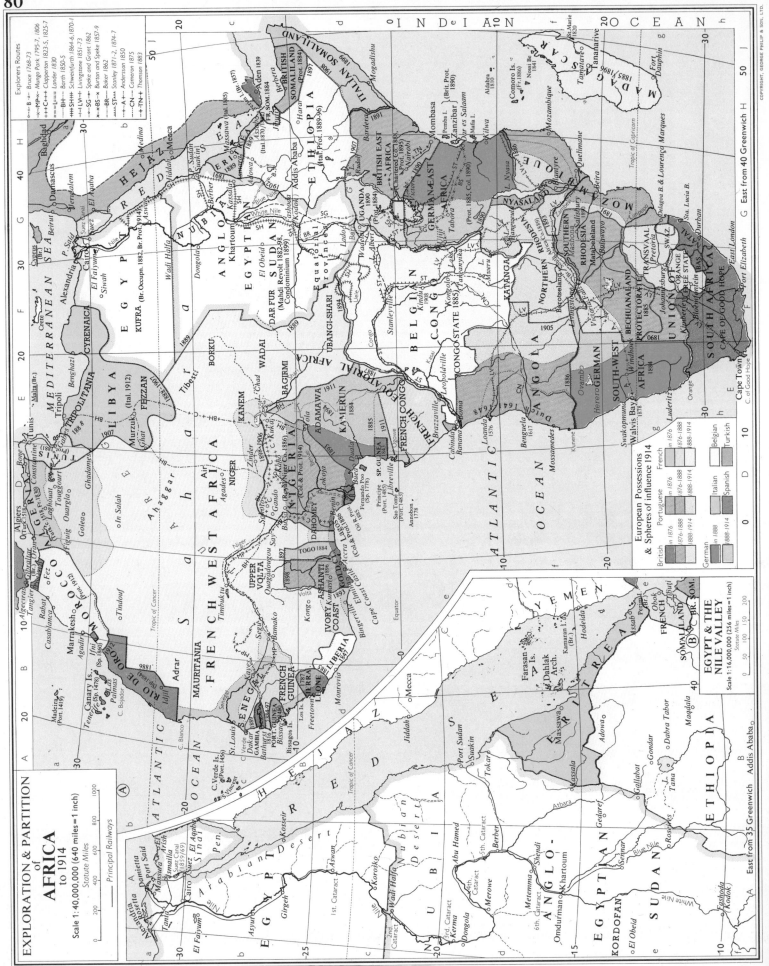

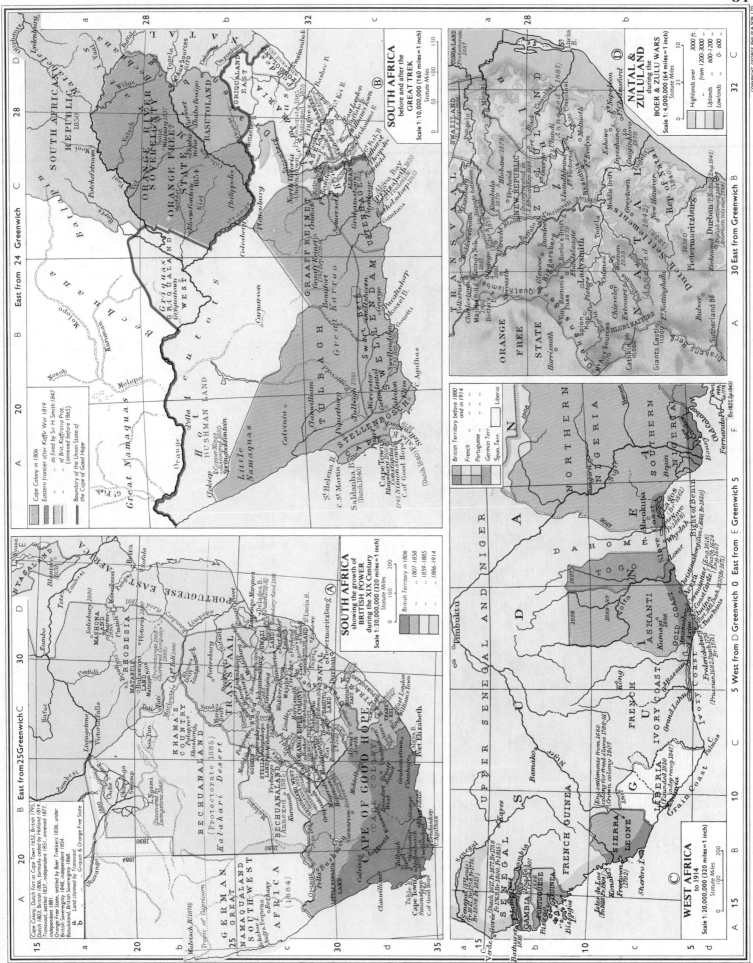

SOUTH AFRICA
before and after the
GREAT TREK

Scale 1:10,000,000 (160 miles=1 inch)

Statute Miles
0   50   100   150

**NATAL &
ZULULAND**
during the
BOER & ZULU WARS

Scale 1:4,000,000 (64 miles=1 inch)

Statute Miles
0   25   50

Highlands over .... 3000 ft.
Uplands .... from 1200-3000
     600-1200
Lowlands 0-600

COPYRIGHT. GEORGE PHILIP & SON, LTD.

Cape Colony in 1806

Eastern frontier after Kaffir War 1819
     .... as fixed by Sir H. Smith 1847
     .... of Brit. Kaffraria Prot.
          (annexed before 1865)

Boundary of the Union State of
the Cape of Good Hope

SOUTH AFRICA
showing the growth of
BRITISH POWER
during the XIX Century

Scale 1:20,000,000 (320 miles=1 inch)

Statute Miles
0   100   200

British Territory in 1806
     1807-1858
     1859-1885
     1886-1914

Cape Colony, Dutch fort at Cape Town 1652, British 1795,
Dutch 1803, British 1806, formally ceded by Holland 1814.
Transvaal, settled 1837, independent 1851, annexed 1877,
independent 1881.
Orange Free State, settled by Boer Trekkers 1836, under
British Sovereignty 1848, independent 1854.
Basutoland, British Sovereignty 1868.
a. Land claimed by Transvaal.
b. .... Griquas & Orange Free State.

WEST AFRICA
to 1914

Scale 1:20,000,000 (320 miles=1 inch)

Statute Miles
100   0   100   200

British Territory before 1880 ....
     and in 1914 ....
French ....
Portuguese ....
German Terr. ....
Span. Terr. ....
Liberia

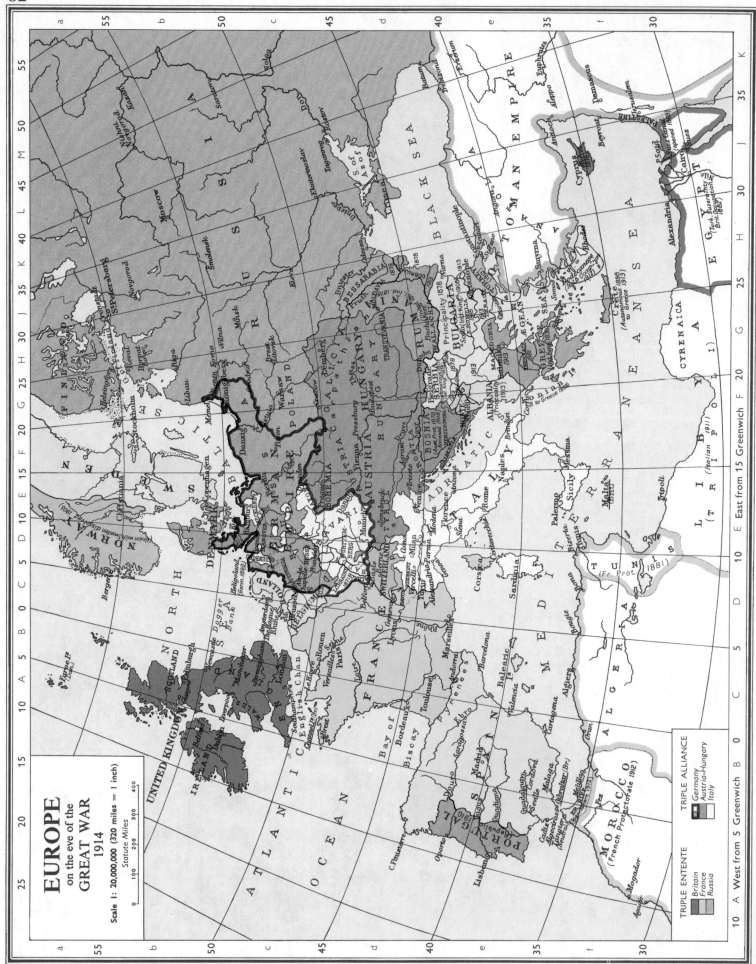

EUROPE
on the eve of the
GREAT WAR
1914

Scale 1: 20,000,000 (320 miles = 1 inch)

Statute Miles

0   100   200   300   400

TRIPLE ENTENTE

Britain
France
Russia

TRIPLE ALLIANCE

Germany
Austria-Hungary
Italy

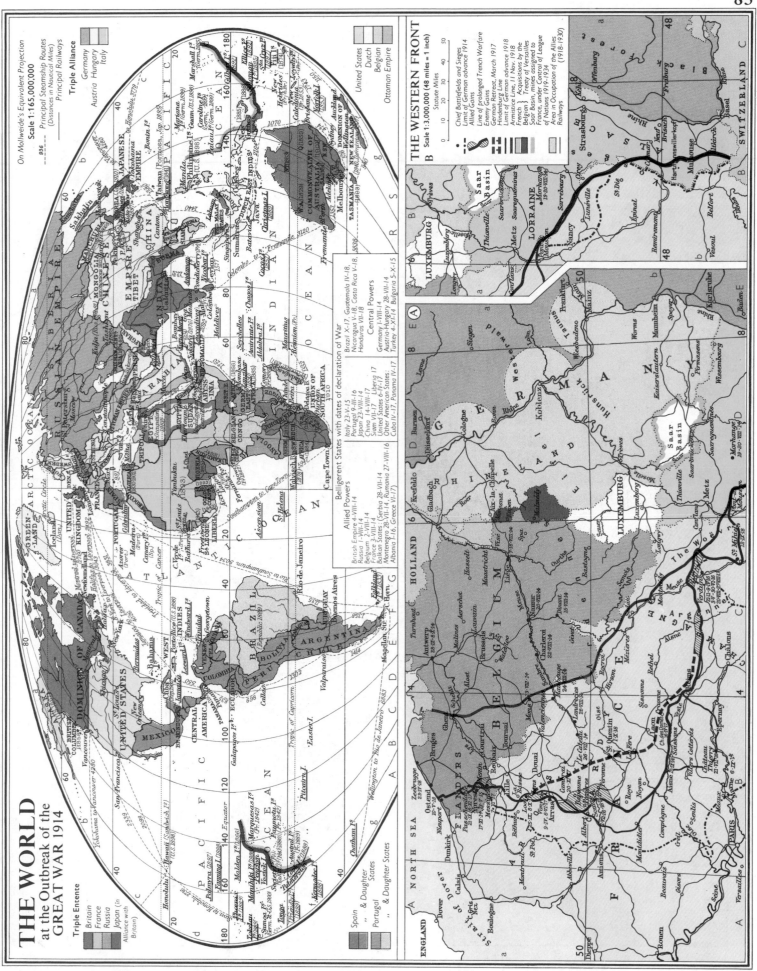

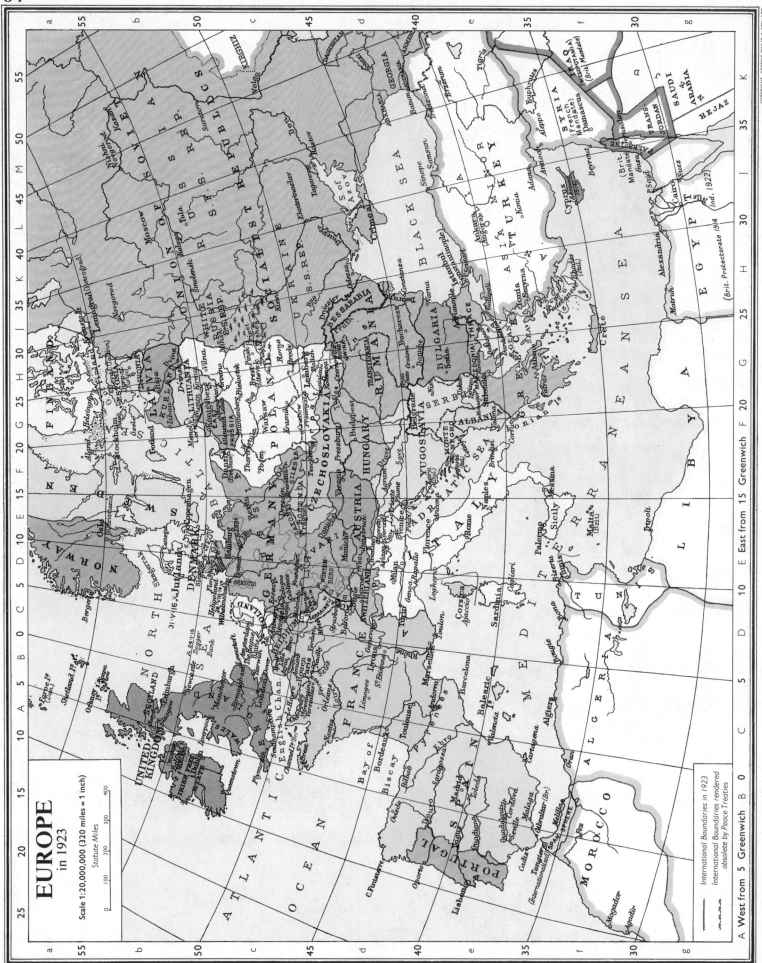

EUROPE
in 1923

Scale 1:20,000,000 (320 miles = 1 inch)

Statute Miles

0   100   200   300   400

International Boundaries in 1923
International Boundaries rendered
obsolete by Peace Treaties

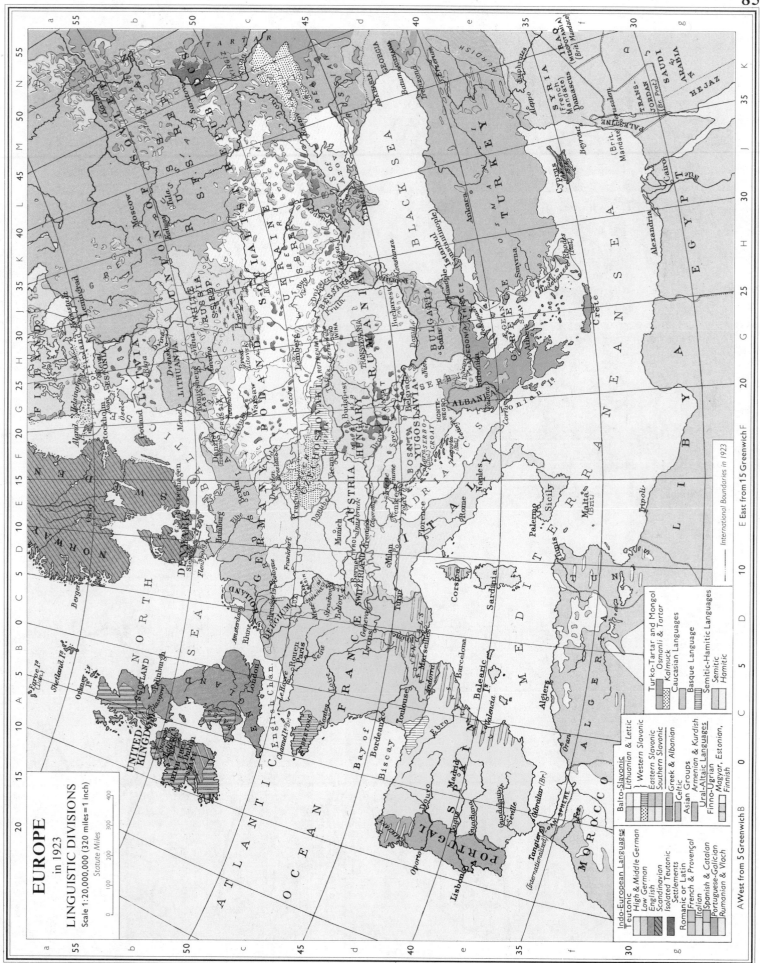

EUROPE
in 1923
LINGUISTIC DIVISIONS

Scale 1:20,000,000 (320 miles=1 inch)

Statute Miles

Indo-European Languages
Teutonic
High & Middle German
Low German
Scandinavian
English
Isolated Teutonic
Settlements
Romanic or Latin
French & Provençal
Italian
Spanish & Catalan
Portuguese-Galician
Rumanian & Vlach

Balto-Slavonic
Lithuanian & Lettic
Western Slavonic
Eastern Slavonic
Southern Slavonic
Greek & Albanian
Celtic
Armenian & Kurdish
Asian Groups
Ural-Altaic Languages
Finno-Ugrian
Magyar, Estonian,
Finnish

Turko-Tartar and Mongol
Osmanli & Tartar
Kalmuck
Caucasian Languages
Basque Language
Semitic-Hamitic Languages
Semitic
Hamitic

International Boundaries in 1923

A West from 5 Greenwich B   E East from 15 Greenwich F

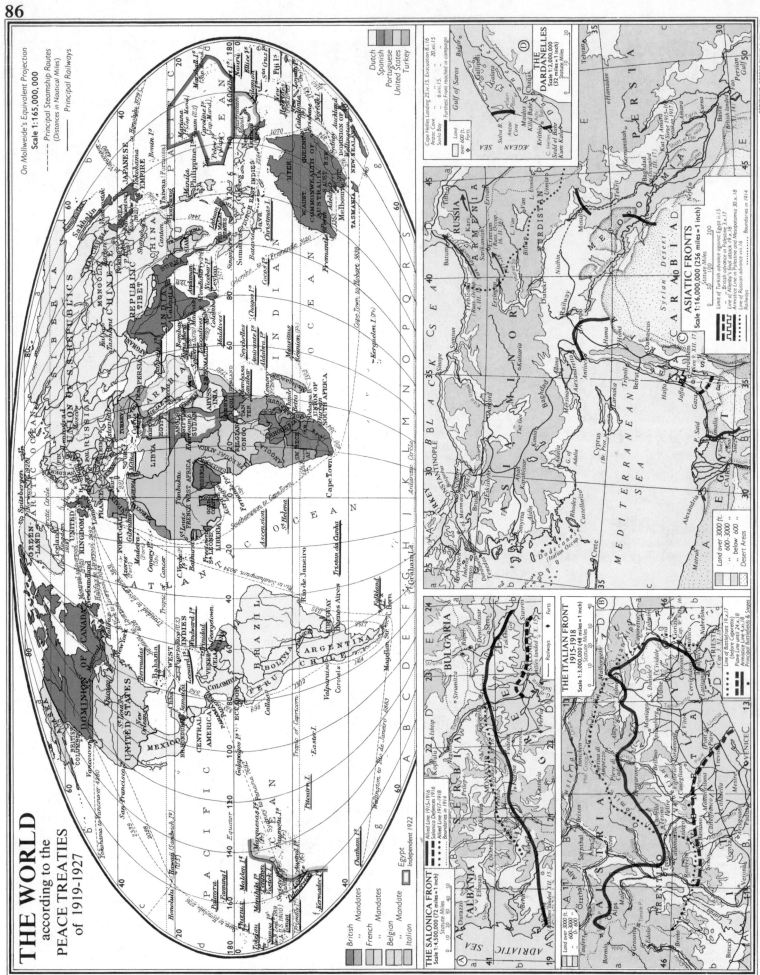

THE WORLD
according to the PEACE TREATIES of 1919-1927

On Mollweide's Equivalent Projection
Scale 1:165,000,000

---- Principal Steamship Routes
(Distances in Nautical Miles)
----- Principal Railways

British Mandates
French Mandates
Belgian Mandate
Italian Mandate

Dutch
Spanish
Portuguese
United States
Turkey

Egypt Independent 1922

THE SALONICA FRONT
Scale 1:4,500,000 (71 miles = 1 inch)
Statute Miles

Allied Line 1915-1916
Salonica Defences 1916
Boundaries in 1914

THE ITALIAN FRONT
1915-1918
Scale 1:3,000,000 (48 miles = 1 inch)
Statute Miles

Line of Battle front (9.x.17 (before Caporetto)
Piave Line until 24.x.18
Armistice Line 4.xi.18
Principal Battlefields & Sieges

Land over 3000 ft.
600-3000 ..
below 600 ..

THE DARDANELLES
Scale 1:2,000,000
(32 miles = 1 inch)
Statute Miles

Land over 600 ft.
Forts

Cape Helles Landing 25.iv.15 Evacuation 8.i.16
Anzac Cove ,, ,, 20.xii.15
Suvla Bay ,, 6.viii.15
,, Furthest Front reached in campaign

ASIATIC FRONTS
Scale 1:16,000,000 (256 miles = 1 inch)
Statute Miles

Limit of Turkish advance against Egypt ii.15
Line of Allenby's final attack 19.ix.18
Armistice Line in Palestine and Mesopotamia 30.x.18
Russian advance 16. iii.18
Russian advance in Palestine xi.17
Boundaries in 1914
Railways

Land over 3000 ft.
600-3000 ..
below 600 ..
Desert Areas

COPYRIGHT. GEORGE PHILIP & SON, LTD.

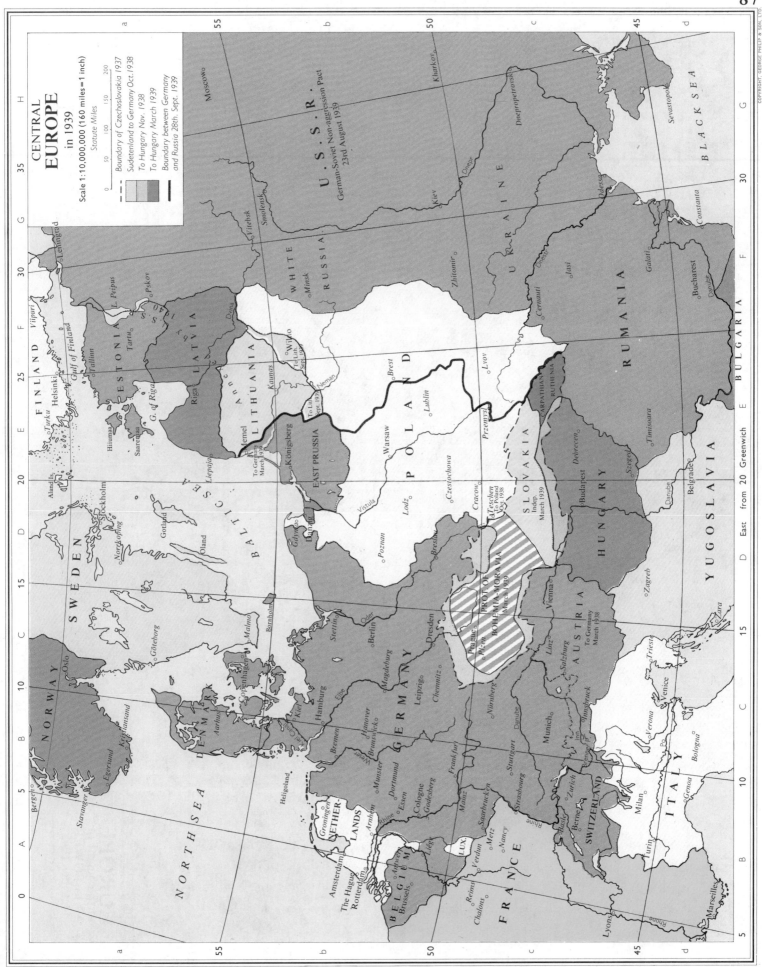

CENTRAL
EUROPE
in 1939

Scale 1:10,000,000 (160 miles=1 inch)

Statute Miles

0   50   100   150   200

Boundary of Czechoslovakia 1937
Sudetenland to Germany Oct.1938
To Hungary Nov. 1938
To Hungary March 1939
Boundary between Germany
and Russia 28th. Sept. 1939

U. S. S. R.

Moscow

Leningrad

WHITE

RUSSIA

Smolensk

Viebsk

Minsk

Kiev

Zhitomir

U K R A I N E

Kharkov

Dnepropetrovsk

Sevastopol

B L A C K   S E A

Constanta

Galati

Bucharest

Danube

BULGARIA

YUGOSLAVIA

Belgrade

Zagreb

Zara

R U M A N I A

Timisoara

Debrecen

Szeged

H U N G A R Y

Budapest

Vienna

A U S T R I A

CARPATHIAN

RUTHENIA

S L O V A K I A

Indep.
March 1939

Cernauti

Jasi

Lvov

Przemysl

P O L A N D

Warsaw

Lublin

Brest

Wilno

Cracow

Teschen
To Poland
Oct. 1938

PROT. OF
BOHEMIA-MORAVIA
March 1939

Prague

Plzen

Czestochowa

Breslau

Lodz

Poznan

Gdynia

Danzig

EAST PRUSSIA

Königsberg

Memel
To Germany
March 1939

Kaunas

LITHUANIA

Riga

L A T V I A

E S T O N I A

Tartu

Tallinn

Saaremaa

Hiiumaa

FINLAND

Viipuri

Helsinki

Turku

Åland Is.

Stockholm

Norrköping

Gotland

Öland

Gdynia

B A L T I C   S E A

Bornholm

Malmö

Copenhagen

Kiel

DENMARK

Aarhus

NORTH SEA

N O R W A Y

Oslo

Bergen

Kristiansand

Egersund

Stavanger

S W E D E N

Göteborg

Oder

Stettin

Berlin

Magdeburg

Hamburg

Bremen

Hanover

Brunswick

Dresden

Leipzig

Chemnitz

G E R M A N Y

Münster

Dortmund

Essen

Cologne

Godesberg

Frankfurt

Mainz

Saarbrücken

Metz

Nürnberg

Stuttgart

Munich

Salzburg

Linz

Innsbruck

SWITZERLAND

Zürich

Basle

Berne

ITALY

Milan

Turin

Genoa

Verona

Venice

Bologna

Trieste

FRANCE

Nancy

Verdun

Reims

Chalons

Strasbourg

Lyons

Marseilles

Rhone

LUX

BELGIUM

Brussels

Antwerp

Liège

NETHER-
LANDS

Amsterdam

The Hague

Rotterdam

Groningen

Arnhem

Helgoland

Vistula

Dnepr

Dniester

Danube

East   from 20   Greenwich

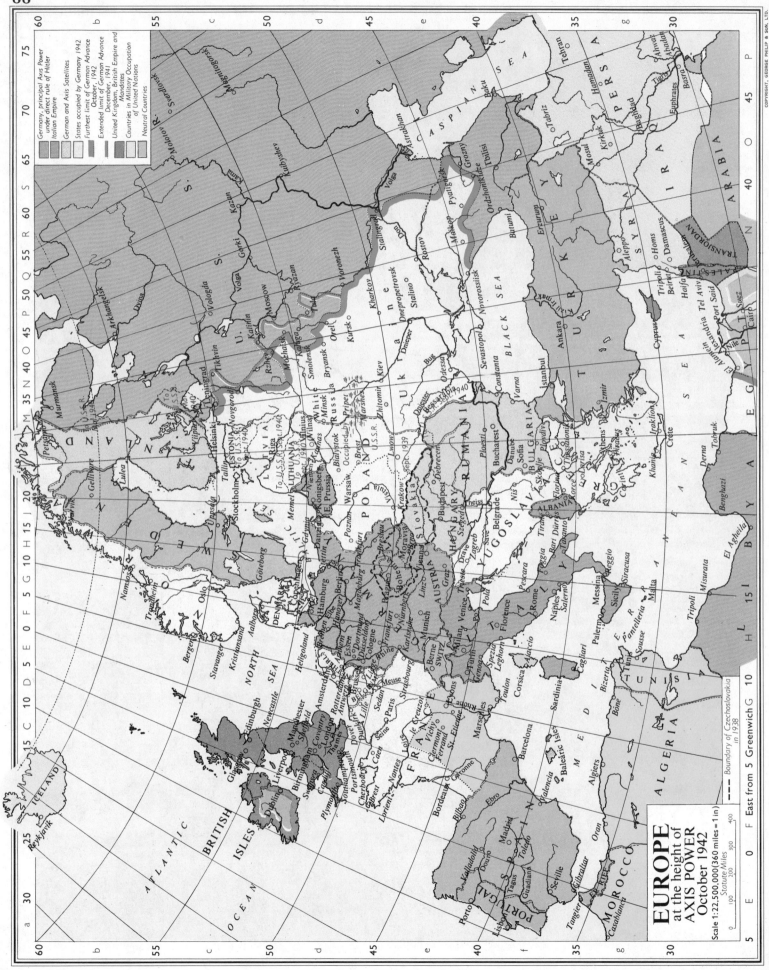

EUROPE
at the height of
AXIS POWER
October 1942

Scale 1:22,500,000(360 miles = 1 in)

Statute Miles
0 100 200 300 400

Germany, principal Axis Power
under direct rule of Hitler
Italian Empire

German and Axis Satellites

States occupied by Germany 1942
Furthest limit of German Advance
October, 1942
Extended limit of German Advance
December, 1941
United Kingdom, British Empire and
Mandates
Countries in Military Occupation
of United Nations
Neutral Countries

Boundary of Czechoslovakia
in 1938

East from 5 Greenwich G

COPYRIGHT, GEORGE PHILIP & SON, LTD.

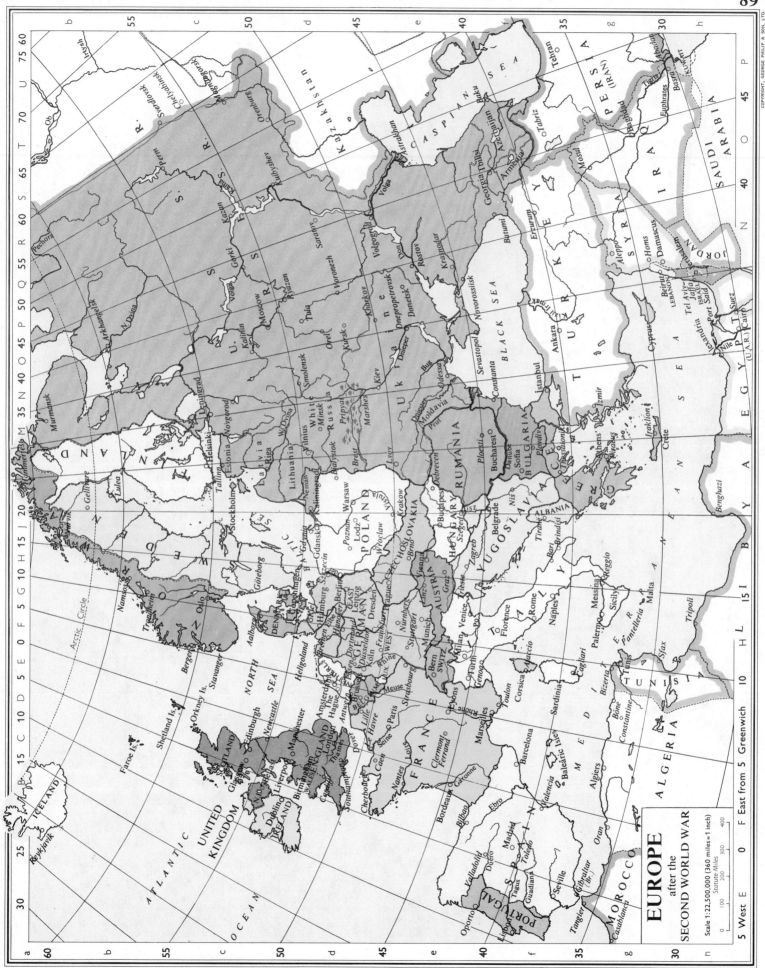

EUROPE
after the
SECOND WORLD WAR

Scale 1:22,500,000 (360 miles = 1 inch)

Statute Miles

0   100   200   300   400

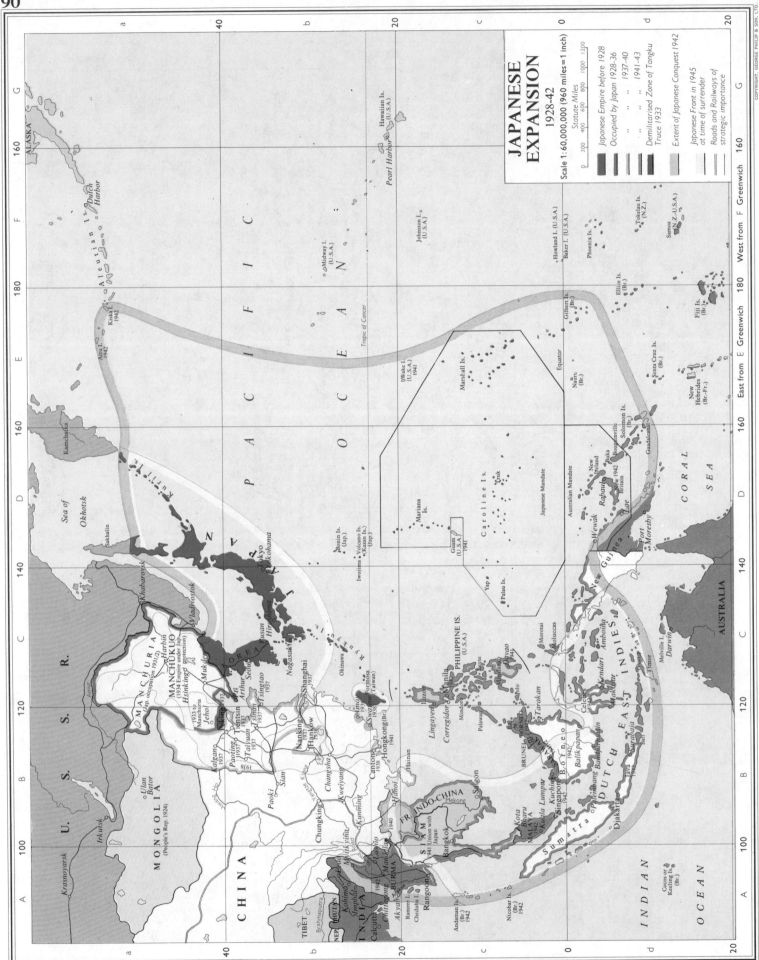

JAPANESE
EXPANSION
1928-42

Scale 1:60,000,000 (960 miles = 1 inch)

Statute Miles
0   200   400   600   800   1000   1200

Japanese Empire before 1928
Occupied by Japan 1928-36
"   "   "   1937-40
"   "   "   1941-43
Demilitarised Zone of Tangku
Truce 1933
Extent of Japanese Conquest 1942

Japanese Front in 1945
at time of surrender
Roads and Railways of
strategic importance

COPYRIGHT, GEORGE PHILIP & SON, LTD.

91

70   A   80   B   90   C   100   D   110   E   120   F   130   G   140   H   150

U.   S.   S.   R.

Omsk   Novosibirsk   Barnaul   Novokuznetsk   Irkutsk   L.   Baikal   Ulan Ude   Chita   Amur   Aleksandrovsk   Sakhalin

Karaganda   Semipalatinsk   Yenisei   Selenga   Khabarovsk

L. Balkhash   MONGOLIA   Ulan Bator   Kerulen   INNER   Harbin   (Pinkiang)   Vladivostok   Sapporo   Hokkaido

Alma Ata   Ili   Urumchi   People's Republic 1924   MONGOLIA   Changchun   Kirin   Hakodate

SINKIANG-ULGUR   Tarim   Hsi-Liao   Mukden   North   SEA   OF   JAPAN   Sendai   Niigata

CHINESE   REPUBLIC   Paotow   Peking   Shenyang   Lü-ta   Cease Fire Line   July 1953   KOREA   Kanazawa   Tokyo

KASHMIR   LADAKH   People's Republic   1949   Lanchow   Tientsin   (Dairen Pt. Arthur)   38th Parallel   Seoul   South   Pusan   Hiroshima   Kobe   Kyoto   Yokohama   Nagoya   Osaka

TIBET   Taiyuan   Tsinan   Tsingtao   Yellow Sea   Kitakyushu   Nagasaki   Kumamoto   Kagoshima

Indus   Invaded by Chinese forces 1950   Hwang-Ho   Sian   EAST   CHINA   SEA

Sutlej   NEPAL   Lhasa   Tsangpo   Nanking   Shanghai

Delhi   Kathmandu   BHUTAN   Chengtu   Yangtze-Kiang   Wuhan   Hangchow

Lucknow   Varanasi   Benares   Ganga   Chungking   Changsha   Nanchang   Foochow   RYUKYUS   Okinawa   (Under U.S. Control 1952)

INDIA   Br. Dom. 1947   Rep. within Commonwealth 1950   Kweiyang   Amoy   Taipei   TAIWAN   (Formosa)   Nationalist China 1950

Nagpur   Howrah   Calcutta   Kunming   Hungshui Ho   Quemoy   PACIFIC

BURMA   Mandalay   Nanning   Si-Kiang   Canton   Tainan   Hongkong   Macao   (Port.)   OCEAN

Bay   of   Bengal   Union of Burma, Indep. Rep. 1948   LAOS   North   Hanoi   Hainan   Luzon   PHILIPPINES   Indep. 1946

Madras   Chiangmai   Luang Prabang   Vientiane   Cease Fire Line   July 1954   Hué   Manila

Pondicherry   (To India 1954)   THAILAND   Bangkok   CAMBODIA   Indep. 1945/54   Phnom Penh   Indep. 1946/54   South   SOUTH   CHINA   SEA   Samar   Mindanao   Davao

CEYLON   (Indep. within the Commonwealth 1948)   Colombo   Saigon-Cholon   Palawan

Nicobar Is.   (to India)   Gulf of Siam   FEDERATION OF MALAYSIA   (1963)   Kota Kinabalu   SABAH   (North Borneo)   Celebes   Sea   Halmahera

MALAYA   Federation 1948, Indep. within Commonwealth 1957   Penang   Kuala Lumpur   Labuan   BRUNEI   Moluccas

Medan   Malacca   Singapore   Kuching   SARAWAK   Borneo   Sulawesi   (Celebes)   Ceram   West Irian

INDIAN   OCEAN   Simeulve   Nias   Padang   Siberut   Kalimantan   Buru

Palembang   INDONESIA   Bandjarmasin   Sumba   Flores   Timor   (Port.)

Djakarta   Semarang   Surabaja   Indep. Republic 1949   Java   Sea   Sunda   Sea   Sumbawa

Djokjakarta   Arafura   Sea

EASTERN
ASIA
1945-1969

Scale 1:30,000,000 (480 miles=1 inch)
Statute Miles
0   100   200   300   400   500
Principal Railways

80   B   90   C   100   East from 110 Greenwich   E   120   F   130   G

COPYRIGHT, GEORGE PHILIP & SON, LTD.

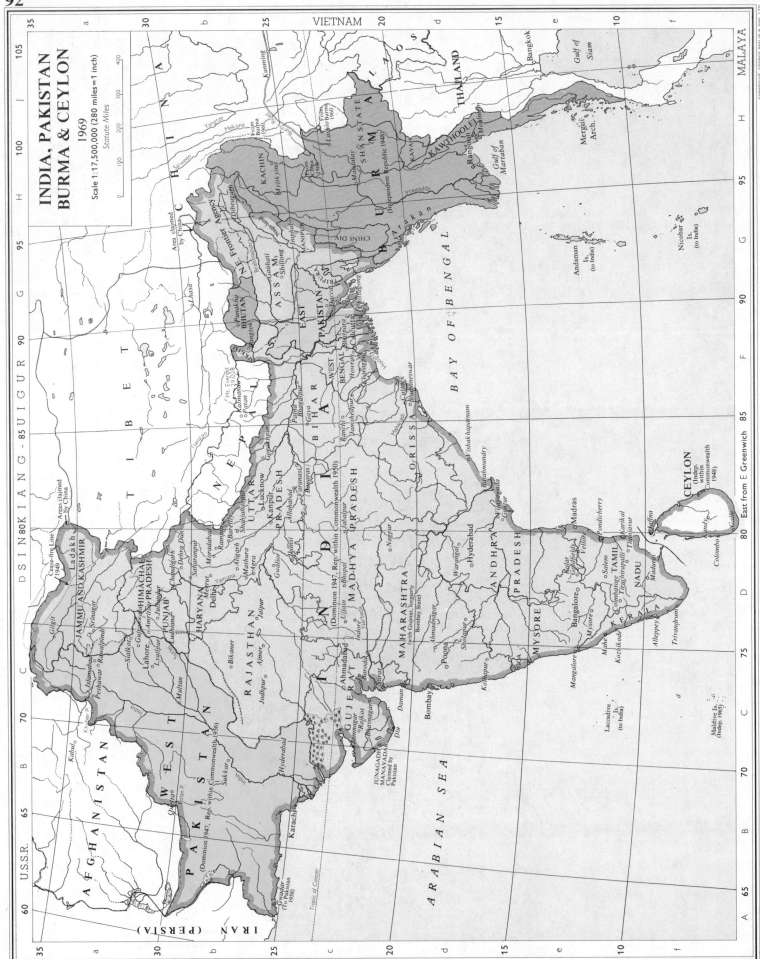

INDIA, PAKISTAN
BURMA & CEYLON
1969
Scale 1:17,500,000 (280 miles = 1 inch)
Statute Miles

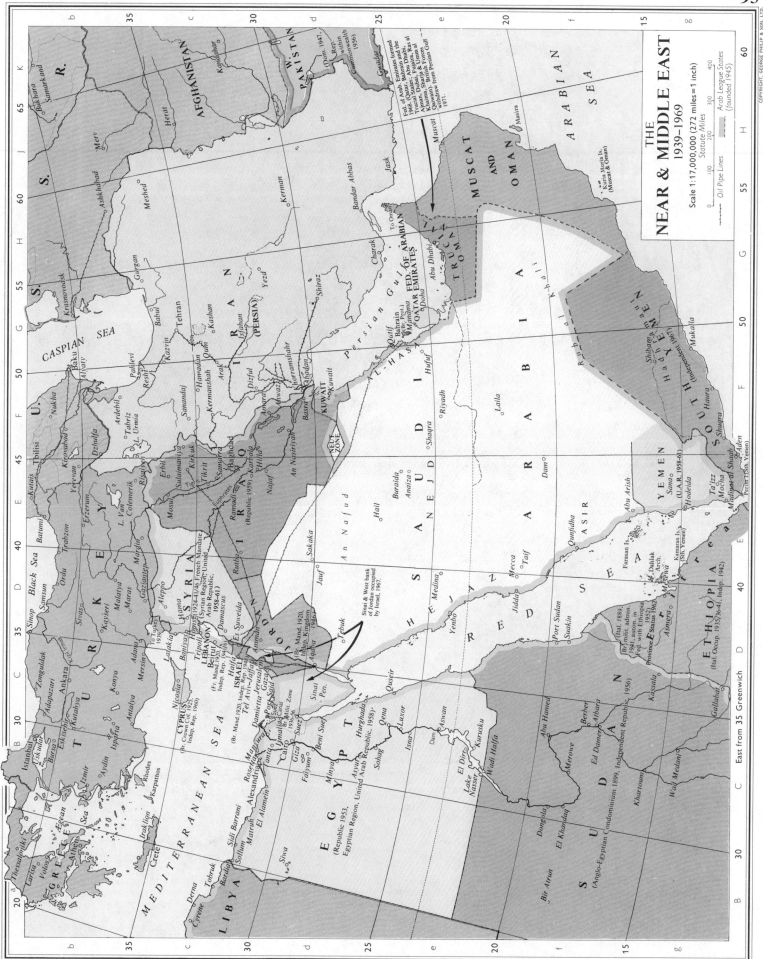

THE NEAR & MIDDLE EAST
1939-1969

Scale 1:17,000,000 (272 miles=1 inch)
Statute Miles

Oil Pipe Lines
Arab League States (founded 1945)

Fed. of Arab. Emirates formed 1971 (Qatar, Bahrain and the Trucial States : Fujaira, Abu Dhabi, Dubai, Sharja & Umm al Qaiwain, Ras al Khaima, British Forces withdraw from Persian Gulf 1971.

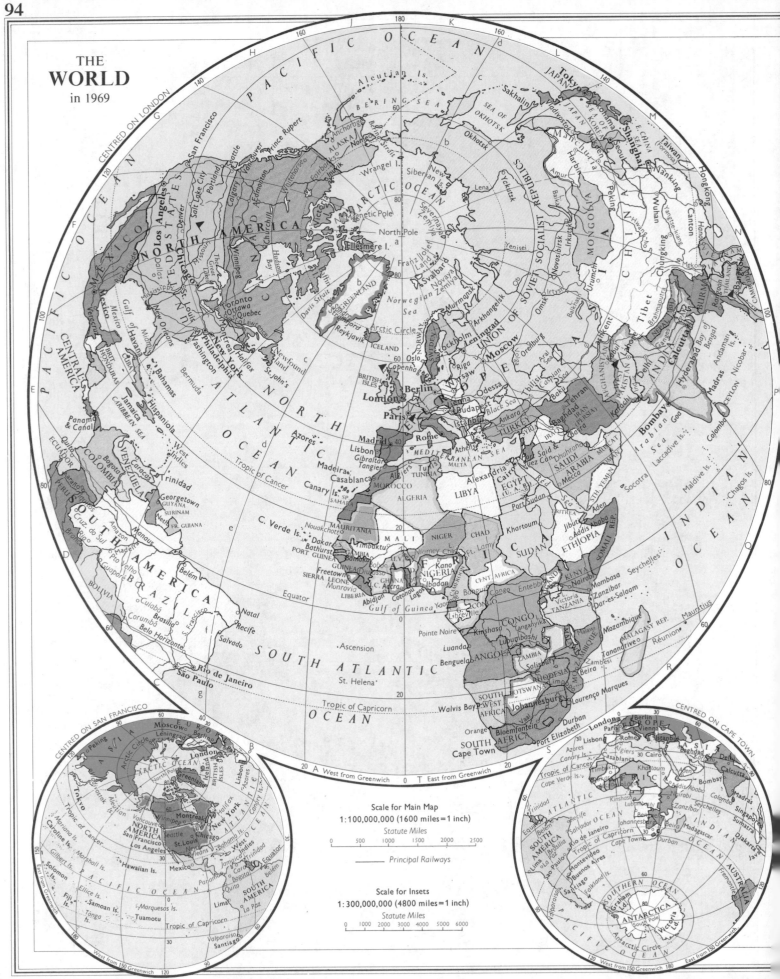

THE
WORLD
in 1969

PACIFIC OCEAN

CENTRED ON LONDON

Scale for Main Map
1:100,000,000 (1600 miles=1 inch)
Statute Miles
0   500   1000   1500   2000   2500

——— *Principal Railways*

Scale for Insets
1:300,000,000 (4800 miles=1 inch)
Statute Miles
0   1000   2000   3000   4000   5000   6000

CENTRED ON SAN FRANCISCO

CENTRED ON CAPE TOWN

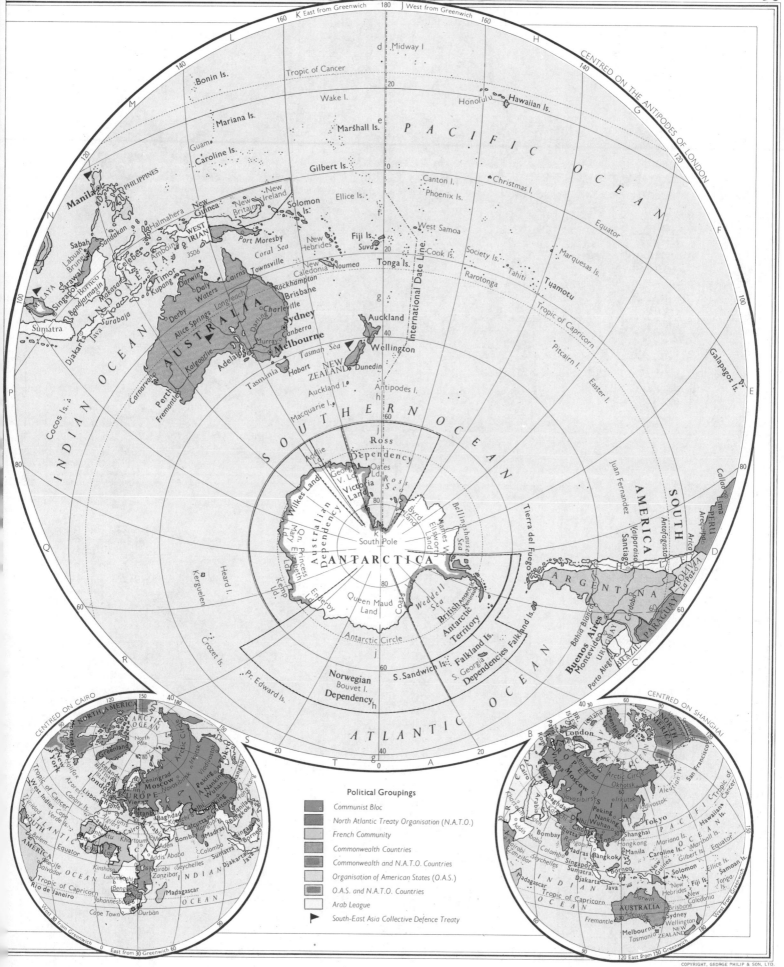

CENTRED ON THE ANTIPODES OF LONDON

East from Greenwich — **West from Greenwich**

PACIFIC OCEAN

d Midway I.

Tropic of Cancer

Bonin Is.

Wake I.

Honolulu • Hawaiian Is.

Mariana Is.

Marshall Is. e

Guam

Caroline Is.

Gilbert Is.

Canton I.

Christmas I.

Equator

Manila

PHILIPPINES

Ellice Is.

Phoenix Is.

Halmahera

New Guinea

New Ireland

Solomon Is.

f

West Samoa

Marquesas Is.

Sabah

Labuan Brunei Sarawak Sandakan

Borneo

WEST IRIAN

New Britain

New Hebrides

Fiji Is.

Society Is.

Tahiti

Tuamotu

MALAYA

Singapore

Bandjarmasin

Celebes Macassar

Amboina 3506

Port Moresby

Coral Sea

New Caledonia

Noumea

Suva

Tonga Is.

Cook Is.

Rarotonga

Tropic of Capricorn

Sumatra

Djakarta Java Surabaja

INDONESIA

Timor Kupang

Darwin Daly Waters

Cairns Townsville

Rockhampton

Brisbane

Galapagos Is.

INDIAN OCEAN

Derby

Nice Springs Longreach

Charleville

AUSTRALIA

Darling Murray

Canberra

Sydney

Melbourne

Auckland

Pitcairn I.

Easter I.

Kalgoorlie

Adelaide

Tasman Sea

Wellington

NEW ZEALAND

Dunedin

SOUTH

AMERICA

Cocos Is.

Carnarvon

Perth Fremantle

Tasmania

Hobart

Auckland I.

Antipodes I.

h

Juan Fernandez

Callao Lima

PERU

Arequipa

Macquarie I.

SOUTHERN OCEAN

Valparaiso Santiago

Antofagasta

Arica

BOLIVIA La Paz

Heard I.

j

Ross

Dependency

Oates Ld

Ross Sea

ARGENTINA

Córdoba

PARAGUAY

Kerguelen

Adélie

George V Ld

Victoria Land

Byrd Land

James W Ellsworth Land

Bellingshausen Sea

Tierra del Fuego

Bahía Blanca

Buenos Aires

URUGUAY

Montevideo

BRAZIL

Porto Alegre

Wilkes Land

Australian Dependency

Princess Mary Ld

Elizabeth Ld

South Pole

k

ANTARCTICA

Weddell Sea

British Antarctic Territory

Crozet Is.

Kemp Ld

Enderby Ld

Queen Maud Land

Coats Ld

Antarctic Peninsula

S. Falkland Is.

Dependencies Falkland Is.

Pt. Edward Is.

Antarctic Circle

j

Norwegian Bouvet I. Dependency h

S. Sandwich Is.

S. Georgia

ATLANTIC OCEAN

Political Groupings

Communist Bloc

North Atlantic Treaty Organisation (N.A.T.O.)

French Community

Commonwealth Countries

Commonwealth and N.A.T.O. Countries

Organisation of American States (O.A.S.)

O.A.S. and N.A.T.O. Countries

Arab League

► South-East Asia Collective Defence Treaty

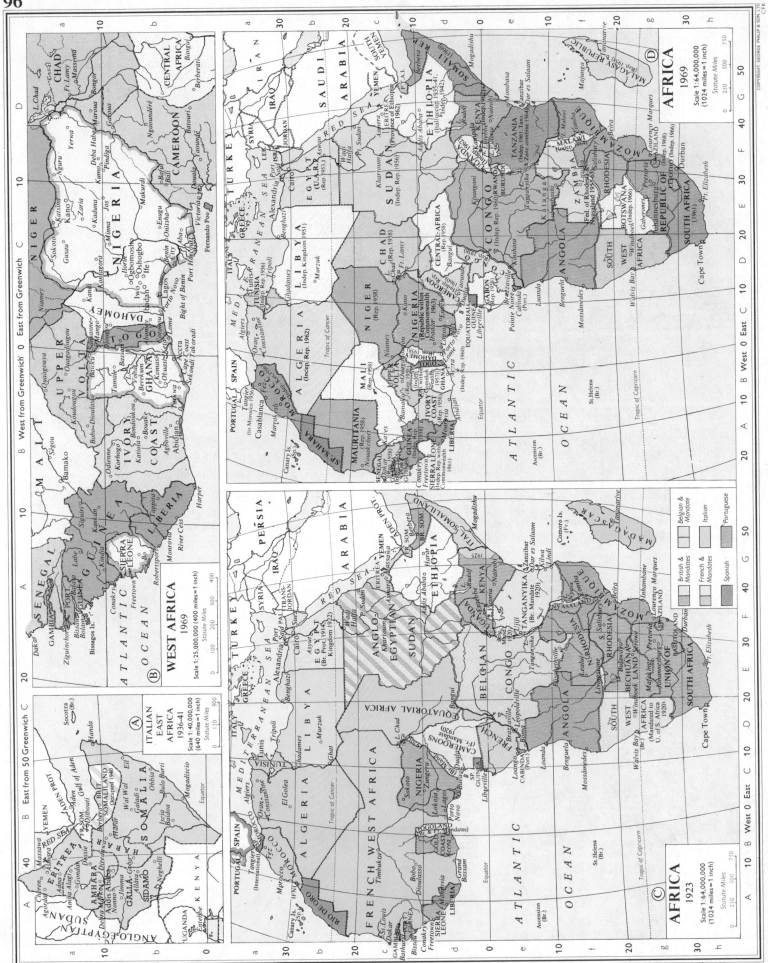

WEST AFRICA
1969

Scale 1:25,000,000 (400 miles=1 inch)

Statute Miles
0 100 200 300 400

ITALIAN EAST AFRICA
1936-41

Scale 1:40,000,000 (640 miles=1 inch)

Statute Miles
0 150 300

AFRICA
1969

Scale 1:64,000,000 (1024 miles=1 inch)

Statute Miles
0 250 500 750

AFRICA
1923

Scale 1:64,000,000 (1024 miles=1 inch)

Statute Miles
0 250 500 750

British & Mandates	Belgian & Mandate
French & Mandates	Italian
Spanish	Portuguese

COPYRIGHT GEORGE PHILIP & SON LTD

CFK

INDEX

Note.—Each map in the Atlas is divided into squares by the lines of latitude and longitude, and these squares are indicated by Reference Letters in the borders of the map. These Reference Letters follow each name in the Index after the Map Number, and indicate in which square each place will be found. Thus: 'Aargau, 29B, Ca' shows that Aargau will be found on Map 29B, in the square indicated by the Reference Letters 'Ca'.

ABBREVIATIONS

Abp. – *Archbishopric*
Arch. – *Archipelago*
B. – *Bay*
Bp. – *Bishopric*
Bur. – *Burgraviate*
C. – *Cape*

Cal. – *Caliphate*
Co. – *County*
D. – *Duchy*
Dist. – *District*
Eccl. – *Ecclesiastical*
Elec. – *Electorate*

G.D. – *Grand Duchy*
I.(s) – *Island(s)*
King. – *Kingdom*
L. – *Lake*
Ld. – *Land*
Land. – *Landgraviate*

M. – *March, Mark*
Marg. – *Margraviate*
Marq. – *Marquisate*
Mt.(s) – *Mount, Mountain(s)*
Mte. – *Monte*
Oc. – *Ocean*

Pr. – *Principality*
Prot. – *Protectorate*
Prov. – *Province*
Pt. – *Point*
R. – *River*
Reg – *Region*

Rep. – *Republic*
S. – *Seigneurie*
Sd. – *Sound*
St. – *State*
Terr. – *Territory*
V. – *Viscounty*

AACHEN, 8, Da; 12, Fd; 38, Gc
Aalborg, 26, Db; 88, Gb
Aalen, 30, Hd; 53, Hc
Aar, R., 29B, Ba
Aarau, 29B, Ca
Aargau, canton, 29B, Ca
Aargau, reg., 10, Ce
Aarhus, 26, Db
Aba, 96B, Cb
Abadan, 93, Fc
Abancay, 68, Bd
Abbasid Caliphate, 8, He
Abbendone (Abingdon), 13, Ee
Abbéville, 38, Dc; 83A, Aa
Abbotsbury, 36, Dg
Abedesberie (Abbotsbury), 13, Df
Abenaki, 56, Fa
Abensberg, 29A, Da
Abeokuta, 81C, Ec
Aberdeen, 14, Fb; 37A, Cb
Aberdeen. co., 37A, Cb
Aberdour, 14, Eb
Aberfeldy, 37A, Cb; 49A, Cb
Aberfoyle, 37A, Bb; 48B, Aa
Abergavenny, 27, Ce
Abergwili, 27, Be; 28A, Bc
Aberlleiniog, 13, Bc
Abernethy, 14, Ec
Abidjan, 96B, Bb
Abingdon, 27, Ee
Abitibi, L., 45A, Ba
Abkhazia, 79, Hb
Åbo, 26, Fa
Abomey, 96B, Cb
Abone (Sea Mills), 3A, De
Abotrites, 8, Ea
Aboukir B., 64, Jf
Abraham, Heights of, 56A
Abrantes, 63, Ac
Abruzzi, reg., 32A, Ec
Abruzzo, 22, Ec
Abu Arish, 93, Ef
Abu Dhabi, 93, Ge
Abu Hamed, 80B, Ad
Abus Fl. (The Humber), 3A, Gc
Abydos, 19, Dd
Abydus, 4B, Hc
Abyssinia (Ethiopia), 6, Ed
Acadia, 45A, Ea; 55B, Db
Acajutla, 55B, Be
Acapulco, 43A, Cc
Accia, 22, Dc
Accompong, 43A, Ec
Accra, 81C, Dc
Acerenza, 22, Fc
Acerenza, eccl. prov., 22, Fc
Achaia, 1, Ed
Achaia, Pr. of, 19, Ce
Achalzich, 79, Hb
Achi Baba, 86D
Achill I., 15, Ac
Achonry, 15, Cb
Achusi (Pensacola), 43A, Da
Acklin I., 43A, Eb
Acqui, 20, Hf; 23B, Bb
Acra (Acre), 13, Gd
Acre, 16, Kf
Acre (Akko), 18C, Cf
Acre, terr., 68, Bc
Acton Burnell, 27, Dd
Actune (Acton), 13, Dc
Adalia, 6, Eb; 86C, Bb
Adalia, G. of, 86C, Bb
Adamawa, 80A, Bd
Adana (Aden), 1, Gf
Adana, Turkey, 18C, Ca
Adapazari, 93, Ca
Adda, R., 5, Bb
Addis Ababa, 96A, Ab
Adelaide, Australia, 77, Fl
Adelaide, S. Africa, 81B, C
Adélie Land, 69C
Adelingle (Athelney), 13, De
Adelsberg, 39, Lf
Aden, 80A, Hc; 93, Fg
Aden, G. of, 96A, Ba
Adige, R., 5, Cb; 86B, Bd
Adirondack Mts., 57, Ea
Admiralty Is., 77, Hb

Adna, 96A, Aa
Adour, R., 11, Ce; 63, Ea
Adowa, 80B, Be
Adramyttium, 19, De
Adrar, 80A, Bb
Adrian, 70, Fc
Adrianople, 78, Fe
Adriatic Sea, 5, Ec
Adwalton Moor, 48A, Cc
Adzharia, 84, Ld
Ægean Sea, 78, Ef
Ægean Theme, 9, He
Ægina, 78, Dg
Ægyptus, 2, Jg
Aegidius & Syagrius, King. of, 8, Ib
Aerschot, 83A, C2
Aesica (Great Chesters), 3C
Aesium, 5B, Bb
Afghan Supremacy, 59A, Ba
Afghanistan, 61B, Bb; 92, Aa
Afiun Karahissar, 86C, Bb
Afyon, 79, Fc
Agades, 80A, Dc
Agadir, 80A, Ba; 82, Af
Agali, 22, Bc
Agamenticus (York), 45B, Db
Agawam (Ipswich), 45B, Db
Agde, 11, Ee
Agder, 12, Fb
Agemundrenesse (Amundreness), 18, Dc
Agen, 11, Dd; 17A, Cd
Agenais, 17, Ff
Aggersborg, 12, Gb
Aggershuus (Christiania), 34, Ea
Aghadoe, 15, Bd
Aghlabids, 8, Dd
Aghlabids, King. of, 6B, Ca
Agincourt, 28D, Da
Agnadello, 32A, Cb
Agordat, 96A, Aa
Agra, 73, Cb
Agraca, Mts., 63B
Agram, 21, Mf; 39, Lf
Agrigentum (Girgenti), 5, Df
Aguilar, 23D, Ca
Agulhas, C., 81B, Bc
Ahausen, 29A, Da
Ahmadabad, 73, Bc; 92, Cc
Ahmadnagar, 59A, Bd; 92, Cd
Ahrensböck, 65F, Ba
Ahwaz, 6A, Db; 93, Fc
Aidin, 78, Fg; 86C, Ab
Aigle, 29B, Ab
Aiguesmortes, 20, Fg
Aiguillon, 53, De
Ailla, 6A, Bc; 18C, Cj
Ailech, 7A, Aa
Ailsa Craig, 49A, Bc
Aimargues, 38, Fg
Ain, R., 29A, Dd
Aintab, 18C, Ea
Air, 80A, Dc
Airds Moss, 49A, Bc
Aire, Flanders, 17, Gc
Aire, Gascony, 22, Bc
Aire, R., 7C, Cb
Airgialla, 7A, Ba
Aisne, R., 17, Hd; 83A, Bb
Aix, 11, Fe
Aix la Chapelle, 10, Bc
Ajaccio, 30, Hg; 84, Dd
Ajmere, 73, Bb
Ajnadain, 6A, Ab
Akaroa, 77A
Akeman Street, 3A, Ee
Akerman, 51, Gd; 78, Hb
Akhaltsikh, 61, Ff
Akhlat, 19, Ge
Akko (Acre), 18C, Cf
Akmolinsk, 74, Fc
Akpatok I., 71, Ha
Akyab, 90, Ac
al Anbar, 6A, cb
al Dahna, 6, Fc

Al-Hasa, 79, Je
al Jawf, 6, Ec
al Kurah, 6A, Cb
al Nufud, 6, Fc
al Raqqah, 6A, Ba
al Ruha, 6A, Ba
Alabama, R., 56, Bd; 57A, Bc
Alabama, st., 72, Cc
Alagoas, 68, Fc
Alais, 30, Ff
Åland Is., 26, Ea
Alamanni, 7A, Fb
Alani, 2, Lc
Alans, 6, Fa; 19, Gd
Alarcos, 23C, Cc
Alasehir, 79, Ec
Alaska, 69B; 71A, Ba
Alaska Pen., 71A, Bb
Alatri, 22A
Alauna (Maryport), 3A, Cb
Alava, 23C, Da
Alba, 5, Ab
Alba de Tormes, 63, Cb
Alban, 7C, Aa; 14, Dc
Albania, 78, Be
Albanian Pr., 24, Fe
Albanians, 18B, Cb
Albano, 22A
Albaracin, 22, Bc; 23C, Eb
Albazin, 74, Lc
Albemarle, 45B, Ae
Albemarle Sd., 57, Ce
Albert, 83A, Ba
Albert, L., 80A, Fd
Alberta, 70, Cb
Albi, 11, Ee; 22, Dc
Albiac, 38, Df
Albis, R., 2, Fc
Albistan, 19, Fe
Albon, 30, Ff
Albret, 17, Ef
Albret, S. of, 30, Cf
Albuera, 23D, Bc; 63, Bb
Albury, 77, Hi
Alcacer do Sal, 23C, Ac
Alcala, 22, Bc; 63, Db
Alcala de Henares, 23C, Db
Alcaniz, 63, Eb
Alcantara, Brazil, 68, Ec
Alcantara, Spain, 23C, Bc; 63, Bc
Alcazar, 34, Be
Alchester, 3A, Ee
Alcira, 23C, Ec
Alclyde, 7B, Aa
Alclyde (Dumbarton), 14, Dd
Alcoboça, 22, Ad
Aldabra, 80A, He
Aldbury, 36, Ff
Aldea de Ponte, 63, Bb
Alderney, 17, Dd
Aleksandrovsk, 91, Ha
Alemquer, 63B
Alemtejo, 23C, Ac; 63, Bc
Alençon, 11, Db
Alençon, D. of, 30, Dd
Alenuihaha Chan., 75D, Cb
Aleppo (Haleb), 18C, Eb
Aleria, 5, Bc; 53, Bf
Alessandria, 32A, Cb
Alet, 11, Bb; 53, Ef
Aleutian Is., 71A, Ab
Alexandretta, 18C, Cb
Alexandria, Egypt, 80B, Aa
Alexandria, Louisiana, 72, Bc
Alexandria, Virginia, 57, Cd
Alexandrovsk, 74, Dd
Alford, 37A, Cb
Algarve, 23C, Ad; 63, Ad
Algarve de Alem Mar, 47, Ae
Algeciras, 23C, Cd; 63A
Algeria, 24, Cf; 80A, Da
Algeria, Pashalik of, 47, Ce
Algiers, 34, Ce; 80A, Da

Al-Hasa
Algiers, Sultanate of, 34, De
Algoa B., 81B, Cc
Algonkins, 45A, Ca
Alhandra, 63B
Alicante, 23C, Ec; 63, Ec
Alice Springs, 77, Ef
Alids, King. of, 6B, Ga
Alife, 21A, Cb; 23B, Ed
Aligarh, 59C, Cb; 92, Db
Aliwal, 73, Ca
Aliwal North, 81A, Cd
Aljubarrota, 23D, Ac
Aljustro, 23C, Ad
Alkmaar, 46A, Db
Allahabad, 73, Db
Allata, 96A, Ab
Allatoona, 72A, Aa
Allegheny Mts., 57, Bd
Allegheny, R., 45A, Ca
Allemanni, 2, Ed; 4A, Db
Allen, Bog of, 15, Ec
Allen, L., 15, Cb
Allenstein, 84, Gb
Alleppey, 92, Df
Aller, R., 10, Cb; 55A, Hb
Allerdale, 28B, Bc
Allier, R., 11, Ed
Allstedt, 39C, Bb
Allumette Is., 45A, Ba
Alma Ata, 91, Ab
Almada, 23D, Ac
Almalik, 25, Hb
Almanza, 47, Be; 63, Ec
Almaraz, 63, Cc
Almeida, 23C, Bb; 63, Bb
Almeria, 22, Bd; 23C, Dd
Almina, C., 63A
Almissa, 22, Fc
Almohad Empire, 18A, Ac
Almonacid, Aragon, 63, Eb
Almonacid, New Castile, 63, Dc
Almora, 73, Cb
Almoravids, 16, Be
Aln, R., 28B, Db
Alnwick, 13, Ea
Alost, 46A, Cd
Alpes, 1, Cc; 2, Fd
Alps, The, 5, Ca; 10, De
Alpuente, 23C, Ec
Alresford, 27, Ee
Alsace, 10, Bd; 39B, Db
Alsace-Lorraine, 65D, Ab
Alsebruge (Axbridge), 13, De
Alsek, R., 71B, Ba
Alsen, 60B, Ba; 65F, Aa
Alsen Sd., 65F, Aa
Alsh, L., 49A, Bb
Alston, 13, Db
Alt, R., 78, Ec
Alt Breisach, 39B, Db
Altenburg, 10, Fd; 21, Kc
Altenkirchen, 53, Gb
Altkirch, 39B, Dc; 83B, Bb
Altmark, 30, Jb; 60A, Cb
Altomünster, 22, Eb
Alton, England, 27, Fe
Alton, Illinois, 72, Cb
Altona, 51, Bc; 65F, Ab
Altorf, 29B, Cb
Altranstadt, 50, Cc
Aluta, R., 19, Cd; 78, Ec
Alvarado, 43A, Cc
Alvertune (Allerton, North-allerton), 13, Eb
Alwar, 73, Cb
Alwinestune (Carisbrooke), 13, Ef
Alyaty, 93, Fb
Alyth, 37A, Cb
Amadeus, L., 77, Ef
Amalfi, 5, Ed
Amami-Oshima, 75, Dc
Amapa, 68, Db
Amara, 86C, Ec; 93, Fc
Amarante, 63, Ab
Amarapura, 73, Gc
Amasia, 9, Kd
Amasra, 24, Je
Amastris, 19, Ed
Amatola Mts., 81B, Cc

Amazon, R., 68, Dc
Amazonas, 68, Cc
Amba Alagi, 96A, Aa
Ambala, 73, Ca
Amberg, 29A, Da
Amboina, 52C, Cb; 90, Cd
Amboise, 11, Dc
Ambra, 32E, Bb
Ambresberie (Amesbury), 13, Ee
Ambur, 59D
Amelia, 57, Ce
Ameland, 46A, Ea
Amelia, 57, Ce
Ameria, 5B, Bb
Amersfoort, 46A, Eb
Amersham, 27, Fe
Amhara, 96A, Aa
Amherst, 73, Gd
Amichel, 43A, Cb
Amida, 2, Mf; 6A, Ca
Amida (Diarbekr), 33A, Fc
Amiens, 11, Eb; 83A, Bb
Amirante Is., 83, Me
Amisus, 18B, Fb; 24, Ke
Amiterno, 21A, Ba
Amman, 79, Gd
Amorgos, 78, Fg
Amorium, 9, Je
Amoy, 91, Ed
Ampezzo, 86B, Ca
Ampurias, 23C, Ga
Amritsar, 73, Ba
Amsterdam, 31A, Ca; 46A, Db
Amsterdam, I., 42B
Amu Darya, R., 61B, Ba
Amur, R., 25, Ma; 91, Fa
An Nafud, 93, Ed
An Nasiriyah, 93, Fc
Anadirsk, 42, Aa
Anadyr, 74, Qb
Anagni, 22A; 32A, Ed
Anahuac, 43A, Cc
Anaiza, 93, Ed
Anamaboe, 81C, Dc
Anapa, 61, Ef
Anas, R., 2, Bf
Anatolia, 33A, Dc; 64, Jf
Anatolic Theme, 9, Je
Ancénis, 20, Ce
Anchialus, 8, Hc
Anchorage, 71A, Ca
Anchu, 76B, Cb
Ancona, 5, Dc
Ancona, M. of, 21, Kg
Ancud, 68, Bg
Ancyra, 2, Ke; 8, Jd
Andalusia, 23C, Cd; 63, Cd
Andaman Is., 73, Fe
Andastes, 45B, Bc
Andechs, 20, Je
Anderida (Pevensey), 3A, Gf
Anderida Silva, 3A, Ff
Andernach, 10, Bc
Anderson, 72, Ec
Andersonville, 72, Dc
Andes, 68, Bc
Andhra, 1, Kf
Andhra Pradesh, 92, Dd
Andorra, 30, Dg; 63, Fa
Andover, 27, Ee
Andredsweald (The Weald), 13, Ge
Andria, 21A, Db
Andros, I., 78, Eg
Andros Is., 43A, Eb
Androscoggin, R., 45B, Da
Andrusov, 50, Gc; 54, Jb
Andujar, 23C, Cc; 63, Cc
Angara, R., 91, Da
Angermanland, 26, Ea
Angers, 11, Cc; 17, Ee
Anghalle, 37B, Dc
Angles, 2A, Ba; 4A, Ba
Anglesey, 27, Bc
Angli, 2, Ec
Anglo-Egyptian Sudan, 80A, Fc
Angol, 68, Bf
Angola, 80A, Ef
Angora, 19, Ee; 86C, Bb

1

Angostura (Ciudad Bolivar), 68, Cb
Angoulême, 11, Dd; 17A, Cd
Angoulême, Co. of, 11, Dd
Angoumois, 17, Ef; 38, Df
Angra Pequena, 81A, Ac
Anguilla, 43A, Fc
Angus, 14, Fc
Anhalt, 20, Jc; 30, Jc
Ani, 9, Ld
Anjala, 51, Fa
Anjou, 28C, Bc; 38, Ce
Anjou, Co. of, 11, Dc; 17, Ee
Ankara, 79, Fb
Anklam, 26, Dc
Ann, 45B, Ad
Annale, R., 49B, Db
Annaly, 15, Dc
Annam, 25, Kd; 74, Jg
Annan, 49A, Cc
Annandale, 14, Ed; 28B, Bb
Annapolis (Port Royal), 45A, Db; 71, Hc
Annecy, 30, Gf
Annobon, 80A, De
Annonay, 30, Ff
Annone, 23B, Bb
Ansbach, 38, Jd
Ansbach, Pr., 53, Jc
Anstruther, 49A, Cb
Antalya, 79, Fc
Antarctic Ocean, 69 C
Antarctica, 95, Ak
Antequera, 23D, Cd
Antibes, 38, Gg
Anticosti, 45A, Ea
Antietam, 72B, Ba
Antigua, 43A, Fc
Antioch, 6A, Ba; 18C, Db
Antioch, Pr. of, 18C, Dc
Antiochia, 16, He
Antipodes I., 69C, 75, Fg
Antivari, 22, Fc; 78, Bd
Antofagasta, 68, Be
Antofagasta, st., 68 ,Ce
Antoing, 46A, Cd
Antrim, co., 37C; 49B, Eb
Antrim, Mts. of, 15, Eb
Antung, 76B, Ca
Antwerp, 17A, Ea; 46A, Dc
Anzac Cove, 86D
Aosta, 5, Ab
Apalachee, 56 ,Cd
Apalachicola, R., 71F, Ba
Apamea (Famia), 18C, Dc
Apcher, 30, Ef
Apennines, 5, Dc
Apia, 75B, Ba
Appalache, 43A, Da
Appalache Bay, 43A, Db
Appalachian Mts., 70, Fd
Appenzell, 29B, Da
Appenzell, canton, 29B, Da
Appin, 49A, Bb
Appleby, 13, Db; 27, Db
Appledore, 7C, Dc
Appomattox Court House, 72, Eb
Appomattox, R., 72B, A6
Apt, 22, Dc; 30, Fg
Apulia, 4B, Fc; 5, Ed
Apulia, D. of, 16, Fd
Apure, R., 43A, Ed
Apurimac, R., 41B, Be
Aqaba, 93, Dd
Aquae (Buxton), 3A, Ec
Aquae Sulis (Bath), 3A, Ec
Aquidaban, 68, De
Aquila, 23B, Dc; 39, Kg
Aqui'eia, 5, Db
Aquileia, eccl. prov., 22, Eb
Aquino, 21A, Bb; 22, Ec
Aquinum, 5B, Bc
Aquitaine, 4A, Cc
Aquitaine, D. of 17, Fe
Aquitania, 2, Dd;
Ar, 65B, Aa
Arabia, 1, Ge; 6, Fc
Arabia Deserta, 1, Ge
Arabia Felix, 1, Fe
Arabian Desert, 80B, Ab
Arabian Sea, 25, Fe
Aracaju, 68, Fd
Aracena, 23D, Bd
Arachosia, 1, Jd
Arad, 33C, Eb
Arafura Sea, 77, Ec; 91, Fg
Aragon, 23C, Ea; 63, Eb
Aragon, King. of, 23C, Eb
Araguaia, R., 68, Dd
Arak, 93, Fc
Arakan, 73, Fc; 92, Gd
Aral, L., 6, Ga; 25, Eb
Aralskoje, 61B, Ba
Aran I., 15, Ca
Aran Is., 15, Dc
Aranda, 63, Db
Aranjuez, 54, Dd
Araraguez, 54, Dd
Aras, R., 19, He
Aravalli Ra., 59C, Bb
Arbe, 22, Ec

Arbo, 23B, Eb
Arboga, 26, Eb
Arborea, 23B, Bd
Arbre Croche, 56, Ca
Arbroath, 37A, Cb
Arc, 28D, Ec
Arcenefeld (Archenfield), 13, De
Arces, 5B, Bc
Archa, 18C, Dd
Arcole, 29A, Dc
Arcos, 23C, Bb
Arcot, 59D; 73, Ce
Arctic Ocean, 69B
Arcugnano, 86B, Bb
Ardagh, 15, Dc
Ardagh, bp., 15A, Bb
Ardebil, 19, He; 93, Fb
Arden, 7B, Cb
Arden, Forest of, 3A, Ed
Ardennes, 11, Fb; 83A, Ca
Ardfert, 15, Bd
Ardfinnan, 15, Dd
Ardgour, 14, Cc
Ardnamurchan Pt., 49A, Ab
Ardoch, 49A, Cb
Ardstraw, bp., 15A, Ba
Arelate (Upper King. of Burgundy), 10, Bf
Aremberg, 53, Gb
Aremburg, 65B, Aa
Arequipa, 68, Bd
Arevallo, 63, Cb
Argaon, 59C, Cc
Argentan, 17, Fd
Argentina, 68, Ce; 83, Ff
Argentine Confederation, 68, Cf
Argentine Rep., 68, Cf
Argenton, 38, De
Arghandab, R., 73, Aa
Argonne, 83A, Cb
Argos, 78, Dg
Argostolion, 78, Cf
Arguin, 35, Hc; 52, Jc
Argyle, bp., 14A, Bb
Argyll, 14, Cc
Argyll, co., 49A, Bb
Argyll and Tarbert, co., 37A, Eb
Aria, 1, Jd
Ariano, 21A, Cb
Arica, 68, Bd
Ariminum (Rimini), 5, Db
Arinos, R., 68, Dd
Arinsol, 23C, Cd
Arisaig, 49A, Bb
Arizona, 70, Cd
Arizona Terr., 67D, Bb
Arkansas, 72, Cc
Arkansas Post, 72, Cc
Arkansas, R., 70, Dd
Arkansas Terr., 67C, Db
Arkhangelsk, 61, Fb; 88, Oa
Arklow, 15, Ed
Arlberg Pass, 29A, Db
Arles, 11, Fe; 17A, Ee
Arles, King. of, 20, Ff
Armagh, 15, Eb
Armagh, co., 37C; 49B, Eb
Armagnac, Co. of, 11, Ce
Armenia, 19, Ge; 79, Hc
Armenia, King. of, 19, Ee
Armeniac Theme, 9, Kd
Armenians, 18C, Ca
Armentieres, 46A, Bd
Armorica, 2, Cd; 4A, Bb
Armstrong, 28B, Bb
Arnhem, 46A, Eb
Arnhem Land, 77, Ed
Arnis, 65F, Aa
Arno, R., 5, Cc: 21B, Bd
Arnsberg, 20, Hc; 38, Hc
Arnstadt, 38, Jc
Arnswalde, 21, Lb
Aroche, 23D, Bd
Aroostook, R., 71E, Bb
Arpinum, 5B, Bc
Arques, 20, Dd
Arran, 14, Cd
Arras, 17, Gc; 46A, Bd
Arroyo de los Molinos, 63, Bc
Arsamosata, 9, Ke
Arsuf, 18C, Bf
Arta, 64, Gf; 78, Cf
Artaxata, 1, Gc
Artenay, 76A, Ab
Artois, 17, Gc; 83A, Ba
Aru Is., 77, Ec
Aruba, 41B, Cb
Arundel, England, 27, Ff
Arundel, Maryland, 45B, Ad
Arve, R., 29B, Ab
Arwystli, 13, Cd
Arzobispo, 63, Cc
Ascalon, 6A, Ab; 18C, Bg
Ascension, 40, Je; 96C, Ae
Aschaffenburg, 29A, Ca
Ascoli, 5, Dc
Ashanti, 81C, Dc
Ashburton, 27, Cf

Ashburton, R., 77, Bf
Ashby-de-la-Zouch, 48A, Cc
Ashdown, 7B, Cc
Ashkhabad, 93, Hb
Ashridge, 36, Ff
Ashuanipi, L., 71, Hb
Asia, cont., 94, Pc
Asia, diocese, 2, Kf
Asia, reg., 1, Ed
Asia Minor, 86C, Bb
Asiago, 84, Ec; 86B, Bb
Asir, 93, Ef
Asirgarh, 73, Cc
Askeaton, 37B, Cd; 49B, Cd
Asmara, 80A, Gc
Asmera, 93, Df
Asoka Empire, 1, Ke
Aspadana, 1, Hd
Aspern, 29A, Ga
Aspinwall, 43D, Ed; 68, Bb
Aspromonte, 32C, Ee
Aspropotamos, R., 78, Cf
Assab, 80B, Ce
Assam, 25, Jd; 73, Fb
Assandun, 12, Ed
Assassins, 18C, Dc
Assaye, 59C, Cc; 69A, Nc
Assiette, Col d', 29A, Bc
Assiniboia, 70, Db
Assisi, 5, Dc
Assuan, 6, Ec
Assynt, 14, Ca
Astarac, Co. of, 11, De
Asterabad, 61, Hg
Asti, 5, Bb; 32A, Cb
Astico, R., 86B, Bb
Astorga, 23C, Ba; 63, Ba
Astrakhan, 19, Hc
Astrakhan, reg., 61, Hd
Asturias, 23C, Ca; 63, Ba
Asuncion, 68, De
Aswan, 80B, Ac; 96D, Fb
Aswan Dam, 93, Ce
Asyut, 80B, Ab
Atacama Desert, 68, Be
Atapuerca, 23C, Da
Atbara, 93, Cf
Atbara, R., 80B, Bd
Atelkuza, 9, Hc
Atella, 32A, Fd
Ath, 46A, Cd; 53, Eb
Athabaska, 70, Cb
Athabaska L., 70, Db
Athabaska, R., 70, Cb
Athboy, 49B, Ec
Athelney, 7C, Bc; 36, Df
Athenae, 2, Hf
Athenry, 37B, Cc; 49B, Cc
Athens, 78, Df
Athens, D. of, 19, Ce
Athens, Barony of, 18B, Cc
Athens, Barony of, 18B, Cc
Athlone, 15, Dc
Atholl, 14, Dc
Athos, Mt., 9, Gd; 18B, Cb
Athy, 15, Ed
Atlanta, 72A, Ab
Atlantic Ocean, 35, Hd
Atrato, R., 43A, Ed
Atrebates, 3A, Ee
Atri, 21, Kg
Atropatene, 2, Nf
Attalia, 19, Ee
Attock, 73, Ba
Attu, I., 90, Ea
Aube, R., 76A, Cb
Auberoche, 28C, Cd
Aubigny, 53, Ed
Auch, 11, De
Auch, eccl. prov., 22, Bc
Auchterarder, 49A, Cb
Auckland, 75, Ff; 77A
Auckland, prov., 77A
Auckland (Waitemata), 77, Ml
Auckland I., 69C; 75, Fg
Auerstädt, 65B, Ba
Aughrim, 49B, Cc
Augsburg, 10, Dd
Augusta (Fort Cornwallis), 57D, Ab
Augusta, Georgia, 72, Dc
Augusta, Maine, 67B, Cd
Augusta Taurinorum (Turin), 5, Ab
Auldearn, 37A, Cb
Aumale, 17, Fd
Aunis, 30, Ce
Aurangabad, 73, Cd
Auray, 28C, Ac; 55A, Be
Aurelian, 2, Dd
Aurillac, 17, Gf; 30, Ef
Aussig, 31, Lc
Aust, 7A, Cb
Austerfield, 7B, Cb
Austerlitz, 29A, Ga
Austin, 70, Ed
Austral (Tubuai) Is., 75, Hf; 83, Bf
Australia, 69A, Qf
Australia, Commonwealth of, 77, Ef
Australian Alps, 77, Hl

Australian Dependency, 95, PJ
Austrasia, 7A, Eb; 8, Da
Austria, 50, Dd; 65A, Cb
Austria, reg., Italy, 5, Cb
Austria, March of, 10, Fd
Austria-Hungary, 82, Fc
Austrian Netherlands, 54, Db
Austrian Silesia, 60A, Fc
Austrian Empire, 62, Fc; 65B, Cb
Autun, 8B, Bb; 11, Fc
Auvergne, 11, Ed; 20, Ef
Auvergne, Co. of, 11, Ed
Auxerre, 11, Ec
Auximum, 5B, Bb
Auximum (Osimo), 5, Dc
Auxonne, 30, Fe
Ava, 41A, Gb; 73, Gc
Avalon, 45A, Ga
Avars, 8, Cd; 9, Fc
Aveiro, 22, Ac
Aventine, 5A
Aversa, 32A, Fd
Avesnes, 46A, Cd
Avignon, 11, Fe; 17, Hf
Avila, 22, Bc; 63, Cb
Avisio, R., 86B, Ba
Avlona, 18A, Ba
Avoca, R., 15, Ed
Avon, R., Bristol, 27, De
Avon, R., Hants., 27, Ef
Avon, R., Warwick, 27, Ed
Avondale, 28B, Ab
Avranches, 11, Cb
Avretone (Overton, Richard's Castle), 13, Dd
Awe, L., 14, Ce
Ax, 11, Ce
Axbridge, 27, De
Axel Heiberg Land, 44, Fa
Axim, 40, Jd; 81C, Dc
Ayacucho, 68, Bd; 69A, Fe
Ayas, 19, Fe
Aydin, 19, De; 93, Bb
Aylesbury, 7A, Cb; 48A, Cd
Aylesford, 7B, Dc
Ayr, co., 37A, Bc; 49A, Bc
Ayr, R., 14, Dd
Ayton, 37A, Cc
Ayubale, 56, Cd
Ayubites, Empire of the, 18B, Ed
Azangarh, 73, Db
Azerbaijan, 79, Jc; 89, Pe
Azores, 55B, Hc
Azov, 24, Kd; 79, Ga
Azov, Sea of, 19, Fc
Aztec Kingdom, 35, Dc
Aztecs, 43A, Bb

BAALBEK, 6A, Bb
Baalbek (Heliopolis), 18C, De
Babul, 93, Gb
Babuyan Is., 75E, Ba
Babylon, 2, Mg
Bacalhaos, 40, Gb.
Bachan, 52C, Cb
Bacharach, 29A, Ba
Bacolod, 75E, Bb
Bactria, 1, Jd
Badajoz, 22, Ad; 63, Bc
Badakshan, 61B, Cb
Baden, 20, Hd; 29B, Ca
Baden, Marg. of, 30, Hd
Baden Baden, 29A, Ca
Badenoch, 14, Eb; 37A, Bb
Badissin, 31, Lc
Baentone (Bampton), 13, Cf
Baeza, 23C, Dd
Bafata, 96B, Aa
Baffin Bay, 44, Ha; 69B
Baffin I., 44, Gd
Bafut, 96B, Db
Bage, 20, Fe
Baghdad, 6A, Cb; 9, Lf
Baghdad, Caliphate of, 18A, Gc
Baghdad Railway, 86C, Bb
Bagirmi, 80A, Ec
Bagnolo, 32D, Bb
Bahama Is., 43A, Eb
Bahawalpur, 73, Bb
Bahia (Salvador), 68, Fd
Bahia, st., 68, Ed
Bahia Blanca, 68, Cf
Bahn, 60A, Eb
Bahrein, 6, Gc; 79, Ke
Baikal, L., 25, Ka; 91, Da
Baker, I., 90, Fd
Bakewell, 7C, Cb
Bakhchisarai, 51, Ge
Baku, 19, Hd; 79, Jb
Balaguer, 23C, Fb
Balaklava, 61, Df
Balasore, 59A, Ec
Balassaghun, 25, Gb
Balaton, L., 31, Me; 33c, Db
Balch, 61B, Bb
Balchik, 78, Gd
Baleares Insulae, 2, Df
Balearic Is., 23C, Gc; 63, Gc

Bali, 96B, Db
Balidon Hill, 28B, Cb
Balikpapan, 90, Bd
Balkans, 78, Ed
Balkh, 6, Hb; 25, Fc
Balkhash, L., 25, Gb; 91, Ab
Ballachuiish, 49A, Bb
Ballater, 49A, Cb
Balleny Is., 95
Ballinamuck, 49B, Dc
Bai.iol. 28B, Db
Ballycastle, 49B, Ea
Ballymena, 49B, Eb
Ballymore, 49B, Ec
Ballyshannon, 49B, Cb
Balneum Regis, 5B, Bb
Balta, 51, Fd; 78, Gb
Baltic Sea, 22, Ea; 26, Eb
Baltimore, Maryland, 57, Cd; 72 B, Ba
Baluchistan, 61B, Bc; 74 Ef
Bamako, 80A, Cc; 81C, Cb
Bamberg, 10, Dd
Banana, 80A, Ee
Banaras (Varanasi), 92, Eb
Banat of Craiova, 33C, Cc
Banat of Temesvar, 33C, Eb
Banbury, 27, Ed
Banda Is, 52 C, Cb
Banda Oriental, 68, Df
Bandar Abbas, 93, Hd
Bandar Maharani, 75A, Cc
Bandjarmasin, 91, Eg
Bandon, 49B, Ce
Bandon, R., 15, Ce
Banff, co., 37A, Cb; 49A, Cb
Bangalore, 73, Ce
Bangaya Is., 52C, Bb
Bangkok, 73, Ge; 92, Je
Bangor, Caernarvon, 13, Bc
Bangor, Flint, 7A, Ca; 13, Dc
Bangor, Ireland, 37B, Fb
Bangor, Maine, 71, Hc
Bangor, bp, 36, Be
Bangtok, 92, Fb
Bangui, 96D, Dd
Bangweulu, L., 80A, Gf
Baniyas, 93, Dd
Banjermassim, 69A, Pe
Bankot, 59A, Bd
Banks I., 44, Ba
Banks Pen., 77, Mj
Bann, R., 15, Eb; 37C
Bannaventa (Whilton Lodge) 3A, Ed
Bannockburn, 28B, Aa
Bannow, B., 15, Ed
Bantam, 41A, He
Bantry B., 15, Be
Bantry B., 15, Be
Banwelle (Banwell), 13, De
Banyaluka, 39, Mf; 78, Ac
Bapaume, 30, Ec; 83A, Ba
Bar, 17A, Eb; 39B, Bb
Bar, D. of, 30, Fd; 39B, Ba
Bar-le-Duc, 17, Hd; 29A, Aa
Bar-sur-Aube, 11, Fb
Bar-sur-Seine, 11, Fb
Bar Hill, 3A, Ba
Bararrahal, 59C, Ce
Baranof I., 71B, Cb
Baranow, 26, Fc
Barataria Bay, 43A, Db
Barawa, 40, Md; 41A, Bd
Barbados, 43A, Gc
Barbarike, I, Je
Barbary, 40, Kc
Barbastre, 22, Cc
Barberton, 81A, Dc
Barbuda, 43A, Fc
Barcastro, 23C, Fa
Barcelona, Spain, 23C, Gb; 63, Gb
Barcelona, Venezuela, 68, Ca
Barcelona, Co. of, 23C, Ga
Barcelona, Co. of (Spanish March) 11, Ce
Barcelonnette, 38, Gf
Barcelos, 63, Cc
Barcoo, R., 77 Gg
Bardera, 80A, Hd
Bardia, 93, Ac
Bardney, 36, Fd
Bardsey, I., 7C, Ab
Bareilly, 73, Cb
Barents Sea, 69B
Barfleur, 28C, Bb; 55A, Cd
Bari, Africa, 80A, Gd
Bari, Italy, 5, Fd; 32A, Gd
Bari Doab, 73, Ba
Barka, 6, Db; 9, Gf
Barking, 13, Ge; 36, Gf
Barletta, 32A, Gd
Barlings, 36, Fd
Barmen, 83A, Da
Barnard Castle, 27, Eb
Barnaul, 91, Ba
Barnstable (Barnstaple), 13, Be

Barnet, 27, Fe
Barnstaple, England, 27, Ce
Barnstable, Massachusetts, 45B, Dc
Baroda, 73, Bc
Barotseland, 80A, Ff
Barra, 43A, Ec
Barra, I., 14, Ac
Barrackpore, 73, Ec
Barranquilla, 68, Ba
Barrois Mouvant, 39B, Bb
Barrosa, 63, Bd
Barrow, Ft., 71A, Ba
Barrow, R., 15, Ed; 37B, Ed
Bartenstein, 60B, Ha
Barth, 31, Ka
Barton-on-Humber, 27, Fc
Bartzo, 23B, Fc
Baruth, 39C, Da
Bärwalde, 39, Lb; 60A, Dc
Basel (Basle), 29B, Ba
Bashee B., 81B, Dc
Basilan, 75E, Bc
Basilicata, 5, Fd
Basing, 7C, Cc; 48A, Cd
Basinges (Basingstoke), 13, Ee
Basingstoke, 27, Ee
Basle (Basel), 29B, Ba
Basle, canton, 29B, Ba
Basle, Bp, of, 29B, Ba
Basques, 8C, Bb
Basra, 6A, Ec
Basra (Bassorah), 41A, Ba
Bass Rock, 28B, Ca
Bass Str., 77, Hi
Bassano, 32D, Bb; 86B, Bb
Bassari, 96B, Cb
Basse, Fontaine, 22, Cb
Bassein, Burma, 73, Fd
Bassein, India, 73, Bd
Bassignano, 32B, Bb; 51, Bd
Bassigny, 39B, Bb
Bassorah, 33A, Gd
Bassorah (Basra), 41A, Ba
Bastarnae, 2, Jc
Bastia, 20, Hg
Bastogne, 83A, Ca
Basutoland, 81B, Db
Batak, 78, Ee
Batangas, 75E, Bb
Batanta, 52C, Db
Batavia, 74, Ji
Batavian Rep., 51, Bc
Bath, England, 27, De
Bath, N. Carolina, 56, Dc
Bath and Wells, bp., 36, Cf
Bathurst, C. Prov., 81B, Cc
Bathurst, Gambia, 81C, Ab
Bathurst, New South Wales, 77, Hh
Bathurst Inlet, 70, Da
Batlapin, 81B, Ca
Batoche, 70, Db
Baton Rouge, 56, Ad
Batouri, 96B, Db
Battle, 12, Ed; 36, Gg
Battleford, 70, Db
Batuchina, 52B, Aa
Batum, 33A, Fb; 79, Hb
Batum, reg., 79, Hb
Batumi, 88, Oe
Baturin, 50, Gc
Baugé, 28D, Bc
Baugy, 38, Ee
Bautzen, 10, Fc; 53, Lb
Bavaria, 10, Ed; 21, Ke
Bavaria, D. of, 30, Jd
Bavaria-Landshut, D. of, 31, Kd
Bavaria-Munich, D. of, 30, Jd
Bavarians, 4A, Eb; 8B, Db
Bawku, 96B, Ba
Bay Is., 43B, Bc
Bayeux, 11, Cb
Baylen, 62, Be; 63, Dc
Bayonne, 11, Ce; 63, Ea
Bayreuth, 20, Jd; 53, Jc
Bayreuth, pr., 38, Jc
Baza, 23C, Dd
Bazarchik, 78, Fd
Bazas, 11, Cd
Beachy Hd., 55A, Dc
Beacon Hill, 56B
Beacons, 27, Ce
Béarn, V. of, 11, Ce
Beaucaire, 17, Hg
Beaufort, France, 38, Ce
Beaufort, Georgia, 57D, Ab
Beaufort, S. Africa, 81B, Bc
Beaufort, Syria, 18C, Ce
Beaufort Bay, 44, Aa
Beaufort Sea, 69B
Beaufort West, 81A, Bd
Beaugency, 20, De; 76A, Ac
Beaujeu, 11, Fc
Beaujeu, S. of, 20, Fe
Beaulieu, England, 36, Eg
Beaulieu, France, 22, Cb
Beauly, 49A, Bb
Beaumaris, 27, Bc
Beaumont, 30, Ed; 76A, Cb
Beaune, 30, Fe

Beaune-la-Rolande, 76A, Bb
Beaupréau, 53, Cd
Beauséjour, 45A, Ea
Beauvais, 11, Eb; 83A, Bb
Beauvais, Co. of, 11, Eb
Beauvale, 36, Ed
Beauvoir, 38, Be
Beaver Dam, 71D
Bebbanburh (Banburgh), 13, Ea
Bec, 17, Fd; 22, Cb
Beccles, 13, Hd
Bechuana, 81B, Ba
Bechuanaland, 81A, Bb; 96C, Eg
Bechuanaland Prot., 80A, Fg; 81A, Bc
Bedale, 27, Eb
Bedeforde (Bedford), 13, Fd
Bedefordscire (Bedfordshire), 13, Fd
Bedford, England, 27, Fd
Bedford, Virginia, 57, Be
Bedford, co., 27, Fd
Bedlington, 27, Ea
Bednore, 59C, Ce
Bedr, 6, Ec
Bedvinde (Great Bedwyn), 13, Ee
Bedwin, 27, Ee
Beeston Castle, 48A, Bc
Bega, 6A, Ec
Beilan, 64, Kf
Beira, 81A, Da
Beira, prov., 63, Ab
Beirut, 79, Gd; 80A, Ga
Beisan, 18C, Cf
Beja, 23C, Bc
Belata, 23C, Ac
Belbuck, 22, Fa
Belcher Is., 70, Fb
Belchite, 63, Eb
Belem, 22, Ad
Belem (Para), 41B, Ed; 68, Ec
Eelerium From., 3A, Af
Belfast, 37B, Fb; 49B, Fb
Belfort, 29A, Bb; 39B, Cb
Belgae, 3A, De
Belgard, 21, Mb
Belgian Congo, 80A, Fe
Belgium, 83A, Ca; 87, Ab
Belgrade, 78, Cc
Belin, 38, Cf
Belinas (Paneas), 18C, Ce
Belize, 43A, Dc
Bellary, 73, Cd
Belle I., Canada, 71, Jb
Belle I., France, 11, Bc
Belle Isle, Str. of., 71, Jb
Belleek, 49B, Cb
Bellegarde, 53, Ef
Bellême, 11, Db; 17, Fd
Belley, 11, Fd; 22, Db
Bellingshausen Sea, 95, Ej
Bellingtun (Bedlington), 13, Ea
Bellinzona, 5, Ba; 29B, Db
Belluno, 5, Da; 86B, Ca
Belmont, U.S.A., 72, Cb
Belo Horizonte, 68, Ee
Belturbet, 49B, Db
Belvedoir (Belvoir), 13, Fd
Belvoir, England, 36, Fe
Belvoir, Syria, 18C, Cf
Belyi, 61, Dc
Bemis Heights, 21, Nc
Benares, 25, Hd; 73, Db
Benauges, 11, Cd
Benavente, 63, Ca
Benbecula, 14, Ab
Benburb, 49B, Eb
Bencoolen, 52, Qe; 75, Ce
Bender, 50, Fd; 78, Gb
Bendigo, 77, Gi
Benedict, 71C, Cc
Benevento (Beneventum), 5, Ed
Benevento, D. of, 23A, Ec
Beneventum (Benevento), 5, Ed
Beneventum, D. of, 4B, Fc
Benfleet, 7C, Dc
Bengal, 25, Hd; 73, Ec
Bengal, Bay of, 25, He
Benghazi, 80A, Ea
Bengkalis, 75A, Ab
Benguela, 80A, Ef
Beni Suef, 93, Cd
Benin, 81C, Fc
Benin City, 96B, Cb
Benin, Bight of, 81C, Ed
Bennington, 57, Eb
Benon, 30, Ce
Bensington, 7B, Cc
Bent's Fort, 70, Dd
Bentheim, 20, Gb
Bentheim, Co. of, 46C, C
Bentonville, 72, Bb
Benue, R., 81C, Fc
Beorn, 12, Dc
Berar, 73, Cc
Berat, 86A, Ab

Berber, 80B, Ad
Berbera, 96A, Ba
Berberati, 96B, Db
Berbers, 6, Bc
Berbice, reg., 41B, Dc
Berbice, R., 68B, Ba
Berchamstede (Berkhamsted), 13, Fe
Berchelai (Berkeley), 13, De
Berchtesgaden, 21, Ke
Bere, 28A, Cb
Bere I., 15, Be
Berea, 81A, Cc
Berekum, 96B, Bb
Beresina, R., 50, Fc
Berezovo, 74, Eb
Berewic (Berwick), 13, Da
Berg, Co. of, 20, Gc
Berg, D. of, 38, Gc; 46C, Cb
Bergamo (Bergamum), 5, Bb
Bergen, Nassau, 29A, Ca
Bergen, Netherlands, 46A, Db
Bergen, Norway, 57, Be
Bergen, Rügen, 22, Ea
Bergen op Zoom, 46A, Dc
Bergerac, 20, Df; 28C, Cd
Bergues, 53, Eb
Berhampore, 73, Ec
Berhampur, 59A, Dd
Beri (Berry Pomeroy), 13, Cf
Bering Sea, 74, Qc
Bering Str., 69B
Berkeley, England, 27, De
Berkeley, Maryland, 45B, Ae
Berkeley, reg., 45A, Bd
Berkhamsted, 27, Fe
Berkshire, 27, Ee
Berkshire Hills, 57, Eb
Berlad, 33A, Ca
Berlin, 21, Kb
Bermejo, R., 68, Ca
Bermuda Hundred, 45B, Ae
Bermuda I., 55B, Dc
Bermudas (Somers Is.), 43A, Fa
Bernardino Pass, 5, Ba
Bernburg, 53, Jb
Berne, 10, Be; 29B, Bb
Berne, canton, 29B, Bb
Bernicia, 7B, Ca; 12, Dc
Bernina, 29A, Db
Berrochescire (Berkshire), 13, Ee
Berry, 17A, Cc
Berry, D. of, 30, Ee
Berthier, 56, Ea
Bervie, 49A, Cb
Berwick, 14, Fd
Berwick, co., 37A, Cc
Berwick upon Tweed, 28B, Cb
Besalú, 22, Cc
Besançon, 11, Gc; 29A, Bb
Besançon, eccl. prov., 22, Bb
Beshbalik, 25, Jb
Bessarabia, 50, Fd; 78, Gb
Bessin, 8, Bb
Bessingen, 20, Hd
Betanzos, 63, Aa
Bethany, 81A, Ac
Bethel, 71A, Aa
Bethelsdorp, 81B, Cc
Bethesda, Pool of, 18D
Bethlehem, 18C, Cg
Bethune, 28B, Ba; 46A, Bd
Betwa, R., 52A, Bb
Beuthen, 21, Nc
Beverley, 27, Fc
Beverley Manor, 56, Dc
Beverlie (Beverley), 13, Fc
Bewcastle, 7B, Ba; 13, Da
Bewdley, 36, Ee
Beyrout, 6A, Bb; 18C, Ce
Béziers, 11, Ee; 17A, De
Bhagalpur, 73, Eb
Bhamo, 73, Gc
Bharatpur, 73, Cb
Bhatpara, 92, Fc
Bhavnagar, 92, Cc
Bhima, R., 73, Cd
Bhonsla's Lands, 73, Cc
Bhopal, 59C, Cc; 73, Cc
Bhubaneswar, 92, Fc
Bhutan, 73, Fb
Bialystok, 51, Ec
Biar, 23C, Ec
Biberach, 20, Hd
Bicocca, 32A, Cb
Bidar, 59C, Cd
Bidassoa, R., 63, Ea
Biddeford, 57, Fb
Bideford, 48A, Ad
Biel (Bienne), 29B, Ba
Biel, L., 29B, Ba
Bielefeld, 30, Hb; 53, Ha
Bielgorod, 19, Fb
Biella, 32A, Cb
Bielostok, 26, Fc; 84, Gb
Bielsk, 61A, Bb
Bienne, 65A, Ab
Bienne (Biel), 29B, Ba
Big, R., 70, Gb
Big Black, R., 72C, Aa
Biggarsberg, 81D, Bb

Bigorre, 17, Fg
Bigorre, Co. of, 11, De
Bihacs, 31, Lf; 39, Lf
Bihar, 73, Eb
Bihar and Orissa, 73A, Bb
Bijapur, 52A, Bc; 73, Cd
Bijayah, 6, Bb
Bikaner, 73, Bb
Billungs, Lds. of the, 10, Db
Billungs, M. of the, 10, Ea
Biloxi, 56, Bd
Binche, 46A, Dd
Binkath, 6, Ha
Bintang, 75A, Bb
Bir Atrun, 93, Bf
Birkenfeld, 39B, Da; 65D, Ab
Birmingham, 64, Bc
Birr, 15, Dc
Birthen, 10, Bc
Biscay, B. of, 11, Bd
Bischofsheim, 20, Jc
Bishop's Stortford, 27, Ge
Bisignano, 21A, Dc
Bismarck (Fort Mandant), 70, Dc
Bismarck Arch., 77, Hb
Bissagos Is., 81C, Ab; 96B, Aa
Bissao, 81C, Ab
Bissau, 96B, Aa
Bistritz, 24, Gd
Bitervum, 5B, Bb
Bithur, 73, Db
Bithynia, 2, Ke; 16, Jd
Bitlis, 9, Le; 86C, Db
Bitolia (Monastir), 78, Ce
Bitonto, 32B, Fd; 54, Fd
Bitsch, 76A, Db
Bizerta, 34, De
Black Castle, 15, Ed
Black Elster, R., 39C, Db
Black Forest, 10, Cd; 29A, Bb
Black Mts., 27, Ce
Black, R., 57, Db
Black River, 43A, Dc
Black Rock, 71D
Black Russia, 50, Ec
Black Sea, 4A, Dc; 19, Ed
Black Umvolosi, R., 81D, Bb
Blacksod B., 49B, Ab
Blackstocks, 57D, Aa
Blackwater, R., Meath. 49B, Ec
Blackwater, R., Munster, 15, Cd
Blackwater, R., Ulster, 15, Db
Bladensburg, 71C, Cc
Blagovyeshchensk, 74, Lc
Blair Atholl, 37A, Cb; 49A, Cb
Blairgowrie, 37A, Cb
Blakeney, 27, Gd
Blamont, 30, Gd; 39B, Cb
Blanc, Mt., 29A, Bc
Blanchegarde, 18C, Bg
Blanco, C., Africa, 80A, Bb
Blanco, C., Oregon, 67C, Aa
Blanco (North), C., 55B, Kc
Blandford, 27, Df
Blankenberghe, 46A, Cc
Blankenburg, 30, Jc
Blantyre, 80A, Gf; 81A, Ea
Blatno, 9, Fc
Blatobulgium, (Birrens), 3A, Ca
Blauwberg, 81B, Ac
Blaye, 17, Ef
Bleichfeld, 10, Dd
Blekinge 26, Eb
Bléneau, 53 Ed
Blenheim, Germany, 29A, Da
Blenheim, New Zealand, 77A
Bletchingley, 27, Fe
Blewfields, 43B, Bc
Blida (Blyth), 13, Ec
Blind B., 77A
Bloemfontein, 81B, Cb
Blois, 11, Dc
Blois, Co. of, 11, Dc
Blood, R., 81D, Ba
Bloody Foreland, 49B, Ca
Blore Heath, 27, Dd
Blue Mts., 77, Ih
Blue Nile, R., 80B, Ae
Blue Ridge Mts., 57, Be
Bluestack, 15, Cb
Blumenau, 68, Ee
Blunkenburg, 30, Jc
Bo, 96B, Ab
Bobbio, 22, Dc
Bobo-Dioulasso, 96B, Ba
Boca de Navios, 43A, Gd
Boca del Toro, 43A, Dd
Bochingeham (Buckingham), 13, Fe
Bochinghamscire (Buckinghamshire), 13, Fe
Böckelheim, 10, Bd
Bodele (Bootle), 13, Cb
Bodmin, 27, Bf
Bodotria Aest. (Firth of Forth), 3A, Da

Bogesund, 26, Db
Boggerah Mts., 15, Bd
Bogota, 68, Bb
Bohemia, King. of, 21, Ld
Bohemia-Moravia, Prot. of, 87, Dc
Bohemian Forest, 60A, Dd
Bohemond, 16, Jd
Bohemond, Castle of, 18E
Bohol, 75E, Bc
Bohun, 28A, Cc
Bohns, 26, Db
Behuslan, 50, Cb
Bois le Duc, 46A, Ec
Boisdale L., 49A, Ab
Boise, 70, Dc
Bojador, C., 55B, Jd
Bokhara, I, Jd; 6, Hb
Bokhara, Khanate of, 61B, B5
Bolama, 96B, Aa
Bolan Pass, 73, Ab; 92, Bb
Bolchen, 39B, Ca
Bolinbroc (Bolingbroke), 13, Gc
Bolingbroke, 27, Fc
Bolivar, 68, Cf
Bolivia, 68, Cd
Bologna (Bononia), 5, Cb
Bolsena, L., 32A, Dc
Bolsover, 13, Ec
Bolton, England, 48A, Bc
Bolton, Mississippi, 72C, Aa
Bolton Abbey, 36, Ed
Bolton Castle, 48A, Cb
Bolzen, 5, Ca
Boma, 80A, Ee
Bombay, 73, Bd
Bona, 16, De; 47, De
Bonacca, 43A, Dc
Bonar Bridge, 49A, Bb
Bonaventure, 45A, Ea
Bonavista, B., 45A, Ga
Bonavista, C., 45A, Ga
Bondoukou, 96B, Bb
Bone, 80A, Da
Bongor, 96B, Da
Boni, 52C, Bb
Bonifacio, 23A, Dc; 53, Bf
Bonin Is., 74, Nf; 90, Db
Bonn, 10, Bc; 83A, Da
Bonny, 81C, Fd
Bononia, 5B, Aa
Booma Pass, 81B, Cc
Boomplaats, 81A, Cc
Boonesboro, 57A, Cb
Boonesborough, 56, Cc
Boonville, 72, Bb
Boothia Pen., 44, Ea
Bopängen, 20, Jd
Boppard, 20, Gc
Bordeaux, 11, Cd
Bordeaux, eccl. prov., 22, Bb
Bordesley, 36, Ee
Börglum, 26, Cb
Borgne, L., 71F, Ba
Borisov, 62, Hb
Borku, 80A, Ec
Bormio, 29B, Eb; 32A, Ba
Borne (Eastbourne), 13, Gf
Borneo, 40, Pd; 91, Ef
Borneo (Java Major), 35, Pd
Bornholm, 26, Eb
Bornhöved, 20, Ja
Borodino, 62, Ka
Boroughbridge, 27, Eb
Borthwick, 37A, Cc
Boshof, 81A, Cc
Bosna, R., 78, Bc
Bosnia, 21, Mf; 78, Ac
Bosporus, 78, Ge; 86C, Aa
Bosra, 6A, Bb
Boston, England, 27, Fd
Boston, Massachusetts, 45B, Db; 56B
Bostra, 18C, Df
Bosworth, 27, Ed
Botany B., 77, Ih
Botha's Pass, 81D, Aa
Bothnia, G. of, 26, Fa
Bothwell, 28B, Ab
Bothwell Bridge, 49A, Bc
Boswana, 96D, Eg
Botzen, 10, Ca
Bouake, 96B, Bb
Boudonitza, 19, Ce
Bougainville, 77, Ic; 90, Dd
Bouillon, 46A, Ee; 53, Fc
Boulogne, 11, Da
Boulonnais, 53, Db
Boundi, 59C, Cb
Bounty I., 75, Fg
Bourbon, 17, Ge; 42, Mf
Bourbon, S. of, 20, Ee
Bourbon l'Ancy, 30, Ee
Bourbon l'Archambault, 53, Ed
Bourbonnais, 17, Ge
Bourg, Guyenne, 20, Cf
Bourg, Savoy, 30, Fe
Bourganeuf, 30, Df
Bourges, 11, Ec
Bourges, eccl. prov., 22, Cb

Bourges, V. of, 11, Ec
Bourgneuf Bay, 28C, Ac
Bourne, 36, Fe
Boutières, 38, Ff
Bouvet I., 95, Th
Bovino, 22, Fc
Bowes, 13, Db
Bowling Green, Virginia, 57, Cd
Bowness, 3C
Boxley, 36, Gf
Boxtel, 46A, Ec
Boyata, 68, Bb
Boyne, R., 15, Ec; 37B, Ec
Brabant, 46A, Dd
Brabant, D. of, 17, Hc; 46, Bb
Bracciano, 39, Kg
Brackley, 27, Ed
Bradeford (Bradford-on-Avon), 13, De
Bradenstock, 36, Ef
Bradford, Wilts., 27, De
Bradford, Yorks., 48A, Cc
Bradninch, 27, Cf
Bradock Down, 48A, Ad
Braemar, 37A, Cb; 49A, Cb
Braga, 22, Ac; 63, Ab
Braga, eccl. prov., 22, Ac
Braganca, Brazil, 68, Fc
Bragança, Portugal, 63, Bb
Brahmanabad, 6, Hc
Brahmaputra (Tsanpo), R., 73, Eb
Braila, 51, Fd; 78, Fc
Bramber and Steyning, 27, Ff
Brampton, 49A, Cc
Branco, R., 68, Cc
Brancepeth, 27, Eb
Brandenburg, Germany, 10, Eb
Brandenburg, Kentucky, 72, Cb
Brandenburg, M. of, 21, Kb
Brandenburg, Abp. of, 30, Hb
Brandon, 45B, Ae
Brandon B., 49B, Ad
Brandon Hill, 15, Ad
Brandywine, R., 57, Dd
Branford, 45B, Cc
Brännkyrka, 26, Eb
Branodunum (Brancester), 3A, Gd
Bras d'Or, L., 45A, Ea
Brashear City, 72, Bd
Brasilia, 68, Ed
Braunau, 21, Kd; 29A, Ea
Braunsberg, 26, Ec; 39, Na
Bravo del Norte (Rio Grande), R., 43A, Bb
Bravoniacum (Kirkby Thore), 3A, Db
Bravonium (Leintwardine), 3A, Dd
Brazil, 41B, Ee; 68, Dd
Brazos, R., 70, Ed
Brazos Santiago, 70, Ee
Brazzaville, 80A, Ee
Brechin, 14, Fc
Brecon, 27, Ce
Breda, 46A, Dc
Breda, Barony of, 46C, Bb
Brederode, 46A, Db
Breedevoort, 46A, Fc
Breedon, 7B, Cb
Breeds Hill, 56B
Breffny, 15, Db
Breisach, 29A, Ba; 38, Gd
Breisgau, 30, Ge; 38, Ge
Breitenfeld, 39, Kc
Breitenwang, 20, Je
Brembre (Bramber), 13, Ff
Bremen, 10, Cb
Bremen, eccl. prov., 22, Da
Bremen, Abp. of, 30, Hb
Bremenium (High Rochester), 3A, Da
Bremerhaven, 55A, Hb; 65D, Aa
Bremetennacum (Ribchester), 3A, Dc
Brenner Pass, 5, Ca; 10, De
Breno, 86B, Ab
Brenta, R., 5, Cb; 86B, Bb
Brentford, 48A, Cd
Brescello, 86B, Ab
Brescia, 5, Cb; 29A, Dc
Breslau, 21, Mc
Bresse, 17A, Ec; 33, Fe
Bressuire, 20, Ce
Brest, 30, Ad
Brest Litovsk, 26, Fc
Breteuil, 11, Eb; 30, Dd
Bretigny, 24, Cd; 28C, Cb
Bretlinton (Bridlington), 13, Fb
Breton C., 45A, Fa
Bretons, 8B, Ab; 85, Dc
Breuckelen, 45B, Cc
Briançon, 20, Gf
Briansk, 26, Hc

Briar Creek, 57D, Ab
Brice's Cross Roads, 72, Cc
Brideport (Bridport), 13, Df
Bridgetown, 43A, Gc
Bridgnorth, 27, Dd
Bridgwater, 27, De
Bridiers, 20, De
Bridlington, 36, Fc
Bridport, 27, Df
Brieg, 31, Mc; 39, Mc
Brienne, 11, Fb
Brienz, 29B, Bb
Brienz, L., 29B, Bb
Briey, 20, Fd; 39B, Ba
Brig, 29B, Bb
Brigantes, 3A, Db
Brighton, 48B, Cd
Brignoles, 20, Gg
Brihuega, 63, Db
Brill, 46A, Dc
Brindisi (Brindisium), 5, Fd
Brioude, 11, Ed
Brisbane, 77, Ig
Brissac, 53, Cd
Bristcl, England, 27, De
Bristol, Rhode I., 57, Fe
Bristol, Tennessee, 72, Db
Bristol, bp., 36, Df
Bristol Channel, 27, Ce
Bristou (Bristol), 13, De
Britain, 2A, Aa
Britannia, 2, Cc
British Columbia, 70, Bb
British East Africa, 80A, Gd
British Guiana, 43D, Gd; 68B, Bb
British Honduras, 55B, Ae
British Isles, 69B
British Kaffraria, 81B, Db
British New Guinea (Terr. of Papua), 77, Gc
British North Borneo, 74, Kh; 90, Bc
British Somaliland, 96A, Bb
British South Africa Company, 80A, Ff
Brittania (Wellington), 77, Nj
Brittany, 7A, Cb
Brittany, D. of, 30, Bd
Brixen, 10, De; 20, Je
Brixworth, 7B, Cb
Broach, 73, Bc
Broad, R., 57D, Aa
Brocavum (Brougham), 3A, Db
Brocolitia (Carrowburgh), 3c
Brod, 78, Ac
Brodick, 37A, Bc
Brody, 50, Fc; 84, Hb
Broken Hill, 77, Gh
Bromberg, 54, Fb; 60A, Fb
Brömsebro, 47, Fa; 50, Db
Bromsgrove, 27, Dd
Bromyard, 27, Dd
Brondolo, 32D, Cb
Bronker's Spruit, 81A, Dc
Brookline, 56B
Brooklyn, 57B
Broom, L., 14, Cb
Broome, 77, Ce
Brosna, R., 15, Dc
Brouage, 53, Ce
Brough, 13, Db; 23B, Cc
Brougham, 28B, Cc
Browns Ferry, 72A, Aa
Bruchhausen, 20, Hb
Bruck, 21, Le
Bruffe, 49B, Cd
Bruges, 17, Gc; 46A, Cc
Bruinsberg, 72C, Ab
Brunanburh, 7C, Ba
Brundisium, 2, Ge
Brunei, 91, Ff
Brunig Pass, 29B, Cb
Brunkeberg, 26, Eb
Brünn, 21, Md; 29A, Ga
Brunnen, 29B, Cb
Brunswick, Georgia, 56, Cd
Brunswick, Germany, 10, Db; 38, Hb
Brunswick, Maine, 57, Gb
Brunswick-Lüneburg, D. of, 20, Jb
Brunswick-Wolfenbüttel, D. of, 30, Hb
Brusa, 19, Dd; 86c, Aa
Brussa, 6, Da
Brussels, 28D, Ea; 46A, Dd
Bruttium, 4B, Fd; 5, Fe
Bryansk, 88, Mc
Brycheiniog, 7B, Bc; 13, Ce
Byron, I., 45A, Ea
Bucaramanga, 68, Bb
Bucellas, 63B
Bucfestre (Buckfastleigh), 13, Cf
Buch, 17, Ef
Buchan, 14, Fb
Buchanan, 48B, Aa

Bucharest, 78, Fc
Buchau, 20, Hd
Buchhorn, 20, He; 53, Hd
Buchy, 76A, Ab
Buckingham, 27, Fe
Buckingham, co., 27, Fe
Buckland (Cornwall), 48A, Bg
Buckland (Somerset), 36, Cf
Buczacz, 50, Fd
Buda, 39, Ne
Budapest, 33C, Db; 87, Dc
Budaun, 73, Cb
Budge Budge, 59A, Ec
Budua, 22, Fc
Budweis, 21, Ld; 29A, Fa
Buea, 80A, Ee
Buelt, 7B, Bb; 13, Cd
Buen Ayre, 43A, Fc
Buenaventura, 41B, Bc
Buenos Aires, 68, Df
Buffalo, 71C, Cb
Buffalo, R., C. Prov., 81B, Cc
Buffalo (Umzimyati), R., 81D, Bb
Bug, R., Poland, 26, Fc; 39, Qb
Bug, R., Ukraine, 9, Jc; 50, Gd
Bugey, 38, Fe
Bugia, 34, De
Builth, 27, Cd
Bujids, King. of, 6B, Gb
Buka, 90, Dd
Bukellarian, Theme, 9, Jd
Bukhara, 93, Jb
Bukkur, 73, Ab
Bukovina, 33C, Fb
Bulair, 78, Fe; 86D
Bulawayo, 81A, Cb
Bulgar, 9, Mb; 19, Ha
Bulgaria, 78, Ed
Bulgaria, King. of, 19, Cd
Bulgarians, 8, Jb
Bulgarians of Kazan, 61, Gd
Bulgars, 8C, Db; 25, Da
Bull Run, 72B, Ba
Bulo Burti, 96A, Bb
Bulun, 74, La
Bulwer, 81D, Ab
Bundelkhand, 73, Cc
Bundoran, 49B, Cb
Bungay, 27, Hd
Bunker Hill, 56B
Bunzlau, 21, Lc
Buraburig, 8A, Ca
Buraida, 93, Ed
Burdas, 9, Mb
Burdekin, R., 77, He
Burdigala, 2, Ce
Burdwan, 59A, Ec; 59B
Burford, 7B, Cc; 27, Ee
Burg, 39, Kb
Burg (Peterborough), 13, Fd
Burgas, 78, Fd
Burgau, 20, Jd
Burgdorf, 29B, Ba
Burgh by Sands, 3C
Burgh on Sands, 28B, Bc
Burgos, 22, Bc; 63, Da
Burgos, eccl. prov., 22, Bc
Burgundian Kingdom, 4A, Db
Burgundians, 2A, Bb; 8C, Bb
Burgundiones, 2, Fd
Burgundy, Co. of, 10, Be; 11, Fc
Burgundy, D. of, 11, Fc
Burgundy, King. of (Arelate), 11, Fd
Burhampur, 59C, Cb
Burke (De Burgh), 37B, Cc
Burkesville, 72, Cb
Burketown, 77, Fe
Burlington, New Jersey, 45B, Bc
Burlington, Vermont, 57, Ea
Burma, 73, Gc
Burma (Mien), 25, Jd
Burma Road, 91, Cd
Burpham, 7C, Cc
Burrium (Usk), 3A, De
Bursa, 93, Bf
Burton upon Trent, 36, Ee
Burtone (Burton), 13, Ed
Buru, 52C, Cb; 91, Fg
Burundi, 96, Ee
Bury St. Edmunds, 27, Gd
Busaco, 63, Ab
Bushman Land, 81B, Ab
Bushmans, R., 81D, Ab
Bushmen, 81A, Ac
Bushy Run, 57, Bc
Bussa, 80A, Dc
Bute, 14, Cd
Bute, co., 37A, Bc
Butera, 21A, Cd
Butler, 37B, Dd
Butley, 36, He
Buton, 52C, Cb
Bütow, 31, Ma
Butte des Mortes, 56, Bb
Butterworth, 48B, Cc
Buttington, 7C, Bb
Buxar, 59A, Dc

Buxtehude, 26, Cc
Buzakha, 6, Fc
Buzancy, 76A, Cb
Buzzard B., 45B, Dc
Byblos (Gibelet), 18C, Cd
Bydgoszcz, 31, Nb
Byelgorod, 61, Ed
Byland, 36, Ec
Byrd Land, 95, Gj
Byzantine Empire, 9, Ge
Byzantium, 1, Ec

Cabellum, 5B, Aa
Cabinda, 80A, Ee
Cabinda, col., 96C, De
Cabot Str., 45A, Fa
Cacabellos, 63, Ba
Caceres, 23C, Bc
Cachoeira, 68, Fd
Caconda, 52, Ke
Cadore, 32A, Ea
Cadiz, 23C, Bd; 63, Bd
Cadodachos, 43A, Ca
Cadzand, 46A, Cc
Caen, 11, Cb
Caer Gai, 3A, Cd
Caer Segeini, 7B, Ab
Caer Segont, 13, Bc
Caer Sws, 3A, Cd
Caerdydd (Cardiff), 13, Ce
Caerlaverock, 28B, Bb
Caerleon, 13, De; 28A, Dc
Caerphilly, 27, Ce; 28A, Cc
Caesar Augusta, 2, Ec
Caesarea, Africa, 2, Df; 4A, Cd
Caesarea, Km. of Jerusalem, 18C, Bf
Caesarea, Syria, 18C, Dc
Caesarea, Turkey, 6, Eb; 19, Fe
Caffraria, 69A, Lf
Cagayan, 75E, Bc
Cagliari, 23A, Bd; 32B, Be
Cagliari, eccl. prov., 22, Dd; 23A, Bd
Cahokia, 56, Ac
Cahors, 11, Dd ;17A, Cd
Caicos, 43A, Eb
Caird Coast, 69C
Cairns, 95, Lf
Cairo (Fustat), 6A, Ab
Cairo, Egypt, 80B, Ab
Cairo, Illinois, 72, Cb
Caistor, Lincs., 3A, Fc
Caistor, Norfolk, 7B, Db
Caithness, 14, Da
Cajamarca, 41B , Bd
Calabria, 5, Fd; 21A, Dc
Calabria Theme, 9, Fe
Calahorra, 22, Bc; 23C, Da
Calais, 17A, Ca; 30, Dc
Calamian Group, 75E, Ab
Calatafimi, 32C, De
Calatayud, 23C, Db; 63, Eb
Calatrava, 22, Bd; 23C, Dc
Calcaria (Tadcaster), 3A, Ec
Calcutta, 59B
Caldera, 68, Be
Caldiero, 29A, Dc
Caldonazzo, 86B, Bb
Calebee, 71F, Ba
Caledon, 81B, Ac
Caledon, R., 81B, Cb
Caledonia, 2, Bb; 14, Eb
Calgary, 70, Cb
Calhoun, 72A, Aa
Cali, 68, Bb
Callao, 68, Bd
Calleva Atrebatum (Silchester), 3A, Ee
Callinicum, 2, Lf; 4B, Kd
Calmar, 26, Eb
Calmar, Union of, 35, Ka
Caine, 27, De
Caltabellotta, 21A, Bd
Caltanisetta, 21A, Cd
Calvi, 32B, Bd
Calvinet, 38, Ef
Calvinia, 81B, Ab
Camaldoli, 22, Ec; 23A, Cb
Camarinal, C., 63A
Cambay, 35, Nc; 73, Bc
Cambay, G. of, 73, Bc
Cambodia, 91, Dc
Camboglanna (Birdoswald), 3C
Cambolu, 35, Pb
Cambrai, 46A, Cc
Cambrai, Bp of, 46C, Ab
Cambrésis, 46A, Cc
Cambridge, England, 27, Gd
Cambridge, Massachusetts, 45B, Db; 56B
Cambridge, co., 27, Gd
Cambridge (Charles), R., 56B
Cambuskenneth, 14, Ec
Camden, Arkansas, 72, Bc
Camden, S. Carolina, 57D, Ab
Camelon, 3A, Ca
Camerino, 5, Dc

Cameron, 37A, Bb
Cameroon, 96D, Dd
Cameroons, 96C, Dd
Cameta, 68, Ec
Camisards, 54, Cd
Campagna, 32A, Ed
Campaldino, 32E, Bb
Campania, 5, Dd
Campbell, 28B, Aa; 37A, Bb
Campbell I., 69C; 75, Fg
Campbeltown, 49A, Bc
Campeche, 43A, Cc
Campeche, st., 43A, Cc
Campeche, G. of, 43A, Cb
Camperdown, 55A, Fb
Campinas, 68, Ee
Campo Formio, 65A, Bb
Campobasso, 32A, Fd
Campos, 68, Ee
Camulodunum (Colchester), 3A, Ge
Canada, 45A, Ba; 69A, Fb
Canadian, R., 70, Dd
Canal Zone, 68, Ab
Canary Is., 80A, Bb
Canaveral, C., 70, Fe
Canberra, 77, Hi
Cancelleria, 5A
Candia, 19, De; 78, Eh
Canea, 78, Eh
Canigou, 22, Cc
Canna, 15, Bb
Cannae, 21A, Db
Cannanore, 59A, Ce
Cannes, 30, Gg
Canossa, 23B, Cb
Canovium (Caerhun), 3A, Cc
Canso, C., 45A, Ea
Cantabria, 4A ,Bc; 8, Bc
Cantabrian Mts., 63, Ca
Canterbury, England, 27, He
Canterbury, N.Z., 77A
Canterbury, bp., 36, Gf
Canterbury, eccl. prov., 22, Ba
Canterbury Plain, 77, Mj
Cantii, 3A, Ge
Canton, China, 25, Ld; 91, Ed
Canton, Mississippi, 72, Bc
Cantuaria (Canterbury), 13, He
Cantware, 7A, Db
Canusium, 5, Fd
Cão, 35, Kf
Cap Francois, 43A, Ec
Capdenac, 38, Ef
Cape, 81B, Ac
Cape Ann (Gloucester), 45B, Db
Cape Breton I., 71, Hc
Cape Breton I. (Ile Royale), 45A, Ea
Cape Coast, 96B, Bb
Cape Coast Castle, 81C, Cc
Cape Cod B., 45B, Dc
Cape Colony, 69A, Lf
Cape Colony (Cape of Good Hope), 81A, Bd
Cape Fear, R., 57, Bf; 57D, Ba
Cape Fear (Charles), R., 45A, Bc
Cape of Good Hope (Cape Colony, 81A), Bd
Cape Porpoise, 45B, Db
Cape Town, 81B, Ac
Caper Verde Is., 80A, Ac
Cape York Pen., 77, Gd
Capetown, 52, Kf
Capitanata, 32A, Fd
Capitol, 5A
Capiz, 75E, Bb
Capo d'Istria, 22, Eb; 32D, Cb
Cappadocia, 2, Lf
Cappadocia Theme, 9, Je
Caporetto, 84, Ec; 86B, Da
Caprera I., 32C, Bd
Capri, 5, Ed
Capsa, 6, Bb
Capua, 5, Ed; 32A, Fd
Capua, D. of, 23A, Ec
Capua, Pr. of, 21A, Cb
Caqueta, R., 68, Bc
Carabobo, 68, Cb
Caracas, 41B, Cc; 68, Cb
Caradeña, 22, Bc
Caralis, 2, Ef
Caramania, 33A, Dc
Caravaggio, 32D, Ab
Carberry House, 37A, Cc
Carbisdale, 37A, Bb
Carcassonne, 11, Ee
Cardaillac, 38, Df
Cardiff, 3A, Ce; 27, Ce
Cardigan, 13, Db; 28A, Bb
Cardigan, co., 27, Bd
Cardigan B., 27, Bd
Carelia, 26, Ha; 47, Ja
Carentan, 38, Cd
Carhaix, 11, Bb
Carham, 14, Fd
Caribbean Sea, 43A, Ec
Caribs, 43A, Fd
Carignano, 29A, Bc; 30, Gf

Carinthia, D. of, 10, Fe; 21, Ke
Carisbrooke Castle, 48B, Cd
Carlat, 17, Gf; 30, Ef
Carleol (Carlisle), 13, Db
Carlingford, 49B, Eb
Carlisle, England, 27, Db
Carlisle, N. America, 57, Cc
Carlisle, bp., 36, Cd
Carlow, 15, Ed
Carlow, co., 37C; 49B, Ed
Carlowitz, 33C, Db; 79, Ca
Carlsbad, 64, Ec; 65C, Ba
Carlsruhe, 65A, Ab
Carmanfa, 1, He
Carmarthen, 27, Be; 36, Bf
Carmarthen, co., 27, Be; 28A, Bc
Carmel, Mt., 18C, Cf
Carmona, 23C, Cd
Carnarvon, Australia, 95, Ng
Carnarvon, S. Africa, 81B, Bb
Carnarvon, Wales, 27, Bc
Carnarvon, co., 27, Bd
Carnatic, 73, Ce
Carnero Pt., 63A
Carnic Alps, 29A, Eb; 86B ,Ca
Carnifex Ferry, 72, Db
Carniola, 10, Ff
Carniola, D. of, 21, Lf
Carnsore Pt., 15, Ed
Carolina, 45A, Ad
Caroline Is., 74, Mg; 90, Dc
Carolines, 40, Rd
Carpathian Mts., 8, Gb; 50, Ed
Carpathian Ruthenia, 87, Ec
Carpatus Mons, 2, Md
Carpentaria, G. of, 77, Fd
Carpentras, 22, Dc
Carpi, 32A, Db
Carrantuohill, 15, Be
Carrara, 32B, Cb
Carrick, Galloway, 14, Dd
Carrick, Leitrim, 49B, Cc
Carrick, Tipperary, 49B, Dd
Carrickfergus, 37B, Fb; 49B, Fb
Carricks Ford, 72, Eb
Carriden, 3A, Ca
Carrig a Foyle, 49B, Bd
Carse of Gowrie, 28B, Ba
Carso, 86B, Db
Cartagena, Columbia, 43A, Ec
Cartagena, Spain, 4A, Bd; 23C, Ed; 63, Ed
Cartago, 41B, Bc
Cartersville, 72A, Aa
Carthage, 4A, Ed; 9, Ee
Carthage, U.S.A., 70, Ed
Carthago, 2, Ff
Carthago Nova, 2, Cf
Cartmel, 28B, Cc; 36, Dc
Carumnassa, R., 59A, Db
Casablanca, 80A, Ca; 96D, Ba
Casale, 32A, Cb
Casalmaggiore, 32D, Bb
Casco B., 57, Fb
Casco (Fort Loyal) (Falmouth), 45B, Db
Caseros, 68, Df
Cashel, 15, Dd
Caspe, 23C, Eb; 23D, Eb
Caspian Sea, 19, Hd; 25, Eb
Cassanitae, 1, Ge
Cassano, Calabria, 22, Fd
Cassano, Lombardy, 29A, Cc
Cassel, Flanders, 20, Fc
Cassel, Thuringia, 20, Hc
Cassett, 30, Ee
Castalla, 63, Ec
Castamon, 18A, Ea
Castanheira, 63B
Castel Branco, 22, Ad
Castel Jaloux, 38, Df
Castel Sardo, 23B, Bd
Castelbaldo, 32D, Bb
Castelfranco, 86B, Bb
Castell Collen, 3A, Cd
Castellamare, 32C, Ed
Castello, 22A
Castello Branco, 63, Bc
Castello Tesino, 86B, Ba
Castellon Alani (Richmond), 13 Eb
Castellon Harundel (Arundel), 13, Ff
Castellon Warham (Corfe Castle), 13 Df
Castelnau, 20, Dg
Castelnaudary, 30, Dg
Castelnuovo, 78, Bd
Castelorizo, 86C, Ab
Castelsagrat, 38, Df
Castets, 38, Cf
Castiglione, Lombardy, 29A, Dc
Castiglione, Tuscany, 20, Jg
Castile, King. of, 23C, Cb
Castilia do Oro, 43A, Dd
Castle I., 56B
Castle Dermot, 49B, Ed

Castle Douglas, 49A, Cc
Castle Flemish, 3A, Be
Castle of St. Angelo, 5A
Castle Rising, 48A, Dc
Castlebar, 49B, Bc
Castlecary, 3A, Ca
Castledykes, 3A, Ca
Castlefinn, 49B, Db
Castlehill, 3A, Ba
Castlejordan, 15, Dc
Castlekevin, 37B, Ec
Castlereagh, 49B, Cc
Castleroe, 37B, Ea
Castlesteads, 3C
Castleton, 57, Eb
Castletown, 48A, Ab
Castra Exploratum (Netherby), 3A, Ca
Castres, 20, Eg; 22, Cc
Castro, 22, Ec; 32B, Cc
Castro Giovanni, 23A, Ef
Castrum Felicitatis, 5B, Ba
Cat I., 43A, Eb
Catalans, 85, Cd
Catalonia, 23C, Fb; 63, Fb
Catalonia, Pr. of, 16, Cd
Catamarca, 68, Ce
Catanduanes, 75E, Bb
Catania, 21A, Cd; 22, Fd
Catanzaro, 22, Fd
Cataractonium (Catterick Bridge), 3A, Eb
Cateau Cambrésis, 34, Cb
Cathay, 25, Kc
Cathkin Peak, 81D, Ab
Catóche, C., 43A, Eb
Catric (Catterick), 13, Eb
Catrone, 22, Dc
Catskill Mts., 57, Db
Cattaro, 22, Fc; 78, Bd
Cattegat, 84, Ea
Catterick, 7A, Ca
Catuvellauni, 3A, Fe
Cauca, R., 68, Bb
Caudebec, 20, Dd
Cauna (Calne), 13, De
Causennae (Ancaster), 3A, Fd
Caus, 13, Dd; 28A, Db
Causse, 38, Eg
Cauvery, R., 73, Ce
Cavan, 49B, Dc
Cavan, co., 37C; 49B, Dc
Cavour, 32C, Ab
Cawnpore, 73, Db
Cawood Castle, 48A, Cc
Cayenne, 43B, Ed; 68, Db
Cayman Is., 43A, Dc
Cayo Romano, 43A, Eb
Cayoan, 52B, Aa
Cayugas, 45A, Bb
Ceara, 41B, Fd
Ceara (Fortaleza), 68, Fc
Ceara, st., 68, Fc
Cebu, 75E, Bb
Cebu, I., 75E, Bb
Ceccanum, 5B, Bc
Cedar Creek, 72B, Aa
Cedar Keys, 72, Dd
Cedar Mountain, 72B, Aa
Cedar Rapids, 57, Ea
Cefalu, 21A, Cc; 22, Fd
Celebes, 52C, Bb; 74, Lj
Celebes (Sulawesi), 91, Eg
Celebes Sea, 91, Ff
Celle, 30, Jb
Celorico, 63, Bb
Celtic Lands, 4A, Aa
Celts, 8C, Aa
Cembala, 19, Ed
Ceneda, 22, Eb
Central Africa, rep., 96D, Dd
Central America, rep., 69A, Ed
Central Australia, 77, Ef
Central Provinces, India, 74, Ff
Cephallenia Theme, 9, Ge
Cephalonia, 78, Cf
Cephalonia, Co. of, 24, Gf
Ceprano, 23B, Dd
Ceram, 52C, Cb; 77, Db; 91, Fg
Cerami, 23A, Ef
Ceramix, 21A, Cd
Cerdagne, 30, Dg
Cerdana, 23C, Ga
Ceredigion (Cardigan), 7B, Ab; 13, Bd
Ceri, 13, Cd
Cerignola, 32A, Fd
Cerigo, 18B, Cc; 78, Dg
Cerisolo, 29A, Bc
Cernauti, 87, Fc
Cerne, 36, Dg
Cerneli (Cerne Abbas), 13, Df
Cerralvo, 43A, Cb
Cerro de Pasco, 68, Bd
Certesyg (Chertsey), 13, Fe
Cervera, 63, Fb
Cervignano, 86B, Db
Cesena, 32A, Eb

Cesenae, 5B, Ba
Cesme, 51, Ff
Cestre (Chester), 13, Dc
Cestrescire (Cheshire), 13, Dc
Cetinje, 78, Bd
Cette, 30, Eg
Ceuta, 23C, Ce; 34, Ac; 63A
Cevennes, 11, Ed
Ceylon, 73, Df
Ceylon (Seilan), 25, Hf
Chabats, 78, Bc
Chablais, 29B, Ab
Chacabuco, 68, Bf
Chaco, 68, Ce
Chaco, L., 96B, Da
Chad, rep., 96D, Dc
Chads Ford, 57, Dd
Chagos Is., 69A, Ne; 94, Qf
Chagres, 43A, Ed
Chalcedon, 2, Je; 8, Hc
Chalchuites, 43A, Bb
Chalcis, 4B, Kd
Chaldea Theme, 9, Kd
Chaldiran, 33A, Fb
Chaleur B., 45A, Da
Chalgrove Field, 48A, Cd
Challon, 29B, Ab
Chalon, 11, Fc
Chalôns, 11, Fb; 83A. Cb
Châlons Camp, 76A, Cb
Chaluz, 17, Ff
Cham, 21, Kd
Chambal, R., 73, Cb
Chambersburg, 72, Eb
Chambéry, 20, Ff; 30, Ff
Chambly, 56, Ea
Champa, 25, Ke
Champagne, 11, Eb; 83A, Cb
Champagne, Co. of, 20, Fb
Champigny, 76A, Bb
Champion's Hill, 72C, Aa
Champlain L., 57, Ea
Chanak, 86D
Chancellorsville, 72B, Ba
Chandax, 9, He
Chandernagore, 59B
Chandière, R., 71E, Ac
Chang-an, 1, Nd
Changchow, 41A, Jb
Changchun, 91, Fb
Changsha, 91, Ed
Changtan, 76B, Ba
Channel Is., 11, Bb
Chantoceaux, 20, Ce
Chapelle St. Lambert, 46B
Charak, 93, Gd
Charcot I., 69C
Chard, 27, Df; 48A, Bd
Charente, R., 17, Ef
Charing Cross, 27A
Charleroi, 46A, Dd
Charles, C., 45B, Be
Charles (Cambridge), R., 56B
Charles, King. of, 8A, Bc
Charles (Cape Fear), R., 45A, Bc
Charles City, 45B, Ae
Charles Fort, 45A, Ad
Charles Town, 45A, Ad
Charleston, Massachusetts, 45B, Db
Charleston, S. Carolina, 57D, Bb
Charleston, W. Virginia, 72, Db
Charleston (Stephen's Fort), 57, Eb
Charlestown, Massachusetts, 56B
Charlestown, Natal, 81D, Aa
Charleville, Australia, 95, Lg
Charleville, France, 53, Fc
Charlotte, 57, Af
Charlottesville, 57, Be
Charlottetown, 71, Hc
Charolais, 30, Fe; 38, Fe
Charolles, 17, He
Charolles, co., 31A, Bd
Charost, 53, Ed
Charroux, 22, Cb
Charsianon Theme, 9, Je
Charter, 81A, Da
Charters Towers, 77 Hf
Chartres, 11, Db; 17A, Cb
Chartreux, 11, Fc
Chatalja, 78, Ge
Château Chinon, 30, Ee
Château Dauphin, 53, Ge
Château d'If, 38, Fg
Château des Dames, 83A, Bb
Château Gaillard, 20, Dd
Château Neuf, 20, Ee
Château Thierry, 17, Gd
Châteaubriant, 38, Ce
Châteaudun, 11, Db
Châteauguay, R., 71C, Da
Châteauroux, 17, Fe
Châteauroux, S. of, 20, De
Châtellerault, 11, Dc
Chatham, 55A, Dc
Chatham I., 75, Gg
Châtillon, 38, Cd; 76A, Cc

Chattahoochee, R., 72, Cc
Chattanooga, 72A, Aa
Chaudière, R., 56, Ea
Chaumont, 20, Fd; 76A, Cb
Chaves, 23C, Bb; 63, Bb
Cheat, R., 57, Bd
Cheduba I., 90, Ac
Chefoo, 74, Le
Chegar, R., 59D
Chelm, 26, Fc; 33C, Ea
Chelmsford, 27, Ge
Chelsea, 56B
Chelyabinsk, 89, Sb
Chelyuskin, C., 69B
Chemnitz, 31, Kc; 53, Kb
Chenab, R., 73, Ba
Chenaresburg (Knaresborough), 13, Eb
Chengtu, 25, Kc; 91, Dc
Chenth (Kent), 13, Ge
Cher, R., 11, Dc; 17, Ge
Chera, 1, Kf
Cherasco, 32B, Ab; 47, Dd
Cheraw, 57D, Ba
Cherbourg, 28D, Bb; 30, Cd
Cherchebi (Kirkby Lonsdale), 13, Db
Cheren, 96A, Aa
Cheriton, 48A, Cd
Cherkassy, 79, Fa
Cherna, R., 86A, Ca
Chernigov, 19, Eb; 26, Hc
Cherokees, 45A. Ac
Cherry Valley, 57, Db
Cherso, 23B, Eb
Cherson, 2A, Eb; 19, Ed
Cherson Theme, 9, Jd
Chertsey, 36, Ff
Chesapeake B., 57, Cd
Chester, England, 27, Dc
Chester, Illinois, 70, Fd
Chester, Pennsylvania, 57, Dd
Chester (Fort New Korsholm), 45B, Bd
Chester, bp., 36, Gd
Chester, Co. Palatine of, 27, Dc
Chesterfield Inlet, 70, Ea
Chesterford, 3A, Gd
Chester-ie-Street, 3A, Eb; 7C, Ca
Chetsteven (Kesteven), 13, Fd
Cheviot Hills, 27, Da; 28B, Cb
Cheyenne, 70, Ea
Chiangmai, 91, Ce
Chiao Chow, 1, Oe
Chiapas, 43A, Cc
Chiavenna, 5, Ba; 23B, Bd
Chiavenna, Co. of, 29B, Db
Chicacole, 59A, Dd
Chicago, 56, Bb
Chichagof I., 71B, Cb
Chichester, 27, Ff
Chichester, bp., 36, Fg
Chickamauga, 72A, Aa
Chickasaw Bluff (Memphis), 71F, Aa
Chickasaws, Alabama,43A,Da,
Chickasaws, W. Virginia, 45A, Ac
Chiclayo, 68, Bc
Chicora, 43A, Da
Chidambaram, 59D
Chidley, C., 71, Ha
Chiem L., 29A, Eb
Chiemsee, 22, Eb
Chiengmai, 73, Gd
Chiese, R., 5, Cb; 86B, Ab
Chieti, 5, Ec
Chieveley, 81D, Ab
Chigirin, 50, Gd
Chignecto, C., 45A, Ea
Chihuahua, 43A, Bb
Chikishlyar, 61B, Ab
Chile, 42, Ff; 68, Be
Chilianwala, 73, Ba
Chilkat B., 71B, Bb
Chillan, 68, Bf
Chillicothe, 56, Cc
Chiloe I., 68, Bg
Chiltern Hills, 27, Fe
Chilternsaetan, 7B, Cc
Chimay, 30, Fc; 46A, Dd
Chimkent, 61B, Ba
China, 41A, Ja; 74, Je
China Sea, 25, Le
Chinampo, 76B, Cb
Chincha Is., 68, Bd
Chinchowfu, 76B, Aa
Chinde, 83, Le
Chindwin, R., 73, Dc
Chinese Eastern Railway, 74, Ld
Chinese Empire, 83, Oc
Chinese Rep., 91, Dc
Ching Chow, 1, Oe
Chingleput, 59D
Chingkiang, 25, Lc; 74, Le
Chinon, 17, Fe; 28C, Cc
Chins Division, 92, Gc
Chinsura, 59B
Chiny, 20, Fd

Chioggia, 32D, Cb
Chios, 24, Hf; 78, Ef
Chippenham, 7C, Bc; 27, De
Chippewa, 71D
Chipping Norton, 27, Ee
Chirbury, 13, Cd
Chirk, 27, Cd
Chisholm, 37A, Bb
Chita, 91, Ea
Chitaldroog, 59A, Ce
Chitor, 25, Gd; 52A, Bb
Chittagong, 92, Gc
Chittagong, st., 73, Fc
Chiusi, 5, Cc
Chobe Swamp, 81A, Ba
Choctaws, 56, Bjd
Choczim, 50, Fd; 54, Hc
Choiseul, E. Indies, 77, Jc
Choiseul, France, 53, Fc
Chola, 1, Kf
Cholas, 25, Ge
Cholula, 43A, Cc
Chongju, 76B, Cb
Chonos Arch., 68, Bg
Chorasmia, 1, Jc
Chorlu (Tzurulum), 19, Dd
Chota Nagpur, 73, Dc
Chotusitz, 29A, Fa
Chowan, R., 45B, Ae
Christchurch, England, 27, Ef
Christchurch, N.Z., 77A
Christiania, 50, Cb; 54, Ea
Christiansand, 26, Cb
Christiansborg, 69A, Kd; 81C, Dc
Christianstad, 51, Cb
Christmas I., Indian Ocean, 83, Pe
Christmas I., Pacific Ocean, 75, Hd
Christopolis, 19, Cd
Chrysopolis, 2, Je; 18E
Chrystler's Farm, 71C, Ca
Chu, R., 91, Ab
Chubut (Rawson), 68, Cg
Chubut, R., 68, Cg
Chudes, 9, Ha
Chulak, 61B, Ba
Chungking, 91, Dd
Chur, 5, Ba; 29B, Cb
Church, States of the, 32A, Ec
Church of the Holy Sepulchre, 18D
Churchill, 70, Eb
Churchill, R., 70, Db
Cibalae, 2, Gd
Cibyrrhaeot Theme, 9, Je
Cicestre (Chichester), 13, Ff
Cilgerran, 28A, Bb
Cilicia, 2A, Ec; 18C, Cb
Cilicia Theme, 2, Kf
Cilli, 21, Le
Cilurnum (Chesters), 3C
Cimarron, R., 70, Ed
Cin, Sea of, 25, Md
Cinbretune (Kinderton), 13,Dc
Cincinnati, 57A, Cb; 71C, Bc
Cintra, 23C, Ac; 63B
Circassia, 61, Ff
Circesium, 2, Mg; 4A, Ld
Circle City, 71A, Ca
Cirencester, 27, Ee
Cirencestre (Cirencester), 13, Ee
Cirey, 83B, Ba
Cirta, 2, Ef
Cisalpine (Italian) Rep., 65A, Ab
Citatea, 78, Dc
Citeaux, 11, Fc
Citra, 32A, Fd
Citronelle, 72, Cd
Citta di Castello, 32A, Ec
Cittadella, 86B, Bb
Cittavecchia, 22, Fc
City Pt., 57, Ce
Ciudad Bolivar (Angostura), 68, Cb
Ciudad Real, 23C, Ce; 63, Dc
Ciudad Rodrigo, 23C, Bb; 63, Bb
Ciudad Victoria, 43A, Cb
Ciudadela, 22, Cc
Cividale, 21, Ke; 86B, Da
Civita, 23B, Bd
Civita Vecchia, 5, Cc
Civitate, 21A, Cb
Civitella, 32A, Ec
Clackmannan, co., 37A, Cb; 49A, Cb
Cladyford, 49B, Db
Clair-sur-Epte, 11, Db
Clairac, 22, Cc; 38, Df
Clairvaux, 11, Fb
Clanwilliam, 81B, Ac
Clara (Clare), 13, Cd
Clare, England, 27, Gd
Clare, Ireland, 37B, Cd
Clare, Wales, 28A, Cc
Clare, co., Ireland, 37C; 49B, Cd
Clare, R., 15, Cc

Clarendon, England, 17, Ec
Clarendon, N. Carolina, 45A, Bd
Classis, 23A, Da
Clausentum (Bitterne), 3A, Ef
Claverhouse, 37A, Cb
Clear, C., 15, Be
Cleeve, 36, Cf
Clermont, Auvergne, 8B, Bb; 11, Ed
Clermont, Champagne, 39B, Ba; 76A, Cb
Clermont, Co. of, 20, Ed; 39B, Ba
Clermont Ferrand, 53, Ee
Cleve, Netherlands, 46A, Fc
Cleve, Co. of, Netherlands, 46A, Fc
Cleveland, Ohio, 71C, Bb
Cleveland, Tennessee, 72A, Aa
Cleves, 53, Gb
Clew B., 15, Bc; 49B, Bc
Clifford, Scotland, 28B, Cc
Clifford, Wales, 13, Cd
Clifford, Co. of., Wales, 28A, Cb
Clifton, 49A, Cc
Clinton, 72C, Aa
Clisson, 28C, Bc
Clissow, 50, Ec
Clogher, 15, Db
Clonard, 15, Dc
Cloncurry, 77, Gf
Clones, 37B, Db; 49B, Db
Clonfert, 15, Cc; 49B, Cc
Clonlish, 49B, Bd
Clonmacnoise, 15, Dc
Clonmel, 37B, Dd; 49B, Dd
Clontarf, 12, Cc; 49B, Ec
Cloudy B., 77A
Cloyne, 15, Ce
Clun, 27, Cd; 28A, Cb
Cluny, 11, Fc
Clydesdale, 14, Ed; 28B, Bb
Clyde, R., 14, Ed; 28B, Ab
Clyde, Firth of, 14, Dd
Clyveland (Cleveland), 13, Eb
Coahuila, 70, Dd
Coats I., 70, Fa
Coats Land, 69C
Cobh (Queenstown), 49B, Ce
Cobija, Bolivia, 68, Cd
Cobija, Chile, 68, Be
Coblenz, 10, Bc; 38, Gc
Coburg, 30, Jc
Cochem, 20, Gc
Cochin, 59A, Ce; 73, Cf
Cochin, st., 59C, Ce; 73, Ce
Cochin China, 74, Jg
Cockburn Chan., 68, Bh
Cockermouth, 27, Cb
Cocos (Keeling) Is., 83, Oe; 90, Ad
Cod, C., 45B, Db
Coevorden, 46A, Fb
Coggeshall, 36, Gf
Cognac, 38, Df
Cohoes, 57, Eb
Coiba I., 43A, Dd
Coigny, 53, Cc
Coimbatore, 73, Ce
Coimbra, 22, Ac; 63, Ab
Colchester, 27, Ge
Cold Harbor, 72B, Bb
Coldstream, 36, Db; 37A, Cc
Colecestra (Colchester), 13, Ge
Colemerik, 93, Eb
Colenso, 81D, Ab
Coleraine, 49B, Ea
Coleroon, R., 52A, Cc; 59D
Colesberg, 81B, Cb
Coligny, 20, Fe
Colima, 43A, Bc
Coll, 14, Bc
Colle, 32E, Bb
Colleton, 45A, Ad
Collioure, 23D, Ga; 53, Ef
Colmar, 8A, Cb; 10, Bd
Colmars, 53, Ge
Cologne, 10, Bc; 83A, Da
Cologne, Abp. of, 46C, Cb
Cologne, eccl. prov., 22, Da
Colombey, 76A, Db
Colombia, 68, Bb
Colombia, Confederation of, 43D, Fd
Colombia, Rep. of, 68, Bb
Colombia, U.S. of, 68, Bb
Colombo, 73, Cf
Colon (Aspinwall), 43D, Ed
Colonea Theme, 9, Kd
Colonia, 68, Df
Colonia Agrippina, 2, Ec
Colonia del Sacramento, 41B, Dg
Colonna, C., 23A, Fd
Colonsay, 14, Bc
Colooney, 49B, Cb
Colorado, R., Argentina, 68, Cf
Colorado, R., U.S.A., 44, Ee
Colorado, st., 70, Dd
Colorado Terr., 67D, Cb

Colosseum, 5A
Columbia, S. Carolina, 57D, Aa
Columbia, Tennessee, 72, Cb
Columbia, Virginia, 56, Dc
Columbia, R., 70, Cb
Columbus, Kentucky, 72, Cb
Columbus, Ohio, 72, Db
Colwyn, 28A, Cb
Comacchio, 5, De
Combermere, 36, De
Comeragh Mts., 15, Dd
Comfort Pt., 67A, Cb
Comiaclum, 5B, Ba
Cominges, 17, Fg; 20, Dg
Cominges, Co. of, 11, De
Commercy, 39B, Bb
Comminges, 22, Cc
Como, 5, Bb; 29A, Cc
Como, L., 5, Ba
Comorin, C., 73, Cf
Comoro Is., 80A, Hf
Compiègne, 17, Gd; 31A, B
Compludo, 22, Ac
Compoalla, 43A, Cc
Compostela, 43A, Bb
Compostela, 16, Ad
Conakry, 96B, Ab
Concepcion, Chile, 68, Bf
Concepcion, Paraguay, 68, De
Concepcion, Uruguay, 68, Df
Concord, 45B, Db
Concordia, 68, Df
Conde, 46A, Cd
Condeixa, 63, Ab
Condercum (Benwell), 3C
Condom, 53, Df
Conegliano, 86B, Db
Conflans, 30, Ed; 83A, Cb
Congaree, R., 57D, Ab
Congo, rep., (formerly Belgian) 96D, Ee
Congo, rep. (formerly French) 96D, De
Congo, R., 80A, Fd
Congo State, 80A, Fe
Coni, 20, Gf
Coningesburg (Conisborough), 13, Ec
Conisborough, 27, Ec
Conjeeveram, 59D
Connacht, 15, Cc
Connaught, 37B, Cc; 49C
Connecticut, 45B, Cc
Connecticut, R., 45A, Cb
Conn, L., 15, Bb; 37B, Bc
Connor, 15, Eb; 49B, Eb
Consentia (Cosenza), 5, Fe
Constance, 10, Ce; 29B, Da
Constance, L. of, 29B, Da
Constanta, 78, Gc
Constantia, 81B, Ac
Constantine, 80A, Da
Constantinople, 18E; 78, Ge
Constantinopolis (Byzantium), 2, Je
Constantsa, 24, He
Constitucion, 68, Bf
Conti, 53, Ec
Convent Garden, 27A
Conversano, 21A, Db
Conway, 27, Cc
Conza, 23, Fc
Cooch Behar, 59C, Eb
Cook Inlet, 71A, Bb
Cook Is., 75, Hf
Cook, Mt., 77, Lj
Cook Str., 77, Mj
Cook's Mill, 71D
Cooktown, 77, Ge
Coolgardie, 77, Ch
Coombe, 36, Ee
Cooper's Creek, 77, Gg
Coorg, 73, Ce
Coosa, R., 56, Bd
Copenhagen, 26, Db
Copiapo, 41B, Bf; 68, Be
Coppermine, R., 70, Ca
Coquet, R., 28B, Db; 48A, Bb
Coquimbo, 68, Bf
Coral Sea, 77, Je; 90, Dd
Corato, 21A, Db
Corbach, 60A, Bc
Corbeil, 11, Eb
Corbet, 28A, Db
Corbie, 11, Eb; 22, Ca
Corbridge, 27, Ea
Cordoba, 68, Cf
Cordova, Alaska, 71A, Ca
Cordova, Spain, 22, Bd; 63, Cd
Cordova, Emirate of, 8, Bd
Corduba, 2, Cf
Corfe Castle, 27, Df
Corfu, 78, Bf
Coria, 22, Ac; 63, Bc
Coringa, 59C, Dd
Corinium (Cirencester), 3A, Ee
Corinth, Greece, 2, Hf
Corinth, U.S.A., 72, Cc
Corinth, G. of, 78, Df
Coritani, 3A, Fc
Cork, 15, Ce
Cork, co., 37C; 49B, Ce

Cork Harbour, 37B, Ce
Cormantine, 81C, Dc
Cormons, 86B, Db
Cornbie (Carn Brea), 13, Af
Corneto, 22A; 23B, Cc
Cornouaille, Co. of, 11, Bb
Cornovii, 3A, Dd
Cornvalge (Cornwall), 13, Bf
Cornwall, Canada, 57, Da
Cornwall, co., 27, Bf
Coro, 43A, Fc
Coromandel, 77A
Coromandel Coast, 59A, De
Coron, 19, Ce
Coronel, 86, Ff
Corpus Christi, 70, Ee
Correggio, 32A, Db
Corregidor, 90, Cc
Corrientes, 68, De
Corrientes, C., Cuba, 43A, Db
Corrientes, C., Mexico, 43A, Bb
Corrieyairack Pass, 49A, Bb
Corsewall Pt., 49A, Ac
Corsica, 5, Bc
Corstopitum (Corbridge), 3C
Cortenuova, 20, Hf
Cortona, Bruttium, 5, Fe
Cortona, Florence, 21, Kg
Corumba, 68, Dd; 94, Cf
Corunna, 23D, Aa; 63, Aa
Corvey, 22, Da; 65B, Aa
Cos, 78, Fg
Cosenza, 23A, Fd
Cosenza (Consentia), 5, Fe
Cossacks, 50, Gd
Cossimbazar, 59B
Costa Rica, 43D, Dc
Côte d'Or, 76A, Cc
Coteau du Lac, 57, Da
Cotentin, 8, Bb; 17, Ed
Cotonou, 94, Te; 96B, Cb
Cotrone, 23A, Fd
Cotswold Hills, 27, De
Cottian Alps, 29A, Bc
Couci, 11, Eb
Couci, S. of, 20, Ed
Coudres, I. aux, 45A, Ca
Coulmiers, 76A, Ac
Countisbury, 7C, Bc
Coupland, 28B, Bc
Couserans, 22, Cc
Courantyne, 68, Db
Courtrai, 28C, Da; 46A, Cd
Coutances, 11, Cb
Coutras, 38, Cf
Covadonga, 22, Bc
Covelong, 59D
Coventreu (Coventry), 13, Ed
Coventry, 27, Ed
Cowal, 14, Cd
Cowans Ford, 57, Af
Cowpens, 56, Cc; 57D, Aa
Cozumel, 43A, Db
Crac de la Pierre (Krak), 18C, Cg
Cracow, 21, Nc
Cracow, Rep. of, 64, Gc
Cradock, 81B, Cc
Craigmillar, 37A, Cc
Crail, 49A, Cb
Cramond, 3A, Ca
Craon, 20, Ce
Craonne, 83A, Bb
Crati, R., 21A, Dc
Crave (Craven), 13, Db
Craven, 45A, Bd
Crawford, 37A, Cc
Crecy, 28C, Ca
Crediton, 27, Cf; 36, Cg
Creeks, 56, Bd; 71F, Ba
Crefeld, 46A, Fc
Creil, 83A, Bb
Crema, 32D, Ab
Cremona, 5, Cd
Creneburne (Cranborne) 13, Ef
Crépy, 53, Ec
Crespy, 38, Ed
Creta, 2, Jf
Crete, 19, Ce; 78, Eh
Crevant, 28D, Dc
Crewkerne, 48B, Bd
Criccieth, 28A, Bb
Crichelade (Cricklade), 13, Ee
Crickhowell, 28A, Cc
Cricklade, 27, Ee
Crim, Khanate of, 79, Ga
Crim Tartary, 33A, Ea
Crimea, 50, Gd
Croagh Patrick, 15, Bc
Croatan I., 45A, Bd
Croatia, 21, Lf
Croats, 9, Fc
Croce, Mte., 86B, Ca
Croceraguel, 36, Bb
Crococalana (Brough), 3A, Fc
Croisic, 55A, Be
Cromarty, 14, Bb; 49A, Bb

Cromarty, co., 37A, Bb
Cromarty Firth, 14, Db
Cropredy Bridge, 48A, Cc
Cross Sd., 71B, Bb
Crossen, 31, Lb
Croton, 57, Ec
Crowland, 7B, Cb; 7C, Cb; 36, Fe
Crown Point, 57, Eb
Crown Princess Martha Land, 69C
Crows Nest Pass, 44, Cd
Croxton, 36, Fe
Crozet Is., 69C
Cruces (Venta Cruz), 43A, Ed
Cruilande (Crowland), 13, Fd
Crussol, 20, Ff
Cruz, C. de, 43A, Ec
Cruzeiro do Sul, 94, Df
Csanad, 19, Gd
Ctesiphon, 1, Gd; 6A, Db
Cuba, 43A, Db
Cuch Behar, 73, Eb
Cucui, 68, Cb
Cucuta, 68, Bb
Cuddalore, 59D
Cuddapah, 73, Ce
Cuenca, Ecuador, 68, Bc
Cuenca, Spain, 22, Bc
Cuiaba, 68, Dd
Cuillins, 14, Bb
Cujavia, 26, Ec; 39, Nb
Culebra B., 43A, Dc
Culiacan, 43A, Bb
Cullen, 49A, Cb
Culloden, 49A, Bb
Culpeper, 72B, Ba
Cumana, 43A, Fc
Cumans, 19, Dc
Cumberland, 71C, Cc
Cumberland, co., 27, Cb
Cumberland Gap, 72, Db
Cumberland House, 44, Dc
Cumberland Mts., 56, Cc
Cumberland, R., 56, Bc
Cumberland Sd., 70, Ha
Cumbria, 7B, Ba; 13, Db
Cumbrian Hills, 27, Cb
Cumnock, 37A, Bc; 49A, Bc
Cuncacestre (Chester-le-Street), 13, Eb
Cuneo, 32A, Bb
Cunningham, 14, Dd
Cupar, 37A, Cb
Curcura, 23B, Fc
Curico, 68, Bf
Curitiba, 68 Ee
Curzola, 22, Fc
Cushendun, 49B, Ea
Cussey, 76A, Cc
Custozza, 32C, Cb
Cutch, 73, Ac
Cuttack, 73, Ec
Cuttack, st., 73, Ec
Cuxhaven, 55A, Hb; 60B, Bb
Cuyo Is., 75E, Bb
Cuyuni, R., 68B, Ba
Cuzco, 68, Bd
Cyclades, 78, Eg
Cydewain, 13, Cd
Cydnus, R., 18C, Ba
Cynllaith, 13, Cd
Cyprus, 2, Kg; 4A, Je; 6A, Ab
Cyprus, King. of, 18A, Eb
Cyprus Theme, 9, Je
Cyrenaica, 1, Ed; 80A, Fa
Cyrene, 2, Hg; 4A, Ge; 93, Ac
Cythnos, 78, Eg
Cyzicus, 8, Hc
Czarnikow, 31, Mb
Czartorysk, 51, Fc
Czaslau, 60A, Ed
Czech, 8C, Cb; 85, Fc
Czechoslovakia, 84, Fc
Czechs, 8, Fb
Czernowitz, 33C, Fb; 78, Ea
Czerwinsk, 26, Fc
Czestochowa, 21, Nc; 87, Db

DABRA TABOR, 80B, Be
Dacca, 59B; 73, Fc
Dachstein, 29A, Eb
Dacia, 2, He
Dacre, 7C, Ba
Dadisleia (Tickhill), 13, Ec
Daghestan, 79, Jb; 84, Md
Dagö, 26, Fb
Dagsburg, 39B, Db
Dagsestune, 14, Ed
Dagupan, 75E, Ba
Dahlak Arch., 80B, Cd
Dahlonega, 72, Dc
Dahomé, 81C, Dc
Dahomey, 96B, Cb
Daibul, 6, Hc
Dairen (Dalny), 76B, Ab
Daix, R., 1, Hb
Dakar, 80A, Bc; 96B, Aa
Dakota Terr., 67D, Ca
Dal, 26, Db

Dal Arridhe, 15, Eb
Dalecarlia, 26, Da
Dalhousie, 71, Hc
Dalkeith, 37A, Cc; 48A, Bb
Dalkey, 37B, Ec
Dallas, Georgia, 72, Dc
Dallas, Texas, 94, Ed
Dalmally, 49A, Bb
Dalmatia, 32A, Gc; 78, Ad
Dalnaspidal, 49A, Bb
Dalny (Dairen), 76b, Ab
Dalriada, 14, Cc; 15, Ea
Dalriada Scots, 7B, Aa
Dalriada Ulaid, 7A, Ba
Dalry, Ayrshire, 37A, Bc
Dalry, Kirkcudbright, 49A, Bc
Dalton, 72A, Aa
Daltune (Dalton), 13, Cb
Dalwhinnie, 49A, Bb
Daly Waters, 95, Mf
Dam, 93, Ee
Daman, 73, Bc
Damariscotta, 45B, Ea
Damascus, 2, Lg; 18C, De
Damascus, Emirs of, 18C, De
Damietta, 6A, Ab; 9, Jf
Damm, 50, Cc
Dammartin, 20, Ed
Damme, 17, Gc, 55, Ec
Damnonii, 3A, Ba
Dampier Arch., 77, Bf
Dampier Str., 77, Hc
Dampierre, 20, Fd
Damvillers, 39B, Ba; 53, Fc
Dan, R., 57, Bc
Danes, 2A, Ca; 7A, Fa; 8, E
Danewerk, 65F, Aa
Danilovski, 61, Eb
Danish Mercia, 7C, Cb
Dankov, 61, Ed
Danube, R., 21, Me; 33C, Ec
Danubius, R., 1, Ec; 2, He
Danubyu, 73, Gd
Danum, (Doncaster), 3A, Ec
Danville, 57, Be
Danzig, 21, Na
Danzig, Rep. of, 60B, Ga
Dar es Salaam, 80A, Ge
Dar Fur, 80A, Fc
Darabjird, 6, Gc
Daras, 4B, Ld
Darbhanga, 73, Eb
Dardanelles, 78, Fe; 86D
Dargun, 22, Ea
Darien, Central America, 43A, Ed
Darien, Georgia, 56, Cd
Darien, G. of, 43A, Ed
Darjeeling, 73, Eb
Darley, 36, Ee
Darling, R., 77, Gh
Darmstadt, 29A, Ca
Daroca, 23C, Eb
Dartford, 36, Gf
Dartmoor, 27, Cf
Dartmouth, England, 27, Cf
Dartmouth, Nova Scotia, 45A, Eb
Dartmouth College, 57, Eb
Darum, 18C, Bg
Darwin, 90, Cd
Dassel, 20, Hc
Dauphiné, 20, Ff; 30, Ff
Davao, 75E, Ce
Davao G., 75E, Cc
Davenport, 7C, Bb
David Comnenus, 18B, Eb
David Street, 18D
David's Gate, 18D
David's Tower, 18D
Davis Str., 44, Jb.; 69B
Davos, 29B, Db
Dawson, 71A, Da
Dax, 22, Bc; 28C, Be; 30, Cg
Dayton, 71C, Bc; 72, Db
De Aveiro, 36, Kd
De Burgh (Burke), 37B, Cc
De Courcy, 17, Ba
De Leuwin, 42B
De Witts Land, 42, Qe
Deabolis, 18A, Ca
Dead Sea, 18C, Cg
Deal, 27, He
Dean, Forest of, 3A, De
Deba Habe, 96B, Da
Debra Markos, 96A, Aa
Debrecen, 87, Ec
Debreczin, 33C, Eb
Decatur, Alabama, 72, Cc
Decatur, Georgia, 72A, Ab
Deccan, 41A, Ec; 73, Cd
Deceangli, 3A, Cc
Decies, 15, Dd
Deddington, 27, Ed
Dedeagach, 78, Ee; 86C, Aa
Dee, R., Aberdeenshire, 14, Fb
Dee, R., Galloway, 36, Bb
Dee, R., Wales, 27, Dc
Deer, 14, Eb
Deer I., 56B
Deerfield, 45B, Cb

Deganwy, 13, Cc; 28A, Ca
Deheubarth, 13, Be; 17, Cc
Dehra Dun, 92, Da
Deira, 7B, Ca
Delagoa B., 81A, Dc
Delaware B., 45B, Bd; 57, Dd
Delaware, R., 45B, Bc; 57, Dc
Delft, 30, Fb; 46A, Db
Delgado, C., 58, Me
Delhi, 25, Gd; 73, Cb
Delhi, Sultanate of, 25, Gd
Demerara (Georgetown), 43D, Gd
Demerara, R., 68B, Ba
Demetae, 3A, Bd
Demirhissar, 86A, Ea
Demmin, 21, Kb; 39, Kb
Demotika, 9, Hd
Denain, 54, Cc
Denbigh, 27, Cc
Dendermonde, 46A, Dc
Dene (Dean), 13, De
Denia, 23C, Fc; 63, Fc
Denmark, 12, Gc
Denmark, King. of, 26, Db
Denmark and Norway, 54, Da
Dennewitz, 60B, Dc
D'Entrecasteaux Is., 77, Ic
Denver, 70, Dd
Deogir, 25, Gd
Deols, 11, Dc
Depenbech, 13, Dc
Deptford, 13, Ge
Derbent, 6, Fa; 19, Hd
Derby, Connecticut, 45B, Cc
Derby, England, 13, Ed
Derby, W. Australia, 77, Ce
Derby, co., 27, Ec
Derbyscire (Derbyshire), 13, Ec
Derevlyans, 9, Hb
Derg, L., 15, Cc
Derg, R., 15, Db
Derlington (Darlington), 13, Eb
Derna, 79, Dd
Derry, 15, Db
Derwent, R., 27, Ec; 48A, Cc
Des Moines, 70, Ec
Deshima, 52, Rc
Desmond, 15, Be
Desna, R., 9, Jb; 61A, Db
Dessie, 96A, Aa
Dessau, 31, Kc; 39, Kc
Desterro (Florianopolis), 68, Ee
Detmold, 10, Cc; 60B, Bc
Detroit, 45A, Ab
Dettingen, 54, Dc; 60A, Bc
Deutsch Brod, 31, Ld
Deva (Chester), 3A, Dc
Devenescire (Devon), 13, Cf
Deventer, 22, Da; 46A, Fb
Devernaki Pass, 78, Dg
Deveron, R., 14, Fb
Devikottai, 59D
Devizes, 27, De
Devol, R., 86A, Bb
Devon, 27, Cf
Devonport, 55A, Ac
Dewalgaon, 73, Cc
Dewas, 73, Cc
Dewsland, 27, Ae
Dhahran, 94, Rd
Dhar, 73, Cc
Dharwar, 73, Cd
Dholpur, 73, Cb
Diakova, 78, Cd
Diamantina, 68, Ed
Diarbekr, 19, Fe
Diarbekr (Amida), 33A, Fc
Dibrugarh, 92, Hb
Die, 11, Fd; 22, Db; 38, Ff
Diedenhofen (Thionville), 10, Bd; 76A, Cb
Diepholz, 30, Hb
Dieppe, 30, Dd; 83A, Ab
Dieren, 46A, Fb
Dieulacres, 36, Dd
Digne, 22, Dc; 38, Gf
Dijon, 11, Fc
Dilawar, 73, Bb
Dimotika, 78, Fe
Dinagat, 75E, Cb
Dinan, 11, Bb
Dinant, 46A, Dd
Dinapore, 73, Db
Dinaric Alps, 78, Ac
Dinas, 28A, Cb
Dinas Brân, 28A, Cb
Dindigul, 59A, Ce
Dinevor, 13, Be
Dingle, 49B, Ad
Dingle B., 15, Ad
Dingwall, 14, Db
Dinkelsbühl, 53, Jc
Dioclea, 9, Fd
Diocletian, Baths of, 5A
Dioscoridis I., 6, Ff
Direldawa, 96A, Bb
Direlton, 28B, Ca
Dirk Hartog I., 77, Ag

Disentis, 20, He; 29B, Cb
Ditmarsh, 26, Cc
Diu, 73, Bc
Dixmude, 46A, Bc
Dixon Entrance, 71B, Cc
Dizful, 93, Fc
Djagatai Empire, 25, Hb
Djakarta, 91, Dg
Djerba, 16, Ef
Djibouti, 96A, Ba
Djokjakarta, 91, Eg
Djougou, 96B, Cb
Dnieper, R., 50, Gc; 87, Gc
Dniester, R., 8, Hb; 87, Fc
Doab, The, 59A, Db
Dobb's Ferry, 57, Ec
Doberan, 22, Ea
Dobruja, 78, Gc
Dobrzyn, 21, Nb
Dobunni, 3A, De
Doce Leguas, Cays de, 43A, Eb
Dodecanese, 79, Ec
Dodinga, 52B, Aa
Dogger Bank, 82, Cb
Doha, 93, Gd
Doiran, 78, De
Dol, 11, Cb; 30, Cd
Dolforwyn, 28A, Cb
Dolomites, 86B, Ba
Dolores, 43C, Ab
Dolwyddelan, 28A, Ca
Dombes, 53, Fd
Domfront, 17, Ed
Dominica, 43A, Fc
Dömitz, 38, Jb
Domrémy, 28D, Eb
Don, R., Russia, 16, Lc; 19, Fb
Don, R., Scotland, 14, Fb
Don Cossacks, 61, Fe
Donauwörth, 29A, Da
Doncaster, 27, Ec
Dondra Hd., 73, Df
Donegal, co., 37C; 49B, Cb
Donegal Abbey, 37B, Cb
Doneham (Dunham Massey), 13, Dc
Donets, R., 19, Fc; 61, Ee
Donetsk, 89, Nd
Dongola, 80B, Ad
Donnington Castle, 48B, Cd
Donzy, 17, Ge; 31A, Bd
Dora Baltea, R., 5, Ab
Dorat, 53, Dd
Dorcestre (Dorchester), 13, Df
Dorchester, Dorset, 27, Df
Dorchester, Massachusetts, 45B, Db; 56B
Dorchester, New Jersey, 45B, Bd
Dorchester, Oxon., 3A, Ee; 7B, Cc
Dorchester Heights, 56B
Dorchester Neck, 56B
Dorchester Pt., 56B
Dordogne, R., 11, Dd
Dore, 7B, Cb
Dorey, 77, Eb
Dordrecht, 26, Bc; 53, Fb
Dornach, 29B, Ba
Dornoch, 37A, Bb; 49A, Cb
Dornoch, bp., 14A, Bb
Dornoch Firth, 14, Eb
Dorostol, 9, Hd
Dorpat, 26, Gb
Dorset, 27, Df
Dorsete (Dorset), 13, Df
Dort, 46A, Dc
Dortmund, 10, Dc
Dorylaeum, 9, Je
Douai, 30, Ec; 46A, Cd
Doubs, R., 11, Fc; 29A, Bb
Douglas, Alaska, 71B, Cb
Douglas, Scotland, 37A, Cc
Douglas, clan, 28B, Bc
Douglas Castle, 28B, Bb
Dourdan, 38, Ed
Douro, R., 22, Ac; 63, Bb
Dover, Delaware, 57, Dd
Dover, England, 27, He
Dover, New England, 45B, Db
Dover, Str. of., 11, Da
Dovere (Dover), 13, He
Down, 15, Fb
Down, co., 37C; 49B, Eb
Downham Market, 48B, Dc
Downpatrick, 37B, Fb; 49B, Fb
Downpatrick, bp., 15A, Ca
Downs, The, 55A, Dc
Downton, 27, Ee
Dragasani, 78, Ec
Dragashan, 78, Ec
Draguignan, 20, Gg; 30, Gg
Draheim, 60A, Fb
Drakens Berg (Quathlamba), 81D, Ab
Drakensberg, 81B, Db
Drangiana, 1, Jd
Draper's Meadow, 56, Cc
Drave, R. 8, Fb; 21, Le
Dregoviches, 9, Gb

Drenthe, 46A, Fb
Dresden, 21, Kc; 31, Kc
Dreux 11, Db; 76A, Ab
Dreznik, 33C, Dc
Drina, R., 78, Bc
Drogheda, 37B, Ec; 49B, Ec
Droitwich, 27, Dd
Dromore, 49B, Eb
Dromore, bp., 15A, Ba
Drumburgh, 3C
Drumclog, 49A, Bc
Dryslwyn, 28A, Bc
Duala, 80A, Dd; 96B, Db
Dubawnt L., 44, Db
Dubienka, 51, Ec
Dubitza, 54, Eb
Dublin, 15, Ec
Dublin, abp., 15A, Bb
Dublin, co., 37C; 49B, Ec
Dübnik, 78, Ed
Dubris (Dover), 3A, He
Ducatus Venetianus, 23B, Db
Ducie I., 75, Jf
Dudelei (Dudley), 13, Dd
Dudley, 27, Dd
Duero, R., 22, Bc; 63, Cb
Duich, L., 49A, Bb
Duisburg, 20, Gc; 46A, Fc
Duiveland, 46A, Cc
Dulce, R., 41B, Cf
Dulcigno, 22, Fc; 78, Be
Duleek, 15, Ec
Dull, 14, Ec
Duluth, 70, Ec
Dumaguete, 75E, Bc
Dumaran, 75E, Ab
Dumbarton, 37A, Bc; 48A, Ab
Dumbarton, co., 37A, Bb; 49A, Bc
Dumdum, 73, Ec
Dumfries, 28B, Bb; 36, Cb
Dumfries, co., 37A, Cc; 49A, Cc
Dumio, 22, Ac
Dumnonii, 3A, Bf
Dun, 20, Ee
Dun Laoghaire (Kingstown), 49B, Ec
Düna, 26, Gb
Dünaburg, 26, Gb
Dunbar, 14, Fc
Dunblane, 14, Ec; 49A, Cb
Duncannon, 49B, Ed
Duncansby Hd., 14, Ea; 49A, Ca
Dundalk, 37B, Ec; 49B, Ec
Dundee, Natal, 81D, Bb
Dundee, Scotland, 28B, Ca; 48A, Ba
Dundonald Castle, 28B, Ab
Dundrennan, 14, Ee
Dundrum, 37B, Fb
Dunedin, 77A
Dunewic (Dunwich), 13, Hd
Dunfermline, 14, Ec
Dungannon, 49B, Eb
Dungarvan, 37B, Dd; 49B, Dd
Dungeness, 55A, Dc
Dungiven, 49B, Db
Dunhevet (Dunheved, Launceston), 13, Bf
Dunholm (Durham), 13, Eb
Dunkeld, 14, Ec
Dunkeswell, 36, Cg
Dunkirk, 46A, Bc
Dunlavin, 49B, Ec
Dunmore Hd., 15, Ad
Dunnet Hd., 14, Ea
Dunnottar, 37A, Cb
Dunois, 30, Dd
Dunrobin, 37A, Cb
Dunrobin Castle, 49A, Cb
Duns, 37A, Cc; 48A, Bb
Dunstable, 27, Fe
Dunstaffnage, 49A, Bb
Dunstanburgh, 27, Ea
Dunster, 27, Ce; 48A, Bd
Dunvegan, 49A, Ab
Dunwich, 27, Hd; 36A
Duppel, 65F, Aa
Dupplin Moor, 28B, Ba
Durance, R., 11, Fe; 29A, Ad
Durango, 43A, Bb
Duras, 53, De
Durazzo, 78, Be
Durban (Port Natal), 81D, Bb
Düren, 20, Gc
Durham, England, 27, Eb
Durham, New Hampshire, 57, Fb
Durham, Bb. of, 28B, Dc; 36, Db
Durham, Palatinate of, 27, Eb
Durinish, 14, Bb
Durlach, 38, Gd
Durnkrüt, 19, Bc
Durness, 14, Da
Durnovaria (Dorchester), 3A, Df
Durobrivae (Rochester), 3A, Ge

Durobrivae (Water Newton), 3A, Fd
Durocobrivae (Dunstable), 3A, Fe
Durolipons (Cambridge), 3A, Gd
Durotriges, 3A, Df
Durovernum (Canterbury), 3A, He
Durovigatum (Godmanchester), 3A, Fd
Dürrenstein, 29A, Fa
Dürres, 88, Je
Durstede, 12, Fc
Dusky B., 77, Lk
Düsseldorf, 38, Gc; 83A, Da
Dutch Brazil, 41B, Ed; 42, He
Dutch East Indies, 74, Kj; 90, Bd
Dutch Harbor, 90, Fa
Dutch New Guinea, 77, Hd
Duxbury, 45B, Db; 57, Fb
Dvina, R., (N.), 61, Fb; 88, Oa
Dvina, R., (W.), 50, Fb; 64, Hb
Dvinsk, 84, Ha
Dyea, 71B, Cb
Dyfed, 7B, Ac; 13, Be
Dyle, R., 46B; 83A, Ca
Dynefwr, 28A, Bc
Dyrrhachium, 2, Ge; 4A, Fc
Dzhulfa, 93, Fb

Ealondscire, (Islandshire), 13, Ea
Eamont, 7C, Ba
Earn, L., 14, Dc
Easby, 7B, Ca
East C., Asia, 69B
East C., New Zealand, 77, Ni
East, Pref. of the., 2, Kf
East Angles, 7A, Dc
East Anglia, 7B, Db; 12, Ec
East China Sea, 91 Fd
East Florida, 71F, Ba
East Franconia, 10, Dd
East Friesland, Co. of, 30, Gb
East Germany, 89, Hc
East London, 81B, Dc
East Main, R., 70, Gb
East March, 28B, Cb
East Mark, 8A, Db
East of March, 27, Cd
East Pakistan, 92, Gc
East Prussia, 39, Pb
East Roman Empire, 2, Kf
East Saxons, 7A, Db
Easter I., 75, Kf
Eastern Association, 48A, Dc
Eastern Bengal and Assam, 73A, Cb
Eastern Ghats, 73, Cd
Eastern Roman Empire, 8, Gd
Eastern Rumelia, 78, Ed
Eastham, 45B, Dc
Easthampton, 45B, Cc
Easton, 57, Dc
Eastphalia, 10, Db
Ebbsfleet, 36, Hf
Ebenezer, 57D, Ab
Eboracum (Evrvic) (York), 13, Eb
Ebro, R., 22, Bc; 63, Da
Eburacum (York), 3A, Ec
Ecbatana, 1, Gd; 6, Fb
Ecclefechan, 49A, Cc
Ecclesia de Labataïlge (Battle), 13, Gf
Echallar, 63, Ea
Echallens, 29B, Ab
Eckernförde, 65F, Aa
Eckmühl, 65B, Bb
Ecuador, 68, Bc
Edam 46A, Eb
Eddisbury, 7C, Bb
Edelsland, 42B; 77, Bh
Eden, R., 7C, Ba; 27, Db
Edenton, 57, Ce
Edessa, 2, Lf; 6, Eb; 19, Fe
Edessa, Co. of, 16, Ke
Edeyrnion, 13, Cd
Edge Hill, 48A, Cc
Edgecot, 27, Ed
Edinburgh (Dunedin), 14, Ed
Edinburgh, co., 49A, Cc
Edington, 36, Df
Edisto, R., 57D, Ab
Edmonton, 70, Cb
Edolo, 86B, Aa
Efferding, 31, Kd
Eger, Bohemia, 21, Kc
Eger, Hungary, 33C, Eb
Eger, R., 21, Kc
Egersund, 87, Ba
Eggmühl, 29A, Ea
Egisheim, 39B, Db
Egitama, 22, Ad
Eglesham (Eynsham), 13, Ee
Egmont, 22, Ca; 46A, Db

Egremont, 27, Cb
Egri Palanka, 78, Dd
Egripo, 78, Df
Egypt, 80A, Fb; 93, Bd
Egypt (Misr), 6, Dc
Egyptian Sudan, 83, Ld
Ehrenbreitstein, 51, Bc
Eia (Eye), 13, Hd
Eichsfeld, 20, Hc
Eichstadt, 10, Dd
Eider, R., 60B, Ba; 65F, Aa
Eifel, 83A, Da
Eigg, 14, Bc
Eight Emirates, 24, Jf
Eil, 95A, Bb
Eilean Donan, 49A, Bb
Einsiedeln, 22, Db; 29B, Ca
Eire, 49B, Dc
Eisenach, 20, Jc; 39C, Ac
Eisenburg, 39C, Bc
Eisenburg (Vasvar), 29A, Gb
Ekaterinoslav, 64, Kd
El Agheila, 88, Jg
El Alamein, 93, Bc
El Aqaba, 80B, Ab
El Bodon, 63, Bb
El Damer, 93, Cf
El Dirr, 93, Ce
El Dorado, 43A, Fd
El Faiyum, 80B, Ab
El Golea, 96C, Ca
El Khandaq, 93, Cf
El Morro, 43A, Db
El Obeid, 80A, Fc
El Paso, 70, Dd
Elands, R., 81A, Cc
Elandslaagte, 81D, Ab
Elassona, 78, Df
Elba, 5, Cc
Elbasan, 86A, Ba
Elbe, R., 10, Cb; 60A, Ac
Elberfeld, 53, Gb; 60B, Ac
Elbeuf, 23C, Cb; 38, Dd
Elbing, 21, Na; 39, Na
Elburz, 19, Je
Elche, 23C, Ec
Elchingen, 22, Eb; 29A, Da
Elderslie, 28B, Ab
Electoral Palatinate, 30, Hd
Eleuthera I., 43A, Eb
Elfael, 13, Cd
Elfsborg, 50, Cb
Elgin, 37A, Cb
Elgin, bp., 14A, Cb
Elgin, co., 49A, Cc
Elgin and Forres. co., 37A, Cb
Elim, 81B, Ac
Elisabethville, 96C, Ef
Elizabeth, New Jersey, 45B, Bc
Elizabeth, Virginia, 45B, Ae
Elizabeth, C., 45B, Db
Elizabethtown, 57B
Elk Hill, 57, Ab
Elkton, 57, Cb
Ellandun, 7B, Cc
Ellesmere, 28A, Db
Ellesmere I., 44, Ga
Ellice Is., 90, Ed
Ellichpur, 52A, Bb
Elliot, 28B, Cb
Elliot Is., 76B, Bb
Ellwangen, 22, Eb
Elmeslae (Helmsley), 13, Eb
Elmet, 7A, Ca
Elmham, 7B, Db; 36A
Elmham, bp., 36A
Elmina, 35, Jd; 81C, Dc
Elmshorn, 65F, Ab
Elne, 11, Ee
Elnestow (Elstow), 13, Fd
Elphin, 15, Cc
Elster, R., 10, Ec
Elstow, 36, Fe
Elten, 65A, Aa
Elvas, 23C, Bc; 63, Bc
Ely, 27, Gd
Ely, bp., 36, Ge
Ely, I. of, 27, Gd
Elyg (Ely), 13, Gd
Embrun, 11, Gd
Emden, 38, Gb; 65D, Aa
Emesa, 9, Ke
Emilia, 32A, Db
Emirs of Damascus, 18C, De
Emly, 15, Cd
Empingham (Losecoat Field), 27, Fd
Empire, The, 16, Dc; 54, Eb
Ems, 60B, Ac
Ems, R., 10, Bb; 38, Gb
Enaghdun, 15, Bc
Encounter B., 77, Fl
Endeavour R., 77, He
Enderby Land, 69C
Engadi, 18C, Cg
Engadin, 29B, Eb
Engelberg, 10, Ce
Engelberg, Abbey of, 29B, Cb
Engern, 10, Cb
Enghien, 46A, Dd

England, 34, Bb; 55A, Cb
England, King. of, 20, Cc
English, R., 70, Eb
English Channel, 7B, Cc
Enkhuizen, 46A, Eb
Enköping, 26, Eb
Ennis, 49B, Cd
Enniscorthy, 15, Ed
Enniskillen, 49B, Db
Enns, R., 29A, Fb
Enos, 78, Fe
Entebbe, 96C, Fd
Entschede, 46A, Fb
Enugu, 96B, Cb
Eperjes, 33C, Eb
Épernay, 83A, Bb
Ephesus, 8, Hd
Epidaurus, 79, Dc
Epidium Prom., 3A, Aa
Epila, 23D, Eb
Épinal, 20, Gd; 83B, Ba
Epirus, 1, Ed; 79, Dc
Epirus, Despctate of, 19, Ce
Eppenstein, 10, Fe
Epworth, 36, Fd
Equatorial Guinea, 96D, Cd
Equatorial Provs., 80A, Fd
Erbach, 38, Hd
Erbil, 93, Eb
Erfurt, 10, Dc; 39C, Bc
Eriboll, 49A, Ba
Ericht, L., 49A Bb
Erie, 70, Fc
Erie, L., 45A, Ab
Eries, 45A, Ab
Eriska, 49A, Ab
Eritrea, 80B, Ce; 96A, Aa
Erivan, 61, Ff; 79, Hb
Erlau, 31, Pe; 33A, Ba
Ermeland. 39, Pb
Ermine Street, 3A, Fd
Erne, L., 15, Db
Erne, Upper L., 49B, Db
Errigal, 15, Ca
Erz Gebirge, 10, Ec
Erzerum, 6, Fb; 79, Hc
Erzingan, 86C, Cb
Es Suweida, 93, Dc
Escewelle (Ashwell), 13, Gd
Escomb, 7B, Ce
Eshowe, 81D, Bb
Eskdale, 14, Ed
Eskisehir, 79, Fc
Eskishehr, 86C, Bb
Esla, R., 63, Cb
Esmeraldas, 68, Bb
Esopus, 45B, Cc
Española(Hispaniola), 43A, Ec
Esperance, 77, Cn
Esperance, C.d', 45A, Ea
Espinosa, 63, Da
Espirito Santo, 68, Ed
Essek, 33C, Db
Essen, 53, Gb; 87, Bb
Essequibo, 41B, Dc
Essequibo, R., 68, Db
Essex, 27, Ge
Essling, 29A, Ga
Esslingen, 30, Hd
Essonnes, 38, Ed
Est-Treding (East Riding), 13, Fc
Estavayer, 29B, Ab
Estcourt, 81D, Ab
Este, 23B, Cb; 32D, Db
Este (D. of Ferrara), 32A, Db
Este (D. of Modena), 32A, Db
Esthonia, 26, Gb
Esthonians, 9, Ha
Estonia, 87, Fa
Estrella, Sierra d', 63, Bb
Estremadura, Portugal, 63, Ac
Estremadura, Spain, 63, Bc
Etampes, 11, Eb; 17, Gd
Étaples, 30 Dc
Ethandun, 7C, Bc
Ethiopia, 6, Ed; 80A, Gd
Etna, Mt., 5 Ef
Etowah, R., 72A, Aa
Ettlingen, 65A, Ab
Ettrick, R., 14, Ed
Ettrick Forest, 28B, Bb
Eu, 11, Db; 17, Fd; 30, Dc
Eucla, 77, Dh
Eugubium, 5B, Bb
Eupàtoria (Kozlov), 50, Gd
Eupen, 83A, Da
Euphrates, R., 2, Mg; 6A, Cb
Eure, R., 76A, Ab
Europa Pt., 63A
Eustria, 8, Gb
Eutaw Springs, 57D, Ab
Evansville, 72, Cb
Evaux, 30, Ee
Everest, Mt., 73, Eb; 92, Fb
Everglades, 43A, Db
Evesham, 13, Ed; 27, Ed
Evora, 22, Ad; 63, Bc
Evora, eccl. prov., 22, Ad
Evreux, 11, Db; 17, Fd

Evrvicscire (Yorkshire), 13, Eb
Ewias, 13, De
Ewisdale, 28B, Bb
Ewyas, 7C, Bc
Ewyas Lacy, 28A, Dc
Exarchate, 5, Cb
Exe, R., 27, Cf; 48B, Bd
Exeter, England, 27, Cf
Exeter, New Hampshire, 45B, Db
Exeter, bp., 36, Bg
Exilles, 38, Gf
Exmoor, 27, Ce
Exonia (Exeter), 13, Cf
Exploring Is. (Lau Group), 75C, Ca
Exsessa (Essex), 13, Ge
Eye, 27, Hd
Eylau, 60A, Ha; 60B, Ha
Eyre, L., 77, Fg

FAENZA, 5, Cb
Faesulae, 5, Cb
Fair Hd., 49B, Ea
Fairbanks, 71A, Ca
Fairfield, Connecticut, 45B, Cc
Fairfield, S. Africa, 81B, Cc
Faiyum, 93, Cd
Fakfak, 77, Eb
Falaise, 11, Cb
Falkenburg, 39B, Ca
Falkenstein, Austria, 33C, Cb
Falkenstein, Swabia, 10, Cd
Falkirk, 28B, Bb; 49A, Cc
Falkland Is., 68, Dh
Falkland Is. Dependencies, 95, Cj
Falköping, 26, Db
Falmouth, England, 55A, Ac
Falmouth, Maine, 57, Fb
Falmouth (Casco) (For Loyal), 45B, Db
False B., 81B, Ac
Falsterbo, 26, Db
Falun, 26, Ea
Famagusta, 16, Je
Famia (Apamea), 18C, Dc
Fanning I., 75, Hd
Fano, 32A, Ec
Fanum, 5B, Bb
Fao, 86C, Ec
Farasan Is., 80B, Cd
Farenam, 27, Ef
Farewell, C., 69B
Farmingham, 45B, Cc
Farnea, Is. (Farne Is.), 13, Ea
Farnham, 27, Fe
Faro, 22, Ad
Faroe Is., 12, Ca; 82, Aa
Farquharson, 37A, Cb
Farrukhabad, 59C, Cb
Fars, 6, Gb
Fashoda (Kodak), 80B, Ae
Fast Castle, 28B, Cb
Fatehgarh, 73, Db
Fatehpur, 73, Db
Fatimite anti-Caliphate, 6B, Ba
Fatimite Caliphs, 16, Jg
Faucigny, 30, Ge
Faventia, 5B, Aa
Faversham, 27, Ge
Fayetteville, N. Carolina, 57, Bf; W. Virginia, 72, Db
Fayum, 6A, Ac
Fear, C., 57D, Bb
Fécamp, 11, Db
Federal District, Brazil, 68, Ed
Federated Malay States, 74, Jh
Fed. of Arabian Emirates, 93, Gd
Fehmarn, 60B, Ca; 65F, Ba
Fehrbellin, 60A, Db
Felipinas, Islas (Philippine Is.), 41A, Kc
Feltre, 5, Ca; 86B, Ba
Fenestrelles, 53, Ge
Fenghwangcheng, 76B, Ca
Fentsch, 39B, Ba
Fer, Pointe au, 57, Ea
Ferette, 31A, Dd
Fergana, 61B, Ca
Ferghana, 6, Ja
Fergus, R., 15, Cd
Ferie (Firle), 13, Gf
Fermanagh, 49B, Db
Fermanagh, co., 37C
Fermo (Firmum), 5, Dc
Fermoy, 49B, Cd
Fernandina, 72, Dc
Fernando Poo, 80A, Dd
Ferns, 15, Ed
Ferozepore, 73, Ba
Ferozeshah, 73, Ba
Ferrara, 5, Cb; 29A, Dc
Ferrara, D. of (Este), 32A, Dc
Ferreus (Orontes), R., 18C, Dc
Ferrol, 55B, Kb; 63, Aa
Ferry Land, 45A, Ga
Ferrybridge, 27, Ec
Feurs, 11, Fd

Fez, 9, Bf; 40, Jc; 80A, Ca
Fez, Sultanate of (Watasios), 34, Be
Fezensac, Co. of, 11, De
Fezzan, 6, Cc; 80A, Eb
Fiesole, 32A, Dc
Fife, 14, Ec
Fife, co., 37A, Cb; 49A, Cb
Fifth Cataract, 80B, Ad
Figeac, 17, Gf
Figueira da Foz, 63, Ab
Figueras, 63, Ga
Figuig, 80A, Ca
Fiji Is., 75C; 77, Ne
Filey, 3A, Fb
Finale, 54, Dd
Findhord, 49A, Cb
Findhorn, R., 37A, Cb
Findon, 49A, Cb
Fingoes, 81B, Dc
Finisterre, C., 63, Aa
Finland, 26, Ga; 88, La
Finland, G. of, 26, Gb
Finnish Peoples, 19, Ca
Finsiaolin, 76B, Ba
Finsteraarhorn, 29B, Cb
Finstingen, 39B, Db
Firmana, 23A, Db
Firmum (Fermo), 5, Dc
First Cataract, 80B, Ac
Fischhausen, 26, Ec
Fishers Hill, 72B, Aa
Fishguard, 55A, Ac
Fishkill, 57, Ec
Fitero, 22, Bc
Fitzalan, 28A, Db; 28B, Dc
Fitzgerald, 37B, Ec
Fitzgibbon, 37B, Cd
Fitzmaurice, 37B, Bd
Fitzroy, R., 77, Cc
Fiume, 39, Lf
Five Forks, 72B, Bb
Fivizzano, 32A, Db
Flanders, 46A, Bd
Flarchheim, 10, Dc
Flatbush, 57B
Flattery, C., 67C, Aa
Flavigny, 22, Cb
Fleet, R., 27A
Flensburg, 26, Cc; 60B, Ba
Fleurus, 38, Fc; 46B
Fleury, Languedoc, 53, Ef
Fleury, Sens, 22, Cb
Flinders, R., 77, Gf
Flint, 28A, Ca
Flint, co., 28A, Ca
Flint, R., 71F, Ca
Flodden, 28B, Cc
Flodden Field, 37A, Cc
Florchingen, 39B, Ca
Florence, Italy, 32E, Bb
Florence, U.S.A., 72, Ec
Florence, Rep. of, 32A, Dc
Flores, Azores, 55B, Hc
Flores, E. Indies, 52C, Bc
Florianopolis (Desterro), 68, Ee
Florida, 56, Bd; 72, Dd
Florida, C., 55B, Bd
Florida Terr., 67C, Ec
Florina, 86A, Cb; 88, Ke
Fluelen, 29B, Cb
Flushing, 46A, Cc
Fochabers, 37A, Db
Focsani, 51, Fd; 78, Fe
Foggia, 23B, Ed; 32A, Fd
Föhr, 65F, Aa
Foix, 11, De; 17, Fg
Folchingeham (Folkingeham), 13, Fd
Folkestone, 13, He; 27, He
Folkstone, 13, He
Fondi, 21A, Bb; 22, Ec
Fonseca, G. of, 43A, Dc
Fontaine, 8A, Bb
Fontainebleau, 47, Cc
Fontanet, 8A, Bb
Fontenay, 30, Ce
Fontenoy, 46A, Cd; 54, Cb
Fontevrault, 17, Ee
Font-Marigny, 22, Cb
Foochow, 25, Ld; 91, Ed
Forbach, 39B, Ca
Forbes, 37A, Dc
Forcalquier, 20, Fg; 30, Fg
Forchheim, 8, Eb, 22, Eb
Ford, 36, Cg
Forden, 3A, Cd
Foresta, 13, De
Forewic (Fordwich), 13, He
Forez, Co. of, 11, Ed
Forfar, 49A, Cb
Forfar, co., 37A, Cb
Forglen, 14, Ed
Forks, The, 69A, Da
Forlì, 32A, Eb
Forlimpopoli, 21, Kf
Formentera, 23C, Fc
Formigny, 28D, Bb
Formosa (Taiwan), 91, Fd
Fornbi (Formby) 13, Cc
Fornovo, 32A, Db
Forres, 37A, Db

Forr, 81D, Bb
Fort Albany, 70, Fb
Fort Alexander, 70, Eb
Fort Amsterdam, 45B, Bc
Fort Ann, 57, Eb
Fort Argyll, 56, Cd
Fort Armstrong, Mississippi Terr., 71F, Ba
Fort Armstrong, Pennsylvania, 57, Bc
Fort Assomption, 57C, Ab
Fort Assumption (Memphis), 56, Bc
Fort Augusta, Georgia, 56, Cd
Fort Augusta, Pennsylvania, 56, Db
Fort Augustus, 37A, Bb
Fort Bard, 65B, Ab
Fort Bariancas, 71F, Ba
Fort Barraux, 38, Ff
Fort Beafort, 81B, Cc
Fort Beauharnais, 56, Ab
Fort Beauregard, 72, Dc
Fort Bedford, 57, Bd
Fort Benton, 70, Cc
Fort Bird, 56, Db
Fort Blakely, 72, Cc
Fort Boise, 44, Cd
Fort Bowyer, 71F, Ba
Fort Brewerton, 57, Cb
Fort Bridger, 70, Cc
Fort Bull, 57, Db
Fort Bute (Manchac), 56, Ad
Fort Butte à la Rose, 72, Bc
Fort Caroline, 43A, Da
Fort Caswell, 72, Ec
Fort Chambly, 57, Ea
Fort Charlotte, 56, Bd
Fort Chartres, 56, Ac
Fort Chelmsford, 81D, Bb
Fort Chequemagon, 56, Ba
Fort Chipewyan, 70, Cb
Fort Chiswell, 57, Ae
Fort Christina (Newcastle), 45B, Bd
Fort Claiborne, 71F, Ba
Fort Clinton, New York, 57, Dc
Fort Clinton, Vermont, 57, Eb
Fort Cornwallis (Augusta), 57D, Ab
Fort Crèvecœur, 56, Ab
Fort Crown Point, 56, Eb
Fort Cumberland, 57, Bd
Fort Dauphin, Canada, 44, Ec
Fort Dauphin, Madagascar, 80A, Hg
Fort de la Presentation, 56, Db 57, Da
Fort de Russy, 72, Bc
Fort Dearborn, 71C, Ab
Fort Delaware, 72, Eb
Fort Deposit, 71F, Ba
Fort des Abitibis, 45A, Ba
Fort Detroit, 56, Cb
Fort Dobbs, 56, Cc
Fort Donelson, 72, Cb
Fort Dummer (Hinsdale), 57, Eb
Fort Duquesne (Fort Pitt), 57, Bc
Fort Edward, 57, Eb
Fort Erie, 71C, Cb; 71D
Fort Esperanza, 72, Ad
Fort Evelyn, 81D, Bb
Fort Frédéric, 56, Eb
Fort Frederica, 56, Cd
Fort Frederick (Port Elizabeth), 81B, Cc
Fort Frontenac, 57, Ca
Fort Gadsden (Negro), 71F, Ba
Fort Gaines, Alabama, 72, Cc
Fort Gaines, Georgia, 71F, Ca
Fort George, British Columbia, 44, Bc
Fort George, Natal, 81D, Bb
Fort George, New York, 57, Eb
Fort George, Ontario, 71D
Fort George, Oregon, 67C, Aa
Fort George, Scotland, 49A, Bb
Fort Gibson, 72, Ab
Fort Granby, 57D, Ab
Fort Halifax, 56, Fb
Fort Hall, 70, Cc
Fort Harris, 57, Cc
Fort Harrison, 71C, Ac
Fort Hatteras, 72, Ec
Fort Henry, Ohio, 56, Cc
Fort Henry, Tennessee, 72, Cb
Fort Herkimer, 57, Db
Fort Hunter, 56 Eb
Fort Independence, 57, Eb
Fort Jackson, Georgia, 72, Dc
Fort Jackson, Louisiana, 72, Cd
Fort Jackson, Mississippi Terr., 71F, Ba
Fort James, 81C, Ab
Fort Jefferson, 72, De

Fort Johnston, 72, Ec
Fort King George, 56, Cd
Fort la Baye, 56, Bb
Fort la Galette, 56, Db
Fort La Reine, 44, Ed
Fort Lamy, 96B, Da
Fort Lamotte, 45A, Cb
Fort Laramie, 67C, Ca
Fort Lawrence, 45A, Ea
Fort le Boeuf, 57, Bc
Fort Leavenworth, 72, Bb
Fort Lee, 57B
Fort Lifou, 52C, Bc
Fort Ligonier, 57, Bc
Fort Livingston, 72, Cd
Fort Loudoun, 56, Cc
Fort Louis, 56, Bd
Fort Loyal (Casco) (Falmouth), 45B, Db
Fort McAllister, 72, Dc
Fort McHenry, 71C, Cc
Fort Mackinac, 56, Ca
Fort McMurray, 70, Cb
Fort Macomb, 72, Cc
Fort Macon, 72, Ec
Fort McRee, 72, Cc
Fort Malden, 71C, Bb
Fort Mandant (Bismarck), 70, Dc
Fort Marion, 72, Dd
Fort Massac, 56, Bc
Fort Massachusetts, 72, Cc
Fort Maurepas, 44, Ec
Fort Meigs, 71C, Bb
Fort Miami, 56, Cb
Fort Mims, 71F, Ba
Fort Mitchell, 71F, Ca
Fort Monroe, 72, Eb
Fort Montgomery, 57, Dc
Fort Moore, 56, Cd
Fort Morgan, 72, Cc
Fort Motte, 57D, Ab
Fort Moultrie, 57D, Bb
Fort Muffin, 57, Dd
Fort Napoleon, 81D, Bb
Fort Nassau, Moluccas, 52B, Aa
Fort Nassau, New Jersey, 45B, Bd
Fort Nassau (Fort Orange), 45B, Cb
Fort Necessity, 57, Bd
Fort New Elfsborg, 45B, Bd
Fort New Gothenburg, 45B, Bd
Fort New Korsholm (Chester), 45B, Bd
Fort Niagara, 57, Bb
Fort Norman, 70, Bb
Fort Nottingham, 81D, Ab
Fort Ontario, 57, Cb
Fort Orange (Fort Nassau), 45B, Cb
Fort Orleans, 56, Ac
Fort Oswego, 57, Cb
Fort Pentagoet (Penobscot), 45B, Ea
Fort Pickens, 72, Cc
Fort Pike, 72, Cc
Fort Pillow, 72, Cb
Fort Pitt (Fort Duquesne), 57, Bc
Fort Pitt (Pittsburgh), 57A, Ca
Fort Powell, 72, Cc
Fort Presqu'ile, 57, Ab
Fort Prince George (Savannah), 56, Cd
Fort Providence, 70, Ca
Fort Prudhomme, 56, Bc
Fort Pulaski, 72, Dc
Fort Quiatanon, 57A, Ba
Fort Rae, 70, Ca
Fort Resolution, 70, Ca
Fort Richelieu, 45A, Ca
Fort Rouille (Fort Toronto), 56, Db
Fort Royal, 43A, Fc
Fort St. David, 59D
Fort St. Esprit (La Pointe), 56, Aa
Fort St. George, 59D
Fort St. Jean, 57, Ea
Fort St. John, 70, Bb
Fort St. Joseph, L. Huron, 45A, Ab
Fort St. Joseph, L. Michigan, 56, Bb
Fort St. Louis, Illinois, 56, Bb
Fort St. Louis, Nova Scotia, 45A, Db
Fort St. Louis, Texas, 43A, Cb
Fort St. Philip, 72, Cd
Fort St. Philippe, 57A, Bd
Fort St. Therese, 45A, Ca
Fort Sandeman, 73, Aa
Fort Sandusky, 56, Cb
Fort Schlosser, 57, Bb
Fort Schuyler, 57, Db
Fort Scott, Georgia, 71F, Ca
Fort Scott, Kansas, 72, Bb
Fort Severn, 70, Fb
Fort Shevchenko, 61B, Aa

Fort Simpson, 70, Ba
Fort Smith, 72, Bb
Fort Snelling, 67C, Da
Fort Stanwix, 57, Db
Fort Stephenson, 71C, Bb
Fort Stoddard, 71F, Ba
Fort Strother, 71F, Ba
Fort Sumter, 72, Ec
Fort Taylor, 72, De
Fort Ticonderoga, 56, Eb
Fort Tombécbé (Fort York), 56, Bd
Fort Toronto (Fort Rouille), 56, Db
Fort Toulouse, 56, Bd
Fort Towson, 72, Ac
Fort Tuli, 81A, Cb
Fort Union, 70, Dc
Fort Vancouver, 44, Bd
Fort Venango, 57, Bc
Fort Victoria, Canada, 44, Bd
Fort Victoria, Natal, 81D, Bb
Fort Wagner, 72, Dc
Fort Walker, 72, Dc
Fort Washington, Maryland, 71C, Cc
Fort Washington, New Jersey, 57B
Fort Washita, 72, Ac
Fort Watson, 57D, Ab
Fort Wayne, 71C, Cc
Fort Wellington, 77, Ed
Fort Western, 56, Fb
Fort William, Bengal, 59C, Ec
Fort William, Canada, 70, Fc
Fort William, Scotland, 37A, Bb
Fort William Henry, 57, Eb
Fort Wiltshire, 81B, Cc
Fort Wrangell, 71B, Cb
Fort York (Fort Tombécbé), 56, Bd
Fort Yukon, 71A, Ca
Fortaleza (Ceara), 68, Fc
Forteviot, 49A, Cb
Forth, R., 28B, Aa
Forth, Firth of, 14, Fc
Fortore, R., 21A, Cb
Fossalta, 20, Jf
Fosse Way, 3A, Ed
Fotheringhay, 27, Fd
Fougères, 20, Cd; 28D, Bb
Fountains, 36, Ec
Four Cantons, L. of the, 29B, Cb
Fourth Cataract, 80B, Ad
Fowey, 48B, Ad
Foyle, L., 15, Da
Foyle, R., 37B, Db
Framlingham, 27, Hd
France, I. de, Indian Ocean, 58, Me
France, King of, 20, De
France Antarctique, 41B, Ef
Franche Comté, 30, Fe
Franci, 2, Ec
Francia, 11, Eb
Franconia, 10, Cc
Frankenthal, 38, Hd
Frankfort, U.S.A., 72, Db
Frankfurt, R. Main, 10, Cc
Frankfurt, R. Oder, 21, Lb
Frankfurt, G.D. of, 65B, Aa
Frankish Empire, 8, Cb
Frankish Kingdom, 4A, Cb
Franklin, 72, Cb
Franklin, terr., 70, Ga
Franks, 2A, Ba; 8C, Ba
Franz Josef Land, 69B
Frascati (Tusculum), 22A
Fraser, R., 70, Bb
Fraserburgh, 49A, Cb
Fraustadt, 31, Mc
Fraxinet, 11, Ge
Fraxinetum, 23A, Ab
Fray Bentos, 68, Df
Frazer, 37A, Bb
Fredericia, 65F, Aa
Frederick, 72B, Ba
Fredericksburg, Virginia, 72B, Ba
Fredericksburg, W. Africa, 81C, Dd
Frederickstown, 57, Cd
Fredericton, 56, Fa; 71, Hc
Frederikssten, 50, Cb
Fredrikshald, 51, Cb
Fredrikshamn, 62, Ha
Freeman's Farm, 57, Eb
Freeport, 70, Fc
Freetown, 81C, Bc
Freiberg, 53, Kb
Freiburg, Germany, 31, Kc
Freiburg, Switzerland, 10, Be; 29A, Ba
Freising, 10, Dd; 31B, Cb
Fréjus, 22, Dc; 38, Gg
Fremantle, 77, Bh
Fremington, 27, Be
French, R., 45A, Aa
French Congo, 80A, Ee
French Empire, 62, Cc

French Equatorial Africa, 80A, Ed
French Frigate I., 75, Gc
French Guiana, 68, Db
French Guinea, 81C, Bb
French Indo-China, 90, Bc
French Ivory Coast, 81C, Cc
French Mills, 57, Da
French Post, 57A, Bc
French Rep., 51, Bd
French Somaliland, 80B, Ce
F. Terr. of Afars and Issas, 96D, Gc
French West Africa, 80A, Cc
Frenchtown, 71C, Bb
Fresnillo, 43A, Bb
Frew, Ford of, 49A, Bb
Fribourg (Freiburg), 29B, Bb
Fribourg, canton, 29B, Bb
Friedberg, Austria, 31, Me
Friedberg, Germany, 53, Hb
Friedland, Bohemia, 47, Fb; East Prussia, 60A, Ha
Friedrich Wilhelmshafen (Madang), 77, Hc
Friedrichstadt, 65F, Aa
Friendly (Tonga) Is., 75, Gf
Friesach, 21, Le
Friesland, 46A, Ea
Frio, C., 68, Ee
Frista, 20, Gb
Frisian Is., 55A, Fb
Frisians, 2A, Ba; 7A, Ea
Frisii, 2, Ec
Fritzlar, 8, Da; 10, Cc
Friuli, 5, Da
Friuli, M. of, 23B, Cb
Frobisher, B., 71, Ha
Frome, 7B, Bc
Fronsac, 11, Cd; 20, Cf
Front Royal, 72B, Aa
Frontenai, 20, Ce
Froschweiler, 76A, Db
Frotesham (Frodsham), 13, Dc
Frutigen, 29B, Bb
Fuego, vol., 43A, Cc
Fuente Guinaldo, 63, Bb
Fuenterrabia, 23C, Ea; 63, Ea
Fuentes, de Onoro, 63, Bb
Fulda, 10, Cc
Fulda, R., 10, Cc; 20, Hc
Fulford, 13, Ec
Fulham, 7C, Cc
Funchal, 55B, Jc
Fundy, B. of, 45A, Da
Fünen, 51, Cb; 65F, Ba
Fünfkirchen, 22, Fb; 39, Ne
Furka Pass, 29B, Cb
Furnes, 46A, Bc
Furness, 36, Cc
Fürstenberg, 30, He
Fürstenwalde, 22, Ea
Fürth, Bavaria, 38, Jd
Fürth, Bohemia, 29A, Ea
Fusan, 74, Le
Fushun, 91, Fb
Füssen, 29A, Db
Futhernesse (Furness), 13, Cb
Futuna Is., 75, Fe
Fyne, L., 14, Cc
Fyvie, 37A, Cb

GABARAS B., 45A, Fa
Gabarret, 20, Dg
Gabbards, 55A, Dc
Gaberones, 96D, Eg
Gabes, 6, Cb; 80A, Da
Gabon, 96D, De
Gabrova, 78, Ed
Gabun, 76, Kd
Gadara, 18C, Cf
Gades, 2, Bf
Gadsden, 72, Cc
Gaeta, 5, Dd
Gaikas, 81B, Cc
Gaikwar, 59A, Bc
Gaines Mill, 72B, Bb
Gainesburg (Gainsborough), 13, Fc
Gainesville, 72B, Ba
Gainsborough, 48A, Cc
Gairloch, 49A, Bb
Galadi, 96A, Bb
Galapagos Is., 75, Le
Galata, 86D
Galati, 61, Be
Galatia, 2, Kf
Galatz, 51, Fd; 78, Fc
Galekas, 81B, Dc
Galford, 7B, Ac
Galich, 19, Cc
Galicia, Poland, 33C, Eb
Galicia, Spain, 63, Ba
Galicians, 85, Ad
Galilee, Sea of, 18C, Cf
Galitch, 19, Ga
Galla, 80A, Gd
Gallabat, 80B, Be
Galla-Sidamo, 96A, Ab
Galle, 92, Ef
Gallegos, 68, Ch
Gallia, 2, Dd

Gallinas, C., 43A, Ec
Gallipoli, Italy, 21A, Eb
Gallipoli, Turkey, 78, Fe
Galloway, 14, De
Gallura, 23B, Bd
Galtellia, 23B, Bd
Galty Mts., 15, Cd
Galveston, 72, Bd
Galway, 37B, Bc; 49B, Bc
Galway, co., 37C, Bc; 49B, Bc
Galway B., 37B, Bc
Gamalama, 52B, Aa
Gambia, 81C, Ab; 96B, Aa
Gambia, R., 81C, Bb
Gambier Is., 75, Jf
Gandersheim, 20, Jb
Gandhara, 1, Kd
Gandia, 23D, Dc
Gando, 80A, Dc
Ganga, R., 91, Bd
Ganganorum Prom., 3A, Bd
Ganges, R., 25, Hd; 73, Ec
Gangra, 16, Jd
Gap, 22, Dc; 30, Gf; 38, Gf
Garamantes, 6, Cc
Garda, L., 5, Cb
Gardelegen, 20, Jb
Gardner, L., 77, Fh
Garfagna, 32E, Ba
Gargano, Mte., 5, Fd
Garhwal, 73, Ca
Garigliano, R., 5, Dd
Garonne, R., 11, Dd
Garoua, 96B, Db
Gartagnana, 23B, Cb
Gartz, 31, Lb; 39, Lb
Gascony, D. of, 11, Ce
Gascoyne, R., 77, Af
Gaspé, 45A, Da
Gaspé, C., 45A, Ea
Gaspereau, 45A, Ea
Gassentino, 32E, Bb
Gastein, 21, Ke
Gatasheved (Gateshead), 13, Eb
Gatinais, 17, Gd
Gatinais, Co. of, 11, Eb
Gatton, 27, Fe
Gauhati, 92, Gb
Gaul, Pref. of, 2, Dd
Gaur, 52A, Cb
Gava, 92, Fc
Gavle, 50, Da
Gavre, 46A, Cd
Gawilgarh, 73, Cc
Gaza, 9, Jf; 18C, Bg; 79, Fd
Gaziantep, 79, Gc
Gdansk, 89, Jc
Gdow, 33C, Eb
Gdynia, 87, Db
Gedaref, 80B, Be
Gedrosia, 1, Je
Geelong, 77, Gi
Geelvink, B., 77, Fb
Geestemünde, 65D, Aa
Gefle, 26, Ea
Geissberg, 76A, Eb
Gelderland, 46A, Eb
Geldern, 20, Gc
Gelligaer, 3A, Ce
Gellivare, 88, Ka
Gelnhausen, 20, Hc; 65A, Aa
Gemar, 39B, Db
Gembloux, 46B
Gemlik, 78, Ge
Gemmi Pass, 29B, Bb
Genadental, 81B, Ac
Genappe, 46B
Generality, Lands of the, 46A, Dc
Geneva, 11, Gc; 29B, Ab
Geneva, L. of, 29B, Ab
Gengenbach, 53, Hc
Genoa (Genova), 5, Bb
Genoa, eccl. prov., 22, Dc
Genoa, G. of, 5, Bb
Genoa, Rep. of, 32A, Cb
Genova (Genoa), 5, Bb
George, 81B, Bc
George, L., 45A, Cb; 57, Eb
George, R., 71, Hb
Georgetown (Demerara), 43D, Gd; 68B, Ba
Georgetown, Delaware, 57, Dd
Georgetown, S. Carolina, 57D, Bb
Georgia, U.S.A., 43C, Ca; 56, Cd
Georgia, U.S.S.R., 19, Gd; 25, Db; 79, Hb
Georgian B., 45A, Aa
Gepidae, 2, Hd; 4A, Gb
Gera, 21, Kc; 65B, Ba
Gerace, 22, Fd
Geraldton, 77, Ag
Gerba, 6, Cb
Geringswalde, 22, Ea
German Confederation, 69A, Kb
German East Africa, 80A, Ge

German Flats, 57, Db
German New Guinea, 77, Hc
German South-West Africa, 81A, Ac
Germani, 1, Db
Germanna, 56, Dc
Germantown, 57, Dc
Germany, 87, Cb
Germany, King. of, 16, Db; 20, Jc
Germiyan, 19, Ee
Gernemutha (Yarmouth), 13, Hd
Gerolstein, 53, Gb
Gerona, 11, Ef; 63, Gb
Gerresheim, 22, Da
Gerrha, 1, He
Gerrhaei, 1, Ge
Gersau, 29B, Ca
Gerstungen, 10, Cc
Gertruidenberg, 46A, Dc
Gesoriacum (Boulogne), 3A, Hf
Gettysburg, 72B, Ba
Gévaudan, Co. of, 11, Ed
Gèvres, 53, Dc
Gex, 38, Fe
Ghadames, 80A, Da; 96C, Cb
Ghana, 96B, Bb
Ghassanids, 6A, Bb
Ghat, 80A, Eb
Ghaznah, 6, Hb
Ghazni, 25, Fc; 73, Aa
Ghent, 17, Gc; 46A, Cc
Gheria, 59A, Ec
Gheriah, 59A, Bd
Ghillinges (Gilling), 13, Eb
Ghomera, 6, Ab
Giants Castle, 81D, Ab
Gibelet (Byblos), 18C, Cd
Gibelin, 18C, Bg
Gibraltar, Europe, 23D, Cd; 63A
Gibraltar, S. America, 43A, Ed
Gibraltar, Str. of, 63A
Gien, 17, Ge; 30, Ee
Giengen, 20, Jd; 38, Jd
Giessen, 60B, Bc
Gifford, 28A, Bc
Gijon, 23D, Ca
Gila, R., 67D, Bb; 70, Cd
Gilbert Is., 90, Ed
Gilbert, R., 77, Ge
Gildeford (Guildford), 13, Fe
Gilgit, 92, Ca
Gilolo, 52C, Ca
Gimborn, 60A, Ac
Gingee, 59D
Ginginhiovo, 81D, Bb
Giornico, 29B, Cb
Giovenazzo, 21A, Db
Gipewiz (Ipswich), 13, Hd
Girgeh, 80B, Ab
Girgenti (Agrigentum), 5, Df
Gironde, R., 17, Ef; 28C, Bd
Girvan, 49A, Bc
Gisborne, 77A
Gisors, 20, Dd; 83A, Ab
Gitschin, 39, Lc
Giurgevo, 78, Ed
Givelcestre (Ilchester), 13, Df
Givet, 53, Fb; 83A, Ca
Giza, 93, Cd
Gjelveju, 86A, Da
Gladbach, 83A, Da
Gladstone, 77, If
Glama, R., 12, Ga
Glandève, 20, Gg; 22, Dc
Glannaventa (Ravenglass), 3A, Cb
Glarus, 29B, Da
Glarus, canton, 29B, Db
Glasgow, 14, Dd
Glasgow, bp., 14A, Bc
Glastingeberie (Glastonbury), 13, De
Glastonbury, 27, De
Glatz, 21, Mc; 39, Mc
Glatz, co., 39, Mc
Glauchau, 39C, Cc; 53, Kb
Gleichen, 39C, Ac
Glen Affric, 14, Db
Glen Coe, 49A, Bb
Glen Elchaig, 49A, Bb
Glen Finnan, 49A, Bb
Glen Garry, 14, Db
Glen Lyon, 49A, Bb
Glen Moriston, 14, Db
Glen Orchy, 49A, Bb
Glen Shiel, 14, Db
Glen Spean, 14, Dc
Glencoe, Natal, 81D, Bb
Glendalough, 15, Ec
Gleniochar, 3A, Bb
Glenluce, 36, Bc; 49A, Bc
Glenmore, 14, Db
Glevum (Gloucester), 3A, De
Glogau, 21, Mc
Glokhov, 19, Eb
Gloucester, England, 27, De
Gloucester, Virginia, 45B, Ae

Gloucester (Cape Ann), 45B, Db; 57, Fb
Gloucester, bp., 36, Df
Gloucester, co., 27, De
Glowecestre (Gloucester), 13, De
Glowecestrescire (Gloucester) shire), 13, De
Glücksburg, 65F, Aa
Glückstadt, 38, Hb
Glywising, 7B, Bc
Gmünd, 20, Hd; 38, Hd
Gmunden, 39, Ke
Gnesen, 21, Mb
Gnesen, eccl. prov., 22, Fa
Goa, 73, Bd
Goba, 96A, Ab
Gobbio, 23B, Dc
Godavari, R., 25, Me; 73, Cd
Godesberg, 87, Bb
Godfrey of Bouillon, 16, Gd
Gödöllő, 33C, Db
Godwin, 12, Dd
Goes, 46A, Cc
Gogra, R., 73, Db
Goias, 68, Dd
Goias, st., 68, Ed
Gok Tepe, 61, Jg
Gokcha, L., 19, Hd
Golconda, 52A, Bc
Golconda Coast, 52A, Cc
Gold Coast, 81C, Dc
Goldelminge, (Godalming), 13, Fe
Golden Gate, Constantinople, 18E
Golden Gate, Jerusalem, 18D
Golden Horde, 25, Da; 61, Fe
Golden Horde, Khanate of the, 19, Gb
Golden Horn, 18E
Golden Vale, 15, Cd
Goldenkron, 22, Eb
Goldsboro, 72, Eb
Goldsborough, 3A, Fb
Golea, 80A, Da
Göllersdorf, 39, Md
Gollheim, 29A, Ba
Gollnow, 26, Ec
Golspie, 49A, Bb
Gommern, 39C, Ba
Gonave, 43A, Ec
Gondar, 80A, Be; 96A, Aa
Gondrecourt, 39B, Bb
Gondwana, 52A, Cb
Gonzaga, 20, Jf
Gonzaga (Marq. of Mantua), 32A, Db
Good Hope, C. of (Tormentoso), 35, Kf; 81B, Ac
Gooshland, 57, Ce
Gooty, 59A, Cd
Gorakhpur, 73, Db
Gordon, 37A, Bc; 37A, Cb
Gordon Castle, 37A, Cb
Gordonsville, 57, Bd; 72B, Aa
Gorée, 81C, Bc
Gorinchem, 46A, Dc
Gorizia, 23B, Db; 84, Ec
Görlitz, 21, Lc
Gorski, 84, Ld
Görz, 21, Kf; 39, Ke
Görz, Co. of, 39, Ke
Gorze, 39B, Ba
Goshen, 81A, Bc
Goslar, 20, Jc
Gosselies, 46B
Göteborg, 87, Ca
Gotha, 30, Jc; 54, Eb
Gothenburg, 47, Ea; 50, Cb
Gothia, Marq. of, 11, Ee
Gotland, 26, Eb; 34, Ea
Gottesgab, 39C, Cc
Göttingen, 26, Dc; 38, Hc
Gottorp, 51, Bc
Gourdon, 17, Ff
Gouritz, R., 81B, Bc
Governors I., 56B
Gower, 27, Be
Gowna, L., 15, Dc
Goya, 68, De
Graaff Reinet, 81B, Cc
Graaff Reinet, dist., 81B, Cc
Gracias á Dios, C., 43A, Dc
Gradisca, 32A, Eb; 86B, Db
Grado, 32D, Cb
Grafenau, 31, Kd
Graham, 37A, Bb
Graham Land, 69C
Grahamstown, 81B, Cc
Graian Alps, 29A, Bc
Grampians, 14, Dc
Gran, 22, Fb; 39, Ne
Gran, eccl. prov., 22, Fb
Gran, R., 31, Nd
Gran Chaco, 68, Ce
Granada, Nicaragua, 43A, Dc
Granada, Spain, 23C, Dd; 63, Dd
Granada, eccl. prov., 22, Bd

Granada, King, of, 23C, Dd
Granadine Confederation, 68, Bb
Granard, 15, Dc
Grand Canal, 25, Lc
Grand Canyon, 70, Cd
Grand Gulf, 72C, Aa
Grand I., New York, 71D
Grand I., Vermont, 57, Ea
Grand Lahu, 81C, Cc
Grand Portage, 44, Ed
Grand Pré, 45A, Ea
Grand, R., 70, Dd
Grand Tartary, 42, Ob
Grande Chartreuse, 22, Db
Grande Gette, R., 46B
Grandpré, 30, Fd
Grandson, 29B, Ab
Granson, 30, Ge
Grant, 37A, Bb
Grantham, 13, Fd
Grantown, 49A, Cb
Granville, 55A, Cd
Grappa, Mt., 86B, Bb
Grasse, 22, Dc
Graudenz, 62, Fb
Grauer Bund, 29B, Db
Graus, 23C, Fa
Grave, 46A, Ec
Gravelines, 46A, Bc
Gravelotte, 76A, Cb
Gravesend, 45B, Cc; 57B
Gravina, 21A, Db
Gravosa, 39, Ng
Gray, 38, Fe; 76A, Cc
Grays Inn, 27A
Graz, 21, Le; 29A, Fb
Great Abaco I., 43A, Eb
Great Australian Bight, 77, Dh
Great Bahama I., 43A, Eb
Great Bear L., 70, Ca
Great Belt, 65F, Ba
Great Bridge, 57, Ce
Great Bulgaria, 19, Jb
Great Cayman, 43A, Dc
Great Dividing Ra., 77, Hf
Great Exuma, 43A, Eb
Great Fish, R., Cape Prov., 81B, Cc
Great Fish, R., S.W. Africa, 81B, Aa
Great Inagua, 43A, Eb
Great Karroo, 81B, Bc
Great Kei, R., 81B, Dc
Great Lakes, 69B
Great Manitoulin I., 45A, Aa
Great Marlow, 48A, Cd
Great Namaqualand, 81A, Ac
Great Namaquas, 81B, Aa
Great Ouse, R., 27, Gd
Great Pedee, R., 45A, Pd
Great Poland, 39, Mb
Great Russian, 85, Kb
Great St. Bernard Pass, 29A, Bc
Great Salt L., 70, Cc
Great Slave L., 70, Ca
Great Slave, R., 70, Ca
Great Whale, R., 70, Gb
Great Zab, R., 6A, Ca
Greater Antilles, 43A, Ec
Greece, 78, Dg
Green B., 56, Ba
Green Mts., 45A, Cb
Green, R., 70, Cd
Green Bay, 70, Fc
Greenbrier, R., 57, Ad
Greencastle, 37B, Eb
Greenland, 69B
Greenlaw, 48A, Bb
Greenock, 49A, Bc
Greensboro, 72, Eb
Greenwich, 45B, Cc
Greifswald, 22, Ea; 39, Ka
Greiz, 39C, Cc; 53, Kb
Grenada, 43A, Fc
Grenadines, 43A, Fc
Grenoble, 11, Fd
Grentebrige (Cambridge), 13, Gd
Grentebrigescire (Cambridge-shire), 13, Gd
Gretna, 28B, Bb; 49A, Cc
Greymouth, 77A
Greytown, 81D, Bb
Grèzes, 17A, Dd
Griffen, 39, Le
Griffin's Wharfe, 56B
Grimesbi (Grimsby), 13, Fc
Grimsby, 27, Fc
Grimsel Pass, 29B, Cb
Grinstead, 27, Fe
Griqualand East, 81B, Db
Griqualand West, 81B, Bb
Griquas, 81B, Bb
Griquatown, 81B, Bb
Gris Nez, C., 55A, Dc
Grislingen, 30, Hd
Grisons (Rhaetian Leagues), 29B, Db
Grobe, 22, Ea
Gröbming, 31, Ke; 39, Ke

Grodno, 26, Fc; 60A, Jb
Groll, 46A, Fb
Groningen, 46A, Fa
Groningen, prov., 46A, Fa
Grosmont, 28A, Dc
Grosotto ,86B, Aa
Gross Jägersdorf, 51, Ec
Gross Mariazell, 22, Fb
Grossbeeren, 60B, Db
Grosseto, 20, Jg; 22, Ec
Grosswardein, 33C, Eb
Grotska, 33C, Ec; 51, Ee
Grozny, 88, Pe
Gruffyd ap Llywelyn, Pr. of, 12, Dc
Gruyères, 29B, Bb
Guadalajara, Mexico, 43A, Bb
Guadalajara, Spain, 63, Db
Guadalcanal, 77, Jc; 90, Dd
Guadalquivir, R., 63, Cd
Guadalupe, 22, Ad
Guadarrama, Sierra de, 63, Db
Guadeloupe, 43A, Fc
Guadenhutten, 56, Cb
Guadiana, R., 63, Bd
Guadix, 22, Bd; 23C, Dd
Guam, 40, Qd; 90, Dc
Guanahani, 40, Fc
Guanajuato, 43A, Bb
Guapora, R., 68, Cd
Guaporé, 94, Df
Guarda, 22, Ac; 63, Bb
Guastalla, 32A, Db
Guatemala, 43A, Cc
Guatulco, 42, Ed
Guaviare, R., 68, Cb
Guayaquil, 68, Ac
Guben, 31, Lc
Guelders, 60A, Ac
Guelders, Co. of, 46C, Ba
Guelders, D. of, 31A, Cb
Gueldres, 46A, Fc
Guérande, 30, Be
Gueret, 30, De
Guermínstr(Warminster),13,Ce
Guernsey, 17, Dd
Guiana, 68, Db
Guienne, D. of (Aquitaine), 11, Dd
Guildford, 27, Fe
Guilford, 45B, Cc
Guilford Court House, 57, Be
Guillon, 28C, Ec
Guimaraes, 23D, Ab
Guinea, 81C, Dc; 96B, Aa
Guinea, G. of, 94, Te
Guinegate, 30, Ec
Guines, 11, Da; 17, Fc
Guingamp, 22, Bb; 38, Bd
Guipuzcoa, 23C, Da
Guise, 17, Gd; 30, Ed; 53, Ec
Gultres, 22, Bb
Gujarat, 25, Gd; 73, Bc
Gujranwala, 92, Ca
Gujrat, 73, Ba
Gumti, R., 73, Db
Gundwana, 59A, Cc
Güns, 39, Me
Guntur, 59A, Cd; 92, Ed
Gurev, 61, He
Gurgan. 93, Gb
Gurganj, 6, Ga
Guria, 79, Hb
Gurk, 22, Eb
Gurkhas, 73, Db
Gurramkonda, 59A, Ce
Gurupa, 41B, Dd
Gusau, 96B, Ca
Güstrow, 39, Kb
Guthrum's King., 7C, Db
Guyana, 68. Db
Guyenne, 20, Df; 28C, Cd
Gwadar, 92, Ab
Gwalior, 25, Gd; 73, Cb
Gwent, 28A, Dc
Gwynedd, 13, Bc; 28A, Dc
Gympie, 77, Ig
Gyrwe (Jarrow), 13, Eb

HAARLEM, 46A, Db
Habitancum (Risingham), 3A, Da
Habsburg, 11, Gc; 29B, Ca
Hackensack, 57B
Haddeby, 12, Gc
Hadby-Schleswig, 12, Gc
Haddington, 49A, Cc
Haddington, co., 49A, Cc
Hadhramaut, 93, Ff
Hadjach, 50, Gc
Hadrianopolis, 2, Je
Hadrian's Wall, 3C
Hafir, 6, Fc
Hafrsfjord, 12, Fb
Hafsids, 24, Eg
Hafsids (Sultanate of Tunis), 34, De
Hagenau, 20, Gd; 29A, Ba
Hagerstown, 72, Ea
Hague, C. de la, 55A, Cd
Hague, The, 46A, Db

Hagustalham (Hexesham) (Hexham), 13, Db
Haifa, 18C, Cf; 93, Cc
Hail, 93, Ed
Hailes, 36, Ef
Hainan, 25, Ke; 91, De
Hainau, 60B, Ec
Hainaut, 10, Ac; 46A, Cd
Haine, R., 46B
Haine's Bluff, 72C, Aa
Haingeham (Hedingham), 13, Gd
Haiti, 43A, Ec
Hakodate, 91, Hb
Halberstadt, 10, Dc
Haleb (Aleppo), 18C, Eb
Halesowen, 36, De
Halifax, England, 48A, Cc
Halifax, N. Carolina, 57, Ce
Halifax, Nova Scotia, 45A, Eb
Hall, 20, Hd; 53, Hc
Halland, 26, Db; 47, Ea
Halle, 10, Ec; 31B, Ca
Hallue, 76A, Bb
Halmahera, 91, Ff
Halmstad, 26, Db
Halton, 27, Dc
Halys, R., 18A, Ea; 24, Jf
Ham, 30, Ed
Hama, 18C, Dc; 93, Db
Hamadan, 6A, Db; 93, Fc
Hamar, 26, Da
Hamburg, 10, Cb
Hamdan, 6, Fd
Hamdanids, King of, 6B, Fa
Hami, 74, Hd
Hamid, 19, Ee
Hamilton, Canada, 70, Fc
Hamilton, Scotland, 37A, Bc
Hamilton Inlet, 71, Jb
Hamilton, R., 71, Hb
Hamm, 60A, Ac
Hammadids, 16, Ce
Hampshire, 27, Ec
Hampton, New Hampshire, 45B, Db
Hampton, Virginia, 45B, Ae
Hampton Roads, 72B, Bb
Hamton, 7B, Cc
Han Dominions, 26, Db
Hanau, 29A, Ca; 30, Hc
Hanchong, 76B, Ba
Han-chung, 1, Nd
Handa, 96A, Ca
Hangchow, 74, Lf; 91, Ec
Hangchow (Quinsay) (Lin-gan), 25, Mc
Hanging Rock, 57D, Aa
Hankow, 74, Ke; 90, Bb
Hanoi, 25, Kd; 91, Dd
Hanover, Germany, 26, Cc
Hanover, Virginia, 57, Ce
Hanover, El., 53, Ha
Hantescire (Hampshire), 13, Ee
Hantune (Southampton), 13, Ef
Harar, 96A, Bb
Harar, prov., 96A, Bb
Harbin (Pinkiang), 90, Ca; 91, Fb
Harcourt, 17, Fd; 53, Cc
Hard Times, 72C, Aa
Hardangerfjord, 12, Fb
Hardknot, 3A, Cb
Harenc, 18C, Db
Harfleur, 30, Dd; 53, Dc
Harlech, 27, Bd
Harmazia, 1, He
Harold, 12, Dd
Harper, 96B, Bb
Harper's Ferry, 56, Dc
Harran, 6A, Ba
Harris, 14, Bb; 37A, Ab
Harrisburg, 72, Ea
Harrismith ,81A, Cc; 81D, Ab
Harrodsburg, 56, Cc
Hartford, 45B, Cc
Hartland, 36 Bg
Hartmannswillerkopf, 83B, Bb
Harts, R., 81A, Cc
Harvard College, 56B
Harwich, 27, He
Haryana, 92, Db
Harz, 60A, Cc
Harz, mts., 10, Dc
Harzburg, 10, Dc
Hasselt, 26, Cc; 83A, Ca
Hastenbeck, 60A, Bb
Hastings, 27, Gf
Hastinges (Hastings), 13, Gf
Hatay, 79, Gc
Hatfield, 7B, Cc
Hatteras, C., 45A, Bf; 57, Df
Hattin, 18C, Cf
Haughmond, 36, De
Haura, 93, Fg
Havana, 43A, Db
Havelberg, 10, Eb; 30, Kb
Havelock, 27, Db; 36A
Haverfordwest, 27, Ae

Haverhill, 45B, Db
Havre, 76A, Ab
Havre de Grâce (Le Havre), 38, Dd
Havre, 93, Ed
Havre de Grace, Maryland, 71C, Cc
Haw, R., 57, Be
Hawaii, 75D, Cc
Hawaiian Is., 90, Gb
Hawarden, 13, Cc; 27, Cc
Hawke B., 77A
Hawkes Bay, 77A
Hawick, 28B, Cb
Hay, 28A, Cb
Hayingen, 30, Hd
Haymarket, 27A
Heard I., 95, Qh
Heathfield, 7A, Ca
Hebrides, 37A, Ab; 49A, Ab
Hebron, Palestine, 18C, Cg
Hebron, Transvaal, 81A, Cc
Hechingen, 60B, Cc; 65B, Ab
Heda (Hythe), 13, He
Hedgley Moor, 27, Da
Hedmark, 12, Ga
Hedon, 27, Fc
Heidelburg, 29A, Ca
Heilbronn, 29A, Ca
Heiligenkreuz, 22, Fb
Heiligerlee, 46A, Fa
Heilsberg, 26, Fc; 60A, Ha
Heinsberg, 46C, Cb
Hejaz, 6, Fc; 80B, Bc
Hejer, 6, Fd
Helder, 46A, Db
Heldernesse (Holderness), 13, Fc
Helena, Arkansas, 72, Bc
Helena, Montana, 70, Cc
Heletune (Halton), 13, Dc
Heligoland, 55A, Ga; 60A, Aa
Heligoland Bight, 55A, Ga
Heliopolis (Baalbek), 18C, De
Hellas, 9, Ge
Helles, C., 86D
Hellespont, 34, He
Hellespontus, 2, Jf
Helluland, 35, Gb
Helmsdale, 49A, Ca
Helsingborg, 26, Db
Helsingfors, 26, Fa
Helsingland, 26, Ea
Helsingor, 26, Lb
Helsinki, 87, Ea
Helston, 27, Af
Helvetian Rep., 65A, Ab
Hemmingstedt, 26, Cc; 30, Ha
Hempstead, 45B, Cc
Hendaye, 53, Cf
Hengistdun, 7B, Ac
Hennebont, 28C, Ac; 55A, Be
Hennersdorf, 60A, Ec
Henrico, 45B, Ae
Henry, C., 45B, Be
Heppenheim, 65C, Ab
Heraclea, Iconium, 16, Je
Heraclea, Nicaea, 19, Ed
Heraklea, 18C, Ba
Herat, 25, Fc; 61B, Bb
Herbertshöhe (Kokopo), 77, Ib
Herculis Prom., 3A, Be
Herdeslege, (Eardisley), 13, Dd
Hereford, 13, Dd
Hereford, bp., 36, De
Hereford, Co., 27, Dd
Herefordscire (Hereford-shire), 13, Dd
Hereke, 33A, Cb
Herero, 80A, Ef
Héricourt, 31A, Dd
Héristal, 7A, Eb; 8, Da
Herjedalen, 26, Da
Hermannstadt (Sibin), 19, Cc
Hermannstadt, Hungary, 24 Gd; 78, Ec
Hermitage, 28B, Cb
Hermon, Mt., 18C, De
Hernösand, 26, Ea
Heruli, 2, Kd
Hersfeld, 10, Cc; 30, Hc
Herteforde (Hertford), 13, Fe
Hertefordscire (Hertford-shire), 13, Fe
Hertford, 27, Fe
Hertford, co., 27, Fe
Hervey Is., 75, He
Herzegovina, 39, Mg; 78, Ad
Hesdin, 53, Eb
Hesse, 10, Cc
Hesse, G. D. of, 65C, Aa
Hesse, Land. of, 30, Hc
Hesse-Cassel, Land., 38, Hc
Hesse-Darmstadt, Land., 38, Hc
Hessen, 60B, Bc
Hevellians, 10, Eb
Heversham, 7B, Ba
Hexham, 27, Db; 36A
Heytesbury, 27, Ee
Hibernia, 2, Bc

Hierapolis, 2, Lf; 4B, Kd
Hierosolyma, 1, Fd
High Bridge, 49A, Bb
High Street, 3A, Db
Hiiumaa, 87, Ea
Hildburghausen, 39C, Ac
Hildesheim, 10, Cb
Hilla, 93, Ec
Hillsborough, 57, Be
Hilo, 75D, Dc
Himachal Pradesh, 92, Da
Himalaya Mts., 73, Ca
Hims, 6A, Bb
Hindon, 27, De
Hindu Kush, 59A, Ba
Hindu States, 25, Ge
Hindustan, 40, Nc
Hingham, 45B, Db
Hinsdale (Fort Dummer), 57, Eb
Hippo, 4A, Dd; 8, Dd
Hippo Regius, 2, Ef
Hira, 6A, Cb
Hiroshima, 91, Gc
Hirschau, 22 Db
Hirschberg, 39, Lc; 60A, Ec
Hirson, 83A, Cb
Hirsova, 78, Fc
Hispania, 2, Be
Hispaniola (Española), 43A, Ec
Hit, 6A, Cb
Hitchin, 36, Ff
Hlobane, 81D, Ba
Hlubi Kaffirs, 81D, Ab
Hobart, 77, Hj
Hobkirk's Hill, 57D, Aa
Hoboken, 45B, Bc
Hochkirch, 60A, Ec
Hochschwab, 29A, Fb
Höchst, 38, Hc
Höchstadt, 29A, Da
Hodeida, 80B, Ce; 93, Eg
Hofburg, 20, Gd
Hog I., 56B
Hohe Tauern, 29A, Eb
Höhen, 10, Ec
Hohenburg, Bavaria, 20, Jd
Hohenburg, Swabia, 20, Hd
Hohenfriedeberg, 60A, Fc
Hohenlinden, 29A, Da
Hohenlohe, 20, Jd
Hohenstein, 60A, Cc
Hohianga B., 77A
Hokkaido, 91, Hb
Holborn, 27A
Holkar, 73, Cc
Holkar and Sindhia, 59A, Cc
Hollabrünn, 29A, Ga
Holland, Co. of, 17, Hb; 46A, Db
Holland, dist., England, 13 Gd
Holland, King. of, 65F, Aa
Holly Springs, 72, Cc
Holme Cultram, 36, Cc
Holme St. Benet, 36, He
Holstein, 10, Ca
Holt, 28A, Da; 48B, Bc
Holy I., 12, Dc; 36, Eb
Holy Roman Empire, 20, Gd
Holy Sepulchre, Church of the, 18D
Holyhead, 3A, Bc
Holyrood, 14, Ed
Homburg, 30, Gc; 39B, Ca
Home, 28B, Cb
Homildon Hill, 27, Da
Homs, 18C, Dd; 79, Gd; 93, Dc
Honduras, 43D, Dc
Honduras, C., 43B, Bc
Honduras, G. of, 43A, Dc
Honfleur, 28D, Cb; 55A, Dd
Hongkong, 91, Ed
Honiton, 27, Cf
Honolulu, 75, Hc; 75D, Cb
Honshu, 91, Hb
Hooghly, 59B
Hooghly, R., 59B; 92, Fc
Hoogstracten, 46A, Dc
Hoorn, 30, Fc; 46A, Eb
Hope, 28A, Ca
Hope Bay, 69C
Hopedale, 71, Hb
Hopetown, 81A, Bc
Hopton Heath, 48A, Bc
Horburg, 39B, Db
Hordaland, 12, Fa
Horgen, 29B, Ca
Horn, 46C, Bb
Horn, C., 68, Ch
Horncastle, 3A, Fc
Horseshoe Bend (Tohopeka), 71F, Ba
Horsham, 27, Fe
Horta, 5B,, Bb
Hostatrich 63, Gb
Hottentots, 81B, Bb
Houdan, 38, Dd
Housatonic, R., 45B, Cc
Houston, 72, Ad

Hovedene (Howden), 13, Fc
Howland I., 90, Gf
Howrah, 92, Fc
Howth, 49B, Ec
Howth Hd., 15, Ec
Hoy, 49A, Ca
Hoya, 20, Hb
Hoysalas, 25, Ge
Hradisch, 22, Fb
Hsi-Liao, R., 91, Fb
Hsinking, 90, Ca
Hsu Chow, 1, Od
Huanuco, 68, Bc
Huaras, 68, Bc
Hubbardton, 57, Eb
Hubertusbrug, 60A, Dc
Hudson B., 70, Fb
Hudson, R., 57, Ec
Hudson (North), R., 45B, Bc
Hudson Str., 70, Ga
Hudson Bay Company Terr., 44, Eb
Hué, 91, De
Huelgas, 22, Bc
Huelva, 23C, Bd
Huesca, Granada, 23D, Dd
Huesca, Saragossa, 23C, Ea
Hufuf, 93, Fd
Hughenden, 77, Gf
Huilier, Fort d', 56, Ab
Hull, 27, Fc
Hulme, 48B, Bc
Hulst, 46A, Dc
Humana, 5B, Bb
Humanita, 68, De
Humber, 27, Gc
Humboldt, R., 70, Cc
Hume Castle, 28B, Cb
Hungarian Ore Mts., 50, Dd
Hungary, 33C, Db; 87, Dc
Hungary, King. of, 16, Fc
Hungshui-Ho, R., 91, Dd
Hun-ho, R., 76B, Ba
Hüningen, 53, Gd
Hunni, 2, Ld
Huns, 2A, Fb
Hunsrück, 83A, Db
Huntcliff, 3A, Fb
Huntedun (Huntingdon), 13, Fd
Huntedunscire (Huntingdon-shire), 13, Fd
Hunter, R., 77, Ih
Huntingdon, 27, Fc
Huntingdon, co., 27, Fd
Huntly, 37A, Cb; 49A, Cb
Huntsville, 72, Cc; 71F, Ba
Huon G., 77, Hc
Hurghada, 93, Cd
Huron, L., 45A, Ab
Huron Mission, 45A, Ab
Hurons, 45A, Ab
Hush, 54, Hc
Hussinetz, 31, Ld
Husum, 65F, Aa
Huy, 53, Fb
Hvitramannaland, 35, Fc
Hwang-ho, R., 25, Lc
Hwicce, 7B, Bc
Hy (Iona), 14, Bc
Hyderabad, Nizam's Dominions, 73, Cd
Hyderabad, Sind, 73, Ab
Hydra, 78, Dg
Hyères, 30, Gg
Hyères, Is. d', 53, Gf
Hyrcania, I, Hd
Hythe, 27, He

IAL, 13, Cc
Iambia, 1, Fe
Iarum (Yarm), 13, Eb
Iasi, 87, Fc
Iazyges, 1, Ec
Ibadan, 96B, Cb
Ibelim, 18C, Bg
Iberia, 19, Gd
Iberus, R., 2, Ce
Ica, 68, Bd
Icaria, 19, De
Iceland, 88, Ba
Iceni, 3A, Gd
Ichaboe I., 81A, Ac
Ichang, 74, Ke
Icknield Way, 3A, Fe
Iconium (Konieh), 18A, Eb; 19, Ee
Iconium (Seljuk Sultanate of Rum), 16, Je
Ida, Mt., 78, Eh
Idaho, 70, Cc
Idaho Terr., 67D, Ba
Idjil, 80A, Bb
Idrisids, 8, Ae
Idrisids, King. of, 6B, Aa
Idstedt, 65F, Aa
Ife, 96B, Cb
Ifni, 80A, Bb
Ifni, col., 96C, Ab
Iganie, 64, Gc
Iglau, 31, Ld; 39, Ld
Ikshids, King. of, 6B, Eb

Ilchester, 27, De
Ile Bouchard, 38, De
Ilfracombe, 48B, Ad
Ilha, 41B, Ee
Ilheus, 68, Fd
Ili, R., 91, Ab
Ilkhan Empire, 25, Ec
Ilkley, 7B, Cb
Ill, R., 39B, Db
Illana B., 75E, Bc
Illapel, 68, Bf
Iller, R., 10, Dd; 29A, Db
Illinois, 56, Bc; 72, Cb
Illinois, R., 56, Bb
Illinois Terr., 71C, Ab
Illyria, King. of, 65C, Bb
Illyria, Pref. of, 2, Hf
Illyrian Prov., 62, Cb
Illyricum, 4A, Gc
Illyricum, Diocese, 2, Gd
Ilmen, L., 26, Hb
Iloilo, 75E, Bb
Ilorin, 96B, Cb
Imbros, 78, Ee
Imeretia, 79, Hb
Imperial Hungary, 39, Me
Imphal, 92, Gc
In Salah, 80A, Db
Inca King., 35, Fe
Inchcolm, 14, Ec
Inchtuthill, 14, Ec
Inde, 43A, Bb
Independence, 70, Ed
India, 92, Dc
Indian Ocean, 35, Ne
Indian Terr., 67D, Db
Indiana, 72, Cb
Indiana Terr., 67B, Aa
Indianapolis, 72, Cb
Indies, 42, Oc
Indonesia, 91, Eg
Indore, 73, Cc
Indraprastha, 1, Ke
Indus, R., 1, Kd; 73, Ab
Ingelheim, 10, Cd
Ingogo, 81D, Aa
Ingolstadt, 22, Eb; 29A, Da
Ingria, 26, Gb; 47, Ha
Inhambane, 96C, Fg
Inis Cathy, 15, Bd
Inishannon, 49B, Ce
Inishowen, 81D, Bb
Inn, R., 20, Je; 29A, Db
Inn Quarter, 33C, Cb; 53, Kc
Inner Mongolia, 91, Eb
Innichen, 86B, Ca
Innsbruck, 29A, Db
Inny, R., 15, Dc
Inter Ripam et Mersham, 13, Dc
Interlaken, 29B, Bb
Inuvik, 94, Gb
Inveraray, 37A, Bb; 49A, Bb
Inveravon, 3A, Ca
Invercargill, 77A
Inveresk, 3A, Ca
Inverey, 49A, Cb
Invergarry, 49A, Bb
Invergordon, 49A, Bb
Invergowrie, 14, Ec
Inverkeithing, 37A, Cb; 48B, Ba
Inverlochy, 49A, Bb
Inverness, 14, Db
Inverness, co., 37A, Bb; 49A, Bb
Inverurie, 49A, Cb
Invola, 32A, Db
Inyati, 81A, Ca
Inyeshane, 81D, Bb
Iona (Hy), 14, Bc; 49A, Ab
Ionia, 84, He
Ionian Is., 62, Ge; 78, Cf
Ionian Sea, 78, Bf
Iowa, 70, Ec
Iowas, 56, Bb
Ipswich (Agawam), 45B, Db; 57, Fb
Ipswich, England, 27, Hd
Iquique, 68, Be
Iquitos, 68, Bc
Iraklion, 88, Lf; 93, Bb
Iran (Persia), 89, Pg; 93, Gc
Iraq, 6A, Db; 79, Hd
Irchester, 3A, Fd
Ireland, 15; 49A
Irish Free State, 84, Ab
Irish Sea, 15, Fc; 28B, Ac
Irkutsk, 91, Da
Iron Gate, 78, Dc
Iroquois, 45A, Bb
Irrawaddy, R., 73, Gc; 92, Hd
Irtapan, 43A, Cc
Irthing, R., 28B, Cc
Irtysh, R., 25, Ga; 91, Aa
Irun, 63, Ea
Irvine, 49A, Bc
Isabella, 43A, Ec
Isandhlwana, 81D, Bb
Isar, R., 10, Ed
Isauria, 2, Kf
Isca (Caerleon), 3A, De

Isca Dumnoniorum (Exeter), 3A, Cf
Ischia, 32B, Dd
Iscia Baidoa, 96A, Bb
Isère, R., 11, Fd; 32A, Bb
Isernia, 22, Ec
Isfahan, 25, Ec; 93, Gc
Ishtip, 86A, Da
Isker, R., 78, Dd
Islamabad, 92, Ca
Island Number Ten, 72, Cb
Islands, B. of, 77A
Islay, 14, Bd
Isle of France, 38, Ed
Isles, King. of the, 14, Bb
Isles, The, bp., 14A, Ab
Ismail, 51, Fd; 78, Gc
Ismailia, 80B, Aa; 86C, Bc
Isna, 93, Cd
Isny, 30, Je
Isola, 32D, Bb
Isonzo, 2A, Cb
Isonzo, R., 5, Db; 86B, Da
Ispahan, 6, Gb
Isparta, 93, Cb
Israel, 89, Mg; 93, Cc
Issoire, 30, Ef
Issoudun, 11, Dc
Istanbul, 93, Ba
Istria, 5, Db; 10, Ef
Isurium (Aldborough), 3A, Eb
Italia, 2, Fe
Italian (Cisalpine) Rep., 65A, Ab
Italian Somaliland, 80A, Hd
Italy, 88, He
Italy, Exarchate of, 4B, Ec
Italy, King. of, 20, Jf
Italy, Pref. of, 2, Fe
Itil, 9, Mc
Ituna Aest. (Solway Firth), 3A, Cb
Itzehoe, 65F, Ab
Iuka, 72, Cc
Iviza, 23C, Fc; 63, Fc
Ivory Coast, 81C, Cd
Ivrea, 5, Ab
Ivry, 38, Dd
Iwo, 96B, Cb
Iwojima, 90, Db
Izborsk, 9, Ha
Izmir, 93, Bb

JABALPUR, 92, Ec
Jabia, 6A, Bb
Jablunkau, 39, Nd
Jaca 22, Bc; 23C, Ea
Jackson, Mississippi, 72C, Aa
Jackson, Tennessee, 72, Cb
Jacksonville, 72, Dc
Jaen, 22, Bd; 23C, Dd
Jaffa, 86C, Bc
Jaffa (Joppa), 18C, Bf
Jaffna, 92, Ef
Jagelions, Lands of the, 31, Md
Jagerndorf, 31, Mc; 33C, Da
Jaintiapur, 73, Fb
Jaipur, 73, Cb
Jaipur, st., 59C, Cb
Jajce, 39, Mf
Jalalabad, 73, Ba
Jalangi, R., 59B
Jalayas, Dominions of the, 24, Mf
Jaleswar, 59B
Jaluit, 75, Fd
Jamaica, 45B, Cc
Jamaica, I., 43A, Ec
Jamaica B., 57B
James B., 70, Fb
James City, 45B, Ae
James W. Ellsworth Land, 69C
Jamestown, 45B, Ae
Jammu and Kashmir, 92, Da
Jamnagar, 92, Cc
Jamshedpur, 92, Fc
Jamtland, 12, Ha
Janer, 31, Mc
Janina, 78, Cf
Jankau, 38, Ld
Japan, 91, Gc
Japan (Zipangu), 25, Nc
Japan, Sea of, 91, Gc
Japanese Empire, 75, Ec
Japura, R., 68, Cc
Jargeau, 28D, Dc
Jarnac, 38, Cf
Jaroslau, 26, Fc
Jaroslavl, 19, Fa
Jarrow, 36, Ec
Jarvis I., 75, He
Jask, 93, Hd
Jassy, 50, Fd; 78, Fb
Jativa, 23C, Ec
Jats, 59A, Cb
Jauf, 93, Dd
Java, 42B; 91, Dg
Java Major (Borneo), 35, Pd
Java Minor (Sumatra), 35, Oe

Java Sea, 91, Eg
Jaxartes, R., 1, Jc
Jebel Hamrin, 19, Ge
Jebel Tarik, 9, Ae
Jeddah, 6, Ec
Jedisan, 50, Gd; 78, Gb
Jefferson City, 72, Bb
Jehol, 90, Ba
Jehoshophat's Gate, 18D
Jelling, 12, Gc
Jemappes, 46A, Cd; 62, Cb
Jemmingen, 46A, Ga
Jemtland, 26, Da
Jena, 30, Jc; 38, Jc; 62, Eb
Jericho, 18C, Cg
Jersey, 17, Dd
Jerusalem, 6A, Bb; 18C, Cg
Jerusalem, Kingdom of, 18C, Cf
Jervaulx, 36, Ee
Jessore, 59B
Jever, 30, Gb; 38, Gb
Jhansi, 73, Cb
Jhelum, R., 73, Ba
Jibuti, 80B, Ce; 94, Re
Jiddah, 80B, Bc
Jimma, 96A, Ab
Jitomir, 50, Fc
Joanna Spring, 77, Cf
Jodhpur, 73, Bb
Johannesburg, 81A, Cc
Johore, 58, Pd
Johore Bahru, 75A, Bb
Johnston, 28B, Bb
Johnston I., 90, Fc
Johnstone, 28B, Bb
Joigny, 11, Ec
Joinville, 17, Hd; 20, Fd
Jolo, 75E, Bc
Jönköping, 26, Db
Joppa, 18A, Bc
Joppa (Jaffa), 18C, Bf
Jordan, 89, Ng; 93, Dc
Jordan, R., 18C, Cf
Jos, 96B, Cb
Joscelin, Lordship of, 18C, Eb
Josselin, 30, Be
Joux, 53, Gd
Juan de Fuca Str., 70, Bc
Juan Fernandez Is., 68, Bf
Jucar, R., 23C, Ec
Juggernaut, 59A, Ed
Jujuy, 41B, Cf
Julian Alps, 86B, Da
Jülich, 20, Gc; 46A, Fd
Jülich, D. of, 46A, Fd
Juliers, Co. of, 46C, Cb
Jullundur, 73, Ca
Jumièges, 22, Cb
Jumna, R., 73, Cb
Junagadh and Manavadar, 92, Cc
Juneau, 71B, Cb
Junin, Argentina, 68, Cf
Junin, Peru, 68, Bd
Junto, Mte., 63B
Jura, I., 14, Cc
Jura, mts., 11, Gc
Jura, Sd. of, 14, Cd
Jurjan, 6, Gb
Jurua, R., 68, Cc
Jussy, 29B, Ab
Justingen, 30, Hd
Jüterbog, 53, Kb
Jutes, 4A, Ba; 7A, Fa
Juti, 2, Eb
Jutland, 55B, La; 84, Da
Juzajan, 6, Hb

KA LAE, pt., 75D, Dc
Kaanbaligh (Peking), 25, Lc
Kabul, 6, Hb; 25, Fc; 73, Aa
Kabul, R., 73, Aa
Kabusi, R., 81B, Cc
Kachin, 92, Hb
Kadisiya, 6A, Cb
Kaduna, 96B, Ca
Kaffa, 19, Fd; 25, Cb
Kaffraria, 81A, Cd
Kagoshima, 91, Gc
Kahoolawe, 75D, Cb
Kaifeng, 25, Lc
Kaiping, 76B, Ba
Kairwan, 8, Ed
Kaisaria, 33A, Ec; 86C, Cb
Kaiser Wilhelm Land, Antarctica, 69C
Kaiser Wilhelms Land (North-East New Guinea), 77, Gc
Kaiserslautern, 29A, Ba
Kaiserswerth, 10, Bc
Kaiwi Chan., 75D, Cb
Kalahari Desert, 81A, Bb
Kalamata, 78, Dg
Kalat, 73, Ab
Kalau, 39C, Db
Kalavryta, 78, Df
Kalgan, 74, Kd; 90, Ba
Kalgoorlie, 77, Ch
Kalimantan, 91, Eg

Kalinga, 1, Lf
Kaliningrad, 89, Kc
Kalinjar, 52A, Cb
Kalisz, 21, Nc; 31, Nc
Kalka, 19, Fc
Kalmuck, 85, Lc
Kalocsa, 22, Fb; 24, Fd
Kalocsa, eccl. prov., 22, Fc
Kalpi, 73, Cb
Kaluga, 24, Kc; 50, Hc
Kama, R., 19, Ja; 88, Qb
Kamakura, 25, Nc
Kamaran, 40, Md
Kamaran I., 80B, Cd; 93, Ef
Kambula, 81D, Ba
Kamchatka, 74, Oc; 90, Da
Kamchik, R., 78, Fd
Kamenets Podolski, 79, Ea
Kamerun, 80A, Ed
Kaminiec, 50, Fd
Kamloops, 70, Bb
Kammin, 21, Lb
Kammin, Bp. of, 31, Ma
Kamp, 22, Da
Kampala, 96D, Fd
Kanara, 59A, Be; 73, Be
Kanauj, 25, Hd
Kanawha, R., 57, Ad
Kanazawa, 91, Gc
Kandahar, 61B, Bb; 73, Aa
Kandavu, 75C, Bb
Kandi, 96B, Ca
Kandy, 73, Df
Kanem, 80A, Ec
Kangaroo I., 77, Fi
Kanizsa, 39, Me
Kankan, 96B, Ba
Kano, 96B, Ca
Kanpur, 92, Eb
Kansas, 70, Ed
Kansas, R., 44, Ee
Kansas City, 72, Bb
Kansas Terr., 67D, Da
Kapolna, 33C, Eb
Kappel, 29B, Cb
Kaprivshtitza, 78, Ed
Kara Kum, 61B, Ab
Kara Kuyunli, 24, Lf
Kara Sea, 74, Ea
Karabagh, 79, Jc
Karachi, 73, Ab
Karafuto, 74, Nd
Karaganda, 91, Ab
Karakakua B., 58, Bd
Karakoram Mts., 59A, Ca
Karakorum, 25, Kb
Karaman, Amirate of, 19, Ee
Karansebes, 33C, Eb
Kara-shahr, 1, Lc
Karassi, 33A, Cc
Karauli, 73, Cb
Karawanken, 29A, Fb
Karbala, 79, Hd
Kardis, 50, Fb; 54, Ha
Kargopol, 61, Eb
Karikal, 59D
Karlovo, 78, Ed
Karlsbad, 31B, Ca
Karlskrona, 51, Db; 54, Fa
Karlsruhe, 83A, Eb
Karmati, King. of, 6B, Fb
Karnul, 73, Cd
Karpathos, 93, Bb
Kars, 19, Gd; 61, Ff; 79, Hb
Karystos, 78, Ef
Karytaena, 78, Dg
Kasai, R., 80A, Ee
Kasalinsk, 61B, Ba
Kaschau, 31, Pd; 50, Ed
Kashan, 93, Gc
Kashgar, 1, Kd
Kashmir, 1, Kd; 73, Ca
Kaskaskia, 56, Bc
Käsmark, 21, Pd
Kasogs (Cherkesses), 9, Lc
Kassa, 33C, Eb
Kassala, 80B, Bd
Kastamuni, 33A, Do
Kastoria, 86A, Cb
Kasvin, 19, He
Kat, R., 81B, Cc
Katanga, 80A, Ff; 96D, Ee
Kath, 6, Ha
Kathiawar, 73, Bc
Katiola, 96B, Bb
Katmandu, 73, Eb
Katrine, L., 14, Dc
Katsina, 96B, Ca
Kattegat, 12, Gb
Katwa, 59B
Kauai, 75D, Bb
Kauai Chan., 75D, Bb
Kaufbeuren, 20, Je
Kaunas, 87, Ea
Kavalla, 78, Ee; 84, Gd
Kawita, 56, Cd
Kawthoolei, 92, Hd
Kayah, 92, Hd
Kayes, 81C, Bb
Kayseri, 79, Gc
Kaysersburg, 39B, Db
Kazam, 19, Ha

Kazan Is., 90, Db
Kazanlik, 78, Ed
Kazanlinsk, 74, Ed
Kazvin, 93, Gb
Ke Chow, 1, Od
Kearney, 70, Ec
Kecskemet, 33C, Db
Kedgeree, 59B
Keeling (Cocos) Is., 90, Ad
Kehl, 39B, Db; 65B, Ab
Kei Is., 52C, Dc
Keiskamma, R., 81B, Cc
Keith, 37A, Cb
Kells, 15, Ec; 49B, Ec
Kelly, 72, Eb
Kelso, 14, Fd; 37A, Cc
Kemi, 26, Fa
Kemp Land, 69C
Kempten, 20, Je
Kenauj, 59C, Cb
Kendal, 27, Db
Kendari, 90, Cd
Kenesaw Mt., 72A, Aa
Kenilworth, 27, Ed
Kenmare, R., 15, Be
Kennebec, R., 45A, Da
Kennedy, 28B, Ab
Kent I., 45B, Ad
Kent, co., 27, Ge
Kentucky, 72, Cb
Kenya, 96C, Fd
Keppel B., 77, If
Kerala, 92, De
Kerbela, 6A, Cb
Kerch, 9, Kc; 79, Ga
Kerguelen I., 69C, 76, Ng
Kerma, 80B, Ad
Kermadec Is., 75, Gf
Kerman, 25, Ed; 93, Hc
Kermanshah, 79, Jd
Kermian, 33A, Cc
Kerrera I., 14, Cc
Kerry, co., 37C; 49B, Bd
Kerulen, R., 91, Eb
Kesselsdorf, 60A, Dc
Keta, 96B, Cb
Kexholm, 50, Ga
Key West, 43A, Db
Keynsham, 36, Df
Khabarovsk, 91, Gb
Khama, 88, Kf
Khama's Country, 81A, Cb
Khanate, 50, Gd
Khandesh, 73, Bc
Kharagpur, 92, Fc
Kharda, 59C, Cd
Kharkov, 9, Kc
Khartoum, 80B, Ad; 96D, Fc
Khazar Empire, 9, Lc
Kherson 8, Jc; 50, Gd
Khiva, 6, Ga; 61B, Ba
Khiva, Khanate of, 61B, Aa
Khmer Empire, 25, Ke
Khmyelnik, 19, Cb
Khodzhent, 61B, Ba
Khojand, 6, Ja
Khokand, 25, Gb; 61B, Ca
Kholm, 61A, Bb
Khorasan, 6, Gb; 25, Ec
Khorramshahr, 93, Fc
Khotan, 1, Ld
Khuzistan, 6, Gb
Khwarizm, 6, Ha; 25, Eb
Khyber Pass, 73, Ba; 74, Fe
Kiakhta, 69A, Pb
Kiaochow, 74, Le
Kichinef, 51, Fd
Kicking Horse Pass, 70, Cb
Kidderminster, 27, Dd
Kidwelly, 27, Be; 28A, Db
Kiel, 26, Dc; 51, Bc; 60B, Ca
Kiel Canal, 87, Bb
Kielce, 21, Pc
Kiev, 19, Eb; 50, Gc; 82, Jb
Kilcullen, 49B, Ec
Kildare, 15, Ec; 49B, Ec
Kildare, co., 37C; 49B, Ec
Kildrummy, 49A, Cb
Kilfenora, 15, Bd; 49B, Bd
Kilia, 51, Fd; 78, Gc
Kilia Mouth, 78, Gc
Kilid Bahr, 86D
Kilimane, 40, Le
Kilkenny, 15, Dd
Kilkenny, co., 37C
Killala, 15, Bb
Killaloe, 15, Cd
Killarney, 49B, Bd
Killarney, Lakes of, 15, Bd
Killiecrankie Pass, 14, Ec
Killybegs, 49B, Cb
Kilmacduagh, 15, Cc
Kilmacrenan, 49B, Da
Kilmallock, 37B, Cd
Kilrush, 49B, Bd
Kilsyth, 37A, Bc; 48B, Ab
Kilwa, 80A, Ge; 96C, Fe
Kimberley, S. Africa, 81A, Bc
Kimberley, W.Australia. 77.De
Kinburn, 51, Gd; 61, De

Kincardine, co., 37A, Cb
Kinchow, 76B, Ab
Kindah, 6, Fc
Kindia, 96B, Aa
Kindu, 80A, Fe
King George Sd., 77, Bi
King George V. Land, 6°C,
King William's Town, 81B,Cc
King's Co., 37C; 49B, Dc
Kings Lynn, 24, Cc; 48A, Dc
Kings Mountain, 56, Cd
Kingston, Canada, 71C, Cb
Kingston, England, 27, Fe
Kingston, Georgia, 56, Cd
Kingston, Jamaica, 43A, Ec
Kingston, New York, 57, Ec
Kingston upon Hull, 36, Fd
Kingstown (Dun Laoghaire),
49B, Ec
Kingswood, 36, Df
Kington, 27, Cd
Kinloss, 14, Eb
Kinross, 37A, Cb
Kinross, co., 49A, Cb
Kinsale, 37B, Ce; 49B, Ce
Kinshasa, 96D, De
Kintore, 37A, Cb
Kintyre, 14, Cd
Kintyre, Mull of, 49A, Bc
Kipchaks (Polovtsi), 19, Gc
Kippure, 15, Ec
Kirchhayn, 30, Hc
Kirensk, 74, Jc
Kirgiz, 25, Ja; 61, Je
Kirin, 91, Fb
Kirk Kilisse, 78, Fe
Kirkcaldy, 49A, Cb
Kirkcudbright, 28B, Bc
Kirkcudbright, co., 37A, Bc
Kirkee, 73, Bd
Kirkham, 36, Fc
Kirkpatrick, 28B, Bb
Kirkstall, 36, Ed
Kirkstead, 36, Fd
Kirkuk, 79, Hc
Kirkwall, 37A, Ca
Kirman, 6, Gc
Kirmisin, 6A, Db
Kirovabad, 93, Fa
Kirriemuir, 37A, Cb
Kisangani, 96D, Ed
Kishinev, 78, Gb
Kiska I., 90, Ea
Kistna, R., 1, Kf; 73, Cd
Kitakyushu, 91, Gc
Kittery, 45B, Db
Kiungchow, 74, Kg
Kiutayeh, 64, Jf
Kizil Ahmadli, Amirate of,
19, Ed
Kizil Irmak, R., 19, Ed
Kizil Kum, 61B, Ba
Kladrau, 21, Kd
Klagenfurt, 29A, Db
Klattau, 21, Kd; 53, Kc
Klausenburg (Kolosvar), 33C,
Eb
Klein Schnellendorf, 60A, Fc
Klip, R., 81A, Cc
Klondyke, 71A, Da
Kloster Zeven, 60A, Bb
Klostergrab, 39, Kc
Klosterneuburg, 22, Fb
Kluane, L., 71B, Ba
Knapdale, 14, Cd; 37A, Bc
Knäred, 50, Cb
Knaresborough, 27, Eb
Knights of the Sword, 34, Ga
Knights Templar, Hospital of
the, 18D
Knin, 22, Fc
Knocke, 46A, Bd
Knockin, 28A, Db
Knockmealdown Mts., 15, Cd
Knocktopher, 49B, Dd
Knoidart, 14, Cb
Knox Land, 69C
Knoxville, 72, Db
Kobdo, 74, Hd
Kobe, 91, Gc
Koblenz, 83A, Da
Kodiak, 71A, Bb
Kodiak I., 71A, Bb
Kodok (Fashoda), 80B, Ae
Kohima, 90, Ab
Kokenhusen, 26, Gb
Kokopo (Herbertshöhe), 77, Ib
Kola, 42, La; 61, Ea
Kolar, 59A, Ce; 59D
Kolar Goldfields, 92, De
Kolberg, 21, La
Kolhapur, 73, Bd
Kolima, R., 69B
Kolin, 29A, Fa; 31, Lc
Kölln, 26, Dc
Köln, 89, Gc
Kolomea, 84, Gc
Kolomna, 19, Fa
Kolozsvar (Klausenburg`,
33C, Eb); 34, Gc
Komati Poort, 81A, Dc
Kommotau, 21, Kd

Komorn, 39, Ne
Konakry, 81C, Bc
Kong, 80A, Cd; 81C, Dc
Kongolo, 80A, Fe
Konia, 24, Jf
Konieh (Iconium), 18A, Eb
Königgratz, 21, Lc; 60A, Ec
Königsau, R., 65F, Aa
Königsberg, Bavaria, 39C, Ac
Königsberg, E. Prussia, 21, Pa
Königstein, 65B, Ba
Konitz, 21, Mb
Konkan, 1, Kf
Konkans, 59A, Bd
Kontagora, 96B, Cc
Konya, 79, Fc
Koonap, R., 81B, Cc
Koporje, 26, Gb
Köprülü, 86A, Ca
Kora, 59A, Db
Kordofan, 80B, Ae
Korcë, 88, Ke
Korhogo, 96B, Bb
Koritza, 86A, Bb
Koro Sea, 75C, Ba
Koroni, 78, Cg
Kororareka, 77, Mi
Korosko, 80B, Ac
Korygaum, 73, Bd
Kosas, 81B, Cc
Kosel, 60A, Gc; 65B, Ca
Koselsk, 19, Fb
Koslin, 31, Ma; 54, Fb
Kosman, I., 77, Id
Kosseir, 80B, Ab
Kossovo, 24, Ge; 78, Cd
Kossovopolye, 50, Ee
Kostroma, 24, Lb; 61, Fc
Kota Bharu, 90, Bc
Kota Kinabalu, 91, Ef
Kotah, 59C, Cb; 73, Cb
Kotchana, 78, De
Kothen, 39C, Bb
Kottbus, 21, Lc; 31, Lc
Koudougou, 96B, Ba
Kovno, 26, Fb
Kowpangtze, 76B, Aa
Kozhikode, 92, De
Kozlov, 61, Fd
Kozlov (Eupatoria), 50, Gd
Kra, 73, Ge
Kraguyevats, 78, Cc
Krak, 18C, Dd; (Crac de la
Pierre), 18C, Cg
Krakow, 88, Kd
Kranganur, 59A, Ce
Krasnik, 26, Fc; 84, Gb
Krasnodar, 89, Md
Krasnovodsk, 61, Hf; 93, Ga
Krasnoyarsk, 74, Hc; 90, Aa
Krefeld, 83A, Da
Kremnitz, 21, Nd
Krems, 10, Fd
Kremsier, 31, Md; 65C, Cb
Kremsmünster, 22, Eb
Kressenbrunn, 21, Md
Kreuznach, 29A, Ba
Kreuzschanze, 46A, Dc
Kriechingen, 39B, Ca
Krim Tartars, 61, Ee
Krishnagar, 59B
Krithia, 86D
Kriviches, 9, Ha
Krcja, 19, Bd
Kronstadt, Hungary, 34, Hc
Kronstadt, Russia, 51, Ga
Krossen, 21, Lb
Krumau, 39, Ld
Krushevatz, 78, Cd
Kuala Lumpur, 91, Df
Kuban, R., 19, Fc
Kubans, 16, Lc
Kublai Khan, Empire of, 25,
Kc
Kucha, 1, Lc
Kuching, 91, Ef
Kufra, 80A, Fb
Kufstein, 39, Ke
Kuibyshev, 88, Qc
Kuka, 80A, Ec
Kuldja, 74, Gd
Kulikovo, 19, Fb
Kulm, Poland, 21, Nb
Kulm, Saxony, 60B, Dc
Kumaon, 73, Ca
Kumarskaya, 74, Lc
Kumasi, 81C, Dc; 96B, Bb
Kumo, 96B, Da
Kumanovo, 78, Cd
Kumamoto, 91, Gc
Kum Kale, 86D
Kuma, R., 33A, Gb
Kumbum, 59B
Kunene, R., 80A, Ef
Kunersdorf, 54, Eb; 60A, Eb
Kunming, 91, Dd
Kuopio, 61, Cb
Kupang, 95, Mf
Kur, R., 33A, Gb
Kura, R., 19, Hd

Kurdish, 85, Le
Kurdistan, 79, Hc
Kurdla, 59A, Cd
Kuria Muria Is., 93, Hf
Kuril Is., 74, Od; 90, Da
Kurland, 26, Fb
Kurna, 86C, Ec
Kursk, 19, Fb; 88, Nc
Kuruman, 81A, Bc
Kuruman, R., 81B, Ba
Kuruska, 93, Ce
Kushan Dominions, 1, Jd
Kuskokwim, R., 71A, Ba
Kuskuskie, 57, Ac
Kustendil, 78, Dd
Küstrin, 31, Lb
Kut-el-Amara, 79, Jd
Kutahya, 33A, Cc; 93, Cb
Kutais, 33A, Fb; 93, Ea
Kutchuk Kainarji, 78, Fd
Kuttenberg, 31, Ld
Kuwait, 79, Je; 93, Fd
Kwangchow, 74, Kf
Kwangtung, 76B, Ab
Kweiyang, 91, Dd
Kyakhta, 74, Jc
Kyburg, 29B, Ca
Kyle, 14, Dd
Kyoto, 25, Nc; 91, Gc
Kyritz, 26, Dc

LA BAHIA, 43C, Bb
La Balize, 56, Be
La Bassee, 83A, Ba
La Belle Alliance, 46B
La Charité, 28D, Dc; 38, Ee
La Colle, 71C, Db
La Colombe, 22, Cb
la Conception, 45A, Ab
La Fère, 28D, Db; 83A, Bb
La Ferté, 22, Db
La Ferté Vidame, 38, Dd
La Garnache, 38, Ce
La Guaira, 43A, Fc
La Haye Sainte, 46B
La Higuera, 23D, Dd
La Hougue, 55A, Cd
La Mancha, 23D, Dc; 63, Dc
La Manche (English Channel),
55A, Dc
La Marche, 39B, Bb
La Marche, Co. of, 11, Dc
La Motte, I., 57, Ea
La Paz, 68, Cd
La Plata, Argentina, 68, Df
La Plata, Bolivia, 41B, Ce
La Plata, dist., 41B, Cf; 42, Ff
La Plata, rep., 69A, Ff
La Plata, Rio de, 68, Df
La Plata, United Provs. of, 68,
Cf
La Pointe (Fort St. Esprit),
56, Aa
La Réole, 17, Ff
La Roche, 53, Cd
La Roche Bernard, 38, Be
La Roche Derien, 28C, Ab
La Rochelle, 11, Cc; 53, Cd
La Serena, 68, Df
La Teste de Buch, 28C, Bd
La Tour, 30, Ef
La Trappe, 22, Cb
La Tremouille, 30, De
Labe, 96B, Aa
Laberge, L., 71B, Ba
Labiau, 39, Pa; 50, Ec
Labrador, 71, Hb
Labrador, Pen. of, 71, Hb
Labuan, 91, Ef
Laccadive Is., 92, Ce
Lachine, 57, Ea
Lachlan, R., 77, Hh
Lactodorum (Towcester), 3A,
Ed
Lacy, 17, Bb
Ladakh, 92, Da
Lade, 12, Ga
Lado, 80A, Gd
Ladoga, 19, Ea
Ladoga, L., 26, Ha
Ladrones, 40, Rd
Ladysmith, 81D, Ab
Lae, 90, Dd
Lafayette, 72A, Aa
Lafayetteville, 56, Dc
Lagan, R., 15, Fb
Lagen, R., 12, Ga
Lagentium (Castleford), 3A, Ec
Laghouat, 80A, Da
Lagos, Nigeria, 80, Dc; 81C, Ec
Lagos, Portugal, 4B, Ad; 23C,
Ad
Lagosta, 84, Fd
Laguna, 68, Ee
Lahave, 45A, Eb
Lahn, R., 10, Cc; 83A, Ea
Lahore, 25, Gc; 73, Ba
Lahr, 30, Gd
Laibach, 10, Fe
Laighin (Leinster), 15, Ed
Laila, 93, Fe
Laing's Nek, 81D, Aa

Lakhmids, 6A, Cb
Lalitpur, 73, Cc
Lamballe, 17, Dd; 20, Bd
Lambertville, 57, Dc
Lambeth, 27A
Lamego, 22, Ac; 23C, Bb
Lammermuir Hill, 14, Fd
Lamon B., 75E. Bb
Lampadar, 27, Bd
Lampsacus, 78, Fe
Lamu, 40, Me
Lanai, 75D, Cb
Lanark, 28B, Bb
Lanark, co., 37A, Cc; 49A, Cc
Lancaster, England, 3A, Db;
27, Db
Lancaster,Pennsylvania,57,Cc
Lancaster, clan, 28B, Db
Lancaster, lordship, 28A, Dc
Lancaster, Co. Palatine of, 27,
Dc
Lancaster Sd., 44, Ga
Lanchow, 91, Dc
Landau, 29A, Ca; 76A, Eb
Landeck, 20, Je
Landeshut, 60A, Ec
Landrecies, 46A, Cd
Landriano, 32A, Cb
Land's End, 55A, Ac
Landsberg, Brandenburg, 21,
Lb
Landsberg, Osterland, 21, Kc
Landshut, 21, Kd
Landstuhl, 39B, Da
Lanercost, 36, Dc
Langarone, 86B, Ca
Langeac, 20, Ef
Langeland, 65F, Ba
Langensalza, 39C, Ab; 60B, Cc
Langford House, 48B, Cd
Langholm, 28B, Cb
Langobardi, 2, Fc
Langport, 27, De
Langres, 11, Fc
Langside, 37A, Bc
Languedoc, 17A, De; 20, Eg
Lanporth (Langport), 13, De
Lansdown, 48A, Bd
Lanshankwan, 76B, Ba
Lanstavetone (Launceston),
13, Bf
Lanthony, 36, Df
Laoag, 75E, Ba
Laodicea, 2, Lf; 18, Cc
Laon, 11, Eb; 83A, Bb
Laos, 91, De
Lapland, 61, Ca
Laprairie, 56, Ea
Laramie, 70, Dc
Larantuka, 52C, Dc
Larche, Col de, 29A, Bc
Laredo, 43A, Cb
Largs, 14, Dd; 37A, Bc
Larino, 22, Ec
Larissa, 19, Ce; 78, Df
Larnaka, 86C, Dc
Laron, 20, Df
Las Navas de Tolosa, 23C, Dc
Las Palmas, 80A, Bb
Las Vegas, 44, Ce; 70, Dd
Lasalle, 70, Fc
Lashio, 92, Hc
Lastingham, 7B, Ca
Laswari, 59C, Cb
Latakia, 79, Gc
Lateran, 5A
Lathom, 48A, Bc
Latin States, 24, Gf
Latins, 8C, Bb
Latisana, 86B, Db
Latvia, 87, Fa
Lau (Eastern) Group, 75C, Ca
Lau Group (Exploring Is.),
75C, Ca
Lauder, 49A, Cc
Lauderdale, 28B, Cb
Laudenburg, Holstein, 20, Jb;
65F, Bb
Lauenburg, Pomerania, 21, Ma
Lauenburg, D., 65F, Bb
Lauenstein, 39C, Dc
Laufen, 29B, Ba
Laun, 39, Kc
Launceston, England, 27, Bf
Launceston, Tasmania, 77, HJ
Laund, 36, Fe
Laupen, 29B, Ba
Laurencekirk, 49A, Cb
Lausanne, 11, Gc; 29B, Ab
Lausitz, 10, Ec
Lausitz, M. of, 21, Lc
Lauter, R., 76A, Eb
Lautrec, 20, Eg
Lavagna, 20, Hf
Laval, 20, Cd
Lavant, 22, Eb
Lavatrae (Bowes), 3A, Eb
Lavaur, 20, Dg
Lavongai(NewHanover), 77. Ib
Lavoro, Terra de, 32A. FJ
Lawes (Lewes), 13, Ff

Lawless, 37B, Bb
Lazica, 19, Gd
Le Cateau, 83A, Ba
Le Creuzot, 88, Fd
Le Havre (Havre de Grace), 38, Dd; 89, Fd
Le Mans, 11, Dc
Le Puiset, 17, Fd
Le Puy, 11, Ed
Lea, R., 7C, Cc
Leaf, R., 70, Gb
League of God's House, 29B, Db
League of Ten Jurisdictions, 29B, Db
Lealui, 96C, Ef
Leavenworth, 70, Ed; 72, Bb
Lebanon, 18C, Ce; 79, Gd
Lebu, 68, Bf
Lebus, 21, Lb; 60A, Eb
Lecce, 5, Gd
Lech, R., 10, De; 30, Jd
Leck, R., 46A, Dc
Lectoure, 11, De
Ledbury, 27, Dd
Ledecestre (Leicester), 13, Ed
Ledecestrescire (Leicester-shire), 13, Ed
Ledo, 90, Ab
Lee, R., 15, Ce
Leeds, Kent, 27, Ge; 36, Gf
Leeds, Yorks, 48A, Cc
Leer 30, Gb
Leesburg, 57, Cd
Leeuwarden, 46A, Ea
Leeuwin, C., 77, Bh
Leghorn, 23B, Cc; 32E, Bb
Legnago, 29A, Dc; 62, Ec
Legnano, 20, Hf
Leicester, 27, Ed
Leicester, co., 27, Ed
Leicester, diocese, 36A
Leighlin, 15, Dd
Leinster, 37B, Dd; 49C
Leinster (Laighin), 15, Ed
Leinster Irish, 49C
Leipzig, 10, Ec
Leire, 12, Gc
Leiria, 23C, Ac; 63, Ac
Leith, 37A, Cc; 48A, Bb
Leitmeritz, 21, Lc
Leitrim, 17, Ba; 49B, Cc
Leitrim, co., 37C; 49B, Cb
Leix, 37B, Dd
Lemberg, 26, Fd; 33C, Eb
Lemnos, 19, De; 78, Ef
Lena, R., 25, Ma; 91, Da
Leningrad, 87, Ga
Lenne, R., 83A, Da
Lennox, 14, Dd
Lens, 17, Gc; 83A, Ba
Lenteurde (Leintwardine), 13, Dd
Lenton, 36, Ee
Leoben, 29A, Fb; 65A, Cb
Leofminstre (Leominster), 13, Dd
Leofric, 12, Dc
Leominster, 27, Dd; 48B, Bc
Léon, France, 11, Ab
Leon, Nicaragua, 43A, Dc
Leon, Spain, 63, Ca
Leon, King. of, 23C, Ba
Leon, prov., 63, Cb
Leon and Castile, King. of, 23C, Cb
Leona, C., 63A
Leonine City, 5A
Leontini, 5, Ef
Leopold Coast, 69C
Leopoldville, 80A, Ee
Lepanto, 18B, Cc; 78, Cf
Lepontine Alps, 29A, Cb
Leptis, 6, Cb
Lerida, 23D, Fb; 63, Fb
Les Clairets, 22, Cb
Lesbos, 19, De
Lescar, 11, Ce
Lesgians, 19, Hd
Lesina, 22, Fc
Lesina, I., 23B, Fc
Lesna, 54, Jb
Lesotho, 96D, Eg
Lesser Antilles, 43A, Fc
Lesser Armenia, 25, Cc
Lessines, 46A, Cd
Lethbridge, 70, Cc
Lethington, 37A, Cc
Letocetum (Wall), 3A, Ed
Letterkenny, 49B, Db
Leucadia, 64, Gf
Leucas, 62, Ge; 78, Cf
Leuchtenburg, 21, Kd
Leuk, 29B, Bb
Leuthen, 54, Fb; 60A, Fc
Leutkirch, 53, Hd
Leutschau, 19, Cc; 31, Pd
Leven, L., Inverness, 14, Cc
Leven, L., Kinross, 14, Ec
Levis, 57C, Ba
Levis, Pt., 56A
Levuka, 75C, Ba

Lewes, 27, Gf
Lewes, R., 71A, Da
Lewis, 14, Ba
Lewiston, 71D
Lexington, Kentucky, 56, Cc
Lexington, Mass., 57, Fb
Lexington, Tennessee, 72, Cb
Leyden, 46A, Db
Leyen, 65B, Ab
Leyre, 22, Bc
Leyte, 75E, Bb
Lhasa, 25, Jd; 73, Fb
Liang Chow, 1, Nd
Liao-ho, R., 76B, Ba
Liao-tung, 76B, Ba
Liaotung, G. of, 76B, Aa
Liaoyang, 76B, Ba
Liard, 70, Ba
Liard, R., 70, Ba
Libau, 51, Fb
Libava, 51, Eb
Liberia, 81C, Cc
Libreville, 80A, Dd
Libya, 80A, Eb; 93, Ac
Licata, 21A, Bd
Licefelle (Lichfield), 13, Ed
Lichfensteig, 29B, Da
Lichfield, 27, Ed
Lichfield, bp., 36, De
Lichsfeld, bp., 30, Jc
Lichtenberg, 39B, Db
Lida, 26, Gc
Liddisdale, 14, Fd; 28B, Cb
Lideforde (Lidford), 13, Bf
Liechtenstein, 65A, Ab
Liège, 46A, Ed
Liège, Bp. of, 46A, Ed
Liegnitz, 19, Db; 21, Mc
Lienz, 31, Ke
Liepaja, 87, Ea
Lier, 46A, Dc
Lierkenshoek, 46A, Dc
Liffey, R., 15, Ec
Lifford, 37B, Db
Liger, R., 2, Dd
Ligny, Belgium, 46B
Ligny, France, 39B, Db
Liguria, 5, Bb; 32C, Bb
Lihue, 75D, Bb
Lille, 28D, Da; 46A, Cd
Lillebonne, 17, Fd
Lillo, 46A, Dc
Lilybaeum, 5, Df
Lima, 68, Bd
Limasol, 18A, Ec
Limburg, Germany, 60A, Bd
Limburg, Netherlands, 46A, Ed
Limburg, Co. of, 46C, Bb
Limerick, 15, Cd
Limerick, co., 37C; 49B, Cd
Limia, 23C, Ab
Limoges, 11, Dd; 84, Cc
Limousin, V. of, 11, Dd
Limoux, 20, Eg
Limpopo, R., 81A, Db
Lincluden, 36, Cb
Lincolescire (Lincolnshire), 13, Fc
Lincolia (Lincoln), 13, Fc
Lincoln, 7B, Cb; 27, Fc
Lincoln, bp., 36, Fe
Lincoln, co., 27, Fc
Lincoln, lordship, 28A, Ca
Lincoln Wolds, 27, Fc
Lincolns Inn, 27A
Lindau, 30, He
Lindi, 96C, Fe
Lindinis (Ilchester), 3A, De
Lindisfarna (Lindisfarne), 13, Ea
Lindisfarne, 36, Eb; 36A
Lindley, 81A, Cc
Lindsay, 28B, Ca; 37A, Cb
Lindsey, 7B, Cb
Lindum (Lincoln), 3A, Fc
Lingan (Quinsay) (Hang-chow), 25, Mc
Lingayen, 75E, Ba
Lingen, 60A, Ab
Lingen, co., 38, Gb
Linköping, 26, Eb
Linlithgow, 28B, Bb
Linlithgow, co., 37A, Cc
Linnhe, L., 14, Cc
Linz, 10, Fd; 33C, Cb
Lion, G. of the, 17, Gg
Lipari Is., 5, Ee
Lippa, 33C, Eb
Lippe, 65D, Aa
Lippe, Co., 30, Hc
Lippe, R., 20, Gc
Lisaine, 76A, Dc
Lisbon, 22, Ad; 23C, Ac; 63B
Lisbon, eccl. prov., 22, Ad
Lisburn, 49B, Eb
Lisieux, 11, Db
Liskeard, 27, Bf
L'Isle Jourdain, 30, Dg
Lismore, Ireland, 15, Dd
Lismore, Scotland, 14, Cc
Lismore, bp., 14A, Bb

Lissa, 32C, Fc
Lithuania, 50, Fc; 87, Ea
Lithuania, G.D. of, 26, Gc
Lithuanians, 9, Ga
Little Belt, 65F, Aa
Little Harbour (Rye), 45B, Db
Little Minch, 14, Bb
Little Namaqua Land, 81A, Ac
Little Namaquas, 81B, Ab
Little Poland, 39, Pc
Little Rock, 72, Bc
Little Russia, 51, Gc
Little Russian, 85, Jc
Little St. Bernard Pass, 5, Ab
Littlechester, 3A, Ed
Litus Saxonicum, 3A, Hd
Livadia, 78, Df
Livenza, R., 86B, Cb
Liverpool, 27, Dc
Livingstone, 81A, Ca
Livonia, 26, Gb
Livonians, 9, Ga
Livorno, 32A, Dc
Livron, 38, Ff
Lixheim, 29A, Ba; 39B, Db
Lizard, 55A, Ac
Llanabadarn, 28A, Bb
Llanbadarn Fawr, 13, Bd
Llandaf (Llandaff), 13, Ce
Llandaff, 27, Ce
Llandaff, bp., 36, Cf
Llandovery, 3A, Cd; 27, Cd
Llanelwy, 13, Cc
Llanfaes, 7B, Aa
Llangollen, 48B, Bc
Llanio, 3A, Bd
Llano Estacado, 44, De
Llanthony, 36, Cf
Llantwit, 28A, Cc
Loanda, 80A, Ee
Loango, 96C, De
Loano, 29A, Cc; 38, Hf
Lobenstein, 39C, Bc
Lobositz, 54, Eb; 60A, Ec
Locarno, 29B, Cb
Loch Inver, 49A, Ba
Lochaber, 14, Dc
Loches, 11, Dc; 17, Fe
Lochmaben, 28B, Bb
Lochnannagh, 49A, Bb
Lockerbie, 49A, Cc
Locri, 5, Fe
Löcse, 39, Pd
Lodève, 11, Ee
Lodi, 32A, Cb
Lodz, 87, Db; 89, Jc
Logan, Mt., 70, Aa
Logans, 56, Cc
Logia Sinus, 3A, Ab
Logrono, 23D, Da; 63, Da
Logstown, 57, Ac
Logudoro, 23B, Bd
Loigny, 76A, Ab
Loir, R., 11, Dc
Loire, R., 11, Cc; 22, Cb
Loitz, 31, Ka
Loja, 68, Bc
Lokoja, 80A, Dd; 96C, Dd
Lombard Alps, 29A, Dc
Lombard King., 5, Bb
Lombards, 4A, Fb
Lombardy, 20, Hf; 32C, Bb
Lombardy, King. of, 23A, Ba
Lombartzyde, 46A, Bc
Lombers, 20, Eg
Lome, 81C, Ec; 94, Te
Lomond, L., 14, Dc
Lonato, 32D, Bb
Loncastre (Lancaster), 13, Db
Londinium (London), 3A, Fe
London, Canada, 70, Fc
London, England, 27, Fe
London, bp., 36, Gf
London Bridge, 27A
Londonderry, co.,37C; 49B, Eb
Long B., 57D, Bb
Long I., Bahamas, 43A, Eb
Long I., Massachusetts, 56B
Long I., New York, 45B, Cc; 56, Eb
Long Island Sound, 57, Ec
Long, L., 14, Dc
Longford, co., 37C; 49B, Dc
Longibardia, 9, Fd
Longjumeau, 38, Ed
Longone, 32B, Cc
Longreach, 95, Lg
Longtown, 49A, Cc
Longueuil, 57, Ea
Longueville, 20, Dd
Longwy, 39B, Ba; 83A, Cb
Lookout Mt., 72A, Aa
Loop Hd., 15, Bd
Loos, 83A, Ba
Lopadium, 19, Dd
Lorch, 8, Eb
Lörchingen, 39B, Db
Lord Howe I., 77, Jh
Loreto, 21, Kg
Loritello, 21A, Cb
Lorne, 14, Cc

Lorne, Firth of, 14, Cc
Lorraine, 83B, Ba
Lorraine, C. de, 45A, Ea
Lorraine, D. of, 20,Gd; 39B,Cb
Lorris, 20, Ee
Lorsch, 8, Db
Los, Is. de, 81C, Bc
Los Adaes, 43A, Ca
Los Angeles, 70, Cd
Los Diabolos, 40, Fc
Los Tiburones, I. de, 40, Be
Losecoat Field (Empingham), 27, Fd
Lostwithiel, 27, Bf
Lot, R., 11, Dd; 22, Cc
Lothar, King. of, 8A, Dc
Lotharingia, 8A, Ca
Lotharingia, D., 10, Ac
Lothian, 14, Ed
Lothian, co., 37A, Cc
Loudoun Hill, 3A, Ba
Loudun, 20, De
Loughbrickland, 49B, Eb
Loughrea, 37B, Cc; 49B, Cc
Louis, King. of, 8A, Db
Louisa, 72, Db
Louisburg, 45A, Fa
Louise, 57, Cd
Louisiade Arch., 77, Id
Louisiana, 56, Bd
Louisiana, st., 72, Bc
Louisville, 72, Cb
Lourenço Marques, 81A, Dc
Lourmarin, 38, Fg
Louth, England, 27, Fc
Louth, Ireland, 37B, Dc
Louth, co., 37C; 49B, Ec
Louvain, 46A, Dd
Lovat, R., 19, Ea
Lovcha, 78, Ed
Lowell, 45B, Db
Lower Alsace, Land. of, 20, Gd
Lower Austria, 65C, Cb
Lower Burgundy (Regnum Provinciae), 11, Fd
Lower California, 42, Dc; 43D Ab
Lower Canada, 71, Gc
Lower Doab, 59C, Db
Lower Lausitz, Marg. of, 31, Lc
Lower Lorraine, 20, Fc
Lower Lotharingia, 10, Ac
Lower Palatinate, 34, Dc; 38, Hd
Lower Peru, 41B, Be
Lower Silesia, 60A, Fc
Lower Tunguska, R., 74, Hb
Lowestoft, 54, Cb; 55A, Db
Loyalty Is., 77, Lf
Loyang, 1, Od
Luang Prabang, 91, Dd
Lübben, 39C, Cb
Lubeck, 10, Db
Lucca, 5, Fe
Lucca, Rep. of, 32A, Dc
Luce, R., 14, De
Lucena, 23D, Cd
Lucera, 5, Fd
Lucerne, 10, Ce; 29B, Ca
Lucerne, canton, 29B, Ca
Luckenwalde, 60A, Db
Lucknow, 73, Db
Luçon, 20, Ce; 47, Bc
Lucy, 28B, Bc
Luderitz, 80A, Eg
Ludes (Louth), 13, Fc
Ludgershall, 27, Ee
Ludhiana, 73, Ca
Ludlow, 13, Dd; 27, Dd
Lug, R., 28A, Db
Lugano, 29B, Cb
Lugdunum, 2, Dd
Luguvalium (Carlisle), 3C
Luitpold Land, 69C
Lujan, 68, Cf
Lu-kiang, R., 73, Gb
Lule Burgas, 78, Fe
Lulea, 88, Ka
Luna, 20, Jf
Lund, 16, Ea; 26, Db
Lund, eccl. prov., 22, Ea
Lundonia (London), 13, Ge
Lundy's Lane, 71D
Lune, R., 48B, Bb
Lüneburg, Germany, 10, Db
Luneburg, Transvaal, 81D, Ba
Lunel, 38, Fg
Lunenburg, 45A, Eb
Lunéville, 10, Bd; 39B, Cb
Lung-Hsi, 1, Nd
Luni, R., 73, Bb
Lunigiana, 32E, Ba
Lünstadt, 20, Gd
Luray, 72B, Aa
Luristan, 79, Jd
Lusatia (Lausitz), 10, Fc
Lusatia, M. of, 16, Eb
Lusatians, 10, Eb

Lusignan. 11, Dc
Lussac, 28C, Cc
Lussina, 23B, Eb
Lutetia, 2, Dd
Lutsk, 19, Db
Lutter, 38, Jc
Lutterberg, 60A, Bc
Lutterworth, 27, Ed
Lützelburg, 39B, Db
Lützelburg (Luxembourg), Co of, 20, Fd
Lützen, 38, Jc; 60B, Dc
Luvre (Oswestry), 13, Cd
Luxembourg, 31A, Dc; 46A, Fe
Luxemburg (Lützelburg), Co. of, 2J, Fd
Luxemburg, co., 46A, Fe
Luxeuil, 10, Be; 39B, Cc
Luxor, 93, Cd
Luynes, 53, Dd
Luzon, 75E, Ba
Lvov, 87, Ec
Lyallpur, 92, Ca
Lycia, 1, Fd
Lydda (St. George), 18C, Dg
Lydenburg, 81B, Da
Lydford, 7C, Ac; 27, Bf
Lydia, 2, Jf
Lykandos, 9, Ke
Lym (Lyme Regis), 13, Df
Lyme Regis, 27, Df
Lynchburg, 57, Be; 72B, Ab
Lynn, 17, Fb; 27, Gd
Lynn Canal, 71B, Cb
Lyonnais, 17, Hf; 38, Ef
Lyons, 11, Fd
Lyons, eccl. prov., 22, Cb
Lyons, Co. of, 11, Fd
Lys, R., 46A, Cd
Lyubech, 9, Jb

Maabar, 35, Nd
Maas, R., 20, Fc; 30, Fc
Maastricht, 83A, Ca
Macae, 1, He
MacAllister, 37A, Bc
Macao, 91, Ed
Macapa, 68, Db
Macaria, 22, Ec
Macassar, 52C, A
McCarthy, 15, Cd
MacCluer G., 77, Eb
MacDonald, 37A, Ab
Macdonald Is., 69C
MacDonald of Clanranald, 37A, Bb
MacDonald of Glencoe, 37A, Bb
MacDonald of Glengarry, 37A, Bb
MacDonald of Inverlochy, 37A, Bb
MacDonald of Keppoch, 37A, Bb
McDonnell, 37B, Ea
Macdonnell Ra., 77, Ef
McDouall, 28B, Ac
Macedonia, 2, Hf; 78, De
Maceio, 68, Fc
Macerata, 22, Ec
Macfie, 37A, Bb
Macgillicuddys Reeks, 15, Bd
McGillipatrick, 15, Dd
Macgregor, 28B, Aa
McGuire, 37B, Db
Machecoul, 30, Ce
Macintosh, 37A, Bb
Mackay, 37A, Ba
MacKenzie, clan, 37A, Bb
Mackenzie, district, 70, Ca
Mackenzie, R., 44, Bb
McKinley, Mt., 71A, Ba
Maclachlan, 37A, Bb
Maclean, 37A, Bb
MacLeod, 37A, Aa
Maclouiste, R., 81A, Cb
MacMahon, 37B, Bd
McMahon, 37B, Eb
MacMurrough, 15, Ed
McMurrough, 37B, Ed
Macnab, 28B, Aa
Mâcon, France, 11, Fc
Macon, U.S.A., 72, Dc
Macpherson, 37A, Bb
Macquarie Is., 69C; 75, Eg
Macroom, 49B, Cc
Mactan, 40, Qd
Madagascar, 80A, Hf
Madang (Friedrich Wilhelm-shafen), 77, Hc
Maddy, L., 49A, Ab
Madeira, 80A, Ba
Madeira, R., 41B, Ce; 68, Cc
Madhya Pradesh, 92, Dc
Madinat al Shaab, 93, Eg
Madras, 59D; 92, Ee
Madre de Dios I., 68, Bh
Madrid, 23C, Db; 63, Db
Madura, 25, Gf; 59A, Cf
Madurai, 92, Df

Maelienydd, 13, Cd
Maelor, 13, Dc
Maeotis Palus, 2, Ld
Maestricht, 46A, Ed
Mafeking, 81A, Cc; 96C, Eg
Mafia I., 80A, Ge
Mafra, 63B
Magadha, I., Le
Magdala, 83, Ld
Magdalen Is., 45A, Ea
Magdalena, R., 68, Bb
Magdalena (Rio Grande), R. 43A, Ed
Magdeburg, 10, Db; 21, Jb
Magdeburg, eccl. prov., 22, Ea
Magdeburg, Abp. of, 30, Jb
Magellan's Str., 68, Bh
Magennis, 37B, Eb
Magenta, 29A; Cc; 32C, Bb
Magersfontein, 81A, Bc
Maggiore, L., 5, Bb
Maghreb, 9, Bf
Maghreb-al-Aqsa, 6, Ab
Maghreb-al-Awsat, 6, Bb
Magnano, 29A, Bc
Magnis (Carvoran), 3C
Magnis (Kenchester), 3A, Dd
Magnitogorsk, 88, Rc
Magnus Portus (Portsmouth Harb.), 3A, Ef
Magog, 57C, Ab
Maguelonne, 11, Ee
Magus Muir, 37A, Cb
Magyar, 85, Fc
Magyars, 8, Hb; 9, Hc
Mahanadi, R., 73, Dc
Maharajpur, 73, Cb
Maharashtra, 92, Dc
Mahé, 73, Ce
Mahon, 63, Hc
Mahra, 6, Gd
Mahratta, 69A, Nc
Mahukona, 75D, Cb
Maida, 62, Fe
Maidenhead, 48B, Cd
Maidos, 86D
Maidstone, 48A, Dd
Maikop, 88, Oe
Maillezais, 22, Bb; 38, Ce
Main, R., Germany, 10, Cd
Main, R., Ireland, 15, Eb
Maine, prov., France, 38, Dd
Maine, st., U.S.A., 71E, Cb
Maine, terr., N.Amer., 45A, Cb
Maine, Co. of., 11, Cb
Mainland, 49A, Ca
Mainz, 10, Cd; 83A, Eb
Mainz, abp., 30, Hc
Mainz, eccl. prov., 22, Ea
Maipu, 68, Bf
Majapahit, 40, Pe
Majorca, 23C, Gc; 63, Gc
Majorca, King. of, 23D, Gc
Majuba Hill, 81D, Aa
Majunga, 96D, Gf
Makasar, 90, Cd
Makran, 6, Hc
Makurdi, 96B, Cb
Makyan, 52B, Aa
Malabar Coast, 59A, Ce
Malacca, 75A, Aa; 91, Df
Malacca, Str. of, 75A, Aa
Malaga, 23C, Cd; 63, Cd
Malagasy Rep., 96D, Gg
Malaita, 77, Kc
Malakand Pass, 73, Ba
Malamocco, 32D, Cb
Malatya, 79, Gc
Malawi, 96D, Ff
Malawi L., 96D, Ff
Malay Pen., 75, Cd
Malaya, 91, Df
Malborgeth, 86B, Da
Malchin, 31, Kb
Malden I., 75, He
Malden, R., 56B
Maldive Is., 92, Cf
Maldon, 27, Ge; 48A, Dd
Maldonado, 68, Df
Malduna (Maldon), 13, Ge
Male, 86B, Aa
Mali, 96D, Bc
Malia, C., 78, Dg
Malik L., 86A, Bb
Malin Hd., 15, Da
Malindi, 69A, Me
Malines, 51, Ac; 83A, Ca
Malling, 36, Gf
Mallow, 49B, Cd
Malmédy, 46A, Kd; 83A, Da
Malmesberie (Malmesbury), 13, De
Malmesbury, 27, De; 48A, Bd
Malmö, 26, Db; 60B, Da
Maloja Pass, 29B, Db
Malolos, 75E, Bb
Malown, 73, Ca
Malpas, 27, Dc
Malplaquet, 46A, Cd; 54, Cb
Malta, 8, Ed; 34, Ee
Malton, 27, Fb
Malvasia, 18B, Cc; 78, Dg

Malvern, England, 36, De
Malvern, Virginia, 57, Ce
Malwa, 1, Ke; 73, Cc
Mamecastre (Manchester), 18, Dc
Mameln, 38, Hb
Mameluke Sultans, 24, Hg
Mamelukes, 25, Cc
Mamistra, 18C, Ca
Mamore, R., 68, Cd
Mamucium (Manchester), 3A, Dc
Man, I. of, 7B, Aa; 34, Bb
Managua, 43D, Dc
Manama, 93, Gd
Manassas Junction, 72B, Ba
Manau, 14, Dc
Manaus, 68, Dc
Manbedj, 18C, Eb
Manchac (Fort Bute), 56, Ad
Manchester, England, 7C, Bb
Manchester, New York, 57, Eb
Manchu, 42, Qb
Manchukuo, 90, Ca
Manchuria, 74, Ld; 90, Ca
Mandalay, 73, Gc
Mandan Village, 44, Dd
Mandeswar, 73, Cb
Manfredonia, 32A, Fd
Mangalore, 73, Be
Mangi, 35, Pc
Mangi (Song Empire), 25, Kd
Manhattan I., 45B, Cc; 57B
Maniago, 86B, Ca
Manihiki, 75, He
Manila, 75E, Bb
Manipur, 73, Fc
Manissa, 78, Ff
Manitoba, 70, Eb
Mannheim, 29A, Ca; 83A, Eb
Manokvary, 77, Eb
Manresa, 23C, Fb; 63, Fb
Mansel, I., 70, Fa
Mansfeld, 20, Jc; 60A, Cc
Mansura, Egypt, 4B, Ld
Mansura, India, 6, Hc
Mansurabad, 6A, Db
Mansurah, 18A, Ec
Mantatis, 81B, Da
Mantes, 17, Fd
Mantua, 5, Cb; 22, Eb
Mantua, Marq. of (Gonzaga), 32A, Db
Manukau Harbour, 77A
Manzanares, 63, Dc
Manzanillo, 43D, Bc
Manzikert, 16, Le
Maputa, R., 81A, Dc
Maqdala, 80B, Be
Mar, 14, Fb
Mar del Plata, 68, Df
Maracaibo, 43A, Bc
Maracaibo, L., 43A, Ed
Marajo I., 68, Ec
Maranhão, 41B, Ed
Maranhao (Sao Luis), 68, Ec
Maranhao, st., 68, Ec
Marañon, R., 68, Bc
Marans, 38, Ce
Marar, G. of, 73, Cf
Maras, 93, Db
Marash, 18C, Da
Maratha, 59A, Cc
Marbella, 23D, Cd
Marble Head, 57, Fb
Marburg, 20, Hc
March, R., 21, Md
Marches, The, 32A, Ec
Marchfield, 21, Md
Marcianopolis, 4A, Hc
Marcomanni, 2, Dc
Mardin, 18A, Gb; 93, Eb
Mare Adriaticum, 2, Ge
Mare Ægæum, 2, Jf
Mare Cantabricum, 1, Bc
Mare Caspium, 1, Gc
Mare Internum, 1, Cd
Mare Ionium, 2, Gf
Mare Suevicum, 2, Gb
Mare Tyrrhenum, 2, Ff
Maree, L., 14, Cb
Marengo, 29A, Cc; 62, Dd
Margam, 7B, Bc
Margarita, 43A, Fc
Margiana, 1, Jd
Margidunum(Castle H.),3A,Fd
Maria, 63, Eb
Maria Van Diemen, C., 77, Mh
Mariana Is., 74, Ng; 90, Dc
Marib, 6, Fd
Marico Drift, 81A, Cb
Marie Byrd Land, 69C
Marie Galante, 43A, Fc
Marienbourg, 46A, Dd
Marienburg, 21, Na
Marienthal, 22, Ea
Marienwalde, 22, Fa
Marienwerder, 21, Nb
Marietta, Georgia, 72A, Ab
Marietta, Ohio, 56, Cc
Mariette, 71C, Ca
Marignano, 29, Cc; 32A, Cb

Marinids, 24, Ag
Maritime Alps, 29A, Bc
Maritza, 78, Ed
Maritza, R., 78, Fe
Mark, 12, Ga
Mark, Co. of, 20, Gc; 46C, Cb
Market Drayton, 48B, Bc
Markirch, 39B, Db
Markland, 35, Fb
Marlborough, England, 27, Ee
Marlborough, N.Z., 77A
Marle, 11, Eb
Marlow, 27, Fe
Marmande, 30, Df
Marmara, Sea of, 78, Ge
Marmolada, 29A, Eb
Marmoutier, 22, Cb
Marne, R., 11, Eb
Maros, R., 33C, Eb; 78, Dc
Maroua, 96B, Da
Marquesas Is., 75, Je
Marra, 18C, Dc
Marrakesh, 80A, Ca; 96D, Db
Marrana, 23B, Cc
Marroqui, C., 63A
Mars Hill, 71E, Cb
Mars la Tour, 76A, Cb
Marsaglia, 29A, Cc
Marsal, 39B, Cb
Marsala, 32C, De
Marsalquivir, 34, Be
Marseilles, 11, Fe; 29A, Ad
Marshall Is., 90, Ec
Marshfield, 45B, Db
Marsi, 21A, Bb
Marsia, 23A, Dc
Marsico, 21A, Cb; 22, Fc
Marston Moor, 48A, Cc
Martaban, G. of, 73, Gd
Martello, The, 86B, Cb
Martha's Vineyard, 45B, Dc
Martigny, 29B, Bb
Martinique, 43A, Fc
Martirano, 21A, Dc
Martyropolis, 4B, Ld
Marvejols, 38, Ef
Maryborough, Australia ,77, Ig
Maryborough, Ireland, 49B, Dc
Maryland, 57, Cd; 72B, Ba
Masan-daran, 61B, Ab
Masbate, 75E, Bb
Mascarenhas, 40, Mf
Mashona, 80A, Gf
Mashona Land, 81A, Da
Masira, 93, He
Mask, L., 15, Bc
Maskat, 41A, Cb; 74, Df
Masmünster, 39B, Dc
Mason and Dixon's Line, 56, Dc
Masovia, 26, Fc
Masper, 45B, Cc
Massa, 22, Ec; 32A, Db
Massachusetts, 45B, Db
Massagetae, 1, Hc
Massawa, 80B, Bd
Massema, 96B, Da
Massikessi, 81A, Da
Massilia, 2, Ee
Masulipatam, 73, Dd
Masurian Lakes, 84, Gb
Matabele, 81B, Da
Matabeleland, 81A, Ca
Matagorda Bay, 43A, Cb
Matamoros, 43A, Db
Matanzas, 43A, Db
Matapan, C., 78, Dg
Matatana, 40, Mf
Matera, India, 59C, Db
Matera, Italy, 21A, Db
Mathura, 92, Db
Mato Grosso (V. Bella), 68, Cd
Mato Grosso, prov., 68, Dd
Matoppo Hills, 81A, Cb
Matruh, 84, Hf; 93, Bc
Mattapony, R., 72B, Ba
Matuku, 75C, Bb
Maturin, 68, Cb
Maubeuge, 46A. Cd
Maui, 75D, Cb
Mauléon, 20, Cg
Maumee, R., 57A, Ca; 71C, Bb
Mauna Loa, 75D, Dc
Mauretania, 2, Df
Mauriac, 20, Ef
Mauritania, 80A, Bc
Mauritania, rep., 96D, Ac
Mauritia (Pernambuco), 42, He
Mauritius, 42, Mf; 69A, Ne
Mauvezin, 38, Dg
Mawddach, R., Bb
Mawson, 69C
Maxen, 60A, Dc
Maxwell, 28B, Bb; 37A, Cc
May, C., 45B, Bd
May, I. of, 28B, Ca
Maya, 63, Ea
Mayas, 43, Ec
Maybole, 28B, Ab
Mayence, 33C, Bb
Mayenne, 17, Ed
Mayenne, R., 53, Cc

Maynooth, 49B, Ec
Mayo, 15, Bc
Mayo, co., 37C; 49B, Bc
Mayorga, 63, Ca
Mazagan, 42, Jc
Mazapil, 43A, Bb
Mazaltan, 43A, Bb
Mazovia, 39, Pb
Mazzara, 21A, Bd; 22, Ed
Mbengga, 75C, Bb
Meander, R., 19, De
Mearns, 14, Fc
Meath, 17, Bb; 37B, Dc
Meath (Midhe), 15, Dc
Meath, co., 49B, Ec
Meaux, England, 36, Fd
Meaux, France, 11, Eb
Mecca, 6, Fc; 25, Dd; 80B, Bc
Mechanicsville, 72B, Bb
Mechlin, 46A, Bc
Mecklenburg, 10, Db
Mecklenburg, D. of, 10, Db
Medan, 91, Cf
Medellin, Colombia, 68, Bb
Medellin, Spain, 63, Cc
Medelpad, 26, Ea
Medeltune (Melton Mowbray), 13, Fd
Media, I., Ed
Medicine Hat, 70, Cb
Medina, 25, Dd; 93, De
Medina (Yathreb), 6, Fc
Medina de Rio Seco, 63, Cb
Medina Sidonia, 23C, Cd
Mediolanum (Milan), 5, Bb
Mediterranean Sea, 8, Fd
Meean Doab, 73, Ca
Meerut, 73, Cb
Mehadia, 78, Dc
Mehidpur, 73, Cc
Meiningen, 20, Jc; 30, Jc
Meirionydd (Merioneth), 13, Db
Meisenheim, 60B, Ad
Meissen, 10, Ec
Meissen, March of, 10, Fc
Mejillones, 68, Be
Mekong, R., 25, Ke; 91, De
Melandra Castle, 3A, Ec
Melbourne, 77, Hi
Melcombe Regis, 27, Df
Meldorf, 20, Ha
Melfi, 21A, Cb; 22, Fc
Melilla, 34, Be; 40, Jc
Melinde, 41A, Be
Melite I., 2, Ff
Melitene, 6A, Ba
Melk, 21, Ld
Mellrichstadt, 10, Dc
Melmoth, 81D, Bb
Melnik, 19, Cd
Meloria I., 24, De
Melrose, 14, Fd; 28B, Cb
Melton Mowbray, 27, Fd
Melun, 11, Eb; 17, Gd
Melville I., Australia, 77, Ed
Melville I., Canada, 44, Ca
Melville Pen., 44, Fb
Memel, 26, Fb; 60A, Ha
Memel, R., 26, Fb
Memleben, 10, Dc
Memmingen, 20, Jd; 29A, Da
Memphis, Egypt, 2, Kh
Memphis, U.S.A., 72, Bb
Memphis (Chickasaw Bluff), 71F, Aa
Memphis (Fort Assumption), 56, Bc
Menado, 52C, Ba
Mende, 11, Ed; 17, Gf
Menderes, R., 24, Hf
Mendip Hills, 27, De
Mendocino, C., 70, Bc
Mendoza, 68, Cf
Mendrisio, 29B, Cc
Menin, 46A, Cd; 53, Eb
Menindee, 77, Gh
Mentana, 32C, Dc
Menteith, 14, Dc
Menteshe, 19, De
Menzies, 37A, Bb
Meonware, 7A, Cb
Meppen, 20, Gb
Mequinenza, 23C, Fb; 63, Fb
Meran, 10, De; 86B, Ba
Mercia, 7B, Cb; 12, Dc
Mercians, 7A, Ca
Mere, 27, De
Meresberie (Maesbury), 13, Cd
Merevale, 36, Ee
Mergui, 73, Ge
Mergui Arch., 92, He
Merida, Spain, 63, Bc
Merida, Venezuela, 43A, Ed
Meridian, 72, Cc
Merioneth, co., 27, Cd
Merleberge (Marlborough), 13, Ee
Meroe, 35, Ld
Merowe, 80B, Ad
Merrimac, R., 45B, Db

Merry Mount (Quincey), 45B, Db
Merse (Mersea I.), 13, Ge
Merse, The, 14, Fd
Mersea, 7C, Dc
Merseburg, 10, Dc; 39C, Bb
Merseburg, M. of, 10, Ec
Mersen, 8A, Ca; 9, Db
Mersey, R., 27, Dc
Mersha, R. (Mersey), 13, Cc
Mersin, 93, Cb
Mersina, 86C, Bb
Mertola, 23C, Bd
Merton, 36, Ff
Merv, 6, Hb; 25, Fc; 61B, Bb
Mesembria, 8, Hc
Mesenheim, 60B, Ad
Methone, 9, Ge
Methven, 28B, Ba
Metis, R., 71E, Ba
Metsovo, 78, Cf
Metz, 10, Bd; 83A, Db
Metz, Bp. of, 30, Gd; 39B, Ca
Meuse, R., 10, Ac, 17, Hc
Meuse, Mouth of the, 46A, Cc
Mexico, city, 43A, Cc
Mexico, st., 43A, Bb
Mexico, G. of, 43A, Cb
Mezen, R., 61, Ga
Mézières, 46A, De, 53, Fc
Miami, 94, Ed
Miami, R., 71C, Bc
Miamis, 45A, Ab; 56, Bb
Miani, 73, Ab
Michigan, 70, Fc
Michigan, L., 56, Bb
Michigan Terr., 67C, Da
Michillimackinac I., 45A, Aa
Michoacan, 43A, Bc
Micmacs, 45A, Da
Mics, 31, Kd
Middelburg, C. of Good Hope, 81A, Bd
Middelburg, Netherlands, 46A, Cc
Middelburg, Tr'vaal, 81A, Cc
Middelfart, 65F, Aa
Middle I. (South I., N.Z.), 77A
Middle Angles, 7A, Ca
Middle Drift, 81D, Bb
Middle March, 28B, Cb
Middle Saxons, 7A, Cb
Middleham, 27, Eb
Middlesex, 27, Fe
Middleton, 37A, Cb
Middletown, Connecticut, 45B Cc
Middletown, New Jersey, 45B, Bc
Midelsexe (Middlesex), 13, Fe
Midhe (Meath), 15, Dc
Midhurst, 27, Fe
Midia, 78, Ge
Midnapore, 59A, Ec; 59B
Midway I., 90, Fb
Miedniki, 26, Fb
Mien (Burma), 25, Jd
Mierdyk, 46A, Dc
Milam, 73, Da
Milan (Mediolanum), 5, Bb
Milan, eccl. prov., 22, Db
Milan, D. of, 32A, Cb
Milazzo, 21A, Cc; 32C, Ee
Milborne Port, 27, Df
Mileburne (Milborne Port), 13, Df
Miletus, 19, De
Milford, Connecticut, 45B, Cc
Milford, Wales, 27, Ae
Milford Haven, 55A, Ac
Milhqu, 11, Ed
Mill Springs, 72, Db
Milledgeville, 72, Dc
Millen, 72, Dc
Millikens Bend, 72C, Aa
Milos, 78, Eg
Milton, 7C, Dc
Milwaukee, 70, Fc
Milzienians, 10, Fc
Min Yueh, 1, Oe
Minaei, 1, Gf
Minas Gerais, 68, Dd
Minch, The, 14, Bb
Mincio, R., 5, Cb
Mindanao, 75E, Bc
Mindelheim, 53, Jc
Minden, 10, Cb
Minden, Bp. of, 60A, Bb
Mindoro, 75E, Bb

Mindoro Str., 75E, Bb
Mingrelia, 61, Ff; 79, Hb
Minho, 63, Ab
Minho, R., 63, Ba
Minna, 96B, Cb
Minneapolis, 70, Ec
Minnesota, 70, Ec
Minnesota Terr., 67D, Da
Minorca, 23C, Gb; 63, Gb
Minsk, 26, Gc; 87, Fb
Minster, 7B, Dc
Minto, L., 70, Gb
Minya, 93, Cd
Miquelon, 45A, Fa
Mirabeau, 17, Fe
Mirabel, 18C, Cf
Mirambeau, 20, Cf
Miramichi B., 45A, Ea
Miranda, Brazil, 68, De
Miranda, Portugal, 22, Ac; 63, Bb
Miranda, Spain, 63, Da
Mirande, 53, Df
Mirandola, 32A, Db
Mirepoix, 22, Cc; 38, Dg
Mirny, 69C
Mirzapur, 59B; 73, Db
Misilmeri, 21A, Bd
Miskolcz, 31, Pd
Misol, 52C, Cb; 77, Eb
Misr (Egypt), 6, Dc
Missassauga Fort, 71D
Missenden, 36, Ff
Missionary Ridge, 72A, Aa
Mississippi, R., 56, Ab; 70, Ec
Mississippi, st., 70, Fd
Mississippi, Delta of the, 43A, Db
Mississippi Terr., 67B, Bb; 71F, Ba
Missolonghi, 78, Cf
Missouri, R., 70, Ec; 72, Bb
Missouri, st., 72, Bb
Missouri Terr., 67C, Ca
Missunde, 65F, Aa
Mistassini, L., 70, Gb
Mistra, 19, Ce
Misurata, 88, Jg
Mitau, 50, Eb; 61A, Ba
Mitchell, R., 77, Ge
Mitchelstown, 49B, Cd
Mittelmark, 31, Kb; 60A, Db
Mitylene, 78, Ef
Mizen Hd., 15, Be
Mkusi, R., 81D, Ba
Mlava, 21, Pb
Moala, 75C, Bb
Mobile, 56, Bd; 67C, Eb
Mocha, 93, Eg
Modbury, 27, Cf
Modder, R., 81B, Cb
Modena, 8A, Dc
Modena (Mutina), 5, Cb
Modena, D. of (Este), 32A, Db
Modon, 78, Cg
Modrusch, 2, Fb
Moesia, 1, Ec; 4A, Gc
Moffat, 37A, Cc
Mogador, 82, Af
Mogadiscio (Mogadishu), 96A, Bb
Mogadishu, 80A, Hd; 96C, Gd
Mogul Empire, 52A, Bb
Moguntiacum, 2, Ec
Mohacs, 33C, Db; 39, Ne
Mohammed Abtin, Dominions of, 24, Kf
Mohawk, R., 57, Db
Mohawks, 45A, Cb; 57, Db
Mohi, 19, Cc
Mohilev, 26, Hc; 50, Gc
Moidart, 14, Cc; 49A, Bb
Mojaisk, 19, Fa
Mold, 27, Cc
Moldau, R., 21, Ld
Moldavia, 50, Fd; 78, Fb
Molème, 22, Cb
Molfetta, 23B, Fd
Molina, 23D, Eb
Mo.1 1s de Rey, 63, Gb
Molise, 23B, Ed; 32A, Fd
Mollendo, 68, Bd
Molloy, 37B, Dc
Mollwitz, 60A, Fc
Molokai, 75D, Cb
Molopo, R., 81B, Ba
Molotov, 88, Rb
Moloyaroslavetz, 62, Ka
Molucca Passage, 52C, Ca
Moluccas, 52C, Cb; 91, Ff
Mölzen, 10, Ec
Mombasa, 80A, Ge; 96D, Fe
Momonia (Mumha) (Munster), 15, Cd
Mömpelgard, 39B, Cc
Mon, I. (Anglesey), 7B, Ab; 13, Bc
Mona (Anglesey), 3A, Ac
Mona Passage, 43A, Fc
Monaco, 32A, Bc
Monaghan, 49B, Eb
Monaghan, co., 37C; 49B, Eb

Monastir (Bitolia), 78, Ce
Monavia (I. of Man), 3A, Bb
Monclova, 43A, Bb
Moncton, 71, Hc
Mondego, R., 63, Ab
Mondoñedo, 22, Ac
Mondovi, 29A, Cc
Mondovia, 32A, Bb
Monemude (Monmouth), 13, De
Monemvasia, 19, Ce
Monfalcone, 86B, Db
Monflanquin, 38, Df
Monforte, 22, Ac
Monghyr, 59A, Eb
Mongol Il-Khans, Empire of the, 19, He
Mongolia, rep., 91, Db
Monks Bretton, 36, Ed
Monks Corner, 57D, Ab
Monmouth, 27, De
Monmouth Court House, 56, Eb; 57, Dc
Monnow, R., 28A, Dc
Monocacy, 72B, Ba
Monocacy, R., 72B, Ba
Monomotapa, 52, Lf
Monongahela, R., 45A, Bb
Monopoli, 32A, Gd
Monreal (Mons Regalis), 18C, Ch
Monreale, 21A, Bc; 22, Ed
Monreale, eccl. prov., 22, Ed
Monroe, 72, Bc
Monrovia, 81C, Bc
Mons, 46A, Cd
Mons Regalis (Monreal), 18C, Ch
Mont Cenis Pass, 5, Ab
Mont de Marsan, 38, Cg
Mont Genèvre Pass, 32A, Bb
Mont Louis, 53, Ef
Mont St. Jean, 46B
Mont St. Michel, 17, Ed
Mont Valerien, 76A, Ab
Montacute, 27, Df
Montagnais, 45A, Ca
Montagud (Montacute), 13, Df
Montalto, 39, Kg
Montana, 70, Dc
Montana Terr., 67D, Ba
Montaperto, 23B, Cc
Montargis, 17, Gd; 38, Ed
Montauban, Provence, 20, Ff
Montauban, Toulouse, 11, Dd
Montaut, 38, Dg
Montbard, 76A, Cc
Montbazon, 53, Dd
Montbéliard, 20, Ge
Montbrison, 30, Ff
Montcenis, 38, Fe
Montdidier, 31A, Bc; 83A, Bb
Monte Cassino, 5, Dd
Monte Peloso, 21A, Db
Monte Redondo, 63B
Monte San Angelo, 21A, Db
Montebello, Milan, 29A, Cc
Montebello, Pavia, 29A, Cc
Montecatini, 32E, Bb
Montefeltro, 32A, Ec
Monteleone, 21A, Dc
Montélimar, 30, Ff
Montendre, 38, Cf
Montenegro, 39, Ng; 78, Bd
Montenotte, 29A, Cc
Montepulciano, 32E, Bb
Montereau, 28D, Db; 31A, Bc
Monterey, California, 70, Bd
Monterey, Mexico, 43A, Bb
Montescaglioso, 21A, Db
Montevideo, 68, Df
Montfaucon, 22, Db
Montferrat, Marq. of, 32A, Cb
Montfort, 11, Db; 30, Dd
Montgomery, Alabama, 72, Cc
Montgomery, Wales, 27, Cd
Montgomery, family, 28B, Ab
Montiel, 23D, Dc
Montlaur, 30, Ef
Montlhéry, 30, Ed; 31A, Bc
Montluçon, 53, Ed
Montmédy, 29A, Aa; 83A, Cb
Montmorency, 53, Ec
Montpellier, 11, Ee
Montpensier, 30, Ee
Montreal, 45A, Ca; 57, Ea
Montreuil, 11, Da; 83A, Aa
Montrose, 49A, Cb
Montserrat, 22, Cc
Montserrat, I., 43A, Fc
Monza, 4B, Eb; 5, Bb
Monzon, 63, Fb
Mooi, R., 81A, Cc
Mook, 46A, Ec
Moore's Creek, R., 57Г, Ba
Moorfields, 27A
Moorfoot Hills, 28B, Bb
Moors, 2A, Ac
Moose, R., 70, Fb
Moose Factory, 70, Fb
Moquegua, 68, Bd
Mora, 26, Da

Moradabad, 73, Cb
Morant, 43A, Ec
Morar, 73, Cb
Morar, L., 14, Cc
Morat, 29B, Bb; 31A, Dd
Morava, R., 78, Cc
Moravia, 8A, Eb; 33C, Db
Moravia, M. of, 21, Md
Moravian Empire, 9, Fc
Moravian Town, 71C, Bb
Moravians, 8, Fb
Moray, 14, Db; 37A, Bb
Moray Firth, 14, Eb
Morea, 78, Dg
Morecambe B., 27, Cc
Morella, 23C, Eb
Morena, Sierra, 63, Cc
Moresnet, 83A, Da
Moret, 20, Ed
Moreton B., 77, Ig
Morgannwg, 7C, Bc; 12, Dd
Morgannwg (Glamorgan), 13, Ce
Morgarten, 29B, Ca
Morhange, 83B, Ba
Moriah, 18D
Moridunum (Carmarthen), 3A. Be
Morimont, 22, Db
Morlaix, 28C, Ab; 38, Bd
Moro, 52B, Aa
Morocco, 96C, Ba
Morocco, King., 80A, Ca
Morotai, 90, Cc
Morpeth, 13, Ea
Morrisburg, 57, Da
Morristown, 57, Dc
Mors, 60A, Ac
Mortagne, 11, Db; 30, Dd
Mortain, 11, Cb
Mortara, 32C, Bb
Mortemart, 53, Dd
Mortie, 52C, Ca
Mortimer, Ireland, 37B, Dd
Mortimer, Wales, 28A, Bc
Mortimers Cross, 27, Dd
Morven, 14, Cc
Mosbach, 20, Hd
Moscow, 19, Fa
Moscow, Pr. of, 24, Kb
Moselle, R., 10, Bd; 39B, Cb
Mosquito Coast, 43A, Dc
Mossamedes, 80A, Ef
Mossel B., 81B, Bc
Mostar, 39, Mg; 78, Ad
Mosul, 6A, Ca; 25, Dc
Motien lin Pass, 76B, Ba
Motir, 52B, Aa
Motrone, 32E, Bb
Moulins, 30, Ee
Moulmein, 73, Gd; 92, Hd
Mount Desert I., 45B, Ee
Mount Grace, 36, Ec
Mount Vernon, 57, Cd
Mountmellick, 49B, Dc
Moura, 23C, Bc
Mourne Mts., 15, Eb
Mourne, R., 15, Db
Moutiers, 11, Gd
Mouzon, 22, Db
Moy, 49A, Bb
Moyenvic, 39B, Cb
Mozambique, 80A, Hf
Mozambique, col., 80A, Gf
Mozdok, 61, Ff
Mozhaisk, 88, Nb
Mscislaw, 51, Gc; 61A, Db
Mstof, 26, Ec
Muck, 14, Bc
Mudania, 79, Eb
Mudki, 73, Ba
Mugello, 32E, Bb
Mügeln, 39C, Db
Mühlberg, 34, Eb; 39C, Db
Mühldorf, 10, Ed
Mühlhausen, 20, Jc
Muiden, 46A, Eb
Muilrea, 15, Bc
Mukalla, 93, Fg
Mukden ,76B, Ba
Mukden (Shenyang), 91, Fb
Mukha, 6, Fd
Muk.aid, 52A, Bc
Mull, 14, Cc
Mullingar, 49B, Dc
Multan, 25, Gc; 73, Ba
Multun, 6, Jb
Mumha (Momonia, Munster), 15, Cd
Muncaster, 13, Cb
Münchengrätz, 60B, Ec
Münden, 53, Hb
Mundelsheim, 29A, Ca
Munich, 29A, Da
Munkacz, 50, Ed; 54, Gc
Münster, Germany, 10, Bc
Munster, Ireland, 37B, Cd

Munster (Mumha, Momonia), 15, Ca
Münster, Bp. of, 30, Gb
Munster Irish, 49C
Munster Thal, 29B, Eb
Münsterberg, 31, Mc
Mur, R., 21, Le
Murad Su, R., 19, Ge
Murat, 30, Ef
Murbach, 20, Ge; 39B, Dc
Murchison, R., 77, Bg
Murcia, 22, Bd; 63, Ed
Murcia, prov., 63, Ec
Muret, 11, De; 22, Cc
Murfreesboro, 72, Cb
Muri, 29B, Ca
Murmansk, 74, Bb; 88, Ma
Murom, 19, Ga
Murom-Riazan, 19, Fb
Murray, 28B, Ba; 37A, Ba
Murray, R., 77, Hi
Murrumbidgee, R., 77, Hh
Mursa, 2, Gd
Murshidabad, 59A, Ec
Murten, 30, Ge
Murviedro, 23C, Ec
Muscat, 40, Mc; 93, He
Muscovy, 35, Mb; 61, Fc
Muskingum, R., 71C, Bb
Musselburgh, 49A, Cc
Mustapha Pasha, 78, Fe
Muta, 6A, Bb
Mutina (Modena), 5, Cb
Muziris, I., Kf
Mweru, L., 80A, Fe
Myitkyina, 92, Hb
Mynyw (St. David's), 13, Ae
Myriocephalon, 18A, Eb
Mysore, 59A, Ce; 73, Ce
Mysore, st., 59D; 73, Ce
Mystic, R., 56B
Myton, 28B, Dc

NAARDEN, 46A, Eb
Naas, 49B, Ec
Nablus, 18C, Cf
Nabresina, 86B, Db
Nachod, 33C, Da
Nafels, 29B, Da
Naga, 75E, Bb
Nagaland, 92, Gb
Nagasaki, 91, Fc
Nagoya, 91, Gc
Nagpur, 73, Cc
Nagy Sarlo, 33C, Db
Nahuas, 43A, Bc
Naiman, 25, Hb
Nain, 71, Hb
Nairn, 37A, Cb
Nairn, co., 37A, Cb; 49A, Cb
Nairn, R., 37A, Cb
Nairobi, 80A, Ge
Naissus, 2, He; 4A, Gc
Najaf, 93, Ec
Najera, 23D, Da; 28C, Ae
Nakhijevan, 9, Me
Namsos, 88, Ha
Namur, 28D, Ea; 46A, Dd
Namur, Co. of, 46C, Bb
Nanaimo, 70, Bc
Nanchang, 91, Ed
Nancy, 10, Bd; 39B, Cb
Nandi, 75C, Aa
Nandidroog, 73, Cc
Nanking, 91, Ec
Nanning, 91, Dd
Nantasket, 45B, Db
Nantes, 11, Cc; 17, Ee
Nantes, Co. of, 11, Cc
Nantucket, 45B, Ec
Nantwich, 48A, Bc
Napier, 77A
Naples (Neapolis), 5, Ed
Naples, King. of, 32A, Fd
Napo, R., 68, Bb
Narbada, R., 25, Gd; 73, Cc
Narberth, 28A, Bc
Narbo, 2, De
Narbonne, 11, Ee
Narbonne, eccl. prov., 22, Cc
Narenta, R., 78, Ad
Narew, R., 31, Pb; 39, Qb
Narke, 50, Db
Narnia, 5B, Bb
Naro, 21A, Bd
Narragansett B., 45B, Dc
Narragh, 15, Ec
Narva, 26, Gb; 54, Ha
Narvik, 88, Ja
Naseby 48B, Cc
Nashborough, 56, Bc
Nashville (Nashborough), 56, Bc
Nass, R., 71B, Dc
Nassau, 43A, Eb
Nassau, Co. of, 20, Hc
Nasser, L., 93, Ce
Natal, Brazil, 68, Fc
Natal, Rep. of, 81D, Bb
Natchez, 56, Ad
Natchitoches, 70, Ed

Nauders, 29A, Db
Naugard, 31, Lb
Naumburg, 21, Jc; 38, Jc
Naumkeag (Salem), 45B, Db
Naupactus, 19, Ce
Nauplia, 78, Dg
Nauplis, 18A, Cb
Nauru, 90, Ed
Nauta, 68, Bc
Navan, 49B, Ec
Navarino, 78, Cg
Navarre, 63, Ea
Navarreins, 38, Cg
Navio (Brough), 3A, Ec
Naworth, 27, Db
Naxos, 78, Eg
Naxos, D. of, 24, Hf; 34, Ge
Naxcuat, 56, Fa
Nay, 38, Cg
Nazareth, Italy, 22, Fc
Nazareth, Palestine, 18C, Cf
Naze, The, 55A, Dc
Neagh, L., 15, Eb
Neapolis, 2, Fe
Neapolis (Naples), 5, Ed
Neath, 28A, Bc
Neath, R., 28A, Bc
Nebbio, 22, Dc
Nebraska, 70, Dc
Nebraska Terr., 67D, Ca
Nechtansmere, 14, Ec
Neckar, R., 10, Cd
Neerwinden, 53, Fb
Negapatam, 59D
Neghelli, 96A, Ab
Negotin, 86A, Da
Negrepelisse, 38, Df
Negro (Fort Gadsden), 71F, Ba
Negro, R., Argentina, 68, Cf
Negro, R., Brazil, 68, Cb
Negroponte, 78, Ef
Negros, 75E, Bb
Nehavend, 6A, Db
Neisse, R., 10, Cc; 60A, Ec
Neisse, R., 10, Cc; 60A, Ec
Neiva, 41B, Bc
Nejd, 6, Fc; 84, Kg; 93, Ed
Nejef, 86C, Dc
Nejran, 6, Fd
Nellore, 52A, Cc
Nelson, 77A
Nelson, prov., 77A
Nelson, R., 70, Eb
Neman, R., 87, Eb
Nemirov, 51, Fd
Nemours, 30, Ed
Nemours, D. of, 30, Ed
Nen, R., 27, Gd; 36, Ge
Nenagh, 37B, Cd; 49B, Cd
Nenana, 71A, Ca
Neocaesarea, 18A, Fa
Nepal, 73, Db
Nephin, 15, Bb
Nepi, 22A
Nepomuk, 22, Eb
Nérac, 38, Df
Nerchinsk, 52, Qb; 74, Kc
Neresheim, 65A, Bb
Nesjar, 12, Gb
Nesle, 20, Ed
Ness, L., 14, Db
Nesse, 13, De
Nessib, 64, Kf
Netherby, 28B, Bb
Netherlands, 46A; 53, Fb
Netherlands, King. of the, 64, Dc
Netherlands Guiana, 68, Db
Netley, 36, Ca
Netz, 65A, Ca
Netze R., 31, Me; 39, Mb
Neu Breisach, 76A, Db
Neu-Sandec, 39, Pd
Neuburg, 38, Jd; 47, Ec
Neuchâtel, 10, Be; 29B, Aa
Neuchâtel, canton, 29B, Aa
Neuchâtel, L. of, 29B, Ab
Neuenburg, 20, Ge
Neuf Brisach, 83B, Ba
Neufchâteau, 29A, Aa
Neufchâtel, 53, Dc
Neuhaüsel, 33C, Db
Neuilly, 84, Cc
Neumark, 31, Lb
Neumarkt, 29A, Db
Neumünster, 65F, Aa
Neuse, R., 56B
Neuss, 46A, Fc
Neustadt, Austria, 21, Me
Neustadt, Hungary, 33C, Db
Neustadt, Moravia, 51, Dd
Neustadt, Palatinate, 39B, Ea
Neustadt, Saxony, 38, Jc
Neustria, France, 4A, Bb
Neustria, Italy, 5, Bb
Neutra, 21, Nd
Neuwerk, 65D, Aa
Neuwied, 53, Gb
Neva, R., 19, Ea
Nevada, 70, Cd
Nevada, Sierra, Spain, 63, Dd
Nevada, Sierra, U.S.A., 70, Bd

Nevada Terr., 67D, Ba
Nevers, 11, Ec
Nevers, Co. of, 11, Ec
Neville, 28B, Cc
Neville's Cross, 27, Eb
Nevis, 43A, Fc
Nevis, L., 49A, Bb
Nevyansk, 61, Kc
New Albion, 42, Dc
New Amsterdam, Guiana, 68B, Ba
New Amsterdam, N. America, 42, Fb
New Archangel (Sitka), 71A, Db
New Biscay, 43A, Bb
New Britain, Canada, 71, Hb
New Britain, I., 90, Dd
New Britain (New Pomerania), I., 77, Ib
New Brunswick, Canada, 71, Hc
New Brunswick, New Jersey, 57, Dc
New Calabar, 81C, Fd
New Caledonia, 70, Bb
New Caledonia, I., 77, Lf
New Castile, 63, Dc
New Dorp, 45B, Bc
New East Prussia, 60A, Hb
New England, 45B, Db
New France, 52, Fb
New Galicia, 43A, Bb
New Granada, Captain-Generalship of, 41B, Bc
New Granada, Rep., of, 68, Bb
New Granada, U.S. of, 68, Bb
New Guinea, 90, Dd
New Guinea, Terr. of, 77, Hb
New Hampshire, 45B, Db
New Hanover, 81D, Bb
New Hanover (Lavongai), 77, Ib
New Haven, 45B, Cc
New Hebrides, 77, Le
New Holland, 42B; 77, Bg
New Ireland, 90, Dd
New Ireland (New Mecklenburg), 77, Ib
New Jersey, 45A, Cc; 57, Dc
New Leinster (Stewart I.), 77A
New Leon, 43A, Cb
New London, 45B, Cc
New Madrid, 72, Cb
New Mecklenburg (New Ireland), 77, Ib
New Mexico, 70, Dd
New Mexico Terr., 67D, Cb
New Munster (South I., N.Z.), 77A
New Navarre, 43A, Aa
New Netherland, 45B, Bc
New Orleans, 56, Ae
New Plymouth, 77A
New Point Comfort, 45B, Ae
New Pomerania, 60B, Da
New Pomerania (New Britain), 77, Ib
New Providence, 43A, Eb
New Republic, 81D, Ba
New Ross, 49B, Ed
New Santander, 43C, Bb
New Siberian Is., 74, Na
New Silesia, 60A, Gc
New South Wales, Australia, 77, Hh
New South Wales, Canada, 70, Eb
New Sweden, 45B, Bd
New Toledo, 41B, Ce
New Ulster (North I., N.Z.), 77A
New York, 57B
New York, st., 57, Db
New Zealand, 77, Nj
Newark, England, 27, Fc
Newark, New York, 57B
Newbattle, 14, Ed
Newbern, 56, Dc
Newburn, 48A, Cb
Newbury, England, 27, Ee
Newbury, Massachusetts, 45B Db
Newburyport, 56, Eb
Newcastle, Delaware, 57, Dd
Newcastle, Leinster, 37B, Ec
Newcastle, Limerick, 49B, Bd
Newcastle, Natal, 81D, Aa
Newcastle, New South Wales, 77, Ih
Newcastle, Ulster, 37B, Ea
Newcastle, Wales, 28A, Bb
Newcastle (Fort Christina), 45B, Bd
Newcastle-under-Lyme, 27, Dc
Newchwang, 74, Ld; 76B, Ba
Newerche (Newark), 13, Fc
Newfoundland, 45A, Fa
Newmarket, 48B, Dc
Newport, I. of W., 27, Ef
Newport, Monmouth, 28A, Cc

Newport, Rhode I., 45B, Dc
Newport, Wales, 28A, Bb
Newport News, 45B, Ae
Newport Pagnell, 48A, Cc
Newry, 49B, Eb
Newstead, 36, Ed
Newtown, 48B, Bc
Newtown Butler, 49B, Db
Newtownards, 49B, Fb
Ngami, L., 81A, Bb
Ngaoundéré, 96B, Db
Ngau, 75C, Ba
Nguru, 96B, Da
Niagara, 70, Gc
Niagara Falls, 57, Bb; 71D
Niamey, 96B, Ca
Nias, 91, Cf
Nicaea, 2, Je; 19, Dd; 79, Eb
Nicaea, Empire of, 19, De
Nicaragua, 43D, Dc
Nicaragua, L., 43D, Dc
Nicastro, 21A, Dc
Nice, 5, Ac; 11, Ge
Nice, Co. of, 38, Gg
Nicholas II Land, 74, Ga
Nickerie, 68B, Ba
Nicobar Is., 92, Gf
Nicomedia, 2, Ke; 19, Ed
Nicopolis, Bulgaria, 78, Ed
Nicopolis, Turkey, 19, Fd
Nicopolis Theme, 9, Ge
Nicosia, 18A, Ec
Nicoya, G. of, 43A, Dd
Nidaros (Trondheim), 26, Da
Nidda, 20, Hc
Nidum (Neath), 3A, Ce
Niebla, 23C, Bd
Niemen, R., 19, Ca; 50, Fc
Nieuport, 46A, Bc
Nieuwveld, 81A, Bd
Niger, rep., 96D, Cc
Niger, R., 81C, Fc
Niger, terr., 80A, Dc
Nigeria, 80A, Dc; 96B, Cb
Nigeria, Federation of, 96D, Cd
Nigritia, 52, Kd
Niigata, 91, Gc
Niihau, 75D, Ab
Nijni Kamchatsk, 52, Sb
Nikolayevsk, 74, Nc
Nikolsburg, 33C, Db; 39, Md
Nile, R., 25, Cd; 80B, Ab
Nilgiri Hills, 73, Ce
Nîmes, 11, Fe
Nimwegen, 20, Fc; 46A, Ec
Ninety Six, 57D, Aa
Ningpo, 41A, Kb; 74, Lf
Ninus, 2, Mf; 4A, Ld
Niort, 30, Ce
Nipigon, L., 70, Fb
Nipissing, L., 45A, Ba
Nis, 88, Ke
Nish (Nissa), 78, Cd
Nishapur, 25, Ec; 61B, Ab
Nishni Novgorod, 19, Ga
Nisibis, 2, Mf; 6A, Ca
Nissa, 8, Gc
Nissa (Nish), 78, Cd
Nith, R., 36, Cb
Nithsdale, 14, Ed; 28B, Bb
Niue (Savage) I., 75, Ge
Nive, R., 63, Ea
Nivelles, 46B
Nivernais, 17, Ge
Nizam's Dominions, 73, Cd
Nizhne Kolymsk, 74, Pb
Nkandhla, mts., 81D, Bb
Noce, R., 86B, Aa
Nocera, 22, Ec
Noddies I., 56B
Nogais, 61, Ee
Nogent le Roi, 30, Dd
Nogent-le-Rotrou, 38, Dd
Nogent-sur-Marne, 76A, Bb
Nogent-sur-Seine, 30, Ed
Noirmoutier, 9, Bc; 53, Dd
Noix, I. aux, 57, Ea
Notley, 36, Ff
Nola, 22, Ec
Noli, 23A, Ba
Nomadic Arab Tribes, 16, Fg
Nombre de Dios, Mexico, 43A, Bb
Nombre de Dios, Panama, 43A, Ed
Nome, 71A, Aa
Nomeny, 39B, Cb
Nona, 22, Fc
Nonette, 20, Ef
Nonno, 96A, Ab
Nootka, 69A, Cb
Norden, 10 Bb
Nordfulc (Norfolk), 13, Gd
Nordgau, Marg. of, 10, Dd
Nordhausen, 10, Dc
Nordheim, 10, Cc
Nördlingen, 29A, Da
Nordmark, 10, Eb
Nordreys, 12, Cb; 14, Bb
Nore, 55A, Dc
Nore, R., 15, Dd
Norfolk, 45B, Ae; 72B, Bb

Norfolk, co., 27, Hd
Norfolk I., 77, Lg
Norham, 27, Da; 28B, Cb
Norhamscire (Norhamshire), 13, Da
Noric Alps, 29A, Fb
Noricum, 2, Fd; 2A, Cb
Norman King., 18A, Bb
Normands, Iles, 17, Dd
Normandy, D. of, 11, Cb
Norrköping, 51, Db; 54, Fa
North C., 69B
North Chan., 14, Cd; 37A, Bc
North I. (New Ulster), 77A
North Pt., 71C, Cc
North (Hudson), R., 45B, Bc
North Sea, 12, Eb; 55A, Eb
North Anna, R., 72B, Bb
North Atlantic Ocean, 94, Cd
North Australia, 77, Ee
North Berwick, 49A, Cb
North Dakota, 70, Dc
North Downs, 27, Ge
North Dvina, R., 89, Oa
North-East Frontier Agency, 91, Cd
North-East New Guinea (Kaiser Wilhelms Land), 77, Gc
North Esk, R., 14, Fc
North Foreland, 55A, Dc
North Frisian Is., 65F, Aa
North Kanara, 52A, Bc
North Konkan, 52A, Bc
North Korea, 91, Fb
North Pacific Ocean, 75, Gc
North Platte, R., 70, Dc
North Pole, 69B
North Potomac, R., 57, Bd
North Saskatchewan, R., 70, Cb
North Somerset I., 44, Ea
North Uist, 14, Ab
North Victoria (Queenstown), 81B, Cb
North Vietnam, 91, Dd
North Wales, 36A
North West Provs., 73, Cb
North West Terr., 67B, Ba
North-West Terrs., 70, Ea
Northallerton, 27, Eb
Northampton, England, 27, Fd
Northampton, Massachusetts, 45B, Cb
Northampton, co., 27, Fd
Northantone (Northampton), 13, Fd
Northantonescire (Northamptonshire), 13, Fd
Northern Circars, 73, Dd
Northern Hiung-nu, 1, Kb
Northern Ireland, 49B, Eb
Northern Nigeria, 81C, Fc
Northern Rhodesia, 80A, Ff
Northern Slav Peoples, 8C, Ca
Northern Terr., Australia, 77, Ee
Northfield, 57, Eb
Northumbria, 7B, Ba
Northymbraland (Northumberland), 13, Da
Norton Sd., 71A, Aa
Nor-Treding (North Riding, Lincolnshire), 13, Fc
Nor-Treding (North Riding, Yorkshire), 13, Eb
Norway, 12, Ga; 82, Aa
Norway, King. of, 26, Da
Norwegian Sea, 94, Tb
Norwic (Norwich), 13, Hd
Norwich, 27, Hd
Norwich, bp., 36, He
Nosob, R., 81B, Ba
Nossi Be, 80A, Hf
Nöteborg, 26, Hb
Notre Dame B., 71, Jc
Notre Dame de la Grasse, 22, Cc
Nottingham, 7C, Cb; 27, Ed
Nottingham, co., 27, Ec
Nouakchott, 96D, Ac
Nouart, 76A, Cb
Noumea, 75, Ff
Nova Coimbra, 41B, De
Nova Foresta (New Forest), 13, Ef
Nova Scotia, 45A, Eb
Novae, 2, Je; 4A, Hc
Novantae, 3A, Bb
Novara, 5, Bb
Novaya Zemlya, 74, Da
Novgorod, Poland, 47, Hb
Novgorod, Russia, 26, Hb
Novgorod, Pr., 61, Eb
Novgorod, Rep. of, 19, Ga
Novgorod Severski, 50, Gc
Novi, 29A. Cc
Novibazar, 78, Cd

Novlomagus (Chichester), 3A, Ff
Novo Alexandrovsk, 61B, Aa
Novogrodek, 26, Gc
Novokuznetsk, 91, Ba
Novorossiisk, 88, Ne
Novosibirsk, 91, Ba; 94, Pc
Noyon, 11, Eb; 83A, Bb
Nubia, 80B, Ac
Nubian Desert, 80B, Ac
Nubians, 6, Ce
Nugent, 37B, Dc
Nuits, 76A, Cc
Nukha, 93, Fa
Nullarbor Plain, 77, Dh
Numidia, 1, Cd; 4B, Dd
Nuneaton, 36, Ee
Nuremberg, 10, Dd
Nuremburg, Bur. of, 30, Jd
Nürnberg, 87, Cc
Nursia, 5, Dc; 23B, Dc
Nyasa, L., 80A, Gf
Nyasaland, 80A, Gf
Nyköping, 26, Eb
Nymphaeum, 19, De
Nymphenburg, 53, Jc
Nyons, 38, Ff
Nystad, 51, Ea; 61, Bb

Oahu, 75D, Cb
Oakham, 27, Fd
Oates Land, 95, KJ
Oaxaca, 43A, Cc
Ob, R., 25, Fa; 61, Lb; 91, Ba
Obbia, 96A, Bb
Ober Selk, 65F, Aa
Oberehnheim, 39B, Db
Oberland, 29B, Bb
Obi, 52C, Cb
Obidos, Brazil, 68, Dc
Obidos, Portugal, 63, Ac
Obok, 80B, Ce; 83, Ld
Obotrites, 10, Db
O'Brien, 15, Cd; 37B, Bd
Obuasi, 96B, Bb
O'Byrne, 37B, Bc
Ocaña, Colombia, 68, Bb
Ocaña, Spain, 62, Bc; 63, Dc
O'Carroll, 15, Db
Ocean I., 75, Fe
Oceanus Atlanticus, 2, Ad
Oceanus Germanicus, 2, Dc
Oceanus Hibernicus (Irish Sea), 3A, Bc
Ochakov, 51, Gd
Ochementone (Okehampton) 13, Bf
Ochil Hills, 28B, Ba
O'Connor, 15, Cc; 37B, Cc
Ocrinum Prom., 3A, Af
Octapitarum Pr., 3A, Ae
O'Dempsey, 15, Dc
Odenburg, 16, Fc
Odense, 26, Db; 65F, Ba
Oder, R., 21, Lb; 31, Lb
Oderberg, 39, Nd
Odessa, 50, Gd; 51, Gd
Odessus, 4B, Gc
Odienne, 96B, Bb
Odiham, 27, Fe
Odoacer, King. of, 2A, Cb
O'Doherty, 37B, Da
O'Donnell, 37B, Cb
O'Donovan, 37B, Ce
O'Dowd, 15, Bb
Oels, 39, Nd
Oenaeum, 19, Fd
Oettingen, 39B, Ca
Ofen, 22, Fb
Ofen Pass, 29B, Eb
Offaly, 15, Dc
Offa's Dyke, 7B, Bb; 13, Cc
Offenburg, 38, Gd; 83B, Ba
O'Flaherty, 15, Cc
O'Flynn, 37B, Bb
Ogbomosho, 96B, Cb
Ogdensburg, 57, Da
Ogeechee, R., 57D, Ab
Oglio, R., 5, Cb
Ogmore, 27, Ce
Ogowe, R., 80A, Ed
O'Hanlon, 37B, Eb
Ohio, 72, Da
Ohio, R., 45A, Ab; 56, Bc
Ohod, Mt., 6, Fc
Oil River Prot., 80A, Dd
Oirghealla (Uriel), 15, Db
Oise, R., 11, Eb
Ojibways, 56, Ba
Oka, R., 61, Fc
Okavango, R., 81A, Aa
Okavango Swamp, 81A, Ba
Okehampton, 27, Bf
O'Kelly, 15, Cc
Okfuskee, 56, Bd
Okhotsk, 42, Qb; 74, Nc
Okhotsk, Sea of, 74, Nc
Okhrida, 78, Cc
Okinawa, 91, Fd
Oklahoma, 70, Ed
Oklahoma Indian Territory 70, Ed

Öland, 26, Eb
Olavarria, 68, Cf
Old Bridge, 49B, Ec
Old Calabar, 81C, Fd
Old Castile, 63, Db
Old Castle, 37B, Db
Old Charles Town, 45A, Bd
Old Fort Franklin, 70, Ba
Old Head of Kinsale, 15, Ce
Old Kilpatrick, 3A, Ba
Old Orsova, 33C, Ec
Old Point Comfort, 45B, Ae
Old Providence I., 43A, Dc
Old Sarai, 25, Db
Old Sarum 27 ,Ee
Oldenburg, 20, Hb; 30, Hb
Oldenburg, Co. of, 38, Hb
Oldenzaal, 46A, Fb
Oléron, 11, Cd
Olicana (Ilkley), 3A, Ec
Olifants, R., 81A, Db
Oliva, 21, Na
Olivenza, 64, Af
Olmütz, 21, Md; 33C, Db
Olonets, 26, Ha
Oloron, 11, Ce; 38, Cg
Öls, 39, Mc
Oltenitza, 78, Fc
Olustee, 57, Dc
Omagh, 37B, Db; 49B, Db
Omaha, 70, Ec
O'Malley, 37B, Bc
Oman, 6, Gc; 25, Ed; 93, He
Oman, G. of, 74, Df
Ombai, 52C, Cb
Omdurman, 80B, Ad
Ominitae, 1, Hf
Ommeyad Emirate, 6B, Aa
Omont, Co. of, 11, Fb
O'More, 37B, Dd
Omsk, 91, Aa
Oneida, L., 57, Cb
Oneidas, 45A, Bb
Onega, L., 26, Ja
Oneglia, 38, Hg
O'Neill, 15, Db
Onitsha, 96B, Cb
Onnum (Halton), 3C
Ono, 75C, Bb
Onondagas, 45A, Bb
Ontario, 70, Fc
Ontario, L., 57, Cb
Oodnadatta, 77, Fg
O'okiep, 81B, Ab
Opland, 12, Ga
Oporto, 23C, Ab; 63, Ab
Oppeln, 21, Mc
Opsikion, 9, Hd
Optimaton, 9, Jd
Oran, 16, Be; 33B, Aa; 80, Ca
Orange, France, 11, Fd
Orange, R., 81B, Ab
Orange Free State, 81B, Cb
Orange River Colony, 81A, Cb
Orange River Sovereignty 81B, Cb
Orangeburg, 57D, Ab
Oranmore, 49B, Cc
Orbe, 9, Dc; 29B, Ab
Orbetello, 32B, Cc; 38, Jg
Orchies, 46A, Cd
Ordovices, 3A, Cd
Ordu, 93, Da
Ordzhonikidze, 88, Oe
Ore Mts., 60A, Dc
Örebro, 26, Eb
Oregon, 70, Bc
Oregon City, 70, Bc
Oregon Country, 70, Cc
Oregon Terr., 67D, Aa
O'Reilly, 15, Dc
Orel, 61, Ed; 88, Nc
Orenburg, 61, Jd; 89, Rc
Orenburg Cossacks, 61, Jd
Orense, 23C, Ba; 63, Ba
Orewyn Bridge, 27, Cd
Orford, 13, Hd, 27, Hd
Oria, 21A, Db
Orientis, 2, Lg
Origny, 22, Dc
Orinoco, Delta of the, 43A, FJ
Orinoco, R., 68, Cb
Oriskany, 57, Db
Orissa, 25, Hd; 73, Ec
Oristano, 22, Dd
Oristano, eccl. prov., 22, Dd
Orizaba, 43A, Cc
Orkney, co., 37A, Ca
Orkney Is., 14, Fa
Orléanais, 38, De
Orléans, 11, Dc; 28C, Dc
Orléans, D. of, 30, Ee
Orléans, I. d', 57C, Ba
Orlov, 61, Jc
Ormoc, 75E, Bb
Ormond, 15, Cd
Ormskirk, 48A, Bc
Ormuz, 25, Ed
Orneau, R., 46B
Orontes, R., 6A, Ba; 18A, Fc
Orontes (Ferreus), R., 18C, Dc
Oropesa, 63, Cc

O'Rourke, 15, Cb
Oroya, 68, Bd
Orsova, 78, Dc
Orsoy, 53, Gb
Orta, 23B, Bd
Ortegal, C., 63, Aa
Ortenau, 33C, Bb
Orthez, 30, Cg; 63, Ea
Ortles, 29A, Db
Ortona, 21, Lg
Oruba, 43A, Fc
Oruro, 68, Cd
Orvieto, 5, Dc
Osaka, 91, Gc
Ösel, 26, Fb
Osero, 22, Ec
O'Shaughnessy, 15, Cc
Oshogbo, 96B, Cb
Osiek, 26, Fc
Osimo, 21, Kg
Osimo (Auximum), 5, Dc
Oslo, 26, Db; 84, Ea
Osma, 22, Bc
Osmanli, 85, Je
Osnabrück, 10, Cb
Ossory, 15, Dd
Ostend, 46A, Bc; 47, Cb
Öster-Götland, 26, Eb
Ostheim, 39C, Ac
Ostia, 5, Dd; 22A
Ostmark, 10, Ec
Ostrach, 29A, Cb
Ostrogothi, 2, Jd
Ostrogothic Kingdom, 4A, Eb
Ostrogoths, 2A, Db
Ostrolenka, 60B, Hb; 64, Gc
Ostrovo L., 86A, Cb
Oswego, 70, Gc; 71C, Cb
Oswestry, 13, Cd; 27, Cd
Otadini, 3A, Da
Otago, 77A
Otaheite, 69A, Be
Otchakov, 54, Jc
Otford, 7B, Dc
Othona (Bradwell), 3A, Ge
O'Toole, 15, Ed; 37B, Ec
Otranto, 5, Gd; 32A, Gd
Otrar, 25, Fb
Ottawa, 70, Gc
Ottawa, R., 45A, Ba; 71C, Ca
Ottawas, 45A, Aa
Otterburn, 27, Da
Ottery St. Mary, 36, Cg
Ottoman Empire, 50, Ee
Ottoman Turks, 24, Hf
Ouagadougou, 96B, Ba
Ouahgouya, 96B, Ba
Ouargla, 80A, Da
Oudenarde, 46A, Cd; 54, Cb
Oudh, 73, Db
Oudon, 20, Ce
Oudtshoorn, 81B, Bc
Ouiatanon, 56, Bb
Oujitsa, 78, Bd
Ourcq, R., 76A, Bb
Ourique, 23C, Ad
Ourthe, R., 83A, Ca
Ouse, R., 27, Ec; 36, Fd
Ovambo, 80A, Ef
Översee, 65F, Aa
Overton, 27, Ee
Overyssel, 46A, Fb
Oviedo, 23C, Ca; 63, Ca
Owen Stanley Ra., 77, Hc
Ox Mts., 15, Cb
Oxeneford (Oxford), 13, Ee
Oxenefordscire (Oxfordshire), 13, Ee
Oxford, England, 27, Ee
Oxford, Maryland, 45B, Ad
Oxford, bp., 36, Ef
Oxford, co., 27, Ee
Oxus, R., 1, Jd; 6, Hb; 25, Fc
Oyster Bay, 45B, Cc
Ozamiz, 75E, Bc

PAARDE BERG, 81A, Cc
Paarl, 81B, Ac
Paauilo, 75D, Db
Pacaltsdorp, 81B, Bc
Pachacamac, 41B, Be
Pacific Ocean, 40, Cd; 75
Padang, 91, Dg
Paderborn, 10, Cc
Padua (Patavium), 5, Cb; 86B, Bb
Paducah, 72, Cb
Paestum, 5, Ed
Pagadian, 75E, Bc
Pagan, 25, Jd; 73, Gc
Pago Pago, 75B, Bb
Pahala, 75D, Dc
Pahang, 41A, Hd
Pahlevi, 93, Fb
Paithan, 1, Kf
Pakhoi, 74, Jf
Palace, Constantinople, 18E
Palapye, 81A, Cb
Palar, R., 59D
Palatine, 5A
Palato, eccl. prov., 22, Fc
Palau Is., 90, Cc

Palawan, 75E, Ac; 90, Bc
Palazzo di Venezia, 5A
Palembang, 91, Dg
Palencia, 22, Bc
Palenque, 43A, Cc
Palermo, eccl. prov., 22, Ed
Palermo (Panormus), 5, De
Palestine, 6A, Ab; 79, Gd
Palestrina, 22A
Palma, 22, Cd; 23C, Gc
Palmas, C., 81C, Cd
Palmella, 23C, Ac
Palmerston I., 75, He
Palmyra, 2, Lg; 4A, Ke
Palmyra I., 75, Hd
Palos, 23D, Bd
Pamiers, 17, Fg; 22, Cc
Pamir, 59A, Ba; 61B, Cb
Pampeluna, 23D, Ea
Pamlico, R., 57, Cf
Pamlico Sound, 45B, Af
Pamphylia, 2, Jf
Pamplona, 22, Bc; 23C, Ea
Panama, 43A, Ed; 68, Bb
Panay, 75E, Bb
Pandhya, 1, Kf
Pandyas, 25, Ge
Paneas (Belinas), 18C, Ce
Panganga, R., 59A, Cd
Panipat, 59A, Cb
Panniar, 73, Cb
Pannonia, 2, Gd; 9, Fc
Panormus (Palermo), 5, De
Pantelleria, 88, Hf
Pantheon, 5A
Panton, 57, Ea
Panuco, 43A, Cb
Panuco, R., 43A, Cb
Paoki, 90, Bb
Paoting, 90, Bb
Paotow, 91, Eb
Papal States, 32B, Dc; 34, Ed
Paphlagonia, 2, Ke; 9, Jd
Papua, G. of, 77, Gc
Papua, Terr. of (British New Guinea), 77, Gc
Para (Belem), 41B, Ed; 68, Ec
Para, st., 68, Dc
Paradies, 22, Fa
Paraguay, 68, De
Paraguay, Jesuit Mission State of, 41B, Df
Paraguay R., 41B, De
Paraiba, 68, Fc
Paraiba, st., 68, Fc
Paramaribo, 68, Db
Parana, 68, Cf
Parana, R., 41B, Df; 68, De
Parana, st., 68, De
Paranagua, 68, Ae
Parchim, 21, Jb
Parenzo, 22, Eb; 23B, Db
Parga, 54, Ge; 78, Cf
Paria, G. of, 43B, Dc
Parintins, 68, Dc
Paris, 11, Eb; 17, Gd
Parisi, 3A, Fc
Parkersburg, 72, Db
Parma, 5, Cb; 38, Jf
Parma, D. of, 38, Jf; 54, Dd
Parnaiba, 68, Ec
Parnaiba, R., 68, Ec
Paros, 78, Eg
Parret, R., 7B, Bc
Parry Is., 69B
Parthenay, 11, Cc
Parthia, 1, Hd
Parthian Empire, 1, Hd
Partenkirchen, 22, Eb
Passamaquoddy B., 45A, Da; 71E, Cc
Passaro, C., 32B, Ee
Passarowitz, 33C, Ec; 78, Cc
Passau, 10, Ed
Passchendaele, 83A, Ba
Passo Fundo, 68, De
Pasto, 68, Bb
Patagonia, 68, Cg
Pataliputra, 1, Le
Patan, 92, Fb
Patavium (Padua), 5, Cb
Patay, 28D, Cb
Patchefstroom, 81A, Cc
Patiala, 73, Ca
Patillos, 68, Be
Patna, 73, Eb
Patras, 78, Cf
Patriarch's Pond, 18D
Patrimonium, 23B, Dd
Patrimony of St. Peter, 16, Ed; 32A, Ed
Patti, 22, Fd
Patzinaks (Pechenegs), 9, Jc
Pau, 30, Cg
Paumotu Arch. (Tuamotu Arch.), 69A, Ce; 75, He
Pavia, 6, Ba
Pavia (Picinum), 5, Bb
Pawtucket, 45B, Dc
Paxo, 62, Ge
Paxton, 57, Cc
Paysandu, 68, Df

Pea Ridge, 72, Bb
Peace, R., 44, Cc; 70, Cb
Peak, The, 27, Ec
Pearl, R., 71F, Ba; 72C, Aa
Pearl Coast, 43A, Fc
Pearl Harbor, 75D, Bb; 90, Gb
Pearl Is., 43A, Ed
Pecfers (Peak), 13, Ec
Pecos, R., 44, De
Pecs, 19, Bc; 33C, Db
Pedee, R., 57D, Ba
Pedir, 40, Od
Peebles, 49A, Cc
Peebles, co., 37A, Cc; 49A, Cc
Peekskill, 57, Ec
Pegu, 25, Je; 73, Gd
Peipus, L., 26, Gb
Peishwa, 59A, Bd
Peking, 91, Ec
Peking (Kaanbaligh), 25, Lc
Pelagonia, 19, Cd
Pelew Is., 74, Mh
Pella, 81B, Ab
Pelly, R., 70, Aa
Peloponnesus, 9, Ge
Pelotas, 68, Df
Pelplin, 22, Fa
Pelusium, 18A, Ec
Pelvoux, Mt., 29A, Bc
Pemaquid, 45A, Db; 45B, Eb
Pemba I., 80A, Ge
Pembroke, 27, Be
Pembroke, Co. Palatine of, 27, Be
Pelim, 61, Kc
Peñafiel, 23D, Cb
Peñan de Alger, 34, Ce
Penang, 91, Df
Penay, 29B, Ab
Penbroc (Pembroke), 13, Be
Pendennis, 48A, Ad
Penedo, 68, Fd
Peneverdant (Penwortham), 13, Dc
Peniscola, 23D, Fb
Penjdeh, 61B, Bb; 74, Ee
Penkridge 13, Dd
Pennal, 3A, Cd
Penner, R., 59D; 73, Ce
Pennine Alps, 29A, Bb
Pennine Chain, 27, Db; 28B, Cc
Pennsylvania, 57, Cc; 72B, Ba
Penobscot (Fort Pentagöet), 45B, Ea
Penobscot B., 45B Ea
Penobscot, R., 45A, Da; 71E, Bc
Penrith, 27, Db
Penryn, 48A, Ad
Penrhyn I., 75, He
Pensacola, 56, Bd; 67B, Bb
Pensacola (Achusi), 43A, Da
Penselwood, 7B Bc
Pentapolis, Africa, 2, Hg; 4B, Ge
Pentapolis, Italy, 5, Dc
Pentegoet, 56, Fb
Penthièvre, 17, Dd
Pentland Firth, 14, Ea
Pentland Hills, 14, Ed
Penukonda, 52A, Bc
Penza, 61, Fd
Peoria, 56, Bb
Pera, 18E; 19, Dd
Perambakan, 59D
Perche, 17, Fd; 30, Dd
Perekop, 51, Gd; 61, De
Perekop, G. of, 61, De
Pereyaslav, 19, Eb
Perigord, Co. of, 11, Dd
Perigueux, 11, Dd
Perim I., 80B, Ce
Pergamum, 9, He; 18A, Db
Perm, 61, Jc; 89, Rb
Pernambuco (Mauritia), 42, He
Pernambuco (Recife), 68, Fc
Pernambuco, st., 68, Fc
Pernau, 26, Fb
Péronne, 11, Eb; 83A, Bb
Perovsk, 61B, Ba
Perpignan, 11, Ee
Perryville, 72, Db
Persarum Regnum, 2, Og
Persepolis, 1, Hd
Pershore, 27, Dd
Persia, 6, Gb; 33A, Hd; 74, Dc
Persia (Iran), 89, Pg; 93, Gc
Persian Empire, 2A, Fc
Persian Gulf, 6, Gc; 93, Gd
Persis, 1, Hd
Persore (Pershore), 13, Dd
Perth, Scotland, 14, Ec
Perth, W. Australia, 77, Bh
Perth, co., 37A, Cb; 49A, Cb
Peru, 68, Bd
Peru, Viceroyalty of, 41B, Be; 42, Ee
Perugia, 5, Dc; 21, Kg
Perusia, 5B, Bb
Pesaro, 8A, Dc; 21, Kg
Pesaro, (Pisaurum), 5, Dc

Pescadores, 75, Cc
Pescara, 32A, Fc
Peschiera, 29A, Dc; 32D, Bb
Peshawar, 25, Gc; 73, Ba
Pessinus, 2, Kf
Pest, 39, Ne
Peterborough, 36, Fe
Peterborough, bp., 36, Fe
Peterhead, 37A, Db
Petersburg, 57, Ce; 72B, Bb
Petersfield, 27, Ef; 48A, Cd
Peterwardein, 50, Dd
Petra, 6A, Bb
Petrianae, 3A, Cb
Petropavlovsk, 58, Rb
Petropolis, 68, Ee
Petsamo, 88, Ma
Pettau, 9, Fc
Petuaria (Brough), 3A, Fc
Pevenesel (Pevensey), 13, Gf
Pevensey, 27, Gf
Pfaffenhofen, 65A, Bb
Pfalzburg, 39B, Db
Pfävers, 29B, Db
Pfirt, 39B, Dc
Pfullendorf, 53, Hd
Pharsalus, 9, Ge
Philadelphia, Nicaea, 19, De
Philadelphia, Pennsylvania, 57, Bd
Philiphaugh, 37A, Cc; 48B, Bb
Philippeville, 46A, Dd
Philippine Is., 74, Lg
Philippine Is. (Felipinas, Islas), 41A, Kc
Philippines (St. Lazaro Arch.), 40, Qd
Philippolis, 81B, Cb
Philippopolis, 2, Je; 78, Ed
Philippsburg, 29A, Ca
Philipstown. 49B, Dc
Philomelion, 18A, Eb
Fhnom, Fenh, 91, De
Phoenicia, 1, Hd
Phoenix Is., 90, Fd
Phrygia, 2, Jf
Piacenza (Placentia), 5, Bb
Piaui, 68, Ec
Piave, R., 5, Db; 86B, Cb
Picardy, 28D, Db; 83A, Bb
Pichincha, 68, Bc
Picinum (Pavia), 5, Bb
Pickawillany, 56, Cb
Pickering, 27, Fb
Pickeringham (Pickering), 13, Fb
Picquigny, 30, Ed
Picti, 2, Cb
Picts, 7B, Ba
Pidurutalagala, 73, Df
Piedmont, 32A, Bb
Piedmont, Pr. of, 38, Gf
Piedra, 22, Bc
Piet Retief, 81A, Dc
Pietermaritzburg, 81D, Bb
Pieters, 81D, Ab
Pietersburg, 81A, Db
Pietra Santa, 38, Jg
Pieve di Cadore, 86B, Ca
Pike's Peak, 70, Dd
Pilar, 68, De
Pilcomayo, R., 68, Ce
Pilica, 60A, Hc
Pilica, R., 31, Fc; 33C, Ea
Pillau, 39, Na
Pillnitz, 60A, Dc
Pilsen, 10, Ed; 39, Kd
Pilten, 26, Fb
Pilton, 7C, Ac
Piltune (Pilton), 13, Be
Pinar del Rio, 43A, Db
Pindari, 73, Cb
Pindiga, 96B, Db
Pindus, 50, Ee
Pine Bluff, 72, Bc
Pinerolo, 32A, Bb
Pines, I. of, 75, Ff
Pines, I. de Cuba, 43A, Db
Pinos, I. de, Panama, 43A, Ed
Pinsk, 34, Hb; 50, Fc; 84, Hb
Piombino, 5, Cc
Pippli, 59B
Piqua, 71C, Bb
Piquetberg, 81B, Ac
Piraeus, 78, Dg; 88, Kf
Pirapora, 68, Ed
Pirmasens, 83A, Db
Pirna, 31, Kc; 39C, Dc
Pirot, 78, Dd
Pisa, 5, Cc; 8A, Dc
Pisaurum, 5B, Bb
Pisaurum (Pesaro), 5, Dc
Piscataqua B. (Portsmouth), 45B, Db
Pisco, 68, Bd
Pisek, 21, Ld; 60A, Ed

Pisidia, 2, Kf
Pisino, 22, Eb
Pistoia, 32E, Ba
Pisuerga, R., 63, Ca
Pitcairn I., 75, Jf
Pitiqui, 43C, Ab
Pitsewo, 76B, Bb
Pittsburg Landing, 72, Cb
Pittsburgh, 71C, Cb
Pittsburgh (Fort Pitt), 57A, Ca
Pityus, 2, Me
Piura, 68, Ac
Placentia, 45A, Ga; 52, Gb
Placentia (Piacenza), 5, Bb
Plaine Selve, 22, Bb
Plancenoit, 46B
Plasencia, 22, Ac; 63, Bb
Plassey, 59A, Ec
Pläswitz, 62, Fb
Platte, R., 70, Dc
Plattsburg, 71, Ea
Plauen, 21, Kc
Plava, 86B, Da
Pleasant Hill, 72, Bc
Plenty, B. of, 77A
Pleshey, 27, Ge
Pless, 31, Nd; 39, Nd
Plessis-les-Tours, 30, De
Plettenburg, 81B, Cb
Pleven, 79, Db
Plevna, 78, Ed
Plintone (Plympton), 13, Bf
Plock, 21, Nb
Ploërmel, 20, Be
Ploesti, 88, Ld
Plön, 65F, Ba
Ploughed Hill, 56B
Plovdiv, 79, Db
Plunket, 37B, Ec
Plymouth, England, 27, Bf
Plymouth, Massachusetts, 45B, Dc
Plympton, 27, Bf; 36, Bg
Pizen, 21, Kc
Po, R., 5, Cb; 21B, Bb; 38, Gf
Poblet, 22, Fc
Poclinton (Pocklington), 13, Fc
Podiebrad, 31, Lc
Podlesia 50, Fc
Podolia, 50, Fd
Poetovia, 2, Gd
Poggibonsi, 32E, Bb
Pohlde, 10, Dc
Pointe Noire, 96D, De
Poissy, 11, Db; 38, Ed
Poitiers, 11, Dc
Poitou, Co. of, 11, Cc
Poitou, 30, Ce
Pola, 5, Db
Poland, 50, Ec; 87, Eb
Poland, King. of, 21, Nc
Poles, 8, Hb; 9, Fb
Polesina, 32D, Bb
Policastro, 32A, Fd
Poligny, 30, Fe
Polillo Is., 75E, Bb
Polling, 10, De
Polotsk, 26, Gb
Polotsk, Pr. of, 19, Db
Polovtsi (Kipchaks), 19, Gc
Poltava, 50, Gd
Polygars, 52A, Bc
Pombal, 63, Ac
Pomerania, D. of, 21, Mb
Pomerania (Pomern), 8, Fa
Pomerelia, 19, Bb; 31, Na
Pompadour, 53, De
Ponape, 75, Ed
Pondicherry, 59D
Pondoland, 81B, Db
Pondos, 81B, Db
Ponferrada, 63, Ba
Pongolo, R., 81D, Da
Poniec, 50, Db
Pons, 20, Cf
Pons Aelius (Newcastle), 3C
Pont à Mousson, 39B, Cb
Pont Audemer, 20, Dd
Pont di Piave, 86B, Cb
Pontarlier, 30, Ge; 76A, Dc
Pontecorvo 32A, Fd
Pontefract, 27, Ec; 48A, Cc
Pontes (Staines), 3A, Fe
Ponthieu, Co. of, 11, Da
Pontica, 2A, Eb
Pontigny, 22, Cb; 28C, Dc
Pontivy, 38, Bd
Pontoise, 20, Ed
Pontremoli, 32A, Cb
Pontus, 2, Kf
Pontus Euxinus, 2, Ke
Pontvallain, 28C, Cc
Ponza, 32A, Ed
Pool, 28A, Cb
Poole, 27, Df
Poole, family, 28A, Cb
Poona, 73, Cc
Popayan, 68, Bb
Popocatopeti, 43A, Cc
Poprad, 31, Pd
Populonium, 5B, Ab

Porcestre (Porchester), 13, Ef
Porcien, Co. of, 11, Fb
Pordenone, 32D, Cb; 86B, Cb
Port Adams, 76B, Bb
Port Antonio, 43A, Ec
Port Arthur, Canada, 70, Fc
Port Arthur, China, 91, Fc
Port au Port, 45A, Fa
Port au Prince, 43C, Dc
Port Augusta, 77, Fh
Port aux Basques, 45A, Fa
Port Bonnel, 18C, Cb
Port Curtis, 77, If
Port Dalrymple, 77, HJ
Port Darwin, 77, Ed
Port Dieu, 29B, Bb
Port Elizabeth (Fort Frederick), 81B, Cc
Port Essington (Port Victoria), 77, Ed
Port Gibson, 72C, Ab
Port Harcourt, 96B, Cb
Port Hudson, 72, Bc
Port Jackson (Sydney), 77, Ih
Port Macquarie, 77, Ih
Port Mahon, 54, Ce
Port Moresby, 77, Hc
Port Mouton, 45A, Eb
Port Natal (Durban), 81D, Bb
Port Nelson, 70, Eb
Port Nicholson, 77A
Port of Spain, 43A, Fc
Port Phillip, 77, Gl
Port Pleasant, 57A, Cb
Port Republic, 72B, Aa
Port Royal (Annapolis), 45A, Db
Port Royal (Stuart Town), 45A, Ad
Port Royal, Jamaica, 43A, Ec
Port Said, 80B, Aa
Port St. Julian, 41B, Ch
Port Simpson, 70, Ab
Port Sudan, 80B, Bd; 96D, Fc
Port Victoria (Port Essington), 77, Ed
Portadown, 49B, Eb
Portage la Prairie, 70, Fb
Portalegre, 22, Ad
Portarlington, 49B, Dc
Portland, England, 77, Bc
Portland, Maine, 56, Eb
Portland, Oregon, 70, Bc
Portland, Victoria, 77, Gl
Portland Canal, 71B, Dc
Portloc (Porlock), 13, Ce
Porto, 22A
Porto Alegre, 68, Df
Porto Novo, India, 59D
Porto Novo, Dahomé, 81C, Ec
Porto Praya, 55B, He
Porto Rico, 43A, Fc
Porto Seguro, 68, Fd
Porto Seguro, prov., 41B, Ee
Porto Velho, 94, Df
Porto Viejo, 68, Ac
Portree, 49A, Ab
Portsmouth (Piscataqua B.), 45B, Db
Portsmouth, England, 27, Ef
Portsmouth, New Hampshire, 45B, Db
Portsmouth, Ohio, 70, Fd
Portsmouth, Rhode I., 45B, Dc
Portsmouth, Virginia, 57, Ce
Portsoy, 49A, Cb
Portugal, 63, Ac
Portugal, Co. of, 23C, Bb
Portugal, King. of, 23D, Bb
Portuguese East Africa, 81A, Db
Portuguese Guinea, 81C, Ab; 96B, Aa
Portus Adurni (Porchester), 3A, Ef
Portus Lemanis (Lympne), 3A, He
Posadas, 68, De
Poschiavo, 29B, Db
Posen, 21, Mb
Posen, reg., 60B, Fb
Potawatomis, 45A, Ab
Potchefstroom, 81B, Ca
Potgieter, 81A, Cc
Poti, 61, Ff; 79, Hb
Potomac, R., 57, Cd; 72B, Ba
Potosi, 68, Cd
Potsdam, 54, Eb; 60A, Db
Poughkeepsie, 57, Ec
Pounanen, 19, De
Poverty B., 77, Nl
Powder, R., 70, Dc
Powderham, 13, Cf
Powhatans, 45A, Bc
Powick Bridge, 48A, Bc
Powys, 7C, Bb; 13, Cd; 27, Cd
Pozières, 83A, Ba
Poznań, 61A, Ab; 87, Db
Praga, 51, Ec
Prague, 21, Lc
Prague, eccl. prov., 22, Fb

Prairie du Chien, 67C, Da
Prairie Grove, 72, Bb
Praslin, 53, Fc
Prato, 20, Jg; 32E, Bb
Prättigau, 29B, Db
Pravadi, 78, Fd
Prayaga, 52A, Cb
Pregel, R., 60A, Ha
Prèmontrè, 22, Cb
Prenzlau, 21, Kb; 65B, Ba
Presba L., 86A, Cb
Presidios, 32B, Cc; 38, Jg
Preslav, 9, Hd
Pressburg, 10, Gd
Preston, 27, Dc
Prestonpans, 49A, Cc
Prestune (Preston), 18, Dc
Pretoria, 80A, Fg; 81A, Cc
Prettin, 39C, Db
Preveza, 78, Cf
Priegnitz, 31B, Ca; 60A, Cb
Prilep, 19, Cd; 86A, Ca
Prince Albert, 70, Eb
Prince Edward I., 71, Hc
Prince Edward I. (Ile de St. Jean), 45A, Ea
Prince Edward Is., 95, Sh
Prince of Wales, C., 71A, Aa
Prince of Wales L., Alaska, 71B, Cc
Prince of Wales L., Canada, 44, Ea
Prince Rupert, 70, Bb
Prince Willem's Is., 42B
Prince William Sd., 71A, Ca
Princess Elizabeth Land, 69C
Princeton, 57, Dc
Principato, 32A, Fd
Principato Salernò, 21A, Cb
Principe, 80A, Dd
Prinkipo Is., 86C, Aa
Pripet, R., 50, Fc
Pripet Marshes, 84, Hb
Prishtina, 78, Cd
Pritzwalk, 21, Kb
Prizren, 19, Cd
Prome, 25, Je; 73, Gd
Prospect Hill, 56B
Prosperous, 49B, Ec
Provencals, 85, Cd
Provence, 8A, Cc; 9, Dd
Provence, Co. of, 11, Gd
Provence, Marq. of, 20, Ff
Providence, Maryland, 45B, Ad
Providence, Rhode I., 45B, Dc
Provincia, 2A, Bb
Provins, 17, Gd
Prüm, 20, Gc
Prussia, 51, Dc; 65A, Ba
Prussians, 8, Ga
Pruth, R., 50, Fd; 78, Fb
Przemysl, 26, Fd; 87, Ec
Psara, 78, Ef
Pskov, 26, Gb
Pueblo, 70, Dd
Puerto Bello, 43A, Ed
Puerto Cabello, 68, Ca
Puerto de Caballos, 43A, Dc
Puerto Deseado, 68, Cg
Puerto Madryn, 68, Cg
Puerto Montt, 68, Bg
Puerto Princesa, 75E, Ac
Puerto Principe, 43A, Eb
Pularoon, 52C, Cb
Pulaski, 72, Cb
Pulaway, 52C, Cb
Pulicat, 59D
Pulicat, L. of, 59D
Pultusk, 31, Pb; 54, Gb
Punakha, 92, Gb
Pungwe, R., 81A, Da
Punjab, 73, Ba; 74, Fe
Puno, 68, Bd
Punta Arenas, 68, Bh
Purdysburg, 57D, Ab
Purnea, 59A, Eb
Purus, R., 68, Cc
Pusan, 91, Fc
Pustat (Cairo), 6A, Ab
Pustertal, 29A, Db; 86B, Ca
Put-in-Bay, 71C, Bb
Putivl, 19, Eb
Puttlingen, 20, Gd; 39B, Da
Putumayo, R., 68, Bc
Puylaurens, 38, Eg
Pwllheli, 28A, Bb
Pyatigorsk, 88, Oe
Pyrenæ Montes, 2, De
Pyrenees, 11, De; 63, Fa
Pyritz, 10, Fb

Qayin, 6, Gb
Qatar, 93, Gd
Qatif, 93, Gd
Qena, 93, Gd
Qivira, 44, Ee
Quadi, 2, Gd
Quatford, 13, Dd

Quathlamba (Drakens Berg), 81D, Ab
Quatre Bras, 46B; 62, Cb
Quebec, 45A, Ca; 56A; 57C, Ba
Quebec, prov., 56, Fc
Quedlinburg, 10, Dc; 65A, Ba
Queen Charlotte Is., 70, Ab
Queen Charlotte Sd., 70, Bb
Queen Mary Land, 69C
Queen Maud Land, 69C
Queen Victoria Spring, 77, Ch
Queen's Co., 37C; 49B, Dd
Queensferry, 49A, Cc
Queensland, 77, Gf
Queenstown (Cobh), 49B, Ce
Queenstown (North Victoria), 81B, Cb
Queenstown, Canada, 71C, Cb
Queenstown, Cape Colony, 81A, Cd
Quelimane, 80A, Gf
Quemoy, 91, Ed
Quensanfu, 25, Kc
Quentovic, 12, Ed
Quercy, 17, Ff; 28C, Cd
Quetta, 61B, Bb; 73, Aa
Quezon City, 75E, Bb
Quiberon, 53, Bd; 55A, Be
Quilon, 59A, Cf
Quimper, 11, Ab
Quimperié, 22, Bb; 28D, Ac
Quincey (Merry Mount), 45B, Db
Quincy, 70, Ed
Quingey, 76A, Cc
Quinsay (Lingan, Hangchow), 25, Mc
Quito, 68, Bc
Qum, 93, Gc
Qunfidha, 93, Ef
Quseir, 93, Cd

Raab, 21, Me
Raab, R., 31, Me; 39, Me
Raasay, 49A, Ab
Rabast, C. de, 45A, Ea
Rabat, 77, Ib; 90, Dd
Raby, 27, Eb
Rabaul, 77, Ib; 90, Dd
Raccoon Ford, 57, Cd
Race, C., 45A, Ga
Radcot Bridge, 27, Ee
Raddenore (Radnor), 13, Cd
Radicofani, 23B, Cc
Radimiches, 9, Jb
Radnor, 27, Cd
Radom, 31, Pc; 39, Pc
Radstadt, 21, Ke
Radzyn, 51, Ec
Raeburnfoot, 3A, Ca
Rageneia (Rayleigh), 13, Ge
Raglan, 48A, Bd
Ragnit, 26, Fb
Ragusa, 39, Ng; 78, Bd
Ragusa, eccl. prov., 22, Fc
Ragusa, Rep. of, 54, Fd
Rain, 29A, Da
Rainy, R., 70, Ec
Rais, 17, Ee; 30, Ce
Raisin, R., 71C, Bb
Rajahahan, 59B
Rajahmundry, 92, Ed
Rajasthan, 92, Cb
Rajkot, 92, Cc
Rajputana, 73, Bb
Rakka, 18A, Fb
Rakonitz, 39, Kc
Ralick Is., 75, Fd
Ralph, 12, Dc
Ramadi, 93, Ec
Ramah, 71, Hb
Ramesyg (Ramsey), 13, Fd
Ramillies, 46A, Dd
Ramle, 18C, Bg
Ramleh, 6A, Ab
Rammekens, 46A, Cc
Ramnagar, 73, Ba
Rampur, 73, Cb
Ramree I., 90, Ac
Rann, The, 73, Bc
Rannoch, L., 49A, Bb
Rannoch Moor, 49A, Bb
Rapa I., 75, Hf
Rapallo, 32A, Cb
Raphoe, 15, Db
Rappahannock, R., 57, Cd
Rapperswyl, 29B, Ca
Rappoltstein, 39B, Db
Raquette, R., 57, Da
Rarotonga, 75, Gf
Ras el Ain, 6A, Ab
Rasgrad, 78, Fd
Rasławice, 51, Dc

Rastatt, 29A, Ca
Rat Portage, 70, Ec
Ratack Is., 75, Fd
Ratae (Leicester), 3A, Ed
Rathfarnham, 49B, Ec
Rathlin I., 15, Ea
Rathmines, 49B, Ec
Rathmore, 37B, Ec
Rathmullan, 49B, Da
Ratibor, 21, Nc
Ratisbon, 8A, Db
Ratisbon (Regensburg), 10, Ed
Ratzeburg, 22, Ea; 30, Jb
Ravenglass, 48B, Bb
Ravenna, 5, Db; 23B, Cb
Ravenna, eccl. prov., 22, Ec
Ravensberg, Co. of, 30, Hb
Ravensburg, 20, He; 30, He
Ravenscar, 3A, Fb
Ravenspur, 27, Gc
Ravenstein, 46A, Ec
Ravi, R., 73, Ba
Rawa, 21, Pc
Rawalpindi, 73, Ba
Rawson (Chubut), 68, Cg
Raymond, 72C, Aa
Raymond of Toulouse, 16, Fd
Ré, I. de, 17, Ee
Reading, England, 27, Fe
Reading, Massachusetts, 57, Cc
Reate, 5, Dc
Recife (Pernambuco), 68, Fc
Recklinghausen, 20, Gc
Reculver, 7B, Dc
Red, R., Canada, 70, Ec
Red, R., U.S.A., 70, Ed
Red River Colony, 70, Ec
Red Russia, 50, Ed
Red Sea, 6, Ec; 25, Cd
Redarians, 10, Eb
Redesdale, 13, Da; 28B, Cb
Redinges (Reading), 13, Ee
Redinha, 63, Ab
Redstone (Fort Burd), 57, Bc
Ree, L., 15, Cb
Regensburg, 8, Eb; 31B, Cb
Reggio (Rhegium), Bruttium, 5, Ee
Reggio (Rhegium), Lombardy, 5, Cb
Reggio, eccl. prov., 22, Fd
Regina, 70, Db
Regni, 3A, Ff
Regulbium (Reculver), 3A, He
Rehdaniya, 33A, Dd
Rei, 19, Je
Reichenau, 22, Db
Reichenbach, 33C, Ca
Reigate, 27, Fe
Reims, 11, Fb; 83A, Db
Reims, eccl. prov., 22, Cb
Remagen, 20, Gc
Remington, 57, Cd
Remiremont, 39B, Cb
Rendsburg, 38, Ha; 65F, Aa
Renfrew, 14, Ed
Renfrew, co., 37A, Bc
Rennel, 77, Kd
Rennes, 11, Cb
Reno, R., 5, Cb; 29A, Dc
Rense, 30, Gc
Rensselaerwyk, 45B, Cb
Requena, 63, Ec
Rerigonius Sinus, 3A, Ba
Resaca, 72A, Aa
Resht, 93, Fb
Resino, 22, Fc
Resolution I., 71, Ha
Rethel, 20, Fd; 31A, Cc
Rethel, Co. of, 30, Kc; 38, Jc
Retford, 27, Fc; 48A, Cc
Réunion, 69A, Mf
Reuss, 39C, Cc
Reuss, Co. of, 30, Kc; 38, Jc
Reuss, R., 29B, Ca
Reutlingen, 20, Hd
Reval, 26, Gb; 54, Ga
Revesby, 36, Fd
Rewah, 73, Dc
Reykjavik, 88, Aa
Reynosa, 63, Ca
Rha, R., 1, Gc
Rhaetia, 2, Fd; 8, Db
Rhætian Alps, 29A, Cb
Rhætian Leagues (Grisons), 29B, Db
Rhagae, 1, Hd
Rhayader, 28A, Cb
Rhegium (Reggio), Bruttium, 5, Ee
Rhegium (Reggio), Lombardy, 5, Cb
Rheinau, 29B, Ca
Rheinberg, 46A, Fc
Rheinfelden, 29A, Bb
Rhenus, R., 2, Ed
Rhine, R., 10, Bc; 46A, Db
Rhine, Confederation of the, 62, Ec
Rhine Prov., 60B, Ac
Rhineland, 83A, Da
Rhodanus, R., 2, De
Rhode Island, 45B, Dc

Rhodes, 78, Gg
Rhodes Drift, 81A, Cb
Rhodesia, 81A, Da; 96D, Ef
Rhodesia and Nyasaland, Federation of, 96D, Ef
Rhodope, 9, Gd; 50, Ee
Rhodri Mawr, Pr. of, 7C, Bb
Rhodus, 2, Jf
Rhône, R., 11, Fd; 30, Ff
Rhos, 13, Cc
Rhuddlan, 27, Cc
Rhufoniog, 13, Cc
Riade, 10, Ec
Ribacoa, 23D, Bb
Ribagorza, 23C, Fa
Ribble, R., 27, Dc
Ribe, 12, Gc; 65F, Aa
Riccall, 12, Dc
Richard's Castle, 28A, Db
Richelieu, 47, Cc; 53, Dd
Richelieu, R., 45A, Ca
Richmond, Canada, 57, Ea
Richmond, Natal, 81D, Bb
Richmond, Surrey, 48B, Cd
Richmond, Virginia, 57, Ce
Richmond, Yorkshire, 27, Eb
Ried, 65B, Bb
Rieneck, 53, Hb
Rienzi, House of, 5A
Rier, R., 81B, Cb
Rieti, 32C, Dc
Rieux, 22, Cc
Riez, 22, Dc
Riga, 26, Fb
Riga, eccl. prov., 22, Ga
Riga, G. of, 26, Fb
Rimini (Ariminum), 5, Db
Rincoede (Ringwood), 13, Ef
Ringgold Is., 75C, Ca
Rio Branco, 94, Df
Rio Branco, prov., 68, Cb
Rio de Janeiro, 68, Ee
Rio de la Hacha, 43A, Ec
Rio de Oro, 80A, Bb
Rio Grande, 68, Df
Rio Grande (Bravo del Norte), R., 43A, Bb
Rio Grande (Magdalena), R., 43A, Ed
Rio Grande, R., Central America, 43A, Dc
Rio Grande do Norte, prov., 68, Fc
Rio Grande do Sul (San Pedro do Rio Grande), 41B, Dg
Rio Grande do Sul, prov., 68, De
Rio Pardo, 68, De
Rio Pecos, R., 70, Dd
Rio Salado, 23D, Bd
Rioja, 23C, Da
Riom, 17, Gf; 20, Ef
Ripa, R. (Ribble), 18, Dc
Ripoll, 22, Cc
Ripon, 27, Eb
Ripuarians, 8b, Ca
Ripuarii, 2, Ec
Ripun (Ripon), 13, Eb
Risaiyeh, 93, Eb
Risti, 22, Ec
Ristovatz, 78, Cd
Ritzebüttel, 30, Hb; 38, Hb
Riva, 20, Jf; 32D, Bb
Rivaulx, 36, Ec
River Cess, 96B, Bb
Riversdale, 81A, Bd
Riviera, 29A, Cc
Rivière du Loup, 45A, Da
Rivoli, Piedmont, 29A, Bc
Rivoli, Veneto, 29A, Dc
Riyadh, 93, Fe
Rjörneborg, 26, Fa
Roanne, 38, Fe
Roanoke, 70, Gd
Roanoke I., 45B, Bf
Roanoke, R., 45A, Bc
Roanoke Sd., 55B, Cc
Robe, R., 15, Bc
Robert of Flanders, 16, Ed
Robertson, 37A, Bb
Robertsport, 96B, Ab
Robogdium Prom., 3A, Aa
Roca, C. da, 63, Ac
Rocca San Casiano, 32E, Ba
Roccasecca, 32A, Ed
Roche, 36, Ed
Rochefort, 30, Cf; 53, Ce
Rochefoucauld, 53, De
Rochester, 27, Ge
Rochester, bp., 36, Gf
Rochingeham (Rockingham), 13, Fd
Rochlitz, 39, Kc; 39C, Cb
Rockhampton, 77, If
Rockhill, 57, Af
Rockingham, 27, Fd
Rockingham B., 77, He
Rockingham Forest, 3A, Fd
Rocky Mount, 57D, Aa
Rocky Mts., 70, Bb
Rocourt, 46A, Ed

Rocroy, 38, Fd
Rodemackern, 39B, Ca
Rodez, 11, Ed
Rodney and de Grasse, 55B, De
Rodosto, 8, Hc; 78, Fe
Roebuck B., 77, Ce
Roelant (Rhuddlan), 13, Cc
Roer, R., 83A, Da
Roeskilde, 26, Db
Rogaland, 12, Fb
Roger's Rock, 57, Eb
Roggeveld. 81B, Bc
Rohan, 17, Dd
Rohilkhand, 73, Cb
Roleca, 63, Ac
Rolla, 72, Bb
Röm, 65F, Aa
Roma (Rome), 2, Fe; 5, Dd
Romagna, 20, Jf; 32A, Ec
Roman Empire, 1, Dc; 4A, Jd
Roman Empire (under Syagrius), 2A, Bb
Romaniola, 23B, Cb
Rome (Roma), 5, Dd
Rome, U.S.A., 72A, Aa
Rome, eccl. prov., 22, Ec
Romenel (Romney), 13, Gf
Romesey (Romsey), 13, Ef
Romney, 27, Gf
Romsey, 36, Eg
Roncaglia, 10, Cf; 20, Hf
Roncesvalles, 8, Bc; 22, Bc
Roncesvalles Pass, 63, Ea
Ronciglione, 39, Kg
Ronda, 23C, Cd; 63, Cd
Rondonia, 68, Cd
Roosebeke, 28D, Da
Roraima, 68B, Aa
Rorke's Drift, 81A, Dc; 81D, Bb
Rosa, Mte., 29A, Bc; 29B, Bc
Rosario, 68, Cf
Rosas, 63, Ga
Roscommon, 15, Cc
Roscommon, co., 37C; 49B, Dd
Roscrea, 37B, Dd; 49B, Dd
Rose Castle, 28B, Bc
Roseires, 80B, Ae
Rosellae, 5B, Ab
Rosemarkie, bp., 14A, Bb
Rosenheim, 53, Kd
Rosetta, 6A, Ab; 80B, Aa
Roskilde, 12, Hc
Rosheim, 39B, Db
Rosnay, 11, Fb
Rosoy, 38, Ed
Ross, England, 27, De
Ross, Ireland, 15, Be
Ross, co., 37A, Bb
Ross, dist., 14, Db
Ross Dependency, 95, Kj
Ross Sea, 69C
Rossano, 22, Fd
Rossbach, 60A, Cc
Rosslyn, 36, Cb
Rostock, 21, Ka; 22, Ea
Rostov (-on-Don), 19, Fc; 79, Ga
Rostov, Suzdal, 19, Fa
Rosyth, 84, Ba
Roteland (Rutland), 13, Fd
Rothbury, 28B, Db
Rothenburg, 20, Jd; 60A, Eb
Rothesay, 37A, Bc
Rotterdam, 46A, Dc
Rotterdam, I., 42B
Rottweil, 20, Hd; 30, Hd
Rotuma I., 75, Fe
Roubaix, 83A, Ba
Roucy, 20, Ed; 30, Ed
Rouecestre (Rochester), 13, Ge
Rouen, 11, Db; 83A, Ab
Rouen, eccl. prov., 22, Cb
Rouergue, Co. of, 11, Ed; 28C, De
Rough Castle, 3A, Ca
Roundway Down, 48A, Cd
Rouses Pt., 57, Ea
Roussillon, Co. of, 11, Ee
Rouvray, 28D, Cb
Roveredo, 32D, Bb
Rovereto, 38, Jf; 86B, Bb
Rovigno, 23B, Db; 32B, Db
Rovigo, 32D, Bb
Rovno, 84, Hb
Rowley, 45B, Db
Rowton, 48B, Bc
Roxburgh, 14, Fd
Roxburgh, co., 37A, Cc; 49A, Cc
Roxbury, 56B
Roxolani, 1, Fc
Royal Niger Company, 80A, Dc
Royal Palace, Jerusalem, 18D
Royale, I. (Cape Breton I.), 45A, Ea
Royan, 38, Cf
Roye, 20, Ed; 81A, Bb
Ruapehu, 77, Ni
Rub al Khali, 93, Gf

Rueda, 63, Cb
Rufford, 36, Ed
Rudolf, L., 80A, Gd
Rudolstadt, 30, Jc; 39C, Bc
Rügen I., 10, Ea
Rügenwalde, 31, Ma
Rugii, 2, Fc; 2, Hd
Ruhr, R., 10, Bc
Rullion Green, 49A, Cc
Rum, I., 14. Bc
Rum, Seljuk Sultanate of (Iconium), 16, Je
Rum or Iconium, King. of, 18A, Fb
Rumania, 78, Ec
Rumelia, 50, Ee
Runcorn, 7C, Bb
Runnymede, 27, Fe
Rupel, 86A, Ea
Rupel Pass, 19, Cd
Rupert, R., 70, Gb
Rupert's Land, 45A, Ba; 70, Fb
Ruphia, R., 78, Cg
Ruppin, 21, Kb
Ruremonde, 46A, Ec
Rus, King. of, 16, Jb
Ruschuk, 78, Ed
Russell, 77A
Russia, 26, Hb; 34, Ja
Russia, Prs. of, 19, Ga
Russian Central Asia, 83, Mc
Russian Empire, 62, Hb; 74, Gc
Russian Soviet Federal Socialist Rep., 84, Lb
Russian States, 24, Kb
Rustenburg, 81A, Cc
Rutba, 93, Ec
Ruthenian, 85, Gc
Rutherglen, 49A, Bc
Ruthin, 27, Cc
Ruthven, 37A, Cb
Ruthwell, 7B, Ba
Rutland, 27, Fd
Rutli, 29B, Cb
Rüttgen, 39B, Ca
Rutupiae (Richborough), 3A, He
Rwanda, 96D, Ee
Ryazan, 19, Fb; 88, Nc
Rye, 13, Gf; 27, Gf
Rye (Little Harbour), 45B, Db
Ryknield Way, 3A, Ed
Rymnik, 61, Ae
Ryswyk, 46A, Db
Ryukyu Is., 91, Fd
Rzeszow, 26, Fc
Rzhev, 61, Dc; 88, Mb

SAALE, R., 10, Dc; 39C, Bb
Saalfeld, 20, Jc; 39C, Bc
Saanen, 29B, Bb
Saar, R., 39B, Ca; 83A, Db
Saar Basin, 83A, Db
Saarbrücken, 10, Bd; 83A, Db
Saareguemines, 83A, Db
Saaremaa, 87, Ea
Saarlonis, 53, Gc; 76A, Db
Saarumon, 76A, Db
Saarwerden, 39B, Db
Saaz, 21, Kc
Saba. 43A, Fc
Sabah, 91, Ef
Sabancuy, 43A, Cc
Sabina, 32A, Ec
Sabina, bp., 22A
Sabine, 72, Bd
Sabine, R., 72, Bc
Sabine Cross Roads, 72, Bc
Sabinensis, 83A, Db
Sabino, 45B, Eb
Sable, C., Florida, 70, Fe
Sable, C., Nova Scotia, 45A, Db
Sable I., 71, Jc
Sabrina Aest. (Severn), 3A, Ce
Sabugal, 63, Bb
Sachsenburg, 53, Kd
Sacile, 29A, Ec
Säckingen, 22, Db; 29B, Ba
Saco, 45B, Db
Saco, R., 45B, Db
Sacramento, California, 70, Bd
Sacramento, Uruguay, 42, Gf
Sacramento, R., 70, Bd
Sada, 6, Fd
Sadowa, 60B, Ec
Saffarids, King. of, 6B, Hb
Sagan, 31, Lc; 39, Lc
Saginaw B., 45A, Ab
Sagitta (Sidon), 18C, Ce
Sagona, 20, Hg
Sagres, 35, Jc
Saguenay, R., 45A, Ca
Sahagun, 22, Ac; 63, Ca
Sahara, 80A, Db
Saharanpur, 92, Db
Saigon, 90, Bc
Saigon-Cholon, 91, De
Sailors Creek, 72B, Ab
Saimatsci, 76B, Ca

St. Achebrannus, 13, Af
St. Aignan, 53, Dd
St. Albans, 27, Fe
St. Amand, 46A. Cd; 46B
St. Amand-Montrond, 38, Ee
St. Andrew I., 43A, Dc
St. Andrews, 14, Fc; 37, Cb
St. Andrews, bp., 14A, Cb; 36, Db
St. Angelo, Castle of, 5A
St. Anne, Church of, 18D
St. Anns, 43A, Ec
St. Antonin, 38, Df
St. Asaph, 27, Cc
St. Asaph, bp., 36, Ce
St. Augustine, 72, Dd
St. Austell, 48B, Ad
St. Avold, 76A, Db
St. Bartholomew, 43A, Fc
St. Bees, 36, Cc
St. Benedictus de Holme (St. Benedict's Abbey), 13, Hd
St. Bernard, Hospice of, 22, Db
St. Berrione (St. Buryan), 13, Af
St. Bertrand, 38, Dg
St. Blazey, 48B, Ad
St. Brieuc, 11, Bb
St. Carentochus (Crantock), 13, Af
St. Cast, 55A, Bd
St. Charles, 56, Ac
St. Charles, R., 56A
St. Christopher, 43B, Dc; 55B, De
St. Clair, 45A, Ab
St. Clair, L., 45A, Ab
St. Claude, 20, Fe
St. Croix, R., 45A, Da; 56, Fa
St. Cuthbertes-Lond, 13, Eb
St. David's, 27, Ae
St. David's, bp., 36, Ce
St. Denis, France, 22, Cb
St. Denis, Louisiana, 56, Bc
St. Dié, 22, Db; 83B, Ba
St. Dizier, 76A, Cb
St. Edmundi (Bury St. Edmunds), 13, Gd
St. Elias, C., 71A, Ca
St. Elias, Mt., 71B, Aa
St. Eustatius, 43A, Fc
St. Fargeau, 20, Ee
St. Flour, 20, Ef; 22, Cc
St. Francis, L., Quebec, 57C, Bb
St. Francis, L., St. Lawrence R., 57, Da
St. Francis, R., 71E, Bb
St. Francis de Sales Mission, 45A, Ca
St. Gall, 10, Ce; 29B, Da
St. Gallen, 29B, Da
St. Geneviève, 56, Ac
St. George (Lydda), 18C, Bg
St. George, Str. of, 18E
St. George's B., 45A, Bd
St. Germain, 53, Dc; 84, Cc
St. Germain, C., 45A, Fa
St. Germans, 36, Bg
St. Germanus, 13, Bf
St. Giles, 27A
St. Gilles, Languedoc, 20, Fg
St. Gilles, Poitou, 53, Cd
St. Goar, 22, Da
St. Gotthard, 29A, Gb; 33C, Db
St. Gotthard Pass, 29B, Cb
St. Helena, 40, Je; 96C, Bf
St. Helena B., 81B, Ac
St. Helens, 55A, Cc
St. Hyacinthe, 57, Ea
St. Ignace Mission, 45A, Aa
St. Ives, Cornwall, 55A, Ac
St. Ives, Hunts, 13, Fd; 48A, Cc
St. Jacob, 30, Ge
St. James Church, Jerusalem, 18D
St. Jean, I. de, (Prince Edward I.), 45A, Ea
St. Jean d'Angely, 20, Cf
St. Jean de Luz, 63, Ea
St. Jean de Maurienne, 11, Gd
St. Jean Pied de Port, 30, Cg; 63, Ea
St. Jehan, I., 45A, Da
St. John, 45A, Da
St. John, Hospital of, 18D
St. John, I., 43A, Fc
St. John, L., 71, Gc
St. John, R., 45A, Da; 71E, Cc
St. John the Baptist, Church of, 18D
St. John's (San Juan), 56, Cd
St. John's, Newfoundland, 45A, Ga
St. Johns, Quebec, 56, Ea
St. John's R., 43A, Da
St. Joseph, 72, Bb
St. Jullian, B. de, 45A, Fa

St. Kitts, 43A, Fc
St. Lawrence, G. of, 45A, Ea
St. Lawrence I., 71A, Aa
St. Lawrence, R., 45A, Da; 57, Da
St. Lazaro Arch. (Philippines), 40, Qd
St. Lizier, 11, De
St. Lo, 22, Bb; 28C, Bb
St. Louis (Senegal), 81C, Aa
St. Louis, Missouri, 56, Ac; 57A, Ab
St. Louis, W. Africa, 80A, Bc; 96C, Ac
St. Loys, C., 45A, Ea
St. Lucia, 43A, Db
St. Lucia B., 81D, Bb
St. Lucia, I., 43A, Fc; 43C, Ec
St. Maixent, 22, Bd; 38, Ce
St. Malo, 20, Cd; 28C, Ab
St. Maria in Mt. Zion, 18D
St. Marie, 80A, Hf
St. Marks, 71F, Ca; 72, Dc
St. Martin, 43A, Fc
St. Martin, C., 81B, Ac
St. Martin, Church of, 18D
St. Mary Magdalen, Church of, 18D
St. Mary's (Santa Maria), 56, Cd
St. Mary's, Canada, 45A, Ba; 56, Db
St. Mary's, Maryland, 45B, Ad
St. Mary's Hospital, 18D
St. Maur, 30, Ed
St. Maurice, R., 57C, Aa
St. Michael (St. Michael's Mount), 13, Af
St. Michael, Alaska, 71A, Aa
St. Mihiel, 83A, Cb
St. Moritz, 29B, Ab
St. Neots, 36, Fe
St. Neotus, 13, Bf
St. Omer, 22, Ca; 46A, Bd
St. Osyth, 36, Hf
St. Paul, France, 22, Cc; 53, Fe
St. Paul, Minnesota, 70, Ec
St. Pauls, 27A
St. Peter, Church of, Jerusalem, 18D
St. Peter's, Rome, 5A
St. Petersburg, 51, Gb; 61, Dc
St. Philippe, 56, Be
St. Pieranus (St. Piran), 13, Af
St. Pierre, 45A, Fa
St. Pierre, L., 57C, Aa
St. Pol, 46A, Bd
St. Pol, prov., 46A, Bd
St. Pol de Leon, 17, Cd
St. Pölten, 21, Ld
St. Probus (Probus), 13, Bf
St. Quentin, 11, Eb; 83A, Bb
St. Regis, 57, Da
St. Riquier, 17, Gc
St. Sauveur, 45A, Db
St. Seurin, 22, Bc
St. Sever, 22, Cc
St. Simon's I., 56, Cd
St. Sophia, 18E
St. Stephen's Gate, 18D
St. Symeon (Seleucia), 18C, Cb
St. Thomas, 43A, Fc
St. Thomas' Tomb, 35, Od
St. Trond, 22, Da; 46A, Ed
St. Urban, 29B, Ba
St. Vaast, 22, Ca; 28C, Bb
St. Valery en Caux, 55A, Dd
St. Valery sur Somme, 28C, Ca
St. Veit, 21, Le
St. Vincent, 80A, Ac
St. Vincent, C., 63, Ad
St. Vincent, I., 43A, Fc
Ste. Foy, 38, Df
Ste. Katherine, 45A, Ga
Saintes, 11, Cd; 30, Cf
Saintonge, 38, Cf
Saintonge, Co. of, 11, Cd
Saipan, 75, Ed
Sajits, King. of, 6B, Fa
Sakaba, 93, Ec
Sakaria, R., 86C, Ba
Sakas, 1, Ke
Sakhalin, 91, Ha
Saladin and the Ayubites, Empire of, 18A, Ee
Salado, R., N. Argentina, 68, Ce
Salado, R., S. Argentina, 68, Cf
Salamanca, 23C, Cb; 63, Cb
Salamis, 9, Je
Salawati, 52C, Db; 77, Eb
Salces, 23D, Ga; 53, Ef
Saldanha, 61, Hd
Saldanha B., 81B, Ac
Salem (Naumkeag), 45B, Db
Salem (Varkinskil), 45B, Bd
Salem, India, 59C, Ce
Salem, Massachusetts, 57, Fb
Salem, Oregon, 70, Bc

Salemi, 32C, De
Salerno (Salernum), 5, Ed
Salerno, D. of, 23A, Ec
Salerno, Pr. of, 21A, Cb
Salernum (Salerno), 5, Ed
Salians, 8B, Ba
Salii, 2, Ec
Salinae (Droitwich), 3A, Dd
Salinesville, 72, Da
Salins, 20, Fe; 31A, Cd
Salisbury, England, 27, Ee
Salisbury, New Hampshire, 45B, Db
Salisbury, North Carolina, 57, Af
Salisbury, Rhodesia, 81A, Da
Salisbury, bp., 36, Ef
Salm, Alsace, 20, Gd
Salm, Luxemburg, 20, Fc
Salm, king., 65B, Aa
Salmon Falls, 45B, Db
Salo, 29A, Dc
Salobrena, 23C, Dd
Salom, 2A, Cb
Salona, Dalmatia, 23B, Fc
Salona, Greece, 19, Ce
Salonae, 2, Ge
Salonica, 78, De
Salonica, G. of, 86A, Db
Salonica, King. of, 19, Ce
Salsette L., 73, Bd
Salt Lake City, 70, Cc
Salt Lakes, 59B
Salta, 68, Ce
Saltillo, 43A, Bb
Saluda, R., 57D, Aa
Saluzzo, 32A, Bb
Saluzzo, Marq. of, 32A, Bb
Salvador, 43D, Dc
Salvador (Bahia), 68, Fd
Salvatierra, 28C, Cb
Salween, R., 25, Jd; 73, Gc
Salza, 20, Jc
Salzach, R., 29A, Eb
Salzburg, 10, Be
Salzburg, eccl. prov., 22, Eb
Salzburg, Abp. of, 31, Ke
Salzwedel, 10, Db; 26, Dc
Samana, C., 43A, Fc
Samandar, 9, Md
Samanids, King. of, 6B, Ha
Samar, 75E, Cb
Samara, 61, Hd
Samarkand, 6, Hb; 25, Fc
Samarra, 6A, Cb; 9, Lf
Sambre, R., 46A, Dd
Samoa, 90, Fd
Samoa Is., 83, Ae
Samogitia, 26, Fb
Samos, I., 78, Fg
Samos, theme, 9, He
Samosata, 8, Kd
Samothrace, 78, Ee
Samsun, 19, Fd; 93, Da
San, R., 19, Cb
San Agostino, 5A
San Ambrosio, 68, Be
San Antonio, 70, Be
San Antonio Bay, 44, Ef
San Antonio, C., 43A, Db
San Bernardino Str., 75E, Bb
San Blas, G. of, 43A, Ed
San Cesareo, 5A
San Christobal, 43A, Cc
San Clemente, 5A
San Cosmo y Damiano, 22, Ac
San Cristoval, 77, Kd
San Daniele, 32D, Ca
San Diego, 70, Cd
San Domingo, 43A, Fc
San Domingo, st., 43A, Ec
San Felipe, Chile, 68, Bf
San Felipe, Venezuela, 43A, Fc
San Felix, 68, Ae
San Fernando, Philippines, 75E, Ba
San Fernando, Venezuela, 68, Cb
San Francisco, 70, Bd
San Germano, 23B, Dd
San Geronimo, 43A, Ba
San Geronimo de Yuste, 22, Ac
San Gimignano, 32E, Bb
San Giovanni, 29A, Cc
San Grisogono, 5A
San Ildefonso, 63, Db
San Jorge, G. de, 68, Cg
San José, 43A, Fc
San Juan (St. John's), 56, Cd
San Juan, Argentina, 68, Cf
San Juan, Mexico, 43A, Bb
San Juan, Porto Rico, 43A, Fc
San Juan de la Peña, 22, Bc
San Juan de los Remedios, 43A, Eb
San Juan de Nicaragua, 43A, Dc
San Juan de Ulloa, 43A, Cc
San Leopoldo, 68, De

San Lorenzo del Escorial, 22, Bc
San Lorenzo Fuori le Mura, 5A
San Lorenzo in Damaso, 5A
San Lorenzo in Lucina, 5A
San Lucas, Mexico, 43A, Bb
San Lucas, Spain, 23C, Bd
San Lucas, C., 43A, Ab
San Luis, Argentina, 42, Ge
San Luis, Brazil, 68, Cf
San Luis, Texas, 43A, Ca
San Luis de Caceres, 68, Dd
San Luis Potosi, 43A, Bb
San Marco, 21A, Dc; 22, Fd
San Marino, 32A, Ec
San Martin, Mexico, 43A, Bb
San Martin, Spain, 22, Cd
San Miguel de Piura, 41B, Bd
San Miniato, 32E, Bb
San Nicolas, 68, Cf
San Pablo, L., 40, Ce
San Pedro do Rio Grande (Rio Grande do Sul), 41B, Dg
San Pietro, 5A
San Prassede, 5A
San Quattro Coronati, 5A
San Rafael, 68, Cf
San Roque, 63A
San Salvador, 43A, Dc
San Salvador, I., 43A, Eb
San Salvador de Bahia, 41B, Fe
San Sebastian, Colombia, 43A, Ed
San Sebastian, Spain, 63, Ea
San Sepolcro, 32E, Cb
San Severina, 22, Fd
San Silvestro, 5A
San Sisto, 5A
San Stefano, Rome, 5A
San Stefano, Turkey, 78, Ge
San Susanna, 5A
San Thomé, 43B, Dd
San Vito, 32D, Cb; 86B, Cb
San Xavier, 43A, Ca
San Zoilo, 22, Bc
Sana, 6, Fd; 93, Ef
Sanandaj, 93, Fb
Sancerre, 17, Ge
Sand, R., 81A, Cb
Sandakan, 95, Ne
Sandal, 27, Ec
Sandalwood I. (Sumba), 52C, Bc
Sanday, 49A, Ca
Sandec, 31, Pd
Sandomir, 31, Pc
Sandusky, 71C, Bb
Sandwic (Sandwich), 13, He
Sandwich, England, 7B, Dc
Sandwich, Massachusetts, 45B, Dc
Sandwich, Michigan Terr., 71C, Bb
Sandwich Is., Antarctic Ocean, 69C
Sandwich Is., Pacific Ocean, 42, Bc
Sandy Hook, 57B
Sangarius, R., 19, Ed
Sangir Is., 52C, Ca
Sanguessa, 63, Ea
Sanquhar, 49A, Cc
Sansanne-Mango, 96B, Ca
Santa Agata, 5A
Santa Balbina, 5A
Santa Barbara, 43A, Bb
Santa Barbara Is., 42, Cc
Santa Catalina, 56, Cd
Santa Catarina, 68, Ee
Santa Catarina, st., 68, De
Santa Cecilia, 5A
Santa Croce, 5A
Santa Cruz, Argentina, 68, Ch
Santa Cruz, Bolivia, 68, Cd
Santa Cruz, Brazil, 41B, Fe
Santa Cruz, Canary Is., 55B, Jd
Santa Cruz, I., Pacific Ocean, 77, Ld
Santa Cruz, I., West Indies, 43A, Fc
Santa Elena B., 43D, Dc
Santa Fé, Argentina, 68, Cf
Santa Fé, Florida, 56, Cd
Santa Fé, New Mexico, 70, Dd
Santa Fé, Spain, 22, Bd
Santa Fé de Bogota, 41B, Bc
Santa Isabel, 68, Cc
Santa Lucia B., 80A Gg
Santa Maura, 68, Dc
Santa Maria (St. Mary's), 56, Cd
Santa Maria in Trastevere, 5A
Santa Maria Maggiore, 5A
Santa Marta, 43A, Bb
Santa Maura, 50, Ef
Santa Prisca, 5A
Santa Rosa, 43A, Bb
Santa Sabina, 5A
Santander, 23C, Da; 63, Da

Santarem, Brazil, 68, Dc
Santarem, Portugal, 63, Ac
Santarem, W. Africa, 35, Kd
Santas Creus, 22, Cc
Santee, R., 45A, Bd; 57D, Bb
Santiago, Chile, 68, Bf
Santiago, San Domingo, 43A, Ec
Santiago, Spain, 63, Aa
Santiago, eccl prov., 22, Ac
Santiago de Compostella, 8, Ac; 22, Ac; 23D, Aa
Santiago de Cuba, 43A, Ec
Santorin, 78, Eg
Santos, 68, Ee
Sao Borja, 68, De
Sao Francisco, 68, Ee
Sao Francisco, R., 68, Ec
Sao José de Rio Negro, 41B, Dd
Sao Luis (Maranhao), 68, Ec
Sao Manuel, 68, Dc
Sao Paulo, 68, Ee
Sao Paulo, st., 68, Ee
Sao Tomé, 80A, Dd
São Vicente, Brazil, 41B, Ef
São Vicente, Portugal, 22, Ad
Saône, R., 11, Fc; 20, Fe
Sapporo, 91, Hb
Saragossa, 23C, Eb; 63, Eb
Saragossa, eccl. prov., 22, Bc
Sarai, 19, Hc; 25, Db; 61, Ge
Sarajevo, 39, Ng; 78, Bd
Saranac, R., 57, Da
Sarandi, 68, Df
Sarangani B., 75E, Cc
Saratoga, 57, Eb
Saratov, 61, Gd
Sarawak, 91, Ef
Sardes, 9, He
Sardica, 4B, Hc; 8, Gc
Sardinia, 5, Bd
Sardinia, King. of, 32B, Ad
Sardis, 18A, Db
Sarepta, 18C, Ce
Sargans, 29B, Da
Sargans, canton, 29B, Db
Sari Bair, 86D
Sarikamish, 86C, Da
Sarisberie (Salisbury), 13, Ee
Sark, 17, Dd
Sarkel, 9, Kc
Sarlat, 20, Df
Sarmatia, 1, Fb
Sarnem, 29B, Cb
Sarnthal Alps, 86B, Ba
Saros, G. of, 86D
Saros-Patak, 33C, Eb
Sarrebourg, 83B, Ba
Sarthe, R., 11, Cc
Sarukham, 33A, Cc
Sarum, 7A, Cb
Sarzana, 22, Dc; 32E, Aa
Saskatchewan, 70, Db
Sassbach, 29A, Ca
Satara, 73, Bd
Satpura Mts., 73, Cc
Saucourt, 9, Cb
Saudi Arabia, 93, Ed; 96D, Gb
Sauer, R., 83A, Dc
Saugerties, 56, Eb
Saugor, 73, Cc
Sault Ste. Marie, 45A, Aa
Saumur, 11, Cc
Saumurois, 53, Cd
Saurashtra, 1, Ke
Sauveterre, 38, Cg
Savage (Niue) I., 75, Ge
Savaii, 75B, Aa
Savana, 22, Ec
Savannah (Fort Prince George), 56, Cd
Savannah, Georgia, 56, Cd; 72, Dc
Savannah, Tenn., 72, Cb
Savannah, R., 56, Cd; 72, Dc
Save, R., 22, Fb; 78, Bc
Savona, 5, Bb
Savoy, 28C, Ed; 32A, Ab
Savoy, Co. of, 11, Fd; 20, Ff
Savoy, D. of, 32A, Bb
Sawantwari, 73, Bd
Sawley, 36, Dd
Saxe-Weimar, 51, Cc
Saxon States, 47, Eb
Saxones, 2, Ec
Saxonia, 12, Gc
Saxons, 4A, Ba; 7A, Fa
Saxony, 10, Cb; 63A, Dc
Saxony, Duchies of, 53, Jb
Saxony, Elec. of, 31, Kc
Say, 80A, Dc
Saybrook, 45B, Cc
Sayda, 39C, Dc
Sayn, 20, Gc
Sayn, Co. of, 30, Gc
Scalea, 21A, Cc
Scandalion, 18C, Ce
Scandia, 2, Fa
Scandinavia, 69B
Scania, 26, Db; 47, Ea
Scapa Flow, 55B, Ka; 84, Ba

Scarboro, 57, Fb
Scarborough, 3A, Fb; 27, Fb
Scardonia, 22, Fc
Scarpanto, 18B, Dc
Sceptesberie (Shaftsbury), 13, De
Schaffhausen, 29B, Ca; 65A, Ab
Schaffhausen, canton, 29B, Ca
Schärding, 21, Kd
Schässburg, 50, Ed
Schauenburg, 20, Hb
Schaumberg, 21, Kd
Scheidungen, 8B, Da
Schelde, R., 46A, Cd
Schemnitz, 31, Nd
Schenectady, 57, Eb
Schenk, 38, Gc
Schesel, 8, Ea
Schio, 86B, Bb
Schirmeck, 39B, Db
Schlei, R., 65F, Ba
Schleiz, 39C, Bc
Schleswig, 26, Cc; 65F, Aa
Schleswig, D., 30, Ha; 65F, Aa
Schleswig, M. of, 10, Ca
Schlettstadt, 20, Gd; 76A, Db
Schleusingen, 39C, Ac
Schmalkalden, 34, Eb
Schmölln, 39C, Cc
Schober Pass, 29A, Fb
Schönhausen, 60B, Cb
Schoodic Lakes, 71E, Bc
Schoonhoven, 46A, Dc
Schouwen, 46A, Cc
Schuylkill, R., 45B, Bc; 57, Dc
Schwarzburg, 39C, Ab
Schwarzburg, Pr., 38, Jc; 39C, Bc
Schwarzenberg, 39C, Cc
Schwarzenburg, 29B, Bb
Schwechat, 33C, Db
Schwedt, 39, Lb
Schweidnitz, 31, Mc; 39, Mc
Schweinfurt, 30, Jc; 38, Jc
Schwerin, 10, Db; 20, Jb
Schwerin, D., 38, Jb
Schwiebus, 39, Lb
Schwyz, 29B, Ca
Schwyz, canton, 29B, Ca
Scilly Is., 55B, Kb
Sciptone (Skipton), 18, Dc
Scireburne (Sherborne), 13, Df
Scireburne (Sherburn), 13, Ec
Sciropesberie (Shrewsbury, 13, Dd
Sciropescire (Shropshire), 13, Dd
Scituate, 45B, Db
Scone, 14, Ec
Scopia, 16, Gd
Scoti, 2, Bc
Scotland, 12, Cb; 34, Ba
Scots, 15, Eb
Scott, 28B, Cb
Scutari, 78, Ge; 86C, Aa
Scutari (Skodra), 78, Bd
Scyros, 78, Ef
Scythia, 1, Kb
Seaford, 27, Gf
Seattle, 70, Bc
Sebago L., 45B, Db
Sebaste, 18C, Cf
Sebastea, 8, Kd; 9, Ke
Sebenico, 31, Lg; 32A, Fc
Secessionville, 72, Dc
Seckau, 22, Eb
Second Cataract, 80B, Ac
Sedalia, 72, Bb
Sedan, 29A, Aa; 88, Fd
Sedberule (Sadbe ge), 13, Eb
Sedd el Bahr, 86D
Sedgemoor, 48B, Bd
Sées, 22, Cb
Segauli, 73, Eb
Segeberg, 22, Ea; 38, Jb
Segedunum (Wallsend), 3C
Segelocum (Littleborough), 3A, Fc
Segni, 22A
Segontium (Caernarvon), 3A, Bc
Segorbe, 22, Bd
Ségou, 96B, Ba
Segovia, 23D, Cb; 63, Cb
Segre, R., 20, Dd
Segu, 80A, Cc
Seilan (Ceylon), 25, Hf
Seine, R., 11, Db; 76A, Cb
Seistan (Sijistan), 6, Hb; 61B, Bb
Seisyllwg, 7C, Ab
Sekondi Takoradi, 96B, Bb
Selby, 36, Ed; 48A, Cc
Selenga, R., 91, Db
Seleucia, 8, Jd; 9, Ke
Seleucia (St. Symeon), 18C, Cb
Selgovae, 3A, Ca
Seljuk Empire, 16, Le
Seljuk Empire of Rum or Iconium, 18B, Ec

Seljuk Kingdom of Rum or Iconium, 19, Fe
Seljuk Turks, 24, Jf
Selkirk, Canada, 70, Eb
Selkirk, Scotland, 14, Fd
Selkirk, co., 37A, Cc
Selma, 72, Cc
Selsey, 7A, Cb; 36A
Selsey, diocese, 36A
Selwood, 7B, Bc
Selymbria, 19, Dd
Selz, 39B, Eb
Semarang, 91, Eg
Semendria, 78, Cc
Semeni, R., 86A, Ab
Semipalatinsk, 91, Ba
Semlin, 78, Cc
Semmering Pass, 29A, Fb
Semoy, R., 46A, Ee
Sempach, 29B, Ca
Sempringham, 36, Fe
Semur, 11, Fc; 30, Fe
Sendai, 91, Hc
Senecas, 45A, Bb
Seneffe, 46A, Dd
Senegal (St. Louis), 81C, Aa
Senegal, rep., 96, Ac
Senegal, terr., 81C, Bb
Senegal, R., 81C, Ba
Senez, 22, Dc
Senigallia, 39, Kg
Senlis, 11, Eb; 83A, Bb
Sennar, 80B, Ae
Senne, R., 46B
Senogalliae, 5B, Bb
Sens, 11, Eb; 17, Gd
Sens, eccl. prov., 22, Cb
Seoul, 91, Fc
Sept Iles, 45A, Da
Septimania, 4A, Cc; 8, Cc
Sequana, R., 2, Dd
Serai, 24, Md
Serampore, 59B
Serbia, 78, Cd
Serbia, King. of, 18B, Bb
Serbs, 9, Fd
Serdica, 2, He; 78A
Sereng, 78, De; 86A, Ea
Sereth, R., 50, Fd; 78, Fb
Sergipe, 68, Fd
Seringapatam, 73, Ce
Seriphos, 78, Eg
Serowe, 96C, Eg
Serpa, 23D, Bd
Serpent's Mouth, 43B, Dc
Serres, 38, Ff
Serrey, 60A, Ja
Servia, 9, Fd; 78, De
Servian Princes, 24, Ge
Seselitre (Seasalter), 13, He
Sesia, R., 29A, Cc
Sessa, 22, Ec
Seteia Aest., 3A., Cc
Setif, 8, Dd
Seton, clan, 28B, Ba; 37A, Cb
Setubal, 63, Ac
Sèvres, 84, Cc
Seward, 71A, Cb
Seychelles, 69A, Me; 94, Rf
Sfax, 89, Hg
Shackleton, 69C
Shaftesbury, 27, Df
Shahjahanpur, 73, Db
Sha-ho, R., 76B, Ba
Shan State, 92, Hc
Shanghai, 91, Fc
Shangtu, 25, Lb
Shannon, R., 15, Cc; 37B, Cc
Shap, 36, Dc; 49A, Cc
Shaqra, 93, Fg
Shari, R., 80A, Ed
Sharks B., 77, Af
Shashi, 74, Ke
Shatt el Hai, R., 86C, Ec
Shawnees, 45B, Bc; 56, Bc
Sheelin, L., 15, Dc
Sheen, 36, Ff
Sheerness, 54, Ce
Sheffield, 27, Ec; 48A, Cc
Shelburne, 71, Hc
Shenandoah, R., 57, Bd; 72B, Aa
Shendi, 80B, Ad
Shenyang (Mukden), 91, Fb
Sheppey, 7C, Dc
Sherborne, 27, Df; 36, Df
Sherborne, diocese, 36A
Sherbro I., 81C, Bc
Sherbrook, 57C, Bb
Sherbrooke, 71, Gc
Sherburn, 48B, Cc
Sheriffmuir, 37A, Cb
Sherman's March, 72, Dc

Sherwood, 7B, Cb
Sherwood Forest, 3A, Ec
Shetland Is., 12, Da; 34, Ba
Shibam, 93, Ff
Shiel, L., 49A, Bb
Shiliho, 76B, Ba
Shillong, 92, Gb
Shiloh, 72, Cb
Shipka Pass, 78, Ed
Shiraz, 6, Gc; 93, Gd
Shirley, 45B, Ae
Shiz, 6A, Da
Shoeburyness, 7C, Dc
Sholanghur, 59A, Ce
Sholapur, 73, Cd
Snoreditch, 27A
Shoreham, England, 27, Ff
Shoreham, Vermont, 57, Eb
Shoshong, 81A, Cb
Shreveport, 70, Ed; 72, Bc
Shrewsbury, England, 27, Dd
Shrewsbury, New Jersey, 45B, Bc
Shropshire, 27, Dd; 28A, Db
Shumla, 62, Hd; 78, Fd
Shuqra, 93, Fg
Shushan (Susa), 6A, Db
Siak, 75A, Ab
Sialkot, 73, Ba
Siam (Thailand), 74, Jg; 90, Bc
Siam, G. of, 91, Dc
Sian, 91, Dc
Sianfu, 74, Je
Siberia, 74, Jb; 83, Pa
Siberut, 91, Cg
Sibin (Hermannstadt), 19, Cc
Sibir, 25, Fa; 40, Na
Sibir, Khanate of, 25, Ga
Sibton, 36, He
Sicilia, 2, Ff
Sicily, 5, Df
Sicily, Co. of, 16, Ee
Sicily, King. of, 23B, Ed
Side, 19, Ee
Sidi Barrani, 93, Bc
Sidlaw Hills, 14, Ec
Sidnacester, 36A
Sidnacester, diocese, 36A
Sidon (Sagitta), 18C, Ce
Siegburg, 20, Gc
Siegen, 53, Hb; 83A, Ea
Siena, 5, Cb
Siena, Rep. of, 32A, Dc
Sieradz, 31, Nc
Sierra Leone, 81C, Bc
Sierra Madre, 43A, Bb
Siffin, 6A, Ba
Sigmaringen, 10, Cd; 60B, Cd
Sigüenza, 22, Bc
Siguiri, 96B, Ba
Sijistan (Seistan), 6, Hb
Sikhs, 59C, Ba
Si-Kiang, R., 91, Ed
Sikkim, 73, Eb; 92, Fb
Sikri, 52A, Bb
Silesia, 33C, Db
Silesia, D. of, 21, Mc
Silistra, 78, Fc
Silistria, 19, Dd
Sillery, 45A, Ca
Silos, 22, Bc
Silures, 3A, Ce
Silves, 22, Ad
Simancas, 23C, Cb
Simbach, 29A, Ea
Simbirsk, 61, Gd
Simcoe, L., 45A, Bb
Simeulve, 91, Cf
Simla, 73, Ca
Simnitza, 78, Ed
Simonstown, 81B, Ac
Simplon Pass, 29B, Cb
Sinai, 6A, Ba
Sinai Peninsula, 18A, Ed; 80B, Ab
Sinaloa, 43A, Bb
Sinclair, 37A, Ca
Sind, 1, Je; 73, Ab
Sindhia, 73, Cc
Singapore, 75A, Bb; 91, Df
Singapore, Str. of, 75A, Bb
Singara, 2, Mf
Singidunum, 4A, Gc
Sinigaglia, 8A, Dc; 32A, Ec
Sinkailin Pass, 76B, Ba
Sinkailin Pass, 76B, Ca
Sinkiang-Uigur, 91, Bc
Sinmintun, 76B, Ba
Sinope, 19, Fd; 79, Gb
Sinsheim, 29A, Ca
Sinus Arabicus, 1, Fe
Sinus Aualites, 1, Gf
Sinus Oxianus, 1, Hc
Sinus Persicus, 1, He
Sion, 11, Gc
Sion (Sitten), 29B, Bb
Siponto, 23B, Ed
Sirhind, 52A, Ba; 73, Ca
Sirji Arjengaon, 73, Cc
Sirmium, 2, Ge; 4A, Fc
Sis, 18C, Ca; 19, Fe
Siscia, 2, Gd

Sissek, 31, Mf; 33A, Aa
Sissonne, 83A, Bb
Sisteron, 22, Dc; 30, Ff
Sistova, 78, Ed
Sita, 19, Fa
Sitabaldi, 73, Cc
Sitcha, 61, De
Sitka, 71B, Cb
Sitka (New Archangel), 71A, Db
Sitten (Sion), 29B, Ba
Sitvatorok, 33C, Db
Siuyen, 76B, Ba
Sivas, 79, Gc
Siwah, 80A, Fb; 93, Bd
Siward, 12, Dc
Siwas, 16, Ke; 18A, Fb
Six Nations, 57, Cb
Sixth Cataract, 80B, Ad
Skagerrak, 12, Gb; 84, Da
Skagway, 71B, Cb
Skara, 26, Db
Skaw, The, 12, Gb
Skeena, R., 70, Bb
Skelleftea, 26, Fa
Skelton, 27, Fb
Skenesboro, 57, Eb
Skenfrith, 28A, Dc
Skeninge, 26, Db
Skhumbi, R., 78, Be
Skipsea, 13, Fc
Skipton, 27, Dc
Skiringssal, 12, Gb
Skodra (Scutari), 78, Bd
Skog, 50, Da
Skopije (Uskub), 78, Cd
Skreen, 15, Ec
Skumbi, R., 86A, Aa
Skye, 14, Bb
Slachter's Nek, 81A, Cd
Slane, 49B, Ec
Slaney, R., 15, Ed; 37B, Ed
Slave Coast, 81C, Dc
Slavinia, 21B, Cb
Slavinia, D. of, 21, Lb
Slavonia, 39, Mf
Slavonic Peoples, 8A, Da
Slavs, 4A, Hb; 8, Ha
Sleat, 14, Cb
Sleat, Sd. of, 14, Cb
Slieve Bloom, 15, Dc
Slieve League, 15, Cb
Sligo, 37B, Cb; 49B, Cb
Sligo, co., 37C; 49B, Cb
Silvnitza, 78, Dd
Slovak, 85, Fc
Slovakia, 87, Ec
Slovenes, 9, Fc
Sluys, 28C, Da; 46A, Cc
Slyne Hd., 49B, Ac
Smaland, 26, Db
Small Saxon States, 65C, Ba
Smerwick, 49B, Ad
Smith Sd., 42, Ga; 69B
Smithfield, 57, Ce
Smithland, 72, Cb
Smolensk, 19, Eb; 26, Hc
Smolensk, Pr., 19, Ea
Smyrna, 78, Ff
Snake, R., 44, Cd; 70, Cc
Snake Hill, 71D
Sneeuw Mts., 77, Fb
Snotingeham (Nottingham), 13, Ed
Snotinghamscire (Nottinghamshire), 13, Fc
Snowdon, 27, Cc
Soa Pan, 81A, Cb
Soana, 23B, Cc
Sobral, 63B
Sobraon, 73, Ba
Sobrarbe, 23C, Ea
Society Is., 75, He
Socorro, 70, Dd
Socotra, 94, Re; 96A, Ca
Söderhamn, 26, Ea
Söderköping, 34, Fa; 50, Db
Södermanland, 26, Eb
Sodor and Man, bp., 36, Bc
Soest, 20, Hc
Sofala, 40, Le; 81A, Db
Sofia, 78, Dd
Sogdiana, 1, Jc; 6, Ha
Sognefjord, 12, Fa
Sohag, 93, Cd
Soignes, Forest of, 46B
Soignies, 46B
Soissons, 11, Eb; 83A, Eb
Sokol, 78, Bc
Sokoto, 96B, Ca
Sokotra, 41A, Cc; 83, Md
Solano, 75E, Ba
Soldaia, 19, Bd
Soldin, 21, Lb
Sole Bay, 55A, Db
Soleure (Solothurn), 29B, Ba
Solferino, 29A, Dc; 32C, Cb
Solikamsk, 61, Jc
Sollum, 93, Cc
Soims, 30, Hc
Solomon Is., 77, Kc; 90, Dd

Solothurn (Soleure), 29B, Ba
Solothurn, canton, 29B, Ba
Solsona, 22, Cc
Solway Firth, 14, Ee
Solway Moss, 37A, Cc
Somali Rep., 96D, Gd
Somalia, 96A, Bb
Somberete, 43A, Bb
Somers Is. (Bermudas), 43A, Fa
Somerset, 27, De
Somerset East, 81B, Cc
Somerton, 7B, Bc
Somme, R., 11, Eb; 83A, Bb
Somnath, 52A, Ab; 25, Gd
Somosierra, 63, Db
Son, R., 73, Dc
Sonchön, 76B, Cb
Soncino, 32D, Ab
Sonderburg, 65F, Aa
Sondershausen, 39C, Ab
Sondre Stromfjord, 94, Cb
Sondrio, 29B, Db
Song Empire (Mangi), 25, Kd
Sonora, 43A, Ab
Sonora, R., 43A, Ab
Soor, 60A, Ec
Sora, 5B, Bc
Sorauren, 63, Ea
Sorbs, 8, Ea
Sorel, 57C, Aa
Soria, 23C, Db; 63, Db
Sorrento, 5, Ed
Sorviodunum (Salisbury), 3A, Ee
Soule, 17, Eg; 30, Cg
Sources, Mont Aux, 81D, Ab
South (Middle) I. (New Munster), 77A
South Africa, Rep. of, 96D, Eh
South Africa, Union of, 80A Fg
South African Republic, 81B, Ca
South Anna, R., 72B, Bb
South Atlantic Ocean, 94, Af
South Australia, 77, Eg
South Beveland, 46A, Cc
South Carolina, 57D, Ab
South China Sea, 91, Ef
South Dakota, 70, Dc
South Downs, 27, Ff
South Esk, R., 14, Fc
South Georgia, 69C
South Ice, 69C
South Kanara, 52A, Bc
South Konkan, 73, Bd
South Korea, 91, Fc
South Manchurian Railway, 74, Ld
South Molton, 27, Cf
South Orkney Is., 69C
South Pacific Ocean, 75, He
South Pass, 44, Dd
South Pole, 69C
South Potomac, R., 57, Bd
South Prussia, 60A, Fb
South Ronaldsay, 49A, Ca
South Saskatchewan, R., 70, Db
South Saxons, 7A, Cb
South Sea, 40, Ed
South Shetland Is., 69C
South Shields, 3C
South Uist, 14, Ab
South Vietnam, 91, De
South West Africa, 96C, Dg
South Yemen, 93, Ff
Southampton, England, 27, Ef
Southampton, Long I., 45B, Cc
Southampton I., 70, Fa
Southern Alps, N.Z., 77, Mj
Southern Hiung-nu, 1, Nc
Southern Nigeria, 81C, Fc
Southern Ocean, 69C
Southern Rhodesia, 80A, Ff
Southern Slavs, 8C, Cb
Southland, 77A
Southold, 45B, Cc
Southwark, 27, Fe; 27A
Southwell, 36, Fd; 48B, Cc
Southwold, 55A, Db
Souvigny, 22, Cb
Sovietskaya, 69C
Sozopolis, 18A, Eb
Sozusa, 4B, Ge
Spa, 46A, Ed
Spain, 34, Bd; 63, Db
Spalato, 5, Fc; 78, Ad
Spalding, 27, Fd
Spallinge (Spalding), 13, Fd
Spandau, 60A, Db
Spanish Fort, 72, Cc
Spanish Guinea, 80A, Dd
Spanish Main, 43A, Ec
Spanish March, 8, Cc
Spanish Morocco, 96D, Ab
Spanish Netherlands, 38, Fc
Spanish Sahara, 96D, Ab
Spanish Town, 43A, Ec
Sparta, 78, Dg
Spartanburg, 72, Dc

Spartel, C., 62, Ae; 63A
Spectacle I., 56B
Spencer G., 77, Fh
Sperrin Mts., 15, Db
Spey, R., 14, Eb
Speyer, 29A, Ca; 83A, Eb
Speyer (Spires), 20, Hd
Spezia, 32A, Cb
Spezzia, 78, Dg
Spichern, 76A, Db
Spilimberg, 86B, Ca
Spinalonga, 79, Ec
Spinis (Speen), 3A, Ee
Spion Kop, 81D, Ab
Spires (Speyer), 20, Hd
Spithead, 55A, Cc
Spitzbergen, 42, Ka; 74, Aa
Spitzbergen Sea, 74, Ba
Splügen Pass, 29B, Db
Spoleto (Spoletium), 5, Dc
Spoleto, D. of, 5, Dc; 21, Kg
Sponheim, 20, Gd
Sporades, 78, Df
Spotsylvania, 72B, Ba
Springbokfontein, 81B, Ab
Springfield, Illinois, 72, Cb
Springfield, Massachusetts, 45B, Cb
Springfield, Missouri, 72, Bb
Spurn Hd., 55A, Db
Squillace, 5, Fe
Srinagar, 25, Gc; 73, Ca
Srivijaya, 25, Jf
Staaten Land, 42, Sf
Stade, 20, Hb
Stadford (Stafford), 13, Dd
Stadfordscire (Staffordshire), 13, Dd
Stadtlohn, 38, Gb
Staete Land, 42B
Staffarda, 29A, Bc; 50, Be
Stafford, 27, Dd
Stafford, co., 27, Dd
Stagno, 22, Fc
Stalingrad, 88, Od
Stalino, 88, Nd
Stamford, Connecticut, 45B, Cc
Stamford, England, 27, Fd
Stamford Bridge, 12, Dc
Standerton, 81A, Cc
Stanes (Staines), 13, Fe
Stanford (Stamford), 13, Fd
Stanfordbrycge (Stamford Bridge), 13, Fb
Stanislau, 84, Gc
Stanleyville, 80A, Fd
Stantune (Long Stanton), 13, Dd
Stanwix, 3C
Stanz, 29B, Cb
Stara Zagora, 78, Ed
Staraya Russa, 61, Dc
S arbuck I., 75, He
Stardub, 19, Ga; 61, Dd
Stargard, 21, Lb; 31, Kb
Starodub, 19, Ga; 61, Dd
Staten I., 45B, Bc; 57B
Stau (Stow), 13, Fc
Staufen, 10, Cd
Staunton, 56, Dc
Staunton, R., 57, Be
Stavanger, 12, Fb; 47, Da
Stavelot, 22, Da; 46A, Ed
Staveren, 26, Cc
Stavropol, Astrakhan, 61, Fe
Sta ropol, Kazan, 61, Gd
Stavros, 86A, Eb
Stavuchanak, 61, Ce
Stayninges (Steyning), 13, Ff
Steelpoort, 81A, Db
Steenkerque, 46A, Dd
Steenwyk, 46A, Fb
Steier, 21, Ld
Steinamanger, 21, Me
Steinau, 39, Mc
Stella Land, 81A, Bc
Stellenbosch, 81B, Ac
Stellenbosch, dist., 81B, Ac
Stelvio Pass, 29B, Eb
Stenay, 38, Fd
Stendal, 20, Jb
Stephen Dushan, Emp. of, 24, Ge
Stephen's Fort (Charleston), 57, Eb
Sternberg, 21, Lb
Stettin, 31, Lb; 39, Cb
Stewart, 28B, Ab; 37A, Bb
Stewart I. (New Leinster), 77A
Stikine, R., 71B, Db
Stiklestad, 12, Ga
Stillwater, 57, Eb
Stirling, 14, Ec; 37A, Cb
Stirling, co., 37A, Bb; 49A, Bb
Stockach, 29A, Cb
Stockholm, 26, Eb
Stoke Courcy, 27, Ce
Stolbova, 47, Ja; 50, Gb
Stollhofen, 29A, Ba
Stolp, 21, Ma

Stolpen, 39C, Eb
Stonehaven, 49A, Cb
Stonington, 45B, Dc
Stony Pt., 57, Dc
Storkow, 31, Kb
Storkyro, 50, Ea
Storm B., 77, Hj
Stormberg, 81B, Cb
Stornoway, 49A, Aa
Stoss Pass, 29B, Da
Stour, R., 27, Ge
Strabane, 49B, Db
Stradella, 29A, Cc
Stralsund, 26, Dc; 31B, Ca
Strand, 27A
Strängnäs, 26, Eb
Stranraer, 49A, Bc
Strasbourg, 7A, Eb; 83B, Ba
Strassburg, 10, Cc
Strata Florida, 36, Cc
Strata Marcella, 36, Ce
Stratford, 45B, Cc
Strath Earn, 14, Ec
Strath Spey, 14, Eb
Strathaven, 28B, Ab
Strathclyde, 14, Ed; 36A
Strathfillan, 49A, Bb
Strathmore, 14, Ec
Strathnaver, 14, Da
Stratton, 48A, Ad
Straubing, 39, Kd
Strelitz, 60B, Db; 65B, Ba
Striguil, 13, De; 28A, Dc
Stromness, 49A, Ca
Stronsay, 49A, Ca
Strumna, R., 78, De; 86A, Ea
Strumnitza, 78, De
Strymon, 9, Gd
Stuart Town (Port Royal), 45A, Ad
Stuhlweissenburg, 33C, Db
Stuhm, 39, Nb
Stuhmsdorf, 50, Dc
Stumitza, 86A, Da
Sturgeon L., 45A, Bb
Stuttgart, 29A, Ca
Styria, 10, Fe
Styria, D. of, 21, Le
Styrian Alps, 29A, Fb
Suakin, 80B, Bd
Suana, 5B, Ab
Subiaco, 22, Ec
Suck, R., 15, Cc
Sucre, 68, Cd
Suda Bay, 79, Dc
Sudan, reg., 81C, Db
Sudan, rep., 96D, Ec
Sudberie (Sudbury), 13, Gd
Sudbury, Canada, 70, Fc
Sudetes, 60A, Fc
Sudfulc (Suffolk), 13, Hd
Sudras, 59D
Sudreys, 12, Cb; 14, Bc
Sudrie (Surrey), 13, Fe
Sudsexe (Sussex), 13, Ff
Sud-Treding (South Riding), 13, Gc
Sudwelle (Southwell), 13, Ec
Sudwerca (Southwark), 13, Fe
Suevi, 2, Ed; 4A, Ac
Suez, 80B, Ab
Suez Canal, 80B, Aa
Suffolk, Virginia, 57, Ce
Suffolk, co., 27, Hd
Sugar Hill, 57, Eb
Suir, R., 15, Dd; 37B, Dd
Sukhumi, 79, Hb
Sukkur, 92, Bb
Sula Is., 52C, Bb
Sula Sea, 75E, Bb
Sulaiman Mts., 73, Aa
Sulaimaniya, 93, Fb
Sulawesi (Celebes), 91, Eg
Sulina, 78, Gc
Sullana, 68, Ac
Sullivan, 15, Be
Sully, 38, Ee
Sulzbach, 21, Jd
Sumatra, 35, Od
Sumatra (Java Minor), 35, Oe
Sumatra, I., 91, Dg
Sumba, 91, Eg
Sumba (Sandelwood I.), 52C, Bc
Sumbawa, 91, Eg
Sumorsete (Somerset), 13, Ce
Sunart, 14, Cc
Sunbury, 56, Cd
Sunda Sea, 91, Fg
Sundarbans, 59B, 73, Ec
Sunday, R., 81D, Bb
Sundgau, 30, Ge; 39B, Dc
Superior, L., 56, Ba; 70, Fc
Supplingenburg, 20, Jb
Sur (Tyre), 18C, Ce
Surabaja, 91, Eg
Surat, 73, Bc
Surinam, 41B, Dc; 42, Gd; 94, Ce
Surrey, 7A, Cb; 27, Fe
Susa, Italy, 5, Ab
Susa, N. Africa, 6, Cb; 24, Ef

Susa (Shushan), 1, Gd; 6A, Db
Susquehanna, R., 45A, Bb; 57, Db
Sussex, 27, Ff
Sutherland, 14, Da
Sutherland Berg, 81D, Ab
Sutlej, R., 73, Da
Sutri, 21, Kg; 23B, Dc
Sutrium, 5, Dc
Suva, 75, Fe; 75C, Bb
Suvla B., 86D
Suwanee, 71F, Ca
Suwanee, R., 71F, Ca
Suzdal, 19, Ga
Suzdal, dist., 19, Ga
Suzzara, 29A, Dc
Svalbard, 94, Rb
Sveaborg, 51, Fa
Svendborg, 26, Db
Sverdlovsk, 74, Ec; 88, Sb
Sverdrup Is., 44, Da
Swaanendael, 45B, Bd
Swabia, 10, Ce; 20, He
Swabian Jura, 10, Cd
Swakopmund, 80A, Eg
Swale, R., 12, Dc
Swan River Colony, 77, Bh
Swanage, 7C, Cc
Swansea, Rhode I., 45B, Dc
Swansea, Wales, 27, Ce; 28A, Bc
Swart Berg, 81B, Bc
Swat, R., 73, Ba
Swatow, 74, Kf; 90, Bb
Swaziland, 80A, Gg; 81A, Dc
Sweden, 26, Ea; 47, Fa; 82, Ea
Sweden and Norway, 64, Ea
Swedish Pomerania, 51, Cc
Sweetheart Abbey, 36, Cc
Swellendam, 81B, Bc
Swellendam, dist., 81B, Bc
Sweyn, 12, Dd
Swilly L., 15, Da
Swiss Confederation, The, 29B; 30, He
Switzerland, 47, Dc; 54, Dc
Sycamore Shoals, 57A, Cb
Sydney (Port Jackson), 77, Ih
Sylt, 65F, Aa
Syr Darya, R., 25, Fb; 61B, Ba
Syracusae, 2, Gf
Syracuse (Syracusa), 5, Ef
Syracuse, New York, 57, Cb; 67B, Ca
Syria, 1, Fd; 6A, Bb; 79, Gc
Syriam, 40, Od
Syrian Desert, 86C, Cc
Syrtis Major, 2, Gg
Syrtis Minor, 2, Fg
Szabacs, 33C, Dc
Szathmar, 33C, Eb
Szcelankemen, 33C, Eb
Szczebrzeszyn, 26, Fc
Szczecin, 89, Hc
Szczekociny, 51, Ec
Sze Chow, 1, Od
Szeged, 87, Ec
Szegedin, 33C, Eb; 39, Pe
Sziget, 33C, Db

TABARISTAN, 6, Gb
Tabasco, 43A, Cc
Tabatinga, 68, Cc
Table B., 81A, Ad
Taboga I., 43A, Ed
Tabor, 31, Ld; 33C, Cb
Tabora, 80A, Ge
Tabriz, 6, Fb; 19, He; 79, Jc
Tacloban, 75E, Bb
Tacna, Chile, 68, Bd
Tacna, Peru, 68, Cd
Tacuba, 43A, Cc
Tacutu, R., 68B, Bb
Tadcaster, 48A, Cc
Tadkin, R., 57, Ae
Tadmor, 6A, Bb; 9, Kf
Tadoussac, 45A, Da; 71, Hc
Tafosoho, 52B, Aa
Taganrog, 61, Ee
Taginae, 5, Dc
Tagliacozzo, 21, Kg
Tagliamento, R., 29A, Ec
Tagus, R., 23C, Ca; 63, Bc
Tahirids, King. of, 6B, Ga
Tahiti, 75, He
Tai Yuan, 1, Od
Taif, 6, Fc; 93, Ee
Taillebourg, 17, Ef
Tain, 37A, Bb; 49A, Bb
Tainan, 91, Fd
Taipei, 91, Fd
Taitze-ho, R., 76B, Ba
Taiwan (Formosa), 91, Fd
Taiyuan, 91, Ec
Ta'iz, 93, Ef
Takhires Gol, L., 86A, Eb
Takrit, 6, Fb
Taku, R., 71B, Cb
Takushan, 76B, Bb
Talangama, 52B, Aa
Talavera, 62, Be; 63, Cc

Talayan, 75E, Bc
Talca, 68, Bf
Talcaguano, 68, Bf
Tali, 25, Kd
Talienwan, 76B, Ab
Talienwan B., 76B, Ab
Talikot, 52A, Bc
Taling Ho, R., 76B, Aa
Talladega, 71F, Ba
Tallahassee, 72, Dc
Tallapoosa, R., 71F, Ba
Tallard, 38, Gf
Tallinn, 87, Fa
Talmont, 20, Ce
Tamale, 96B, Bb
Tamar, R., 27, Be
Tamatave, 80A, Hf
Tambof, 61, Fd
Tamesis (R. Thames), 3A, Ge
Tamil Nadu, 92, De
Tampa, 72, Dd
Tampa B., 44, Ff; 70, Fe
Tampico, 43A, Cb
Tamrush, 78, Ee
Tamworde (Tamworth), 13, Ed
Tamworth, 7B, Cb; 48A, Cc
Tana, India, 35, Nd
Tana, Russia, 19, Fc
Tana, L., 80B, Be
Tananarive, 80A, Hf
Tanaro, R., 29A, Bc
Tancrids Tower, 18D
Tandil, 68, Df
Tandjungpinang, 75A, Bb
Tanega Shima, 41A, La
Tanganyika, 96C, Fe
Tanganyika, L., 80A, Fe
Tangermünde, 30, Kb
Tangier, 23D, Ce; 63A
Tanjore, 59D
Tann, 29A, Ea
Tannenberg, 31, Pb; 84, Gb
Tanner's Gate, 18D
Tanta, 80B, Aa
Tantallon Castle, 28B, Ca
Tantone (Taunton), 13, Ce
Tanzania, 96D, Fe
Taormina, 21A, Cd
Taormina (Tauromenium), 5, Ef
Tapajos, 68, Cd
Tappita, 96B, Bb
Tapti, R., 73, Bc
Tara, 15, Ec
Tarakan, 90, Bc
Taranaki, 77A
Taranto, 32A, Gd
Taranto, G. of, 32B, Fd
Tarapaca, Chile, 68, Cd
Tarapaca, Colombia, 68, Cc
Tarascon, 38, Dg
Tarasp, 29B, Eb
Tarazona, 22, Bc; 23C, Eb
Tarbes, 11, Ce; 63, Fa
Tarentaise, 22, Db
Tarentaise, eccl. prov., 22, Db
Targowica, 51, Gd
Tarifa, 23D, Cd; 63A
Tarija, 68, Ce
Tarim, R., 25, Hb; 91, Bb
Tarki, 19, Hd
Tarkwa, 96B, Bb
Tarlac, 75E, Ba
Tarn, R., 11, Ed
Tarnof, 26, Fc
Tarnopol, 33C, Fb; 62, Hc
Tarnow, 33C, Ea
Taron, 18C, Ce
Tarraco, 2, De
Tarragona, 23C, Fb; 63, Fb
Tarragona, eccl. prov., 22, Cc
Tarsus, 6A, Ba; 18C, Bb
Tartar, 85, Mb
Tartary, 35, Nb; 69A, Nb
Tartas, 30, Cg
Tartu, 87, Fa
Tashihkiao, 76B, Ba
Tashkent, 25, Fb; 61B, Ba
Tasman Sea, 77, Kl
Tasmania, 77, Gj
Tateshale (Tanshelf), 13, Ec
Tati, 81A, Cb
Tati, R., 81A, Cb
Tattershall, 27, Fc
Tatungkow, 76B, Cb
Taufers, 86B, Aa
Taunton, England, 27, Ce
Taunton, Rhode I., 45B, Dc
Taunus, 83A, Ea
Taurica, 2, Kd
Tauroggen, 60A, Ja
Tauromenium (Taormina), 5, Ef
Taurus, 2, Kf; 19, Ee
Taus, 31, Kd
Tavastehus, 26, Fa
Tavestoche (Tavistock), 13, Bf
Tavira, 23C, Bd
Tavistock, 27, Bf
Tavoy, 73, Ge
Tavua, 75C, Aa

Tawarik, 6, Bc
Taxila, 1, Kd
Tay, Firth of, 14, Fc
Tay, L., 14, Dc
Tay, R., 14, Ec
Tbilisi, 93, Ea
Tchirman, 33A, Cb
Tebuk, 93, Dd
Tecklenburg, 20, Gb
Tecklenburg, co., 46C, Ca
Tees, R., 27, Eb
Teesdale, 28B, Cc
Tefe, 68, Cc
Tegeingl, 13, Cc
Tegesta, 43A, Db
Tehama, 6, Fd
Tehran, 93, Gb
Tehri, 73, Cc
Tehuantepec, 43A, Cc
Tehuantepec, Isthmus of, 43A, Cc
Teifi, R., 27, Bd
Teith, R., 14, Dc
Tekke, Amirate of, 19, Ee
Tekrit, 86C, Dc
Tel Aviv-Jaffa, 79, Fd
Tell-basher (Turbessel), 18C, Eb
Teller, 71A, Aa
Tellicherri, 73, Ce
Tembuland, 81A, Cd
Tembus, 81B, Cb
Teme, R., 28A, Cb
Temesvar, 33C, Eb
Temple, Jerusalem, 18D
Temple, London, 27A
Temple Bar, 27A
Templeborough, 3A, Ec
Templin, 31, Kb
Temuco, 68, Bf
Tenasserim, 73, Ge
Tenby, 27, Be
Tenda, 32A, Bb
Tenda, Coc di, 29A, Bc
Tenedos, 78, Ef; 86C, Ab
Tenerife, 80A, Bb
Tenes, 16, Ce
Tengri Nor, L., 73, Ca
Tennessee, R., 56, Bd
Tennessee, st., 72, Cb
Tenterden, 27, Ge
Teodekesberie (Tewkesbury), 13, De
Teofilo-Otoni, 68, Ed
Tephrik, 16, Ke
Tepl, 22, Eb
Teplitz, 33C, Ca; 60B, Dc
Terek, R., 19, Hd; 61, Ff
Terek Cossacks, 61, Gf
Teresina, 68, Ec
Tergovist, 24, Hd
Terminal Pt., 76B, Bb
Termoli, 32A, Fc
Ternate, 52B, Aa
Terni, 22, Ec; 39, Kg
Ternova, 78, Ed
Terracina, 5, Dd; 22A
Terschelling, 46A, Ea
Tertry, 7A, Db; 8B, Bb
Teruel, 22, Bc; 23C, Eb
Teschen, 21, Nd; 87, Dc
Teslin, L., 70, Aa
Teslin, R., 71B, Ca
Tete, 42, Le; 81A, Da
Tetford (Thetford), 13, Gd
Tettenhall, 7C, Bb; 13, Dd
Tetuan, 16, Ae
Teupitz, 60A, Db
Teutonic Knights, 21B, Db; 26, Gb
Teviot, R., 48A, Bb
Teviotdale, 28B, Cb
Tewkesbury, 27, De; 36, Df
Texas, 70, Fd
Texel, 46A, Da
Tezcuco, 43A, Cc
Thaba Bosigo, 81B, Cb
Thabanchu, 81B, Cb
Thailand, 91, Dc
Thame, 36, Ff
Thames, R., Canada, 45A, Ab
Thames, R., Connecticut, 45B, Cc
Thames, R., England, 27, Ee
Thanet, 7B, Dc
Thanjavur, 92, De
Thann, 39B, Dc
Thapsus, 2, Ff
Thar Desert, 59A, Bb
Tharandt, 39C, Dc
Thasos, 78, Ee
The Forks, 69A, Da
The Hague, 46A, Db
Theanum, 5B, Bc
Thebes, 19, Ce
Theiss, R., 22, Gb; 33C, Eb
Thelwall, 7C, Bb
Theodosiopolis (Erzerum), 4A, Ld
Theopolis, 81B, Cc
Thérouanne, 22, Ca; 46A, Bd
Thessalonica, 8, Gc; 9, Gd
Thessalonica Theme, 9, Gd

Thessaly, 78, Df
Thetford, 7C, Db; 36, Ge
Thiers, 30, Ef
Thikombia, 75C, Ca
Thimer, 11, Db
Thionville, 29A, Ba; 83A, Db
Third Cataract, 80B, Ad
Thirsk, 27, Eb
Tholen, 46A, Dc
Thooley, 39B, Da
Thomar, 23C, Ac; 63, Ac
Thomastown, 49B, Cd
Thomond, 15, Cd
Thompsons I., 56B
Thorn, 21, Nb
Thorney, 36, Fe
Thouars, 11, Cc
Thousand Is., L. of, 57, Ca
Thrace, 8, Hc; 78, Fe
Thrace Theme, 9, Hd
Thracesian Theme, 9, He
Thracia, 2, Je
Threave, 14, Fe
Threave Castle, 28B, Ac
Three Kings I., 75, Ff
Three Points, C., 81C, Dd
Three Rivers, 57C, Aa
Thun, 29B, Bb
Thun, L., 29B, Bb
Thur, R., 29B, Ca
Thurgau, 10, Ce; 29B, Da
Thuringia, 10, Dc; 39C, Ad
Thuringia, Land. of, 21B, Cb
Thuringia, March of, 10, Fc
Thuringian Forest, 10, Dc
Thuringians, 4A, Ea; 7A, Fb
Thurles, 49B, Dd
Thurso, 37A, Ca
Tibbu, 6, Cc
Tiber, R., 5, Dc; 32A, Ec
Tiberias, 18C, Cf
Tibesti, 80A, Eb
Tibet, 25, Hc; 92, Fa
Tiburon, C., 43A, Ec
Ticino, canton, 29B, Cb
Ticino, R., 5, Bb
Tickhill, 27, Ec
Ticonderoga, 57, Eb
Tidor, 52B, Aa
Tientsin, 74, Ke; 91, Ec
Tierra del Fuego, 68, Ch
Tierra Firme, 43A, Fd
Tiflis, 19, Gd; 79, Hb
Tigris, R., 2, Mg; 6A, Ca
Tikhvin, 88, Mb
Tikrit, 93, Ec
Till, R., 28B, Cb; 48A, Cb
Tilsit, 60A, Ha; 61, Bc
Timahoe, 15, Dd
Timaru, 77A
Timbuktu, 81C, Da
Timbuktu (Tombuto), 35, Jd
Timisoara, 87, Ec
Timor, 52C, Cc; 91, Fg
Timor Laut, 52C, Dc
Tinchebrai, 17, Ed
Tindouf, 80A, Cb
Tinemuthe (Tynem'th), 13, Ea
Tingitana, 2, Cg
Tinnevelly, 73, Cf
Tinos, 78, Eg
Tintagel, 13, Bf; 27, Bf
Tintern, 36, Df
Tioga, 56, Db
Tippecanoe, 71C, Ab
Tipperah, 73, Fc
Tipperary, 37B, Cd
Tipperary, co., 49B, Dd
Tippermuir, 37A, Cb
Tiranë, 88, Je
Tirlemont, 46A, Dd
Tirnova, 78, Ed
Tiruchirapalli, 92, De
Tisz, R., 89, Kd
Titicaca, L., 68, Cd
Titus, Baths of, 5A
Tivli, 22A; 32A, Ed
Tiverton, 27, Cf
Tivoli, 22A; 32A, Ed
Tlaxcala, 43A, Cc
Tiemsen, 6, Ab; 9, Bf
Tmatarakhan, 9, Kc
Tobago, 43A, Fc
Tobermory, 49A, Ab
Tobolsk, 74, Ec
Tobruk, 93, Ac
Tocantins, R., 68, Ec
Toce, R., 29B, Cb
Togean Is., 52C, Bb
Togo, 81C, Ec; 96B, Cb
Togoland, 96C, Cd
Tohopeka (Horseshoe Bend), 71F, Ba
Tokar, 80B, Bd
Tokat, 33A, Eb
Tokay, 33C, Eb
Tokelau Is., 83, Ae; 90, Fd
Tokelau (Union) Is., 75, Ge
Tokyo, 91, Ec
Toledo, Ohio, 70, Fc

Toledo, Spain, 23C, Cc; 63, Cc
Toledo, eccl. prov., 22, Bc
Toledo, Mts. of, 63, Cc
Toliman, 52B, Ab
To.lhuys, 53, Gb
Tolmezzo, 86B, Da
Tolmino, 86B, Da
Tolosa, 2, De
Tols, 53, Jd
Tolu, 43A, Ed
Tombigbee, R., 43A, Da
Tomen-y-mur, 3A, Cd
Tomini, Gulf of, 52C, Bb
Tomsk, 42, Ob; 74, Gc
Tonale Pass, 29A, Db
Tonbridge, 27, Ge
Tondern, 65F, Aa
Tonebridge (Tonbridge), 13, Ge
Tonga (Friendly) Is., 75, Gf
Tonga Land, 81D, Ca
Tongatabu, 75, Gf
Tongking, 74, Jf
Tongue, Kyle of, 49A, Ba
Tongueland, 36, Bc
Tonk, 73, Cb
Tonnai, 20, Cf
Tonnerre, 11, Fc; 17A, Dc
Tönning, 65F, Aa
Tonsberg, 26, Db
Toome, 37B, Eb
Topeka, 10, Ed
Tor B., 55A, Bc
Torchesey (Torksey), 13, Fc
Tordesillas, 23D, Cb; 63, Cb
Torgau, 21, Kc; 39C, Cb
Torjok, 19, Ea
Torksey, 7C, Cb
Tormentoso, C. (C. of Good Hope), 35, Kf
Tormes, R., 63, Bb
Torni (Thorney), 13, Fd
Toro, 23C, Cb; 63, Cb
Toronto, 70, Gc
Toronto (York), 71C, Cb
Toropets, 19, Ea
Torre, Devon, 36, Cg
Torre, Somerset, 13, Ce
Torrens, L., 77, Fh
Torres, 23B, Bd
Torres, eccl. prov., 22, Dc
Torres Str., 77, Gc
Torres Vedras, 63B
Torridon, L., 14, Cb
Torrington, 27, Bf
Tortola, 43A, Fc
Tortona, 5, Bb
Tortosa, 23C, Fb; 63, Fb
Tortue (Tortuga), 43D, Eb
Tortuga, I., Haiti, 43A, Eb
Tortuga, I., Venezuela, 43A, Fc
Tory I., 15, Ca
Tostar, 6A, Db
Toteberie (Tutbury), 13, Ed
Totenais (Totnes), 13, Cf
Totnes, 27, Cf
Totoya, 75C, Cb
Touggourt, 80A, Da
Toul, 10, Ad; 39B, Bb
Toulon, 11, Fe; 29A, Ad
Toulouse, 11, De
Toulouse, Co. of, 11, De
Touraine, 11, Dc
Tourcoing, 46A, Cd
Tournai, 46A, Cd
Tournon, 17, Hf; 38, Df
Tours, 11, Dc
Tours, eccl. prov., 22, Bb
Toury, 76A, Ab
Towcester, 7C, Cb; 48B, Cc
Tower, 27A
Townsville, 77, He
Towton, 27, Ec
Towy, R., 28A, Cb
Toxandria, 8b, Ba
Trabzon, 93, Da
Trafalgar, 55B, Kc; 69A, Jc
Trafalgar, C., 63A
Trajan's Wall, 78, Gc
Tralee, 37B, Bd; 49B, Bd
Trani, 32A, Gd
Tranquebar, 42, Od; 59D
Trans Tiberis, 5A
Trans-Caspian Rail'y, 74, Dd
Trans-Jordan, 79, Gd
Transkei, 81B, Dc
Transmarine Algarve, 35, Jc
Transvaal, 81A, Db
Transylvania, Europe, 33C, Eb
Transylvania, N. America, 57A, Bb
Transylvanian Alps, 50, Ed
Trapani, 5, Dc
Trapezus, 2, Le; 4A, Kc
Traquair, 28B, Bb
Tras os Montes, 63, Bb
Trasimene, L., 5, Dc
Trastamara, 23D, Aa

Trau, 22, Fc
Traungau, 10, Fd
Traunstein, 53, Kd
Trautenau, 60B, Ec
Travancore, 73, Cf
Travnik, 78, Ac
Trebbio, R., 5, Bb
Trebizond, 19, Fd; 79, Gb
Trebizond, Empir of, 19, Fd
Trebnitz, 22, Ia
Tregony, 27, Bf
Tréguier, 11, Bb
Trelleborg, 12, Gc
Tremetone (Trematon), 13, Bf
Trencsen, 21, Nd
Trent, 5, Ca
Trent, Bp. of, 30, Je; 33C, Cb
Trent, R., 27, Ec
Trentino, 84, Ec; 86B, Aa
Trenton, 45A, Cb; 57, Dc
Tresch (Thirsk), 13, Eb
Trèves, 10, Bd; 83A, Db
Trèves, Abp. of, 22, Db; 46C, Cb
Treviglio, 32A, Cb
Treviso, 5, Db; 86B, Cb
Treviso, M. of, 23B, Cb
Trévoux, 53, Fe
Tribulation, C., 77, He
Tribur, 10, Cd
Trichinopoly, 59D
Triebl, 39, Kd
Trier, 31A, Dc; 76A, Db
Trieste, 5, Db
Triglav, 29A, Fb
Trim, 15, Ec; 49B, Ec
Trim, bp., 15A, Bb
Trimontium (Newstead), 3A, Da
Trincomali, 73, Df
Trinidad, Bolivia, 68, Cd
Trinidad, Cuba, 43A, Eb
Trinidad, I., 43A, Fc
Trinity B., 45A, Ga
Trinovantes, 3A, Ge
Tripoli, Libya, 6, Cb; 80A, Ea
Tripoli, Syria, 6A, Bb; 18C, Cd
Tripoli, Volhynia, 19, Dc
Tripolis, 2, Fg
Tripolitana, 4B, Ee
Tripolitania, 80A, Ea
Tripolitza, 78, Dg
Tripura, 92, Gc
Trisameron, 4B, Dd
Trisanna, R., 29B, Ea
Tristan da Cunha, 69A, Jf
Trivadee, 59D
Trivandrum, 73, Cf
Trivento, 22, Ec
Trobriand Is., 77, Ic
Trocala, 5, Df
Troia, 21A, Cb
Troina, 21A, Cd
Troitskoye, 61, Ec
Trondelag, 12, Ga
Trondheim (Nidaros), 26, Da; 88, Ha
Trondhjem, 50, Ca
Trondhjem, prov., 50, Ca
Tronto, R., 21A, Ba
Troppau, 31, Md; 39, Md
Tropea, 22, Fd
Trostan, 15, Ea
Trotternish, 14, Bb
Troy, 57, Eb
Troyes, 2, Dd; 28D, Db
Troyes, Co. of, 11, Eb
Trucial Oman, 93, Ge
Trujillo, Peru, 68, Bc
Trujillo, Spain, 23C, Cc; 63, Cc
Trujillo, Venezuela, 68, Bb
Truk, 90, Dc
Truro, 27, Af
Truxillo, 43A, Dc
Tsang-Wu, 16, Ka
Tsanpo (Brahmaputra), R., 73, Eb
Tsaribrod, 78, Dd
Tschaslau, 31, Ld
Tsinan, 91, Ec
Tsingtao, 91, Fc
Tsympe, 33A, Cb
Tuam, 15, Cc
Tuamotu Arch. (Paumotu Arch.), 75, He
Tuareg, 80A, Db
Tübingen, 10, Cd; 64, Dd
Tubual (Austral) Is., 75, Hf
Tucson, 70, Cd
Tucuman, 41B, Cf; 68, Ce
Tudela, 23C, Ea; 63, Ea
Tuder, 5, Dd
Tugela, R., 81D, Bb
Tukharistan, 6, Jb
Tula, 84, Kb; 88, Nc
Tulbagh, 81B, Ae
Tulbagh, dist., 81B, Bc
Tulcea, 78, Gc
Tullagh, 37B, Ec

Tullahoma, 72, Cb
Tullamore, 49B, Dc
Tulle, 22, Cb; 30, Df
Tulunid Dominions, 9, Hf
Tulunids, King. of, 6B, Db
Tumbez, 68, Ac
Tummel, R., 49A, Bb
Tun, 6, Gb
Tunga Bhadra, R., 73, Cd
Tungchow, 74, Kd
Tunis, 24, Df; 80A, Da
Tunis, prot., 80A, Da
Tunis, Pashalik of, 47, De
Tunis, Sultanate of (Hafsids)
34, De
Tunisia, 96C, Ca; 96D, Ca
Tunja, 68, Bb
Tunja, R., 78, Fd
Tupelo, 72, Cc
Turbessel (Tell-basher), 18C,
Eb
Turenne, 11, Dd
Turenne, V. of, 11, Dd
Turgai, 74, Ed
Turkestan, 61B, Ba
Turkestan, reg., 61B, Ba
Turkey, 93, Db
Turkheim, 29A, Ba; 39B, Db
Turkish Hungary, 39, Ne
Turkomans, 24, Lf
Turks Is., 43A, Eb
Turku, 87, Ea
Turin, 20, Gf; 32C, Ab
Turin (Augusta Taurinorum),
5, Ab
Turmid, 6, Hb
Turnberry, 14, Dd
Turneffe, 43A, Dc
Turnham Green, 48A, Cd
Turnhout, 46A, Dc
Turov, 26, Gc
Turriff, 37A, Cb
Turukhansk, 74, Gb
Tus, 6, Hb
Tuscaloosa, 72, Cc
Tuscan Presidios, 47, Ed
Tuscana, 5B, Ab
Tuscany, 5, Ce
Tuscany, D. of, 23A, Cb
Tuscany, G. D. of, 32B, Cc;
38, Jg
Tuscaroras, 45A, Bc
Tusculum (Frascati), 22A
Tuscumbia, 72, Cc
Tutbury, 27, Ed
Tutuila, 75, Ge; 75B, Bb
Tuva, 74, Hc
Tuy, 22, Ac; 23C, Aa
Tuz Gol, L., 86C, Bb
Tuzi, 78, Bd
Tver, 19, Fa
Tvinam (Twineham, Christ-
church), 13, Df
Tweed, R., 14, Ed; 28B, Bb
Twelve Pins, 15, Bc
Two Sicilies, King. of, 18B,
Bc; 21, Kg; 32B, Ed
Tyburn, 27A
Tyne, R., 27, Eb; 28B, Dc
Tynedale, 13, Db
Tynedale, Franchise of, 28B,
Cb
Tynemouth, 27, Ea
Tyr Connell, 15, Cb
Tyr Owen, 15, Db
Tyras, R., 2, Jd
Tyre, 2, Lg; 16, Kf
Tyre (Sur), 18C, Ce
Tyrnau, 39, Md
Tyrol, 20, Je
Tyrol, Co. of, 20, Je
Tyrone, 37B, Db
Tyrone, co., 49B, Db
Tyrrell, 37B, Dc
Tyrrhenian Sea, 5, Dd
Tyumen, 74, Ec
Tzurulum (Chorlu), 19, Dd

UBANGI-SHARI, 80A, Fd
Ubeda, 23C, Dc
Uberaba, 68, Ed
Uberlingen, 20, He
Ucayali, R., 68, Bc
Uch, 25, Gd
Uckermark, 31B, Ca
Ucles, 23C, Dc
Udaipur, 73, Bc
Udine, 22, Eb; 29A, Eb
Udskot, 74, Mc
Uele, R., 80A, Fd
Uexküll, 26, Fb
Ufa, 61, Jd
Ufa, R., 19, Ka
Uganda, 80A, Gd
Uighur, 25, Hb
Uitenhage, 81A, Cd
Uitenhage, dist., 81B, Cc
Ujiji, 80A, Fe
Ujjain, 1, Ke; 92, Db
Ukermark, 60A, Db
Ukraine, 19, Eb; 50, Gd

Ukraine Soviet Socialist Rep.,
84, Jc
Ukrians, 10, Eb
Uladh (Ultonia, Ulster), 15, Db
Ulan Bator, 91, Db
Ulan Ude, 91, Da
Uleåborg, 61, Cb
Ullapool, 49A, Bb
Ulm, 10, Cd; 29A, Ca
Ulster, 37B, Db; 49C
Ulster (Uladh, Ultonia), 15, Db
Ulster Irish, 49C
Ultonia (Uladh, Ulster), 15, Db
Ulundi, 81D, Bb
Ülzen, 26, Dc
Umarkot, 52A, Ab
Umbria, 5, Dc; 32A, Ec
Umeå, 26, Fa
Umfraville, 28B, Cb
Unfuli, R., 81A, Ca
Umkomaas, R., 81B, Db
Umtali, 81A, Da
Umzimkulu, R., 81B, Db
Umzimvubu, R., 81B, Db
Umzimyati (Buffalo), R.,
81D, Bb
Una, R., 33C, Dc
Ungava, 70, Gb
Ungava B., 44, Hc; 71, Hb
Union (Tokelau) Is., 75, Ge
Union of Soviet Socialist
Republics, 94, Qc
United Arab Republic, 96D,
Fb
United Kingdom, 64, Ab
United Provinces, Rep. of, 38,
Fb
United St. of America, 70–71
United States of Brazil, 68, Dd
Unkiar Skelessi, 79, Eb
Unterwalden, 29B, Cb
Upland, New Sweden, 45B, Bd
Upland, Sweden, 26, Ea
Upolu, 75B, Ba
Upper Alsace, 31A, Dd
Upper Alsace, Land. of, 20, Ge
Upper Austria, 65C, Bb
Upper Burgundy (Regnum
Jurense), 11, Gc
Upper Burma, 74, Hf
Upper Canada, 71C, Ca
Upper Doab, 59C, Cb
Upper Lausitz, Marg. of, 31,
Lc
Upper Lorraine, 20, Gd
Upper Lotharingia, 10, Bd
Upper Palatinate, 30, Jd
Upper Peru, 41B, Ce
Upper Senegal and Niger, 81C,
Da
Upper Silesia, 60A, Fc
Upper Volta, 80A, Cc
Upper Volta, St., 96B, Bc
Upsala, 26, Eb
Uraba, G. of, 43A, Ed
Ural Mts., 19, Ka
Ural, R., 19, Kb; 61, Hd
Uralsk, 61, Hd
Urbino, 5, Dc; 8A, Dc
Urbinum, 5B, Bb
Urfa, 79, Gc
Urga, 74, Jd
Urgel, 11, De; 23C, Fa
Urgenj, 25, Eb
Uri, 29B, Cb
Uriel, 37B, Db
Uriel (Oirghealla), 15, Db
Urmia, 86C, Db
Urmia, L., 6A, Da
Urseren, 29B, Cb
Uruguaiana, 68, De
Uruguay, 68, Df
Uruguay, R., 68, De
Urumchi, 91, Bb
Usak, 79, Ec
Usedom, 10, Eb; 31, Kb
Ushant, 11, Ab
Usingen, 65B, Aa
Usk, 28A, Cc
Usk, R., 27, De; 28, Cb
Uskub (Skoplje), 78, Cd
Uskudar, 93, Ba
Ust Yurt, 61, Jf
Ustyug, 61, Gb
Utah, 70, Cd
Utah L., 44, Cd
Utah Terr., 67D, Bb
Utica, Mississippi, 72C, Aa
Utica, New York, 57, Db
Utrecht, Natal, 81D, Ba
Utrecht, Netherlands, 46A, Eb
Utrecht, prov., 46A, Eb
Utrecht, Bp. of, 46C, Ca
Uttar Pradesh, 92, Eb
Uttoxeter, 48B, Cd
Uxbridge, 48B, Cd
Uyuni, 68, Ce
Uzés, 11, Fe
Uzes (Cumans), 9, Mc
Uznach, 29B, Da

VAAL, R., 81A, Cc

Vabres, 22, Cc
Vadstena, 26, Db
Vaduz, 38, He
Vaigeu, 52C, Db
Vaison, 22, Dc
Val d'Aran, 23D, Fa
Val Leventina, 29B, Cb
Val Maggia, 29B, Cb
Valais, 29B, Bb
Valais, Co. of, 11, Gc
Valcour I., 57, Ea
Valdemoni, 21A, Cc
Valdez, 71A, Ca
Vale Royal, 36, Dd
Valence, 11, Fd
Valence, family, 37B, Ed
Valencia, Spain, 63, Ec
Valencia, Venezuela, 68, Cb
Valencia, eccl. prov., 22, Bd
Valencia, prov., 63, Ec
Valenciennes, 46A, Cd
Valentia I., 49B, Ae
Valladolid, 23C, Cb; 63, Cb
Valle Crucis, 36, Ce
Valley Forge, 57, Dc
Vallombrosa, 32A, Dc
Valls, 63, Fb
Vallum Antonini, 3A, Ba
Valognes, 11, Cb
Valois, 17, Gd
Valois, Co. of, 11, Eb
Valona, 16, Fd; 78, Be
Valparaiso, 68, Bf
Valromey, 53, Fe
Valsainte, 29B, Bb
Valsch, R., 81B, Ca
Valtellina, 29B, Db
Valverde, 23D, Bc
Van, 19, Ge; 86C, Db
Van, L., 6A, Ca
Van Diemen's Land, 77, Gj
Van Reenen's Pass, 81D, Ab
Vancouver, Canada, 70, Bc
Vancouver, U.S.A., 70, Bc
Vancouver I., 70, Bc
Vandal Kingdom, 4A, Dd
Vandali, 2, Gc
Vandalia, 67C, Eb
Vandals, 2A, Ac
Vannes, 11, Bc
Vanua Levu, 75C, Ba
Var, R., 29A, Bd
Värälä, 51, Fa
Varanasi (Banaras), 92, Eb
Varazdin, 21, Me
Vardar, R., 78, De; 86A, Da
Varennes, 29A, Aa; 31A, Cc
Varey, 20, Ff
Varilhes, 38, Dg
Varkinskil (Salem), 45B, Bd
Varna, 78, Fd
Vasa, 26, Fa
Vasconia, 4A, Bc
Vassy, 38, Fd
Vasvar, 33C, Db
Vasvar (Eisenburg), 29A, Gb
Vaternish, 14, Bb
Vatersay, 49A, Ab
Vatican, 5A
Vatter, L., 26, Db
Vaucouleurs, 28D, Eb
Vaud, 29B, Ab
Vaud, Co. of, 11, Gc
Vaudemont, 20, Fd; 39B, Cb
Vaudreuil, 57, Da
Vechte, R., 46A, Gb
Vectis (I. of Wight), 3A, Ef
Veglia, 22, Eb
Veile, 65F, Aa
Velay, Co. of, 11, Fd
Velikie Luki, 61, Dc
Velletri, 32B, Dd
Vellinghausen, 60A, Ac
Vellore, 59D
Venaissin, 30, Ff
Vendée, 53, Cd; 62, Bc
Venden, 26, Gb
Vendôme, 11, Dc
Venedae, 1, Fb
Vener, L., 26, Db
Venetia, 5, Db; 32C, Db
Venetian Alps, 29A, Dc
Venezuela, 43C, Ed; 68, Db
Venezuela, G. of, 43A, Ec
Venice, 32D, Cb
Venice, D. of, 10, Ef
Venice, G. of, 29A, Ec
Venlo, 46A, Fc
Venonae (High Cross), 3A, Ed
Venta Belgarum (Winchester),
3A, Ee
Venta Cruz (Cruces), 43A, Ed
Venta Icenorum (Caister), 3A,
Hd
Venta Silurum (Caerwent),
3A, De
Ventadour, 17, Gf; 53, Ee
Ventersdorp, 81A, Cc

Ventimiglia, 5, Ac; 20, Gg
Vera Cruz, 43A, Cc
Vera Cruz, Terra da, 40, He
Veragua, 43A, Dd
Veragua, prov., 43A, Dd
Vercelli, 5, Bb; 29A, Cc
Verchères, 57, Ea
Vercovicium (Housesteads),
3C
Verde, C., 80A, Bc; 81C, Ab
Verden, 10, Cb; 60A, Ac
Verden, Bp. of, 38, Hb
Verdon, R., 29A, Bd
Verdun, Gascony, 38, Dg
Verdun, Lotharingia, 10, Ad
Verdun, Bp. of, 39B, Ba
Vereeniging, 81A, Cc
Veria, 78, De
Verkhne Kolymsk, 74, Ob
Verkhne Udinsk, 74, Jc
Verkhoyansk, 74, Mb
Verkne Chusovoi, 61, Jc
Vermandois, Co. of, 11, Eb
Vermland, 26, Db
Vermont, 67C, Fa; 71, Gc
Vernemetum (Willoughby),
3A, Ed
Verneuil, 17, Fd
Verny, 74, Fd
Verona, 5, Cb; 32D, Bb
Verona, M. of, 10, Ef; 20, Jf
Verria, 86A, Dc
Versailles, 53, Ec; 76A, Bb
Verterae (Brough), 3A, Cc
Vertus, 30, Ed
Veruela, 22, Bc
Verulamium (St. Albans), 3A,
Fe
Verviers, 46A, Ed
Vervins, 38, Ed
Vesle, R., 83A, Bb
Vesoul, 20, Ge; 83B, Bb
Vester-Götland, 26, Db
Vesterås, 26, Eb
Vesterbotten, 26, Fa
Vestmanland, 26, Eb
Veszprem, 21, Me
Vet (Sand), R., 81A, Cc
Vevey, 29B, Ab
Vexin, Co. of, 11, Db
Vexins, 38, Ce
Vézelay, 20, Ee; 31A, Bd
Via Dolorosa, 18D
Viadua, R., 2, Gc
Vianen, 46A, Ec
Vianna, 23D, Ab; 63, Ab
Viatka, 19, Ha
Viborg, Denmark, 26, Cb
Viborg, Finland, 26, Ga
Vic, 39B, Cb
Vic Bigorre, 63, Fa
Vicenza, 5, Cb; 38, Jf
Vich, 11, Ef
Vichy, 88, Fd
Vicksburg, 72C, Aa
Victoria, British Columbia,
70, Bc
Victoria, Cameroon, 96B, Cb
Victoria, Rhodesia, 81A, Db
Victoria, dist., S. Africa, 81B,
Cc
Victoria Falls, 81A, Ca
Victoria I., Canada, 44, Ca
Victoria, I., Moluccas, 52C, Cb
Victoria, L., 80A, Ge
Victoria Land, 69C
Victoria, R., 77, Ee
Victoria, st., 77, Gi
Vidin, 33A, Bb
Viedma, 68, Cg
Vienna, Austria, 10, Gd
Vienna, Gaul, 2, Dd
Vienne, 11, Fd; 17A, Ed
Vienne, eccl. prov., 22, Db
Vienne, R., 11, Dc; 30, De
Vientiane, 91, De
Viervoet, 81B, Cb
Vierzon, 28C, Dc; 76A, Bc
Vietnam, 91, De
Vigan, 75E, Ba
Vigo, 63, Aa
Viipuri, 87, Fa
Vijayanagar, 52A, Bc
Vijayanagar, king., 41A, Ec
Vijayawada, 92, Ed
Viken, 12, Gb
Vilagos, 33C, Eb
Vilaine, R., 30, Be
Vilkomir, 26, Fb
Villa Bella (Mato Grosso), 68,
Cd
Villa do Conde, 63, Ab
Villa Dolores, 68, Cf
Villa St. Albani (St. Albans),
13, Fe
Villa Viciosa, Portugal, 63, Bc
Villa Viciosa, Spain, 63, Db
Villach, 10, Ee; 29A, Eb
Villafranca, Italy, 32C, Cb
Villafranca, Spain, 63, Ba
Villarrica, 68, De

Villefranche, Guyenne, 53, Ee
Villefranche, Lyonnais, 53, Fe
Villemaur, 31A, Bc
Villena, 23C, Ec; 63, Ec
Villeneuve, 20, Df
Viliers Bretonneux, 76A, Bb
Villers Cotterets, 83A, Bb
Villersexel, 76A, Dc
Vilna, 26, Gc
Vilnius (Vilna), 88, Lc
Vimiero, 63, Ac
Viminacium, 2, He
Vimy, 83A, Ba
Vincennes, 56, Bc
Vindhya Mts., 73, Cc
Vindocladia (Badbury), 3A, Df
Vindolanda (Chesterholm), 3C
Vindomora (Ebchester), 3C
Vindovala (Rudchester), 3C
Vinegar Hill, 49B, Ed
Vinland, 35, Fb
Vinnitsa, 79, Ea
Vinovia (Binchester), 3A, Eb
Vionville, 76A, Cb
Vire, 53, Cc
Virgin Is., 43A, Fc
Virginia, 57, Ce; 72B, Bb
Virginia Colony, Raleigh's,
45A, Bc
Viroconium (Wroxeter), 3A,
Dd
Visconti, Lands of, 24, Dd
Visé, 83A, Ca
Viseu, 23C, Ab
Vishakhapatnam, 92, Ed
Vishegorod, 19, Da
Visigothi, 2, Hd
Visigothic Kingdom, 4A, Bc
Viso, Mte., 29A, Bc
Visp, 29B, Bb
Vistula, R., 31, Pc; 33C, Ea
Viterbo, 5, Dc
Viti Levu, 75C, Aa
Vitichev, 9, Jb
Vitoria, Brazil, 68, Ee
Vitoria, Spain, 63, Da
Vitoria la Conguista, 68, Ed
Vitré, 20, Cd
Vitry, 11, Fb
Vitry, Co. of, 11, Fb
Vittoria, 4B, Bc
Vittorio, 86B, Cb
Viviers, 11, Fd; 17, Hf
Vizagapatam, 73, Dd
Vizcaya, 23C, Da
Vizeu, 22, Ac; 63, Bb
Vizianagram, 59A, Dd
Vizye, 19, Dd
Vlach, 8C, Db
Vlachs, 19, Ec
Vladikavkaz, 61, Ff
Vladimir, Poland, 26, Fc
Vladimir, Russia, 19, Ga
Vladimir Volinski, 19, Cb
Vladivostok, 91, Gb
Vlieland, 46A, Da
Vodena, 86A, Db
Vogtland, 21, Kc
Volcano Is., 90, Db
Volga, R., 19, Hc; 24, Md
Volgograd, 89, Od
Volhynia, 50, Fc
Volkovisk, 62, Gb
Volksrust, 81D, Aa
Volmeringen, 39B, Ca
Vologda, 19, Fa
Volos, 78, Df
Volta, L., 96B, Bb
Volta, R., 81C, Dc
Volterra, 32E, Bb
Volturno, R., 32C, Dd
Voltutara, 22, Fc
Vorarlberg, 33C, Cb
Voronezh, 61, Ed; 88, Nc
Vosges, 10, Bd; 83B, Ba
Vostok I., 83, Be
Votyaks, 19, Ja
Vouillé, 4A, Bb; 8B, Ab
Vrania, 78, Cd
Vryburg, 81A, Bc
Vryheid, 81A, Dc; 81D, Ba
Vyatiches, 9, Ka
Vyazma, 19, Ea

WAAG, R., 21, Nd
Waal, R., 46A, Ec
Wabash, R., 56, Bc; 57A, Bb
Wachefeld (Wakefield), 13, Ec
Wad Medani, 93, Cg
Wadai, 80A, Ec
Wadelai, 80A, Gd
Wadern, 76A, Db
Wadi Halfa, 80B, Ac
Wagram, 29A, Ga
Wagrians, 10, Da
Wahlstatt, 60B, Fc
Waianae, 75D, Bb
Waiblingen, 10, Cd
Waidhaus, 39, Kd
Waidhofen, 21, Le
Waigen, 77, Eb

Waikato, R., 77A
Wailuku, 75D, Cb
Waimea, 75D, Bb
Waitara, 77A
Waitemata (Auckland), 77, Ml
Waitzen, 22, Fb
Wake I., 90, Ec
Wakefield, 27, Ec
Wakkerstroom, 81D, Ba
Wal Wal, 96A, Bb
Walachia, 78, Ec
Walcheren, 46A, Cc
Waldeck, 30, Hc
Waldeck, co., 38, Hc
Walden, 36, Ge
Waldsassen, 22, Eb
Waledana (Saffron Walden), 13, Gd
Walenstadt, 29B, Da
Wales, 28A; 34, Bb; 55A, Bb
Wales, Pr. of, 27, Cd
Wales, The March of, 17, Dc
Walila, 6, Ab
Walingeford (Wallingford), 13, Ee
Walla Walla, 70, Cc
Wallhof, 50, Eb
Wallingford, 27, Ee
Wallis Is., 75, Ge
Walpole, 57, Eb
Walsingham, 36, Ge
Walsleben, 10, Db
Waltham, 13, Ge; 36, Gf
Walton Castle, 3A, He
Walvis Bay, 80A, Eg
Walvisch B., 81A, Ab
Wandatin, 76B, Bb
Wandiwash, 59D
Wangama, 77A
Wanganui, 77, NJ
Wangen, 30, He
Wantage, 7C, Cc; 48B, Cd
Warangal, 25, Ge; 92, Dd
Warberg, 26, Db
Wardha, R., 59C, Cc
Wardour Castle, 48A, Bd
Wareham, 27, Df
Wargaon, 59A, Bd
Warham (Wareham), 13, Df
Wark, 27, Da; 28B, Cb
Warkworth, 27, Ea
Warnabians, 10, Eb
Warneton, 46A, Bd
Warnstedt, 10, Dc
Warren, 28A, Ca
Warrington, 3A, Dc; 48A, Bc
Warsaw, 21, Pb
Warsaw, G. D. of, 62, Gb
Warta, R., 21B, Db; 31, Db
Wartburg, 20, Jc; 39C, Ac
Warthe, R., 21, Lb; 22, Fa
Warwic (Warwick), 13, Ed
Warwick, England, 27, Ed
Warwick, Rhode I., 45B, Dc
Warwick, co., 27, Ed
Warwicscire (Warwickshire), 13, Ed
Wash, The, 27, Gd; 36, Ge
Washington, Arkansas, 72, Bc
Washington, Dist. of Columbia, 71C, Cc; 72B, Ba
Washington, st., 70, Bc
Washington I., 75, Hd
Washington Terr., 67D, Aa
Wasit, 6A, Db
Watasios (Sultanate of Fez), 34, Be
Watchet, 27, Ce
Waterboer's Land, 81A, Bc
Wateree, R., 57D, Aa
Waterford, 15, Dd
Waterford, co., 49B, Dd
Waterloo, 46B
Watford, 48B, Cd
Watkins Pt., 45B, Be
Watling Street, 3A, Ed
Wattignies, 46A, Dd
Watton, 36, Fd
Waverley, 36, Ff
Wavre, 46A, Dd; 46B
Waxhaw Creek, 57, Af
Weardale, 28B, Cc
Weare, 27, De
Wearmouth, 36, Ec
Weddell Sea, 69C
Wedmore, 7C, Bc
Wedone (Weedon), 13, Ed
Weenen, 81D, Bb
Wehlau, 39, Pa; 50, Ec
Weiden, 38, Jd
Weihaiwei, 74, Le
Weil, 30, Hd; 38, Hd
Weilerthal, 39B, Db
Weimar, 10, Dc
Weinsberg, 10, Cd
Weissenburg, Alsace, 39B, Da
Weissenburg, Germany, 20, Jd; 29A, Da
Weissenfels, 39C, Bb
Weitburg, 65B, Aa

Welbeck, 36, Ed
Weldon, 72, Eb
Welfesholz, 10, Dc
Wella (Wells), 13, Gd
Welland, R., 27, Fd
Welle (Wells), 13, De
Wellesley, 37B, Ec
Wellesley Is., 77, Fe
Wellington, 75, Fg
Wellington (Brittania), 77, NJ
Wellington, prov., 77A
Wells, 27, De
Welshpool, 27, Cd
Wenchow, 74, Lf
Wendover, 27, Fe
Wener, L., 12, Hb
Wenloch (Wenlock), 13, Dd
Wenlock, 27, Dd
Weobley, 27, Dd; 23, Db
Werben, 10, Db; 38, Jb
Werc (Wark), 13, Da
Werdenfels, 53, Jd
Weremuthe (Wearmouth), 13, Eb
Werle, 21, Kb
Wernigerode, 60A, Dc
Werra, R., 10, Dc; 20, Hc
Wertheim, 53, Hc
Wes-Treding (West Riding, Lincolnshire), 13, Fc
Wes-Treding (West Riding, Yorkshire), 13, Ec
Wesel, 20, Gc; 60A, Ec
Wesel (Oberwesel), 20, Gc
Weser, R., 10, Cb; 30, Hb
Wessaugusset (Weymouth), 45B, Db
Wessex, 7B, Bc; 12, Dd
West Bengal, 92, Fc
West Dvina, R., 89, Lb
West Florida, 56, Bd
West Franconia, 10, Cd
West Germany, 89, Gd
West Indies, 55B, Dd
West Irian, 91, Gg
West Looe, 27, Bf
West March, 28B, Bb
West Meath, co., 49B, Dc
West New Jersey, 45A, Cc
West Pakistan, 92, Bb
West Point, 57, Dc
West Prussia, 31, Nb
West Roman Empire, 2, Fe
West Saxons, 7A, Cb
West Schelde, R., 54, Cb
West Virginia, 72, Db
West Wales, 7B, Ac; 36A
Westderbei (West Derby), 18, Dc
Wester Wald, 10, Cc
Western Australia, 77, Cg
Western Ghats, 73, Bd
Western Pomerania, 39, Kb
Western Samoa, 75, Ge; 75B
Westerwald, 83A, Da
Westland, 77A
Westmeath, co., 37C
Westminster, 27A; 36, Ff
Westminster, Palace of, 27A
Westminster Abbey, 27A
Westmonasterium (Westminster), 13, Fe
Westmorland, 27, Db
Westover, 45B, Ae; 57, Ce
Westphalia, 10, Bb; 20, Hc
Westport, Missouri, 70, Ec
Westport, New Zealand, 77A
Westray, 49A, Ca
Wetherby, 48B, Cc
Wethersfield, 45B, Cc
Wetter, I., 52C, Cc
Wettin, 10, Dc; 39C, Bb
Wettingen, 29B, Ca
Wetzlar, 10, Cc
Wewak, 90, Dd
Wexford, 15, Ed
Wexford, co., 37C; 49B, Ed
Wexio, 26, Db
Weymouth, 27, Df; 55A, Bc
Weymouth (Wessaugusset), 45B, Db
Weymouth B., 77, Gd
Whalley, 36, Dd
Wheeling, 57, Ac
Wherwell, 36, Ef
Whitby, 27, Fb
Whitchurch, 48B, Cd
White Castle, 28A, Dc
White Croats, 9, Gb
White Horse, 71B, Ca
White House, 72B, Bb
White Huns, 6, Ha
White Marsh, 57, Dc
White Mts., 45A, Cb
White Nile, R., 80B, Ae
White Pass, 71B, Cb
White Plains, 57, Ec
White Russia, 51, Gc
White Sea, 61, Ea
White Umvolosi, R., 81D, Bb

Whitehall, 27A
Whitern, 7B, Aa
Whithorn, 14, De
Whitland, 36, Bf
Whitsand B., 55A, Ac
Whydah 81C, Ec
Wiceford (Witchford), 13, Gd
Wich (Nantwich), 13, Dc
Wiche (Droitwich), 13, Dd
Wick, 49A, Ca
Wicklow, 15, Ed
Wicklow, co., 37C; 49B, Ed
Wicklow Hd., 15, Ed
Wicklow Mts., 15, Ed
Wicumbe (High Wycombe), 13, Fe
Widin, 19, Cd; 78, Dc
Wied, 20, Gc
Wielun, 61A, Ab
Wiesbaden, 60B, Bc; 83A, Ea
Wiesloch, 38, Hd
Wigan, 3A, Dc; 27, Dc
Wigemor (Wigmore), 13, Cd
Wight, I. of, 27, Ef
Wigmore, 28A, Db
Wigtown, 14, De
Wigtown, co., 37A, Bc
Wigtown B., 28B, Ac
Wiht, Is. de (I. of Wight), 13, Ef
Wiju, 76B, Ca
Wildhaus, 29B, Da
Wildspitze, 29A, Db
Wilge, R., 81B, Da
Wilhelmshaven, 55A, Hb
Wilkes Land, 69C
Wilkesbarre, 56, Db
Willebroek, 46A, Dc
Willemstadt, 52B, Aa
Williamsburg, 57, Ce
Williamsport, 70, Gc
Willis Creek, 56B
Willmanstrand, 51, Fa
Willsboro, 57, Ea
Wilmington, Delaware, 57, Dd
Wilmington, North Carolina, 57D, Ba
Wilno, 87, Fb
Wilson's Creek, 72, Bb
Wiltberg, 20, Jc
Wilten, 10, De
Wiltescire (Wiltshire), 13, Ee
Wilton, 27, Ee
Wiltshire, 27, Ee
Wiltunie (Wilton), 13, Ee
Wiltzes, 8, Ea; 10, Eb
Wimborne, 7C, Cc
Wimpfen, 10, Cd
Winburg, 81A, Cc
Winburne (Wimborne Minster), 13, Ef
Winceby, 48A, Cc
Wincelcumbe (Winchcomb), 13, Ee
Winchelsea, 17, Fc; 27, Gf
Winchester, England, 27, Ee
Winchester, Virginia, 57, Bd
Winchester, bp., 36, Ef
Windau, 26, Fb
Windesores (Windsor), 13, Fe
Windhoek, 80A, Ec
Windsheim, 22, Eb; 30, Jd
Windsor, Connecticut, 45B, Cc
Windsor, England, 27, Fe
Windward Passage, 43A, Ec
Winnebago, L., 56, Bb
Winnepesaukee, L., 45B, Db
Winnipeg, 70, Ec
Winnipeg, L., 70, Eb
Winnipegosis, L., 70, Eb
Winnisimet, 56B
Winnsboto, 57D, Aa
Winter Hill, 56B
Winterberg Mts., 81B, Cc
Winterthur, 29B, Ca
Wintonia (Winchester), 13, Ee
Wirecestre (Worcester), 13, Ed
Wirecestrescire (Worcestershire), 13, Dd
Wisbeche (Wisbech), 13, Gd
Wisby, 26, Eb
Wischehrad, 31, Lc
Wisconsin, 70, Ec
Wisconsin, R., 56, Bb
Wislica, 31, Pc
Wismar, 26, Dc; 31B, Ca
Wissembourg, 29A, Ba
Witebi (Whitby), 13, Fb
Witham, Essex, 7C, Dc
Witham, Wiltshire, 36, Df
Witham, R., 27, Fc
Witney, 27, Ee
Witteland, 42B
Witteland West, 77, Bf
Wittelsbach, 20, Jd
Wittenberg, 21, Kc; 31B, Ca
Wittenberg, mts., 81B, Cb
Wittgenstein, 30, Hc
Wittstock, 21, Kb
Wloclawek, 22, Fa

Woburn, 36, Ff
Woerden, 46A, Db
Woëvre, The, 83A, Cb
Wohlau, 39, Mc
Wolfenbüttel, 20, Jb
Wolgast, 21, Ka
Wollin (Jomsburg), 10, Fb
Wolmar, 50, Fb
Wölpe, 20, Hb
Woods, L. of the, 70, Ec
Woodstock, England, 27, Ee
Wooler, 49A, Cc
Worcester, England, 27, Dd
Worcester, Massachusetts, 57, Fb
Worcester, S. Africa, 81B, Ac
Worcester, bp., 36, De
Worcester, co., 27, Dd
Wordingborg, 26, Db
Worksop, 36, Ed
Worms, 10, Cd; 83A, Eb
Wörth, 39B, Ea; 76A, Db
Wrangel I., 74, Qa; 94, Jb
Wrath, C., 14, Ca
Wrexham, 48B, Bc
Wroclaw, 89, Jc
Wuhan, 91, Ec
Wuhu, 74, Ke
Württemberg, 10, Cd; 20, Hd
Würzburg, 10, Cd; 29A, Da
Wurzburg, G. D. of, 65B, Ba
Wurzen, 39C, Cb
Wychwood, 7B, Cc
Wycombe, 27, Fe
Wye, R., 27, De; 36, De
Wymondham, 36, He
Wynaad Malabar, 73, Ce
Wyndham, 77, De
Wynendael, 46A, Bc
Wyoming, 57, Cc
Wyoming, st., 70, Dc

Xanten, 46A, Fc
Xeres, 23C, Bd; 63, Bd
Xingu, R., 68, Dc

Y Gaer, 3A, Cd
Yadavas, 25, Gd
Yakutat B., 71B, Bb
Yakutsk, 74, Lb
Yalu, R., 76B, Ca
Yamasees, 45A, Bc
Yamuna, R., 92, Db
Yanaon, 73, Dd
Yanbu, 6, Ec
Yandabu, 73, Gc
Yandua, 75C, Ba
Yang Chow, 1, Oe
Yangtze-Kiang, R., 91, Dc
Yanselin Pass, 76B, Ba
Yantra, R., 78, Ed
Yaoundé, 96B, Db
Yap, 90, Cc
Yaqui, Pico de, 43D, Ec
Yarkand, 1, Kd; 74, Fe
Yarm, 27, Eb
Yarmak, 6A, Bb
Yarmouth, I. of W., 27, Ef
Yarmouth, Maine, 57, Fb
Yarmouth, Massachusetts, 45B, Dc
Yarmouth, Norfolk, 27, Hd
Yarmouth, Nova Scotia, 56, Fb
Yasawa Is., 75C, Aa
Yathreb (Medina), 6, Fc
Yavanas, 1, Je
Yazoo, R., 56, Ad; 72C, Aa
Yecla, 63, Ec
Yeddo, 69A, Qc
Yekaterinburg, 61, Kc
Yekaterinoslav, 51, Gd
Yellow Ford, 49B, Eb
Yellow Sea, 91, Fc
Yellowhead Pass, 44, Cc
Yellowstone, R., 70, Dc
Yellowstone National Park, 70, Dc
Yemen, 6, Fd; 25, De; 93, Ef
Yenbo, 93, De
Yenisei, R., 25, Ha
Yeniseisk, 74, Hc
Yentowwa B., 76B, Bb
Yerevan, 93, Ea
Yerwa, 96B, Da
Yeu, 53, Bd
Yewin, 77, Bg
Yezd, 6, Gb; 93, Gc
Yih Chow, 1, Nd
Yingkow, 76B, Ba
Ynys Enlli, 7B, Ab
Yokohama, 91, Gc
Yola, 80A, Ed
Yonne, R., 11, Ec
York (Agamenticus), 45B, Db
York, England, 27, Ec; 36A
York, Maine, 57, Fb
York, Pennsylvania, 57, Cd
York (Toronto), 71C, Cb
York, abp., 36, Ed

York, C., 77, Gd
York, eccl. prov., 22, Ba
York, Norse King. of, 7C, Ca
York, R., 72B, Bb
York Factory, 70, Eb
York Moors, 27, Fb
York Wolds, 27, Fb
Yorkshire, 27, Eb
Yorktown, 57, Ce; 72B, Bb
Youghal, 37B, De; 49B, De
Ypres, 17, Gc; 46A, Bd
Ysabel, 77, Jc
Ystrad Towy, 7B, Ac
Ythancester, 7B, Dc
Yu Chow, 1, Od
Yucatan, 43A, Db
Yu-chang, 1, Oe
Yugoslavia, 84, Fd
Yukon, 71B, Ba
Yukon, R., 71A, Ba
Yunnan, 74, Jf
Yun-nan, prov., 73, Gb
Yverdon, 29B, Ab
Yxninga (Exning), 13, Gd

Zabern, 38, Gd
Zablat, 39, Ld
Zabid, 6, Fd
Zacatecas, 43A, Bb
Zacatula, 43A, Bc
Zacynthos (Zante) I., 78, Cg
Zafra, 63, Bc
Zagreb, 16, Fc
Zahringen, 10, Bd; 20, Gd
Zaitun. 25, Ld; 35, Pc
Zallaca, 23C, Bc
Zambesi, R., 81A, Da
Zambia, 96D, Ef
Zamboanga, 75E, Bc
Zamora, 23C, Cp; 63, Cb
Zamosc, 50, Ec; 62, Gb
Zanesville, 71C, Bc
Zanj, 6, Fd
Zante, 78, Cg
Zante (Zacynthos) I., 78, Cg
Zanzibar, 80A, Ge
Zapetra, 8, Kd
Zara, 5, Eb; 32A, Fb
Zara, eccl. prov., 22, Ec
Zaranj, 6, Hb
Zaria, 96B, Ca
Zator, 31, Nd
Zduny, 26, Ec
Zealand, 65F, Ba
Zeebrugge, 83A, Ba
Zeeland, Denmark, 51, Cb
Zeeland, Netherlands, 46A, Cc
Zehdenick, 22, Ea
Zeila, 40, Md
Zeitz, 21, Kc; 39C, Cb
Zeitz, March of, 10, Ec
Zell, 53, Hc
Zengg, 21, Lf
Zenta, 33C, Eb
Zerbst, 21, Kc
Zettin, 33C, Db
Zevenbergen, 46A, Dc
Zhitomir, 87, Fb
Zidon, 18A, Fc
Ziegenhain, 20, Hc
Zierikzee, 46A, Cc
Ziguinchor, 96B, Aa
Zinder, 80A, Dc
Zion Gate, 18D
Zipangu (Japan), 25, Nc
Zips, 24, Gd; 33C, Eb; 50, Ed
Zirids, 16, Df
Zittau, 21, Lc
Ziyanids, 24, Cg
Znaim, 21, Md; 31B, Db
Zobor, 9, Fc
Zollern, 10, Cd; 30, Hd
Zomba, 96C, Ff
Zonguldak, 79, Fb
Zorndorf, 54, Eb; 60A, Eb
Zornoza, 63, Da
Zossen, 60A, Db
Zoutpansberg, 81A, Cb
Zug, 29B, Ca
Zug, canton, 29B, Ca
Zug, L., 29B, Ca
Zuider Zee, 46A, Eb
Zullichau, 60A, Eb
Zulpich, 4B, Da
Zulu, 81D, Bb
Zululand, 81D, Bb
Zumbo, 81A, Da
Zungeru, 81C, Fc; 96C, Cd
Zurawno, 50, Ed
Zürich, 10, Ce; 29B, Ca
Zürich, canton, 29B, Ca
Zürich, L. of, 29B, Ca
Zutphen, 46A, Fb
Zutphen, prov., 46A, Fb
Zvenigorod, 10, Ec
Zweibrücken, 29A, Ba
Zweibrucken, Pr. of, 53, Gc
Zwettl, 39, Ld
Zwickau, 21, Kc; 39C, Cc
Zwolle, 46A, Fb

PRINTED IN GREAT BRITAIN BY GEORGE PHILIP PRINTERS, LIMITED, LONDON